Handbook of Forensic Social Work

Handbook of Forensic Social Work

Theory, Policy, and Fields of Practice

EDITED BY

David Axlyn McLeod,
Anthony P. Natale,
Kristin W. Mapson

OXFORD
UNIVERSITY PRESS

OXFORD
UNIVERSITY PRESS

Oxford University Press is a department of the University of Oxford. It furthers
the University's objective of excellence in research, scholarship, and education
by publishing worldwide. Oxford is a registered trade mark of Oxford University
Press in the UK and certain other countries.

Published in the United States of America by Oxford University Press
198 Madison Avenue, New York, NY 10016, United States of America.

Library of Congress Cataloging-in-Publication Data
Names: McLeod, David Axlyn, author. | Natale, Anthony P., author. |
Mapson, Kristin W., author.
Title: Handbook of forensic social work : theory, policy, and fields of practice /
David Axlyn McLeod, Anthony P. Natale, Kristin W. Mapson.
Description: New York, NY : Oxford University Press, [2024] |
Includes bibliographical references.
Identifiers: LCCN 2023009081 (print) | LCCN 2023009082 (ebook) |
ISBN 9780197694732 (paperback) | ISBN 9780197694749 (epub) |
ISBN 9780197694763
Subjects: LCSH: Social work with criminals—United States. |
Social work with juvenile delinquents—United States. |
Social work with children—United States. |
Criminal justice, Administration of—Psychological aspects. |
Criminal justice, Administration of—Social aspects—United States.
Classification: LCC HV7428 .M353 2023 (print) | LCC HV7428 (ebook) |
DDC 365/.660973—dc23/eng/20230607
LC record available at https://lccn.loc.gov/2023009081
LC ebook record available at https://lccn.loc.gov/2023009082

DOI: 10.1093/oso/9780197694732.001.0001

Printed by Marquis Book Printing, Canada

Contents

List of Contributors

Soonok An
University of Illinois at
Urbana-Champaign

Meredith Canada, MSW, MPA, LCSW
Indiana University

John Carl, PhD
University of Oklahoma

Rachel C. Casey, PhD, MSW
University of Southern Maine

Oscar A. Chacon
Alianza Americas

Constance L. Chapple, PhD
University of Oklahoma

Angelique Day, PhD, MSW
University of Washington

Vanessa Drew, EdD, MSW
Elon University

Zackery D.O. Dunnells, MSW
University of Oklahoma

Leigh-Anne Francis, PhD
The College of New Jersey

John R. Gallagher, PhD, LCSW, LCAC
Morgan State University

Leah E. Gatlin, PhD, MSW
The University of Oklahoma

Bonni Goodwin, PhD, LCSW
University of Oklahoma

Kirsten Havig, PhD, MSW
University of Illinois

Trina L. Hope, PhD
University of Oklahoma

Elizabeth A. Justesen, Esq, MSW
Legal Aid Society of Suffolk County

Hannah E. Karpman, PhD, MSW
Smith School for Social Work

Stephanie C. Kennedy, PhD, MSW
Council on Criminal Justice

George S. Leibowitz, PhD, MSW
Stony Brook University

Margaret B. Leonard, MSW, MPH, MDiv
The Andrew Young School of Policy
Studies at Georgia State University

Heather M. Lepper-Pappan, MS
University of Oklahoma

Matthew S. Lofflin, PhD
University of Oklahoma

Erin. J. Maher, PhD
University of Oklahoma

Kristin W. Mapson, PhD, MSW
University of North Carolina Wilmington

Jason Matejkowski, MSW, PhD
University of Kansas

Keshawn Mathews, BSW
University of North Carolina at Charlotte

Susan McCarter, PhD
The University of North Carolina at
Charlotte

David Axlyn McLeod, PhD, MSW
University of Oklahoma

Sujeeta E. Menon, PhD
Civic Heart Community Services

Carmen Monico, PhD, MSW, MS, SEP
North Carolina Agricultural and
Technical State University

Anthony P. Natale, PhD, MSW
University of Oklahoma

Andrea Nichols, PhD
St. Louis Community College
Forest Park

Anne Nordberg, PhD, MSW
University of Texas at Arlington

Neema Olagbemiro, MPH
North Carolina Agricultural and
Technical State University

Burcu Ozturk, PhD, MSW
Wichita State University

Carrie Pettus, PhD, MSW
Justice System Partners & Wellbeing &
Equity Innovations

Angela B. Pharris, PhD, MSW
University of Oklahoma

Steven W. Pharris, MSW, JD, LCSW
National Association of Social Workers

Mark Plassmeyer, PhD, MSW
University of Arkansas

Kathleen M. Preble, PhD, MSW
University of Missouri Columbia

Dana Prescott, PhD, MSW, JD
Boston College School of Social Work
Prescott Jamieson & Murphy Law
Group, LLC

Kathleen Ray, PhD, LCSW
Ramapo College

Sophia P. Sarantakos, PhD, MSW
University of Denver

Saliseah Scales, MSW
UNC Charolette

Anna M. Scheyett, PhD, MSW
University of Georgia

Paula S. Schonauer, MSW
Private Practice

Shannon M. Sliva, PhD
University of Denver

Carly Sommers, Esq.

Jessica D. Strong, PhD, LMSW
Blue Star Families

Faye S. Taxman, PhD
George Mason University

Kris Taylor, MSW, LCSW
University of North Carolina at Charlotte

Maria E. Torres, PhD
Stony Brook University School of
Social Welfare

Kelechi Wright, PhD
University of Kansas

Introduction to Forensic Social Work

Anthony P. Natale, David Axlyn McLeod, and
Kristin W. Mapson

Introduction to the *Handbook of Forensic Social Work Practice*

Forensic social work is a unique practice field that interfaces with criminal justice or legal systems at the micro, mezzo, and macro levels of practice. This *Handbook* provides important reference content while exploring the multiple facets of the justice system; the differential nature of people, families, and communities navigating it; and the various ways social workers interface with the criminal justice system and associated client populations. The *Handbook* is an accessible resource for social workers that synthesizes current research and practice in forensic areas. The *Handbook* provides a comprehensive tool for social workers engaged in forensic practice to assist in knowledge and skill acquisition, which can help deliver effective social work services.

Forensic Social Work Practice

The authors of this text rely upon the National Organization for Forensic Social Work (NOFSW) to help define and detail the scope of social work practice in forensics. According to the NOFSW, forensic social work applies social work to law and legal systems, questions, and issues and, more broadly, social work practice relative to legal matters and litigation in criminal or civil cases (NOFSW, n.d.). Examples of fields of practice within that frame include separation and divorce; child custody; neglect and termination of parental rights; juvenile and adult justice services; corrections; and court-mandated treatment. The NOFSW

Anthony P. Natale, David Axlyn McLeod, and Kristin W. Mapson, *Introduction to Forensic Social Work* In: *Handbook of Forensic Social Work*. Edited by: David Axlyn McLeod, Anthony P. Natale, and Kristin W. Mapson, Oxford University Press. © Oxford University Press 2024. DOI: 10.1093/oso/9780197694732.003.0001 indicates that social workers engaged in forensic practice must have specialized knowledge, including familiarity with the law, to deduce appropriate conclusions and recommendations for critical review within legal systems. Without advanced and technical skills, social workers practicing forensics in criminal and civil justice systems will be minimally effective (NOFSW, n.d.).

The tasks of forensic social workers are diverse and include consultation, education, and training for members of the civil and criminal justice systems and the public. Additional duties include providing diagnosis, treatment, and professional recommendations for criminal and juvenile justice and child welfare populations and law enforcement or other criminal justice personnel. Finally, forensic social workers may be engaged in policy program development, mediation, arbitration, or behavioral science research and analysis (NOFSW, n.d.).

Forensic Social Work as Interprofessional Practice

Forensic social work occupies an interprofessional space in our culture and the broader profession, distinguishing this type of practice from others. Atop the list of the primary challenges in this *dual citizenship* is a constant negation for forensic social workers regarding balancing multiple client systems at every turn. Forensic social workers are constantly working to facilitate the ethical delivery of services to their direct client or client system while often being aware of their moral responsibility to the broader community's safety, which is usually no easy task.

In addition to managing the existential complexities of providing competent social work practice to direct clients and the community, forensic social workers often do so in *host settings*. For example, a social worker providing mental health services to incarcerated individuals could likely spend much of their time immersed in an organizational culture where they feel alienated, particularly regarding the profession's values. Forensic social workers face challenges with responding in these settings; managing the delivery of competent, ethical practice; advocating for their clients and client systems in alignment with professional values; and realistically maintaining their professional standing within the organization. Due to the potential for significant organizational culture issues, forensic social workers may find themselves in challenging workforce-related situations more often than their nonforensically associated peers.

Historically, social work practitioners have served in various interprofessional settings, including schools, hospitals, and mental health clinics. Forensic social work provides a unique opportunity for social work practitioners to interface with individuals who work in criminal justice settings, such as police officers, lawyers, judges, probation officers, and correctional workers. Forensic social workers need to understand the unique and dynamic organizational structures in the criminal justice system as it allows them to navigate and operate in a way that will most effectively serve their client population. This text will explore the varying aspects of the criminal justice system that work in settings for forensic social workers. Below you will find some examples of the fields of practice as well as the role of the social worker.

Brief Criminal Justice History

Criminological scholars have long studied how communities and governments developed and maintained social control systems. Much of our knowledge related to the evolution of the criminal justice system in the United States stems from historical analyses and influences of past societal, systemic, and judicial norms. Friedman (1993), in the widely influential text *Crime and Punishment in American History*, describes crime and criminal activity as socially abhorrent and unacceptable behaviors that are direct products of a social context. In other words, communities, either latently or explicitly, define acceptable and unacceptable behavior and employ various enforcement tactics to influence community members toward compliance. American history thoroughly documents the disproportionate and differential deployment of legal mechanisms, in the United States, based on socially accepted norms of a time and place. For example, the forced migration of native populations, slavery, Jim Crow, and women's voting rights were all seen (in their time) as socially acceptable by those in power to employ and enforce the law.

Common Law and Subjective Application

Several influences assisted in the early development of justice systems in the United States. As will be further expanded later in this text, the United States' legal systems were initially developed, structurally and conceptually, based on models from Great Britain and highly influenced by the concepts of *common law* and civil and criminal procedures (discussed later). Common law is a system that came to be in the Middle Ages of Europe and focuses on *case law* and *precedent*, which means that judges and juries focus the standards of their decisions on previously resolved legal examples. In other words, if the court decided to wage a specific penalty for specific behavior in the past, that same penalty should be applied to future cases. This system could theoretically ensure fairness, but that does not always occur. Due to the historical carryover, the common law system can be particularly problematic in resolving social problems as social mood evolves (Milsom, 1981). Additionally, when the metric for controlling social behavior is connected to the specific past perspectives of appropriateness derived from the opinions of those in power, the opportunity for disproportionate and differential experiences is systemic.

Dominant Cultural Influences of the Time

Another critical example to note is the influence of the Puritans. Some legal scholars call this the "Puritan Revolution" in English law (Black, 1984). Specifically, this movement led to an infusion of religion and law and provided an excellent example of developing a system reliant on common law. Using judicial precedent rather than statutes can be problematic because the interpretation of the law and its applications to humans is often inherently flawed and, at a minimum, changes over time. For example, historically, the United States' legal systems were dominated by individuals who held views of differential worthiness, human fallibility, and a strong belief in *predestination*. In the dominant Puritan culture of early New England, a core construct of early American thought was that people's lives, behaviors, and interactions were all predetermined and controlled through the sovereignty of a higher power (Rutman & Rutman, 1994). As translated to the legal systems that could be interpreted to suggest the general social mood, people interfacing with the legal system were there because they *deserved* to be, if for no other reason than their nature. In this culture, crime was equated to sin, and the sinner was reviled and worthy of severe punishment.

This origin story is an important one for several reasons. The first is associated with the need to recognize the subjective nature of applying the U.S. justice system. Social mood, public perception, and the norms of a time and place all play a role in how justice is defined and distributed. Secondly, the system's goals may have shifted over time, but the residual impact from past interpretations lingers in our courts today. As we move forward, it is of incredible importance that, as a culture, we assess the ethical application of our legal systems and the intended objectives imparted in these spaces.

Criminal Justice: Punishment or Rehabilitation

An important question is whether the criminal justice system's overarching goal is to punish or rehabilitate. The answer to that question depends on who responds and the time frame under consideration. In a broad sense, the current criminal justice system contains various punishments in the form of fines, corporate punishment, or custodial sentences intended to encourage and enforce societal behavior norms (Sanders et al., 2010). Historically, the criminal justice system featured four purposes: (a) retribution, which is intended as punishment for past crimes by limiting the freedoms of the offender; (b) incapacitation, which is intended to remove offenders from society so that they cannot engage in criminal activity; (c) deterrence; which is linked to the previous two purposes and is intended to reduce the likelihood that the offender will engage in additional criminal acts; and (d) rehabilitation, which is intended to provide the offender with additional psychological and occupational skills to reduce the likelihood of recidivism (Reiman & Leighton, 2015).

For most of American history, rehabilitation has been an essential component of the criminal justice system. However, many factors emerged in the early 1970s that forced a move away from rehabilitation and ushered in a new era that was "tough on crime" (Lynch, 2002). The 1960s had been a tumultuous decade for the United States, with war, increased substance abuse, and civil rights challenging Americanism's wholesome image. The zeitgeist quickly changed, and public policy shortly after that reflected those central societal problems resulting from drug use and a lenient criminal justice system that upended the country's moral code experienced in the 1950s (Lynch, 2002).

The convergence of factors that had facilitated a shift toward a tough-on-crime stance was cemented in the early 1970s (Martinson, 1974). Specifically, Martinson concluded that rehabilitation programs did not affect recidivism (Martinson, 1974). Also, federal and state budget shortfalls further exacerbated the findings of this study. Together, the study findings, *get-tough-on-crime* approach, and fiscal realities supported a new narrative that would guide criminal justice activities for the next four decades, becoming known as the nothing works doctrine (Andrews & Bonta, 2010). In this approach, punishment is the primary function of the criminal justice system. It is reflected in the evolution of laws that have led to the most extensive incarceration system in the world. Travis et al. (2014) noted that in 1972, the U.S. incarceration rate was 161 per 100,000 and had quintupled in growth to 707 per 100,000 by 2012.

Simultaneously, as the new get-tough-on-crime approach took hold in the criminal justice system's custodial aspects, the noncustodial aspects also moved away from rehabilitation. They were replaced with an increased focus on punishment (Phelps, 2013). The emphasis on punishment is evident in the evolving roles of corrections counselors, whose work was once intended to facilitate the development of occupational, social support, and psychological development and came to feature a focus on drug testing, probation fees, and electronic monitoring (Taxman et al., 2010). In the past 5 years, serious consideration of the impacts of the tough-on-crime stance has emerged for custodial and noncustodial components of the criminal justice system. Whether this will usher in a new series of approaches to criminal behavior remains unknown. What is becoming clear is that abandoning rehabilitative aspects of the system did not advance justice and that individual-centered approaches to crime prevention that are complemented by community-based approaches such as work programs, education, and psychotherapy do aid in community reintegration, reduce recidivism, and hold the promise for restorative justice (Andrews & Bonta, 2010).

Current Challenges in Forensic Social Work

Like any field of social work, forensic social work has evolving challenges that address the micro, mezzo, and macro levels. These will be covered throughout the text, and several are highlighted below. Figure 1.1 presents current challenges to social workers in forensic practice.

Social work, as a profession, is guided by a set of values and a code of ethics. Among these, for example, is acknowledging all people's dignity, worth, and value (National Association of Social Workers [NASW], 2017). This is an easy concept in theory or conversation, but it can become more difficult to practice when applied to work with people who may have hurt others. To add to the complexity of this, often, forensic social workers are challenged with not only providing services to people who may have behavioral histories that are in contrast to their belief system(s), morality, and, more broadly, the values of the profession but also to do so despite our own biases or reactions to these populations. In short, it is often an emotionally challenging scenario to manage.

In 2013, the American Academy of Social Work and Social Welfare began to focus the nation's scientific and practical energy on meeting society's most significant social problems, culminating in the 12 grand challenges for social work (Uehara et al., 2013). The challenges were designed to represent areas amenable to measurable change within 10 years and fall into three broad categories: individual and family well-being, stronger social fabric, and just society (Barth et al., 2014). Under a just society, the domain lays the grand challenge to Promote Smart Decarceration.

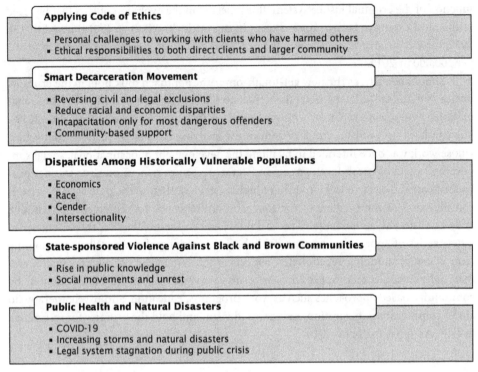

Applying Code of Ethics
- Personal challenges to working with clients who have harmed others
- Ethical responsibilities to both direct clients and larger community

Smart Decarceration Movement
- Reversing civil and legal exclusions
- Reduce racial and economic disparities
- Incapacitation only for most dangerous offenders
- Community-based support

Disparities Among Historically Vulnerable Populations
- Economics
- Race
- Gender
- Intersectionality

State-sponsored Violence Against Black and Brown Communities
- Rise in public knowledge
- Social movements and unrest

Public Health and Natural Disasters
- COVID-19
- Increasing storms and natural disasters
- Legal system stagnation during public crisis

FIGURE 1.1 Current Challenges in Forensic Social Work

At the heart of the smart decarceration grand challenge is recognizing that mass incarceration coupled with failed rehabilitation has resulted in enormous economic and human costs (Pettus-Davis & Epperson, 2015). The challenge is to develop a proactive, comprehensive, evidence-based strategy to reduce the number of people imprisoned while embracing a practical and just public safety approach ("Promote Smart Decarceration," n.d.). The stated societal goal of the smart decarceration grand challenge is to reduce the prison population by 1 million people in the next decade ("Promote Smart Decarceration," n.d.). Additional vital outcomes include redressing racial, economic, and behavioral health disparities among incarcerated women while maximizing public safety and community well-being.

This grand challenge includes critical strategies for achieving these outcomes (Pettus-Davis & Epperson, 2015). The first strategy focuses on reversing civic and legal exclusions for offenders. The second strategy focuses on reducing racial and economic disparities in the criminal justice system. The third strategy focuses on incapacitation for only the most dangerous offenders. The fourth and final strategy focuses on community-based support resource reallocations (Pettus-Davis & Epperson, 2015).

Throughout this *Handbook*, many chapters will detail specific challenges facing historically marginalized populations during their intersection with legal systems. From issues of economics and income inequality to disparities based on gender, race, age, or other identities, social workers often must address the complexity of how marginalized people interact with legal systems. Social workers have been working to alleviate the marginalization of distinct populations since the profession's inception. In forensic social work, this is particularly important due to the stakes involved. When people encounter legal systems or events that could lead to their interaction with these systems, the implications of the interactions they face could be severe and lifelong.

One of the most critical challenges facing forensic social work at this time is the impact of state-sponsored violence against Black and Brown communities. With advances in modern communication technology, the world has seen first-hand what many from these communities already knew; their experience and interaction with state agencies was far different from those who lived in predominantly White spaces. Social workers have an ethical obligation to be on the frontline of advocating for change in this space and utilizing strategies that empower Black and Brown individuals, families, and communities during their interactions with state and federal systems.

In addition to the many challenges social workers face with significant historical ties, the COVID-19 pandemic brought to bear the importance of understanding how social work practice, and in this case forensic social work, can be complicated by public health and natural disasters. These phenomena complicate social work with people in carceral spaces for multiple reasons—not the least of which is the inability of many incarcerated people to come and go freely or isolate themselves for public health safety reasons. In addition, these events can initiate chain reactions that slow and even completely stall legal proceedings and the process many people depend on for safety and justice.

The specific challenges listed above will be difficult to solve, and many will continue to linger for years. Some of these have been with us since the profession's origin, and others have more recently brought to light critical systemic weaknesses that must be addressed in policy and practice. While the challenges forensic social workers face are often complicated and significant, the impact forensic social workers make on our communities in the face of these challenges is essential. Throughout this text, many problems will be highlighted as these are explored, to remember that intersectionality often is present in these spaces. For example, not only must a person or jurisdiction deal with the complications of a global pandemic, but also they may be doing so while trying to resolve issues of racial tension and address disparities in the legal process.

How to Use This *Handbook*
Purpose

Regardless of the field of practice, social workers aid marginalized and oppressed populations in solving individual, family, group, and community problems that cut across pressing social issues, including direct work with people in jails or prisons, noncustodial work in state or local corrections systems, or providing primary health or mental health care through community-based social service agencies that serve offenders or their families (Maschi & Killiam, 2011). Additionally, social workers may be called upon to participate in criminal or civil court proceedings involving offenders or their families. At some point in their careers, most social workers will engage in forensic social work directly or indirectly. They must develop a framework and essential skills to engage in professional practice (Barker & Branson, 2014). The authors believe that forensic social work is not a boutique topic; therefore, it represents a core aspect of professional social work practice that requires specialized knowledge and skills regardless of the social workers' chosen field of practice.

Who Should Use the *Handbook*

A number of key groups can benefit from this *Handbook*, including:

- forensic social work students who are emerged in learning about forensics and connections between various fields of practice within it,
- forensic social workers who desire to enhance their performance through knowledge acquisition and application of tools for improving performance,
- forensic social workers who seek to better understand a field of practice outside of their own,
- administrators who supervise forensic social workers, and
- interprofessional practice colleagues interested in gaining insight into social work within forensic systems.

Organization of the *Handbook*

The *Handbook of Forensic Social Work Practice* is organized into six sections. Below are the section descriptions and the corresponding chapters for that section.

Section I: Introduction—The chapter authors in this section present the fundamentals of the *Handbook of Social Work Practice*. Each of these section chapters provides key concept overviews, discusses current challenges, and addresses future directions for social work.

1. Introduction to Forensic Social Work
2. Introduction to the U.S. Court System
3. Introduction to the Development of Social Policy
4. Ethics in Forensic Social Work

Section II: Vulnerable Populations—The chapter authors in this section seek to highlight and emphasize specific structural barriers and injustices experienced by the highlighted population across forensic settings. Chapter authors offer a broad scope of social workers' challenges and associated roles in engaging with these groups in practice settings.

5. Women in Forensic Settings
6. Older Adults in Forensic Settings
7. Sexual Orientation in Forensic Settings
8. Transgender and Gender Nonconforming People in Forensic Social Work Practice
9. Addressing Racial and Ethnic Disparities: Ethical and Legal Frameworks to Guide Forensic Social Work Practice
10. Mental Health in Forensic Settings

Section III: Criminology Theories—The chapter authors in this section explore criminological theory by providing a comprehensive historical overview of the theory in addition to debating the intellectual sources, knowledge, evidence base, value, and impact of each theory. Chapter authors share how the theory covered has historically and currently informs criminology and/or the criminal justice system and the practical application of these theories.

11. History of Criminal Justice Theory
12. Trauma-Informed Theory in Criminal Justice

Section IV: Forensic Policy—The chapter authors in this section explore criminal justice policy. This section provides a comprehensive historical overview of forensic policies in the United States, with a debate about each policy's knowledge and evidence base, value, and impact. Chapter authors discuss how policies influence current social work practice.

13. Major Policies Impacting Child Welfare
14. Mass Incarceration and For-Profit Prisons
15. Immigration Policy
16. Drug Policy
17. Capital Punishment
18. Mental Health Policies
19. Juvenile Justice Policy
20. Civil Commitment Policies
21. Intimate Partner Violence Policies

Section V: Fields of Practice—The chapter authors in this section explore current fields of practice in forensic social work. These chapters are intended to provide an introduction and overview of the area of practice and a series of critical reviews of the existing literature, each focusing on distinct populations. Chapter authors provide an overview of (1) the theoretical foundations and empirical bases for treatment programs; (2) populations or subgroups for which an evidence base has emerged, including discussion of settings (e.g., secure corrections, community services, and mental health systems) and gender issues; and (3) evaluation research methodologies that have been utilized. Finally, the chapter authors provide examples of the role of social workers (highlighting knowledge, skills, and ethical dilemmas) in this area, as well as a case study.

22. Reentry Challenges, Collateral Consequences, and Advocacy for Returning Community Members
23. Child Welfare
24. Domestic and Relational Violence
25. Juvenile Justice
26. Drug Court

Each chapter includes an abstract and keywords to guide knowledge acquisition. The practical applications are intended to reflect a social worker's knowledge, skills, and tasks within a given field of practice that integrates a forensic social work perspective. For example, the knowledge and skills required for a child welfare worker testifying in court differ from the specific practice knowledge and skills required of a community-based rehabilitation social worker focused on developing offender occupational and reintegration skills. Professional and ethical dilemmas are also presented to assist the social worker in decision-making between at least two possible moral imperatives.

References

Andrews, D. A., & Bonta, J. (2010). Rehabilitating criminal justice policy and practice. *Psychology, Public Policy, and Law*, 16(1), 39.

Barker, R. L., & Branson, D. M. (2014). *Forensic social work: Legal aspects of professional practice*. Routledge.

Barth, R. P., Gilmore, G. C., Flynn, M. S., Fraser, M. W., & Brekke, J. S. (2014). The American Academy of Social Work and Social Welfare: History and grand challenges. *Research on Social Work Practice*, 24(4), 495–500.

Black, B. (1984). Aspects of puritan jurisprudence: Comment on the puritan revolution and English law. *Valparaiso University Law Review*, 18(3), 651–664.

Friedman, L. M. (1993). *Crime and punishment in American history*. Basic Books.

Lynch, M. (2002). The culture of control: Crime and social order in contemporary society. *PoLAR: Political and Legal Anthropology Review*, 25(2), 109–112.

Martinson, R. (1974). What works? Questions and answers about prison reform. *Public Interest*, 35, 22.

Maschi, T., & Killian, M. L. (2011). The evolution of forensic social work in the United States: Implications for 21st-century practice. *Journal of Forensic Social Work*, 1(1), 8–36.

Milsom, S. F. C. (1981). *Historical foundations of the common law*. Butterworth-Heinemann.

National Association of Social Workers (NASW). (2017). *Code of ethics*. NASW Distribution Center.

National Organization of Forensic Social Work (NOFSW). (n.d.). *Forensic social work*. https://nofsw.org/?page_id=10

Pettus-Davis, C., & Epperson, M. W. (2015). *From mass incarceration to smart decarceration* (Grand Challenges for Social Work Initiative Working Paper No. 4). American Academy of Social Work and Social Welfare.

Phelps, M. S. (2013). The paradox of probation: Community supervision in the age of mass incarceration. *Law & Policy*, 35(1–2), 51–80.

Promote Smart Decarceration. (n.d.). *Policy recommendations for meeting the grand challenge to promote smart decarceration*. https://csd.wustl.edu/Publications/Documents/PB9.pdf

Reiman, J., & Leighton, P. (2015). *Rich get richer and the poor get prison: Ideology, class, and criminal justice*. Routledge.

Rutman, D. B., & Rutman, A. H. (1994). *Small worlds, large questions: Explorations in early American social history, 1600–1850*. University Press of Virginia, Charlottesville.

Sanders, A., Young, R., & Burton, M. (2010). *Criminal justice*. Oxford University Press.

Taxman, F. S., Henderson, C., & Lerch, J. (2010). The socio-political context of reforms in probation agencies: Impact on adoption of evidence-based practices. In F. McNeill, P. Raynor, & C. Trotter (Eds.), *Offender supervision: New directions in theory, research, and practice* (pp. 336–378). Routledge.

Travis, J., Western, B., & Redburn, F. S. (2014). *The growth of incarceration in the United States: Exploring causes and consequences*. The National Academies Press.

Uehara, E., Flynn, M., Fong, R., Brekke, J., Barth, R. P., Coulton, C., . . . Walters, K. (2013). Grand challenges for social work. *Journal of the Society for Social Work and Research, 4*(3), 165–170.

2

Introduction to the U.S. Court System

Steven W. Pharris and Angela B. Pharris

Overviewing the U.S. Court System

The courts have a fundamental and vital role as one of the three distinct branches of the U.S. government. Courts are essential for upholding the rules of law that govern people and organizations fairly, and they monitor the government to ensure it follows constitutional and other regulations and serves to protect individual rights. In many ways, courts operate on principles that have been established for decades, even centuries. However, courts are also socially constructed, shaped, and changed by history, culture, and norms, making them both a fixed and yet remarkably fluid institution. Before examining the courts, it is essential to understand three distinct constitutional rules that guide the courts. Courts are part of the balance of government power and are established to oversee equal protection of citizens by the government, outlined in the Fifth and 14th Amendments of the U.S. Constitution. Next, courts must uphold the constitutional requirement of due process outlined in the Fifth Amendment. Finally, courts are governed by their jurisdiction and common law and are assigned the task to ensure that the individuals or groups that come to the court have standing or a right to bring cases before the court.

The framers of the Constitution and the government recognized an inherent tension between individual rights and freedoms and the state's interest. No individual or group of people should be arbitrarily held to government authority. Additionally, no person is above the law. To remedy this dilemma, the courts are governed by equal protection laws, which means that a government body may not deny people equal protection under the law. Equal protection does not mean that everyone will be treated the same. Instead, the court is obligated to treat people the same if they have similar circumstances. The process of classifying the conditions that fit equal protection is not always organized or straightforward, nor do

Steven W. Pharris and Angela B. Pharris, *Introduction to the U.S. Court System* In: *Handbook of Forensic Social Work*. Edited by: David Axlyn McLeod, Anthony P. Natale, and Kristin W. Mapson, Oxford University Press. © Oxford University Press 2024. DOI: 10.1093/oso/9780197694732.003.0002 the Constitution and law include all groups of people for equal protection (i.e., rights for certain gender identities or sexual orientations), so the court may make a decision that is later appealed in higher courts. When a law infringes on freedom, such as an individual right to free speech or the right to parent a biological child, there must also be evidence that the state has a compelling interest to infringe on that personal right. The equal protection clause requires the state to practice equal protection; therefore, the equal protection clause is central to civil rights protections.

The Fifth and 14th Amendments of the U.S. Constitution require that part of an individual's equal protection is due process. To properly understand the legal system, you must first understand what due process is and how legal proceedings operate under established rules and principles. Due process provides that no state shall deprive any person of life, liberty, or property without the law's due process. Due process is respect for an individual's legal rights, a balance of power, and protection of individuals from government harm. Due process is often thought of as a legal process to ensure fair procedures are used by the court and that judges can determine fairness, justice, and liberty. For example, many people are aware of the legal requirement of law enforcement to notify a suspect during a police interrogation of their Miranda warning, which advises them of the right to remain silent, the right to refuse to answer questions, and the right to legal representation during questioning.

The federal, tribal, state, and municipal courts all have a defined jurisdiction or official power or authority to make legal decisions and judgments. To have jurisdiction, a court must have authority over the subject matter of the case (subject matter jurisdiction), or it must be able to exercise control over the defendant or the property (personal jurisdiction) involved (American Bar Association [ABA], 2021). For example, the juvenile courts have subject matter jurisdiction over the delinquency charges of a person under 18 but cannot hear auto theft claims by an adult. The law sets the extent of the court's jurisdiction. The first step in all legal proceedings is to determine which level of the court has jurisdiction over the matters at hand.

The U.S. court system is intentionally adversarial. Lawyers are counselors and advocates for their clients and are assigned to be champions and advocate for their interest against the opposing counsel. While lawyers cannot act in an illegal or unethical way, they do not hold any obligation to consider all sides of the case or the complex and interchanging systems in which the client exists in the way social workers trained in an ecosystems perspective are. In court, lawyers' function is to win the case and minimize personal freedom or property loss. For lawyers, their assignment is to assess the law on behalf of the client, not to think about and act on behalf of others or society. Lawyers are willing to compromise but should only do so when it is in the client's best interest. The courts' adversarial role is a unique and very different from the training, values, and ethics of a social work professional.

This chapter highlights the courts' similarities and differences, explores how the courts determine jurisdiction, and provides an overview on how they apply equal protection under the law. The court systems have a hierarchy that we use to structure the chapter. First, we examine the federal courts and the United States' highest court, the Supreme Court, and their responsibilities. Second, we discuss the unique and essential characteristics and jurisdiction of tribal courts. Next, we will review the state courts, both civil and criminal, and briefly examine some state courts' challenges. Finally, we explore the lower courts, which are local and municipal. The concepts presented in this chapter are part of legal training for lawyers and law enforcement and are part of their decision-making process. Forensic social workers should be familiar with the concepts in this chapter to practice effectively in the multidisciplinary setting.

Federal Courts and Supreme Court of the United States

The United States' highest courts are the federal courts, with the U.S. Supreme Court the highest. Figure 2.1 illustrates the U.S. court structure. The federal court system has three distinct levels. The U.S. district courts have nationwide jurisdiction over certain types of criminal and civil cases. There are 94 federal judicial districts, including one in each state, the District of Columbia, Puerto Rico, and the U.S. territories (Virgin Islands, Guam, Northern Mariana Islands). The federal circuit court is the next level of court and is divided into 13 circuits whose primary assignment is to hear appeals from the federal district courts. These 13 appellate courts sit below the U.S. Supreme Court, the United States' highest court and final appeal court. Federal judges and Supreme Court justices are all appointed by the U.S. president and confirmed by the U.S. Senate. Once selected, the justice or judge may hold that appointed position until they elect to retire or resign from the post. Figure 2.2 illustrates the geographic boundaries of U.S. federal courts.

Federal courts are considered courts of limited jurisdiction, meaning they only hear and decide cases that dissolve federal disputes or claims that involve a violation of the U.S. Constitution. The federal courts hear cases involving violations of federal laws, lawsuits between states, lawsuits involving parties from two different states, or suits filed against the U.S. government. The federal courts will also hear claims against foreign diplomats and disputes involving treaties and disputes from foreign governments. At times, there can be some overlap between state and federal courts, but most often, cases involving a violation of a state law remain in the state court.

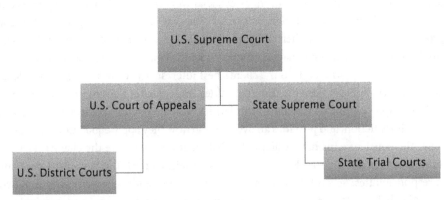

FIGURE 2.1 The U.S. Court Structure

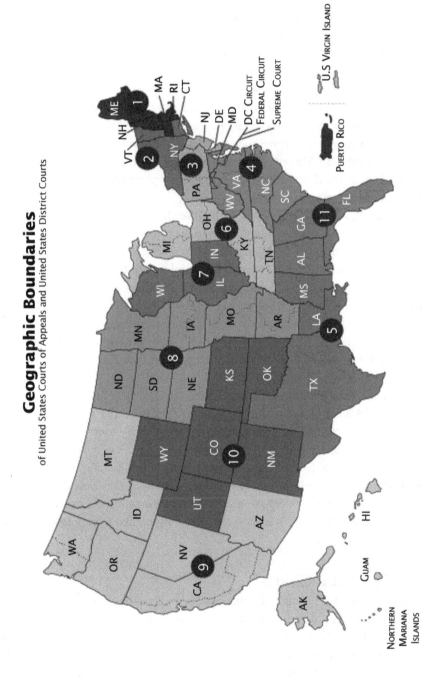

Geographic Boundaries
of United States Courts of Appeals and United States District Courts

FIGURE 2.2 Geographical Boundaries of the Federal Courts Retrieved from uscourts.gov/about-federal-courts/federal-courts-public/court-website-links

Despite the federal courts' narrow jurisdiction, they still hear a variety of civil and criminal cases. Examples of cases in the federal civil courts involve taxes or a contract dispute, such as a hospital filing a claim against Medicare or Medicaid for reimbursement costs. The federal district courts also hear criminal cases. Criminal allegations are more likely to be brought to the federal courts if the alleged crime occurred in two different states or territories or if a federal agent (like the Drug Enforcement Agency) was involved in the arrest. Drug offenses can be both a state and federal crime (see Title 21 U.S.C. Controlled Substance Act). Cases involving drug offenses are more likely tried in federal courts if they involve an extensive investigation and raid for drug sales or the possession of larger quantities of illegal substances intended for distribution. Likewise, certain weapons and firearms charges such as the unlawful sale of weapons, possession of stolen firearms or explosives, or the use of a gun or weapons in a school zone are likely to be heard in federal district courts (U.S. Attorney's Office, n.d.). The federal courts also hear cases involving *white-collar crimes* such as embezzlement, fraud, or tax evasion. Federal laws typically have stricter and harsher sentencing than state courts.

One unique aspect of federal courts is that they hear cases involving hate crimes. Hate crimes are one of the federal courts' highest priorities and are investigated by the Federal Bureau of Investigations (FBI). In part, hate crimes are heard in the federal courts because of local and state law enforcement's historical failure to act on cases involving crimes motivated by hate. Hate crimes are any willful bodily injury, threat, or conspiracy to harm any person motivated in whole or in part by the offenders' bias against an actual or perceived race, national origin, color, relation, gender, gender identity, sexual orientation, or disability (18 U.S. Code § 249 Hate Crimes Act). The law also includes similar threats against a religious property (mosque, synagogue, or church) or actions that block someone's access to exercise their religious beliefs. When a crime is committed and identified as a hate crime, the FBI becomes the lead investigative agency (FBI, n.d.). Hate crime laws allow the federal courts to use enhanced sentencing and stricter penalties, but the crime must be proven beyond a reasonable doubt, which is the court's highest scrutiny level. Most states also have passed laws for certain hate crimes, but most do not use the same criteria as the federal law and have a lot of variation. Additionally, states may have difficulty providing the expertise to build a legal case to identify the crime as a hate crime and are at risk of policing bias in determining if a crime was motivated by hate. Even if a state does not have specific hate crime laws, the federal laws make it possible to report the crime to the FBI.

The U.S. Supreme Court

The U.S. Supreme Court is the highest in the judicial system. The Supreme Court can decide appeals of all cases brought in federal court or cases brought in state court that focus on issues of federal law (U.S. Department of Justice, District of Utah, n.d.). Once the circuit court or state supreme court rules on a case, either party may appeal the decision to the Supreme Court. However, the Supreme Court is not required to hear the appeal, and less than 1% of appeals sent to the highest court are heard by the justices (U.S. Courts, n.d.).

The Supreme Court's unique responsibility is the power of judicial rule to void acts of Congress that conflict with the Constitution. As a result, there are certain circumstances where the court has the unique status of also being the court of original jurisdiction. Article II of the Constitution declares that the Supreme Court has original jurisdiction for suits between two states or a claim between a state and a foreign government. The Supreme Court often settles disputes with a national outcome; examples include marriage equality rights, appeals to state voter registration laws, and cases that challenge gender inequality. In all, the Supreme Court hears about 80 cases a year. Cases are determined by the "rule of four," in which four of the nine justices must decide that the case has value and merit. A legal order is issued to the lower court to send the records of the case for review, called a *writ of certiorari* (Judicial Learning Center, n.d.). In the case of *Marbury v. Madison*, the Supreme Court affirmed that the courts must uphold Article VI of the Constitution as the "supreme law of the land" and over time asserted the Supreme Court as an equal branch of the U.S. government and the chief interpreter of the Constitution (Nelson, 2018).

Tribal Courts

Native American and Alaska Native nations constitute one of the three types of sovereign governments within the U.S. justice system (O'Connor, 1997). According to the U.S. Census Bureau, an estimated 5.6 million people, or 1.5% of the U.S. population, are American Indian or Alaska Natives (U.S. Census Bureau, 2019). At this time, 575 recognized American Indian or Alaska Native tribal entities have a government-to-government relationship with the United States between two distinct and sovereign nations. As a recognized sovereign government, a tribe has the right to establish their own government, make and enforce laws, collect taxes, establish and determine citizenship, and license and regulate activities.

The Indian Reorganization Act of 1934 (25 U.S.C. 501 et seq.) was intended to stop the breakup of reservations and revitalize the economies and governmental institutions for tribes. The law encouraged tribal nations to enact laws and establish courts, so long as they mirrored the many elements of federal and state systems (Kickingbird, 2009). Unfortunately, by 1934 many tribes were not in a position to replicate the federal and state government's robust justice system, nor did they have the government's financial support. In 1953, Congress enacted Public Law 83-280 (67 Stat. 588) to grant certain criminal jurisdictions over American Indians residing on reservations. In 1991, the U.S. Civil Rights Commission found that despite the legal mandate of Congress to fund tribal courts, they have remained significantly underfunded since the laws were passed and the funds were authorized from Congress (U.S. Commission on Civil Rights, 1991). Congress affirmed that the government failed to live up to past trust obligations and had a legal responsibility to assist tribal governments in developing judicial systems. This led to the Indian Tribal Justice Act of 1993, which authorized $58 million annually for 5 years and a $50 million annual appropriation for ongoing funding. But the funding has never been allocated as directed by the law, and to date, only $5 million has been appropriated (Tribal Court Clearinghouse, n.d.). Future public policies may attempt to remedy the lack of funding for criminal justice systems. Data reveals that allocating funding to tribal criminal justice systems at the same rate as federal and state systems may significantly reduce crime (U.S. Commission on Civil Rights, 2018) while also upholding the sovereignty of the tribal nations.

Tribal courts operate similarly to federal and state courts in many ways but may also use the tribes' traditional dispute resolution processes in their court systems. Tribal courts use testimony, maintain records of proceedings, and use judges and juries to decide cases (Jones, 2000). Tribal courts use a variety of structures for sentencing that follow colonized systems but also include options for dispute resolution techniques such as peacemaking, the use of sentencing circles, and other methods of resolutions that have been influential in the nations for generations (Jones, 2000).

Tribal courts do have some significant limitations. Standing in tribal court is often limited to citizens of the tribe. Standing is a legal term used to describe whether a party bringing a lawsuit has the right to do so or if the case is in the correct court. State courts have the authority to act when any crime or violation of the law is committed within the state regardless of the accused's citizenship. This authority is not the same for tribal courts. In *Oliphant v. Suquamish,* the Supreme Court ruled that Indian tribes lack the inherent authority to regulate the criminal conduct of non-Indians (Jones, 2020); therefore, the tribe has no criminal jurisdiction over non-Indians committing crimes in Indian country. Thus, if a non-Indian commits a crime in Indian country, the case is transferred or handled in the federal district courts, which determine if they want to take up the case. This creates some significant and troublesome gaps in protecting victims of crime when the federal courts do not enforce or pursue criminal prosecution. Federal courts lack the resources to pursue charges when a crime does not meet the standard for felony criminal prosecution. Most notably, domestic violence charges are often classified as lower status offenses (misdemeanors) and federal courts are significantly less likely to take legal action in these cases (Mikkanen, 2010).

One clear exception to the jurisdiction of tribal courts is in the protection of children. The Indian Child Welfare Act (ICWA) is one of the most critical child welfare protections for the sovereignty of tribes and their right to make judicial determinations on behalf of their children and citizens. When court cases involve American Indian or Alaska Native children, tribal courts have the right to intervene in state court actions that are covered by the ICWA. This includes the right to make the determination of out-of-home placement such as foster care and the right for tribal courts to oversee proceedings for the termination of parental rights and in the judgment of legal adoption, even if only one parent is recognized as a citizen of the tribe and the other is not. Many advocates, policy experts, and legal scholars consider the ICWA to be the *gold standard* of law explaining the relationship between the tribes and the U.S. government because it protects tribes' and tribal courts' sovereignty in child and family court cases and beyond. While the implementation of the ICWA is not always consistent in child welfare and adoption practices, its affirmation of the importance of tribal sovereignty and their courts is essential. Table 2.1 provides an overview

TABLE 2.1 Jurisdiction Guidelines for Tribal Courts

Identity of the Offender	Identity of the Victim	Jurisdiction
Indian	Indian	If the offense is listed in the Major Crimes Act, as amended, (18 U.S.C. §1152), the tribal and federal government have jurisdiction; the states do not. If the offense is not listed in the Major Crimes Act, tribal jurisdiction is **exclusive.**
Indian	Non-Indian	If the offense is listed in the Major Crimes Act, the tribal and federal government have jurisdiction; the states do not. If the offense is not listed in the Major Crimes Act, under the General Crimes Act, the tribal and federal governments have jurisdiction; the states to not.
Non-Indian	Indian	Federal jurisdiction is **exclusive**; tribal and state governments do not have jurisdiction.
Non-Indian	Non-Indian	States have **exclusive** jurisdiction; tribal and federal governments do not have jurisdiction.

Source: U.S. Attorney's Manual and the U.S. Government Accountability Office analysis of relevant statutory provisions. See U.S. Government Accountability Office. (2011, February). *Indian country criminal justice: Departments of the Interior and Justice should strengthen coordination to support of tribal courts.* https://www.gao.gov/new.items/d11252/pdf

of jurisdiction guidelines that are used in tribal courts including offender and victim type and jurisdiction.

State Courts

The U.S. Constitution established an independent court system in every state with jurisdiction over civil and criminal cases. State trial courts handled over 83.5 million cases in 2018, down from the highest point of 106.1 million in 2008 (Court Statistics Project, 2020). State criminal courts make up about 20% of the cases, and a significant majority of those cases are for crimes considered to be misdemeanors by state law. Only 25% of cases heard in criminal courts are for felony crimes (Court Statistics Project, 2020). National data shows that overall, caseloads reported by state trial and criminal courts have been on a steady decline over the last decade. Civil court cases involve private rights and make up approximately 20% of the cases in state trial courts. Examples of civil court cases include contract disputes, small claims, probate, and estate claims. State trial courts also have jurisdiction for cases involving domestic relationships. Approximately 6% of state trial cases include divorce, custody, paternity, adoption, and other domestic issues such as civil protection orders. State courts also hear juvenile court delinquency and dependency caseloads, including abuse and neglect cases, which account for 1% of cases. The most considerable portion of state trial court caseloads is noncriminal traffic courts, which account for 53% of state trial court case activity (Court Statistics Project, 2020). Figure 2.3 illustrates the distribution of incoming criminal cases.

State civil and criminal courts use a system established to be adversarial. In this system, opposing attorneys are specifically charged with advancing the personal interests of

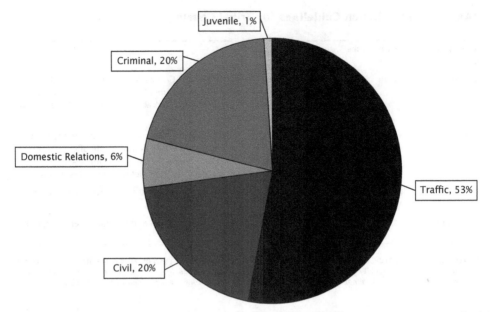

FIGURE 2.3 Distribution of Incoming Criminal Cases Source: Court Statistics Project. *State court caseload digest, 2018 data.* https://www.courtstatistics.org/__data/assets/pdf_file/0014/40820/2018-Digest.pdf

their clients. These adversarial systems' goals are to protect the citizen accused of the crime and protect the presumption of innocence.

State Criminal Courts

Criminal courts represent a robust system designed to respond to criminal law violations. Criminal courts hear cases that are considered offenses against the community and involve cases such as homicide or assault, property cases, drug cases, weapons cases, and other activities or behaviors defined as criminal by state laws and statutes. State criminal courts have jurisdiction to interpret the state's current laws and statutes in the context of alleged illegal activity. In criminal cases, only the state or government can initiate a charge against a person alleged to have committed a crime, typically through a lawyer representing the state, often called the district attorney, prosecuting attorney, or county attorney.

In a criminal case, the state prosecutor acts on behalf of the state to prove the defendant is guilty based on the evidence presented. The defendant, who is the person accused of the crime, has a defense attorney, whose assignment is to acquit the defendant by forcing the state to present compelling (strong) evidence. Therefore, in state criminal courts, the burden of proof is assigned to the state to present evidence that can override the presumption of innocence and prove guilt beyond a *reasonable doubt*, which is the expected standard in criminal trials.

State Civil Courts

State laws also allow individuals to pursue a legal claim against another person, business, or other entity. The government or state is not involved in bringing a charge or making a civil court claim, as jail time is not a civil case remedy. Civil cases involve conflict between people or institutions such as businesses and occur most often when some dispute cannot be solved between the individuals without court intervention. Civil claims may involve personal injury, property damage, contract disputes such as housing evictions, professional malpractice, or other small claims such as collecting bad debt.

In civil cases, the person who made a claim is called the plaintiff. The plaintiff has the burden of proving their case by demonstrating a preponderance of the evidence which is a very different standard from the burden of proof in a criminal case. A *preponderance of the evidence* is to find that one party has more substantial evidence than the other. This level of proof does not require the evidence presented to leave the judge or jury without any doubt.

State Civil and Criminal Court Phases

There are three distinct court phases: the pretrial phase, the trial phase, and the sentencing or decision process. Each phase of the court process has essential tasks assigned to protect constitutional rights. The first step in the court process, the pretrial hearing, occurs very soon after an arrest or a charge is made against an individual of a criminal act. Very few cases advance through the entire court process and steps for a trial. In a civil case, the complaint states the plaintiff's version of the facts. Most civil cases are settled with an agreement between parties even before the lawsuit is filed or are moved to an alternative dispute resolution process such as mediation (ABA, 2021).

The steps of a criminal trial are illustrated above in Figure 2.4. Criminal cases have a unique process for the pretrial phase. During the pretrial hearing, the defendant is informed of the charges against them and is provided access to legal representation. During this phase, the defendant will be asked to enter a plea (guilty/not guilty) as the case begins to move to the trial phase. During the pretrial hearing, the judge reviews the arrest reports, considers if the report meets the definition of probable cause for arrest, and determines if the defendant should be detained while awaiting a trial.

The court may determine that the defendant can remain in the community while awaiting trial. The defendant may be asked to provide bail or bond or be required to participate in some other form of pretrial monitoring. During this time, the defendant will encounter one of the unique features of the criminal court system, the use of plea bargaining. During the pretrial hearing, the defendant is informed of the potential maximum sentence or punishment that could occur if found guilty during a trial. The state's prosecuting attorney often presents the defendant with an alternative if they agree to enter a plea of guilty during a pretrial hearing. While no exact data is available, the Bureau of Justice Statistics estimates that between 90% and 95% of defendants accept the offer at this pretrial hearing and do not progress to trial (Devers, 2011). Often, defendants will be offered certain conditions during the state attorney plea bargain, such as a more lenient sentence or reducing the severity of charges in exchange for the guilty plea. This process saves the state from the burden and costs of trials that would otherwise cause a significant lag in our court system's expediency. Critics of plea bargaining argue that the process may be subject to constitutional error, permits sloppy and unfair policing, is

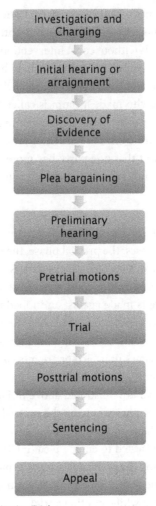

FIGURE 2.4 Steps in the Criminal Justice Trial

prone to disproportional outcomes by race, and is a primary contributor to prison and jail overcrowding (Bibas, 2012).

The next phase of the court process is the trial, a formal evaluation of evidence and legal claims. In some cases, this can be a long process that involves many events. Generally, the steps include selection of a jury, examination of the evidence, cross-examination, presentation of evidence by the defense, a rebuttal, final motions, and a closing argument. Although not required, most trials consist of juries of six to 12 persons selected from a jury pool. In most states, candidates for a jury are pooled from a voter registration list or the driver's license registry. The jury requirements vary from state to state and may vary for different types of criminal hearings. After jury selection, the trial begins. For trials without a jury, referred to as bench trials, the judge will decide the fact questions (evidence) and law questions. In criminal trials, the state makes its case and has the responsibility for the burden of proof, to prove beyond a reasonable doubt the defendant is guilty. Generally, there must be a *preponderance of the evidence* (greater weight of evidence), but the burden of proof is far more significant in criminal trials than in civil trials. At the end of the trial, after deliberation from the jury, a verdict of "guilty" or "not guilty" will be delivered; in civil cases the jury will find for the plaintiff or defendant. After the ruling, the trial is concluded, and the case moves to the final stage of sentencing.

The Lower Courts

The lower courts make up the most extensive system of courts in the United States. There is considerable variation in the organization and structure of lower courts, which may also be called municipal courts, district courts, superior courts, or courts of limited jurisdiction. In many states, the lower courts of the state criminal courts and the courts for local municipal governments are organized under one umbrella. For this chapter, we will use the term "municipal courts" to reference any local court with limited jurisdiction and authority to hear and adjudicate state misdemeanor offenses and municipal codes. Municipal codes can include local city ordinances, traffic laws, property evictions, noise violations, and other charges that do not meet the standard for jurisdiction for state criminal courts. Municipal courts, therefore, have limited jurisdiction, and the most serious allegations of illegal activity that can be heard in municipal courts are crimes that are punishable by 1 year or less. Typically, municipal courts issue punishments that can range from a few days or months of punishment by jail, but they often levy fines and costs between $500 and $2,500 (Natapoff, 2020).

Because municipal courts do not have a standard reporting mechanism to collect data or operate under any central authority type, it is extremely difficult to determine municipal courts' full impact. One of the most comprehensive reports on the municipal courts' collective impact collected data for over 7,500 municipal courts across 30 states and found that altogether, those courts processed over 3.5 million criminal cases in 1 year (Natapoff, 2020). From the data collected in the study, those municipal courts alone collected as much as $3.1 billion in revenues from hearing outcomes. The income reported does not include estimates related to traffic courts, which would significantly increase the collection of fines (Natapoff, 2020). The municipal courts' fees fund the courts and other local government budget operations for many municipal governments, such as law enforcement and local detention centers.

The structure and organization of municipal courts vary by jurisdiction. Municipal courts may or may not be presided over by judges with law degrees, and they do not have consistent legal representation for many of the hearings. Judges may be appointed by the mayor or the elected official of the city government. The judges may work full time for the courts, but the presence of a defense attorney is rare (Natapoff, 2020). Municipal courts, in many ways, seem to be exempt from the separation of power established in the other state and federal systems. "The Supreme Court, government officials, and scholars alike too often dismiss these courts as inferior and their cases as minor, and fail to scrutinize their operations or protect their defendants who pass through them" (Natapoff, 2020, p. 973).

The lower courts, and specifically municipal government courts, have received significant criticism in recent years. There is growing evidence to suggest that municipal courts may be one of the worst civil rights offenders of the court system as municipalities have changed their function from public safety to that of a revenue mechanism to fund local government and law enforcement (National Association of Criminal Defense Lawyers [NACDL], 2016). An examination of the summary courts, a type of municipal court in South Carolina, conducted by the NACDL and the American Civil Liberties Union found that the courts had several constitutional violations, including the consistent absence of lawyers in criminal proceedings and police frequently acting as the prosecutor. The report also noted that the courts lacked adequate legal counsel before a trial and that the accused are often not informed of their right to have a lawyer. They observed that many defendants were offered a choice to pay a fine or spend time in jail for the accused crime. If the judge determined that the charged could not pay the fine, the judge would often decide to force the defendant to accept a jail sentence (NACDL, 2016).

Another criticism of municipal courts is their shift from public safety to a municipal government funding mechanism. After the death of Michael Brown in 2014, the Civil Rights Division of the U.S. Department of Justice released a study finding that the law enforcement practices in Ferguson, MO, are consciously revenue driven and discriminate against African Americans (U.S. Department of Justice Civil Rights Division, 2015). The report explicitly cites the municipal government court for using judicial authority to compel payments to produce revenue for the city's finances. The court did not act as the neutral arbiter of the law or function as a check on Ferguson police conduct. The lack of oversight and accountability coupled with the motivation to generate revenue has left municipal courts as significant barriers to justice and at risk of sustaining and perpetuating racism, implementing dehumanizing practices, and criminalizing poverty (Natapoff, 2020). Table 2.2 illustrates the U.S. court system by its structure, cases heard, and how its judges are chosen.

Social Work and the Courts

The role of social workers in courts has evolved tremendously in recent years. Once, the social work profession lacked expertise and scientific rigor in the courts' eyes. With influence from social work organizations such as the National Association of Social Workers (NASW) and the profession's growth, social workers are now often considered expert witnesses, have established client–social worker privileged communication, and have a significant role in helping courts reach conclusions of justice. The social work profession has even made a significant impact on state and federal laws via legal advocacy strategies that have influenced cases concerning same-sex marriage, health care, adoption, and other issues

TABLE 2.2 The U.S. Court System

	Court Structure	Types of Cases	Judicial
The Federal Courts	Article III of the Constitution creates the Supreme Court and gives Congress the right to establish a federal court system. The Constitution states that federal judges must be nominated by the president and confirmed by the Senate. There are 13 U.S. courts of appeals and 94 U.S. district and trial courts.	• Cases that deal with the constitutionality of the law • Cases involving U.S. treaties • Cases involving U.S. ambassadors • Disputes between two or more states • Criminal and civil cases for federal laws	Federal judges and Supreme Court Justices hold those positions for life after appointment.
The State Courts	State courts hear cases involving state laws. State supreme court decisions may be appealed to the U.S. Supreme Court. State courts have specific courts for different legal matters (e.g., probate court, criminal court, juvenile court).	• Criminal cases for state laws • Contract disputes • Personal injury • Marriage, divorces, adoption, and other family law issues • Probate (wills and estates)	State court judges can be selected in many ways, all according to the state law. This includes election, voting, appointment for life, and appointment for a term.
The Lower Courts (Municipal Courts)	The lower courts have limited jurisdiction over cases and can only hear cases that are specific to a community, city, county, or district code or law.	• Traffic citations • Violations of city ordinances • Some misdemeanor cases that involve no more than 1 year minimum, if found guilty • Domestic violence order of protection	There is significant variation in how the lower courts establish a judge. They may be voted or appointed. The lower courts have significant variation in the training requirements for judges.

through filings of an *amicus curiae*, or a person not party to a suit but having a strong interest in the subject matter.[1]

Testifying as a Professional Witness

Social workers are often called upon to testify or provide case records related to a client in judicial proceedings. Written communication such as case notes, clinical notes, assessments, and other documents are frequently requested by lawyers or even subpoenaed by the courts. In *Martha S. v. State of Alaska*, the courts expanded social workers' role as expert professional witnesses by allowing testimony of second-hand knowledge gathered during clinical practice, increasing the likelihood of social work practice records being requested by the courts. The NASW Code of Ethics (2017) in standards section 1.7 shows that social workers

1. For a detailed list of amicus briefs visit the NASW Legal Defense Fund Database at https://www.socialworkers.org/About/Legal/Legal-Briefs/About-the-Amicus-Brief-Database.

must obtain valid consent from the client before disclosing any confidential information. The Supreme Court case *Jaffee v. Redmond* formally recognized the importance of confidentiality in social worker–client relationships. The extension of privileged communication to social workers provided clients with the protection that social workers cannot be required to testify against them without their consent. Even with a subpoena, social workers in court settings are required to pursue the standards for consent and confidentiality. Courts have recognized that privileged communication protects information in the therapeutic relationship between professionals and their clients. Social work professionals should work with their client and their legal representation to determine what information to release.

Social workers are often called upon to serve as expert witnesses in court proceedings—the legal team employs the social worker/expert witness to provide professional expertise about the case, but they do not have a direct professional practice relationship with the defendant or plaintiff. The courts recognize experts as those who, through education or experience, have the skills and knowledge to form an opinion to assist in the trial. When a social worker is serving as an expert witness, they are not a witness to the facts or events but are there to help explain to the courts what the facts of the case mean, given their experience, skills, and knowledge of the subject matter (Bullis, 2013). It is important that any social work professional who has agreed to serve as an expert witness work closely with the legal team to prepare for the testimony and only give testimony to subject matter about which they have competence and expertise. There are many courses and continuing education opportunities designed to help social workers build their competency and skills during testimony. Social work professionals should only agree to act as expert witnesses when they have been carefully trained to perform the task.

Conclusion

This chapter examined the jurisdictions and other key features of federal, tribal, state, and lower courts. There are many similarities and yet many unique characteristics for each level of the court. As the social work profession's influence and involvement in the courts continue to increase, the legal system has found many areas outside of the courtroom for social workers to utilize their education, skills, and application of scientific rigor to restore communities, groups, and individuals. Specialty courts, such as drug courts, veterans' treatment courts, mental health courts, etc., rely on social workers' expertise to adjudicate offenses in a rehabilitative or restorative manner. The increased prevalence of social workers engaged and employed within the boundaries of the legal profession and courts is evidenced by the increase of social work schools providing courses in law, criminal justice, and child welfare—in some instances offering a dual degree in social work and law—making forensic social work a large field of interest for many.

References

American Bar Association (ABA). (2021). *How courts work.* https://www.americanbar.org/groups/public_education/resources/law_related_education_network/how_courts_work/

Bibas, S. (2012). Incompetent plea bargaining and extrajudicial reforms. *Harvard Law Review, 126*, 150.

Bullis, R. K. (2013). *The narrative edge: A guide for social work expert witness.* Council on Social Work Education.

Court Statistics Project. (2020). *State court caseload digest: 2018 data.* National Center for State Courts. https://www.courtstatistics.org/__data/assets/pdf_file/0014/40820/2018-Digest.pdf

Devers, L. (2011). Plea and charge bargaining. Bureau of Justice Statistics. *Research Summary, 1*, 1–6.

Federal Bureau of Investigations (FBI). (n.d.). *What we investigate: Hate crimes.* https://www.fbi.gov/investigate/civil-rights/hate-crimes

Jones, B. J. (2000). Role of Indian tribal courts in the justice system. US Department of Justice, Office of Justice Programs, Office for Victims of Crime.

Judicial Learning Center. (n.d.). *The U.S. Supreme Court.* https://judiciallearningcenter.org/the-us-supreme-court/

Kickingbird, K. (2009). Striving for the Independence of Native American Tribal Courts. *Human Rights, 36*, 16.

Mikkanen, A. Q. (2010). *Indian country criminal jurisdiction chart.* U.S. Attorney's Office, Western District of Oklahoma. https://www.justice.gov/sites/default/files/usao-wdok/legacy/2014/03/25/Indian%20Country%20Criminal%20Jurisdiction%20ChartColor2010.pdf

Natapoff, A. (2020). Criminal Municipal Courts. *Harvard Law Review, 134*, 964.

National Association of Criminal Defense Lawyers (NACDL). (2016). *Summary injustice: A look at constitutional deficiencies in South Carolina's summary courts.* http://www.nacdl.org/summaryinjustice

National Association of Social Workers (NASW). (2017). *Code of ethics.* NASW Press.

Nelson, W. E. (2018). *Marbury v. Madison: The origins and legacy of judicial review* (2nd ed., revised and expanded). University Press of Kansas.

O'Connor, S. D. (1997). Lessons from the third sovereign: Indian Tribal courts. *Tulsa Law Journal, 33*(1), 1.

Tribal Court Clearinghouse. (n.d.). *Federal laws: Chapter 38- Indian Tribal Justice Act.* https://www.tribal-institute.org/lists/fed_laws.htm

U.S. Attorney's Office. (n.d.). *Quick reference to federal firearm laws.* https://www.justice.gov/sites/default/files/usao-ut/legacy/2013/06/03/guncard.pdf

U.S. Census Bureau. (2019). *American Indian and Alaska Native alone or in combination with one or more other races* (Table B0210). American Community Survey. https://data.census.gov/cedsci/table?q=American%20Indian%20and%20Alaska%20Native&tid=ACSDT1Y2019.B02010&hidePreview=false

U.S. Commission on Civil Rights. (1991). *The Indian Civil Rights Act: A report to the United States Commission on Civil Rights.*

U.S. Commission on Civil Rights. (2018). *Broken promises: Continuing federal funding shortfall for Native Americans. Briefing before the United States Commission on Civil Rights.* https://www.usccr.gov/pubs/2018/12-20-Broken-Promises.pdf

U.S. Courts. (n.d.). *About the Supreme Court.* https://www.uscourts.gov/about-federal-courts/educational-resources/about-educational-outreach/activity-resources/aboutU.S. Department of Justice Civil Rights Division. (2015). *Investigation of the Ferguson police department.* https://www.justice.gov/sites/default/files/opa/press-releases/attachments/2015/03/04/ferguson_police_department_report.pdf

U.S. Department of Justice, District of Utah. (n.d.). *Introduction to the federal court system.* Offices of the United States Attorneys. https://www.justice.gov/usao/justice-101/federal-courts

3

Introduction to the Development of Social Policy

Angela B. Pharris and Anthony P. Natale

Public policy is a course of action adopted by governments at various levels in the form of laws, regulations, procedures, administrative actions, and practices. The welfare of people is the focus of social welfare policy, one subset of public policy. Social policies govern many broad dimensions, including food, education, income, labor, housing, health and mental health, and family (Karger & Stoesz, 2013). In addition to these overall dimensions, of particular interest to forensic social workers are policies that govern juvenile and criminal justice, child welfare, civil commitment, capital punishment, immigration, mental health, sexual offenses, and diversion. In the third section of this handbook, these domains are explored in more depth.

In this chapter, we provide foundational knowledge and key concepts to understand the vast array of social policies that impact forensic science workers. Vital terms are overviewed to achieve this aim. Next, we describe the policymaking process at distinct levels, including federal, state, county, and municipal. We then discuss the policymaking process at each stage: agenda setting, policy formation, adoption, implementation, and evaluation. This discussion is followed by a description of five classifications or types of social welfare policy: distributing and redistributing resources and goods, regulating behavior, meeting constituent expectations, and holding the function of symbolism. We conclude with a discussion of critical considerations for social workers in the development of social policy.

Key Social Policy Terms

In addition to public policy and social policy described above, there are several critical terms essential to understanding social policy development. Table 3.1 provides an overview of these key terms, definitions, and source locations.

Angela B. Pharris and Anthony P. Natale, *Introduction to the Development of Social Policy* In: *Handbook of Forensic Social Work.*
Edited by: David Axlyn McLeod, Anthony P. Natale, and Kristin W. Mapson, Oxford University Press. © Oxford University Press 2024.
DOI: 10.1093/oso/9780197694732.003.0003

TABLE 3.1 Definition of Key Terms and Source Locations

Key Terms	Definition	Source Locations
Bills	Proposed legislation under consideration	▪ Federal Bills: https://www.govtrack.us/ ▪ State Bills: https://www.congress.gov/state-legislature-websites
Laws	Legislation that has passed the legislature and is approved by the executive (override veto is the exception)	▪ U.S. Code (general and permanent laws): https://www.govinfo.gov/app/collection/uscode ▪ Statutes at Large (new laws): https://www.loc.gov/law/help/statutes-at-large/ ▪ County Codes (too many to list here): local websites or county courthouses ▪ Municipal Code: https://library.municode.com/
Executive Orders	Directives initiated by the executive that can create committees and organizations and manage operations	▪ Federal Orders, Federal Register: https://www.federalregister.gov/ ▪ State Orders, Law Library of Congress (state laws and regulations): https://www.loc.gov/law/
Judicial Decisions	Interpretation by a system of hierarchical courts of the constitutionality of legislative and executive actions	▪ U.S. Supreme Court Reports: https://www.loc.gov/law/help/us-reports.php ▪ State Supreme Courts (too many to list here): each maintains an online site ▪ District Courts: variable
Regulations	Issued by agencies, boards, and commissions to explain how agencies plan to carry out laws	▪ Federal Register: https://www.federalregister.gov/ ▪ Code of Federal Regulations: https://www.govinfo.gov/app/collection/cfr ▪ Law Library of Congress (state laws and regulations): https://www.loc.gov/law/

Policymaking Levels

Differentiating government levels in the policymaking process is essential to understanding how the policies are developed, function, and support, and intersect across levels. There are crucial distinctions in the scope and range of federal, state, and local laws, including counties, cities, townships, and villages.

Everyone in the United States must comply with federal laws. Examples of federal laws that impact social workers include anti-discrimination and civil rights laws that apply in various settings, including juvenile and criminal justice, child welfare, and aging services. States can enact policy and laws within their jurisdiction for the people who live or work in a particular state, commonwealth, or territory (American Samoa, Guam, the Northern Mariana Islands, Puerto Rico, or the U.S. Virgin Islands). States and territories too can provide additional anti-discrimination and civil rights laws. Local laws apply to those who live or work in particular counties, cities, municipalities, towns, townships, or villages. Examples of local laws include rent, zoning, and regional safety. Local laws may also consist of anti-discrimination and civil rights ordinances.

From Ideas to Laws

To understand social policy development, it is essential to review how ideas transform into social policies. In social work terms, laws are macro interventions designed to impact vulnerable people challenged by a large-scale social problem (e.g., poverty, abuse, discrimination). Federal and state governments move from ideas to laws in similar ways. Ideas come from various sources, including constituent groups, special interest groups, individual citizens, or elected officials (Karger & Stoesz, 2013). Next, the idea is transformed into a bill and introduced by a sponsor from either the House of Representatives or Senate (Nebraska is the exception given that it has a unicameral body). If a bill requires raising any revenue in the federal government, the bill must start in the House of Representatives. The House of Representatives in Congress is larger and proportional to the population and thought to represent the country more.

The next step is for the bill to go to a small committee of elected officials to research, discuss, and edit for changes. A vote to accept or reject the bill and its changes is made, or the bill is referred to a subcommittee for further research. If scheduled, the bill is then debated on the House or Senate floor, along with proposed changes and amendments, before a vote. If a majority favors the bill, it moves to the opposite chamber to repeat many of the same committee review processes, debates, and voting steps. Both the House of Representatives and the Senate must agree on the same version of the final bill, which requires a conference committee, where members of each house negotiate the final bill to get it passed in both chambers (Karger & Stoesz, 2013).

Once the House and Senate have passed a bill, it reaches the executive branch, the president, or, in the case of state policy, the governor's desk. There are four options available to the executive. The first is to approve and pass the bill by officially signing it into law. The second is to take *no action*, where the bill automatically becomes law because the president has not acted, despite Congress remaining in session for 10 days. A third option is to *veto* the bill, where the president rejects the bill and returns it to Congress (Congress can override a presidential veto with a two-thirds vote from both chambers). The final option is a *pocket veto*, which occurs when Congress adjourns without giving the president 10 days to consider the bill and the executive chooses not to sign it (Karger & Stoesz, 2013).

Local legislators include city, town, and county council members, as outlined in each state constitution. Local legislators have the authority to enact local law (Gilbert et al., 2013). Policymaking at the local level follows a similar process. For example, a proposal being considered by the city council can be referred to various subcommittees for examination and analysis. Those committees can then place the proposal on the committee agenda for further investigation or expert testimony. The committee makes recommendations on the proposal for full consideration by the city council. The council may approve, disapprove, or modify the suggestions brought forth. If the proposal passes the council, it is sent to the mayor, who can approve or disapprove of the council's actions (Gilbert et al., 2013).

Policymaking Process

Familiarity with the policymaking process, key stages, and knowledge of using specific pressure points for advocacy is essential for forensic social work practice. Howlett et al. (2009) offer a five-stage policymaking process model (Figure 3.1) that is instructive, including the stages of agenda forming, policy formation, adoption, implementation, and

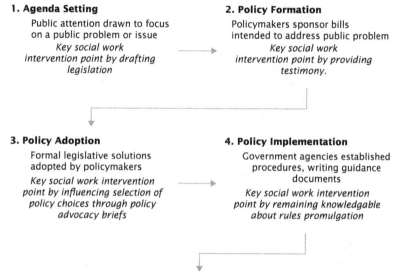

FIGURE 3.1 Policy Development Stages

evaluation. An essential principle of this policymaking model is that the process is cyclical and begins, ends, and starts anew.

Agenda Setting

In a pluralistic society where there are competing social, political, economic, and environmental issues, the agenda-setting stage in policy development is critical. Given the limited capacity to consider and address these complex challenges, only the most salient issues will impact the agenda (Howlett, Ramesh, & Perl, 2009). These complex issues must become agenda items for consideration by policymaking bodies to initiate the policy development process. Policymaking bodies exist at all levels, including city, county, state, federal, and administrative agencies such as health departments or county corrections departments.

Even if an issue is placed on the policy agenda, a strong chance exists that the issue will not move forward to complete the policy process by becoming a law. Several challenges can keep an issue from moving forward into law, including economic resources, displacement of the issue by a competing crisis, and public opinion changes. The pressing issues that can withstand those challenges hold the greatest chance of making it to policy formation, the next stage of the policymaking process (Howlett et al., 2009).

Many factors impact agenda setting. Of no surprise to social workers, power is the first factor that influences agenda setting. Those with access to legislators can directly lobby for solutions to their problems so that small interest groups without the same political currency are denied. Another factor that impacts agenda setting is the amount of public support or outcry an issue receives. Public protests against state-sanctioned violence in the summer of 2020 resulted in policing reform bills proposed on local, state, and federal policymaking agendas (Howlett et al., 2009).

The media's power in shaping an issue's relevance is also necessary to consider in agenda setting. While media coverage of problems can raise a sense of urgency about the issue, not covering public concerns can also effectively minimize the importance of a topic, thereby deeming it unworthy of being placed on the policy agenda. Singular significant events also shape the policymaking agenda. For example, there are many bills named after individual cases that generated considerable media interest and affected public opinion and legislation (examples include Sara's law—sex offender registry; the Matthew Shepard and James Byrd Jr. Hates Crimes Act—expands federal hate crime laws; and Pamela's law—bans the sale and possession of substances used for ingesting bath salts).

Policy Formation

The second stage of the policy development process is policy formation, in which a range of solutions to issues emerges and are considered. It should come as no surprise that issue solutions are often impacted by political ideology, with preferences for certain types of solutions preceding others. Many times, all political parties may agree that a problem at hand needs to be addressed, but the pathways they select in the policy formulation will be vastly different. For example, a conservative ideological solution to intimate partner violence issues may include an increase in local law enforcement resources and training to intervene, along with stricter sentencing for offenders. In contrast, a more liberal ideology is reflected in a bill that enhances community-based services and emergency shelter funding and provides access to counseling services. Policy formation is best done after analyzing the viable policy solutions to a problem and identifying the solution with the most significant potential to resolve or lessen the issue. Social policy is often formed incrementally, meaning it may take several laws to provide a comprehensive solution to the social problem. Incremental policymaking is the most common approach to policy formation, where the policy solution offered is a small, incremental step from the previous policy solutions in place. Incremental policymaking is common when the nature and scope of the problem are enormous and enduring.

It is also noteworthy that social work activism has the greatest influence at the policy formation stage. Social workers are best positioned when they're engaged in this stage of the policymaking process by providing text for legislation, providing expert testimony, and organizing community groups to influence the selection of the proposed issue solutions. Policy solutions must contain two essential features. First, the solution must be valid, efficient, and feasible for addressing the issue. Second, the policy must be politically feasible; recognizing that power imbalances in a policymaking body must be navigated deftly if the proposal has a chance of becoming adopted.

Policy Adoption

The third phase of the policy development process is policy adoption, in which government bodies adopt policies for future implementation. The government's relevant institutions must adopt proposed solutions to public issues to grant them effect. Sometimes the public issue at hand is a crisis and the policy may take effect immediately. An example of this is the Patriot Act, which was passed in response to the terrorist attacks of September 11, 2001, and intended to transform national security through broad security reforms. In other cases, policies are designed to set the path forward, sometimes charting course years out, as is the case with the Social Security retirement age.

Mayors can adopt policies to bring about change at the local level, county commissioners can do so at the county level, and governors can do so at the state level, but only the president can adopt national policies. Once adopted, the relevant government bodies move into policy implementation, the next phase of the policy development process.

Policy Implementation

The fourth phase of the policy development process, implementation, is when adopted policies are put into action. The point of implementation is the time at which the intervention concept is tested against reality.

There are three general criteria for successful policy implementation:

1. The policy must be communicated from the relevant legislative or executive body to the appropriate governing body with the power to enact it.
2. There must be clear interpretation of policy intentions; ambiguity can lead to policy challenges, ineffectiveness, and failure. Clear instructions also prevent judicial involvement due to ambiguous language, forcing legislators to reconsider the policy.
3. The resources needed to implement the policy entirely exist, and the agencies' processes and priorities serve as the governing body. Implementation also includes integration, minimizing disruption, competition, or conflict with existing governing agency priorities.

Given that legislation is often a negotiation process, agencies can struggle to interpret policies in ways that are actionable. Consequently, vague policies impose a great deal of confusion and require discretion for agencies tasked with administering them. Also, many policies require implementation across many levels of government (a federal policy that is enacted in the state) or across systems (a new foster care policy that is administered by both the Children's Bureau and Medicaid divisions). Implementation is one of the most challenging aspects of policymaking and often results in considerable variation from the original policy design as the policy is implemented. This is especially true if the new policy does not have accountability for implementation or future outputs or outcomes. The governing agencies tasked with administering policies may have apathy or disagreement toward the new policy and program, slowing the implementation and changes. Governing agencies are also not immune from scandals, employee ineptitude, and bureaucratic incompetence.

Policy Evaluation

The final stage of the policy development process is a policy evaluation. At this stage, policies, once enacted, must be evaluated to understand their impact. Evaluation comes in several forms, including anecdotes and stories, feedback from those affected by the policies, formal research using empirical evidence to determine effectiveness, and scientific research, which provides comparative statistics to evaluate a policy's causal results. The evaluation takes place at different times depending on the administrative agencies. The point of implementation or soon after is an ideal time for policy evaluation to begin, given the ability to recalibrate if it's determined the current activities are not likely to meet the intended outcomes. Public policies can be challenging to access, mainly if they intend to accomplish broad conceptual goals subject to different interpretations. Policing reforms, for example, could be challenging to define in ways that are universally accepted. A debate also exists whether a policy is deemed successful for accomplishing some of its intended objectives or whether it must meet all goals to meet success criteria. The evaluation also provides policy feedback opportunities to inform future policy agenda items. Social workers are often involved in both policy implementation and evaluation processes of policymaking.

Policy Types

What does it mean for a public policy or law to be fair? Who gets to determine the fairness or equity of any public policy? Our collective ideas on "fairness" drive a lot of policy choices. For example, imposing across-the-board gasoline tax increases creates an equal distribution of the burden among all people who purchase gasoline for their cars. But for lower income earners, the tax increase creates an unequal burden. The way citizens and policymakers view fairness has a lasting impact on policymaking, including which problems get attention by policymakers and which issues are set on the agenda. It also impacts which solutions to the problems are used, as well as which issues are ignored.

In many ways, public policy comes down to determining the distribution, allocation, and enjoyment of public goods. Two broad questions that policymakers must (or should) consider is what is going to be the cost of this policy, and who will bear it? They must also account for who benefits. Each of the types of policies described provides a way to categorize public policy and assess the kind of power by examining the policy's costs and benefits. Every public policy outcome has individuals, groups, and communities who will benefit from the policy outcomes. Each type of policy has a set of costs, which are left out of the policy outcome or may result in a loss because of the policy. There are many ways of classifying public policy described by researchers, but the most used types are distributive policy, redistributive policy, regulatory policy, constituent policy, and symbolic policy (Lowi, 1972). Table 3.2 illustrates the policy types and their intended beneficiaries.

Distributive Policy

The distributive policy is the most frequent type of public policy used in the current policy process. Distributive public policies are ones in which there are narrowly defined benefits to a small group of people or groups of people but they are done at all taxpayers' expense. So distributive policy has high costs with very concentrated benefits. The costs are often widely spread out across all taxpayers to keep conflict or opposition at bay. Some examples

TABLE 3.2 Policy Type, Beneficiaries and Costs, and Examples

Policy Type	Beneficiaries and Costs	Examples
Distributive Policy	• Costs are diffused to many. • Benefits are to a narrow group.	Interstate highway, public universities
Regulatory Policy	• Costs are concentrated to a few. • Benefits are diffused to many.	Occupational license, environmental policy
Redistributive Policy	• Costs are concentrated to a few. • Benefits are concentrated to a few.	Poverty reduction policy like SNAP or Medicaid
Constituent Policy	• Costs and benefits are created to favor the government.	Policy to deploy services in the Department of Homeland Security
Symbolic Policy	• Costs are minimal or do not exist. • Benefits are symbolic and convey political meaning.	A law to have "In God we Trust" in a motto

of distributive policy are the interstate highway systems that are funded by tax revenues but primarily benefit corporations that need the efficient transportation system for cargo shipment and delivery, and public universities that are funded from both state and federal revenues but only benefit those who work or study there.

Regulatory Policy

Regulatory policy is another policy type used by policymakers to address issues. Regulatory policies are rules and policies designed to protect health, safety, and the environment and are often used to control or safeguard common resources (water, air, fuel, etc.). Regulatory policies have very concentrated and sometimes even private costs but have extensive and diffused benefits to many. Influential interest groups often govern regulatory policy and have a direct interest in the regulatory policy outcomes. At times they can be a singular issue, such as the National Association of Social Workers, which functions as a professional organization that lobbies for policies and laws that protect and govern the profession of social work and social work licensure and ensure that the public is protected from poor-performing and unethical social workers. There can also be regulatory policies that have competing interest groups. Consider the policies that go into environmental and climate regulations, including oil and gas companies, manufacturing industries, wind and solar energy, and transportation industries interested in the regulations that govern their world. Regulatory policy is created to manage the damages resulting from unchecked production or careless operations in these industries and ensure that their output does not decrease air quality and water safety. Regulatory policies often come with a lot of criticism, but they do function to protect individuals from influential groups by acting in the best interest of many.

Redistributive Policy

Another type of policy is created to redistribute the resources of society from one group to another. Redistributive policies have very concentrated and narrow costs and benefits and are often designed to avoid corruption or harm. Some refer to this policy type as a "Robin Hood" effect, where an identifiable group of citizens wins at the expense of an identifiable group who loses. We often think of social welfare programs as examples of this type of policy, where resources from taxes are used to create programs that buffer poverty effects, such as Supplemental Nutrition Assistance Program (SNAP) and other food programs, housing assistance policies, or other poverty elimination programs. Social welfare policy is not the only policy that fits this type and is a narrow view of redistributive policy. It is not uncommon for redistributive policies to provide benefits to the wealthy at others' cost. Another example is a mass transit bill that will fund a rail system connecting two major urban communities. The identifiable group who benefits from this policy lives in the urban communities that would use the rail system. In contrast, individuals who live in rural communities receive no or a minimal benefit from that public policy.

Constituent and Symbolic Policy

The final types of public policies are constituent and symbolic policies. Constituent policies are comprehensive policies that typically do not focus on individuals and groups specifically and are more often created to favor the government for the people. The policies tend to direct the government to act, guide government agencies and other institutions' decisions and actions, or shape the purpose and function of the government. For example, in 1992, a constituent policy created the Department of Substance Abuse and Mental Health as a centralized government agency to manage government resources to address substance abuse and mental health.

The final type of public policies is those which are considered to be symbolic. They are generally a type of policy that defines and reflects values and upholds government principles with high symbolic value. Still, the policy itself has no actual effect in terms of money involved and rarely has procedural or structural changes associated with the policy. Symbolic policies can be highly influential as they are often created to both advance and disrupt social movements. Politicians may use symbolic policies to send a signal of control to voters or other governments worldwide. Examples of symbolic policies are prohibition of flag burning and a no-smoking policy on a college campus. Occasionally, a policy that appears to be symbolic may have significant consequences and should be monitored and examined like any other policy type.

Issues for Social Workers in Policy Practice

Social work professionals have the important task of advocating for policy reform of the systems, institutions, and policies that shape the forensic practice environment. Our Code of Ethics centers social work professionals on the value of pursuing social change (National Association of Social Workers, 2017). Likewise, social work education programs focus on training students to identify, assess, and apply critical thinking to policies that formulate and advocate for better practices that advance human rights (Council on Social Work Education, 2015). As the authors of future chapters in this text will examine in more detail, forensic policy and the systems it creates are deeply integrated into systems of oppression and racism. Yet at the same time, forensic programming is slowly shifting to interventions that reflect a trauma-informed and rehabilitative social work approach with the emergence of specialized courts, restorative justice practices, community-based alternatives to sentencing, and the use of more trauma-informed practices.

The infusion of practical reform in criminal justice settings will begin at the policy level. Social work professionals must be integrated into and a partner in the various criminal justice system settings, including the policymaking process. Your social work studies are the beginning of a multistep process to learning and engaging in effective policy practice. Knowing how to find current laws and policies in use at the federal, state, tribal, and local government levels is essential. Knowing what the policy is that exists and the impact the policy is having is a key to change. Also, professionals need to take an active role in understanding the economic setting and the budget process for policies that create programming and guide interventions to ensure that resources are devoted to necessary system reforms and desired outcomes.

Social workers are community organizers and have essential skills to mobilize voters and deploy citizens for collective action. Understanding the policies' power and the values and ideologies that guide policy preferences will help advance the policy agenda and reforms. Social workers should understand how problems are framed and how to find solutions within that framing for policy action. Adopting a political lens helps in crafting arguments that are palpable to decision makers across party lines. Research on the policy formulation process has shown that policy agendas are set by the individual or group advocates who are ready to bring policy solutions when a window of opportunity becomes available (Kingdon & Stano, 1984). Social workers should act as policy entrepreneurs who can tell the story behind the policy issue, produce feasible solutions to problems, and adapt strategies to advance the issue when the window of opportunity opens (Cairney, 2018).

References

Cairney, P. (2018). Three habits of successful policy entrepreneurs. *Policy & Politics, 46*(2), 199–215. https://bristoluniversitypressdigital.com/downloadpdf/journals/pp/46/2/article-p199.pdf

Council on Social Work Education. (2015). *Educational policy and accreditation standards.* https://www.cswe.org/getattachment/Accreditation/Standards-and-Policies/2015-EPAS/2015EPASandGlossary.pdf

Gilbert, R., Stevenson, D., Girardet, H., & Stren, R. (2013). *Making cities work: Role of local authorities in the urban environment.* Routledge. https://doi.org/10.4324/9781315066431

Howlett, M., Ramesh, M., & Perl, A. (2009). *Studying public policy: Policy cycles and policy subsystems* (Vol. 3). Oxford: Oxford University Press. https://www.sfu.ca/~howlett/documents/j.1541-0072.1998.tb01913.x.pdf

Karger, H. J., & Stoesz, D. (2013). *American social welfare policy: A pluralist approach, Brief Edition.* Pearson.

Kingdon, J. W., & Stano, E. (1984). *Agendas, alternatives, and public policies* (Vol. 45, pp. 165–169). Little, Brown. https://scholar.google.com/citations?view_op=view_citation&hl=en&user=3nuovy0AAAAJ&citation_for_view=3nuovy0AAAAJ:YOwf2qJgpHMC

Lowi, T. J. (1972). Four systems of policy, politics, and choice. *Public Administration Review, 32*(4), 298–310. https://edisciplinas.usp.br/pluginfile.php/4286588/mod_resource/content/1/lowi-four-systems-of-policy%201972.pdf

National Association of Social Workers. (2017). *Code of ethics.* NASW Press. https://www.socialworkers.org/About/Ethics/Code-of-Ethics/Code-of-Ethics-English

4

Ethics in Forensic Social Work

David Axlyn McLeod, Burcu Ozturk, and
Zackery D.O. Dunnells

Practicing Ethically in Forensic Social Work

Professional ethics is described as combining broad goals with specific rules of conduct (Congress, 1999). Ethics includes matters of rights, responsibilities, and well-being (Banks, 2015). Nearly 100 years ago, Mary Richmond was credited with developing the first social work code of ethics (McLeod, 2017). Since the inception of the profession, ethics has been at the core of social work practice. According to the National Association of Social Workers (NASW) Code of Ethics (found at http://www.socialworkers.org/About/Ethics/Code-of-Ethics), social workers are expected to provide competent service in these crucial, complex professional roles considering the array of possible interactions with a legal system that is as dynamic and diverse.

The contexts in which forensic social workers function unambiguously differentiate them from other social workers in many ways. Forensic social workers must simultaneously provide competent services to their clients while safeguarding the larger community and ensuring the legal system's laws and regulations are upheld. The luxury of devoting all their professional energy and attention to a single individual or entity is rarely afforded to social workers in general. It can become even more complex in forensic and legal settings. Social workers must balance providing ethical and legal service to all individuals and systems involved while also advocating for the development of fair laws and reformation of laws that they deem unjust by the profession's standards. This task may seem daunting, but it is a task that forensic social workers are uniquely prepared to accomplish. By nature, forensic social workers must continually navigate competent service delivery provisions in conjunction with criminal and civil legal systems while also abiding by a professional code of ethics. The National Organization of Forensic Social Workers (NOFSW) created a code of ethics for its members in 1987 (Butters & Vaughan-Eden, 2011). According to the NOFSW, all forensic

David Axlyn McLeod, Burcu Ozturk, and Zackery D.O. Dunnells, *Ethics in Forensic Social Work* In: *Handbook of Forensic Social Work*. Edited by: David Axlyn McLeod, Anthony P. Natale, and Kristin W. Mapson, Oxford University Press. © Oxford University Press 2024. DOI: 10.1093/oso/9780197694732.003.0004 social workers should promote well-being, encourage the equal availability of quality forensic social work services to all, and minimize potential harm (Butter & Vaughan-Eden, 2011). The NOFSW code of ethics aims to provide more specific guidelines to resolve ethical dilemmas when forensic social workers have a challenge.

Some roles for forensic social workers include child abuse and neglect workers, child custody and divorce specialists, social workers who provide sexual offender or mandated batterer treatment, mental health or substance abuse clinicians, and even mitigation specialists focused on biopsychosocial reporting for court systems before sentencing. The application of evidence-based ethical decision-making has been at the center of service delivery (Congress et al., 2009). With that said, ethical decision-making within forensic social work practice is paramount as forensic social workers interact with various parts of the legal system throughout the entirety of the legal process. It is common for social workers in these roles to face complex ethical dilemmas that warrant a decision that will significantly impact their clients' lives and the broader community (Forgey & Colarossi, 2003). A typical example of this is a forensic psychiatric social worker in the role of a competency evaluation. This type of social worker is tasked with evaluating the client's psychiatric ability to stand trial for the charges against them. Utilizing the social worker's ongoing assessment of the client's psychological state, the social worker must determine whether psychological impairment has impacted the client's ability to conduct themselves within the confines of the law. This example brings up the dual nature of responsibility that a forensic social worker carries as their decision-making will affect their client and the community. Navigating situations like these underscores the importance of understanding the basics of ethics and ethical decision-making, mainly how these processes are applied to social work at the intersections between social work and the legal system.

The purpose of this chapter is to explain ethics in forensic social work and explore the relationship between ethics and law and the role of legal professionals in the criminal justice system. In addition, we highlight ethical decision-making models as a resource and how forensic social workers apply ethics and utilize ethical decision-making models to resolve complex decisions in practice.

The Social Work Code of Ethics

Values

When exploring the application of ethics to social work practice, values are often confused for ethics. By its nature, the social work profession is value-driven. Brown (1968) suggests that no other profession places more emphasis on the importance of values, which can be defined as deeply held ideas or beliefs that are often a reflection of personal and professional experiences, external or societal influences, and time and context. Social work as a profession has valued service and social justice, the importance of human relationships, the dignity and worth of all people, and integrity and competence in practice.

Ethics tend to be deducted from values concerned with what is suitable and desirable in each context. This deduction comes from the application of those values of what is appropriate or desirable. Thus, ethical behavior can be measured and prescriptive, while values tend to be more of a broad and general construct.

Ethical Principles

According to the NASW Code of Ethics (2006), social work ethical principles are based on social work's core values of service, social justice, dignity and worth of the person, importance of human relationship, integrity, and competence. Social work ethical principles include that (NASW, 2006):

1. The primary goal of social workers is to assist people in need and address social problems.
2. Social workers focus on social injustice issues such as poverty, discrimination, and other forms of social injustice to ensure everyone has equal opportunities.
3. Social workers treat all individuals with respect and are mindful of people's differences.
4. Social workers understand the relationship among people and engage people as partners in the helping process.
5. Social workers are aware of the profession's mission, ethical principles, and ethical standards and act honestly.
6. Social workers aim to enhance their professional expertise and increase their knowledge and skills.

Ethical Standards

Social work ethical standards are relevant to social workers' professional activities. Social workers' ethical standards focus on (a) ethical responsibilities to clients, (b) ethical responsibilities to colleagues, (c) ethical responsibilities in practice, (d) ethical responsibilities as professionals, (e) ethical responsibilities to the social work profession, and (f) ethical responsibilities to the broader society (NASW, 2006).

Unethical Versus Unprofessional

The central social work value that all people are deserving of dignity and respect is an example of deducting ethical behavior from a given value. When entering a relationship with clients or a client system, social workers need to be aware of biases. A forensic social worker providing treatment for a juvenile sex offender must be mindful of potential negative feelings or thoughts related to the client's prior conduct. An example of ethical behavior would be the social worker referencing specific ethical standards principles within the NASW Code of Ethics as a guide for finding ways to maintain positive and appropriate interactions between themselves and the client despite their aversion to the client's conduct. On the other hand, it would be unethical for the social worker to allow their biases to impact or mitigate the services provided to this client. This example demonstrates how ethical behavior can be more nuanced and individualized than the brief appearance of the connection between values and ethics. This is because (a) people do not always behave in a manner reflective of their values and (b) people can hold a wide range of differing and conflicting values by nature.

Lowenberg et al. (2000) suggest that professional ethics are derived from the actual values of the profession rather than the values of an individual practitioner. Social workers can use the awareness of this distinction to avoid projecting their values on the client or the client system. To help navigate these complexities, the NASW Code of Ethics ethical standards assist social workers in upholding the behavioral expectations for the profession. Thinking about ethical decision-making deliberately and intentionally is paramount in social work.

Ethics Versus Law

The noncongruence between ethical behavior and the law is a common point of confusion. Ethics are connected to a specific set of applied behaviors in practice settings as it relates to social work. On the other hand, the law defines expectations of how citizens should interact with the government and one another and the consequences if those expectations are not met (Albert, 1986; Black, 1972; Van Hoose & Kottler, 1985). Complex decision-making in social work practice tends to function within indistinct shades of gray compared to the law's black-and-white expectations, further complicating the distinction between the two. Similarly, conformity to moral decision-making and ethical behavior is most associated with professional or personal value structures and respect. In contrast, legal expectations are most connected to and enforced by an externalized threat of punishment (Lowenberg et al., 2000).

Serious conflicts can arise between ethics and the law (McLeod, 2017). Although it is not necessarily illegal for a social worker to treat a client disrespectfully, it is most definitely unethical. Specifically, for forensic social workers, their practice's venue often overlaps with the legal system, thus requiring that the facilitation of their service delivery abide by the dynamic code of the law—making this area extremely difficult to navigate. This brings up another distinction between unethical versus unprofessional interactions. Behavior can be unethical, unprofessional, or both. While unethical behavior is subject to professional sanction, unprofessional behavior is subject to civil and criminal lawsuits.

Legal Responsibilities

Forensic social workers are commonly required to make complicated decisions at the intersection of ethics and law. For example, mandated reporting related to individual and family safety by social workers to the police or child welfare entities may be dictated by statutory law in the jurisdiction to which the social worker is practicing. Yet, the social worker must still examine those laws related to confidentiality, client autonomy, and overall ethical service delivery. It is possible for social workers in legal settings to find themselves in scenarios where their legal obligations could be seen as unethical or their professional behaviors aligned with social work could be seen as illegal.

Adversarial System

Courtrooms within the legal system in the United States employ an adversarial process, meaning there are ultimately two sides in any case. Each side is represented by a lawyer responsible for entirely arguing their side's legal case. In the criminal court system, one side brings forward prosecution when a legal statute has been violated. The other side brings forward a defense of that prosecution. An impartial third party, whether a judge or jury, is responsible for hearing both sides of the case and concluding whether guilt can be determined based upon a particular threshold of evidence. The system can foster an organizational culture focused more on winning an argument than ethically exploring a situation.

Prosecution Ethics

In the existing literature, many studies mention that law and social work professions collaborate within an interdisciplinary context (Benson, 2007; Coleman, 2001; Taylor, 2006). In the forensic social work setting, forensic social workers often collaborate and communicate with a large team of law enforcement, lawyers, and court systems to provide services to their clients. Prosecutors are part of the professional team in the legal system and are the people's legal representatives to enhance the laws being prosecuted. Prosecutors should act ethically and professionally in the criminal justice system. According to American Bar Association (ABA), the primary goal of the prosecutor is not only to convict but also to seek justice in the law (found in the Standards for the Prosecution Function at http://www.americanbar.org). The prosecutor should be aware of all individuals' constitutional and legal rights, including suspects and defendants, and be respectful to all persons.

Social workers are responsible for advocating for their clients, including those accused or convicted of a crime. In the juvenile justice system, they can testify in court on behalf of both defendants and litigants (Maschi & Killian, 2011). According to the NASW Code of Ethics (2006), social workers promote clients' well-being and use understandable language for their services. Especially in legal practice, legal language can be challenging to understand, so social workers should inform the clients of their rights, provide detailed information, and arrange effective translators when necessary. Social workers should prepare victims and witnesses for the court process and provide assistance, knowledge, and referrals to them. Also, social workers should assist in developing training and education for internal staff and external stakeholders concerning victims and witnesses involved in prosecutions matters.

Additionally, social workers have an ethical responsibility to their colleagues, and they should treat each other with respect. Social workers should collaborate with other professionals and contribute to decisions that affect the well-being of clients. Forensic social workers can assist other members of the legal system in understanding the offenders and victims. While social workers consider the client's environment, well-being, and relationship with various systems, prosecutors and lawyers value the client as an individual and ensure safety for the community (Cole, 2012). Hence, the duties and responsibilities of each professional as an advocate can have different ethical considerations. Therefore, forensic social workers should be aware of other professionals' values in the legal setting to be effective team partners.

Defense Ethics

Forensic social worker practice has a history in forensic practice, but social workers' role in this setting remains new and unclear (Buchanan & Nooe, 2017; Hisle et al., 2012). Although the state's administration, funding, and operations are different, each state has a defense system (Owens et al., 2014). After the public defense system arose, several studies found social work in a few public defense practices beginning in the early 1970s (Senna, 1975; Wald, 1972). The National Association for Public Defense (2017) highlighted that efficient public defense depends on social workers being part of the defense team. In defense settings, collaboration with social workers is fundamental in understanding and relating clients' needs and identifying and advocating for appropriate services (Buchanan & Nooe, 2017). In the interdisciplinary context among social workers and legal professionals, it is significant to know the perceptions held by other professionals. Forensic social workers work closely with prosecutors, defense attorneys, and other legal professionals. Hence, it is beneficial to understand defense lawyers' responsibilities and ethics while also considering social work ethics.

In the criminal justice system, defense lawyers serve many purposes to ensure that the court does not wrongfully convict defendants. The defense lawyer must act professionally and ethically when dealing with the judge and the prosecutor. In the criminal process, defense lawyers and counsels should respect the client's dignity by helping enforce their rights (Simon, 1992). The defense lawyer should provide adequate defense for poor and rich defendants alike and offer equal benefits to all individual defendants (Simon, 1992). Defense lawyers can inform clients of the privilege against self-incrimination and assist them in this (Simon, 1992). However, defense lawyers should not misrepresent the client in court and should not follow any unethical or illegal information given by the defendant. Defense lawyers should consider the principle of confidentiality when they communicate with clients and social workers.

During collaboration, ethical dilemmas and conflicts between social workers and attorneys may arise when legal and psychosocial needs clash (Buchanan & Nooe, 2017). A lack of understanding of other professions' roles in the team is expected. Therefore, clarifying professionals' roles and boundaries is key to acting ethically in forensic social work and other practice settings.

Civil Practice Ethics

Civil law covers many branches, including family law, property law, tort law, and contract law (Merryman & Pérez-Perdomo, 2018). Social workers may have clients involved in child custody disputes, domestic violence issues, and neglect and child abuse cases. Also, social workers might work on adoption cases and with foster families when children have been removed from the home due to domestic violence or neglect. Likewise, social workers often can be called to testify as expert witnesses in the court system, and witnesses can be a significant source of the case in court, so they have a role in civil practice settings.

According to the NASW Code of Ethics (2006), social workers should behave honestly and responsibly, promoting ethical practices on the part of the agency with which they are affiliated. Social workers should consider their client's privacy and protect the confidentiality of all information obtained, except for compelling professional reasons. When forensic social workers deal with child abuse and neglect issues, they should provide the child abuse reports to authorities. Also, social workers should take the responsibility of safeguarding clients' interests and rights. Sometimes social workers may face ethical dilemmas in civil practice, where they maintain client confidentiality and only disclose certain information to authorities. Social workers should consider NASW Code of Ethics principles and laws in those circumstances to resolve these dilemmas. Additionally, forensic social workers can use alternative dispute resolution (ADR) when dealing with civil practice cases, including resolving disputes without litigation through negotiation, arbitration, and mediation (Kelly, 2016).

Ethical Decision-Making Models

Over the years, scholars from social work have created many ethical decision-making frameworks (Úriz Pemán et al., 2017). In social work practice, ethical decision-making models can be helpful for social workers in resolving ethical dilemmas (Buck et al., 2016; Úriz Pemán et al., 2017). Multiple tools should be considered to manage the complicated nature of many cross-system ethical decisions that forensic social workers encounter frequently. Furthermore, the authors argue that utilizing these tools during ethical decision-making should be central to practice and not merely an afterthought. For this text, we highlight the ETHICA model of ethical decision-making as a resource to utilize when making some of these complex decisions.

ETHICA Model

Elaine Congress (2009) developed the ETHICA model in response to calls from Reamer (1995), among others, to shift the focus of ethical decision-making from a concentration on the morality of the client or client system to the ethical behavior of the practitioner. This model suggests that when social workers assess an ethical dilemma, they must work through six distinct steps to make a conscious decision about behaving ethically in a given situation. The ETHICA model's first step is to examine relevant values, including personal, social, cultural, client, and professional values, and look for alignment. This is followed by considering the NASW Code of Ethics and relevant laws, regulations, and agency policies related to their specific provision area(s). Next, one is to hypothesize potential scenarios based on the available decisions to be made. The model then helps a worker identify the level of vulnerability and potential harm for all affected by the possible decision outcomes. At this point, if the practitioner has not been able to make a decision, they should then consult available colleagues and supervisors. Lastly, the model suggests that the practitioner should then advocate for systemic change related to their agency, profession, and the larger community to avoid any similar ethical dilemmas arising in the future. This last step is critical because, as previously discussed, forensic social workers are responsible to both the client and the larger community.

Decisions made by forensic social workers have far-reaching and long-lasting ramifications on individuals, families, the community, and the safety of all parties involved. *One example is a forensic social worker helping clients in a diversion program avoid prison for substance use charges by working toward substance use treatment goals. In addition to evaluating the community's safety, this social worker must continually assess the client's fidelity to the diversion process and the associated behavioral and treatment expectations.*

TABLE 4.1 ETHICA Model

	Actions to Take in ETHICA Model
E	Examine values (personal, social, cultural, client, and professional)
T	Think about the NASW Code of Ethics, laws, regulations, and agency policies
H	Hypothesize about different scenarios
I	Identify who is most vulnerable and who will be harmed
C	Consult with supervisors and colleagues
A	Advocate for agency, profession, community, and systemic change

Ethical Principles Screen

The ethical principles screen created by Lowenberg et al. (2000) is an example of a useful screening tool aimed at helping social workers make decisions regarding vulnerability, safety, and potential for harm. The first step in the process is to apply what the authors call the *ethical rules screen*. As seen in Figure 4.1, the ethical rules screen is quite simple. It suggests a social worker should first identify if, and to what degree, any of the rules from the NASW Code of Ethics could be used or applied to the situation. The Code should take precedence over the social worker's value system. If one or more of the rules from the code of ethics do apply, the screen suggests you follow those. If the NASW Code of Ethics does not address the specific problem, it is recommended that the worker move forward to the more extensive ethical principles screen.

Lowenberg and Dolgoff designed the ethical principles screen to help social workers make decisions if the scenario they are dealing with does not seem to be covered clearly in the NASW Code of Ethics or when one or more ethical principles conflict with each other. The screen (depicted in Figure 4.2) starts with the "most important" ethical principle, the protection of human life, and continues with the principle of equality and inequality; the principle of autonomy, independence, and freedom; the principle of least harm; the

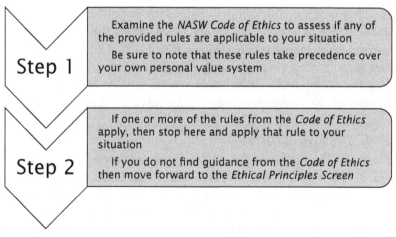

Step 1
Examine the *NASW Code of Ethics* to assess if any of the provided rules are applicable to your situation

Be sure to note that these rules take precedence over your own personal value system

Step 2
If one or more of the rules from the *Code of Ethics* apply, then stop here and apply that rule to your situation

If you do not find guidance from the *Code of Ethics* then move forward to the *Ethical Principles Screen*

FIGURE 4.1 Ethical Rules Screen

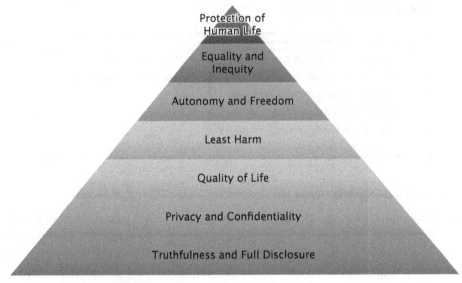

FIGURE 4.2 Ethical Principles Screen

principle of quality of life; the principle of a person's right to privacy; and the principle of full disclosure (Lowenberg et al., 2000).

Of particular importance to social workers, this framework suggests that protection of human life take precedence over any other ethical obligation of the social worker. Social workers should start with ethical principle 1 and work their way down to the last while continually evaluating the given predicament. For example, suppose a social worker knew that they would violate privacy and confidentiality to protect human life in their situation. In that case, the ethical principles screen could provide a process to help the worker make that choice. Each level is organized and depicted further in Table 4.2. While all ethical principles are essential, the ethical principles screen can be used to help manage a situation and allow the social worker to focus on the "most important" issues first while keeping in mind all other ancillary details and their importance and relevance to the more significant situation and the decision to be made. Specifically, this screening tool can help forensic social workers process the implications of deciding in the context of intersecting systems by allowing them to process those implications in order of importance. It can also promote critical thinking and reflection to assist social workers in combating ambiguity when making ethical decisions and assist in documentation and justification of decision-making.

Deeper Considerations

Having a code of ethics helps social workers define the profession and provide guidelines in finding a solution when dealing with ethical practice dilemmas. Forensic social workers most often collaborate with other professionals in the criminal justice system and are involved with emotionally charged criminal and civil cases that require special attention to ethics (Butters & Vaughan-Eden, 2011). Within the legal system, forensic social workers may face sensitive roles, boundaries, and power differences with potential tensions between clients' rights and those of the larger society (Butters & Vaughan-Eden, 2011).

TABLE 4.2 Ethical Principles Screen Components

Principles Rank Ordered	Ethical Principles
Principle 1	The *protection of human life* applies to all persons, both to the life of a client and to the lives of others. This principle takes precedence over every other obligation.
Principle 2	The *principle of equality and inequality* suggests that equal persons have the right to be treated equally, and nonequal persons have the right to be treated differently if the inequality is relevant to the issue in question. Child abuse is one area where this principle applies: Children are not equal to adults.
Principle 3	A social worker should make practice decisions that *foster a person's autonomy, independence, and freedom*. A person does not have the right to decide to harm themselves or anyone else because the right to make such a decision is their autonomous right.
Principle 4	A social worker should always choose the option that will *cause the least harm*, the least permanent harm, and/or the most easily reversible harm.
Principle 5	A social worker should choose the option that *promotes a better quality of life* for all people, the individual, and the community.
Principle 6	A social worker should make practice decisions that strengthen every person's *right to privacy*. Keeping confidential information intact is a direct derivative of this obligation.
Principle 7	A social worker should make practice decisions that permit them to *speak the truth* and *fully disclose* all relevant information to the client and others.

Social work in legal settings is an area of growing importance. Barker and Branson (2014) suggest an increasing need for social workers who understand navigating the judiciary system (Cole, 2012). With newly found space in these areas, the NASW Code of Ethics calls social workers to advocate for policy and legislation changes that promote social justice in civil and criminal arenas. Forensic social workers can serve as a bridge between the legal system and human service agencies. They can be experts in various settings, such as prisons, court systems, child welfare, mental health agencies, rehabilitation centers, hospitals, and faith-based institutions. Forensic social workers can also serve an essential role in expanding the profession's knowledge base regarding current legal frameworks and their influences on clients' lives (Naessens & Raeymaeckers, 2020).

Overall, collaboration provides benefits for clients (Maschi & Killian, 2011). Lawyers have emphasized that social workers help address clients' psychosocial needs (Pierce, Gleasonwynn, & Miller, 2001). Also, many researchers have found that having social workers and lawyers together allows clients to feel safe and secure while providing an extra layer of protection (Pierce et al., 2001). Forensic social workers address clients' well-being with a psychosocial and justice (law and policy) lens (Maschi & Killian, 2011). They aim to simultaneously help people, families, and society by collaborating with various professions to solve problems in legally related areas (Abramson & Rosenthal, 1995; Maschi & Killian, 2011).

Conclusion

This chapter explored ethics in forensic social work, including the relationship between ethics and law and legal professionals' role in the criminal justice system. We discussed varying roles and ethical considerations for social workers and their relationship with legal professionals in criminal justice. Forensic work has been evolving for decades and is defined broadly concerning the criminal and civil justice system. Forensic social workers have various roles in the criminal and civil justice system to provide mental health services, conduct risk assessments, provide expert witness testimony, conduct custody evaluation, and administer victim or offender services. Often forensic social workers also collaborate with other professionals in the legal system. Social workers must be aware of different professional values and conflicts between ethics and law in interdisciplinary settings. Having various roles and responsibilities and collaborating with multiple professionals can cause issues and raise essential questions among social workers.

The NASW Code of Ethics assists social workers in defining their profession and providing guidelines to resolve challenges when they face dilemmas. Social workers should be aware of these dilemmas and determine their roles, responsibilities, and priorities to maintain professional ethics. When social workers grapple with ethical dilemmas in practice, reviewing the NASW Code of Ethics guidelines is crucial. However, there may be times when the NASW Code of Ethics guidelines are not helpful in specifically resolving dilemmas, causing conflicting guidance. Consequently, social workers might find other ways to resolve these dilemmas, including peer, colleague, or supervisor consultation, as well as using ethical decision-making models.

Several models of ethical decision-making have been proposed. This chapter discussed ethical decision models as a resource for forensic social workers to resolve complex decisions. Social workers are encouraged to use ethical decision models to think critically and promote the client's well-being. ETHICA (Congress, 2009) is one of the models appropriate for social workers and can be used in various situations in social work practice. The ETHICA model recommends six distinct steps for social workers to make proper decisions and choose ethically when faced with dilemmas. Also, Lowenberg et al. (2000) developed the ethical principles screen to help social workers make decisions regarding vulnerability, safety, and potential harm. The ethical principles screen tool has a hierarchical ranking, including different social work values, to help social workers make the most ethical decisions.

In summary, ethical decision-making is a crucial factor among professional social work practitioners. In addition to utilizing an ethical decision-making tool, social workers should consider professional judgment and consult with supervisors or colleagues and other professionals involved in the case as needed. According to the NASW Code of Ethics, social workers' primary goal is to help people in need and challenge social injustice. Social workers have an advocacy role in protecting the client's rights and should engage in social and political action to ensure people have access to resources. In the 21st century, combining forensic social workers' practice skills and legal knowledge will benefit clients' well-being and create a unique role in forensic social work practice. In the next century, an increase in expectations from forensic social workers is probable. Consequently, it is essential to understand the ethics and roles of forensic social workers in legal settings.

References

Abramson, J. S., & Rosenthal, B. S. (1995). Interdisciplinary and inter-organizational collaboration. In R. L. Edwards (Ed.), *Encyclopedia of social work* (19th ed., pp. 1479–1489). NASW Press.

Albert, R. (1986). *Law and social work practice*. Springer Publishing.

Banks, S. (2015). Social work ethics. *International Encyclopedia of the Social & Behavioral Sciences, 22*, 782–788. https://doi.org/10.1016/B978-0-08-097086-8.28030-6

Barker, R. L., & Branson, D. M. (2014). *Forensic social work: Legal aspects of professional practice*. Routledge. https://doi.org/10.4324/9781315821573

Black, D. (1972). The boundaries of legal sociology. *Yale Law Journal, 81*, 1086–1101.

Benson, S. R. (2007). Beyond protecting orders: Interdisciplinary domestic violence clinics facilitate social change. *Cardozo Journal of Law & Gender, 14*, 1.

Brown, B. (1968). *Social change: A professional challenge*. Unpublished paper.

Buchanan, S., & Nooe, R. M. (2017). Defining social work within holistic public defense: Challenges and implications for practice. *Social Work, 62*(4), 333–339. https://doi.org/10.1093/sw/swx032

Buck, P. W., Fletcher, P., & Bradley, J. (2016). Decision-making in social work field education: A "good enough" framework. *Social Work Education, 35*(4), 402–413. https://doi.org/10.1080/02615479.2015.1109073

Butters, R. P., & Vaughan-Eden, V. (2011). The ethics of practicing forensic social work. *Journal of Forensic Social Work, 1*(1), 61–72. https://doi.org/10.1080/1936928X.2011.541202Cole, P. L. (2012). The role of perceptions in collaborative relationships: Implications for forensic social work practice. *Journal of Forensic Social Work, 2*(1), 3–24. https://doi.org/10.1080/1936928X.2012.658750

Coleman, B. (2001). Lawyers who are also social workers: How to effectively combine two different disciplines to better serve clients. *Washington University Journal of Law & Policy, 7*, 131.

Congress, E. P. (1999). *Social work values and ethics: Identifying and resolving professional dilemmas*. Wadsworth Group/Thompson Learning.

Congress, E. (2009). *ETHICA: Expanding the ETHIC model to include advocacy* [Paper presentation]. CSWE Baccalaureate Program Directors Meeting, Phoenix, AZ.

Congress, E., Black, N., & Strom-Gottfried, K. (2009). *Teaching social work values and ethics: A curriculum resource* (2nd ed.). CSWE Press.

Forgey, M. L., & Colarossi, L. (2003). Interdisciplinary social work and the law: A model domestic violence curriculum. *Journal of Social Work Education, 39*, 459–476. https://doi.org/10.1080/10437797.2003.10779149

Hisle, B., Shdaimah, C. S., & Finegar, N. (2012). Neighborhood Defenders Program: An evaluation of Maryland's holistic representation program. *Journal of Forensic Social Work, 2*(2–3), 122–140. https://doi.org/10.1080/1936928X.2012.743868

Kelly, D. R. (2016). *NASW law note: Social workers and alternative dispute resolution*. https://doi.org/10.1093/sw/sww004

Lowenberg, F., Dolgoff, R., & Harrington, D. (2000). *Ethical decisions for social work practice* (6th ed.). Peacock.

Maschi, T., & Killian, M. L. (2011). The evolution of forensic social work in the United States: Implications for 21st century practice. *Journal of Forensic Social Work, 1*(1), 8–36. https://doi.org/10.1080/1936928X.2011.541198

McLeod, D. A. (2017). Social work and the law: An overview of ethics, social work, & civil and criminal law. In T. Maschi & G. Leibowitz (Eds.), *Forensic practice: Psychosocial and legal Issues across diverse populations and settings* (2nd ed., pp. 63–81). Springer Publishing Company.

Merryman, J. H., & Pérez-Perdomo, R. (2018). *The civil law tradition: An introduction to the legal systems of Europe and Latin America*. Stanford University Press.

Naessens, L., & Raeymaeckers, P. (2020). A generalist approach to forensic social work: A qualitative analysis. *Journal of Social Work, 20*(4), 501–517. https://doi.org/10.1177%2F1468017319826740

National Association for Public Defense. (2017). *Foundational principles*. https://www.publicdefenders.us/foundationalprinciples

National Association of Social Workers. (n.d.). *NASW code of ethics*. https://www.socialworkers.org/About/Ethics/Code-of-Ethics/Code-of-Ethics-English

Owens, S., Accetta, E., Charles, J., & Shoemaker, S. (2014). *Indigent defense services in the United States, FY 2008–2012*. Office of Justice Programs Bureau of Justice Statistics US Department of Justice. http://www.bjs.gov

Pierce, C. T., Gleasonwynn, P., & Miller, M. G. (2001). Social work and law: A model for implementing social services in a law office. *Journal of Gerontological Social Work, 34*(3), 61–71.

Reamer, F. (1995). Malpractice claims against social workers: First facts. *Social Work, 40*, 595601. https://doi.org/10.1093/sw/40.5.595

Senna, J. J. (1975). Social workers in public defender programs. *Social Work, 20*(4), 271–277. https://doi.org/10.1093/sw/20.4.271

Simon, W. H. (1992). The ethics of criminal defense. *Michigan Law Review, 91*, 1703. https://repository.law.umich.edu/mlr/vol91/iss7/3

Taylor, S. (2006). Educating future practitioners of social work and law: Exploring the origins of inter-professional misunderstanding. *Children and Youth Services Review, 28*(6), 638–653. https://doi.org/10.1016/j.childyouth.2005.06.006

Úriz Pemán, M. J., Idareta Goldaracena, F., Viscarret Garro, J. J., & Ballestero Izquierdo, A. (2017). Methodologies for ethical decision making in social work. *Annual of Social Work, 24*(1), 33–54. https://doi.org/10.3935/ljsr.v24i1.124

Van Hoose, W., & Kottler, J. (1985). *Ethical and legal issues in counseling and psychotherapy* (2nd ed.). Jossey-Bass.

Wald, M. (1972). *The use of social workers in a public defender office: An evaluation of the Offender Rehabilitation Project of the Public Defender Office for Santa Clara County, California*. Office of the Public Defender.

5

Women in Forensic Settings

David Axlyn McLeod, Zackery D.O. Dunnells, and Burcu Ozturk

Introduction

Before delving too deeply into women's experiences in forensic settings, it is essential to create a frame of reference by which we will explore this phenomenon. With over 230,000 women and girls in carceral facilities across the United States, and nearly a million involved in the criminal justice system as a whole, this is a topic of great importance and nuance (American Civil Liberties Union [ACLU], 2021; Kajstura, 2019). The primary approach we will use to examine women's experiences in forensics settings will be *feminist pathways*. These (feminist pathways) approaches to understanding women's interactions with crime and the criminal justice system have long been studied and are well validated. Repeatedly, what has often been found through research on the topic is that when women engage in criminal activity, they usually have complicated backstories, perhaps beginning with their abuse in childhood (Acoca, 1998; Belknap & Holsinger, 2006; DeHart, 2008; McDaniels-Wilson & Belknap, 2008; Salisbury & Van Voorhis, 2009). Many times, in these women's lives, their abusive childhood transitions into abusive relationships in adulthood, where these women are further victimized through male-dominated violence (McLeod et al., 2019). These experiences can often lead girls and young women to flee their homes with an absence of resources and subject themselves to the risks of life on the street (Acoca, 1998; Belknap & Holsinger, 2006; DeHart et al., 2014; Goodkind et al., 2006; Greene et al., 2000), which Daly (1992) suggests may place a woman at a higher risk of encountering delinquent peers, criminal genic men, and other circumstances that could lead to prolonged and more severe victimization and exposure to alcohol abuse and illicit drug use.

The survival skills that often accompany these scenarios could include engaging in theft, gang involvement, or other criminal activity such as prostitution or drug sales (Daly, 1992; DeHart, 2008; DeHart & Moran, 2015). The possibilities and risks for these women

David Axlyn McLeod, Zackery D.O. Dunnells, and Burcu Ozturk, *Women in Forensic Settings* In: *Handbook of Forensic Social Work*. Edited by: David Axlyn McLeod, Anthony P. Natale, and Kristin W. Mapson, Oxford University Press. © Oxford University Press 2024. DOI: 10.1093/oso/9780197694732.003.0005

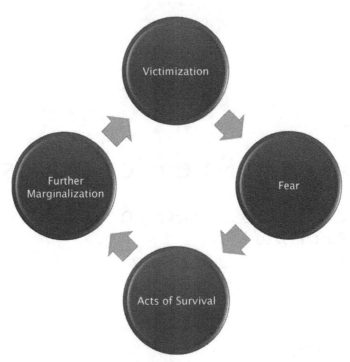

FIGURE 5.1 The Cycle of Victimization and Marginalization That Criminally Justice-Involved Women Experience

are endless. Researchers have shown that leaving abusive homes often places women in circumstances that increase their likelihood for differential experiences of oppression, marginalization, disempowerment, vulnerability, and further abuse (Belknap & Holsinger, 2006; Daly, 1992; Owen, 1998; White & Widom, 2003). This phenomenon is perhaps best described by Barbara Owen (1998) in her research with criminal justice–involved women. She found the *multiplicity of abuse* these women suffered throughout their lives directly influenced their *spiraling marginality* and subsequent criminality. Figure 5.1 visualizes this process and its potential cyclical nature. After experiencing victimization, women often experience tremendous fear, leading them to engage in survival acts, which puts them at higher risk for marginalization, leading to further victimization. While some women may find their way out of the cycle, researchers suggest that women who engage in criminal activity have a background of complicated marginalization, which feeds their levels of risk and increases their exposure to other interpersonal and systemic oppression (McLeod et al., 2019). Over time, this cycle compounds, necessitating understanding this phenomenon to competently work with criminal justice–involved women.

Gender Impacts in Forensic Settings

National Landscape

The incarceration rates of women in the United States have risen by twice that of men since 1985, creating a national reality that women are now the fastest growing segment of the U.S. incarcerated population (ACLU, 2021). The most significant rises in these rates are seen in local jails and state prison systems, and the explosive levels of women's involvement are likely tethered to the largely criticized *war on drugs* (Bureau Justice Statistics, 2020; Sentencing Project, 2020). If community sentencing (probation) is included in the estimate, upwards of 1 million women are under the control of correctional systems in the United States at the time of this text going to press (Sentencing Project, 2020).

The *National Resource Center on Justice-Involved Women* produced a critical report in 2012, highlighting important points to recognize when working with criminal justice–involved women. While a link to the full report is available in this chapter's resources section, Table 5.1 organizes the report's 10 salient points with essential facts associated with

TABLE 5.1 Ten Truths About Working With Justice-Involved Women

Truth about Incarcerated Women	Additional Context
1. Women pose a lower public safety risk than men.	▪ Women are more likely to enter the criminal justice system for nonviolent crimes. ▪ Justice-involved women are less likely to have extensive criminal histories. ▪ Women have lower recidivism rates.
2. Women present risk and need factors that signal different intervention needs.	▪ Women are more likely to have experienced sexual abuse and other forms of victimization. ▪ Women are more likely to experience co-occurring disorders; in particular, substance abuse problems tend to be interlinked with trauma and/or mental illness. ▪ Economic hardship, lower educational attainment, fewer vocational skills, underemployment, and employment instability are common among women.
3. Women's engagement in criminal behavior is often related to their relationships, connections, and disconnections with others.	▪ Women in the criminal justice system often have experienced abuse and neglect from the individuals closest to them; these experiences contribute to difficulties throughout their lives. ▪ The desire to preserve and maintain relationships can be linked to the very reasons that women commit crimes.
4. Traditional criminal justice systems were designed for men, not women.	▪ The programs and services that are available to women within institutional and community settings and to support them during transition and reentry may not adequately meet their needs. ▪ Access to appropriate health care for incarcerated women may not be adequate. ▪ Reentry services for women do not always consider the unique challenges that women face.
5. Women often report histories of sexual victimization and trauma, and they continue to be vulnerable to such victimization within correctional settings.	▪ Trauma is linked to mental health, substance abuse, and relationship difficulties. ▪ Individuals who are exposed to trauma do not easily recover from those experiences. ▪ Incarcerated women with a history of trauma and accompanying mental health concerns are more likely to have difficulties with prison adjustment. ▪ Correctional policies and procedures can trigger PTSD and hinder recovery.
6. Traditional prison classification systems tend to result in unreliable custody designations for incarcerated women.	▪ Classification tools are generally normed on male offender populations and are not validated on women, yet they are often used to guide key housing decisions for women. ▪ Traditional classification instruments typically do not incorporate factors linked to misconduct, prison adjustment, and recidivism among women.

(continued)

TABLE 5.1 Continued

Truth about Incarcerated Women	Additional Context
7. Gender-responsive assessment tools can enhance case management efforts with justice involved women.	▪ Gender-informed tools include both gender-neutral and gender-responsive factors that are specifically linked to outcomes for women (e.g., depression, psychotic symptoms, housing safety, parental stress). ▪ Gender-informed assessments consider a woman's strengths, which in turn play a protective role and mitigate the risk of negative outcomes.
8. Women are more likely to respond favorably when criminal justice staff adhere to evidence-based gender-responsive principles.	▪ Staff are more likely to achieve successful outcomes if they understand and apply the research literature on evidence-based and gender-informed practices. ▪ Interventions are most effective when their dosage and intensity are based on risk level. ▪ Staff who understand the importance of developing a professional working relationship with women and have the skills necessary to engage them appropriately are more successful. ▪ When staff recognize women's strengths, provide feedback, and help women mobilize their personal and social supports, they realize more positive outcomes.
9. Incarceration and reentry are particularly challenging for justice-involved mothers of minor children.	▪ A key source of stress for women while incarcerated, and during reentry, is the limited ability to maintain a connection with their minor children. ▪ Another significant challenge for mothers involved in the criminal justice system is their experience with poverty and economic marginalization.
10. The costs of overly involving women in the criminal justice system are high.	▪ Repeated exposure to the criminal justice system is detrimental to both women and their children. ▪ Costs can be avoided to state and local criminal justice systems, women, and their families, not to mention taxpayers.

each. As you review the table, be sure to recognize the recurring themes connected to feminist pathways. Among these points are that justice-involved women have disproportionate experiences of trauma and abuse across their lifespan. These experiences have led them to prison and interaction in the criminal justice system. Also, recognize that in working with these women, gender-specific trauma-informed approaches are the most efficacious. Finally, we must acknowledge in the recommendations that empirical evidence supports the point that women typically differ from men in how they have come into the criminal justice system and their levels of violence and likelihood for reoffending.

Trauma Among Criminal Justice–Involved Women

The discussion of criminal justice–involved women cannot be had without understanding the impact of trauma across the lifespan. There is perhaps no more prominent contributing factor to their criminal justice system's involvement than trauma: either facing or dealing with legal charges or experiencing victimization. While trauma can originate from many sources, which is discussed later in this chapter, understanding trauma and how it impacts people multidimensionally is essential when developing a quality standard of practice for women in forensic settings.

Trauma has been defined as the experience of any situation that can be shocking, terrifying, or overwhelming and produce feelings of fear or helplessness (Gillece, 2009). Research suggests that trauma need not be physically experienced to create a neurobiological impact. If a person believes themself to be in a situation producing eminent fear or threat of harm, the brain responds as if that harm is physiologically proximal and immediately present (Perry & Pollard, 1998; Perry & Szalavitz, 2007). Biological responses to trauma include increases in blood pressure and other hyperarousal markers, including releasing stress hormones like cortisol, dopamine, epinephrine, and norepinephrine (Perry & Szalavitz, 2007). These biologically driven hormonal responses can contribute to significant mental health issues such as posttraumatic stress disorder (PTSD) or *dissociation*, which can be observed through an emotional or mental detachment from events, up to and including an absence of recollection or personal connection to activities and experiences (Carrion & Steiner, 2000; DePrince & Freyd, 2007).

The negative impacts of trauma can be the product of a single disturbing or threatening event; however, it is more likely for trauma to be *complex* in the lives of system-involved women. This prolonged and repeated exposure to stress hormones and rapid neurotransmitter activity can result in brain cell death and impaired brain and physiological functioning over time (Gillece, 2009; Perry & Pollard, 1998). These repeated acute trauma experiences have been associated with lifelong maladaptive coping mechanisms (Alisic et al., 2011). These can include decreases in executive functioning, cognitive processing, logic and reasoning abilities, resulting in inhibited problem-solving skills (Pflugradt & Allen, 2010). Trauma survivors have been shown to have significant biological impacts and feel terror, which may cause them to act violently (Solomon & Heide, 2005).

Adverse Childhood Experiences and Violent Adult Relationships

Most incarcerated women in the United States have a significant history of trauma that begins in childhood. These trauma histories directly connect to PTSD and other behavioral and emotional problems associated with these women's presence in the criminal justice system (Jones et al., 2017). Without a doubt, the linkages between physical, sexual, and emotional abuse in childhood, as well as other dysfunctional household factors, have been shown to have a profound impact on the trajectories of these women's lives (Jones et al., 2017).

The adverse childhood experiences (ACEs) study (Felitti et al., 1998) has provided decades worth of data to help frame conversations and inform the later life experiences of people who experienced abusive, neglectful, and chaotic home/life experiences during childhood. The 10 unique ACE categories are divided into two specific clusters. The first cluster includes direct acts such as physical abuse, sexual abuse, or emotional abuse. In contrast, the second cluster consists of five categories of household dysfunction or chaos, such as having an incarcerated parent, having divorced parents, or having experienced domestic violence between parents. Possible ACE scores can range from 0 to 10. To learn more about the ACEs studies, visit the Centers for Disease Control and Prevention (CDC) website at https://www.cdc.gov/violenceprevention/aces/index.html.

Importantly, not all women who experience trauma in childhood find themselves involved in the criminal justice system as adults, yet when we examine the backgrounds of women involved in the criminal justice system, there is an overwhelming presence of childhood adversity in their personal histories. In many cases, the experiences of abuse, neglect, and household dysfunction in childhood placed these women on a path toward maladaptive coping mechanisms, drug and alcohol abuse, trauma-based high-risk decision-making, and other problematic adverse longitudinal life outcomes (Dong et al., 2004; Dube et al., 2002; Whitfield et al., 2003).

Jones et al. (2018) indicate that the presence and accumulation of ACEs, higher levels of ACE scores, and multiple clusters of ACEs are directly linked to relationship-based violence for criminal justice–involved women. Examples include simple assault, aggravated assault, sexual abuse, and psychological abuse in adult relationships. Data have continually shown that as the numbers of these women's ACE scores rise, so does their likelihood of being physically, sexually, and emotionally abused in their adult, preprison relationships (Jones et al., 2018). When working with women involved in the criminal justice system, it is vitally important for social workers to understand that the pathways that brought these women into the criminal justice system have been riddled with pain and trauma and that higher levels of trauma experienced in childhood are correlated with higher levels of victimization they have endured in their romantic relationships before criminal justice involvement. This is a complex phenomenon that we will continue to unpack further.

Continuing to think about this phenomenon from a trauma-informed lens, we understand that trauma can be actualized or perceived. Either way, it has a significant influence on an individual's brain activity and physiological functioning. To place this in context with childhood abuse and relational violence for women, numerous researchers have revealed that these phenomena are compounding (Cook & Goodman, 2006; Stark, 2007; Swan & Snow, 2002). Childhood abuse sets the stage for a higher impact of relationship-based violence, particularly *coercive control*, defined as nonphysical strategies by abusers to maintain power and control over their partners. This is characterized by intimidation, surveillance, isolation, economic control, and threats of harm, which are often enforced when an abused party does not comply with the demands of the abusive party in a relationship (Cook & Goodman, 2006; Stark, 2007; Swan & Snow, 2002). Abusers use this pattern of behavior to control their abused partners through marginalization and actively reduce a person's liberty, freedom, and self-efficacy (Stark, 2007).

These types of abusive tactics are overrepresented in women's preprison relationships and have profound and significant behavioral effects (McLeod et al., 2019). In one study, over 66% of incarcerated women reported being involved in a violent relationship at the time of their arrest, with over 43% meeting full diagnostic criteria for PTSD (Sharp et al., 2014). These violent and controlling relationships are not fictional or imaginary. For women from this same population, threats of harm related to behavioral control in their relationships are correlated almost perfectly with enacted physical and sexual violence with a statistically significant Pearson's correlation level of $r = .94$, representing a strong association

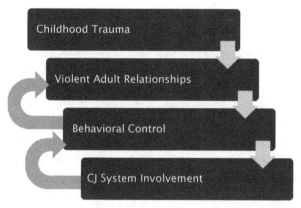

FIGURE 5.2 The Path of the Complex Trauma Criminal Justice-Involved Women Endure

(McLeod et al., 2019). With that said, criminal justice–involved women are more likely than not to be in an abusive relationship at the time of their arrest, and their partner is more likely than not to actively control their behavior. That control is then enforced with physical and sexual violence in the event of their noncompliance.

The complex trauma the criminal justice–involved women endure is represented in the path described in Figure 5.2. What begins as adversity and trauma in childhood transitions into violent adult relationships, which then, in turn, adds to the complex nature of these women's trauma. In the next step, the women in these violent relationships are directly associated with behavioral control within the relationship's context, continuing earlier trauma and further accentuating the loss of autonomy and self-control. This cycle leads to a series of unhealthy relationships, or more directly to criminal justice system involvement. When involved with the criminal justice system, rather than rehabilitation of trauma, women experience additional behavioral control layers, which accentuates their trauma experience, further disempowering them. This takes away from their ability to make changes that assert control of their lives, counterproductive to the rehabilitative process.

Understanding the complex nature of trauma and how it impacts females neurologically and behaviorally is paramount to improving quality of life. Extensive training on trauma-informed work and the development of new best practice models are essential to advance this field forward. Many other areas will be addressed throughout the remainder of this chapter, as related to the experiences of women who are engaged in forensic settings. Still, all of them will be connected in one way or another to histories of trauma and the ways that these women have interacted with the world.

Mental Health and Substance Abuse Issues

It should be no surprise when looking at system-involved women's complicated histories that they often suffer from mental health and substance abuse problems. Depending on where the data are drawn from, it can be seen that at least half of individuals in jail and prison are struggling with mental health problems, with up to one-quarter of those presenting symptoms of severe psychological distress (Bronson & Berzofsky, 2017). These rates are upwards of five times higher than in the general population. Female prisoners experience mental health problems at roughly double the rate of men, approaching 70% to 80% of the incarcerated female population (Bronson & Berzofsky, 2017; Jordan et al., 1996; Teplin et al., 1996). Additionally, researchers found that female state prisoners met the criteria for drug or alcohol dependence at a rate of almost 70% (Bronson et al., 2017). Just over 70% of women in state prisons, and nearly 50% of those in federal facilities, are documented to have used illegal drugs before incarceration (Mumola, 1999).

PTSD ranks as one of the highest mental health problems experienced by incarcerated women (Bloom & Covington, 2008). Considering the above discussion of trauma and our understanding of complex trauma histories for criminal justice–involved women, this should come as no surprise. In addition to other mental health conditions, PTSD can present as anxiety or depression and is often medicated through alcohol or illicit drug use. These connections are often intertwined with the experiences of criminal justice–involved women. It is not that their experience of mental health problems is related only to the trauma background. Instead, the trauma and marginalization that system-involved women have experienced have had a profound impact on their mental state and ability to lead the kinds of lives they aspire to. Correctional facilities, and the criminal justice experience in general, can have exacerbating effects on people experiencing PTSD. Thus, specific attention should be paid to engaging in a trauma-informed way and the complication of a co-morbid mental health and substance abuse diagnosis.

The Feminization of Poverty

Income and Debt

In addition to the trauma of adverse childhood experiences and adult relationships, system-involved women often come from circumstances of socioeconomic marginalization. Research has continually shown how women in the United States live at higher poverty rates than men (Bleiweis et al., 2020). Intersectionality complicates this phenomenon even further and shows how women of color tend to be disproportionately impoverished and that one in four unmarried mothers in the United States lives in poverty (Bleiweis et al., 2020). This is not something that starts later in life, as the data suggest that women begin living in poverty rates higher than men as early as the age of 5 (Bleiweis et al., 2020). In essence, the feminization of poverty begins in early childhood and continues across many women's lifespan. Not only is poverty associated with incarceration and criminal justice system involvement, but also the associations are powerful. When examining base-level income before incarceration, incarcerated people in the United States earn 41% less than nonincarcerated people in their similar demographic brackets (Rabuy & Kopf, 2015). Adding this to the reality that women in the United States still earn $.82 on the dollar compared to their male counterparts, this is particularly problematic and exponentially impactful (Bleiweis, 2020).

This finding is further compounding when examining income disparities across racial lines. Compared to White, non-Hispanic men, Asian American and Pacific Islander women in the United States earn an average of $.92 on the dollar, Black women $.62, Native American women $.57, and Latina women $.54 (Bleiweis, 2020). Furthermore, LGBTQ women experience higher rates of poverty than cisgender straight women, with around 18% of lesbian, almost 30% of bisexual cisgender women, and about 30% of transgender women living in poverty in the United States compared to approximately 18% of cisgender women and 13% of cisgender men (Badget et al., 2019).

Income disparities are not the only problem for women in social economics and poverty. Access to education and the debt accumulated to earn higher education disproportionately affect women in the United States, particularly women of color. While student loan debt is a widespread problem affecting many segments of the population, Black women tend to borrow closer to $38,000 to finance their educations, whereas White women tend to borrow closer to $31,000 (Chang, 2015). While higher education may not be one of the eminent risk factors that leads people into involvement with the criminal justice system, it is one of the most vital protective factors to keep people from becoming involved in the criminal justice system in the first place or to allow them to rise above previous criminal justice interactions (Wilkinson & Lantos, 2018). The reality is that these options are further from reach for most women in the United States, which is essential to recognize when working with these populations.

Income and debt are two substantial factors in these women's lives, but not the only ones. Women are also more likely to be caregivers. This means they are also responsible for the added costs and burdens caregiving places on the entire household. The lack of supportive employment policies and lower wages in traditionally feminized professions further complicate and accentuate this problem. In short, women in the United States are more likely to have higher levels of debt, more likely to have lower income levels, and more likely to have higher household and family responsibility levels, which translate into monthly financial obligations. This is also further complicated by intersectionality along race, sexual orientation, gender identity, and several other factors.

Legal Representation, Advice, and Decision-Making

Directly related to income is the lack of access to adequate, quality legal representation. It is easy to understand how women have lower income levels, more debt, and less essential access to socioeconomic resources. They also have restricted access to private representation within the criminal justice system, increasing the likelihood of relying on public defenders more often than men. The Bureau of Justice Statistics found that around 73% of county-based public defender offices exhibited a trend of exceeding maximum recommended cases per attorney (Farole, & Langston, 2007). This overloaded public defense system translates into a reality that, for many women, means they do not have access to an attorney who has the time or resources to investigate, research, and prosecute their case. The American Bar Association (ABA) has argued that this overwhelmed system creates and continually fosters an inability to properly serve poor and disadvantaged populations, which in turn is in direct violation of the constitutional right to counsel in criminal proceedings, as deemed by the Supreme Court (2004).

The overwhelming volume of cases handled by public defender's offices creates a scenario where defendants are encouraged to engage in plea bargaining. In exchange for pleading guilty to their charges, they can receive reduced charges or sentencing. This process has been well documented to have differential effects. The most negative of these differentially impact people of color, who are less likely to have their original charges reduced at the same levels as White people (Berdejo, 2019). When we investigate the recommendation and encouragement for a plea bargain from a trauma-informed perspective, there are even more differential effects on these women.

As noted earlier in this chapter, system-involved women tend to have complex personal histories with multiple levels of marginalization across their lifespan. They have likely been survivors of childhood abuse and male maltreatment and have a higher-than-typical likelihood of being involved in violent romantic relationships just before being charged with a criminal offense. All these factors contribute to the potential for them to follow the public defender's suggestions even against their wishes, which is a behavior that has been reinforced throughout their lives. Trauma-informed practice helps us understand that the decision-making process of women involved in the criminal justice system is directly related to their past experiences of abuse and marginalization. Briefly, these women have experienced across their lifespan that if they do not follow the directions of a person in power and authority over them, they will reap dire consequences. Further research is needed to reveal how women engage in the plea-bargaining process and how to modify policy considering these realities.

Female-Specific Intervention Features

With full consideration of all the realities described above, treatment and intervention are perhaps some of the most important aspects of working with women in forensic settings. A few specific barriers remain regarding therapeutic success regardless of a woman's needs (mental health, substance abuse, or co-occurring related and wraparound treatment). Among the most important of these is the difficulty in establishing a positive therapeutic relationship. The complex trauma history of criminal justice–involved women impacts their ability to have appropriate positive attachment and counter the therapeutic relationship (Motz, 2019). Before the onset of interventions, social workers need to be aware of and familiar with the most recent empirical literature on engaging clients and sustaining the therapeutic relationship in a trauma-informed way. It can often be the exact, reactive types of behaviors such as rapid breathing, muscle tension, and guilty feelings that we should expect to see from trauma survivors that will then serve as a barrier to women's access to treatment in correctional settings.

Co-occurring disorders, the combination of mental health and substance abuse issues, are often present in criminal justice–involved women and have specific ties to experiences of trauma and marginalization across the lifespan. Seventy-five percent of women in state prisons struggle with co-occurring disorders (James & Glaze, 2006). Studies have also long shown how the combined effects of PTSD (the most common condition in women's carceral populations along with depression), coupled with substance abuse, creates a substantially higher level of mental disorders, medical problems, psychological symptoms, noncompliance with treatment, and a host of maladaptive life problems (Najavits et al., 1997).

TABLE 5.2 The Primary Structural Elements and Their Components in Existing Gender-Specific Evidence-Based Treatment Programs

Structural Element	Components
1. Individualized Treatment	• Each client is unique, and their individual story must be validated • Develop personalized goals and priorities • Treatment should be flexible and adaptive to the individual's pattern of recovery
2. Women-Only Groups	• Women benefit from the relational aspects of group work • Women are more likely to engage in group work than men • Women do not work as openly when men are present • High rates of empirical success

3. The Physical Environment	• Treatment strategies must be designed to the dysfunctional systems women have already experienced
	• Trauma-informed therapeutic culture
	  • *Attachment:* culture of belonging
	  • *Containment:* culture of safety
	  • *Communication:* Culture of openness
	  • *Involvement:* culture of participation and citizenship
	  • *Agency:* culture of empowerment

4. Strengths-Based Treatment	• Work based on individual assets rather than deficits • Work toward client identification of strengths and skills • Nonconfrontational

Many therapeutic programs currently exist while more are evaluated each day; however, a few common threads have been observed in the most successful programs for criminal justice–involved women. Covington and Bloom (2007) identified and organized the primary structural elements in existing gender-specific evidence-based treatment programs (see Table 5.2). Strengths-based and trauma-informed approaches are crucial in treatment with criminal justice–involved women. Particular attention is paid to the psychological environment, where developing a culture of belonging, safety, openness, participation, and empowerment is vital to operational and therapeutic success. While many specific therapeutic programs or approaches can be used, the structural elements identified here provide the most direct pathway to these women's success.

Some of the more critical facets explored in this collection of structural elements are related to relational components. From the support and sense of community fostered through women-specific group participation to the cultivation of a culture of belonging and citizenship, the relationships that women develop are paramount to their success, posttraumatic growth, and empowerment to escape the cycle of interaction with the criminal justice system. Women in forensic settings benefit from female-specific programming in mental health, substance abuse, co-occurring, or relational contexts. This could be specifically related to the impact of trauma history and problematic relationships before system involvement.

System-Involved Women With Children

Although an entirely separate topic in and of its own, the discussion of women in forensic settings cannot be had without also addressing women as caregivers for minor children, which creates and exacerbates the cyclical problem of intergenerational incarceration. There are over 2.7 million children who have incarcerated parents in the United States, which is one in 28 children (Pew Charitable Trusts, 2010). Fifty-four percent of inmates are parents with children ages 0 to 7, including more than 120,000 mothers and 1.1 million fathers (Pew Charitable Trusts, 2010).

According to the most recent available data of the Adoption and Foster Care Analysis and Reporting System (AFCARS), parental incarceration was why 7% of children entered foster care in 2019 (Children's Bureau, 2020). Children might have additional trauma when their parents are involved in criminal activities and have witnessed the arrest or been questioned by the prosecutor (Peterson et al., 2015; Poehlmann-Tynan et al., 2017). In addition, children can experience sadness, shame, isolation, concern for the parent's well-being, and anger toward the parent or the system when their parents are incarcerated (Corinne Wolfe Children's Law Center et al., 2011). Furthermore, parental incarceration can cause long-term negative impacts on child well-being outcomes such as the risk for learning disabilities and developmental delays (Turney, 2014), low level of school performance (Murphey & Cooper, 2015), and antisocial behaviors (Murray et al., 2012).

The children in the ACEs study were exposed to higher levels of childhood adversity than the general population. They receive one ACE score just by the nature of their mother's incarceration. However, when considering the experience of the mother's life and the likelihood of substance abuse, violent relationships, and other hardships, the potential ACE scores rise for these children. This is further complicated by the additional trauma they experience due to child welfare system involvement and estrangement from parental figures. These children start life with significant disadvantages, so it is no wonder that children follow their parents' pathways into the criminal justice system. Children of incarcerated parents are, without any doubt, one of the highest risk populations in our society regarding exposure to adversity, and specific intervention is needed to address their current needs and set them up for positive trajectories in life (Berger et al., 2016). The incarceration of any family member can have a direct and lasting impact on all other family system parts.

Conclusion

In this chapter, we have explored some specific facets of social work with systems-involved women. We recognize that women find their pathways into the criminal justice system in distinctly different ways than men. The outcomes of interventions working with these women both in the system and along the pathways into and out of the system are better when engaging in trauma-informed and gender-specific practice. Trauma-informed practice is becoming more of a staple of social work, and reliance on that and evidence-based strategies is crucial to working with this population.

Moving forward in the text, we will discuss several significant trends. Diversion courts, for example, are a significant evidence-based advancement in social work with women in forensic settings. Additionally, domestic violence courts, substance abuse courts, family courts, and other alternative programs give women the tools to seek recovery (in various contexts) rather than institutionalization. These programs need to be further developed and enhanced, as they have proven effective and fiscally efficient. It is also essential to focus on gender-specific programming for women. This chapter outlines several vital criteria to identify existing gender-specific programming and modify and create programming to help women succeed.

From a policy perspective, several macro interventions are needed. Specific reform to our court systems and the process of public defense is among the most important for women. As mentioned above, women involved in the criminal justice system are less likely to have financial resources and more likely to be forced to trust the overwhelmed public defense system with their case. A great deal of criticism has come about for the public defense system, with particular attention paid to caseloads and public defenders' inability to prepare for their clients' adversarial defense adequately. This leads to practice and consistent courtroom dependence on plea bargaining. We can connect through evidence-based trauma-informed research to a specific disadvantage in the decision-making process for women who have likely experienced coercive and controlling relationships throughout their lives.

Working with women in forensic settings is an area of practice that is growing exponentially. We need to recognize the unique ways women have ended up in these situations and the complexity it would take to help them work their way into a healthier future. Some mechanisms exist to help us address these things clinically; however, the larger social constructs of sexism in the marginalization of women and intersectionality in the complex and multilayered oppression of people in our society must be addressed to remedy these problems fully. Micro-level approaches are essential clinically, and macro-level systemic change is vital to move this area forward.

Resources

- Ten Truths That Matter When Working With Justice-Involved Women
  - https://cjinvolvedwomen.org/wp-content/uploads/2015/09/Ten_Truths.pdf
- Incarcerated Women and Girls
  - https://www.sentencingproject.org/publications/incarcerated-women-and-girls/
- Sesame Street Resources for Children of Incarcerated Parents
  - https://sesamestreetincommunities.org/topics/incarceration/

Case Study

You work in management at a local nonprofit agency in a midsized city in the United States. Your agency does incredible work, but like many nonprofits, it suffers from a lack of funding and its service to a primarily impoverished community section. The agency's primary goal is to foster healthy reentry and system integration for people who have had criminal justice involvement. Your agency is relatively well connected to other service providers in the community and primarily serves Latinx individuals and families. The local, state, and national political environment has made it increasingly difficult to serve these families due to increased levels of marginalization and scrutiny that many of them have come to experience daily.

You have a new client on your caseload. Marlow is a 28-year-old Latina woman who has just been released from the corrections department after serving 18 months on controlled substance–related charges. She is a mother of two young children (3 and 6 years old) currently in state custody. She has some ties to family in the community; however, many family members who are not presently documented are hesitant to work with social service agencies out of fear of being reported to the government. Marlow has some history of associations with people who are gang involved. She reports some history of violence in childhood, which led to her running away at 14. She has previously worked in home-based childcare but has no formal job training or advanced education and did not complete high school. Since she was released early, she will have to report to parole, and probation will have a strict set of guidelines by which she has to live her daily life. Your job is to help her meet her goals and objectives and reintegrate into the community in a healthy and successful way.

Questions for Discussion

1. What are some of the first steps you need to take to organize and work with Marlow on her reentry?
2. What are some specific challenges that you can foresee and will need to plan for?
3. What are some potential areas of strength that you will work to identify?
4. What types of services and interventions would you prioritize, and in what order would you prioritize them?

References

Acoca, L. (1998). Outside/inside: The violation of American girls at home, on the streets, and in the juvenile justice system. *Crime & Delinquency, 44*(4), 561–589. https://doi.org/10.1177%2F0011128798044004006

Alisic, E., Jongmans, M. J., van Wesel, F., & Kleber, R. J. (2011). Building child trauma theory from longitudinal studies: A meta-analysis. *Clinical Psychology Review, 31*(5), 736–747. https://doi.org/10.1016/j.cpr.2011.03.001

American Bar Association. (2004, December). *Gideons broken promise: Americas continuing quest for equal justice*. A Report on the American Bar Association's Hearings on the Right to Counsel in Criminal Proceedings. American Bar Association Standing Committee on Legal Aid and Indigent Defendants. https://www.americanbar.org/content/dam/aba/administrative/legal_aid_indigent_defendants/ls_sclaid_def_bp_right_to_counsel_in_criminal_proceedings.authcheckdam.pdf

American Civil Liberties Union. (2021). *Facts about over-incarceration of women in the United States.* https://www.aclu.org/other/facts-about-over-incarceration-women-united-states

Badgett, M. V., Choi, S. K., & Wilson, B. D. (2019). *LGBT poverty in the United States: A study of differences between sexual orientation and gender identity groups.* https://williamsinstitute.law.ucla.edu/wp-content/uploads/National-LGBT-Poverty-Oct-2019.pdf

Belknap, J., & Holsinger, K. (2006). The gendered nature of risk factors for delinquency. *Feminist Criminology, 1*(1), 48–71. https://doi.org/10.1177/1557085105282897

Berdejo, C. (2019). *Gender disparities in plea bargaining. Indiana Law Journal, 94*, 1247. https://www.repository.law.indiana.edu/ilj/vol94/iss4/1

Berger, L. M., Cancian, M., Cuesta, L., & Noyes, J. L. (2016). Families at the intersection of the criminal justice and child protective services systems. *Annals of the American Academy of Political and Social Science, 665*(1), 171–194. https://doi.org/10.1177%2F0002716216633058

Bleiweis, R. (2020, March 24). *Quick facts about the gender wage gap*. Center for American Progress. https://www.americanprogress.org/issues/women/reports/2020/03/24/482141/quick-facts-gender-wage-gap/

Bleiweis, R., Boesch, D., & Gaines, A. C. (2020. August 3). *The basic facts about women in poverty*. Center or American Progress. https://cdn.americanprogress.org/content/uploads/2020/08/07060425/Women-IPoverty-UPDATE.pdf?_ga=2.145082544.500453984.1610463609-1045554167.1610463609

Bloom, B. E., & Covington, S. (2008). Addressing the mental health needs of women offenders. *Women's Mental Health Issues Across the Criminal Justice System*, 160–176.

Bronson, J., & Berzofsky, M. E. (2017). *Indicators of mental health problems reported by prisoners and jail inmates, 2011–12*. Bureau Justice Statistics. https://www.bjs.gov/index.cfm?ty=pbdetail&iid=5946

Bronson, J., Stroop, J., Zimmer, S., & Berzofsky, M. (2017). *Drug use, dependence, and abuse among state prisoners and jail inmates, 2007–2009* (NCJ 250546). Bureau of Justice Statistics. https://www.bjs.gov/content/pub/pdf/dudaspji0709.pdf

Bureau Justice Statistics. (2020). *Prisoners in 2019*. https://www.bjs.gov/index.cfm?ty=pbdetail&iid=7106

Carrion, V. G., & Steiner, H. (2000). Trauma and dissociation in delinquent adolescents. *Journal of the American Academy of Child & Adolescent Psychiatry*, *39*(3), 353–359. https://doi.org/10.1097/00004583-200003000-00018

Chang, M. (2015). *Women and wealth: Insights for grantmakers*. Asset Funders Network. https://assetfunders.org/wp-content/uploads/Women_Wealth_-Insights_Grantmakers_brief_15.pdf

Children's Bureau. (2020). *The AFCARS report: Preliminary F.Y. 2019 estimates as of June 23,2020—No. 27*. U.S. Department of Health and Human Services, Administration for Children and Families, Children's Bureau. https://www.acf.hhs.gov/cb/resource/afcars-report-27

Cook, S. L., & Goodman, L. A. (2006). Beyond frequency and severity: Development and validation of the brief coercion and conflict scales. *Violence Against Women*, *12*(11), 1050–1072. https://doi.org/10.1177%2F1077801206293333

Corinne Wolfe Children's Law Center; Advocacy Inc.; New Mexico Children, Youth & Families Department; New Mexico CASA Network; New Mexico Citizens Review Board; & New Mexico Children's Court Improvement Commission. (2011). *Connecting children with incarcerated parents*. https://childlaw.unm.edu/assets/docs/best-practices/Connecting-children-with-incarceratedparents-2011.pdf

Covington, S. S., & Bloom, B. E. (2007). Gender responsive treatment and services in correctional settings. *Women & Therapy*, *29*(3–4), 9–33. https://doi.org/10.1300/J015v29n03_02

Daly, K. (1992). Women's pathways to felony court: Feminist theories of lawbreaking and problems of representation. *Southern California Review of Law & Women's Studies*, *2*, 11.

DeHart, D. D. (2008). Pathways to prison: Impact of victimization in the lives of incarcerated women. *Violence Against Women*, *14*(12), 1362–1381. https://doi.org/10.1177%2F1077801208327018

DeHart, D., Lynch, S., Belknap, J., Dass-Brailsford, P., & Green, B. (2014). Life history models of female offending: The roles of serious mental illness and trauma in women's pathways to jail. *Psychology of Women Quarterly*, *38*(1), 138–151. https://doi.org/10.1177%2F0361684313494357

DeHart, D. D., & Moran, R. (2015). Poly-victimization among girls in the justice system: Trajectories of risk and associations to juvenile offending. *Violence Against women*, *21*(3), 291–312. https://doi.org/10.1177%2F1077801214568355

DePrince, A. P., & Freyd, J. J. (2007). Trauma-induced dissociation. In M. J. Friedman, T. M. Keane, & P. A. Resick (Eds.), *Handbook of PTSD: Science and practice* (pp. 135–150). Guilford Press.

Dong, M., Anda, R. F., Felitti, V. J., Dube, S. R., Williamson, D. F., Thompson, T. J., Loo, C. M., & Giles, W. H. (2004). The interrelatedness of multiple forms of childhood abuse, neglect, and household dysfunction. *Childhood Abuse & Neglect*, *28*, 771–784. https://doi.org/10.1016/j.chiabu.2004.01.008

Dube, S. R., Anda, R. F., Felitti, V. J., Edwards, V. J., & Croff, J. B. (2002). Adverse childhood experiences and personal alcohol abuse as an adult. *Addictive Behavior*, *27*, 713–725. https://doi.org/10.1016/S0306-4603(01)00204-0

Farole Jr, D. J., & Langston, L. (2007). County-based and Local Public Defender Offices. Retrieved from https://bjs.ojp.gov/content/pub/pdf/clpdo07.pdf

Felitti, V. J., Anda, R. F., Nordenberg, D., Williamson, D. F., Spitz, A. M., Edwards, V., Koss, M. P., & Marks, J. S. (1998). Relationship of childhood abuse and household dysfunction to many of the leading causes of death in adults: The adverse childhood experience (ACE) study. *American Journal of Preventative Medicine, 14*, 245–258. https://doi.org/10.1016/S0749-3797(98)00017-8

Gillece, J. B. (2009). Understanding the effects of trauma on lives of offenders. *Corrections Today, 71*(10), 48–51. https://www.thefreelibrary.com/Understanding+the+effects+of+trauma+on+lives+of+offenders.-a0196927757

Goodkind, S., Ng, I., & Sarri, R. C. (2006). The impact of sexual abuse in the lives of young women involved or at risk of involvement with the juvenile justice system. *Violence Against Women, 12*(5), 456–477. https://doi.org/10.1177%2F1077801206288142

Greene, S., Haney, C., & Hurtado, A. (2000). Cycles of pain: Risk factors in the lives of incarcerated mothers and their children. *Prison Journal, 80*(1), 3–23. https://doi.org/10.1177%2F0032885500080001001

James, D., & Glaze, L. (2006). *Mental health problems of prison and jail inmates* (NCJ 213600). Bureau of Justice Statistics. https://ojp.gov

Jones, M. S., Worthen, M. G., Sharp, S. F., & McLeod, D. A. (2018). Bruised inside out: The adverse and abusive life histories of incarcerated women as pathways to PTSD and illicit drug use. *Justice Quarterly, 35*(6), 1004–1029. https://doi.org/10.1080/07418825.2017.1355009

Jones, M., Worthen, M., Sharp, S., & McLeod, D. A. (2018). Life as she knows it: The effects of adverse childhood experiences on intimate partner violence among women prisoners. *Child Abuse and Neglect.* https://doi.org/10.1016/j.chiabu.2018.08.005

Jordan, B., Schlenger, W., Fairbank, J., & Caddell, J. (1996). Prevalence of psychiatric disorders among incarcerated women. *Archives of General Psychiatry, 53*(6), 1048–1060. https://doi:10.1001/archpsyc.1996.

Kajstura, A. (2019, October 29). *Women's mass incarceration: The whole pie.* Prison Policy Initiative. https://www.prisonpolicy.org/reports/pie2019women.html.

McDaniels-Wilson, C., & Belknap, J. (2008). The extensive sexual violation and sexual abuse histories of incarcerated women. *Violence Against Women, 14*(10), 1090–1127. https://doi.org/10.1177%2F1077801208323160

McLeod, D. A., Jones, M., Sharp, S., & Gatlin, L. (2019). No idle threat: Coercive control and enacted violence in the pre-prison relationships of incarcerated women. *Violence & Victims, 34*(3). https://doi.org/10.1891/0886-6708.VV-D-17-00023

Motz, A. (2019). Engaging women in forensic clinical interviews: The impact of gender. *International Journal of Forensic Mental Health, 18*(1), 21–34. https://doi.org/10.1080/14999013.2019.1567625

Murphey, D., & Cooper, P. M. (2015). *Parents behind bars: What happens to their children?* Child Trends.

Murray, J., Farrington, D. P., & Sekol, I. (2012). Children's antisocial behavior, mental health, drug use, and educational performance after parental incarceration: A systematic review and meta-analysis. *Psychological Bulletin, 138*, 175–210. https://www.doi.org/10.1037/a0026407

Najavits, L., Weiss, R., & Shaw, S. (1997). The link between substance abuse and post- traumatic stress disorder in women: A research review. *American Journal of Addictions 6*(4), 273–283. https://doi.org/10.1111/j.1521-0391.1997.tb00408.x

Owen, B. (1998). *In the mix: Struggle and survival in a women's prison.* SUNY Press.

Perry, B. D., & Pollard, R. (1998). Homeostasis, stress, trauma, and adaptation: A neurodevelopmental view of childhood trauma. *Child and Adolescent Psychiatric Clinics of North America, 7*(1), 33–51. https://doi.org/10.1016/S1056-4993(18)30258-XPerry, B. D., & Szalavitz, M. (2007). *The boy who was raised as a dog: And other stories from a child psychiatrist's notebook—What traumatized children can teach us about loss, love and healing.* Basic Books.

Peterson, B., Fontaine, J., Kurs, E., & Cramer, L. (2015). *Children of incarcerated parents framework document: Promising practices, challenges, and recommendations for the field.* Urban Institute.

Pew Charitable Trusts. (2010). *Collateral costs: Incarceration's effect on economic mobility.*

Pflugradt, D. M., & Allen, B. P. (2010). An exploratory analysis of executive functioning for female sexual offenders: A comparison of characteristics across offense typologies. *Journal of Child Sexual Abuse, 19*(4), 434–449. https://doi.org/10.1080/10538712.2010.495701

Poehlmann-Tynan, J., Burnson, C., Runion, H., & Weymouth, L. A. (2017). Attachment in young children with incarcerated fathers. *Development and Psychopathology, 29*, 389–404. https://doi.org/10.1017/S0954579417000062

Rabuy, B., & Kopf, D. (2015). *Prisons of poverty: Uncovering the pre-incarceration incomes of the imprisoned.* Prison Policy Initiative, *9.*

Salisbury, E. J., & Van Voorhis, P. (2009). Gendered pathways: A quantitative investigation of women probationers' paths to incarceration. *Criminal Justice and Behavior, 36*(6), 541–566. https://doi.org/10.1177%2F0093854809334076

Sentencing Project. (2020). *Incarcerated women and girls.* https://www.sentencingproject.org/publications/incarcerated-women-and-girls/

Sharp, S., Jones, M., & McLeod, D. A. (2014). *Oklahoma study of incarcerated mothers and their children.* Oklahoma Commission on Children and Youth, George Kiser Family Foundation, and The Oklahoma Department of Corrections.

Solomon, E. P., & Heide, K. M. (2005). The biology of trauma: Implications for treatment. *Journal of Interpersonal Violence, 20*(1), 51–60. https://doi.org/10.1177/0886260504268119

Stark, E. (2007). *Coercive control: How men entrap women in personal life.* Oxford Press.

Swan, S. C., & Snow, D. L. (2002). A typology of women's use of violence in intimate relationships. *Violence Against Women, 8*(3), 286–319. https://psycnet.apa.org/doi/10.1177/10778010222183071

Teplin, L., Abram, K., & McClellan, G. (1996). Prevalence of psychiatric disorders among incarcerated women: 1. Pretrial detainees. *Archives of General Psychiatry, 53*(6), 505–512. https://doi.org/10.1001/archpsyc.1996.01830060047007

Turney, K. (2014). Stress proliferation across generations? Examining the relationship between parental incarceration and childhood health. *Journal of Health and Social Behavior, 55*(3), 302–319.

White, H. R., & Widom, C. S. (2003). Intimate partner violence among abused and neglected children in young adulthood: The mediating effects of early aggression, antisocial personality, hostility and alcohol problems. *Aggressive Behavior: Official Journal of the International Society for Research on Aggression, 29*(4), 332–345. https://doi.org/10.1002/ab.10074

Whitfield, C. L., Anda, R. F., Dube, S. R., & Felitti, V. J. (2003). Violent childhood experiences and the risk of intimate partner violence in adults: Assessment in a large health maintenance organization. *Journal of Interpersonal Violence, 18,* 166–185. https://doi.org/10.1177%2F0886260502238733

Wilkinson, A., & Lantos, H. (2018). *How school, family, and community protective factors can help youth who have experienced maltreatment.* Child Trends.

6

Older Adults in Forensic Settings

Dana Prescott

Demographics and Host Environments

The profession of social work has historically acted in the roles of case managers, advocates, and clinicians working in the shadow of *host environments*: prisons, schools, courts, and hospitals (Prescott, 2013). Broadly defined for the purposes of this chapter, adults and children in the United States may find it difficult to live through life stages and avoid the experience of, and intersectionality with, these host environments. For older adults especially, not only may these host environments involve mental health, medical, prison, and legal systems, but also this same vulnerable demographic may be raising grandchildren, have adult children living with them, or be facing poverty and homelessness themselves (Canham, Custodio, Mauboules, Good, & Bosma, 2020; M. Choi et al., 2016). Given the expansion of this population over the next few decades, forensic social workers need to acquire specialized knowledge relevant to forensic assessment and interventions for clients.

In the United States, older adults, defined by the U.S. Census Bureau as over 65 years old, are a growing segment of the population (U.S. Census Bureau, 2020). Increases in life expectancy (among some but not all demographics) present a challenge to forensic social work at all macro and clinical practice levels. The 2016 American Community Survey (ACS) estimated the number of people in the United States aged 65 and over as 49.2 million (Roberts, Ogunwole, Blakeslee, & Rabe, 2018). Many remain in their own households instead of retirement or assisted care communities, even living as caregivers to grandchildren. Of that group, more than half were aged 65 to 74. The 75- to 84-year-old age group consists of approximately 14.3 million, or 29%. There were more females than males among the older population, with the disparity in numbers between the sexes increasing with age. The ACS also reported that more than three-quarters of the 49.2 million older population

Dana Prescott, *Older Adults in Forensic Settings* In: *Handbook of Forensic Social Work.* Edited by: David Axlyn McLeod, Anthony P. Natale, and Kristin W. Mapson, Oxford University Press. © Oxford University Press 2024. DOI: 10.1093/oso/9780197694732.003.0006 was White. The proportions of older populations for groups identified by races other than White in the ACS were statistically smaller than their respective representations in the total population (Roberts et al., 2018).

This chapter is organized by forensic roles for older adults in the context of capacity and competency, criminal responsibility and sentencing mitigation, and grandparents as primary caregivers of children in child custody and child protection cases. It is imperative to understand that, traditionally, forensic social workers have operated in these ecosystems as experts in adversarial judicial and administrative proceedings, such as competency or end of life and workers' compensation or Social Security eligibility, respectively. In this role, historically, forensic social workers have transferred and transformed complex and relevant research-based and scientific knowledge to decision makers (Gothard, 1989; Maschi & Killian, 2011; Roberts & Brownell, 1999).

Throughout this chapter, it is critical to remember that forensic social workers hold a specific ethical and legal responsibility to consider cultural, racial, immigration, or refugee status and socioeconomic differences and disparities when working with any population (Butters & Vaughan-Eden, 2011; Evans & Hass, 2018; Maschi & Leibowitz, 2017). These obligations should be not only observed after licensure and in the field but also introduced during the education and training of social workers in any degree program (Kheibari et al., 2021; Prescott, 2020). Therefore, the brief foundation to follow is intended to provide an understanding of the specific roles and duties of forensic social workers in transferring and transforming knowledge while always maintaining their ethical responsibilities to vulnerable older adults as the touchstone.

Social Work Ethics in Forensic Practice With Older Adults

Since the founding of social work at the turn of the 20th century, social workers have had a duty to apply the best science of the day to better understand and alter the biological, political, and social forces that shape individual outcomes (Fook et al., 1997). Social work has evolved for more than a century from an intersection of frameworks: generalist, community, individual needs, human rights, and social justice (Kam, 2014). These frameworks ever adapt, shift, and merge, and then re-emerge with new obligations and new theories, along with new evidence-based practices. As Reamer (1998) summarized on the 100th anniversary, the evolution of social work from community advocacy to more specialized individual services meant that the profession could "no longer afford to have only a vague understanding of prevailing ethical standards" (p. 489).

Modern social work thereby required and acquired its own code of ethics that emphasized the core value of social justice and the duties of competence and integrity (Barsky, 2019; National Association of Social Workers, n.d.). However, the practice of forensics across disciplines and ethical codes generates specific challenges related to respect for the individual and truth telling to share research and data with decision makers. Among those challenges is the notion that a profession, by definition, requires compartmentalized learning and specialization. Given the generalist model of social work at its roots, specialization or compartmentalization at the academic and practice levels may have serious consequences to social work research, practice, and the public good, an argument that is not new to the profession (Leighninger, 1980). Yet, as Gilgun (2005) so aptly summarizes, "No social worker states that we should not use research when it is available. No one can put up a respectable argument that we should fly by the seat of our pants and use untested assumptions on clients" (p. 59).

Maschi and Leibowitz (2017) support that proposition by arguing that forensic social work has "affected the social work profession with a call to fulfill its long-forgotten mission to respond and advocate for justice reform and health and public safety" (p. xv). Rigid training, institutional and professional gain, and narrow thinking increase the potential for confirmation, allegiance, and selection bias (Dror, 2020; Neal et al., 2019; Sovacool, 2008; Zapf & Dror, 2017). A consequence (foreseeable and unforeseeable) of this conflation of biases may skew expert opinions at significant risk to vulnerable groups. Moreover, there is an affirmative duty to organize parsimoniously and adapt specialized knowledge and skills (Banks, 2020; Barker & Branson, 2014; Barsky, 2019). These duties merge with an overarching obligation to avoid "deception, exploitation, or needless invasion of the privacy of the people whom we examine or about whom we testify" (Appelbaum, 2008, p. 197).

As Applebaum wisely (2008) noted, "Professional ethics cannot contradict or subtract from the ordinary obligations shared by all human beings" but must constitute "an addition to that corpus of duties" (p. 196). In that sense, he wrote, principles specific to specialty codes for forensics should derive from an analysis of the functional roles performed for society, including the administration of justice, and an applicable ethics code should facilitate and protect that role. Avoidance of bias in the forensic role derives from testimony and reports that accurately reflect scientific data that is generalizable and relevant to the subject and the consensus of that field. Anything that stretches data or controverts generally accepted professional standards drawn from replicated and independent research may be an unethical deviation of both shared ethics and the corpus of duties specific to forensic social work.

Therefore, for forensic social workers, working with clients in host environments is coextensive with the competency and integrity required to organize and adapt specialized knowledge and skills (Banks, 2020; Barker & Branson, 2014; Barsky, 2019). In a seminal article, Dane and Simon (1991) recognized (and warned) that once social work was organized as a formal profession, as Reamer suggests, these host settings were dominated by organizations with people who were not social workers, such that social workers must provide evidence "on a regular basis of their indispensability to either the mission or overall welfare of the host" (p. 208). Clinical and case management presents enough challenges when working within organizations in terms of professional turf, educational training, and dissemination of knowledge (Dane & Simon, 1991; Germain & Gitterman, 1980).

In this manner, much may be written about those challenges even into the 21st century. The various interdisciplinary and transdisciplinary challenges for professional social workers, however, in more traditional or nonforensic roles are beyond the scope of this chapter (Bellamy et al., 2013; Satterfield et al., 2009). However, one of those relevant challenges is the concern that social workers do not maintain current knowledge of evidence-based practices, such as the modern development of neuroscience, that are critical to understanding and assisting older adults subject to the legal system. For a forensic social worker working with older adults with cognitive and biological vulnerabilities, this duty of competency and integrity is especially important ethically and legally.

In one recent study, social work practitioners viewed neuroscientific knowledge as based "on a passive uptake, rather than active knowledge seeking," with the rationale of a lack of "initiative for practitioners" because of a lack of time and resources, a "different perspective on 'knowledge,'" and "their own understanding of the role of a social worker" (Plafky, 2016, p. 1511). What these quotations may reflect is a different attitude concerning evidence-based and -informed practice as relatively new terms in social work settings and, therefore, "not as ingrained in practice as it is, for example, for psychologists or medicine where guidelines and protocols seem to be more rigorous" (p. 1512). This is not simply a passing criticism because research reveals the complex relationship for social workers maintaining current knowledge of new sciences that may impact intervention design for clients.

Therefore, the strengths and impediments that apply to clinical and macro social work apply even more to forensic social work's ethical practice. As defined by its long history in medicine, psychology, and social work, the specialty of forensics is the very act of rigorously applying scientific and policy knowledge to individuals living in organic and adaptive systems. That act of agency on behalf of clients and organizations requires current knowledge across disciplines and ethical frameworks for critically analyzing and accurately and precisely translating science and specialized knowledge to host environments.

Forensic Practice With Older Adults Considerations

Forensic social work has a precise role identification and correlative duty. The practice of forensics generally refers to any subdiscipline (e.g., clinical, developmental, social, cognitive) when applying scientific, technical, or specialized knowledge to assist in addressing legal matters (American Psychological Association, 2013). Forensic social work includes specialized knowledge, "painstaking evaluation, and objective criteria associated with treatment outcomes" (Roesch, 2015, p. 187). A partial list of being forensic for social workers includes identifying, assessing, and labeling by diagnoses, competency, criminal responsibility, disability, sentencing mitigation, elder guardianships, hospitalization, suicide risk, and other matters that profoundly influence everything from loss of liberty to the right to the least restrictive treatment and access to interventions (Maschi & Leibowitz, 2017).

The National Association of Social Workers (NASW) Code of Ethics (n.d.) does not, however, specifically define forensic social work as a specialization, nor has the NASW adopted, unlike the American Psychological Association, specialty guidelines. However, the NASW Code of Ethics does guide any social worker in Section 1.04(c). When "generally recognized standards do not exist with respect to an emerging area of practice, social

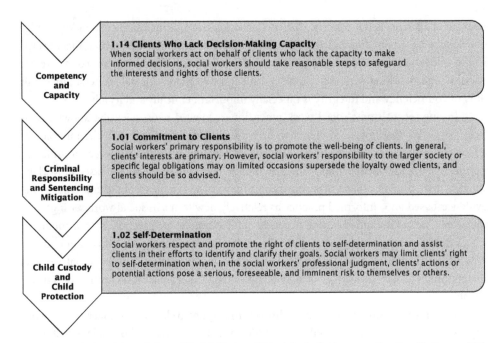

Competency and Capacity

1.14 Clients Who Lack Decision-Making Capacity
When social workers act on behalf of clients who lack the capacity to make informed decisions, social workers should take reasonable steps to safeguard the interests and rights of those clients.

Criminal Responsibility and Sentencing Mitigation

1.01 Commitment to Clients
Social workers' primary responsibility is to promote the well-being of clients. In general, clients' interests are primary. However, social workers' responsibility to the larger society or specific legal obligations may on limited occasions supersede the loyalty owed clients, and clients should be so advised.

Child Custody and Child Protection

1.02 Self-Determination
Social workers respect and promote the right of clients to self-determination and assist clients in their efforts to identify and clarify their goals. Social workers may limit clients' right to self-determination when, in the social workers' professional judgment, clients' actions or potential actions pose a serious, foreseeable, and imminent risk to themselves or others.

FIGURE 6.1 National Association of Social Workers Ethical Code Guidance on Practice Challenges With Older Adults

workers should exercise careful judgment and take responsible steps (including appropriate education, research, training, consultation, and supervision) to ensure the competence of their work and to protect clients from harm" (p. 9). Thus, the ethical duty to offer competent and evidence-informed opinions within the scope of their knowledge and experience is itself an ethical obligation of social workers to integrity drawn from truthful and transparent expert opinion (Reamer, 2013). Figure 6.1 presents ethical challenges in forensic social work practice with older adults and corresponding guidance from the NASW Code of Ethics.

As Maschi and Killian (2011) summarize, "Effective forensic social work requires an integrated yet two-pronged approach that addresses well-being (psychosocial) and justice (law and policy) to help individuals, families, and communities" (p. 13). This two-pronged strategy, or analytical model, is important because transmuting conceptual frameworks, theories, or hypotheses with observations from testing and clinical interviews as a predictive funnel is intended to minimize errors from unguided guesswork or intuitive or reflexive decision-making (Cashmore & Parkinson, 2014). This very act of expressing agency to an authority about another person is, by definition, acting in a forensic role. After all, there is always the potential for implicit bias, even for trained professionals and those who have the power to judge others, when life experience and heuristics trump intelligent and reflective observation (Dror, 2020; Hodgson & Watts, 2017; Kheibari et al., 2021; Scherr & Dror, 2021).

Reliance on the phrase "evidence-informed practice," like evidence-based practice, inadequately describes the competency and integrity required to share expert data and generalizable and relevant research. For example, in some organizations, forensic social work practice may mean commonly writing court reports without any citations and references to the specific data, like police charges, medical records, domestic abuse complaints and orders, child protection investigations, or other current testing (Plafky, 2016). These samples matter because for forensic psychologists or pathologists, among other specialties, explicit reference to this information and related research may help the fact finder classify as "scientifically valid" the conclusions of the expert.

When assessing or opining about an older adult, thus impacting their rights to self-determination and autonomy, it is appropriate to differentiate this "hierarchy of evidence (namely theories, research evidence, and practical/legal evidence)" (Plafky, 2016, p. 1213) in host environments. Grounding forensic conclusions on neuroscientific research knowledge for an older adult with cognitive and organic disabilities like dementia means explaining the connection to that condition and the interventions and restrictions a court may impose. These forms of knowledge translation in forensic practice encourage social workers to apply, adapt, and utilize scientific knowledge, which then becomes what Plafky identifies as *professional knowledge* or *knowledge-for-practice*.

It is not possible (or wise) to review all forensic practice areas related to older adults. Nor is it feasible to review the distinctions between forensic social work in jury and nonjury cases. However, there is value to recognizing that most cases related to older adults occur in probate and family courts or in administrative proceedings that do not have juries. The next section's discussion is intended to highlight concepts and terms that a forensic social worker should be familiar with when working with a population with its unique vulnerabilities. Moreover, by legislation and policy, these areas are areas in which forensic social workers who are granted legal authority to "decide" the mental status of older adults in host environments will be providing or interpreting data from other professions.

Older Adult Forensic Demographics

Existing and earlier studies suggest that at least half of elderly prisoners and forensic evaluees have a diagnosable psychiatric disorder, and up to 80% of older offenders have had psychiatric hospitalization for issues including dementia, alcohol abuse and dependence, substance use addictions, depression, and personality disorders (Argyriou, Um, Carron, & Cyders, 2018; N. G. Choi et al., 2019; Lewis et al., 2006). Arrests for violent offense among older adults have been associated with male gender, minority status, immigration status, low socioeconomic status, and history of past violent offenses, which, in turn, have been linked to elder competency (Lewis et al., 2006; Reyes et al., 2021). This data's consistency suggests that social workers adapt specialized knowledge that might include recognizing when a partner may consent to sexual activity or be victimized and unsafe from criminal or economic predators within or outside a family system (Cook, 2015; Werner & Doron, 2016).

Of concern with this population, dementia and other cognitive disorders such as Alzheimer's are progressive neurodegenerative syndromes that cause an irreversible decline in cognitive function (based upon current science) with limitations in language and memory executive function, orientation, and thinking processes. Individuals with dementia also experience significant physical limitations, including motor deficits and gait and balance disturbance, and may also include a range of behaviors, including agitation, physical and verbal aggression, paranoia and delusion, depression, apathy, and anxiety (Park, Howard, Tolea, & Galvin, 2020).

These social and biological problems' vulnerabilities are still to be foreseen with the epidemiological crisis of COVID-19 and its stress on institutions and family systems. The possibility of higher rates of elder abuse and neglect, interpersonal violence, and mental health disorders is coupled with health care disparities in nursing homes, prisons, and veteran's facilities (Altendorf et al., 2020; Cordasco et al., 2020). The risk for severe COVID-19 aftereffects and death escalates with older age but is especially likely for those who are immunocompromised or have underlying health conditions, including diabetes, cancer, and heart and respiratory diseases, particularly if residing in institutional settings (Chaimowitz et al., 2021; Xiang et al., 2020).

Whether in the criminal or civil arenas, neuroscience developments are critical to any analysis by forensic social workers of competency, capacity, or risk of harm to self or others (Cipriani, Danti, Carlesi, & Di Fiorino, 2017; Park et al., 2020). Although these measures are drawn frequently from criminal populations, the prevalence of intersection with older adults' legal system coincides with many of the same mental health and social determinants described (Holzer et al., 2020). The negative implications for older adults may be even greater when factoring in these risk factors and the potential for bias in an assessment of lesbian, gay, bisexual, and transgender older adults (Maschi & Aday, 2014; Orel, 2014).

Forensic Practice Examples With Older Adults

A number of social work practice challenges exist when working with older adults. Each challenge is detailed next and also captured in Table 6.1 by social work practice challenges, fields of practice impacted, and navigation tips.

Competency and Capacity

Historically, the terms "capacity" and "competency" existed in different environments. *Capacity* is a clinical practice term related to retaining people's power to make decisions for themselves (Moye et al., 2013). *Competency* is a legal determination that implicates rights in the criminal and civil sense, such as the ability to stand trial or the imposition of a guardianship or conservatorship, and is typically defined at the state and federal level by legislation (American Bar Association Commission on Law and Aging, 2008; American Psychological Association, 2005, 2006, 2008; Moye et al., 2013; Siegel, 2008).[1] The distinction may be less

---

1. A guardianship generally refers to the right to make day-to-day decisions about things like medications, housing, travel, and other activities. A conservatorship relates to the capacity to manage and spend money without oversight. An adult can be competent to make daily life decisions but not manage money without the risk of being taken advantage of. Thus, an older adult may have one or both with limitations (Gassoumis et al., 2015; Glen, 2012).

TABLE 6.1 Older Adult Forensic Social Work Challenges, Fields of Practice, and Navigation Tips

Practice Challenge	Impacted Fields of Practice	Challenge Navigation Tips
Competency and Capacity	▪ Medical, psychiatric, and psychological evaluations are required under state law as a foundation for determining competency or capacity and appointment of guardians, conservators, or institutionalization. ▪ Knowledge of the neurological, biological, and environmental impact of aging, its association with emotional and economic stress, and the implications of poverty and delayed retirement without adequate home-based social services or the income and savings to maintain stability in the home and community.	▪ Knowledge of interdisciplinary and transdisciplinary professional disciplines and their intersection with state law and courts is critical to advocating for the safety and autonomy of older adults. ▪ Knowing one part without the other leaves older adults vulnerable to losing the least restrictive services, maintaining dignity, and protecting civil rights.
Criminal Responsibility and Sentencing Mitigation	▪ Legal proceedings with the federal and state prosecutors, judges, and probation staff should connect clinical and community social work knowledge of family systems and dynamics, poverty, mental health, bias, and the availability of community services for alternative sentencing or mitigation of incarceration. ▪ This impacts the duty of social work to protect victims of abuse and interpersonal violence, as well as community safety.	▪ Risk assessments and competency evaluations are areas that social workers should advocate for but as independent from the state and for purposes of including alternative sentencing and evidence-informed interventions for consideration by judges, prosecutors, and defense attorneys. ▪ Learning to advocate using research and data to assist the courts to differentiate risk for an older adult and to ensure that cultural, racial, and economic disparities do not enhance the risk of inequitable sentencing or prevent access to services.
Child Custody and Child Protection	▪ The economic and emotional stressors associated with older adults caring for their children, or the children of their children, implicate clinical and macro knowledge of addiction, interpersonal violence, adoption, standards for best interests of the child, jeopardy, and termination of parental rights. ▪ The availability of clinical and community resources, intergenerational poverty, and patterns of familial abuse and violence, and the implicit and explicit biases that make older adults and children more vulnerable to epistemic injustice.	▪ Understanding strength-based perspectives that do not treat individuals and family systems as "clients" but as part of the solution, which in turn implicates a focus on coping and resilience rather than blame-and-shame labeling and diagnosis. ▪ Including a deeper understanding of the research related to ACEs and trauma-informed and multisystemic interventions, and advocacy against bias in the removal and placement of children subject to safety and stability in homes with older adults as parents.

useful today than in the past, but the precise definition is critical to forensic practice because, like the referral questions in a parental capacity evaluation or risk assessment, the role of the forensic social worker *is defined by what the law requires to be answered,* as defined by the law relevant to a case. Any meanderings outside that lane have the potential for ethical or legal liability.

For example, if an older adult is faced with criminal charges that may involve the risk of incarceration, the court may order a pretrial competency evaluation. In the criminal arena, most states have adopted a test similar to federal code 18 USC §4241(d):

> If, after the hearing, the court finds by a preponderance of the evidence that the defendant is presently suffering from a mental disease or defect rendering him mentally incompetent to the extent that he is unable to understand the nature and consequences of the proceedings against him or to assist properly in his defense, the court shall commit the defendant to the custody of the Attorney General.

An observer might then see that the person has pressured speech, makes odd statements, and seems disconnected during a mental status examination as part of an evaluation (Burgess, 2013; Hall, 2009).[2] One may conclude from that data that there is a problem with capacity or competency for immediate treatment or risk of suicide, but does that rise to the level required to stand trial in a criminal case as defined by the law? A fundamental duty of the forensic social worker is to frame the investigation from multiple data sources in the context of the specific law that a judge must apply to the person standing before a court.

The test for competently making life decisions, such as executing a will and powers of attorney and health care or advance directives, as well as managing personal finances, may be completely different such that competence or capacity in one environment may not be the same (or even close for that matter) in another (Crampton, 2004; Eggenberger, Luck, Howard, & Prescott, 2019; Whitman, 2012). The field of capacity assessment is dominated by a complex tension between two core ethical principles: autonomy (self-determination) and protection (beneficence; Berg, Appelbaum, Lidz, & Parker, 2001). Although there are nuanced differences from state to state, the past decade has seen the generation of a balancing test between disability, cognition, and functionality (which is the capacity to engage in self-care in a specific environment). Grey (2018) summarizes this more modern approach as follows:

> The goal of competency determinations in guardianship proceedings is to allow individuals as much autonomy as possible, only interfering when cognitive and behavioral incapacity puts them at too great a risk of harm to themselves or their property. Thus, knowing the precise law or the precise referral questions dictates the assessment tools and the type of structured or unstructured interview which may be undertaken. (p. 741)

Ultimately, and for social work in particular, competence and capacity are at the core functions of informed consent before being compelled to accept a loss of autonomy, possibly in addition to liberty and property rights. Underpinning this fundamental principle is

2. As a matter of revealing the bias of the writer, I prefer the strength-based approach to identifying individuals by their status as people rather than as clients or patients we observe, label, or define by the problem. I am grateful to social worker and educator Dr. Walter Kisthardt for this lesson many years ago (Weick et al., 1989). This point is especially relevant for report writing and testimony by forensic social workers.

the obligation to respect self-determination as the fountainhead of informed consent, as it means the right "to participate fully in decisions made about them to 'promote individual autonomy' and 'encourage rational decision making'" (Regehr & Antle, 1997, p. 302). In this context, the dimensions of science, ethics, and law share, in host environments, a common root for forensic social work: *volenti non fit injuria* ("to one who is willing, no wrong is done"; Levy, 1983, p. 4). This means that forensic social workers who provide assessments and expert opinions about older adults accurately reveal strengths and limitations before more wrong is done by misuse of research, overdiagnosis, or implicit bias more supportive of the institutions than human rights.

Criminal Responsibility and Sentencing Mitigation

Researchers and policymakers have recognized that the various combinations of health, cognitive functioning, and age of individuals involved with the justice system can have significant mitigation implications for the aging population's sentencing. As sentencing procedures have evolved, the relevance of these factors and the development of comprehensive historical data may increase the chance that these elements can significantly affect the sentence disposition and better ensure the humanitarian treatment of aging populations (Ryon, Chiricos, Siennick, Barrick, & Bales, 2017; Tussey, 2018). Aging is but one of many factors that may implicate the intersectionality of conviction and punishment on the effects of race, ethnicity, gender, age, and other social characteristics and environmental history on the inequality of outcomes (Steffensmeier et al., 2017). When a condition is diagnosable, such as dementia and its variants, there is a legitimate concern that criminal law and health policy should no longer be "treated as two separate worlds" but that criminal responsibility needs to be reconsidered in light of modern scientific and social change (Arias & Flicker, 2020).

In the United States, *criminal responsibility* (CR) "presupposes a prohibited voluntary conduct (intentional bodily movements) or *actus reus* but also requires a 'subjective element' or *mens rea*" (Tsimploulis, Niveau, Eytan, Giannakopoulos, & Sentissi, 2018, p. 372). Conversely, competency is fluid—or organic—as the status can change over time such that a person may not be competent to stand trial or needs a guardianship one day and 6 months later is deemed competent to stand trial or have the guardianship terminated. CR, however, concerns the intent to commit a criminal act at that moment in time. Criminal responsibility thereby

> mixes different meanings (practical and capacity) but applies especially to social and legal norms (normative meaning). More specifically, a person is *prima facie* criminally responsible when he or she commits a crime while validating its constitutive elements: the *actus reus* and the *mens rea*. The *actus reus* is the material element of a crime, which is to say the act that is being reprimanded, and the *mens rea* is the mental element, which is to say the state of mind of the accused at the moment of committing that act. (Bigenwald & Chambon, 2019, p. 1407)

For purposes of this brief review of criminal responsibility, it is important to keep in mind that insanity is a legal and not a psychiatric term and by no means is interchangeable (Tsimploulis et al., 2018). Some have argued, for example, that personality disorders or other psychopathological diagnoses may negate the material elements of a crime, but that argument does not yet carry policy weight (Kinscherff, 2010). This discussion at the outset is relevant because, again, the law defines the forensic social work role in a case, not personal values or wishing that the law were different.

CR commonly arises in death penalty cases and many other criminal charges when the state must prove any intent. The battle of experts in the arena is particularly acute given the highest stakes of liberty or life (Ratliff & Willins, 2018; Ricciardelli, 2020). Forensic social workers have a powerful role in trial strategies and outcomes given that older adults charged with serious crimes have comorbid mental and legal issues related to substance misuse, mental illness or trauma, and other social problems that require alternative sentencing plans apart from incarceration (Kheibari et al., 2021). When employed to gather mitigating evidence or offer an expert opinion, forensic social workers need to be very aware of the risks of ingroup bias and its implications in wrongful convictions and exonerations (Scherr & Dror, 2021).

These forensic activities can be grouped under the broad heading of mitigation practice, which has, of necessity, grown in conjunction with massive incarceration rates, the New Jim Crow, and drug interdiction and criminalization of much of American law over the past 40 years (Alexander, 2020; Scheyett, Pettus-Davis, McCarter, & Brigham, 2012). Mitigation practice is a subspecialty of forensic behavioral health, which includes assessment, treatment, consultation, and other services on behalf of individuals involved with the criminal justice system (Kheibari et al., 2021). Of critical importance, these services are integral to interdisciplinary legal and mental health teams and, thereby, encourage forensic social workers to convey data in a manner that meets the requirements of the court and is accessible by the team (Guin et al., 2003; Patterson, 2019).

This section concludes with a historical reference of significance to forensic social work. It is important to recognize that change in sentencing mitigation practice was built on original and collaborative efforts between forensic social workers and defense lawyers (Cooley, 2005). This was not the given so many may take for granted today. Readers may be unaware of the U.S. Supreme Court decision in *Wiggins v. Smith*, 539 U.S. 510 (2003). In *Wiggins*, the court's 7–2 majority opinion specifically relied on the work of a clinical social worker, Hans Selvog, as a basis for vacating a conviction due to ineffective assistance of counsel in a capital sentencing case.

In 1993, Wiggins sought postconviction relief in Baltimore County Circuit Court and challenged the adequacy of his representation at sentencing, arguing that his attorneys had rendered constitutionally defective assistance by failing to investigate and present mitigating evidence of his dysfunctional background. To support that claim, the petitioner presented Hans Selvog's expert testimony concerning an elaborate social-history report Selvog had prepared that included evidence of the severe physical and sexual abuse the petitioner suffered at the hands of his mother, foster parents, and other authority figures.

Relying on state social service, medical, and school records, as well as interviews with the petitioner and numerous family members, Selvog chronicled the petitioner's bleak and horrific life history from childhood. The court vacated the conviction. As the majority concluded, "Wiggins' sentencing jury heard only one significant mitigating factor—that

Wiggins had no prior convictions. Had the jury been able to place petitioner's excruciating life history on the mitigating side of the scale, there is a reasonable probability that at least one juror would have struck a different balance" (*Wiggins v. Smith*, 2003, p. 537). This tier of forensic social work will become even more valuable as Americans live longer, "excruciating" life stories become prolongated, and biological and social conditions connect older adults to host environments.

Child Custody and Child Protection

It may seem odd to include this topic, as this chapter pertains to adults over 65. Forensic social workers, however, are grounded in the biopsychosocial obligations to understand and explain family systems. The same older adults with the risk of degenerative mental and physical health are now raising grandchildren caught in child protection and child custody cases. These circumstances are relevant to forensic social workers providing information and data in cases that may involve child protection services and, concomitantly, complaints of interpersonal violence in a home headed by an older adult as part of the placement. In addition, these older adults, now with diminishing capacities and raising grandchildren, may themselves have been trauma victims or have a history of inflicting trauma as parents or caregivers.

Approximately 7.6 million children in the United States live in households headed by kin defined as a grandparent, uncle, aunt, or other relatives. More than 2.6 million children live with grandparents, relatives, or close family friends without either of their parents in the home (Sneed & Schulz, 2019). The public health crisis related to opioid addiction, mass incarceration, and economic deprivation and instability of housing and income has accelerated the rates of placement from court orders and private decision-making by families. While caregivers might be aunts, uncles, siblings, or other relatives, most are grandparents, and many of them are the primary if not sole caregivers. Sneed and Schulz (2019) revealed that 41% are older than age 60, approximately 57% are in the workforce, approximately 69% are married, nearly two-thirds are female, nearly one in five lives in poverty, and more than a quarter have a disability. A slim majority, 53%, are White; approximately 20% are Black or African American; 20% are of Hispanic or Latino origin; 3% are Asian; and 2% are American Indian or Alaska Native.

Therefore, the child welfare system relies heavily on kinship care providers, which has consequences for older adult caregivers' population. Studies that focus on grandparents raising grandchildren as custodial caregivers generally associate this form of support with numerous adverse physical health outcomes, including poorer self-rated health, increased frailty, and greater coronary heart disease risk (Sneed & Schulz, 2019). Many struggle with their own mental health issues. These can stem from feelings of shame, loss, or guilt about their adult child's inability to parent. Some older adults suffer from social isolation and depression because they do not want their peers to know about their situation; or they are grieving a host of losses, including losing the traditional grandparent role or losing control over their future, financial security, and leisure time (Cox, 2020; Lent & Otto, 2018; Sprang, Choi, Eslinger, & Whitt-Woosley, 2015). For older populations especially, kinship care, by default or court order, arising from absent parents because of addiction or mass incarcerations may exacerbate quality of life and stressors that impact preexisting health disparities as well as intergenerational violence and poverty (Kelley et al., 2013; Xu et al., 2020).

As identified in the prior subsections, forensic social workers may profoundly influence older adults' trajectory by understanding the intergenerational, economic, and environmental stressors that are now impacted by declining health. The history and experiences of these older adults as parents and children may have a much greater influence on the commission of violence, the misuse of medication, the capacity for self-care and the care of others like grandchildren, or forms of depression and despair that lead to hospitalization and even suicide. This is the reality testing, grounded in data and research, required when exercising the specialized knowledge of forensic social work to explain how an older adult went from one point in life to another and what interventions may be effective.

Conclusion

Vulnerable and oppressed populations in the United States inevitably intersect with one or more host environments over a lifespan. Those interactions' frequency and severity might differ depending on race, culture, immigration status, socioeconomic status, gender, or other demographic and economic variables. In host environments working with older adults, social workers are held to a standard of competent and ethical practices that requires much more than instincts or personal feelings about right and wrong. These environments require multiple sources of data and multiple hypotheses, as well as explanations for explicitly why "I know what I know" and how a particular way of knowing is supported by intellectual rigor, emotional objectivity, and expert opinions drawn from a transparent analysis of data.

Webb (2001), for example, described this need in the context of teaching a rational actor model for evidence-based social workers. Arguing for a more "sweeping critique of the evidence-based models" for social work, he recognized that social workers, as "agents of change," require a deeper understanding of deliberation and choice when making decisions (p. 67). As he succinctly noted, "Notoriously, social workers make decisions not only because of the ways things are but because of the way they would like things to be" (p. 67). Forensic social work encourages intentionality when social workers act as agents in open and adaptive systems in which there are consequences to clients from reactive or value-laden decisions disconnected from data and research (Prescott, 2007).

I have argued elsewhere that social work is unique as a profession: Social workers are intrinsically and unavoidably forensic because social workers' core values require that social workers undertake and employ macro and specialized knowledge at all levels of service (Prescott, 2020). This pertains to pursuing social justice to ensure people's dignity and worth and the protection of personal autonomy and self-determination. In actuality, the power and privilege of being a forensic social worker require expert opinions drawn from population data, generalizable and relevant research, and a keen understanding of the influence those variables have on the statutory dimensions or referral questions before any decision maker.

The examples in this chapter are selective, of course, and do not come close to all the material covered in this book. However, a social worker's engagement is not the benign (even if well-intentioned) transfer of information about a person or group to a government authority with the power to sanction or reward. Rather, the forensic social worker's role is an intentional act of agency, or *praxis*, between a vulnerable individual, from whom, willingly or not, information is transferred and transformed to an authority with the power to render judgment with attendant consequences to vulnerable older adults.

This praxis is much more than reflexive (Payne, 1998). This praxis means, in the deepest ethical and moral sense, that *becoming* a competent forensic social worker who practices with integrity requires targeting the specialization of forensic social work, "a practice specialization that speaks to the heart, head, and hands (i.e., knowledge, values, and skills) of social work using a human rights and social justice approach integrated with a forensic lens" (Maschi & Leibowitz, 2017, p. xv). Given the growing population of older adults in the United States (and globally for that matter) and the historical oppression of minorities and vulnerable populations within that population, the need for forensic social workers who can navigate those needs and vulnerabilities is especially acute.

Others have suggested the need for more specialized education and postdegree training in forensics or other fields to protect vulnerable populations (Sheehan, 2016). These moral and legal duties are grounded in the very core of the integrity and competence required to exercise specialized power thoughtfully and with cultural sensitivity and intellectual depth. Social work is, of necessity and core values, a rigor-driven chameleon in its delivery of service to clients and victims of oppression in host environments; and that chameleon quality characterizes social workers as integral and ethically grounded members of interdisciplinary teams (Cole, 2012; Colvin et al., 2011). Becoming and being forensic means those social workers accept responsibility for older adults living in diverse organizations and social environments.

References

Alexander, M. (2020). *The New Jim Crow: Mass incarceration in the age of colorblindness.* New Press. https://www.ojp.gov/ncjrs/virtual-library/abstracts/new-jim-crow-mass-incarceration-age-colorblindness

Altendorf, A., Draper, B., Wijeratne, C., Schreiber, J., & Kanareck, D. (2020). Neglect of older people: touching on forensic and pathophysiological aspects. *The Gerontologist,* 60(6), e449–e465. https://doi.org/10.1093/geront/gnz084

American Bar Association Commission on Law and Aging & American Psychological Association. (2005). *Assessment of older adults with diminished capacity: A handbook for lawyers* (2nd ed.). https://www.apa.org/pi/aging/resources/guides/diminished-capacity.pdf

American Bar Association Commission on Law & Aging and American Psychological Association. (2008). *Assessment of older adults with diminished capacity: A handbook for psychologists.* https://www.apa.org/pi/aging/resources/guides/diminished-capacity.pdf

American Psychological Association. (2013). Specialty guidelines for forensic experts. *American Psychologist,* 68(1), 7–19. https://psycnet.apa.org/doiLanding?doi=10.1037%2Fa0029889

Appelbaum, P. S. (2008). Ethics and forensic psychiatry: Translating principles into practice. *Journal of the American Academy of Psychiatry and the Law Online,* 36(2), 195–200. http://jaapl.org/content/jaapl/36/2/195.full.pdf

Argyriou, E., Um, M., Carron, C., & Cyders, M. A. (2018). Age and impulsive behavior in drug addiction: A review of past research and future directions. *Pharmacology Biochemistry and Behavior, 164*, 106–117. https://doi.org/10.1016/j.pbb.2017.07.013

Arias, J. J., & Flicker, L. S. (2020). A matter of intent: A social obligation to improve criminal procedures for individuals with dementia. *Journal of Law, Medicine & Ethics, 48*(2), 318–327. https://doi.org/10.1177/1073110520935345

Banks, S. (2020). *Ethics and values in social work*. Bloomsbury Publishing. https://www.google.com/books/edition/Ethics_and_Values_in_Social_Work/6RxHEAAAQBAJ?hl=en&gbpv=1&dq=Ethics+and+values+in+social+work.&pg=PR9&printsec=frontcover

Barker, R. L., & Branson, D. M. (2014). *Forensic social work: Legal aspects of professional practice* (2nd ed.). Routledge. https://doi.org/10.4324/9781315821573

Barsky, A. E. (2019). *Ethics and values in social work: An integrated approach for a comprehensive curriculum* (2nd ed.). https://global.oup.com/academic/product/ethics-and-values-in-social-work-9780190678111?cc=us&lang=en&

Bellamy, J. L., Mullen, E. J., Satterfield, J. M., Newhouse, R. P., Ferguson, M., Brownson, R. C., & Spring, B. (2013). Implementing evidence-based practice education in social work: A transdisciplinary approach. *Research on Social Work Practice, 23*(4), 426–436. https://doi.org/10.1177%2F1049731513480528

Berg, J. W., Appelbaum, P. S., Lidz, C. W., & Parker, L. S. (2001). *Informed consent: Legal theory and clinical practice*. Oxford University Press. https://www.google.com/books/edition/Informed_Consent/b6w7V7gCkSIC?hl=en&gbpv=1&dq=Berg,+J.+W.,+et+al.+(2001).+Informed+consent:+Legal+theory+and+clinical+practice.+Oxford+University+Press.&pg=PR11&printsec=frontcover

Bigenwald, A., & Chambon, V. (2019). Criminal responsibility and neuroscience: No revolution yet. *Frontiers in Psychology, 10*, 1406. https://doi.org/10.3389/fpsyg.2019.01406

Burgess, W. (2013). *Mental status examination: 52 challenging cases, DSM and ICD-10 interviews, questionnaires and cognitive tests for diagnosis and treatment* (3rd ed.). https://www.amazon.com/Mental-Status-Examination-Challenging-Questionnaires/dp/1482552957?asin=1482552957&revisionId=&format=4&depth=1

Butters, R. P., & Vaughan-Eden, V. (2011). The ethics of practicing forensic social work. *Journal of Forensic Social Work, 1*(1), 61–72. https://doi.org/10.1080/1936928X.2011.541202

Canham, S. L., Custodio, K., Mauboules, C., Good, C., & Bosma, H. (2020). Health and psychosocial needs of older adults who are experiencing homelessness following hospital discharge. *The Gerontologist, 60*(4), 715–724. https://doi.org/10.1093/geront/gnz078

Cashmore, J., & Parkinson, P. (2014). The use and abuse of social science research evidence in children's cases. *Psychology, Public Policy, and Law, 20*(3), 239.

Chaimowitz, G. A., Upfold, C., Géa, L. P., Qureshi, A., Moulden, H. M., Mamak, M., & Bradford, J. M. W. (2021). Stigmatization of psychiatric and justice-involved populations during the COVID-19 pandemic. *Progress in Neuro-Psychopharmacology and Biological Psychiatry, 106*, 110150. https://doi.org/10.1016/j.pnpbp.2020.110150

Choi, M., Sprang, G., & Eslinger, J. G. (2016). Grandparents raising grandchildren: A synthetic review and theoretical model for interventions. *Family & Community Health, 39*(2), 120–128. https://journals.lww.com/familyandcommunityhealth/Abstract/2016/04000/Grandparents_Raising_Grandchildren__A_Synthetic.7.aspx

Choi, N. G., Dinitto, D. M., & Arndt, S. (2019). Marijuana use among older adults: Harms may outweigh benefits. *Innovation in Aging, 3*(Suppl 1), S204. https://doi.org/10.1093/geroni/igz038.740 http

Cipriani, G., Danti, S., Carlesi, C., & Di Fiorino, M. (2017). Armed and aging: Dementia and firearms do not mix! *Journal of Gerontological Social Work, 60*(8), 647–660. https://doi.org/10.1080/01634372.2017.1376240

Cole, P. L. (2012). You want me to do what? Ethical practice within interdisciplinary collaborations. *Journal of Social Work Values and Ethics, 9*(1), 26–39. https://www.semanticscholar.org/paper/You-want-me-to-do-what-Ethical-practice-within-Cole/274cae0e73bb88eeb64449483becd288ed38503

cColvin, J. D., Nelson, B., & Cronin, K. (2011). Integrating social workers into medical–legal partnerships: Comprehensive problem solving for patients. *Social Work, 57*(4), 333–341. https://doi.org/10.1093/sw/sws012

Cook, J. (2015). When one spouse has it: Dementia and the permissibility of marital sex under criminal statute. *Journal of Marshall Law Review, 49*, 1225–1258. https://scholar.google.com/citations?view_op=view_citation&hl=en&user=1WlyTSMAAAAJ&citation_for_view=1WlyTSMAAAAJ:u-x6o8ySG0sC

Cooley, C. M. (2005). Mapping the monster's mental health and social history: Why capital defense attorneys and public defender death penalty units require the services of mitigation specialists. *Oklahoma City University Law Review, 30*, 23–41. https://heinonline.org/HOL/LandingPage?handle=hein.journals/okcu30&div=8&id=&page=

Cordasco, F., Scalise, C., Sacco, M. A., Bonetta, C. F., Zibetti, A., Cacciatore, G., ... Aquila, I. (2020). The silent deaths of the elderly in long-term care facilities during the Covid-19 pandemic: The role of forensic pathology. *Medico-Legal Journal, 88*(2), 66–68. https://doi.org/10.1177%2F0025817220930552

Cox, C. (2020). Older adults and COVID 19: Social justice, disparities, and social work practice. *Journal of Gerontological Social Work, 63*(6–7), 611–624. https://doi.org/10.1080/01634372.2020.1808141

Crampton, A. (2004). The importance of adult guardianship for social work practice. *Journal of Gerontological Social Work, 43*(2–3), 117–129. https://doi.org/10.1300/J083v43n02_08

Dane, B. O., & Simon, B. L. (1991). Resident guests: Social workers in host settings. *Social Work, 36*(3), 208–213. https://psycnet.apa.org/record/1991-28704-001

Dror, I. E. (2020). Cognitive and human factors in expert decision making: Six fallacies and the eight sources of bias. *Analytical Chemistry, 92*(12), 7998–8004. https://www.researchgate.net/publication/341793979_Cognitive_and_Human_Factors_in_Expert_Decision_Making_Six_Fallacies_and_the_Eight_Sources_of_Bias#read

Eggenberger, T., Luck, G. R., Howard, H., & Prescott, D. E. (2019). Advanced directives and family practice: Implications and ethics for "greying" family systems and interdisciplinary collaboration. *Journal of the American Academy of Matrimonial Lawyers, 32*, 1–28. https://cdn.ymaws.com/aaml.org/resource/collection/52E2F025-4275-4FEC-ACDD-6AADA46E6951/AdvancedDirectivesandFamilyPractice2.pdf

Evans, B. F., & Hass, G. A. (2018). *Forensic psychological assessment in immigration court: A guidebook for evidence-based and ethical practice.* Routledge.

Fook, J., Ryan, M., & Hawkins, L. (1997). Towards a theory of social work expertise. *British Journal of Social Work, 27*(3), 399–417. https://www.researchgate.net/profile/Linette-Hawkins/publication/31105399_Towards_a_Theory_of_Social_Work_Expertise/links/57ad897008ae42ba52b32f4f/Towards-a-Theory-of-Social-Work-Expertise.pdf

Germain, C., & Gitterman, A. (1980). *The life model of social work practice.* Columbia University Press. https://www.jstor.org/stable/10.7312/gitt13998

Gilgun, J. F. (2005). The four cornerstones of evidence-based practice in social work. *Research on Social Work Practice, 15*(1), 52–61. https://doi.org/10.1177%2F1049731504269581

Gothard, S. (1989). Power in the court: The social worker as an expert witness. *Social Work, 34*(1), 65–67. https://doi.org/10.1093/sw/34.1.65

Grey, B. J. (2018). Aging in the 21st century: Using neuroscience to assess competency in guardianships. *Wisconsin Law Review, 2018*, 735–781. https://uwlaw-omeka.s3.us-east-2.amazonaws.com/original/3da3b625d2523ab1ee7f9653e6394ebba111d693.pdf

Guin, C. C., Noble, D. N., & Merrill, T. S. (2003). From misery to mission: Forensic social workers on multidisciplinary mitigation teams. *Social Work, 48*(3), 362–371. https://doi.org/10.1093/sw/48.3.362

Hall, R. C. (2009). Mental status: Examination. In A. Jamieson & A. A. Moenssens (Eds.), *Wiley encyclopedia of forensic science* (1st ed., pp. 1–8). Wiley & Sons. https://doi.org/10.1002/9780470061589.fsa287

Hodgson, D., & Watts, L. (2017). *Key concepts and theory in social work.* Bloomsbury Publishing.

Holzer, K. J., AbiNader, M. A., Vaughn, M. G., Salas-Wright, C. P., & Oh, S. (2022). Crime and violence in older adults: Findings from the 2002 to 2017 national survey on drug use and health. *Journal of Interpersonal Violence, 37*(1-2), 764–781. https://doi.org/10.1177%2F0886260520913652

Kam, P. K. (2014). Back to the "social" of social work: Reviving the social work profession's contribution to the promotion of social justice. *International Social Work, 57*(6), 723–740.

Kelley, S. J., Whitley, D. M., & Campos, P. E. (2013). Psychological distress in African American grandmothers raising grandchildren: The contribution of child behavior problems, physical health, and family resources. *Research in Nursing & Health, 36*(4), 373–385. https://doi.org/10.1002/nur.21542

Kheibari, A., Walker, R. J., Clark, J., Victor III, G., & Monahan, E. (2021). Forensic Social Work: Why Social Work Education Should Change. *Journal of Social Work Education, 57*(2), 332–341. https://doi.org/10.1080/10437797.2019.1671257

Kinscherff, R. (2010). Proposition: A personality disorder may nullify responsibility for a criminal act. *Journal of Law, Medicine & Ethics, 38*(4), 745–759. https://doi.org/10.1111/j.1748-720X.2010.00528.x

Leighninger, L. (1980). The generalist-specialist debate in social work. *Social Service Review, 54*(1), 1–12. https://www.journals.uchicago.edu/doi/abs/10.1086/643800

Lent, J. P., & Otto, A. (2018). Grandparents, grandchildren, and caregiving: The impacts of America's substance use crisis. *Generations, 42*(3), 15–22. https://www.ingentaconnect.com/content/asag/gen/2018/00000042/00000003/art00004

Levy, C. L. (1983). *The human body and the law: Legal and ethical considerations in human experimentation* (2nd ed.). Legal Almanac Series. Oceana Publications.

Lewis, C. F., Fields, C., & Rainey, E. (2006). A study of geriatric forensic evaluees: Who are the violent elderly? *Journal of the American Academy of Psychiatry and the Law, 34*(3), 324–332. http://jaapl.org/content/34/3/324

Maschi, T., & Aday, R. H. (2014). The social determinants of health and justice and the aging in prison crisis: A call for human rights action. *International Journal of Social Work, 1*(1), 15–33. http://dx.doi.org/10.5296/ijsw.v1i1.4914

Maschi, T., & Killian, M. L. (2011). The evolution of forensic social work in the United States: Implications for 21st century practice. *Journal of Forensic Social Work, 1*(1), 8–36. https://doi.org/10.1080/1936928X.2011.541198

Maschi, T., & Leibowitz, G. S. (Eds.). (2017). *Forensic social work: Psychosocial and legal issues across diverse populations and settings* (2nd ed.). Springer Publishing.

Moye, J., Marson, D. C., & Edelstein, B. (2013). Assessment of capacity in an aging society. *American Psychologist, 68*(3), 158. https://psycnet.apa.org/doi/10.1037/a0032159 https://psycnet.apa.org/record/2013-12501-004

National Association of Social Workers (NASW). (n.d.). *Code of ethics of the National Association of Social Workers*. NASW Press. https://www.socialworkers.org/About/Ethics/Code-of-Ethics

Orel, N. A. (2014). Investigating the needs and concerns of lesbian, gay, bisexual, and transgender older adults: The use of qualitative and quantitative methodology. *Journal of Homosexuality, 61*(1), 53–78. https://doi.org/10.1080/00918369.2013.835236

Park, J., Howard, H., Tolea, M. I., & Galvin, J. E. (2020). Perceived benefits of using nonpharmacological interventions in older adults with Alzheimer's disease or dementia with Lewy bodies. *Journal of Gerontological Nursing, 46*(1), 37–46. https://doi.org/10.3928/00989134-20191217-01

Patterson, G. T. (2019). *Social work practice in the criminal justice system* (2nd ed.). Routledge.

Payne, M. (1998). Social work theories and reflective practice. In R. Adams, L. Dominelli, M. Payne, & J. Campling (Eds.), *Social work: Themes, issues and critical debates* (3rd ed., pp. 119–137). Springer. https://www.google.com/books/edition/Social_Work_Themes_Issues_and_Critical_D/aSNIEAAAQBAJ?hl=en&gbpv=1&dq=R.+Adams,+L.+et+al.+(Eds.),+Social+work:+Themes,+issues+and+critical+debates&pg=PR10&printsec=frontcover

Plafky, C. S. (2016). From neuroscientific research findings to social work practice: A critical description of the knowledge utilisation process. *British Journal of Social Work, 46*(6), 1502–1519. https://doi.org/10.1093/bjsw/bcv082

Prescott, D. E. (2007). The act of lawyering and the art of communication: An essay on families-in-crisis, the adversarial tradition, and the social work model. *Legal Ethics, 10*(2), 176–192. https://doi.org/10.1080/1460728X.2007.11423891

Prescott, D. E. (2013). Social workers as "experts" in the family court system: Is evidence-based practice a missing link or host-created knowledge? *Journal of Evidence-Based Social Work, 10*(5), 466–481. https://doi.org/10.1080/15433714.2012.759844

Prescott, D. E. (2020). Flexner's thesis was prescient: Ethical practices for social workers "in the trenches" requires forensic knowledge. *Journal of Social Work Values & Ethics, 16*(2), 40–52. http://jswve.org/download/fall_2019_volume_16_no._2/articles/40-Flexners-thesis-was-prescient-16-2-Fall-2019-JSWVE.pdf

Ratliff, A., & Willins, M. (Eds.). (2018). *Criminal defense-based forensic social work*. Routledge. https://doi.org/10.4324/9781315410173

Reamer, F. G. (1998). The evolution of social work ethics. *Social Work, 43*(6), 488–500. https://doi.org/10.1093/sw/43.6.488

Reamer, F. G. (2013). *Social work values and ethics*. Columbia University Press.

Regehr, C., & Antle, B. (1997). Coercive influences: Informed consent in court-mandated social work practices. *Social Work, 42*, 300–306. https://doi.org/10.1093/sw/42.3.300

Reyes, L., Treitler, P., & Peterson, N. A. (2021). Testing relationships between racial-ethnic identity, racial-ethnic discrimination, and substance misuse among Black and Latinx older adults in a nationally representative sample. *Research on Aging, 44*(1), 96–106. https://doi.org/10.1177/0164027520986952

Ricciardelli, L. A. (Ed.). (2020). *Social work, criminal justice, and the death penalty*. Oxford University Press. https://www.google.com/books/edition/Social_Work_Criminal_Justice_and_the_Dea/wvUTE AAAQBAJ?hl=en&gbpv=1&dq=Ricciardelli,+L.+A.+(Ed.).+(2020).+Social+work,+criminal+justice,+ and+the+death+penalty.+Oxford+University+Press.&pg=PP1&printsec=frontcoverRoberts, A. R., & Brownell, P. (1999). A century of forensic social work: Bridging the past to the present. *Social Work, 44*(4), 359–369. https://doi.org/10.1093/sw/44.4.359

Roberts, A. W., Ogunwole, S. U., Blakeslee, L., & Rabe, M. A. (2018). *The population 65 years and older in the United States: 2016*. Suitland, MD, USA: US Department of Commerce, Economics and Statistics Administration, US Census Bureau. https://www.census.gov/content/dam/Census/library/publications/2018/acs/ACS-38.pdf

Roesch, R. (2015). Social worker assessments of competency to stand trial. *Journal of Forensic Social Work, 5*(1–3), 186–200. https://doi.org/10.1080/1936928X.2015.1109398

Rome, S. H. (2013). *Social work and law: Judicial policy and forensic practice*. Pearson Education.

Ryon, S. B., Chiricos, T., Siennick, S. E., Barrick, K., & Bales, W. (2017). Sentencing in light of collateral consequences: Does age matter? *Journal of Criminal Justice, 53*, 1–11. https://doi.org/10.1016/j.jcrimjus.2017.07.009

Satterfield, J. M., Spring, B., Brownson, R. C., Mullen, E. J., Newhouse, R. P., Walker, B. B., & Whitlock, E. P. (2009). Toward a transdisciplinary model of evidence-based practice. *Milbank Quarterly, 87*(2), 368–390. https://doi.org/10.1111/j.1468-0009.2009.00561.x

Scherr, K. C., & Dror, I. E. (2021). Ingroup biases of forensic experts: Perceptions of wrongful convictions versus exonerations. *Psychology, Crime & Law, 27*(1), 89–104. https://doi.org/10.1080/1068316X.2020.1774591

Scheyett, A., Pettus-Davis, C., McCarter, S., & Brigham, R. (2012). Social work and criminal justice: Are we meeting in the field? *Journal of Teaching in Social Work, 32*(4), 438–450. https://doi.org/10.1080/08841233.2012.705241Sheehan, R. (2016). Forensic social work: Implementing specialist social work education. *Journal of Social Work, 16*(6), 726–741. https://doi.org/10.1177%2F1468017316635491

Siegel, D. M. (2008). The growing admissibility of expert testimony by clinical social workers on competence to stand trial. *Social Work, 53*(2), 153–163. https://doi.org/10.1093/sw/53.2.153 https://academic.oup.com/sw/article-

Sneed, R. S., & Schulz, R. (2019). Grandparent caregiving, race, and cognitive functioning in a population-based sample of older adults. *Journal of Aging and Health, 31*(3), 415–438. https://doi.org/10.1177%2F0898264317733362

Sovacool, B. K. (2008). Exploring scientific misconduct: Isolated individuals, impure institutions, or an inevitable idiom of modern science? *Journal of Bioethical Inquiry, 5*(4), 271–282. http://hdl.handle.net/10822/953929

Sprang, G., Choi, M., Eslinger, J. G., & Whitt-Woosley, A. L. (2015). The pathway to grandparenting stress: Trauma, relational conflict, and emotional well-being. *Aging & Mental Health, 19*(4), 315–324. https://doi.org/10.1080/13607863.2014.938606

Steffensmeier, D., Painter-Davis, N., & Ulmer, J. (2017). Intersectionality of race, ethnicity, gender, and age on criminal punishment. *Sociological Perspectives, 60*(4), 810–833. https://doi.org/10.1177%2F07311 21416679371

Tsimploulis, G., Niveau, G., Eytan, A., Giannakopoulos, P., & Sentissi, O. (2018). Schizophrenia and criminal responsibility: A systematic review. *Journal of Nervous and Mental Disease, 206*(5), 370–377.

https://journals.lww.com/jonmd/Abstract/2018/05000/Schizophrenia_and_Criminal_Responsibility__A.10.aspx

Tussey, C. M. (2018). Mitigating effects of age-related issues on sentencing and housing placements. In S. S. Bush & A. L. Heck (Eds.), *Forensic geropsychology: Practice essentials* (pp. 281–300). American Psychological Association. https://psycnet.apa.org/doi/10.1037/0000082-014 https://psycnet.apa.org/record/2018-07513-014

U.S. Census Bureau. (2020, June). *65 and older population grows rapidly as baby boomers age* [Press release]. https://www.census.gov/newsroom/press-releases/2020/65-older-population-grows.html

Webb, S. A. (2001). Some considerations on the validity of evidence-based practice in social work. *British Journal of Social Work*, *31*(1), 57–79. https://psycnet.apa.org/doi/10.1093/bjsw/31.1.57 https://psycnet.apa.org/record/2001-03098-005

Werner, P., & Doron, I. (2016). The legal system and Alzheimer's disease: Social workers and lawyers' perceptions and experiences. *Journal of Gerontological Social Work*, *59*(6), 478–491. https://doi.org/10.1080/01634372.2016.1239235

Whitman, R. (2012). Capacity for lifetime and estate planning. *Pennsylvania State Law Review*, *117*(4), 1061–1080. http://www.pennstatelawreview.org/117/4/2-Whitman%20(final).pdf

Wiggins v. Smith, 539 U.S. 510 (2003). Retrieved from https://supreme.justia.com/cases/federal/us/539/510/

Xiang, X., Ning, Y., & Kayser, J. (2020). The implications of COVID-19 for the mental health care of older adults: Insights from emergency department social workers. *Journal of Gerontological Social Work*, *63*(6–7), 662–664. https://doi.org/10.1080/01634372.2020.1779160

Xu, Y., Wu, Q., Jedwab, M., & Levkoff, S. E. (2020). Understanding the relationships between parenting stress and mental health with grandparent kinship caregivers' risky parenting behaviors in the time of COVID-19. *Journal of Family Violence*, 1–13. https://www.ncbi.nlm.nih.gov/pmc/articles/PMC7682691/

Zapf, P. A., & Dror, I. E. (2017). Understanding and mitigating bias in forensic evaluation: Lessons from forensic science. *International Journal of Forensic Mental Health*, *16*(3), 227–238. https://psycnet.apa.org/doi/10.1080/14999013.2017.1317302

7

Sexual Orientation in Forensic Settings

Anthony P. Natale

Background and Context

Lesbian, gay, and bisexual (LGB) people's unique needs in their interactions with forensic social workers are essential to consider. For context, it is necessary to remember that the criminalization of sodomy, involving sexual acts engaged in routinely by gay men, was only deemed unconstitutional by the Supreme Court in 2004 in *Bowers v. Hardwick*. Consequently, for most of the country's history, homosexuality was a criminal offense punishable by jail. At the end of 2020, 68 countries worldwide continue to criminalize homosexual behavior, with 11 of those deeming the act punishable by death (Human Rights Watch, 2020). Despite the decriminalization of homosexuality in the United States, the civil rights of LGB people have been slow to emerge. Among those civil rights protections deemed essential to the American experience are employment, housing, education, income, health, family, and relationships. LGB individuals have only been able to access a federally recognized marriage since 2013 and employment discrimination protections since 2020.

Discrimination and harassment of LGB community members by law enforcement officers have been well documented in the literature (Mallory et al., 2015) and are not the focus of this chapter. Instead, education, child welfare, juvenile justice, and adult correctional systems are institutions where trauma is commonplace for LGB people and are the focus of this chapter. For example, Irvine and Canfield (2015) warn that despite the disproportionately high rates of LGB youth in juvenile justice systems, forensic staff, including social workers, overlook the unique experiences and challenges of LGB youth. Meyer et al. (2017) indicate that LGB people are more likely to end up in jail and face abuse while in jail in the general population. Forms of abuse come as verbal slurs, humiliation, intimidation,

Anthony P. Natale, *Sexual Orientation in Forensic Settings* In: *Handbook of Forensic Social Work*. Edited by: David Axlyn McLeod, Anthony P. Natale, and Kristin W. Mapson, Oxford University Press. © Oxford University Press 2024. DOI: 10.1093/oso/9780197694732.003.0007 threats, and different forms of abuse (physical, sexual, emotional). Solitary confinement, a means for dispensing additional harsh treatment, is commonly given to LGB people, sometimes for months or years, as a means to manage prison design or understaffing, not to handle a behavior (Lara, 2009). Solitary confinement comes with a host of physical and mental disorders, including complex trauma (Ahalt et al., 2017).

This chapter aims to provide definitions and examples for key terms relative to LGB people and the oppression resulting from societal response to their sexual orientation. Next, it provides an overview of rates and trends of LGB people and engagement with forensic institutions. Then, it discusses fundamental constitutional rights afforded to incarcerated people followed by rights legislated by Congress. It then details pathways influenced by heterosexism that illuminate LGB overrepresentation in forensic institutions. The chapter closes with a listing of crucial reforms needed relative to LGB experiences with forensic settings, along with critical strategies for social workers to accomplish these goals.

Sexual Orientation and Forensics: Important Concepts

Sexual Orientation

Sexual orientation is an enduring romantic, emotional, or sexual attraction to others. Sexual orientation has several variations along a continuum and is quite diverse. Sexual orientation includes heterosexual (attraction to the opposite sex), homosexual (attracted to the same sex), bisexual (attracted to more than one sex), and asexual (without romantic, emotional, or physical attraction). While often conflated, sexual orientation is distinct from gender identity. Sexual orientation refers to who people are attracted to, while gender identity refers to an individual's self-concept of being nonbinary, female, or male. This chapter will focus on sexual orientation, with the following chapter focusing on gender identity (Human Rights Campaign [HRC], 2014).

Homophobia and Biphobia

Homophobia is best understood when examined by its linguistic roots. *Phobia* refers to fear, whereas *homo* refers to homosexual people; the words combined are the fear of homosexual people. Biphobia, then, is fear of bisexual people. Homophobia and biphobia can arise from limited contacts with LGB people, media-reinforced stereotypes, and religious depictions (HRC, 2014).

Homohatred

Homohatred is similarly best understood when examined by its linguistic roots, which, when joined together, is the hatred of homosexuals. Homohatred is an intense fear of homosexual people, resulting in acts of violence directed at LGB people (HRC, 2014). Examples include threats of neglect and emotional, physical, and sexual abuse. Macro examples include local, state, and national policies that use sexual orientation for discriminatory purposes.

Internalized Homophobia, Biphobia, and Homohatred

Internalized homophobia, biphobia, and homohatred are fears and hatred that LGB people direct toward themselves and other LGB people due to internalizing society's negative perceptions, stereotypes, stigma, intolerance, dehumanization, and hostility toward LGB people (HRC, 2014). Internalized homophobia, biphobia, and homohatred manifest in several ways, including stigma, shame, and self-hatred. Each also displays clinical diagnoses such as depression or anxiety, in examples of closeted policymakers utilizing their elected power to support anti-LGB policy or, perhaps most strikingly and severe, the number of LGB people who die by suicide (Frost & Meyer, 2009).

Suicide risk is high among Lesbian, Gay, Bisexual and Transgender (LGBT) people, representing their second leading cause of death, with nearly 30% of LGB high school students reporting attempted suicide compared to 6.5% of their non-LGB-identified peers (Kann et al., 2016). Bisexual people are more likely to experience suicidality when compared to their lesbian and gay peers (Kann et al., 2011).

Heterosexism

Heterosexism is a system of privileges and power acts for heterosexual people that operates with prejudice, bias, and discriminatory behavior by defining homosexuality and bisexuality as atypical and therefore subordinate within a social hierarchy (HRC, 2014). Examples of heterosexism are assessments of human sexuality assuming heterosexuality (Utamsingh et al., 2016), higher rates of severe punishments for LGB students (Himmelstein & Brückner, 2011; Kosciw et al., 2012; Kosciw et al., 2013; Mallett, 2016) and foster children, and higher rates of solitary confinement for LBG people incarcerated in juvenile or correctional institutions (Kunzel, 2008).

Structural Heterosexism

Structural heterosexism occurs due to institutional prejudice, bias, and discriminatory policies and practices that subordinate homosexuality and bisexuality to heterosexuality (HRC, 2014). Structural heterosexism is the compounded discrimination that occurs across time due to linkages between institutions (e.g., education, housing, employment, health care). For example, while the Supreme Court has granted LGB individuals the right to work and marriage without discrimination, the same does not apply to health care, education, or housing institutions (Movement Advancement Project, 2021). As a result, LGB individuals receive more limited civil rights, which holds implications for LGB individuals interfacing with forensic social workers.

Intersectionality

Intersectionality was coined by Kimberlé Crenshaw (1989) while describing how the courts had a hard time viewing the compounded oppression that occurs to individuals at the intersections of different forms of structural oppression, racism, and sexism in the case she was analyzing. Crenshaw recognizes that individuals can sit at multiple intersections in addition to the two in the case, such as ableism, ageism, heterosexism, cisgenderism, and classism.

While structural heterosexism is a robust set of forces that enforces LGB-directed discrimination and oppression, individuals are not their sexuality alone. Intersectionality reminds the social worker that LGB people can occupy multiple intersections (ableism, ageism, cisgenderism). Individuals can experience the compounded and synergistic effects of each structure of oppression—structural racism, structural sexism, and structural cisgenderism. Intersectional social work practice, then, is essential when working with LGBT individuals to consider the additional intersections that support the current problem and provide guidance to problem-solving and systemic intervention selection.

LGB People and Forensic Involvement Background and Context

Rates and Trends

The incarceration rate of self-identified LGB persons was more than three times that of the U.S. adult population for 2011–2012 (Meyer et al., 2017). LGB people are more likely to have been sexually victimized as children, incarcerated, experienced solitary confinement, and reported current psychological distress compared to straight inmates (McCauley & Brinkley-Rubinstein, 2017). Meyer et al. (2017) explain that forensic staff use an individual's sexual orientation as a rationale for solitary confinement, purportedly for personal protection. To be exact, solitary confinement is a form of punishment. Solitary confinement includes up to 23 hours a day in lockdown, exclusion from all programming, and denial of visitation. Researchers have well documented these conditions as promoting severe psychological distress (Ahalt et al., 2017; Clark, 2017; Meyer et al., 2017).

LGB people, particularly those of color or low income, are disproportionately represented in contacts with the criminal justice system (Movement Advancement Project and Center for American Progress, 2016). Many factors contribute to the disproportionate contacts, including poverty, discrimination in schools and workplaces, and the history of bias, abuse, and profiling of LGBT people. The criminalization of poverty, homelessness, and sex work disproportionately impacts LGB people, and again disproportionately affects LGB communities of color (Movement Advancement Project and Center for American Progress, 2016).

Researchers have demonstrated that LGB inmates are overrepresented in jails and federal prisons and are three times more likely to be incarcerated than the general population. Lesbian or bisexual women represent 40% of incarcerated women. Estimates include LGBT youth as between 12% and 20% of the juvenile detention population, despite making up only 7% of the overall youth population (Kann et al., 2011). LGBT youth are vulnerable to many factors, including family rejection that manifests as homelessness and hostility in the foster care system or other safety net systems, which often serve as a pathway to the juvenile justice system (Mitchum & Moodie-Mills, 2014).

The United States incarcerates more people than any other country in the world, and jail and prison facilities' conditions vary. What is less variable is physical and sexual violence aimed at LGB people. These systems exacerbate abuse and mistreatment, leading to posttraumatic stress disorder, depression, and substance abuse. In penal institutions, LGBT prisoners face blatant forms of abuse, including humiliation and degradation from staff and prisoners and being placed in indefinite solitary confinement—conditions that cause harm and trauma (Ahalt et al., 2017). Ignoring LGBT prisoners' requests for temporary custody puts them at immediate risk for physical or sexual harm.

Policies That Protect the Rights of Incarcerated People

Mogul et al. (2011) revealed that LGB individuals are disproportionately represented in penal institutions compared to the general population. Heterosexism bias is common in these institutions, which reaps discrimination for LGB people, especially LGB people of color. Examples include physical abuse, verbal harassment, sexual abuse, threats, and enforcement of solitary confinement. A series of constitutional amendments and federal laws protect vulnerable populations, including LGB people.

U.S. Constitutional Rights

The First Amendment. The First Amendment of the U.S. Constitution contains rights concerning religion, free expression, the press, assembly, and petition for grievance. Incarcerated individuals retain the rights to religion and free expression during incarceration periods.

The Fifth Amendment. The Fifth Amendment to the Constitution notes that the *federal government* provides due process in life, liberty, and the pursuit of happiness, which intends to describe a set of fair procedures for use during legal obligations.

The Eighth Amendment. The Eighth Amendment to the Constitution indicates that excessive bail shall not be required, nor excessive fines imposed or cruel and unusual punishments inflicted. The amendment provides all incarcerated individuals freedom from cruel and unusual punishment. Freedom from cruel and unusual punishment is the basis for supporting several rights for incarcerated people; among these are the right to be safe, the right to privacy, the right to free expression, the right to religion, the right to necessary medical care, and the right to equal access. These rights operate in more limited ways for incarcerated people.

The 14th Amendment. The 14th Amendment's equal protection clause requires that *state governments* practice equal protection, which intends to describe a set of legal obligations to ensure the use of fair procedures. The right to safety, for example, encourages incarceration officials to acknowledge the vulnerability of LGB individuals and to mitigate risk and increase safety. The right to health care includes decisions about necessary medical treatment, such as HIV care and solitary confinement. A limited right to privacy exists for protected information such as health status or sexual orientation, indicating the information is only shareable when a legitimate purpose exists. Figure 7.1 provides an overview of the constitutional rights of incarcerated people.

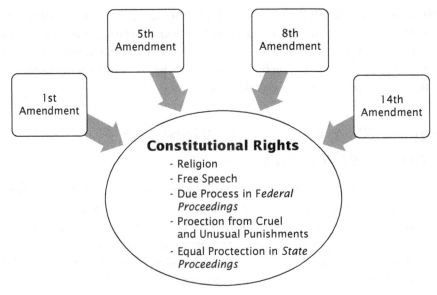

FIGURE 7.1 Constitutional Rights of Incarcerated People

U.S. Legislated Rights

Education Amendments of 1972—Title IX. Title IX of the Education Amendments of 1972 protects individuals from discrimination based on sex in education programs or activities that receive federal financial assistance. Incarcerated persons are guaranteed these protections, just like all students. Title IX complaints have successfully been used, as in *Jeldness v. Pearce*, to rectify the discrimination in the number and variety of curriculum options for male versus female prisoners (Cohen, 2005).

The **Rehabilitation Act of 1973—Section 504.** The Rehabilitation Act of 1973 prohibits disability discrimination in federal agency programs receiving federal assistance, in federal employment, and in federal contractors' practices. Unlike the Americans with Disabilities Act, which does not allow incarcerated individuals to sue the federal government, under Section 504 of the Rehabilitation Act of 1973, incarcerated individuals can sue for an injunction, a court order requiring the prison or agency to correct the violation (Ginsberg, 2009).

Americans with Disabilities Act (ADA) of 1990—Title II. The ADA prohibits discrimination in employment, public services, public accommodations, and telecommunications. Eight years after its passage, the Supreme Court ruled in *Pennsylvania DOC v. Yeskey* that Title II applies to incarcerated persons with disabilities, thereby guaranteeing them access to reasonable accommodations. Functionally, this means that incarcerated persons with disabilities received access to grab bars, wheelchair ramps, and particular adaptations (for those who are deaf or have a cognitive disability) in educational or treatment-related programs (Greifinger, 2006).

Prison Litigation Reform Act (PLRA) of 1996. The PLRA is a federal law that places several restrictions on incarcerated persons to file lawsuits about their confinement

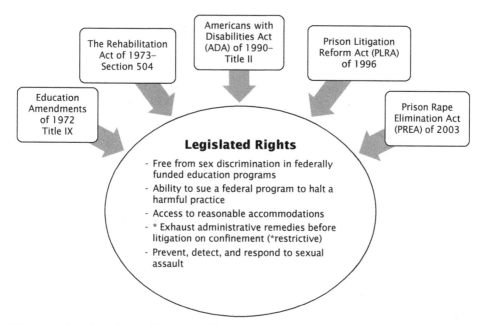

FIGURE 7.2 Legislated Rights of Incarcerated People

conditions. The law requires prisoners to have *exhausted* administrative remedies before they can sue about their confinement. Functionally, this means that incarcerated persons must go through the institutions' formal grievance processes, including all possible appeal processes, to allow correctional officials the ability to address the problems before litigation can begin. This grievance process places an undue burden upon the incarcerated individual and results in an estimated 2.3 million incarcerated people's restricted access to the courts (Human Rights Watch, 2020).

Prison Rape Elimination Act (PREA) of 2003. The PREA contains the federal rules to address aspects of preventing, detecting, and responding to sexual abuse in federal facilities. In 2012, the Department of Justice issued its previous standards with different versions of the standards applying to different types of forensic facilities. As federal standards, they are legally binding on federation prisons. State prison systems can lose federal funding if not in compliance. The PREA regulations include several protections for LGBT individuals, including consideration of a person's identity or status in risk for sexual victimization and unique concerns for the housing of intersex individuals. The PREA has been critiqued as limited and unclear and used to justify the mistreatment of LGBT individuals, such as consensual physical contact between LGBT prisoners (Moster & Jeglic, 2009). Figure 7.2 provides an overview of the legislated rights of incarcerated people.

LGB People Are Overrepresented in Forensic Institutions

Heterosexism produces disproportionate rates of LGB involvement across all institutional settings. Figure 7.3 illustrates a conceptual model of the pathways toward the disproportionality of LBG people in forensic settings. These pathways begin early in the lives of LGB

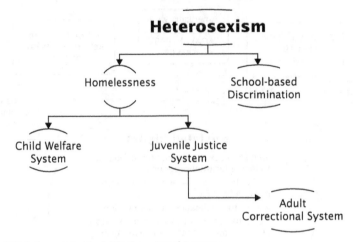

FIGURE 7.3 LGB Pathway Into the Adult Correctional System

youth who face discrimination and harassment in their schools and sometimes even more so in their homes.

In the home, LGB youth can face physical abuse, sexual abuse, emotional abuse, threats of outing sexual orientation, and denial of basic safety, including food and shelter. Over a quarter of LGB youth become homeless when their sexual orientation is disclosed or discovered (Durso & Gates, 2012). Threats of safety do not end there, however, as one study found that 78% of LGBTQ youth were removed or ran away from their foster placements due to sexual orientation or gender identity hostility (Forge et al., 2018). Homelessness for LGB youth is a pathway into child welfare or juvenile justice systems, and sometimes both (Mallett, 2017; Mitchum & Moodie-Mills, 2014). Compared to other system-involved youth, LGBTQ youth of color have longer stays in both the child welfare and juvenile justice systems and face an elevated risk of discrimination and violence.

LGB youth also face school settings that feature heterosexism, which contributes to disproportionate rates of school detentions and punishments, especially for LBG youth of color, and lower high school completion rates for LGBT youth compared to their heterosexual peers (Mallett, 2017; Mitchum & Moodie-Mills, 2014). Beck et al. (2013) estimate that LGBT youth prevalence at around 4.3%, compared to between 5% and 10% of the total foster youth population who are LGB.

The juvenile justice system features an overrepresentation of LGBT youth, with nearly 300,000 gay and transgender youth detained annually. More than 60% are Black or Latino, with between 13% and 15% of the juvenile justice system represented by LGBT youth (Movement Advancement Project and Center for American Progress, 2016). LGBT people experience abuse and harassment; improper placement, including solitary confinement; and denials of programming and essential health care (Fathi, 2009). It is here where solitary confinement patterns first appear due to safety concerns for the individual, and they will often carry over into adult institutions. This practice continues even though there is clear evidence that indicates solitary confinement increases trauma precipitously, particularly for youth whose sequential and hierarchical development is ongoing.

Meyer and colleagues (2017) used a probability sample of inmates in U.S. prisons and jails who completed the National Inmate Survey, 2011–2012, and reported that the LGB incarceration rate is more than three times the already high national incarceration rate (1,882 vs. 662 per 100,000). Further, the data revealed that 9.3% of men in prison, 6.2% of men in jail, 42.1% of women in prison, and 35.7% of women in jail engaged in sexual activities with same-sex partners. The authors noted that LGB individuals have longer sentences in comparison to their heterosexual counterparts and concluded with a set of recommendations to address LGB disproportionality, mistreatment, harsh punishment, and sexual victimization (Meyer et al., 2017).

Needed LGB Forensic Institutional Reforms

Education System

Hostile school environments, which feature intolerance, prejudice, and verbal and physical aggression, have profound negative impacts on LGB youth achievement outcomes (Kosciw et al., 2012). Casey et al. (2019) found agreement in their data. They indicated that the pervasive instructor and peer-based discrimination common for LGB individuals in the K–12 system extends to the higher education system as well.

Several school-based reforms for LGBT students could impact their inclusion and safety experiences while at school. It begins with recognizing the pervasiveness of heteronormativity in the classroom and school-level policies, procedures, and practices (Snapp et al., 2015). Concerning policy, explicit guidelines with specific language prohibiting harassment and discriminatory behavior based on sexual orientation are recommended, along with clear examples of harassment based on actual or perceived sexual orientation (Marksamer & Tobin, 2014).

Explicit anti-bullying policies that include sexual orientation need to become the norm, with training provided for students and education staff on the causes and consequences of bullying, along with clear expectations for behavior (Gower et al., 2018). Any successful anti-bullying campaign depends on clearly articulated standards, a clear reporting structure, and clear consequences for violation. Beyond anti-bullying training, education staff needs ongoing in-service training on the unique barriers of LGB youth in educational attainment, including high rates of homelessness, substance abuse, and suicide. Schools need to provide explicit privacy guidelines to education staff on LGB students' sexual orientation in full recognition of the grave consequences that can arise from unauthorized disclosure (Snapp et al., 2015).

Instructors should review classroom-level policies, procedures, and practices to ensure they are free from heteronormative bias. Examples include a review of language used in the curriculum and course examples. Also, merely using the words "gay," "bisexual," and "lesbian" in class signals comfort with the issue. In a growing trend, some states have moved to the inclusion of LGB history-themed weeks as part of the state curriculum (Steck & Perry, 2018; Toomey et al., 2012).

Child Welfare System

The child welfare system's paradox is that LGBT youth removed from their family of origin due to their sexual orientation routinely find the same homophobia and heteronormative standards placed on them again, but this time mandated by the state. As mentioned previously, not only are LGB youth overrepresented in foster care, but also they often report receiving less support and more challenges in their placements. Ultimately, LGB youth are less likely to receive a permanent placement before they age out of care (McCormick et al., 2017).

Many child welfare reforms for LGB youth could impact their inclusion and safety experiences while engaged in this system. The most critical reforms involve the recruitment, training, and orientation of foster care and kinship placements to support LGBT youth in the foster care system. The home study process must assess the goodness of fit between members of the home and their ability to support LGB youth in addressing their developmental needs, including their sexual health (Elze, 2014).

Given the unique needs and risks of the LGB youth in foster care settings, caseworkers need to engage in consistent contact for ongoing assessment of LGB youth's safety and inclusion (Dettlaff et al., 2018). Frequent visits allow LGB youth and their foster or kinship families to assess needs continuously. An ongoing assessment allows time for making linkages to immediate and long-term services.

Like all youth in the foster care system, a focus on family preservation and permanency is of paramount importance, but this is especially true for LGB youth. Lack of permanency promotes the likelihood of homelessness and engagement in survival commercial sex work, becoming a pathway into the juvenile or adult correctional systems or both for LGB youth. Elze (2012) recommends expanding support services to families of LGB youth before and after disruptions occur when reunification remains viable. With appropriate support, families may be able to weather the initial crisis of sexual orientation disclosure with guidance and counseling on how to support positive adolescent development in human sexuality and improve family communication and functioning (Wilber et al., 2006).

When there are no other options than out-of-home placement for LGBT youth, support services by caseworkers for the child and foster family toward permanency are essential. Foster families need assistance to identify services, supports, and resources for LGB youth. Those LGB youth who will not reach permanency while in the foster care system need clear pathways to independence to reverse the trend of aging out of foster care into correctional settings (Forge et al., 2018).

Like the education system, that child welfare system needs reform, starting with training requirements (Wilber et al., 2006). All participants engaged in support of LGB youth in the child welfare system should receive ongoing training on the unique needs of LGB development across the lifespan, including their sexual orientation. In addition to the risk factors identified, specific LGB inclusion strategies for foster care placements are needed. LGB youth need a greater understanding of child welfare workers' failings in the system relative to LGB needs and the link to their involvement in the juvenile justice or adult correctional system. This training must develop strategies to disrupt these pathways into incarceration facilities (Wilber et al., 2006).

Reforming child welfare policies, practices, and procedures toward the inclusion of LGB youth begins with examining heteronormativity and how it manifests within the child welfare system. Antidiscrimination policies are an essential pathway but only one of a necessary torrent of guidelines that need reform for the safety and inclusion of LGB youth, including privacy policies, health care treatment policies, and mental health intervention policies (McCormick et al., 2017).

Juvenile Justice System

The juvenile justice system is a different experience from the child welfare or education systems for a couple of distinct reasons. Their involvement with the justice system limits LGB youth's freedoms. LGB youth inappropriately receive the *sex offender* label, which can have profound social consequences among correctional staff and incarcerated youth alike (Estrada & Marksamer, 2006).

Like the two systems reviewed already, heteronormativity is pervasive in the juvenile justice system as well. Examples of discriminatory sexual orientation pathways into this system include detention for consensual, age-appropriate, same-sex behavior and survival sex work while homeless (Estrada & Marksamer, 2006). Comparatively to the other two systems reviewed, LGB anti-discrimination policies and practices are uncommon in these institutions.

Many juvenile justice reforms for LGB youth could impact their inclusion and safety experiences while engaged in this system (Hunt & Moodie-Mills, 2012). The training needs for both the education and child welfare systems, including fostering safe and supportive environments for youth and appropriately addressing harassment, discrimination, and all forms of abuse, remain relevant in this system. A particular training need in the juvenile justice system focuses on the short- and long-term consequences of solitary confinement, with specific attention paid to the traumatization or retraumatization of LGB individuals who receive solitary confinement solely because of their sexual orientation (Hunt & Moodie-Mills, 2012).

To that end, solitary confinement, or the separation of LGB people as policy, needs to be eradicated. The practice is inhumane and clearly produces trauma for LGB youth, and so long as no guidance forbids it, the method will remain. Despite the obvious questions about cruel and unusual punishment, LGB youth are generally powerless to raise concerns about their confinement or advocate for themselves through the system, in which there is disproportionate power stacked against them at every turn (Majd et al., 2009).

Adult Corrections System

The adult correctional system is a different experience from the three other systems as it represents the most extraordinary restrictions on the individual rights of LGB people. By the time individuals make their way into the adult corrections system, their pathways for life have been altered, for some in minor ways, but for some in significant ways that can include life in prison. Like the three systems reviewed already, heteronormativity is pervasive in the adult correctional system, and LGB anti-discrimination policies and practices are common in these institutions. An example in the adult penal system is solitary confinement or separation due to sexual orientation, under the guise that it is a safety measure for the LGB individual. Solitary confinement produces more harm than it could ever mitigate for LGB individuals and should not be used to accommodate institutional shortcomings in staffing or culture and climate (Hanssens et al., 2014).

Many reforms to the adult corrections system could impact LGB inclusion and safety experiences while they are engaged in this system (Brown & Jenness, 2020). It is safe to assume that all of the training needs for the education, child welfare, and juvenile justice systems are relevant here. Staff training should emphasize the unique needs of LGB incarcerated people, foster safe and supportive environments for LGB folks, and appropriately address harassment and discrimination and all forms of abuse (Brown & Jenness, 2020).

At the policy, procedure, and practice levels, there are several needed reforms. The first needed practice reform is to perform individualized assessments as individuals make their way into corrections institutions. Individual assessments that inquire about sexual orientation can help identify essential health and mental health needs and supports or an appropriate housing plan for LGB individuals (Brown & Jenness, 2020).

The second reform focuses on limiting the use of segregation. Current best practices about segregation policies must include adhered-to timelines for reviewing the usefulness of segregation, required rationale identification, and examples of alternatives considered before individuals are placed in segregation for protective purposes. Also, so long as individuals are in segregation, they should have equal access to all resources available to others, including programs, privileges, visitation, recreation, and council. For example, suppose the reason for separation is the individual's fear for their safety. In that case, a policy statement that allows those LGB individuals to remain in protective custody is the best approach (Brown & Jenness, 2020).

The third reform focuses on nondiscrimination statements that address the conditions of confinement for LGB people. Such statements should expressly prohibit discrimination and verbal, physical, and sexual harassment of LGB individuals based on the actual or perceived sexual orientation. The policy should apply to all correctional staff, volunteers, contractors, and fellow incarcerated people (Brown & Jenness, 2020).

This chapter aims to provide definitions and examples for key terms relative to LGB people and the oppression resulting from societal response to their sexual orientation. The chapter reviewed the rates and trends of LGB engagement with forensic institutions. It provided an overview of the fundamental constitutional rights afforded to incarcerated people, followed by crucial legislated rights. It also detailed the pathways to overrepresentation in forensic settings, which results from heterosexism. The chapter closed with a listing of critical reforms needed relative to LGB experiences within forensic settings.

References

Ahalt, C., Haney, C., Rios, S., Fox, M. P., Farabee, D., & Williams, B. (2017). Reducing the use and impact of solitary confinement in corrections. *International Journal of Prisoner Health*, *13*(1), 41–48. https://doi.org/10.1108/ijph-08-2016-0040

Beck, A., Berzofsky, M., Caspar, R., & Krebs, C. (2013). *Sexual victimization in prisons and jails reported by inmates, 2011–2012.* https://www.bjs.gov/content/pub/pdf/svpjri1112.pdf

Brown, J. A., & Jenness, V. (2020). LGBT people in prison: Management strategies, human rights violations, and political mobilization. In *Oxford research encyclopedia of criminology and criminal justice.* https://doi.org/10.1093/acrefore/9780190264079.013.647

Casey, L. S., Reisner, S. L., Findling, M. G., Blendon, R. J., Benson, J. M., Sayde, J. M., & Miller, C. (2019). Discrimination in the United States: Experiences of lesbian, gay, bisexual, transgender, and queer Americans. *Health Services Research, 54,* 1454–1466.

Clark, A. B. (2017). Juvenile solitary confinement is a form of child abuse. *Journal of the American Academy of Psychiatry and the Law, 45*(3), 350–357. https://pubmed.ncbi.nlm.nih.gov/28939734/

Cohen, D. S. (2005). Title IX: Beyond equal protection. *Harvard Journal of Law & Gender, 28*(2), 217. http://ssrn.com/abstract=1019652

Crenshaw, K. (1989). Demarginalizing the intersection of race and sex: A black feminist critique of antidiscrimination doctrine, feminist theory, and antiracist politics. *University of Chicago Legal Forum, 1989*(1), 139. http://chicagounbound.edu/uclf/vol1989/iss1.8

Dettlaff, A. J., & Washburn, M. (2018). Lesbian, gay, and bisexual (LGB) youth within in welfare: prevalence, risk, and outcomes. *Child Abuse & Neglect, 80,* 183–193. https://doi.org/10.1016/j.chiabu.2018.03.009

Durso, L. E., & Gates, G. J. (2012). *Serving our youth: Findings from a national survey of service providers working with lesbian, gay, bisexual, and transgender youth who are homeless or at risk of becoming homeless.* Los Angeles: The Williams Institute with True Colors Fund and The Palette Fund.

Elze, D. E. (2012). *In-home services for families of LGBTQ youth.* National Resource Center for Youth. https://clas.uiowa.edu/sites/clas.uiowa.edu.nrcfcp/files/5LGBTissuebriefwithpractice.pdf

Elze, D. (2014). LGBT youth and their families. In G. P. Mallon & P. M. Hess (Eds.), *Child welfare for the twenty-first century: A handbook of practices, policies, and programs* (pp. 158–178). Columbia University Press. https://psycnet.apa.org/record/2014-48855-007

Estrada, R., & Marksamer, J. (2006). Lesbian, gay, bisexual, and transgender young people in state custody: Making the child welfare and juvenile justice systems safe for all youth through litigation, advocacy, and education. *Temple Law Review, 79,* 415. Retrieved May 25, 2021, from https://static1.squarespace.com/static/566c7f0c2399a3bdabb57553/t/566cadd75a5668242bb2132a/1449962967872/2006-LGBT-Young-People-in-State-Custody.pdf

Fathi, D. (2009). *No equal justice: The prison litigation reform act in the United States.* Human Rights Watch. https://www.hrw.org/report/2009/06/16/no-equal-justice/prison-litigation-reform-act-united-states#

Forge, N., Hartinger-Saunders, R., Wright, E., & Ruel, E. (2018). Out of the System and onto the Streets. *Child Welfare, 96*(2), 47–74. https://housingis.org/resource/out-system-and-streets

Frost, D. M., & Meyer, I. H. (2009). Internalized homophobia and relationship quality among lesbians, gay men, and bisexuals. *Journal of Counseling Psychology, 56*(1), 97. https://psycnet.apa.org/doi/10.1037/a0012844

Ginsberg, B. (2009). Out with the new, in with the old: The importance of Section 504 of the Rehabilitation Act to prisoners with disabilities. *Fordham Urban Law Journal, 36,* 713. http://ir.lawnet.fordham.edu/ulj/vol36/iss4/4

Gower, A. L., Forster, M., Gloppen, K., Johnson, A. Z., Eisenberg, M. E., Connett, J. E., & Borowsky, I. W. (2018). School practices to foster LGBT-supportive climate: Associations with adolescent bullying involvement. *Prevention Science, 19*(6), 813–821. https://psycnet.apa.org/doi/10.1007/s11121-017-0847-4

Greifinger, R. B. (2006). Commentary: Disabled prisoners and reasonable accommodation. *Criminal Justice Ethics, 25*(1), 2–55.

Hanssens, C., Moodie-Mills, A. C., Ritchie, A. J., Spade, D., & Vaid, U. (2014). *A roadmap for change: Federal policy recommendations for addressing the criminalization of LGBT people and people living with HIV.* Center for Gender & Sexuality Law at Columbia Law School. https://www.hivlawandpolicy.org/sites/default/files/Roadmap_For_Change_full_report.pdf

Himmelstein, K. E., & Brückner, H. (2011). Criminal-justice and school sanctions against nonheterosexual youth: A national longitudinal study. *Pediatrics, 127*(1), 49–57. http://doi.org/10.1542/peds.2009-2306

Human Rights Campaign. (2014). *Glossary of terms.* http://www.hrc.org/resources/glossary-of-terms

Human Rights Watch. (2020) *Country profiles: Sexual orientation and gender identity.* https://www.hrw.org/video-photos/interactive/2020/06/22/human-rights-watch-country-profiles-sexual-orientation-and-gender-identy

Hunt, J., & Moodie-Mills, A. (2012). The unfair criminalization of gay and transgender youth: An overview of the experiences of LGBT youth in the juvenile justice system. *Center for American Progress, 29,* 1–12. https://cdn.americanprogress.org/wp-content/uploads/issues/2012/06/pdf/juvenile_justice.pdf

Irvine, A., & Canfield, A. (2015). The overrepresentation of lesbian, gay, bisexual, questioning, gender nonconforming and transgender youth within the child welfare to juvenile justice crossover population. *American University Journal of Gender, Social Policy & Law, 24,* 243. https://digitalcommons.wcl.american.edu/cgi/viewcontent.cgi?article=1679&context=jgspl

Kann, L., Olsen, E. O. M., McManus, T., Harris, W. A., Shanklin, S. L., Flint, K. H., Queen, B., Lowry, R., Chyen, D., Whittle, J. T., Lim, C., Yamakawa, Y., Brener, N., & Zaza, S. (2016). Sexual identity, sex of sexual contacts, and health-related behaviors among students in grades 9–12—United States and selected sites, 2015. *Morbidity and Mortality Weekly Report: Surveillance Summaries, 65*(9), 1–202. https://www.cdc.gov/mmwr/volumes/65/ss/ss6509a1.htm

Kann, L., Olsen, E. O., McManus, T., Kinchen, S., Chyen, D., Harris, W. A., Wechsler, H., & Centers for Disease Control and Prevention (CDC). (2011). Sexual identity, sex of sexual contacts, and health-risk behaviors among students in grades 9–12—Youth risk behavior surveillance, selected sites, United States, 2001–2009. *Morbidity and Mortality Weekly Report: Surveillance Summaries, 60*(7), 1–133. https://pubmed.ncbi.nlm.nih.gov/21659985/

Kosciw, J. G., Greytak, E. A., Bartkiewicz, M. J., Boesen, M. J., & Palmer, N. A. (2012). *The 2011 National School Climate Survey: The experiences of lesbian, gay, bisexual and transgender youth in our nation's schools.* Gay, Lesbian and Straight Education Network (GLSEN). https://www.glsen.org/sites/default/files/2020-04/2011%20GLSEN%20National%20School%20Climate%20Survey.pdf

Kosciw, J. G., Palmer, N. A., Kull, R. M., & Greytak, E. A. (2013). The effect of negative school climate on academic outcomes for LGBT youth and the role of in-school supports. *Journal of School Violence, 12*(1), 45–63. http://doi.org/10.1080/15388220;2012.732546

Kunzel, R. (2008). Lessons in being gay: Queer encounters in gay and lesbian prison activism. *Radical History Review, 2008*(100), 11–37. https://doi.org/10.1215/01636545-2007-020

Lara, A. (2009). Forced integration of gay, bisexual and transgender inmates in California state prisons: From protected minority to exposed victims. *Southern California Interdisciplinary Law Journal, 19,* 589. https://gould.usc.edu/why/students/orgs/ilj/assets/docs/19-3%20Lar.pdf

Majd, K., Marksamer, J., & Reyes, C. (2009). *Hidden injustice: Lesbian, gay, bisexual, and transgender youth in juvenile courts.* Equity Project. https://www.nclrights.org/wp-content/uploads/2014/06/hidden_injustice.pdf

Mallett, C. A. (2017). The school-to-prison pipeline: Disproportionate impact on vulnerable children and adolescents. *Education and Urban Society, 49*(6), 563–592. https://doi.org/10.1080/1045988X.2016.1144554

Mallory, C., Hasenbush, A., & Sears, B. (2015). *Discrimination and harassment by law enforcement officers in the LGBT community.* https://williamsinstitute.law.ucla.edu/wp-content/uploads/LGBT-Discrimination-by-Law-Enforcement-Mar-2015.pdf

Marksamer, J., & Tobin, H. J. (2014). *Standing with LGBT prisoners: An advocate's guide to ending abuse and combating imprisonment.* https://transequality.org/issues/resources/standing-lgbt-prisoners-advocate-s-guide-ending-abuse-and-combating-imprisonment

McCauley, E., & Brinkley-Rubinstein, L. (2017). Institutionalization and incarceration of LGBT individuals. In K. Eckstand, & J. Potter (Eds.), *Trauma, resilience, and health promotion in LGBT patients* (pp. 149–161). Springer. https://link.springer.com/chapter/10.1007%2F978-3-319-54509-7_13

McCormick, A., Schmidt, K., & Terrazas, S. (2017). LGBTQ youth in the child welfare system: An overview of research, practice, and policy. *Journal of Public Child Welfare, 11*(1), 27–39. https://www.tandfonline.com/doi/full/10.1080/15548732.2016.1221368

Meyer, I. H., Flores, A. R., Stemple, L., Romero, A. P., Wilson, B. D., & Herman, J. L. (2017). Incarceration rates and traits of sexual minorities in the United States: National Inmate Survey, 2011–2012. *American Journal of Public Health, 107*(2), 267–273. https://www.ncbi.nlm.nih.gov/pmc/articles/PMC5227944/

Mogul, J. L., Ritchie, A. J., & Whitlock, K. (2011). *Queer (in) justice: The criminalization of LGBT people in the United States* (Vol. 5). Beacon Press.

Mitchum, P., & Moodie-Mills, A. C. (2014). *Beyond bullying: How hostile school climate perpetuates the school-to-prison pipeline for LGBT youth.* Center for American Progress. https://www.ojp.gov/ncjrs/virt ual-library/abstracts/beyond-bullying-how-hostile-school-climate-perpetuates-school

Moster, A. N., & Jeglic, E. L. (2009). Prison warden attitudes toward prison rape and sexual assault: Findings since the Prison Rape Elimination Act (PREA). *Prison Journal, 89*(1), 65–78. https://www.ojp.gov/ncjrs/ virtual-library/abstracts/prison-warden-attitudes-toward-prison-rape-and-sexual-assault

Movement Advancement Project. (2021, January 15). *Snapshot: LGBTQ equality by state.* https://www.lgbt map.org/equality-maps

Movement Advancement Project and Center for American Progress. (2016). Unjust: *How the broken criminal justice system fails LGBT people of color.* https://www.lgbtmap.org/policy-and-issue-analysis/ criminal-justice-poc

Snapp, S. D., Watson, R. J., Russell, S. T., Diaz, R. M., & Ryan, C. (2015). Social support networks for LGBT young adults: Low cost strategies for positive adjustment. *Family Relations, 64*(3), 420–430.

Steck, A. K., & Perry, D. (2018). Challenging heteronormativity: Creating a safe and inclusive environment for LGBTQ students. *Journal of School Violence, 17*(2), 227–243. https://www.tandfonline.com/doi/full/ 10.1080/15388220.2017.1308255

Toomey, R. B., McGuire, J. K., & Russell, S. T. (2012). Heteronormativity, school climates, and perceived safety for gender nonconforming peers. *Journal of Adolescence, 35*(1), 187–196. https://doi.org/10.1016/ j.adolescence.2011.03.001

Utamsingh, P. D., Richman, L. S., Martin, J. L., Lattanner, M. R., & Chaikind, J. R. (2016). Heteronormativity and practitioner–patient interaction. *Health Communication, 31*(5), 566–574. https://www.tandfonline. com/doi/full/10.1080/10410236.2014.979975

Wilber, S., Reyes, C., & Marksamer, J. (2006). The Model Standards Project: Creating inclusive systems for LGBT youth in out-of-home care. *Child Welfare*, 133–149. https://pubmed.ncbi.nlm.nih.gov/16846109/

8

Transgender and Gender Nonconforming People in Forensic Social Work Practice

Paula S. Schonauer

Background and Context of Transgender and Gender Nonconforming Populations

In 2016, the Republican majority in the North Carolina General Assembly passed the Public Facilities Privacy and Security Act, also known as House Bill 2 or *HB2*. Governor Pat McCrory signed the bill into law, stipulating that individuals must use the restroom that corresponds with the designated sex listed on their birth certificates. In addition, HB2 provided criminal penalties for transgender people who use restrooms consistent with their expressed and innate gender identities. As a result, HB2 sparked a national debate about transgender access to restrooms and other public accommodations.

This legislation and the surrounding debate are strident attempts to prohibit transgender and gender nonconforming (TGNC) people from participating in the public sphere, essentially criminalizing forays into public spaces. Without safe and legal access to public accommodations such as restrooms, transgender people would face significant challenges to their civil rights while participating in economic activities such as buying groceries or searching for employment. In addition, they would be unable to use public spaces for entertainment, education, and political participation without risking criminal penalties, including fines and/or imprisonment.

Essentially, Senator Cruz and like-minded people are trying to advocate the disappearance of transgender Americans from public view with laws like North Carolina's HB2. But unfortunately, inclusion is not a new problem for people who do not identify with

Paula S. Schonauer, *Transgender and Gender Nonconforming People in Forensic Social Work Practice* In: *Handbook of Forensic Social Work*. Edited by: David Axlyn McLeod, Anthony P. Natale, and Kristin W. Mapson, Oxford University Press. © Oxford University Press 2024.
DOI: 10.1093/oso/9780197694732.003.0008

mainstream ideas about gender roles, identity, and expression, especially when framed in binary terms like male and female and masculine and feminine.

This chapter provides an overview of critical issues for TGNC people. To begin, terminology applicable to transgender/nonbinary/gender nonconforming people is introduced for basic understanding. The caveat is that terms are fluid and ever-changing as the transgender community evolves. Next, the chapter explores histories of oppressive forensic systems designed to target transgender or gender nonconforming people through interactions with police, courts, and correctional institutions. Subsequently, the chapter closes with observations and commentary about the current state of affairs governing TGNC people's interactions with forensic institutions.

Gender Identity and Expression Key Terms

Sex

Sex is often regarded as an immutable condition of biology based on the appearance of external genitalia. Sex tends to be used as a predetermining factor for most parents and society at large, dictating how a child is treated from the day of birth throughout the child's life. Sex is commonly defined in binary terms—male and female—but there is another category that is lesser known, called intersex.

Intersex

In some cases, external genitalia is ambiguous or includes other factors (i.e., internal genitalia, chromosomal patterns, and hormonal sex) that differ from what might be seen as conclusive factors in assigning sex. However, people who have been designated as intersex have many of the same challenges TGNC people have. Their concerns address the medical establishment, which has historically performed interventional surgeries to assign an intersex child a sex that conforms to the usual binary expectations for boys and girls.

According to InterAct, an advocacy organization for intersex youth, most of these surgeries (i.e., creating a vagina, reducing a clitoris, moving a urethra, or removing testes) occur before the age of 2, before a child can determine gender identity for themselves. InterAct wants to make sure all surgeries to change sex traits are the concerned person's choice ("What Is Intersex?," 2022).

Transgender

Trans (on the other side of) gender is often used as an umbrella term to describe a range of identities, expressions, and/or gender roles that are not typically associated with a person's sex at birth. However, while the term "transgender" is commonly accepted, not all TGNC people self-identify as transgender (Human Rights Campaign [HRC], 2014).

Cisgender

Cis (on this side of) gender is an adjective used to describe a person whose gender identity and gender expression align with the sex assigned at birth—a person who is not TGNC (HRC, 2014).

Sexual Orientation

Sexual orientation, acknowledged as a vital component of identity, refers to a person's sexual, romantic, and emotional attraction to another person (HRC, 2014).

A person's gender identity does not predict that person's sexual orientation. People may describe their sexual orientations using various terms: gay, lesbian, straight, heterosexual, bisexual, queer, pansexual, or asexual, among others. In addition, they may find themselves attracted to men, women, both, neither, or people who are transgender, nonbinary, or gender nonconforming. For a thorough discussion of sexual orientation in forensic social work, see Chapter 7.

Sex Assigned at Birth

One of the first things parents want to know about their children is the biological sex (boy or girl). Due to technologies like ultrasound, many parents no longer wait for birth to know the biological sex, often having a gender-reveal party to celebrate the anticipated sex of a child. However, a child's outward sex characteristics do not always predict a child's gender identity.

Sex assigned at birth refers to the designation of a child's sex document at the time of birth (birth certificate), often the first and determinative identity document a child receives. TGNC people describe this documentation as assigning a gender at birth. Most people's gender identity and sex assigned at birth are congruent. TGNC individuals have gender identities that differ from the sex assigned to them at birth to varying degrees (HRC, 2014).

Gender

Gender refers to the attitudes, feelings, and behaviors most often associated with a person's biological sex. People are often expected to express themselves and behave according to cultural expectations based on one's biological sex. People who can successfully live up to these expectations are gender normative. Conversely, those whose behavior and expressions are incompatible with these expectations are often referred to as gender nonconforming (American Psychological Association, 2022).

Gender Identity

Gender identity refers to a person's deeply felt sense of being a boy, a man, or a male, or a girl, a woman, or a female. In addition, some people identify as an alternative gender (e.g., genderqueer, gender nonconforming, gender neutral, gender nonbinary). These identities may or may not correspond to a person's sex assigned at birth or to a person's primary or secondary sex characteristics (HRC, 2014).

Gender identity does not predict one's gender expression. Many self-identified transgender people have not taken steps to transition medically or socially. An affirmed gender identity refers to a person's gender identity after coming out as TGNC.

Historically, the word "transgender" has been used as an umbrella term encompassing a spectrum of gender identities and expressions. However, in recent years, the idea of a transgender umbrella has become a subject of debate. For example, there have been efforts to exclude drag performers and crossdressers from inclusion beneath the transgender umbrella. Such persons often do not report feelings of gender dysphoria, relegating their behaviors to expression alone without an overarching identity issue.

The existence of gender identities and expressions outside the binary expectations for most men and women in our society indicates that gender identity involves a spectrum or continuum of behaviors and expressions and the possibility of fluidity in the various ways people engage the world.

Nonbinary (Genderqueer/Nonconforming)

Nonbinary describes a person whose gender identity does not align with a binary understanding of gender, male or female (HRC, 2014). Nonbinary people reject traditional social roles, expectations, and modes of expression, redefining gender for themselves or identifying as a third or fourth gender category. For example, they may see themselves as both man and woman (bigender, pangender, androgyne, genderqueer), neither man nor woman (genderless, gender neutral, agender), or moving between genders (gender fluid).

Transphobia

Transphobia is the fear of people who are or are thought to be transgender, or whose gender expression isn't traditional (Planned Parenthood, 2021). Transphobia is often associated with irrational fear and misunderstanding of transgender people and is accompanied by negative attitudes and beliefs, aversion to and prejudice against transgender people. Acts of violence, discrimination, derogatory language, and microaggressions such as using inappropriate pronouns are often transphobic.

Cissexism

Cissexism is a term that looks beyond the transphobic, irrational fears of individual people to describe systemic oppression (Zambon, 2021). Simply, cissexism refers to attitudes and behaviors that indicate a lack of recognition of TGNC people as valid human beings with real experiences, challenges, and achievements. People influenced by cissexism often engage in acts of violence, discrimination, derogatory language, and a host of microaggressions.

Systemic Cissexism

Systemic cissexism impacts the mental and physical health, welfare, and life expectancy of TGNC people through denials of gender-affirming care in health care settings, housing, employment, education, and public accommodations (James et al., 2016). Very often, systemic cissexism comes from the official invisibility of gender diversity in our society: the binary designations of male and female on official documents; the lack of recognition of gender-diverse people in law and policy, which employers, government officials, and educational institutions can exploit to avoid liability; and the implacable resistance of religious institutions to recognize TGNC people as valid human beings. In many cases, religious institutions deny TGNC people access to vital services such as emergency housing, access to nutrition and health care, and employment. For example, many homeless shelters are run by religious organizations and feeding programs such as soup kitchens. Additionally, many hospitals are owned and run by religious organizations, which often refuse to provide treatment to TGNC people based upon sincerely held convictions backed by the Religious Freedom Restoration Act of 1993. Authored by Chuck Schumer, then a representative from the New York Ninth Congressional District, the act prohibits the government from substantially burdening a person's exercise of religion (H.R. 1308—103rd Congress, 1993). Commonly, charity programs, employment programs, and substance use treatment programs will not serve TGNC people unless they effectively renounce their gender identities and conform to traditional modes of expression aligning with their sex assigned at birth.

TGNC people commonly suffer from minority stress, depression, anxiety, and posttraumatic stress disorder because of the significant barriers encountered while trying to survive in hostile environments. Often, lack of education, skills, and support leave TGNC people vulnerable to exploitation, or they lack legitimate access to the economic means to support their lives, transitions, and aspirations.

Without legitimate access to economic resources, many TGNC people must negotiate the treacherous territory of black markets, criminal enterprises, and dangerous personal encounters to meet their basic needs, afford medical expenses, and gain access to hormone treatment, often administered without medical supervision, which is yet another potential danger. In addition, TGNC people of color are particularly vulnerable to exploitation and survival behaviors such as sex work because of the intersectional oppressions they face in daily life (James et al., 2016).

Transgender and Gender Nonconforming Forensic Interactions

Historical Context

TGNC people and law enforcement have been at odds in the United States since the mid-19th century, when various cities began passing municipal ordinances that made it illegal for a man or a woman to appear in public dressed in a manner not consistent with his or her sex assigned at birth (Stryker, 2009). An even more extended history prohibiting crossdressing dates back to the colonial period. These ordinances and laws banned the wearing of clothing associated with a particular rank in society or a profession. Other laws prohibited White people from impersonating Native Americans or Black people while prohibiting Black people and Native Americans from impersonating White people. According to Susan Stryker (2009) in her book *Transgender History*, the focus on gendered crossdressing emerged from how Americans lived their lives within the context of cities. Sears (2005) provides an example of such an ordinance from the Revised Orders of the City and County of San Francisco.

This ordinance was typical throughout many cities in the United States, beginning with New York City in 1845 and Columbus, Ohio, in 1848, through Cincinnati, Ohio, in 1974 (Sears, 2005). It is not documented why gendered crossdressing became an issue in the mid-19th century. Still, the emergence of urban, industrialized communities likely provided a respite from the close observation experienced in tight-knit rural communities where privacy and anonymity were much more challenging to achieve (Stryker, 2009). Another factor possibly influencing such laws and ordinances was the emergence of first wave feminists in the 19th century, some of whom advocated that traditional women's garments kept women in bondage. Amelia Bloomer proposed that women wear pants-like garments for more comfort and mobility (Stryker, 2009). The backlash against first wave feminism included concerns that people would no longer distinguish men from women.

Though these laws and ordinances had been designed to regulate gender expression, they became tools of oppression for law enforcement officers who patrolled inner cities and neighborhoods with higher proportions of people identified as homosexual. Furthermore, in the 1850s, the separate terms used to identify modern LGBTQ communities had less meaning as homosexuality and variant gender expressions were seen to be inversions of heterosexuality. Thus, men attracted to other men were seen as acting like women, while women attracted to other women were seen as acting like men (Stryker, 2009). Also, the grouping of crossdressing with lewd and lascivious behaviors added more stigma to variant gender expressions, creating an association that has plagued TGNC people through the present day, labeling them as engaging in perverse and predatory behaviors.

Three-Article Rule

According to Kate Redburn, a JD/PhD candidate at Yale University, there are many accounts of a *three-article rule* used by police throughout the United States to determine if people were crossdressing (Ryan, 2019). Source material in memoirs and interviews asserts that the three-article rule was bona fide law. For example, Aleshia Brevard (2001), in her memoir about her male-to-female transition, *The Woman I Was Not Born to Be: A Transsexual Journey*, recalls being subject to arrest for not wearing at least three gender-appropriate articles of clothing.

Rusty Brown, who had worked as a machinist during World War II, found herself out of work at the end of the war. She began dressing as a man to continue working as a machinist but found herself drawn to the world of drag, working as a drag king in New York City. The three-article rule was regarded as law by the very people oppressed by it. It was reported as a factor in Greenwich Village in the weeks and months leading up to the Stone Wall Riots (Ryan, 2019). According to Susan Stryker, similar circumstances contributed to the Compton Cafeteria Riot in August 1966, the first known protest by transgender people, primarily transgender women and drag performers, against police abuse. Police humiliated those arrested in front of other prisoners, forcibly shaved their heads, or placed them in solitary confinement. All too often, these transgender women, who still had male genitalia, would be housed in male jail facilities where their femininity would make them vulnerable to attacks, sexual assaults, and murder (Stryker, 2009).

Despite the widespread impression that the three-article rule was an existing law, it was merely revamping old masquerade laws dating back to the 1840s to target LGBTQ people throughout the 1940s, '50s, and '60s (Ryan, 2019). Some of these laws, as mentioned previously, were not designed to police sexuality and gender identity/expression but were often used by police as a pretext for stopping TGNC individuals in public spaces. So, perhaps the three-article rule was a tool that law enforcement used to seem objective when engaging in discriminatory practices or a term used by the LGBTQ community to keep each other safe (Ryan, 2019).

Walking While Trans

Though the three-article rule and the accompanying masquerade laws once used to target gender nonconforming people have declined in use since the 1970s, law enforcement officers continue to target and stop TGNC people and regularly demand identification, give orders to disperse, and subject them to arrest for minor offenses associated with suspicions of prostitution. These activities disproportionately affect transgender women, particularly transgender women of color, and have become colloquially labeled by the TGNC community as "walking while trans" (Carpenter & Marshall, 2017).

Starting in the late 1960s, criminal defendants began challenging crossdressing laws in numerous cities throughout the United States. Through their success in seeking judicial remedies, many of these crossdressing bans were either stricken from the books or no longer enforced (Redburn, 2018). However, crossdressing and gender nonconformity being associated with sexual deviance and sex work has contributed to a higher number of TGNC people being stopped by police. For example, according to the 2015 U.S. Transgender Survey, police frequently stop transgender women for suspicion of prostitution even when they are not engaging in sex work. Eleven percent of respondents reported being stopped by police for walking while trans, with transgender women of color reporting substantially higher rates (James et al., 2016).

Community-generated survey data and an impressive collection of anecdotal evidence point to a substantial problem with police profiling of TGNC people, especially transgender women of color (Figure 8.1; Carpenter & Marshall, 2017). However, police departments remain reluctant to acknowledge this data, relying instead on their data collection, which, like the criminal justice system, is based upon a binary view of sex and gender. As a result, police-generated statistics do not capture the transgender status of field contacts or arrestees. Because of this, it is difficult to establish a pattern of profiling and harassment (Carpenter & Marshall, 2017).

A contributing factor to the walking while trans problem is the high rate at which TGNC people participate in the underground economy, including dealing drugs, stealing and/or fencing property, and engaging in sex work. The commercial sex trade includes participation in the pornography industry, escort services, and street-level sex work (James et al., 2016). In addition to money, TGNC people may exchange sex for a place to sleep, food, or a variety of other goods and services. Family rejection, poverty, or unequal opportunities in employment, housing, and education are all reasons transgender folks participate in this kind of work (James et al., 2016). According to the U.S. Transgender Survey, 20% of respondents who identify as TGNC have at some point participated in activities associated with the sex trade (James et al., 2016). This contributes to a pattern of engagement that places TGNC people at higher risk than the general population for adverse outcomes when interacting with police and the criminal justice system.

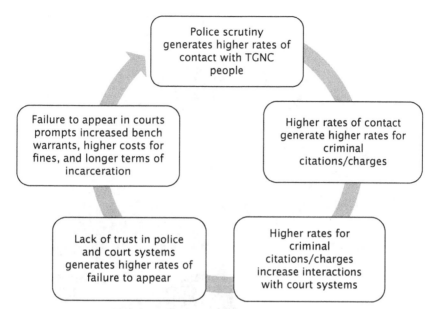

FIGURE 8.1 Race/Ethnicity of Trans Women Stopped by Police for Sex Work

Discomfort and Fear of Law Enforcement Officers

The impact of police profiling and harassment is a crisis for the TGNC community in the United States. This condition places TGNC people, a vulnerable population, at the wrong end of police activities, where they are more likely to experience threats to their well-being than to feel protected. TGNC people report a high incidence of negative interactions with police, which has greatly diminished their trust in law enforcement personnel. According to the U.S. Transgender Survey, 57% of respondents reported they were never or were only sometimes treated respectfully by police officers who thought or knew they were TGNC. Additionally, 58% reported maltreatment by police officers, with incidents ranging from being referred to as the wrong gender to verbally harassed to physically and/or sexually assaulted. Fifty-seven percent of respondents reported they were either somewhat or very uncomfortable asking for police assistance (James et al., 2016). Figure 8.2 which illustrates Transgender, Nonbinary, or Gender Nonconforming (TGNC) Cycle of Criminal Justice System Encounters.

Policies That Protect the Rights of Incarcerated People

One of the challenges for TGNC people involves the lack of consistency in laws regarding the recognition and welfare of TGNC people in federal, state, and local jurisdictions. As a result, in many forensic settings, TGNC people do not benefit from the applicable laws and policies that protect the rights and dignity of people who encounter authorities associated with the criminal justice system.

In many cases, laws that apply to gay, lesbian, and bisexual people can apply to TGNC people as well, especially regarding the First, Fifth, Eighth, and 14th Amendments of the U.S. Constitution (though one must acknowledge that originalist interpretations of the U.S.

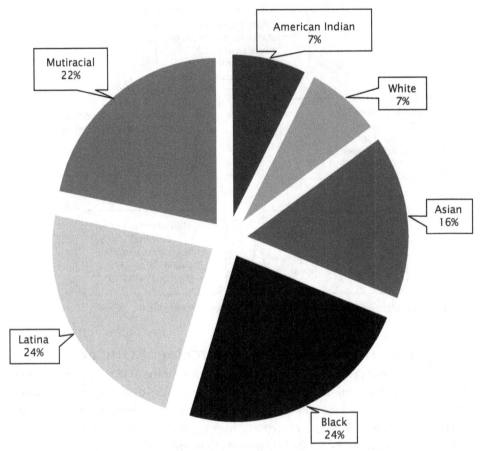

FIGURE 8.2 Transgender, Nonbinary, or Gender Nonconforming (TGNC) Cycle of Criminal Justice System Encounters

Constitution may not recognize any person on the LGBTQ spectrum). Additionally, the Prison Rape Elimination Act of 2003 (PREA) broadly applies to TGNC people. Still, it has been established that TGNC people are particularly vulnerable to sexual assault in forensic settings, with the additional problems of intransigent institutions failing to use all measures possible to protect TGNC people from physical and sexual assault, often blaming TGNC people for their victimization and refusing to take grievance reports seriously (James et al., 2016).

A common response to TGNC people in forensic settings is to place them in solitary confinement for protection, while other inmates experience solitary confinement as a punishment. In recent years, solitary confinement has received challenges in state and federal courts, citing it as a cruel and unusual punishment prohibited under the Eighth Amendment.

According to the National Equality Map published by the Movement Advancement Project (MAP), protections for TGNC people are not consistent or pervasive throughout the United States. A majority of states and territories—29—have a low or negative rating regarding laws and policies regarding protections for gender identity and expression. At the same time, 21 states and territories have a low or negative rating for protections based upon sexual orientation (Movement Advancement Project, 2022).

In some states with negative or low rating on the National Equality Map, some of the larger cities have adopted municipal ordinances protecting TGNC people from discrimination in housing, employment, and access to public accommodations and have worked with their respective police agencies to develop training and policies concerning the treatment of TGNC people. One example is Norman, Oklahoma, which passed a comprehensive nondiscrimination ordinance (including gender identity and expression) in 2019 (Riley, 2019), prompting efforts in the Oklahoma state legislature to restrict cities and towns from adopting such protections, attempting to nullify Norman's effort to recognize the full equality of LGBTQ people.

Transgender and Gender Nonconforming Forensic Challenges

Identity Documents

TGNC people encounter obstacles in U.S. court systems, in both civil and criminal courts, on a routine basis with judges and prosecutors who are not informed about or do not care about the specific challenges TGNC people face when seeking redress in court. It is often evident that cultural, religious, and personal values impact outcomes for TGNC people when interacting with court systems. For example, in a 2012 case in Oklahoma City, Oklahoma, district court judge Bill Graves denied a transgender woman's petition to change her name based on the judge's religious beliefs. In his decision to deny the petitioner, Judge Graves accused the transgender woman of perpetrating fraud and cited biblical scripture:

> To grant a name change, in this case, would be to assist that which is fraudulent. Notably, Genesis 1:27–28 states: So, God created man in his own image, in the image of God created he him; male and female created he them. And God blessed them, and God said unto them, Be fruitful, and multiply, and replenish the earth. The DNA code shows God meant for them to stay male and female (Clay, 2012)

The transgender woman, in this case, appealed to the Oklahoma Court of Civil Appeals regarding Judge Graves's decision. They returned a favorable response, calling Judge Graves's behavior *judicial abuse*. The transgender plaintiff spent $18,000 in legal fees to appeal Judge Graves's decision, surpassing the means of most transgender women in the United States (Clay, 2012).

The barriers to legally changing personal documentation are numerous in the United States, and there are no laws that consistently apply from state to state. For example, according to the U.S. Transgender Survey, only 11% had preferred names and gender on all IDs and records. As much as 68% reported being unable to put names and gender on any of their documentation (James et al., 2016). The barriers are often financial, but various jurisdictions prohibit changing personal documents ranging from birth certificates to unique IDs, driver's licenses, and, in recent years, passports.

The inability to obtain personal documentation of one's gender identity places TGNC people at risk for harassment and discrimination, requiring TGNC people to out themselves during encounters with law enforcement. Showing an ID that does not match one's gender presentation invites harassment (25% reported), denial of services and benefits (16% reported), requests to leave an establishment (9% reported), and assault or attack (2% reported; James et al., 2016). It is worth considering that conflicting documents often inhibit TGNC people from accessing vital services such as emergency shelters, increasing the chances of having adverse encounters with law enforcement.

Criminal Justice System Mistrust

In their article "Walking While Trans: Profiling of Transgender Women by Law Enforcement, and the Problem of Proof," Carpenter and Marshall (2017) detail that continual and often unwarranted police contact dramatically increases the rate at which transgender women must engage with criminal courts and the rate at which they are incarcerated. In both survey data and anecdotal reports, many TGNC people report being arrested because they are TGNC. According to the National Transgender Discrimination Survey, of the 2% of respondents arrested by police, 22% reported believing they were detained because they were transgender (James et al., 2016).

A 2005 Amnesty International report revealed unfair police profiling of transgender sex workers and that TGNC people are under intense scrutiny by police (Amnesty International, 2005). In 2015, the National Transgender Discrimination Survey supported a pattern of profiling transgender women as sex workers, especially transgender women of color, which is a pervasive problem spanning decades even as the transgender community has become more visible and politically relevant (James et al., 2016).

Continual scrutiny of TGNC people by police leads to higher arrest rates, creating higher contact rates with criminal courts. Higher arrest rates produce higher rates of incarceration. Because TGNC people lack trust in the criminal justice system, they frequently fail to appear for scheduled hearings and related events associated with charges brought from walking while trans violations (Carpenter & Marshall, 2017). Failure to appear in court prompts the issuance of bench warrants, increases the cost of fines, and results in longer jail terms. So often, what beings as a minor citation can become a continuous cycle of interactions with the criminal justice system.

The cycle of contact can render TGNC people helpless in the face of debt, stigmatized by arrest records, and more likely to engage in underground economic activities like sex work and selling street drugs (Carpenter & Marshall, 2017). Engaging in felonious activities can eventually lead TGNC people into the prison system, where they face physical abuse, sexual assault, denial of medical care, constant harassment by both staff and fellow inmates, and solitary confinement (protective custody), which has a significant impact on mental and physical well-being (Grassian, 2006). Though protective custody, in these cases, is not meant to be a punishment, it has the same effects as solitary confinement, mainly by inhibiting TGNC people from engaging in rehabilitative activities such as work, education, and recovery programs (James et al., 2016).

Failures From Cops to Courts

According to the National Transgender Discrimination Survey, 58% of respondents (who reported that police knew or suspected they were TGNC) reported verbal harassment, physical assault, sexual assault, or other mistreatment by police and/or other law enforcement officials (James et al., 2016). Additionally, 57% of respondents reported feeling somewhat uncomfortable or very uncomfortable asking the police for help, with 15% reporting feeling neutral and only 29% feeling comfortable (James et al., 2016).

It is easy to conclude that crimes against TGNC people are underreported. Moreover, when TGNC people report crimes committed against them, they often report a lack of sympathy or seriousness by responding police officers and/or investigators (Buist & Stone, 2014).

In a well-known case involving Brandon Teena in 1993, attackers kidnapped him and drove him to a remote area in Nebraska, where they brutally raped him. The local sheriff's office failed to respond promptly after the crime was reported and physical evidence was provided via a rape kit. Records reveal Brandon Teena's insensitive treatment from Sheriff Charles Laux, including questions about Brandon's genitalia and whether he stuffed his underwear with a sock and referring to him as "it" (Buist & Stone, 2014). A week after Brandon reported the rape, suspects John Lotter and Tom Nissen murdered Brandon and two witnesses to the crime. The lack of response by authorities sparked outrage, a great deal of public sympathy, and a major motion picture in 1999, *Boys Don't Cry*, featuring Hilary Swank as Brandon, a role that won Hilary Swank critical acclaim and an Academy Award for Best Actress in a Leading Role.

In 2002, Gwen Araujo, a 17-year-old preoperative transgender woman, was murdered at a party by four young men who went to school with her. Rumors had abounded at school that Gwen was transgender. Her assailants forced her into a bathroom to reveal her *real sex* and later that evening beat her with their fists and a shovel, strangled her, and buried her in the remote California wilderness (Bettcher, 2007).

Party participants did not report the crime. When Gwen's mother reported her missing the next day, the police did not respond with concern, considering Gwen's transgender status as evidence she was likely to engage in defiant and risky behavior. When the crime came to light, law enforcement and court officials considered Gwen at least partially responsible for what happened to her, accusing Gwen of being deceptive about her transgender status, which facilitated a *trans panic defense*. Despite the brutal way she died, it took two trials to achieve convictions, which were not commensurate to the crime: second-degree murder and voluntary manslaughter (Bettcher, 2007).

The elements of both crimes indicate that the resultant death was unintentional despite Gwen being lured into a trap to be exposed and beaten. In California, the necessary element to establish a charge of second-degree murder is unconsidered rash impulse. The intentional element marking the differences between first-degree (premeditated) murder and second-degree murder had been debated in the first trial, which resulted in a hung jury and a declared mistrial. The voluntary manslaughter charge had been a plea deal after the second trial when jurors could not reach a verdict about one of the defendants. Some of the jurors in both trials, according to Bettcher (2007), admitted they considered *sexual provocation* as a factor that led to the murder. In addition, the jurors in both trials did not favor a hate crime enhancement for the accused despite testimony involving anti-trans epithets used by the defendants (Bettcher, 2007).

While the United States was embroiled in a debate about whether George Zimmerman had been justified in killing Trayvon Martin in February 2012, CeCe McDonald, an African American transgender woman, pleaded guilty to second-degree manslaughter in June 2012, receiving 41 months in prison. Though some of the elements of her case differ from Zimmerman's case, the similarities are noteworthy. Both defendants claimed self-defense. Both defendants claimed to fear for their lives. However, the circumstances that led to CeCe McDonald's use of a pair of scissors to defend herself are readily apparent, as CeCe was injured from an attack with a broken bottle and assaulted by multiple people. In the Zimmerman case, an element of concern revolved around whether he ignored advice from a dispatcher by initiating a confrontation with Trayvon Martin. However, prosecutors in CeCe McDonald's case would not consider a self-defense plea even though Minnesota law establishes that an act of self-defense occurs when a person is repelling a real or perceived threat of bodily harm or there is a defensive response from the defender (Buist & Stone, 2014). CeCe McDonald entered a plea to avoid a possible 20-year sentence (Buist & Stone, 2014).

According to Bettcher (2007), CeCe McDonald understood her circumstances. As a transgender woman of color, she knew that she was more likely to experience hostility from court officials and, perhaps, a lack of due care and concern on the part of her public defender. She likely understood she would have had difficulty overcoming the prejudice of jurors who may blame transgender victims, viewing their gender expression as provocative (Bettcher, 2007). Because of her intersecting identities, she could not trust the criminal justice system with her life (Buist & Stone, 2014). In contrast, Zimmerman, a cisgender heterosexual male armed with a gun, had enough confidence in the system to endure a jury trial. He received an acquittal on all charges in July 2013.

Systemic Erasure: Invisibility in Forensic Settings

Double Hard Time

CeCe McDonald served 19 months of a 41-month sentence, slightly less than half the time she had been given. Considering the circumstances TGNC people face in prison, one could argue she served every bit of her sentence without reprieve. Because CeCe McDonald had not had gender affirmation surgery, she was sent to Minnesota Correctional Facility-St. Cloud, a men's prison. For many trans women, being housed in a men's prison is a living nightmare. In addition to the near-constant sexual harassment, trans women in men's facilities are repeatedly targeted for sexual assault and physical abuse (Jenness & Gerlinger, 2020).

The National Transgender Discrimination Survey reports a high physical and sexual assault rate aimed at TGNC people in jails and prisons. Nearly one-third of respondents who had been incarcerated (30%) reported being physically and/or sexually assaulted by facility staff or other inmates (James et al., 2016). In addition to these hazards, TGNC people face a total institution, which defines all aspects of members' lives. As total institutions, prisons are rigidly binary regarding gender segregation, predominantly defining people as either male or female based upon genitalia and often disregarding the lived experiences and the development of secondary sex characteristics (i.e., chest development, facial hair, deepened voice) of TGNC people sentenced to prison.

Incarcerated TGNC people frequently report being denied adequate medical care, hormone therapy, and other gender-affirming medical procedures, which could help reduce the impact of gender dysphoria and the attendant mental health challenges associated with institutional denials of personal identity. For example, the National Transgender Discrimination Survey reports that 37% of respondents taking hormones before being incarcerated were denied hormone therapy after incarceration (James et al., 2016).

The high-profile case of Ashley Diamond, highlighted in the *New York Times* in 2015, asserted that prison provides a context for the deliberate defeminizing of transgender women. The story also reported that Ashley Diamond was forced to strip alongside male inmates and that she hugged her breasts protectively while doing so (Sontag, 2015). Commenting about being denied hormone therapy, Ashley Diamond noted, "The State of Georgia would make a man out of me" (McCray, 2017, p. 1).

Protective custody, often used to safeguard inmates who may be targeted for violence and harassment, can have detrimental effects on TGNC inmates because it resembles solitary confinement. In recent years solitary confinement has been increasingly recognized as a cruel and unusual punishment. Grassian (2006) details the debilitating psychiatric effects on prisoners, including "severe exacerbation or recurrence of existing illness, or the appearance of an acute mental illness in individuals who had been previously free of any such illness" (p. 333). Symptoms of mental illness include hyperresponsivity to external stimuli; perceptual distortions, illusions, and hallucinations; panic attacks; difficulties with thinking, concentration, and memory; intrusive obsessional thoughts, often experienced through the emergence of primitive aggressive ruminations; overt paranoia; and problems with impulse control (Grassian, 2006).

The National Transgender Discrimination Survey reports that 52% of respondents who had been incarcerated were subjected to isolation in one or more ways. Some respondents (17%) reported being held in a separate area for transgender, lesbian, gay, and bisexual people, such as a pod, unit, tank, or other housing areas. In comparison, others (42%) reported being held in solitary confinement (James et al., 2016). Those in solitary confinement reported a range of times in which they had been held in isolation: 40% for 14 days or less, 28% for 1 to 3 months, and 14% for over 6 months (James et al., 2016).

Transgender Men and Incarceration

The documentation of transgender men and their experiences in corrections systems is virtually nonexistent. Much of the data derives from anecdotal sources and many studies that are difficult to quantify beyond their specific parameters. The documentation of TGNC people in corrections institutions is dependent upon studies and surveys produced by advocacy organizations and educational institutions, which often limit the study of incarcerated

persons because they are often not fully able to consent to such studies. However, the anecdotal evidence is compelling.

The National Transgender Discrimination Survey reports that TGNC people are incarcerated at a rate of 16% compared to 2.7% for the general population. In addition, transgender men are incarcerated at a rate of 10%, compared to a rate of 4.9% for all men (James
et al., 2016).

Transgender men experience many issues reported by transgender women in corrections settings: the invalidation of gender identity; compulsory conformity to institutional expectations of gender expression; denial of medical treatment, including hormone
therapy; and various forms of isolation. For example, transgender men in prison are often
compelled to shave if they have facial hair, which is challenging because of restrictive access
to razors and other shaving implements. Transgender men are often issued women's underwear and subjected to discipline if they gain access to and wear men's briefs and boxers.
They are often forced to wear institutional dresses if more androgynous clothing is unavailable (Lawliet, 2016).

Though women's prisons are seen as less violent, transgender men report a high physical and sexual abuse rate frequently provoked and initiated by facility staff. Detention staff
have been reported as challenging and abusing transgender men as they would other men
to treat them like the men they think they are and sexually harassing and assaulting them to
remind them they are women (Lawliet, 2016).

With only 6% of transgender men having obtained gender-affirming bottom surgery
(Lawliet, 2016), transgender men have a smaller chance of avoiding incarceration in women's
prisons than do transgender women avoiding being held in men's prisons if they have had
gender affirmation surgery. Though speculative because of lack of study, transgender men
being incarcerated in men's prisons may not be a suitable alternative due to the prevailing
lack of physical stature among most transgender men. Men of smaller stature are frequently
subjected to physical and sexual abuse in men's prisons (Wolff & Shi, 2009). If their transgender status becomes known in a men's prison population, they may be marked as targets.

Systemic Forensic Social Work Practice Challenges

The primary obstacle to obtaining meaningful reform regarding the treatment of TGNC
people in the criminal justice system is the lack of comprehensive study regarding the
unique challenges they face when dealing with policing organizations, courts, and correctional institutions. Because of the rigidity of the gender binary in the criminal justice
system, it is difficult to determine the degree of police profiling applied to TGNC people
and the level of discrimination when police officers decide to cite, detain, and arrest people
who do not fit into the predominant gender binary of male and female.

Criminal courts, including prosecutors, defense attorneys, juries, and judges, have
shown significant resistance to being educated regarding the needs and vulnerabilities of
TGNC people, often making decisions that place TGNC people in harmful situations and
subject to inhumane treatment. Some of this resistance is societal, reflective of the ideas
prevalent in mainstream discourse. The jury pool, for instance, will be knowledgeable about
the lives and needs of TGNC people to the degree they see TGNC people portrayed in local

and national media and based upon personal experiences with TGNC people they may have met and know. Police and other law enforcement personnel often have exposure to the LGBTQ community through diversity training. However, their views may not necessarily reflect material presented in the training but rather the attitudes and beliefs about TGNC people that predominate within the cultures of the various agencies. Likewise, prosecutors and defense attorneys will know only as much as they are exposed to regarding TGNC people in personal experience and/or legal training. Judges may or may not understand the TGNC community, but their function is to make sure cases presented before them adhere to the law legislated through representative government. Proper jurisprudence should preclude judges from inserting personal opinions into a court decision, but, as is well known, judges often make rulings based upon personal belief systems outside of the law, such as Judge Bill Graves when he ruled against transgender women changing their names based upon his understanding of biblical teachings.

According to Carpenter and Marshall (2018) in "Walking While Trans: Profiling of Transgender Women by Law Enforcement, and the Problem of Proof," a significant challenge to collecting more quantitative data addressing the profiling of, targeting of, and discrimination against TGNC people is the criminal justice system itself. The rigid adherence to binary views about gender makes it difficult to quantify how often police officers interact with TGNC people. For example, field contact reports have two designations for a person's sex (male or female) at birth or the officers' perceptions of a person's sex. The lack of other choices contributes to a sense of TGNC people being erased or rendered invisible when contacting the criminal justice system.

Carpenter and Marshall (2018) also point out that it is difficult to add choices to field contact reports because of concerns about TGNC people's medical and personal privacy. Many TGNC people do not want their gender history reflected in official public records, especially those generated by law enforcement officials. Also, it is awkward to require police officers to question people about their gender status without seeming intrusive or invasive in their approach to soliciting such information.

Law enforcement agencies and other criminal justice institutions are suspicious of data generated outside their purview. As a result, they will effectively gaslight people and organizations trying to question how they fulfill their duties. If it cannot be quantified in their own experience and/or measurement, they will tend to disregard concerns brought before them by TGNC people, advocates, and allies.

Recommendations

A significant challenge for TGNC people is the process toward greater visibility in society. As observed in recent years, the increased visibility of transgender people has promoted more awareness about TGNC people, and this awareness has spurred a greater degree of cultural relevance, which gives mainstream people more opportunities to learn about the lives and challenges of TGNC people and their attempts to access mainstream benefits and responsibilities.

However, increased visibility has generated a backlash of hate and violence directed at TGNC people. There has also been a significant disinformation campaign trying to discredit the existence of TGNC people, some of which are being promoted by people touting themselves as medical and mental health care professionals. Such tactics are difficult to counter in the best of conditions, but it is impossible when TGNC people avoid being visible and refrain from telling their stories.

Understanding how challenging it is to stand against cultural ignorance, TGNC advocates maintain that visibility and developing a voice to engage people are entirely necessary. Many people in society do not know what to think about TGNC people. They are not necessarily predisposed to reject TGNC people, nor will they accept them without learning who they are. In common political parlance, they are the moveable middle, which can be reached through advocacy and education.

As with the movement toward marriage equality in the United States, developing allies in the struggle for equality is necessary. Embracing allies builds a coalition of support. Likewise, TGNC people need to be good allies in support of other movements, emphasizing common experiences and the sharing of aspirations. Through these efforts, coalitions can hold criminal justice officials more accountable for their behavior and influence the development of more inclusive and sensitive policies.

References

American Psychological Association. (2022). *Gender.* https://apastyle.apa.org/style-grammar-guidelines/bias-free-language/gender

Amnesty International. (2005). *United States of America: Stonewalled: Police abuse and misconduct against lesbian, gay, bisexual and transgender people in the U.S.*

Bettcher, T. M. (2007). Evil deceivers and make-believers: On transphobic violence and the politics of illusion. *Hypatia, 22*(3), 43–65. https://doi.org/10.1111/j.1527-2001.

Brevard, A. (2001). *The woman I was not born to be: A transsexual journey.* Temple University Press. https://muse.jhu.edu/book/45898

Buist, C. L., & Stone, C. (2014). Transgender victims and offenders: Failures of the United States criminal justice system and the necessity of queer criminology. *Critical Criminology, 22*(1), 35–47. https://www.semanticscholar.org/paper/Transgender-Victims-and-Offenders%3A-Failures-of-the-Buist-Stone/476cd1f10fb2ac1f110d07ed4b95a39aefc5ac82

Carpenter, L. F., & Marshall, R. B. (2017). Walking while trans: Profiling of transgender women by law enforcement, and the problem of proof. *William & Mary Journal of Women & the Law, 24*, 5. https://www.semanticscholar.org/paper/Walking-While-Trans%3A-Profiling-of-Transgender-Women-Carpenter-Marshall/e1f612583b65ec08934d286aa90c78b3d3d558dd#paper-header

Clay, N. (2012, November 20). Oklahoma appeals court orders name change in transgender case. *The Oklahoman.* https://www.oklahoman.com/story/news/columns/2012/11/20/oklahoma-appeals-court-orders-name-change-in-transgender-case/61027039007

Grassian, S. (2006). Psychiatric effects of solitary confinement. *Washington University Journal of Law & Policy, 22*, 325. https://heinonline.org/HOL/LandingPage?handle=hein.journals/wajlp22&div=26&id=&page=

H.R. 1308—103rd Congress (1993–1994): Religious Freedom Restoration Act of 1993. (1993, November 16). Library of Congress. https://www.congress.gov/bill/103rd-congress/house-bill/1308 https://www.congress.gov/103/statute/STATUTE-107/STATUTE-107-Pg1488.pdf

Human Rights Campaign. (2014). *Glossary of terms.* https://www.hrc.org/resources/glossary-of-terms

James, S., Herman, J.L., Rankin, S., Keisling, M., Mottet, L., & Anafi, M. (2016). *The report of the 2015 US transgender survey.* Washington, DC: National Center for Transgender Equality. https://transequality.org/sites/default/files/docs/usts/USTS-Full-Report-Dec17.pdf

Jenness, V., & Gerlinger, J. (2020). The feminization of transgender women in prisons for men: How prison as a total institution shapes gender. *Journal of Contemporary Criminal Justice, 36*(2), 182–205. https://doi. org/10.1177%2F1043986219894422

Lawliet, E. (2016). Criminal erasure: Interactions between transgender men and the American criminal justice system. *Aleph, UCLA Undergraduate Research Journal for the Humanities and Social Sciences, 13,* 11–39. https://doi.org/10.5070/L6131040223

McCray, R. (2017, February). *After decades in prison, this transwoman is finally getting gender confirmation surgery.* https://www.vice.com/en/article/xy7q94/after-30-years-in-prison-this-trans-woman-is-finally-getting-gender-confirmation-surgery

Movement Advancement Project (MAP). (2022). *Snapshot: LGBTQ equality by state.* https://www.lgbtmap.org/equality-maps

Planned Parenthood. (2021). *What's transphobia?* https://www.plannedparenthood.org/learn/gender-identity/transgender/whats-transphobia

Redburn, K. (2018, April). *Before equal protection: The fall of anti-crossdressing laws and the origins of the transgender legal movement 1964–1980.* https://papers.ssrn.com/sol3/papers.cfm?abstract_id=3199904

Riley, J. (2019, August). Oklahoma's Norman city council passes state's first LGBTQ nondiscrimination ordinance. *Metro Weekly.* https://www.metroweekly.com/2019/08/oklahomas-norman-city-council-passes-lgbtq-nondiscrimination-ordinance/

Ryan, H. (2019, June). *How dressing in drag was labeled a crime in the 20th century.* https://www.history.com/news/stonewall-riots-lgbtq-drag-three-article-rule

Sears, C. (2005). *"A dress not belonging to his or her sex": Crossdressing law in San Francisco, 1860–1900.* University of California, Santa Cruz. https://www.academia.edu/31670727/Review_of_Clare_Sears_Arresting_Dress_Cross_Dressing_Law_and_Fascination_in_Nineteenth_Century_San_Francisco_in_the_Committee_on_Lesbian_Gay_Bisexual_and_Transgender_History_Newsletter_Spring_2016

Sontag, D. (2015, April 5). Transgender woman cites attacks and abuse in men's prison. *New York Times.* https://www.nytimes.com/2015/04/06/us/ashley-diamond-transgender-inmate-cites-attacks-and-abuse-in-mens-prison.htmlStryker, S. (2009). *Transgender history.* Seal Press. https://www.amazon.com/Transgender-History-second-Todays-Revolution/dp/158005689X?asin=158005689X&revisionId=&format=4&depth=1

What is intersex? (2022). https://medlineplus.gov/ency/article/001669.htm

Wolff, N., & Shi, J. (2009). Contextualization of physical and sexual assault in male prisons: Incidents and their aftermath. *Journal of Correctional Health Care, 15*(1), 58–77. https://doi.org/10.1177/1078345808326622

Zambon, V. (2021, February). *Transphobia: Definition, effects on health, and seeking help.* https://www.medicalnewstoday.com/articles/transphobia#effects-on-physical-health

9

Addressing Racial and Ethnic Disparities

Ethical and Legal Frameworks to Guide Forensic Social Work Practice

Maria E. Torres, Hannah E. Karpman,
Leigh-Anne Francis, and George S. Leibowitz

> Where, after all, do universal human rights begin? In small places, close to home—so close and so small that they cannot be seen on any maps of the world. Yet they are the world of the individual person; the neighborhood he lives in; the school or college he attends; the factory, farm, or office where he works. Such are the places where every man, woman, and child seek equal justice, equal opportunity, and equal dignity without discrimination. Unless these rights have meaning there, they have little meaning anywhere. Without concerted citizen action to uphold them close to home, we shall look in vain for progress in the larger world.
>
> —Eleanor Roosevelt (1958, speaking on
> the UN Declaration of Human Rights)

Introduction

Involvement with the law or legal issues is the hallmark of forensic social work. Given the far reach and impact of the law in everyday life, this means that forensic social workers are often working across systems and settings, interacting with multiple institutions or systems when addressing their clients' needs (e.g., health and mental health care facilities, child welfare agencies, school systems, or elder care facilities). They may be part of a legal defense team working on mitigation strategies for a death penalty case; working at a community reentry program, child welfare, or juvenile justice agency; or serving as an expert

Maria E. Torres, Hannah E. Karpman, Leigh-Anne Francis, and George S. Leibowitz, *Addressing Racial and Ethnic Disparities*
In: *Handbook of Forensic Social Work*. Edited by: David Axlyn McLeod, Anthony P. Natale, and Kristin W. Mapson, Oxford University Press.
© Oxford University Press 2024. DOI: 10.1093/oso/9780197694732.003.0009

witness in a legal proceeding. Regardless of the job or context, a crucial aspect of forensic social work is its foundational focus on social justice, equity, and human rights (Maschi & Leibowitz, 2018).

Racial and/or ethnic disparities exist when a racial/ethnic group within the forensic system is larger than the proportion of those groups in the general population (Schrantz & McElroy, 2000). Racial and ethnic disparities in entry to and treatment within the forensic system have been well documented in the United States since the very beginning of the system itself (Mauer, 2010; Miller et al., 2018). Despite the longstanding trends in disparate treatment of people of color and immigrant communities by the forensic system, recent events have created a window of opportunity for real change to these systems.

Technological advances, especially the advent of cell phones with video-recording capacity, have allowed individuals to document their lives in real time. The proliferation of social media platforms allows these experiences to be readily shared. Organizers from Black Lives Matter (BLM) and other racial justice leaders have successfully harnessed these technologies to focus national and international attention on the policies that impact the lives of people of color—precisely, policies related to policing and incarceration (Mundt et al., 2018). In 2014, videos and images of violence against Black men by police were widely circulated, drawing national and international outrage. To be clear, the violence experienced by Black men at the hands of police is not a new phenomenon. It is merely that documenting and sharing these incidents has become more accessible. While technology is part of why the BLM movement successfully drew attention to disparities in the forensic system, that is only part of the story. BLM organizers are incredibly effective at strategic engagement with individuals and systems, including politicians and the press. The movement offered a clear policy agenda with specific actions and targets, providing clear leadership for concrete change (Nardini, Rank-Christman, Bublitz, Cross, & Peracchio, 2021).

This racial justice movement occurred in parallel with the rise of Trumpism. Trumpism is marked by racialized and nationalist sentiment, used to generate fear of the "other" to support political agendas (De Matas, 2017). The impact of this ideology was evidenced by the policies arising out of the Trump administration and the effect of these policies on those who hold marginalized identities. Research suggests Trumpism resulted in fear among marginalized communities at the individual level, for both their rights and safety (Serwer, 2018). These fears are not unfounded, given the targeting of communities of color and immigrants by the police and other law enforcement personnel and an increase in hate crimes (Warren-Gordon & Rhineberger, 2021).

Finally, the COVID pandemic brought renewed focus on identity-related disparities. Older individuals, those with chronic health conditions, those living in institutions (including the carceral system), and those who were racial or ethnic minorities were more likely to contract COVID and less likely to receive adequate care, resulting in higher mortality rates (Alcendor, 2020; Razai, Kankam, Majeed, Esmail, & Williams, 2021). The reasons for these disparities are complicated and highlight the intersection of economic insecurity, housing insecurity, systemic racism, and the health risks of being institutionalized.

First, this chapter highlights the history of slavery in this country and how its roots are tightly connected to the present-day forensic system. To understand the disparities, we see in today's forensic system the long shadow of slavery on U.S. culture, viewing it as a marker of the deeply held White supremacist attitudes and beliefs that extended to all Indigenous persons, non-White immigrants, refugees, and ethnic minorities. By focusing on Black Americans, we set the stage for how we came to the current disparities in the forensic system. However, the chapter authors also explore how systemic racism impacts all people of color. We then explore theoretical and research frameworks that can help us examine how present-day racial and ethnic disparities in the forensic system can be understood and mitigated, applying them to current statistics on disparities in access to, type of interaction with, and outcomes of forensic involvement. Finally, we discuss how these current-day dilemmas should inform forensic social workers at the micro, mezzo, and macro levels, engaging both practical and ethical dilemmas in our discussion.

Origins of Racial and Ethnic Disparities in the Forensic System: From Slavery to Mass Incarceration

> The slave went free; stood a brief moment in the sun; then moved back toward slavery.
>
> —DuBois (1966)

U.S. forensics systems generate, are complicit in, and comprise multiple intersecting oppressions, including White supremacy/anti-Blackness and economic inequity. An exploration of anti-Blackness in the forensics system reveals how the forensics system has sustained White supremacist systems of power in the form of slavery, the post–Civil War South's for-profit prison system, and mass incarceration in the New Jim Crow era (the 1970s to present). These power systems have relentlessly worked to keep Black Americans disproportionately impoverished, hindering opportunities for economic growth or stability at every turn in poor Black communities. Centering Black people in our exploration of the forensics system requires us to analyze and understand slavery as the first system of mass incarceration.

The earliest phases of chattel slavery as a carceral process involved the brutal forced migration of over 12 million Africans in the early 1500s to a landmass that European invaders would call "the Americas" (Digital History, 2021). European colonialism, a White male Christian campaign of genocide, mass rape, and mass land theft, facilitated slavery's expansion (Alexander, 2010; Smith, 2007). Slavery, an institution older than the United States at the time of this writing, was legal since the nation's founding. Over 10 generations, it is estimated that 15 million Black men, women, and children were enslaved (Davis, 2016). The racist terrorism at the heart of the slavery system was many-pronged: White men's rape of Black women and girls, White women's rape of Black men and boys, forced reproduction, whipping, branding, and the dehumanization of being legally defined as chattel, put on display, corporally inspected, bought and sold at slave markets, forced to do backbreaking labor, and forced family separation (Foster, 2011; White, 1999). Tragically, systemic carceral practices did not end with destroying the slavery system (Schwalm, 1997). Many of the acts of violence described above persisted well after slavery's destruction as core features of the post–Civil War South's prisons and the legal system.

In the wake of slavery's destruction, a for-profit penal system emerged in the South. The South's previously majority White male prison population was deliberately repopulated with formerly enslaved Black people, most of them Black men. In the post–Civil War South, White male legal officials targeted Black people for mass arrests that transformed a mass incarceration system of chattel enslavement into a mass incarceration system constituted by prisons. In Atlanta, for example, in the late 1890s and early 1900s, over 60,000 arrests were made against Black people (LeFlouria, 2015).

Not only was the penal system a racialized apparatus of social control, but also it was a means of re-ensnaring emancipated Black people in a system of compulsory labor. Because the *13th Amendment* abolished slavery and involuntary servitude *except as a punishment for a crime* (Alexander, 2010), the South's incarcerated Black men, women, and children were forced to labor in the fields and homes of former slave-owning White families, for state governments as well as corporations, and on plantation farms controlled by wealthy White male southerners and northerners (Blackmon, 2008; Curtin, 2000).

It is critical to emphasize that *most* of the South's imprisoned Black people were *wrongly* arrested and convicted. White male legal officials—sheriffs, bailiffs, judges, and more—pocketed the fees and fines by Black folks who could pay. When the state prisons needed workers, many Black people were rounded up and incarcerated without charges or convictions (Blackmon, 2008). In addition to the extraction of unpaid labor, the mass incarceration system was used to strip Black men of key citizenship rights, of which they gained recognition under Reconstruction. Black men with felony convictions were barred from voting (Curtin, 2000; Holloway, 2009).

Since the dissolution of racial segregation laws in the 1960s, in what can be understood as the start of the New Jim Crow era, systemic racism in forensics systems and beyond has created and maintained a mass incarceration crisis in poor African American communities. Scholars and activists call the mass incarceration system the "New Jim Crow" because, as Michelle Alexander writes, just like Jim Crow, it is a racial caste system that uses the law and custom to lock into place an inferior position for stigmatized groups (Alexander, 2010). While Jim Crow laws subjugated Black people en masse, post-1970s New Jim Crow systems used "a web of" ostensibly race-neutral "laws, rules, policies, and customs" to target and control Black people that are branded "criminals" inside and outside of jails and prisons. The impacts of these laws, rules, and policies are profound and far-reaching. Black people convicted of a crime, as well as those who merely come to the attention of law enforcement and are never convicted, are legally denied jobs, professional licenses, housing, the ability to vote, welfare benefits, and education and are excluded from juries, perpetuating the cycle of hardship, poverty, and oppression to which Black Americans are disproportionately subjected. Incarcerated Black men, women, and children labored under brutal and deadly conditions. Black men worked in the waist- or neck-high water in prison mines, became sick or died from poisonous and explosive gasses, and were viscously whipped for failing to meet their quotas (Curtin, 2000). White male guards whipped, raped, and otherwise tortured Black women and girls whether they were laboring on chain gangs or confined in cells (LeFlouria, 2015).

Southern prisons institutionalized the anti-Black violence that structured Black–White relations in the South. In the post–Civil War decades, White violence was ubiquitous and unchecked by a legal system that White men controlled and administered (Litwack, 1999). State officials—police officers, senators, and more—were among the perpetrators of racist mob violence. While most lynching victims were Black men and boys, mobs of White people of all genders, ages, and economic statuses also lynched Black women and girls and entire Black families. They carried out murderous rampages on entire towns of Black people. Lynchings evolved into spectacles of violence where Whites in pairs and groups ranging from five to over 20,000 mutilated, dismembered, and burned their victims while still alive (Litwack, 1999). White men and boys conducted individual and collective spontaneous and organized rape campaigns against Black women and girls (Freedman, 2013; Hunter, 1998; LeFlouria, 2015). Even as Black people defended themselves from, survived, and perished due to savage forms of White state and vigilante violence, they persisted in building schools, churches, and businesses and, during the Reconstruction period (1867 to 1877), ran for political office and voted in the successful elections of White male and Black male Republicans (Curtin, 2000; Freedman, 2013). White violence was frequently a response to Black people's progress. When a minority of Black people achieved middle- and upper-income status, Black-owned businesses and homes were either destroyed or seized by White-owned banks, merchants, and other Whites (Litwack, 1999). Anti-Black violence inside and outside the post–Civil War South's mass incarceration system, perpetuated, justified, or ignored by forensics officials, was crucial to maintaining White supremacy into and throughout the Jim Crow era.

In the late 1960s and early 1970s, just after the Jim Crow period came to a close, the Central Intelligence Agency (CIA) and Federal Bureau of Investigation (FBI) colluded with police departments nationwide to infiltrate and dismantle Black and Brown liberation movements; Nixon positioned himself as a *law and order* president and declared a *war on drugs* backed by relatively few policy changes and resources (Alexander, 2010; Charles, 2016; Haas, 2019). When the Reagan administration picked up the mantle of drug war law and order politics in 1981, there were roughly 300,000 people in state and federal prisons (Bureau of Justice Statistics, 1982). Eight years later, upon Reagan's departure from office, there were over 1 million people in state and federal prisons and local jails. At the end of President Clinton's reign in 2001, that number ballooned to approximately 2 million (Snell & Bureau of Justice Statistics, 1995). As the prison population drastically increased in the 1980s, crime in general and drug crime expressly declined. After a peak in crime rates from the mid-1980s to the early 1990s, the overall crime rate was again on the decline (Alexander, 2010; Gramlich, 2020). Since 1991, the national crime rate has plummeted by approximately 50%, yet the carceral population has soared by 500% (Gramlich, 2020; Sentencing Project, 2021). While it is tempting to assume that harsher sentencing, policing, and the prison boom caused the decrease in crime, exhaustive research studies prove that is not the case, pointing to socioeconomic factors that include lower unemployment rates, income growth, and an aging population as factors precipitating the national decline in crime rates (Roeder, Eisen, Bowling, Stiglitz, & Chettiar, 2015).

Between 1981 and 1987, federal, state, and local taxpayer dollars financing the criminal punishment system jumped from $24.4 billion to $34.2 billion. By 1997, taxpayer funding soared to $63.9 billion (Kahn, 2018). Government and law enforcement officials pointed to violent crime in poor Black urban areas as the motivation for the dramatic funding increases for policing and prisons even as violent crime rates *dropped* and rates of violent victimization were *equivalent* in urban and suburban communities (Wise, 2003). The continued surge in government spending corresponded with deep funding cuts to housing, food, cash aid, and health care programs for impoverished people. These were the same programs to address economic inequities that yielded disproportionate poverty rates among Black, Indigenous, and people of color (BIPOC). These government programs functioned as a concrete alternative to crime in impoverished communities, crimes that are often rooted in economic survival (Sudbury, 2010).

To understand how the earliest mass incarceration systems—that is, slavery, post–Civil War penal systems, and Jim Crow—are alive in today's forensics systems, it is helpful to consider how drug policy and drug policing are linked to the New Jim Crow era explosion in the carceral population. The implementation of draconian mandatory minimum and truth-in-sentencing laws, as well as three-strikes- and one-strike-you're-out public housing policies, intensified the more extreme poverty in which Black people lived (compared to poor Whites; Wise, 2003) and disproportionately and more severely punished the minority of poor Black people who turned to crime, in part, due to the deprivation of structural alternatives such as job training programs, equitably resourced schools, and the living-wage jobs that were a casualty of deindustrialization, globalization, welfare cuts, and government neglect (Sudbury, 2010). In response, political change agents aim for the variety of systemic forces responsible for Black people's high incarceration rate: disproportionate poverty, the lack or absence of living-wage jobs, environmental racism, health care inequity, housing segregation, underresourced schools, discriminatory policing, draconian mandatory minimum sentencing, and overincarceration.

Today's New Jim Crow

In the wake of the video-recorded police murders of Breonna Taylor and George Floyd and the White vigilante murder of Ahmaud Arbery (Baptiste, 2020; Cyrus, 2021), more and more White and non-Black people of color are awakening to the reality that White supremacy is at the heart of the United States' policing and prison systems. Growing numbers of people view policing and prisons as apparatuses of organized state violence against poor Black communities. Before cell phone videos, body camera footage, and social media were commonplace, the absence of explicitly racist rhetoric in law, policy, and the speech of law enforcement officials had marginalized anti-racist critiques of the carceral system, erecting roadblocks to activist groups and people working inside systems of power to create change. These critiques can no longer be ignored and are supported by the data.

For example, White people commit *most* nonviolent and violent crimes, including drug-related offenses. Yet, the incarcerated population is majority BIPOC, with Black people constituting the largest imprisoned racial group at roughly 40% of the United States' incarcerated population (Sawyer & Wagner, 2020). Most arrests of Black people have been for drug-related offenses (Howell, Skoczylas, & DeVaughn, 2019). Black people are arrested and incarcerated at grossly disproportionate rates for drug crimes than White people who actually commit the majority of drug offenses. Most drug users and dealers are White, and White people are more likely to possess drugs than Black people. In addition to dealing drugs at higher rates, White youth use heroin, cocaine, and crack at seven to eight times the rate of Black youth. In light of these facts, the overpolicing of poor Black communities for drug crimes makes little sense and exposes the persisting White supremacist ideologies and structural practices that cast Black communities as havens of crime (Alexander, 2010).

Black people were regarded as inferior by genetic design, inherently criminal, and therefore eligible for enslavement, a condition defined through the absence of citizenship and the rights locked to that status, including the right to vote, the right to testify against a White person in court and serve on a jury, and the right to an education. In the post-Reconstruction South, and under Jim Crow, African Americans were barred from voting, excluded from juries, denied access to health care and an equitable education, subjected to housing and job discrimination, and stigmatized as inherently criminal. Today, for Black people who are labeled "criminals" with felony convictions and those who are merely arrested though not convicted of a crime, alienation from citizenship rights persists as incarcerated people and returning citizens are legally denied the fundamental human rights that were nonexistent for Black people living under racial segregation.

Wrongful Incarceration

The number of cases involving people of color spending their lives in prison, many of whom are on death row and wrongfully incarcerated, is emblematic of cumulative criminal justice system flaws. In 2021, Yucato Briley was exonerated after years of corresponding with defense lawyers and innocence projects, having been wrongly charged with armed robbery and possession of a gun. The average age of incarceration is 27, and the average age of exoneration is 42 (Vera Institute for Justice, 2021). The example above garnered national attention and illustrated the devastating consequences of racism and human rights violations and the withholding of evidence that could exonerate the wrongfully convicted. In these cases, after conviction, the burden of proof is high to exonerate upon appeal.

Theoretical Frameworks for Understanding Contemporary Disparities in the Forensic System

The National Organization of Forensic Social Workers (NOFSW) has a stated commitment to viewing the client's experiences and the social worker's role within the system through a social justice and human rights lens (NOFSW, 2020). Achieving this goal when working with clients who may identify as racial or ethnic minorities, may be living in

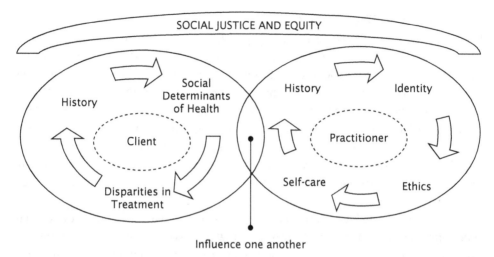

FIGURE 9.1 Conceptualizing Forensic Social Work Practice

poverty, are immigrants or refugees, identify as queer or transgender, or hold any other marginalized identity or combination of marginalized identities requires knowledge of their experiences, historically and in today's environment. Recognizing the complexity of the issues that bring a person into contact with a forensic social worker, a practitioner must move beyond a fundamental person-in-environment analysis of the situation to one that invites greater complexity. This is best accomplished via a multitheoretical approach that allows the practitioner to explore, understand, and then work to mitigate the impacts of inequalities on this client's life and their experiences with the legal, health care, education, and other systems.

Ecological Systems Model

Bronfenbrenner's ecological systems model provides an ideal organizing framework for this task, allowing us to identify theoretical frameworks focused on disparities or inequities at the micro-, meso-, and macrosystem levels (Bronfenbrenner, 1992). Figure 9.1 provides a roadmap to the frameworks we have chosen to highlight for this task. Running alongside these frameworks focused on the client experience, we draw attention to the experience of the social work practitioner, raising vital questions related to ethical practice and self-care. We recognize the social worker as a complex entity that comes to this work not as a blank slate, but as an individual with their historical context, biases, and experiences.

As we work our way through the identified frameworks, we will identify contemporary examples of salient issues that forensic social workers encounter. Recognizing that individuals and their circumstances are infinitely more complex than any description, we are sensitive to the risk of being too reductionistic of an individual or their community. The choice to use a multitheoretical approach for this work is in response to this risk and is designed to build your capacity and confidence to engage with difference. However, that is defined in your practice.

The Social Justice System

Using our discussion of slavery and the legacy of slavery in the United States as a jumping-off point, we start unpacking frameworks at the macrosystems level, starting with history. Understanding the historical journey of the individual or community being served in terms of the experience of the oppressed and that of the oppressor cannot be understated. In addition to an exploration of the African American experience, it is crucial to understand the journey of the many other marginalized groups (e.g., Indigenous peoples, other racial/ethnic minorities, immigrants, refugees, those living with any kind of disability, the mentally ill, etc.), taking into consideration how White supremacist ideals and perceptions of threats, rights, and privileges have caused harm at the individual, community, and societal level.

There is no way to know the history of every population you work with. However, it is your responsibility to learn as much as you can. That process begins by showing genuine curiosity and interest in your client, exercising thoughtful and respectful inquiry, and having the patience to understand that it may take time for the client to trust you enough to share aspects of themselves or their experiences. The social justice system (SJS) approach described by Maschi and Killian (2011) centers on human rights. It is informed by a belief that the same rights, protections, opportunities, obligations, and social benefits are available to all members of a society (Barker, 2003; Maschi & Killian, 2011; Maschi & Leibowitz, 2018). The SJS approach explicitly recognizes the existence of a *justice environment*—exploring its influence on the individual and their community. A forensic social worker's role within the justice environment is to address the individual-level impacts of macro-level laws or policies. This could include legal issues that arise when an interaction with rules or policies restricts or negatively impacts the individual, resulting in contact with the legal system as a resolution is sought out.

One example with profound ramifications is the impact of legislation that excludes some people with criminal records, and sometimes even those with pending charges, from serving on a jury (Jackson-Gleich, 2021). Every state in the nation has some form of jury exclusion based on criminal conviction (Jackson-Gleich, 2021). Given what we know about the disproportionally high incarceration rates for Black and Latinx populations, it is logical to assume that they would be less likely to serve on a jury. A 2017 study estimated that one-third of Black men in the United States had a felony conviction (Shannon et al., 2017). This data was unavailable for Latino men due to inconsistencies in reporting Latino ethnicity. In addition, because the ability to serve on a jury requires the ability to absorb the costs associated with answering a summons to appear for jury duty, those who are poor are also less likely to participate. Therefore, the defense attorney is more likely to face a jury that consists of a majority of White, middle- and upper-class individuals (Joshi & Kline, 2015). This is despite researchers showing that racially mixed juries "raised more case facts, made fewer factual errors, and were more amenable to discussions of race-related issues" (Sommers, 2006, p. 13). Other examples of justice environments include legislation that impacts access to employment or housing for those with a disability or a criminal record, advocating for an incarcerated person with severe mental illness who should be in a treatment facility but is in prison, zoning laws that impact the environment and health of those living in poor neighborhoods, or an immigrant child in a detention center who could be with family members across the country.

The Social Determinants of Health

The social determinants of health (SDOH) is a framework used globally in the health care arena that acknowledges the patterns of inequity in the larger environment, which influences health outcomes (Marmot, 2005). The SDOH takes into consideration the non-medical factors that influence health and well-being by focusing on where people live, work, and age via an inquiry regarding one's neighborhood and built environment (e.g., crime rate, green space, access to public transportation), the economic stability of the community and the individual (e.g., employment opportunities and ability to earn a living wage), the social and community context (e.g., access to social network and community connections), access to education and educational attainment (e.g., quality of K–12 education, access to higher education, and ability to pursue desired educational opportunities), and finally one's overall health and access to health care services (e.g., physical health, access to needed medical care, and feeling able/welcome to seek needed services; Marmot, 2005). The SDOH is shaped by the more significant state and federal policy environment and often reflects the wealth inequalities, income gaps, and other intersecting systems (education, health care, workplace) we observe in the United States today. Even in the same community, the experiences of those who have resources are markedly different from those who do not. To understand the lived experience of their clients, particularly racial/ethnic minority clients, exploring the SDOH can provide significant insights that will inform your practice.

For example, we can apply the SDOH framework to understand better the individual- and community-level impacts of overcriminalization and overreliance on the police. The United States incarcerates or detains more people than any other nation (Sawyer & Wagner, 2020). Data from the Vera Institute show that every 3 seconds, someone in the United States is being arrested (Vera Institute for Justice, 2021). Although prisons are often the focus, the number of admissions in local jails is also significantly higher than other nations (Western et al., 2021). Mass incarceration is a result of *tough on crime* policies that led to the overcriminalization of drug use and other behaviors through overly harsh sentencing guidelines that disproportionately impacted Black and Latinx communities and poor communities (Alexander, 2010; Sawyer & Wagner, 2020; Vera Institute for Justice, 2021). Feeding into this situation but distinct from it is our overreliance on the police as the first response line for all distressing situations. Of the 240 million calls made to 911, only 1% are for serious violent crimes. The overwhelming majority of calls were nonemergency calls related to quality-of-life issues, including homelessness, substance use, and mental health emergencies—situations that do not involve a crime—or nuisance calls (e.g., noise complaints, disturbance of the peace, animal complaints).

This data raises important questions in terms of the appropriate allocation of resources. Police officers are trained to address a wide range of situations. However, deploying them for all situations, particularly when another cadre of workers with training specific to the population or context is available should be reconsidered.

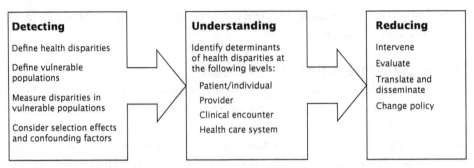

FIGURE 9.2 Kilbourne's Health Disparities Framework

Health Disparities

The health disparities frameworks used by health service researchers help both frame the issues facing practitioners within forensic social work and consider potential responses to disparities within it. The research shows that what individuals experience when interacting with the health and behavioral health care system is largely influenced by their identity. For example, suppose you are a person of color, LGBTQ, poor, or a member of other marginalized groups. It is more likely that you have limited access to care and that your treatment would be significantly worse than it would be for your White-identified, heterosexual, cisgender colleagues (Braveman et al., 2011; Chang, 2019; Ren et al., 1999). Researchers demonstrate that these same disparities exist within the juvenile justice (Robles-Ramamurthy & Watson, 2019), jail and prison (Freiburger & Sheeran, 2020), probation and parole (Jannetta et al., 2014; Phelps, 2019), and child welfare systems (Huggins-Hoyt et al., 2019).

The Kilbourne framework is one of the most popular for examining disparities in the health system (Kilbourne, Switzer, Hyman, Crowley-Matoka, & Fine, 2006). It asserts that research on systemic health disparities should occur in three phases, as detailed in Figure 9.2. The first phase helps identify and document the disparity, the second phase seeks to understand the disparity and the mechanisms by which it occurs, and the third phase aims to alleviate the disparity. This way of approaching racial and ethnic disparities in health care is easily translatable to the field of forensics. Research on disparities in the forensic system can borrow this trajectory to move from identifying racial and ethnic disparities to work that eliminates them.

A Focus on the Clinical Interaction

Kilbourne's team (2006) recognizes the institution's role and the impact of interactions within the clinical relationship on exacerbating or mitigating disparities. This framework is beneficial for thinking about the clinical interaction between a social worker and a client within the forensic system. Kilbourne argues that both the clinician and the client bring a set of cultural assumptions and experiences to the interaction, shaping its outcome. The environment within which this interaction occurs cannot be ignored. This framework offers an ecological perspective on disparities and their relationship to clinical interaction, as detailed in Figure 9.3.

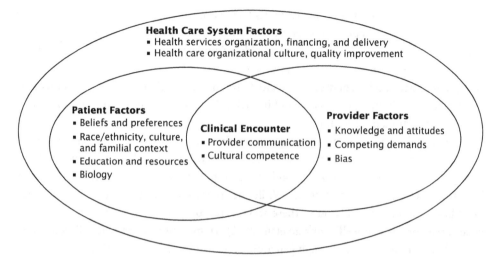

FIGURE 9.3 Kilbourne's Ecological Perspective on Health Disparities

Ameliorating Disparities

Regardless of whether a social worker decides to work in forensics, our profession and its professional mandates require engaging in efforts to reimagine the field of forensics. Some have also argued that the goal of forensics itself, to define right and wrong, is in itself against the principles of a profession focused on bringing people together (Young, 2015). Many organizations are working on issues related to race and racism and the role of forensic settings and can provide specific guidance or opportunities to get involved in change efforts. As a professional social worker, it will be up to you to decide whether you want to work within this system. The practice section below is designed to help inform both your decision and your practice should you choose to do so.

Forensic Social Work: Practice Considerations

The goal for this chapter is to provide the historical context for the present-day forensic system and frameworks to understand the system in its current state to inform social work practice. Practitioners must engage in forensic work with a keen understanding of the history of chattel slavery in the United States and its connections to the present-day forensic system. This understanding presents an ethical dilemma for those who consider forensic work. For those who decide to engage in forensic work, using the frameworks discussed above can help guide how we choose to engage and inform constant reflection about our choices and their impacts.

Frameworks to Guide Practice

Historical Lenses

We are just learning about the profound and long-lasting impact of community-level trauma on the individuals who directly experience that trauma and their offspring. The experience of trauma—for instance, the pervasive, violent, violating, multiple and intersecting traumas of slavery—alters the developing brain and the neurobiological responses of an individual. These altered responses impact individuals' understanding of themselves and their world and have lifelong effects. The adverse childhood experiences study (Hughes et al., 2017) demonstrates a link between exposure to trauma in childhood and adverse outcomes in adulthood, including poor health and behavioral health outcomes. Exposure to trauma is a social determinant of health.

Trauma does not just impact a single generation but is transmitted intergenerationally. For example, researchers suggest that exposure to adverse childhood events significantly affects parenting, increasing the likelihood of exposure to trauma for children of those who have themselves experienced trauma. While the transmission of trauma through generations has been long understood in these ways, it has only recently been understood as a genetic phenomenon as well (Narayan et al., 2021). Trauma alters an individual's genes, and those alterations are passed through generations (Conching & Thayer, 2019).

It is essential to understand trauma and the history of slavery and the carceral system. The problem is not located within the individual but is best understood as a problem created and maintained by systemic structures. This requires understanding the role of a clinician in addressing structural elements of an individual's life and orienting them to the impact of those structures rather than blaming the individual.

Racialized trauma is not just a historical phenomenon. Being a person of color in the United States means constant exposure to structural racism and its impacts. Therefore, clinicians must learn to name the realities of structural racism, illuminate them to clients, and actively engage in understanding how individual clients in their clinical interactions experience these structures.

Social Determinants of Health

The SDOH framework encourages a focus on the structural elements of society that contribute to a particular outcome for an individual. Therefore, when working with individuals within the forensic system, we must attend to the structures within which they live that have impacted their current situation. This kind of focus demands that we center the outcomes for individuals not on their choices or behaviors but on the contexts in which they must survive. When working with clients, this means getting a complete history of their experience with attention to how systems of oppression have impacted and continue to impact their lives and opportunities.

The liberation health framework (Martinez & Fleck Henderson, 2014) is both a theory and a practice model that attends to the SDOH. The practice theory argues that human difficulties cannot be understood in isolation from the conditions in which they live, including economic, political, historical, social, and cultural factors. This theory is highly consistent with the SDOH framework and a helpful translation of this framework into social work practice. The liberation health practice model argues that the social worker's role is to help individuals and families understand how these oppressive systems contribute to the conditions of their lives and support them in finding their liberation from both internal and external oppression (Martinez & Fleck Henderson, 2014).

Kilbourne's Health Disparity Model

Kilbourne's models highlight the need to examine the systems in which we work, how our clients receive services, and the dynamics of structural forces on clinical interaction. This requires that a clinician focus dually on the context in which they work and the factors that influence their client and themselves. In a classic or traditional sense, this may be framed as attention to transference or countertransference, that is, how a client responds to us and how we, in turn, respond to a client (Parth, Datz, Seidman, & Löffler-Stastka, 2017). However, contemporary scholars have attended to the context of a racialized society within the dynamics of the therapeutic dyad, raising how deeply internalized ideas about race and both perceived and understood identities may impact this interaction (Stoute, 2020). Reading this literature and using it to interrogate how our practice is influenced by racism and identity is critical to working within the forensic system.

Williams et al. (2019) offer a framework for understanding racism in the health and mental health systems. This framework helps both articulate the practice issues for social workers within forensics and consider potential responses. Williams et al. assert that social workers must examine three types of racism: (a) structural or institutional racism, (b) cultural racism, and (c) discrimination. Structural/institutional racism reflects the laws, policies, and practices of a society that enforce the privileging of one group of individuals over another. Cultural racism refers to the creation and enforcement of superiority/inferiority in a larger society's values, language, imagery, symbols, and unstated assumptions. Cultural racism manifests itself in media, stereotyping, and norms within society and institutions. Discrimination from an organizational lens includes the inclusive world of acts of an individual or institution, whether with or without intent, that result in inequitable treatment of two racial groups. A subset of those acts is articulated or reported by the individuals they target and constitute discrimination. This framework helps a social worker in the forensic field consider the needed knowledge and skills they require to understand and ideally mitigate the impact of their interactions on racial disparities.

Ethical Considerations for Working Within an Unjust System

So far, this chapter has discussed how carceral and policing systems are actors in systemic racism. We close the chapter by highlighting ethical dilemmas posed by working within these systems. Social workers often find themselves in settings whose mission is not social work driven. Examples of host settings like this include hospitals, schools, courts, and many institutions within the forensic system. In some cases, the mission of these host settings is in direct conflict with how we understand the profession of social work. Some forensic settings fall in this category.

The National Association of Social Workers (NASW) Code of Ethics is unambiguous concerning the expectation of social workers when it comes to discrimination:

> Social workers should not practice, condone, facilitate, or collaborate with any form of discrimination based on race, ethnicity, national origin, color, sex, sexual orientation, gender identity or expression, age, marital status, political belief,

religion, immigration status, or mental or physical ability. (NASW, 2021, Social Workers' Ethical Responsibilities as Professionals section, para. 4)

This statement, taken from the Code of Ethics, outlines the responsibility of social workers to refuse to engage in acts of discrimination. However, given that discrimination is rampant, systemic, and in many cases unconscious, how to interpret this statement is complicated. Many of the systems we work in are discriminatory. For instance, data on the child welfare system regularly indicates the impact of discrimination at every system level. This results in children of color being referred to child welfare services, placed outside of their homes, and lingering in placement instability much longer than their White peers (Becker et al., 2007; Cheng & Li, 2012; LaBrenz et al., 2021; Leathers, Falconnier, & Spielfogel, 2010; Maguire-Jack et al., 2020). One could argue that any social worker engaged in child welfare violates the NASW Code of Ethics (Dettlaff et al., 2020).

The same is true for forensic systems. We know that forensic systems not only discriminate but also actively enforce systemic racism. The Code of Ethics, if taken literally, might suggest that social workers refuse to work within these systems. Yet, if we refuse to work in such systems, those currently caught in these systems may lose access to our advocacy and support. Others believe that the best way to change and influence a system is from within and choose to work in forensics so that they can be active participants in transformation.

For those who choose to work in forensics, the NOFSW is one organization that seeks to provide support and guidance in ethics (NOFSW, 2020). In 2020, the organization updated its code of ethics to specifically include directives for conducting anti-racist work, encouraging social workers to educate and confront injustices:

2.01 Equity, Justice, and Anti-Racism.
Forensic social work professionals know that their acts of commission or omission have implications for equity and justice across legal and human service systems. Forensic social work practitioners elevate issues that promote clients' equal access to navigate systems. Forensic social work professionals recognize that silence is complicit action and raise awareness and challenge injustice in a productive, pragmatic, and problem-solving manner. Forensic social work practitioners attest to the discrimination and oppression that occurs but is not limited to race, ethnicity, national origin, color, class, sex, sexual orientation, gender identity or expression, age, marital status, political belief, religion, immigration status, and mental or physical ability. Forensic social work professionals acknowledge both historical and modern-day oppression and injustices within legal and human service systems, work to dismantle these policies and practices and demonstrate an active and constant commitment to anti-racism and anti-oppressive professional practice. (NOFSW, 2020, pp. 7–8)

The codes of our profession offer an impossible mandate, with little guidance about how it could be achieved. Social workers are left to their own devices to determine whether they believe it is ethical to work within the forensic system and, if so, whether parts of forensics may be ethical. Vital in this consideration is a recognition that whether intentional or not, individuals will be complicit in the work of the organization in which they work, and those with privilege will engage in implicit bias regardless of intent or desire. Social workers must make individual decisions based on their understanding of the code of ethics, their commitments, and the roles and institutions in which they may be working. Creating a set of ethical guidelines for oneself when considering such positions is likely a helpful process. Forensic social workers can use these principles to guide decisions about where to situate themselves within or outside the system and when making in-the-moment decisions about the ethical implications of specific requests often driven by social work staff.

References

Alcindor, D. J. (2020, July 30). Racial disparities-associated Covid-19 mortality among minority populations in the U.S. *Journal of Clinical Medicine, 9*(8), 2442. https://doi.org/10.3390/jcm9082442 https://www.mdpi.com/2077-0383/9/8/2442

Alexander, M. (2010). *The new Jim Crow: Mass incarceration in the age of colorblindness.* New Press.

Baptiste, N. (2020). *There are no Black victims in Donald Trump's America.* Mother Jones. https://www.motherjones.com/anti-racism-police-protest/2020/09/there-are-no-black-victims-in-donald-trumps-america/

Barker, R. L. (2003). *The social work dictionary.* NASW Press.

Becker, M. A., Jordan, N., & Larsen, R. (2007). Predictors of successful permanency planning and length of stay in foster care: The role of race, diagnosis, and place of residence. *Children & Youth Services Review, 29*(8), 1102–1113. https://doi.org/10.1016/j.childyouth.2007.04.009

Bureau of Justice Statistics (1982). *State and Federal Prisoners, 1925–1985.* Retrieved from https://bjs.ojp.gov/content/pub/pdf/sfp2585.pdf

Blackmon, D. A. (2008). *Slavery by another name: The re-enslavement of black Americans from the Civil War to World War II.* Doubleday.

Braveman, P. A., Kumanyika, S., Fielding, J., Laveist, T., Borrell, L. N., Manderscheid, R., & Troutman, A. (2011, December). Health disparities and health equity: The issue is justice. *American Journal of Public Health, 101*(Suppl 1), S149–S155. https://doi.org/10.2105/ajph.2010.300062

Bronfenbrenner, U. (1992). Ecological systems theory. In R. Vasta (Ed.), *Six theories of child development: Revised formations and current issues* (pp. 187–249). Kingsley.

Chang, C. D. (2019, January). Social determinants of health and health disparities among immigrants and their children. *Current Problems in Pediatric and Adolescent Health Care, 49*(1), 23–30. https://doi.org/10.1016/j.cppeds.2018.11.009

Charles, D. M. (2016). Frank J. Rafalko, MH/CHAOS: The CIA's campaign against the radical new left and the Black Panthers Book review]. *Intelligence & National Security, 31*(3), 455–456. https://doi.org/10.1080/02684527.2015.1013730

Cheng, T. C., & Li, A. X. (2012). Maltreatment and families' receipt of services: Associations with reunification, kinship care, and adoption. *Families in Society: Journal of Contemporary Social Services, 93*(3), 189–195. https://doi.org/10.1606/1044-3894.4215

Conching, A. K. S., & Thayer, Z. (2019). Biological pathways for historical trauma to affect health: A conceptual model focusing on epigenetic modifications. *Social Science & Medicine, 230,* 74–82. https://doi.org/10.1016/j.socscimed.2019.04.001

Curtin, M. E. (2000). *Black prisoners and their world, Alabama, 1865–1900.* University Press of Virginia.

Cyrus, R. (2021). *How the George Floyd uprising was framed for white eyes.* Mother Jones. https://www.motherjones.com/politics/2021/06/george-floyd-protest-photography-white-liberals/

Davis, L. E. (2016). *Why are they angry with us? Essays on race.* Lyceum Books.

De Matas, J. (2017). Making the nation great again: Trumpism, Euro-scepticism and the surge of populist nationalism. *Journal of Comparative Politics, 10*(2), 19–36. http://www.jofcp.org/assets/jcp/JCP-July-2017.pdf#page=19

Dettlaff, A. J., Weber, K., Pendleton, M., Boyd, R., Bettencourt, B., & Burton, L. (2020). It is not a broken system, it is a system that needs to be broken: The upEND movement to abolish the child welfare system. *Journal of Public Child Welfare, 14*(5), 500–517.

Digital History. (2021). *The middle passage.* DH ID 3034. https://www.digitalhistory.uh.edu/disp_textbook.cfm?smtid=2&psid=3034

Du Bois, W. E. B. (2014). *Black reconstruction in America (the Oxford WEB Du Bois): An essay toward a history of the part which Black folk played in the attempt to reconstruct democracy in America, 1860–1880.* Oxford University Press.

Foster, T. (2011). The sexual abuse of Black men under American slavery. *Journal of the History of Sexuality, 20*(3), 445–464. https://muse.jhu.edu/article/448992/summary

Freedman, E. B. (2013). *Redefining rape.* Harvard University Press. https://books.google.com/books?hl=en&lr=&id=oQjeAAAAQBAJ&oi=fnd&pg=PP8&dq=Freedman,+E.+B.+(2013).+Redefining+rape.+Harvard+University+Press

Freiburger, T. L., & Sheeran, A. M. (2020). The joint effects of race, ethnicity, gender, and age on the incarceration and sentence length decisions. *Race and Justice, 10*(2), 203–222. https://doi.org/10.1177%2F2153368717739676

Gramlich, J. (2020, November). *What the data says (and doesn't say) about crime in the United States.* Pew Research Center. https://sentencing.typepad.com/sentencing_law_and_policy/2020/11/what-the-data-says-and-doesnt-say-about-crime-in-the-united-states.html

Haas, M. (2019). Gridlock in Washington. *Why democracies flounder and fail* (pp. 139–227). Palgrave. http+://doi.org.10.1007/978-3-319-74070-6

Howell, J., Skoczylas, M., & DeVaughn, S. (2019). living while black. *Contexts, 18*(2), 68–69.

Holloway, P. (2009). "A chicken-stealer shall lose his vote": Disfranchisement for larceny in the south, 1874–1890. *Journal of Southern History, 75*(4), 931–962. http://www.jstor.org/stable/27779119

Huggins-Hoyt, K. Y., Briggs, H. E., Mowbray, O., & Allen, J. L. (2019). Privatization, racial disproportionality and disparity in child welfare: Outcomes for foster children of color. *Children and Youth Services Review, 99*, 125–131. https://doi.org/10.1016/j.childyouth.2019.01.041

Hughes, K., Bellis, M. A., Hardcastle, K. A., Sethi, D., Butchart, A., Mikton, C., Jones, L.,& Dunne, M. P. (2017). The effect of multiple adverse childhood experiences on health: a systematic review and meta-analysis. *The Lancet Public Health, 2*(8), e356–e366. https://www.thelancet.com/pdfs/journals/lanpub/PIIS2468-2667(17)30118-4.pdf

Hunter, T. W. (1998, December). To 'joy my freedom: Southern black women's lives and labors after the Civil War. *American Historical Review, 103*(5), 1702. https://doi.org/10.1086/ahr/103.5.1702

Jackson-Gleich, G. (2021). *Rigging the jury: How each state reduces jury diversity by excluding people with criminal records.* https://www.prisonpolicy.org/reports/juryexclusion.html

Jannetta, J., Breaux, J., Ho, H., & Porter, J. (2016). Examining racial and ethnic disparities in probation revocation: Summary findings and implications from a multisite study. https://nicic.gov/examining-racial-and-ethnic-disparities-probation-revocation-summary-findings-and-implications

Joshi, A. S., & Kline, C. T. (2015). *Lack of jury diversity: A national problem with individual consequences.* American Bar Association (ABA). https://www.americanbar.org/groups/litigation/committees/diversity-inclusion/articles/2015/lack-of-jury-diversity-national-problem-individual-consequences/

Kahn, R. S. (2018). *Other people's blood: US immigration prisons in the Reagan decade.* Routledge.

Kilbourne, A. M., Switzer, G., Hyman, K., Crowley-Matoka, M., & Fine, M. J. (2006). Advancing health disparities research within the health care system: A conceptual framework. *American Journal of Public Health, 96*(12), 2113–2121. https://ajph.aphapublications.org/doi/abs/10.2105/AJPH.2005.077628

LaBrenz, C. A., Findley, E., Graaf, G., Baiden, P., Kim, J., Choi, M. J., & Chakravarty, S. (2021). Racial/ethnic disproportionality in reunification across U.S. child welfare systems. *Child Abuse & Neglect, 114*, 104894. https://doi.org/10.1016/j.chiabu.2020.104894 https://www.sciencedirect.com/science/article/abs/pii/S0145213420305494?via%3Dihub

Leathers, S. J., Falconnier, L., & Spielfogel, J. E. (2010). Predicting family reunification, adoption, and subsidized guardianship among adolescents in foster care. *American Journal of Orthopsychiatry, 80*(3), 422–431. https://doi.org/10.1111/j.1939-

LeFlouria, T. L. (2015). *Chained in silence: Black women and convict labor in the new South*. UNC Press Books. https://uncpress.org/book/9781469630007/chained-in-silence/

Litwack, O. F. (1999). *Trouble in mind: Black southerners in the age of Jim Crow*. Vintage. https://books.goo gle.com/books/about/Trouble_in_Mind.html?id=wmE9DwAAQBAJ

Maguire-Jack, K., Font, S. A., & Dillard, R. (2020). Child protective services decision-making: The role of children's race and county factors. *American Journal of Orthopsychiatry*, *90*(1), 48–62. https://doi.apa. org/record/2019-26291-001

Marmot, M. (2005, March). Social determinants of health inequalities. *Lancet*, *365*(9464), 1099–1104. https://doi.org/10.1016/s0140-6736(05)71146-6

Martinez, D. B., & Fleck-Henderson, A. (2014). Introduction: Why liberation health social work? In A. Fleck-Henderson, & D. B. Martinez (Eds.), *Social justice in clinical practice* (pp. 11–15). Routledge. https://www.book2look.com/embed/9781317800453

Maschi, T., & Killian, M. L. (2011). The evolution of forensic social work in the United States: Implications for 21st century practice. *Journal of Forensic Social Work*, *1*(1), 8–36. https://doi.org/10.1080/19369 28X.2011.541198

Maschi, T., & Leibowitz, G. S. (Eds.). (2018). *Forensic social work: Psychosocial and legal issues across diverse populations and settings* (2nd ed.). Springer. https://books.google.com/books?hl=en&lr=&id=iMypD gAAQBAJ&oi=fnd&pg=PP1&dq=Forensic+social++work:+Psychosocial+and+legal+issues+across+ diverse+populations+and+settings+(2nd+Ed.)

Mauer, M. (2010). *Justice for all? Challenging racial disparities in the criminal justice system*. https://www. prisonpolicy.org/scans/sp/Justice-for-All-Challenging-Racial-Disparities-in-the-Criminal-Justice-System.pdf

Miller, R. J., Kern, L. J., & Williams, A. (2018). The front end of the carceral state: Police stops, court fines, and the racialization of due process. *Social Service Review*, *92*(2), 290–303. https://doi.org/10.1086/697905

Mundt, M., Ross, K., & Burnett, C. M. (2018). Scaling social movements through social media: The case of Black Lives Matter. *Social Media+ Society*, *4*(4), 2056305118807911. https://doi.org/10.1177%2F20563 05118807911

Narayan, A. J., Lieberman, A. F., & Masten, A. S. (2021). Intergenerational transmission and prevention of adverse childhood experiences (ACEs). *Clinical Psychology Review*, *85*, 101997. https://doi.org/10.1016/ j.cpr.2021.101997

Nardini, G., Rank-Christman, T., Bublitz, M. G., Cross, S. N., & Peracchio, L. A. (2021). Together we rise: How social movements succeed. *Journal of Consumer Psychology*, *31*(1), 112–145. https://doi.org/ 10.1002/jcpy.1201

National Association of Social Workers (NASW). (2021). *Code of ethics of the National Association of Social Workers*. https://www.socialworkers.org/About/Ethics/Code-of-Ethics/Code-of-Ethics-English

National Organization of Forensic Social Work (NOFSW). (2020, August). *Specialty guidelines for values and ethics*. https://4251f553-c8e8-439c-83bb-61068f7fb2c6.filesusr.com/ugd/f468b9_20e60b0830ed4 a51808154902b7e9f20.pdf

Parth, K., Datz, F., Seidman, C., & Löffler-Stastka, H. (2017). Transference and countertransference: A review. *Bulletin of the Menninger Clinic*, *81*(2), 167–211. https://doi.org/10.1521/bumc.2017.81.2.167

Phelps, M. S. (2019). Mass probation and inequality: Race, class, and gender disparities in supervision and revocation. In J. T. Ulmer, & M. S. Bradly (Eds.), *Handbook on punishment decisions* (p. 43). Routledge. https://www.routledge.com/Handbook-on-Punishment-Decisions-Locations-of-Disparity/Ulmer-Brad ley/p/book/9780367405168

Razai, M. S., Kankam, H. K., Majeed, A., Esmail, A., & Williams, D. R. (2021). Mitigating ethnic disparities in Covid-19 and beyond. *BMJ*, *372*, m4921. https://doi.org/10.1136/bmj.m4921

Ren, X. S., Amick, B. C., & Williams, D. R. (1999, Spring–Summer). Racial/ethnic disparities in health: The interplay between discrimination and socioeconomic status. *Ethnicity and Disease*, *9*(2), 151–165. https://europepmc.org/article/med/10421078

Robles-Ramamurthy, B., & Watson, C. (2019). Examining racial disparities in juvenile justice. *Journal of the American Academy of Psychiatry and the Law*, *47*(1), 48–52. https://doi.org/10.29158/JAAPL.003 828-19

Roeder, O. K., Eisen, L. B., Bowling, J., Stiglitz, J. E., & Chettiar, I. M. (2015). *What caused the crime decline?* Columbia Business School Research Paper (pp. 15–28). Brennan Center of Justice. https://nicic. gov/what-caused-crime-decline

Roosevelt, E. (1958, March 27). *Remarks to the United Nations.* https://erpapers.columbian.gwu.edu/quo tations

Sawyer, W., & Wagner, P. (2020, March). *Mass incarceration: The whole pie 2020* [Press release]. https://www. prisonpolicy.org/reports/pie2020.html

Schrantz, D., & McElroy, J. (2000). *Reducing racial disparity in the criminal justice system: A manual for practitioners and policymakers.* https://web.archive.org/web/20060601225204/http://www.sentencingproject. org/pdfs/5079.pdf

Schwalm, L. A. (1997). *A hard fight for we: Women's transition from slavery to freedom in South Carolina* (Vol. 145). University of Illinois Press.

Sentencing Project. (2021). *Fact sheet: Trends in U.S. corrections* https://www.sentencingproject.org/publi cations/trends-in-u-s-corrections/

Serwer, A. (2018). *Trumpism, realized.* https://www.theatlantic.com/ideas/archive/2018/06/child-separat ion/563252/

Shannon, S. K., Uggen, C., Schnittker, J., Thompson, M., Wakefield, S., & Massoglia, M. (2017). The growth, scope, and spatial distribution of people with felony records in the United States, 1948–2010. *Demography, 54*(5), 1795–1818. https://doi.org/10.1007/s13524-017-0611-1

Smith, B. V. (2017). Sexual abuse of women in United States prisons: A modern corollary of slavery 1. In P. L. Ellman (Ed.), *The courage to fight violence against women: psychoanalytic and multidisciplinary perspectives* (pp. 107–128). https://www.taylorfrancis.com/chapters/edit/10.4324/9780429481390-13/sex ual-abuse-women-united-states-prisons-modern-corollary-slavery-1-brenda-smith?

Snell, T. L., & Bureau of Justice Statistics (BJS). (1995). *Correctional populations in the United States, 1993* (NCJ-156675). DOJ Statistics. https://bjs.ojp.gov/content/pub/pdf/cpus93ex.pdf

Sommers, S. R. (2006). On racial diversity and group decision making: Identifying multiple effects of racial composition on jury deliberations. *Journal of Personality & Social Psychology, 90*(4), 597–612. https://doi. org/10.1037/0022-3514.90.4.597

Stoute, B. J. (2020) Racism: A challenge for the therapeutic dyad. *American Journal of Psychotherapy, 73*(3), 69–71. https://europepmc.org/article/med/32927960

Sudbury, J. (2010). Unpacking the crisis: Women of color, globalization and the prison-industrial complex. In *Interrupted life: Experiences of incarcerated women in the United States* (pp. 11–25). University of California Press.

Vera Institute for Justice. (2021). *Annual report 2020: Reckoning with justice.* https://www.vera.org/annual-report-2020-reckoning-with-justice

Warren-Gordon, K., & Rhineberger, G. (2021). The "Trump effect" on hate crime reporting: Media coverage before and after the 2016 presidential election. *Journal of Ethnicity in Criminal Justice, 19*(1), 25–45. https://doi.org/10.1080/15377938.2021.1895944

Western, B., Davis, J., Ganter, F., & Smith, N. (2021). The cumulative risk of jail incarceration. *Proceedings of the National Academy of Sciences, 118*(16), e2023429118. https://doi.org/10.1073/pnas.2023429118

White, D. G. (1999). *Aren't I a woman? Female slaves in the plantation South* (rev. ed.). Norton & Company.

Williams, D. R., Lawrence, J. A., & Davis, B. A. (2019, April). Racism and health: Evidence and needed research. *Annual Review of Public Health, 40*, 105–125. https://doi.org/10.1146/annurev-publhealth-040 218-043750

Wise, T. (2003). *Coloring crime: Race, violence and media manipulation.* http://www.timwise.org/2003/06/ coloring-crime-race-violence-and-media-manipulation/

Young, D. S. (2015). Lived challenges to ethical social work practice in criminal justice settings. *Journal of Forensic Social Work, 5*(1–3), 98–115.

10

Mental Health in Forensic Settings

Jason Matejkowski and Kelechi Wright

Definitions of forensic social work have broadened over time from specific social work roles with offenders and victims of crime to work "with diverse populations impacted by legal issues both civil and/or criminal" (Maschi & Killian, 2011, p. 12). As such, forensic mental health services can involve those related to involuntary civil commitment, hospitalization or outpatient treatment, child welfare and family services, and coordinated systems of care across the interface of criminal justice and mental health services (Kennedy et al., 2019; National Association of State Mental Health Program Directors, 2014). Civil commitment, a process where a person with mental illness is assessed for involuntary treatment, receives its own treatment in Chapter 20 of this *Handbook*. Given space limitations, the focus here is more narrowly on the services and supports for people with mental health problems who contact criminal law enforcement.

Adults who have a mental illness interface with the American criminal justice system at higher rates than adults who do not have mental health challenges. This observation is sustained through multiple studies despite differing methods for measuring prevalence in particular forensic settings. For example, compared to 5% in the general population, 26% of adults incarcerated in jail and 14% in prison have serious mental illness symptoms. Nine percent of persons released from jail and 7% released from prison on postrelease supervision have been diagnosed with a serious mental illness (Bronson & Berzofsky, 2017). There is a need for social work to address these disparities through both clinical and policy practice.

Social work in forensic settings should be guided by theory that postulates the reasons behind the high rates of adults with mental illness in the criminal justice system. Evidence from testing these theories can identify promising clinical and policy approaches aimed at alleviating this problem. Three prominent and rigorously tested

Jason Matejkowski and Kelechi Wright, *Mental Health in Forensic Settings* In: *Handbook of Forensic Social Work*. Edited by: David Axlyn McLeod, Anthony P. Natale, and Kristin W. Mapson, Oxford University Press. © Oxford University Press 2024. DOI: 10.1093/oso/9780197694732.003.0010 theories explaining the high rates of justice system contact among this population are briefly discussed in this chapter: the criminalization hypothesis, general personality and cognitive social learning theory (i.e., the risk-need-responsivity model), and focal concerns theory addressing stigma and discrimination. Through the lens of these theories, the chapter identifies the needs (and contributors to the needs) of adults with mental illness along with the settings in which social workers are called upon to address these needs, either through direct clinical intervention or through the enactment of agency- and system-level policy reform.

Forensic Mental Health Settings and Theories for Practice With Adults Who Have Criminal Justice System Contact

The sequential intercept model (Munetz & Griffin, 2006) provides a framework to study how people with mental illnesses interface with the criminal justice system. The model identifies a series of points within criminal justice system processing at which an intervention can be employed to divert individuals from penetrating further into this system. These intercepts constitute the settings for mental health forensic social work covered in this chapter. In addition to community-based preventative behavioral health supports and activities (termed "Intercept 0"), the sequential intercept model identifies Intercept 1 as Law Enforcement and Emergency Services; Intercept 2 as Initial Hearings and Initial Detention; Intercept 3 as Jails and Courts; Intercept 4 as Reentry from Jails, Prisons, and Hospitals; and Intercept 5 as Community Corrections and Community Support Services (Figure 10.1).

Criminalization Hypothesis

The criminal justice system involvement of persons with mental health problems has been explained as the result of law enforcement authorities displacing treatment providers in the role of responding to disruptive and potentially dangerous behaviors of persons with mental illness, thereby criminalizing mental illness (Lamb & Weinberger, 1998). At the root of the criminalization hypothesis are the tremendous changes that occurred to the public mental health system in the United States during the latter part of the 20th century and continue to be borne out today. These include the unavailability of long-term hospital beds for persons with chronic and severe mental illness, the lack of adequate community mental health supports, and difficulties accessing these supports. As a result, the criminal justice system began filling these voids. Criminalization theory has been influential in shaping policy and services for people with mental illness who are criminally involved (Skeem et al., 2011). Indeed, an array of programs for this population, such as mental health courts (see Matejkowski, 2019) and specialty probation (e.g., Skeem et al., 2017), focus on using criminal justice involvement to leverage mental health treatment, based on the notion that treating a person's mental illness will result in reduced criminal behaviors and reduced justice system contact.

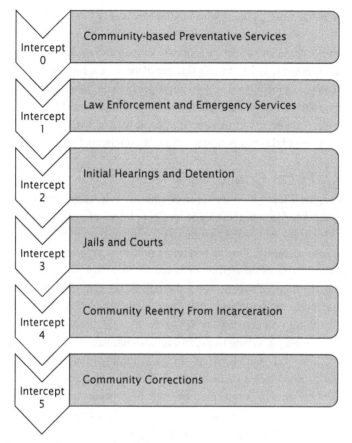

FIGURE 10.1 Depiction of Munetz and Griffin's (2006) Sequential Intercept Model

Risk-Needs-Responsivity Model

The general personality and cognitive social learning model draws upon social learning principles to explain criminal behavior (Bonta & Andrews, 2016). Couched within this broader theory is a major approach to offender rehabilitation today, the risk-needs-responsivity (RNR) model. This model is based on the following three principles: (a) a person's level of risk for criminal involvement is measurable, and treatment services should be proportional to this risk level; (b) this treatment is targeted to alleviate criminal risk factors (termed "criminogenic needs"); and (c) this treatment is delivered in an evidence-based way (termed "general responsivity") as well as responsive to an individual's learning abilities and preferences (termed "specific responsivity").

While the criminalization hypothesis suggests that mental health treatment should be primary when attempting to reduce criminal involvement of people with mental illness, the RNR model has identified a set of "central eight" risk factors that predict criminal involvement reliably. These central risk factors should be the target of treatment (for a review, see Bonta & Andrews, 2016). Indeed, research has shown that these criminogenic needs are strongly predictive of criminal behavior among adults regardless of the presence of a mental health problem (Bonta et al., 2014), and a growing body of research suggests that higher levels of criminogenic needs among people with mental illness may be contributing to their over-representation in the criminal justice system (Matejkowski & Ostermann, 2015; Wilson et al., 2020). Importantly, stigma and social exclusion accompanying mental illness may contribute to heightened criminogenic needs among this population. Few supportive familial relationships and low levels of school, work, and prosocial leisure and recreational involvement—all members of the group of central eight risk factors and all influenced by discriminatory attitudes and behaviors—are more common among people with mental illness than those without and are likely the result of discrimination toward this population (Matejkowski, 2010).

Stigma and Focal Concerns Theory

Rüsch and colleagues (2005) identify three components of stigma to include stereotypes (i.e., commonly accepted [not necessarily accurate] opinions about a group of people), prejudice (i.e., negative attitudes toward a group of people based upon belief in relevant stereotypes), and discrimination (i.e., hostile behaviors reflecting prejudice). They further define public stigma as consisting of these three elements within a system of power differences that leads to negative treatment of the stigmatized group by the general public. As an extension of public stigma, focal concerns theory has been posited to explain racial and gender disparities in justice system outcomes (Ray & Dollar, 2013; Steffensmeier & Demuth, 2006). However, this theory may also help to explain the mechanisms behind the overrepresentation of people with mental health problems in the criminal justice system.

Specifically, focal concerns theory states that criminal justice authorities' imposition of sanctions and punishment is informed by their perceptions of the blameworthiness of people suspected or convicted of a crime, their beliefs about how best to protect the community, and their understanding of the availability of resources and agency constraints in responding to given situations (Steffensmeier et al., 1998). Focal concerns theory can be considered to incorporate elements of the criminalization hypothesis in that both theories posit that the interactions of criminal justice authorities with people who have mental health needs are influenced by the availability of mental health services. However, in addition to resource scarcity, focal concerns theory also suggests that authorities often rely on stereotypes to determine the culpability of the person being scrutinized, given their limited knowledge of the individual's characteristics and circumstances. These stereotypes often reflect the beliefs that people with mental illness are more dangerous than people without mental health problems (Batastini et al., 2018; Pescosolido et al., 2019). Focal concerns theory suggests that as a result of this prejudice, criminal justice system actors can discriminate against people with mental health problems whom they come into contact with so as to more frequently and more severely impose sanctions and reduce the liberties of persons with mental illness compared to those without a mental health problem.

Social Work Strategies for Addressing Forensic Mental Health Problems and Challenges

Guided by the theoretical models just described and within the forensic settings identified by the sequential intercept model, we present here some of the structural barriers, injustices,

TABLE 10.1 Summary of Associated Challenges and Social Worker Roles

Intercept	Challenges	Roles
Policing	▪ Improper de-escalation of people in crisis ▪ Lack of crisis services ▪ Public health vs. public safety approaches ▪ Lack of community programming that targets criminogenic needs ▪ Perceptions of people with mental illness as dangerous	▪ De-escalation training, co-responding and sole responding to crises ▪ Crisis stabilization, screening and assessment, and referral services ▪ Providing interventions that target criminogenic and mental health needs ▪ Advocating and boundary-spanning ▪ Anti-stigma training
Initial Detention and Jails	▪ Reluctance to reveal mental health symptoms ▪ Misinterpretation of symptoms as behavioral problems ▪ Overreliance on medications for treatment	▪ Developing safe environments free of victimization ▪ Advocating to increase access to treatment and to decrease use of disciplinary responses ▪ Providing individual and group therapy and addressing criminogenic needs
Reentry from Jails and Prisons	▪ Lack of services for persons with complex needs; fragmented, siloed services ▪ Stigma against people with criminal histories	▪ Linking, referring, and case managing services ▪ Altering policy, lobbying for changes to policy and budget priorities
Community Corrections	▪ Denial of community supervision ▪ Numerous, onerous supervision mandates ▪ High rates of technical violations while under community supervision	▪ Providing courts, parole boards with accurate information ▪ Tailoring supervision requirements ▪ Problem-solving supervision violations

and challenges experienced by people with mental illness and how they relate to the overrepresentation of this population within the criminal justice system. Within this discussion of challenges, we focus on the specific implications of mental health that are important for social workers to consider within their forensic practice roles. A summary is presented in Table 10.1.

Policing

In an age where "defund the police" has become a controversial yet common call to action (Jacobs et al., 2020), law enforcement practices have come under increased scrutiny. In addition to police interactions with people of color, law enforcement practices pertaining to persons with mental health and substance use problems have also been highlighted as needing reform. As the criminalization hypothesis would suggest, a substantial amount of law enforcement involves responding to people with mental health problems, with estimates ranging from 10% to 20% of police contacts with the public involving people with a mental illness (Cordner, 2006; Kaminski et al., 2004). Further, research reveals the criminal justice system is a major referral source to mental health treatment services (Matejkowski, Lee, & Han, 2014; Nam et al., 2016).

Policing Challenges

Police are often not trained to safely de-escalate people experiencing a mental health crisis. This deficit in policing tactics is significant in that many officers resort to arresting those exhibiting mental health–related problems rather than resolving concerns on-site or making referrals for more appropriate treatment and support services (Munetz & Griffin, 2006). Contributing to this problem is a lack of community resources to which people in crisis can be referred (Kuehn, 2014). Some precincts operate within communities where mental health services are scarce, resulting in law enforcement having to either jail those with mental health problems or release them back into communities without needed supports (Watson et al., 2011). Another challenge is the often-tense relations between law enforcement and mental health agencies. Police and mental health therapists and clinicians hail from disciplines that differ philosophically; their training and practice can strongly diverge paradigmatically. The mental health field typically views problems from a treatment-oriented lens, whereas the law enforcement field gives primacy to public safety. These fundamental differences can explain the struggle in collaborating among law enforcement and mental health professionals (Lamberti, 2016). This proves difficult for those living with mental health diagnoses as poor collaborative efforts can result in persons falling through the cracks. Rather than having an organized and connected referral system, those struggling with mental health crises are met with a muddled and ineffective response and shuttled back and forth between correctional and treatment settings.

Somewhat counter to the criminalization hypothesis is the observation that people with mental health problems often do not come into contact with law enforcement solely as a result of a lack of mental health treatment or due to symptoms related to their psychiatric condition. Research has suggested that anywhere from 10% to 20% of lethal (Matejkowski et al., 2008) and nonlethal crimes (Peterson et al., 2014) committed by people with a diagnosed mental health problem can be attributed to symptoms of a mental illness. Further, mental illness may also play a role in the development of criminogenic needs (e.g., antisocial personality, antisocial cognitions, antisocial relations, substance use disorders) and, through various mechanisms, lead to antisocial behaviors and encounters with law enforcement. The RNR model suggests that programs targeting these criminogenic needs would be a more suitable response than treatment solely aimed at alleviating psychiatric symptoms. However, though models and means have been suggested to integrate programming that targets criminogenic needs into behavioral health services (see Bonfine et al., 2020; Osher et al., 2012), the availability of such resources to law enforcement is minimal, perhaps due to stigma and the reluctance of community treatment providers to serve those who are justice involved (Bandara et al., 2018).

In addition to its presence among treatment providers, mental health stigma and focal concerns would suggest that law enforcement contacts are impressed with perceptions of persons with mental illness as dangerous and unpredictable (Watson et al., 2004), leading to differential treatment by law enforcement. Indeed, many people in the mental health community report discrimination from law enforcement (Thornicroft et al., 2009) and have experienced higher rates of use of force than people without mental health problems (Rossler & Terrill, 2017). Social workers have a role in changing these perceptions and practices.

Social Work Roles in Policing

Then president-elect Joe Biden was quoted by the *Washington Post* stating that it is "really, really important that psychologists and social workers join police on calls involving mentally ill people to de-escalate the circumstance, to deal with talking them down" (Kindy et al., 2020). These remarks came after a host of community protests challenging the justice system to reform after unarmed individuals with mental health problems (e.g., Daniel Prude and Stacy Kenny) were killed by law enforcement officers (Kindy et al., 2020). Indeed, social workers play vital roles in law enforcement efforts to assist the mental health community and prevent such grave injustices.

Specialty programs have been developed that utilize differing combinations of law enforcement and social workers to respond to persons experiencing a behavioral health crisis. These include law enforcement officers trained in crisis intervention (Compton et al., 2014), co-responder teams that pair officers with mental health social workers (Dempsey et al., 2020), and teams of social workers trained to replace police officers in crisis response calls (National Public Radio, 2020). When paired together, social workers are present to help triage a mental health crisis and assist law enforcement officers in referring people in need of appropriate treatment and support services (Watson & Fulambarker, 2012). Social workers also work in "drop-off" locations, a key part of diversion programming where those experiencing mental health crises can be transported for a temporary period to avoid arrest or jail (Steadman et al., 2000). In this role, social workers provide crisis stabilization, screening and assessment, and referral services.

Social workers may also provide direct mental health training to law enforcement, equipping them to service populations facing psychological disorders. As Hansson and Markström (2014) state:

> The police force have in several studies been pointed to as an important source of perceived discrimination, which makes the development of anti-stigma interventions focusing [on] the police being of importance in conjunction to other efforts to diminish the burden of stigma and discrimination on people with a mental illness. (p. 7)

Such training interventions can be effective at increasing law enforcement officers' knowledge about mental illness and improving attitudes, and reducing stigma toward people with mental illness (Watson et al., 2017)—all of which, according to focal concerns theory, could reduce the problem of high rates of people with mental illness penetrating the criminal justice system.

From a macro perspective, social workers are trained to network and create partnerships in various entities. They can navigate the challenges and rifts between police and mental health entities, creating bridges between the institutions and services that span law enforcement and mental health service providers. Social workers can take public policy and advocacy positions pressing for criminal justice reform and re-evaluating community law enforcement tactics. As mental health agency administrators and in clinical leadership roles, they can promote anti-stigma efforts to increase acceptance of and services with clients with criminal histories and those who are currently justice involved. In addition, they can incorporate into their services treatments and supports that address important criminogenic needs among this population to reduce further justice system involvement.

Initial Detention and Jails

Following an arrest, an individual is typically booked into a local city or county jail to await an initial hearing of charges that have been filed against them. At this arraignment, the defendant is made aware of their rights, arrangements for legal representation are made, a plea may be entered, and, assuming the defendant pleads not guilty, the court will determine whether detention until a trial is warranted and the amount of bail that may be required to be released from detention before trial. While jails hold persons convicted of crimes (typically, for less than a year), most people leave jail in less than a month, and in many cases, they are released within days (Zeng, 2020). Social work within prison settings (other than reentry services) is excluded from the current discussion as it represents ultimate penetration into the criminal justice system and is therefore not identified as a diversion point in the sequential intercept model (Munetz & Griffin, 2006). For an overview of social work in prison, the reader is referred to Matejkowski, Johnson, and Severson's review (2014).

Initial Detention and Jail Challenges

Social workers in jails often assess new arrivals, and this aids in the identification of psychiatric and substance use disorders, the risk for suicide, and educational and vocational needs among inmates. They develop treatment and support plans for inmates; provide individual therapy and psychosocial, educational support groups; provide referrals to medical or mental health services; and monitor inmates' progress and compliance in treatment. During the assessment phase, the social worker determines the inmate's eligibility for services and treatment and begins to plan for the inmate's discharge. In addition to their short stay and often unexpected releases, challenges to conducting these assessments among the jail population include reluctance by some detainees to reveal the psychiatric symptoms they are experiencing, often because of the stigma associated with being labeled with a mental illness and of concerns of being perceived as weak and fears of being victimized by predatory inmates.

People incarcerated with mental illnesses report more complex histories than do those without mental illness, including homelessness, unemployment, physical and sexual abuse histories, and co-occurring substance use disorders (James & Glaze, 2006). However, jails are not well equipped to respond to the myriad needs of persons with mental health problems. Mental health training for correctional officers is minimal and may contribute to the higher rates of disciplinary infractions reported among inmates with mental illness (Bronson & Berzofsky, 2017; Callahan, 2004). For example, suicide is the leading cause of death in jails (Carson & Cowhig, 2020), and, not surprisingly, having a serious mental illness is a significant predictor of self-harm (Fazel et al., 2016). Although self-harm attempts by those incarcerated may indicate a psychiatric crisis, they tend to be interpreted as behavioral problems and treated as institutional infractions (Comartin et al., 2020) or as reasons to have medications and treatment "forced" onto inmates (Callahan, 2004, p. 46), potentially extending the jail stays of inmates with mental health problems.

Social Work Roles in Initial Detention and Jail

Rehabilitation services within jails reflect tenets from both the criminalization hypothesis (i.e., mental health treatment) and the RNR model (i.e., programs that target criminogenic needs). Basic jail services for persons with mental illness focus on their stabilization so that they can function safely within the jail. However, mental health treatment is rare and tends to consist solely of prescription medication (Bronson & Berzofsky, 2017). When services other than medication are available, jail social workers may be called upon to provide individual and group psychotherapy services to inmates with mental health problems. Individual psychotherapy is less common than group therapy and tends to focus on symptom reduction and adaptation to the carceral environment, while group psychotherapy services are more problem focused and can include topics on anger and stress management and problem-solving (Metzner et al., 2000; Morgan, 2003).

In addition to mental health treatment, jails may offer programming that targets the criminogenic needs of persons housed therein. Jails offer varying amounts of these services, such as cognitive skills training to address antisocial thinking patterns, vocational rehabilitation, and educational programming. According to the RNR model, the presence of a mental illness is a characteristic of program participants that must be addressed if these types of programming are to be effective (Bonta & Andrews, 2016). In this regard, inmates with mental illnesses may have difficulty paying attention to or concentrating on particular tasks, remembering and recalling information, or relating to and communicating with other people (Wilson et al., 2018). Although taking into consideration these special needs may improve program outcomes, responsivity to the special needs of mentally ill inmates is rarely taken into account in correctional programming (Van Voorhis & Lester, 1997). As a result, these institutional programs have low rates of initiation and retention and are not highly effective at providing inmates with mental illness the skills and tools necessary to improve their adjustment to jail or their chances of successful community reintegration upon their release.

Social workers possess a unique set of skills that can be used to increase the ability of jails to enroll and retain inmates in effective institutional programs (e.g., motivational interviewing). Trained in evidence-based practices, social workers should identify programming with rigorous empirical support for alleviating a specific type of problem common among jail detainees. Once identified, the social worker can advocate for the implementation of these programs. After their implementation, social workers can advocate for institutional procedures to facilitate access to programming among those with psychiatric disorders. This can include helping staff rethink classification and program entry criteria or modifying the criteria and program delivery to better accommodate persons with mental illnesses. Such efforts may smooth the way for recovery and skills attainment conducive to successful community reentry.

Reentry From Jails and Prisons

The process of returning to the community accompanies a host of challenges, including obtaining employment, locating a residence, organizing finances, and personal complications with reconnecting with prosocial family, friends, and other natural supports. Persons with mental illness leaving incarceration tend to face these challenges to a higher degree than those without a mental health problem (Mallik-Kane & Visher, 2008) and, as a result, return to custody at higher rates and more quickly (Baillargeon et al., 2009).

In their review of legal and ethical standards requiring health and mental health care for inmates and how these standards have evolved to include transitional planning, Mellow and Greifinger (2008) state:

> The recent emphasis on post-release planning is based in the reality that the correctional system does not have a rehabilitative effect. The high rate of rearrest and reincarceration is a strong indicator that nearly half of the released inmates are not positively reintegrating into their home communities. . . . A coordinated discharge planning process may help decrease the number of readmissions. (pp. 22–23)

Indeed, transition or reentry planning that begins before release and continues with support into the community is seen as crucial for maintaining stable community tenure (Bowman & Travis, 2012). Complicating matters for persons with mental illness returning to their communities are both the complex needs and the dual stigma related to a criminal record and a mental health diagnosis.

Reentry From Jails and Prisons Challenges

One of the major challenges associated with reentry for those with mental illness is ensuring that connections to treatment and formal supports are solidified and maintained. Making and maintaining these connections are complicated by a host of challenges, including a lack of available services, fragmented and siloed services, and a reluctance and inexperience among treatment providers to serve persons with complex needs. Limited options, costs, long waits, and perceived stigma are common barriers to accessing treatment (Cohen Veterans Network & National Council for Behavioral Health, 2018). For example, while substance use disorders are common among people with mental health problems who are justice involved, many treatment providers will limit clients served to "pure types" who have either a mental health or substance use problem, but not both (Lurigio et al., 2004). Among mental health providers, lower levels of perceived similarity with and respect for clients with criminal justice involvement (as compared to clients without such involvement) likely results in an unwelcoming treatment experience, further reducing treatment engagement (Baillargeon et al., 2010; Bandara et al., 2018). Indeed, in substance use treatment settings, Sung and colleagues (2001) found that persons with criminal involvement were readily expelled from treatment, often for behaviors common among those seeking treatment for addiction (e.g., relapse, missed programming).

The exclusionary attitude toward those reentering the community can apply to a host of needed resources to address criminogenic needs, including access to housing, employment, education, and prosocial supports such as families and peers (Draine et al., 2005). Social workers can ease this process by working with communities and individuals to identify sources of social, economic, and cultural capital inherent in both that can slow the *revolving door* of incarceration and reincarceration.

Social Work Roles in Reentry From Jails and Prisons

Social workers stand to assist those under criminal justice supervision with mental health problems by setting up services, including Medicaid coverage (Slate & Johnson, 2009), before release. Social workers trained in case management and referral skills can assist with arranging mental health appointments and other resources in a proactive effort to keep those who have been released from *slipping through the cracks*. Within prerelease programs, social workers can provide job placement assistance, psychoeducational courses, group therapy, and addiction management supportive services (Matejkowski, Johnson, & Severson, 2014). Some of these programs focus on criminogenic needs that can assist people with mental illness to feel more prepared to reintegrate and be more successful once released.

Failure to rectify the structural problems associated with reentry leaves those with mental illness in a vulnerable place. Social workers should lead efforts to identify common barriers to persons incarcerated to gain access to needed community supports and problem-solving methods for overcoming and removing such obstacles. These efforts should include all relevant stakeholders, from public and nonprofit administrators to frontline service providers and persons previously incarcerated. Social workers and these stakeholders can work together to accurately identify common challenges and, in response to these challenges, to alter policy and lobby for changes to agency, local state, and federal policy and budget priorities. Through their recurrent entry and exit through jails and prisons, those with mental illness will fail to benefit from the programs that could further their success if they find the web of formal supports confusing and disorganized. Attempts to reform the criminal justice system for those facing mental illness must involve coordinated efforts, ranging from the institutional discharge process to the treatment and support services within the communities of those released.

Community Corrections and Community Support Services

Probation refers to a court-ordered period of correctional supervision in the community, either as an alternative to incarceration or involving a combined sentence of incarceration followed by a period of community supervision. Parole consists of a term of community supervision following a period of confinement in state or federal prison (Kaeble & Alper, 2020). At year end 2018, there were approximately 4.4 million adults in the United States under law enforcement supervision in the community through either probation or parole (together, termed "community corrections"; Kaeble & Alper, 2020).

Community Corrections and Community Support Services Challenges

When compared to a sentence to jail or prison, a term of community supervision may be considered preferable. However, persons convicted of a crime who have a mental illness often encounter unique and substantial challenges to success under community supervision, not the least of which is being granted the opportunity to serve out a sentence (or portion of a sentence) in the community in the first place. For example, early research examining the impact of mental illness on parole release decisions showed enormous detrimental effects of a psychiatric history on release decisions. In one study by Feder (1994), 79% of inmates without a history of psychiatric hospitalization while incarcerated received favorable parole release decisions, while only 21% with a psychiatric hospitalization were paroled. The stigma associated with psychiatric disabilities and, in this case, perceptions of dangerousness and instability were asserted to explain high rates of parole denial (e.g., Feder, 1994). However, as parole board decision-making embraced more actuarial approaches to risk assessment, researchers moved from framing their studies of decision-making regarding stigma and discrimination based solely on petitioners' mental health status to an RNR framework. This more recent research began to provide observations that, compared to those without mental illness, higher levels of assessed risk and criminogenic needs among people with mental health problems were negatively impacting release to community corrections (Houser et al., 2019; Matejkowski et al., 2010).

Many under community supervision are returned to custody for a new offense or violating their supervision conditions. National research indicates that over half of parolees are rearrested within 2 years of being released (A. Solomon et al., 2005). Of the more than 445,000 adults who exited parole in the United States during 2018, 25.0% (111,651) exited via return to incarceration. The same is true for 15.9% of the 1,853,462 adults who exited probation in 2018 (Kaeble & Alper, 2020). Specific to revocations due to technical violations, researchers have indicated that parolees with mental illness are more likely to have their parole revoked due to a technical violation than parolees without mental illness (Ostermann & Matejkowski, 2014; Pew Center on the States, 2011). These higher rates of technical violations among people with mental illness may result from stigma toward people with mental illness. For example, research conducted with probation officers revealed that officers would opt for more punitive responses when responding to a probation violation by a person with a mental illness than they would with probationers without a mental illness, even when the probationers had been assessed at the same public safety risk level (Eno Louden et al., 2018).

The burdens of community supervision are often higher among persons with mental illness. For example, in addition to standard conditions, supervision mandates often include participation in mental health or substance use treatment or housing programs and adherence to these specialty treatment providers' recommendations. These additional mandates placed upon persons with mental illness, along with limited availability of services (Van Deinse et al., 2018), may contribute to technical violations while under supervision or a desire to avoid community supervision altogether (Matejkowski & Ostermann, 2020).

In sum, a considerable portion of adults under correctional supervision in the community have a mental illness. These people face potential discrimination based upon their mental health status in terms of being granted community supervision as early release from (or instead of) custody. Once granted community supervision, they face differential treatment in the form of more severe sanctions that returns them to incarceration at higher rates than what is seen among those under supervision who do not have a mental illness. Further, due to heightened criminogenic needs and a tendency to overinflate the role of mental health treatment in criminal risk reduction, this population is saddled with onerous community supervision conditions that can lead to increased surveillance and risk for violation of technical conditions of supervision and return to incarceration.

Social Work Roles in Community Corrections and Community Support Services

From a focal concerns' perspective, social workers can provide courts and parole boards with accurate information about the weak link between mental illness and public safety risk. Doing so may increase the chances that individuals with mental illness are provided the opportunity to serve out sentences (or portions of their sentences) in the least restrictive setting. Social workers can also provide these authorities information about the person's risks and needs for use in release decision-making and supervision planning.

Reflecting the RNR model and the criminalization hypothesis, social workers use evidence-based assessment tools to assess inmates' level of risk for criminal behavior following release and tools to assess needs for mental health and addiction care. Social workers summarize the information gleaned from these instruments and offer recommendations for sentencing, release, and case planning to courts and the parole board. Specific to the RNR model's risk principle, social workers should advocate that community supervision conditions should be minimal for those assessed at low risk for criminal involvement (and higher for those assessed as higher risk). Community supervision conditions should also be limited and targeted to the identified criminogenic needs of parolees. Requiring low-risk offenders to engage in risk reduction programming can be counterproductive, and requiring offenders to engage in treatment and services that do not have evidence in reducing their criminogenic needs is unnecessarily costly and burdensome and contributes to technical violations and further incarceration.

Community corrections officers who do not take a therapeutic approach to supervision and a problem-solving approach to community violations have been found to contribute to recidivism through closer monitoring, resulting in increased technical violations (Petersilia & Turner, 1993; P. Solomon et al., 2002). Incorporating social work approaches into community supervision can improve responses to problematic behaviors of those supervised with mental illness. When supervision violations are a function of mental illness, social workers can advocate for services rather than sanctions and encourage community corrections officers to view violations as "opportunities to build closer alliances" and to assist them in "avoiding future, and more serious, problems" (Lurigio, 2001, p. 457). Therapeutic responses built on a strong working alliance and positive regard, rather than strategies aimed at control and deterrence, are associated with greater participation in treatment and rehabilitation programs and improved client outcomes (Norcross, 2011; Rogers, 1951). Extending these social work values to the community corrections setting is likely to reduce risks for reincarceration and increase treatment access and adherence for individuals with mental health problems.

Special Note on Coercion and Social Work Values

There is a genuine tension underlying social work within criminal justice forensic settings where core social work values (e.g., the dignity and worth of the person, the importance of human relationships) that encompass the doctrine of self-determination pull a practitioner in one direction while public safety mandates that often involve authoritarian approaches pull in opposition. Nowhere is this conflict more likely to become apparent than working with individuals with mental illnesses under justice supervision. Criminal justice diversion, correctional, and community supervision programs serving people with mental health problems are often structured and function in a way that leverages the legal system to motivate those supervised toward utilization of mandated treatment services. For example, community corrections often leverage their authority to promote compliance among those they supervise (Bogue, Nandi, & Berghuis, 2003). Problem-solving courts (e.g., mental health courts) that divert incarceration of mentally ill individuals charged with criminal offenses also often rely on sanctions or the threat of sanctions (including incarceration) to motivate individuals' adherence to prescribed treatment services (Matejkowski et al., 2020).

Erroneous assumptions of incompetence and flawed character combine to compel some actors in these settings to behave paternalistically, if not despotically. Matejkowski and Severson (2020) point out that throughout the settings identified in the sequential intercept model are professionals who maintain a

> disbelief about recovery, be it recovery from mental illness (Roberts & Boardman, 2013) or recovery from criminality (Cullen, 2013). Such skepticism about recovery, that is, thinking that recovery is not possible, translates to authoritarian and coercive approaches to treatment and supervision. (p. 7)

This disbelief and resultant perceptions of such persons as incapable or *lesser than* contribute to the proliferation of system mandates for compliance sought through fear of punishment or restriction of freedoms. These coercive practices conflict with social work's ethical principle of respecting the person's inherent dignity and worth.

Social Workers Roles in Addressing Coercion

There is growing room within criminal forensic settings for more egalitarian policies and practices, including shared decision-making (SDM). SDM is a collaborative process between providers/supervisors and consumers/supervisees that involves sharing of information (e.g., treatment options, evidence of treatment efficacy, and associated outcomes along with consumers' treatment preferences and values) and consensus building as features of the preferred course of treatment/supervision (Matejkowski et al., 2018). Borne out of mental health and health care, the involvement of those supervised in developing and evaluating their progress in their supervision is also beginning to be realized as an important contributor to improved outcomes for those involved in the criminal justice system (Taxman, 2013).

More effective incorporation of SDM throughout the criminal justice system continuum (when public and personal safety allow) can reduce coercion and better align criminal justice system services with the social work profession's values and enhance procedural justice. Procedural justice is essentially a belief in the fairness of legal procedures (Tyler, 1988) that can contribute to a person's willingness to accept and engage in legal and mandated treatment service (Redlich & Han, 2014). Social workers can promote procedural justice in these settings through transparency and communication and SDM. Taxman (2013) points out:

> This requires the supervision agency to provide the offender with: 1) results from the risk and need assessment, including an explanation of factors that affect these risk and need assessments and choices that can be made that can facilitate change; 2) options regarding programming, services, controls, with a preference for the offender selecting the best option; 3) review of progress, where the offender is asked to assess how well he or she has done; and 4) changes in the supervision plan based on the offender (and the officer in a shared decision-making model) input. (p. 84)

It will be necessary to change perceptions through education and training so that criminal justice practices and policies progress toward increased procedural justice. Training can be framed to effectively impart that people with mental illness can recover. Endorsement of recovery as something possible can reduce negative perceptions and social othering of people with mental illness. Training that specifically promotes awareness of fundamental commonalities among those under criminal justice supervision and their supervisors and that emphasizes a view of mental illness as a disease that, while sometimes disabling, would not necessarily prevent someone from giving input to and participating in decisions about the terms under which they will live could help to promote these changes.

Summary

Social work with persons experiencing mental health problems and criminal justice system involvement is often complicated by the extent and severity of the myriad needs of this population. From a clinical standpoint, the criminalization hypothesis prioritizes the need for mental health treatment among this group of people, while the RNR model identifies employment and education involvement, enhancement of prosocial supports, reduction in antisocial thinking patterns, and other criminogenic needs as targets for intervention. Indeed, the research indicates that both approaches and attention to fundamental human needs (i.e., housing, health care, financial supports) are necessary to reduce justice system contact and improve quality of life among this population.

Unfortunately, the research also indicates these resources are scarce, and when they are present, they are often uncoordinated, unidimensional, and exclusionary. Treatment to address mental health and criminogenic needs, either while incarcerated or through a diversion program, is supplied far less than demand requires. Further, these services are siloed from each other and are often coordinated neither within the community nor across carceral and community settings. The dual stigma of a mental health diagnosis and a criminal record further limits access and engagement in services, with mental health problems serving as a barrier to in-custody and reentry programs, and criminal histories and dual diagnoses precluding access to humane community treatment. Pair these obstacles with mandates on those supervised to engage in services to obtain or maintain their freedom, and what results is a system that functions to continue to incarcerate and reincarcerate individuals with mental health problems.

It is difficult to identify other settings or populations where social workers' skills and principles could be of more value. Social workers should be involved in each of the forensic settings identified in the sequential intercept model to provide and coordinate needed services and supports for this population. This will require a straddling of systems that involves understanding diverse, often opposing, theory, policy, and clinical approaches. Understanding these varying perspectives will improve the social worker's ability to advocate for appropriate responses to the needs of this group of people. As promoters and providers of evidence-based practices, social workers should also identify services with rigorous empirical support for alleviating the specific problems common within this population. Once identified, the social worker should advocate for policies and procedures that will facilitate their availability. Finally, provision of services in a way that respects the dignity and worth of those served, that are built on a strong therapeutic relationship and respect, rather than on fear and coercion, are associated with greater participation in treatment and rehabilitation programs and improved client outcomes. As such, the promotion of these social work values throughout forensic settings may increase treatment access and adherence for individuals with mental health problems, reduce risks for reincarceration, and ultimately improve both public health and safety (Matejkowski, Johnson, & Severson, 2014).

Failure to address the disparities that those with mental health problems and criminal histories face in the criminal justice and community mental health systems not only puts this vulnerable population at risk for further marginalization but also remains costly and burdensome to society. The theories surrounding forensic social work discussed here provide strong frameworks for addressing these negative outcomes. Adequately understanding the roles social workers can play requires a proactive and reactive lens. Proactive attention requires an understanding of the policies that have contributed to the justice involvement of those with mental health diagnoses (e.g., deinstitutionalization) to craft alternatives that prevent the criminalization of people with mental health problems. Reactive measures involve continuous evaluation of the effectiveness of existing clinical and policy practices to rid the space of those that are ineffective and to identify and promote those that can help reduce the overrepresentation of this population in criminal justice settings (i.e., those that serve to reduce criminogenic needs). In these efforts, through competent and compassionate advocacy and intervention that is based firmly upon social work values, social workers can serve to reduce the unjust treatment of people with mental health problems that accompanies their plummeting into a criminal justice system that was designed neither for their rehabilitation nor treatment.

References

Baillargeon, J., Binswanger, I. A., Penn, J. V., Williams, B. A., & Murray, O. J. (2009). Psychiatric disorders and repeat incarcerations: The revolving prison door. *American Journal of Psychiatry*, *166*(1), 103–109. https://doi.org/10.1176/appi.ajp.2008.08030416

Baillargeon, J., Hoge, S. K., & Penn, J. V. (2010). Addressing the challenge of community reentry among released inmates with serious mental illness. *American Journal of Community Psychology, 46*(3–4), 361–375. https://doi.org/10.1007/s10464-010-9345-6

Bandara, S. N., Daumit, G. L., Kennedy-Hendricks, A., Linden, S., Choksy, S., & McGinty, E. E. (2018). Mental health providers' attitudes about criminal justice–involved clients with serious mental illness. *Psychiatric Services, 69*(4), 472–475. https://doi.org/10.1176/appi.ps.201700321

Batastini, A. B., Lester, M. E., & Thompson, R. A. (2018). Mental illness in the eyes of the law: Examining perceptions of stigma among judges and attorneys. *Psychology, Crime & Law, 24*(7), 673–686. https://doi.org/10.1080/1068316X.2017.1406092

Bogue, B. M., Nandi, A., & Berghuis, D. J. (2003). *The probation and parole treatment planner* (Vol. 172). John Wiley & Sons.

Bonfine, N., Wilson, A. B., & Munetz, M. R. (2020). Meeting the needs of justice-involved people with serious mental illness within community behavioral health systems. *Psychiatric Services, 71*(4), 355–363. https://doi.org/10.1176/appi.ps.201900453

Bonta, J., & Andrews, D. A. (2016). *The psychology of criminal conduct.* Taylor & Francis.

Bonta, J., Blais, J., & Wilson, H. A. (2014). A theoretically informed meta-analysis of the risk for general and violent recidivism for mentally disordered offenders. *Aggression and Violent Behavior, 19*(3), 278–287. https://doi.org/10.1016/j.avb.2014.04.014

Bowman, S. W., & Travis, R., Jr. (2012). Prisoner reentry and recidivism according to the formerly incarcerated and reentry service providers: A verbal behavior approach. *Behavior Analyst Today, 13*(3–4), 9. http://dx.doi.org/10.1037/h0100726

Bronson, J., & Berzofsky, M. (2017). *Indicators of mental health problems reported by prisoners and jail Inmates, 2011–12.* http://www.bjs.gov/content/pub/pdf/imhprpji1112.pdf

Callahan, L. (2004). Correctional officer attitudes toward inmates with mental disorders. *International Journal of Forensic Mental Health, 3*, 37–54. https://doi.org/10.1080/14999013.2004.10471195

Carson, E., & Cowhig, M. (2020). *Mortality in local jails, 2000–2016: Statistical tables.* https://www.bjs.gov/content/pub/pdf/mlj0016st.pdf

Cohen Veterans Network & National Council for Behavioral Health. (2018). *America's mental health 2018.* https://www.cohenveteransnetwork.org/AmericasMentalHealth/

Comartin, E. B., Nelson, V., Smith, S., & Kubiak, S. (2020). The criminal/legal experiences of individuals with mental illness along the sequential intercept model: An eight-site study. *Criminal Justice and Behavior, 48*(1), 76–95. https://doi.org/10.1177%2F0093854820943917

Compton, M. T., Bakeman, R., Broussard, B., Hankerson-Dyson, D., Husbands, L., Krishan, S., Stewart-Hutto, T., D'Orio, B. M., Olivia, J. R., Thompson, N. J., & Watson, A. C. (2014). The police-based crisis intervention team (CIT) model: II. Effects on level of force and resolution, referral, and arrest. *Psychiatric Services, 65*(4), 523–529. https://doi.org/10.1176/appi.ps.201300108

Cordner, G. (2006). *People with mental illness: Problem-oriented guides for police.* https://cops.usdoj.gov/RIC/Publications/cops-p103-pub.pdf

Cullen, F. T. (2013). Rehabilitation: Beyond nothing works. *Crime and Justice, 42*(1), 299–376.

Dempsey, C., Quanbeck, C., Bush, C., & Kruger, K. (2020). Decriminalizing mental illness: Specialized policing responses. *CNS Spectrums, 25*(2), 181–195. https://doi.org/10.1017/S1092852919001640

Draine, J., Wolff, N., Jacoby, J. E., Hartwell, S., & Duclos, C. (2005). Understanding community re-entry of former prisoners with mental illness: A conceptual model to guide new research. *Behavioral Sciences & the Law, 23*(5), 689–707.

Eno Louden, J., Manchak, S. M., Ricks, E. P., & Kennealy, P. J. (2018). The role of stigma toward mental illness in probation officers' perceptions of risk and case management decisions. *Criminal Justice and Behavior, 45*(5), 573–588. doi:10.1177/0093854818756148

Fazel, S., Hayes, A. J., Bartellas, K., Clerici, M., & Trestman, R. (2016). Mental health of prisoners: Prevalence, adverse outcomes, and interventions. *Lancet Psychiatry, 3*(9), 871–881. https://dx.doi.org/10.1016%2FS2215-0366(16)30142-0

Feder, L. (1994). Psychiatric hospitalization history and parole decisions. *Law and Human Behavior, 18*, 395–410.

Hansson, L., & Markström, U. (2014). The effectiveness of an anti-stigma intervention in a basic police officer training programme: A controlled study. *BMC Psychiatry, 14*(1), 55. https://doi.org/10.1186/1471-244X-14-55

Houser, K. A., Vîlcică, E., Saum, C. A., & Hiller, M. L. (2019). Mental health risk factors and parole decisions: Does inmate mental health status affect who gets released. *International Journal of Environmental Research and Public Health, 16*(16), 2950. https://doi.org/10.3390/ijerph16162950

Jacobs, L. A., Kim, M. E., Whitfield, D. L., Gartner, R. E., Panichelli, M., Kattari, S. K., . . . Mountz, S. E. (2021). Defund the police: Moving towards an anti-carceral social work. *Journal of Progressive Human Services, 32*(1), 37–62. doi:10.1080/10428232.2020.1852865

James, D. J., & Glaze, L. E. (2006). *Mental health problems of prison and jail inmates.* https://www.bjs.gov/content/pub/pdf/mhppji.pdf

Kaeble, D., & Alper, M. (2020). *Probation and parole in the United States, 2017–2018.* U.S. Department of Justice.

Kaminski, R. J., Digiovanni, C., & Downs, R. (2004). The use of force between the police and persons with impaired judgment. *Police Quarterly, 7*(3), 311–338. https://doi.org/10.1177/1098611103253456

Kennedy, H. G., Simpson, A. I. F., & Haque, Q. (2019). Perspective on excellence in forensic mental health services: What we can learn from oncology and other medical services. *Frontiers in Psychiatry, 10*, 733. https://doi.org/10.3389/fpsyt.2019.00733

Kindy, K., Tate, J., Jenkins, J., & Mellnik, T. (2020, October 17). Fatal police shootings of mentally ill people are 39 percent more likely to take place in small and midsized areas. *Washington Post.* https://www.washingtonpost.com/national/police-mentally-ill-deaths/2020/10/17/8dd5bcf6-0245-11eb-b7ed-141dd88560ea_story.html

Kuehn, B. M. (2014). Criminal justice becomes front line for mental health care. *JAMA, 311*(19), 1953–1954. https://doi.org/10.1001/jama.2014.4578

Lamb, H. R., & Weinberger, L., E. (1998). Persons with severe mental illness in jails and prisons: A review. *Psychiatric Services, 49*(4), 483–492.

Lamberti, J. S. (2016). Preventing criminal recidivism through mental health and criminal justice collaboration. *Psychiatric Services, 67*(11), 1206–1212. doi:10.1176/appi.ps.201500384

Lurigio, A. J. (2001). Effective services for parolees with mental illnesses. *Crime and Delinquency, 47*, 446–461. https://doi.org/10.1177/0011128701047003009

Lurigio, A. J., Rollins, A., & Fallon, J. (2004). The effects of serious mental illness on offender reentry. *Federal Probation, 68*(2), 45–52.

Mallik-Kane, K., & Visher, C. A. (2008). *Health and prisoner reentry: How physical, mental, and substance abuse conditions shape the process of reintegration.* Urban Institute.

Maschi, T., & Killian, M. L. (2011). The evolution of forensic social work in the United States: Implications for 21st century practice. *Journal of Forensic Social Work, 1*(1), 8–36.

Matejkowski, J. (2010). *"Differential treatment" of persons with mental illness in parole release decisions?* [Doctoral dissertation]. University of Pennsylvania, Philadelphia, PA.

Matejkowski, J. (2019). Mental Health Courts. *Criminology.* doi:10.1093/obo/9780195396607-0271

Matejkowski, J., Caplan, J. M., & Cullen, S. W. (2010). The impact of severe mental illness on parole decisions: Social integration within a prison setting. *Criminal Justice and Behavior, 37*(9), 1005–1029. https://doi.org/10.1177/0093854810372898

Matejkowski, J., Cullen, S. W., & Solomon, P. L. (2008). Characteristics of persons with severe mental illness who have been incarcerated for murder. *Journal of the American Academy of Psychiatry and the Law, 36*(1), 74–86.

Matejkowski, J., Han, W., & Conrad, A. (2020). Voluntariness of treatment, mental health service utilization, and quality of life among mental health court participants. *Psychology, Public Policy, and Law, 26*(2), 185. https://doi.org/10.1037/law0000227

Matejkowski, J., Johnson, T., & Severson, M. E. (2014). Prison social work. *Encyclopedia of Social Work.* https://oxfordre.com/socialwork/view/10.1093/acrefore/9780199975839.001.0001/acrefore-9780199975839-e-1002

Matejkowski, J., Lee, S., & Han, W. (2014). The association between criminal history and mental health service use among people with serious mental illness. *Psychiatric Quarterly, 85*, 9–24. https://doi.org/10.1007/s11126-013-9266-2

Matejkowski, J., Lee, S., & Severson, M. E. (2018). Validation of a tool to measure attitudes among community corrections officers toward shared decision making with formerly incarcerated persons with mental illness. *Criminal Justice and Behavior, 45*(5), 612–627. https://doi.org/10.1177/0093854818761991

Matejkowski, J., & Ostermann, M. (2015). Serious mental illness, criminal risk, parole supervision, and recidivism: Testing of conditional effects. *Law and Human Behavior, 39*(1), 75–86. https://doi.org/10.1037/lhb0000094

Matejkowski, J., & Ostermann, M. (2021). The Waiving of Parole Consideration by Inmates With Mental Illness and Recidivism Outcomes. *Criminal Justice and Behavior, 48*(8), 1052–1071. https://doi.org/10.1177/0093854820972162

Matejkowski, J., & Severson, M. E. (2020). Predictors of shared decision making with people who have a serious mental illness and who are under justice supervision in the community. *International Journal of Law and Psychiatry, 70*, 101568. https://doi.org/10.1016/j.ijlp.2020.101568

Mellow, J., & Greifinger, R. (2008). The evolving standard of decency: Postrelease planning? *Journal of Correctional Health Care, 14*(1), 21–30. doi:10.1177/1078345807309617

Metzner, J. L., Cohen, F., Grossman, L. S., & Wettstein, R. M. (2000). Treatment in jails and prisons. In R. M. Wettstein (Ed.), *Treatment of offenders with mental disorders* (pp. 211–264). Guilford.

Morgan, R. (2003). Basic mental health services: Services and issues. In T. J. Fagan & R. K. Ax (Eds.), *Correctional mental health handbook* (pp. 303–327). Sage.

Munetz, M., & Griffin, P. (2006). Use of the sequential intercept model as an approach to decriminalization of people with serious mental illness. *Psychiatric Services, 57*(4), 544–549.

Nam, E., Matejkowski, J., & Lee, S. (2016). Criminal justice contact and treatment utilization among people with mental illness and substance use disorders. *Psychiatric Services, 67*(10), 1149–1151. https://doi.org/10.1176/appi.ps.201500381

National Association of State Mental Health Program Directors. (2014). *Forensic mental health services in the United States: 2014.* https://www.nasmhpd.org/sites/default/files/Assessment%203%20-%20Updated%20Forensic%20Mental%20Health%20Services.pdf

National Public Radio. (2020). *"CAHOOTS": How social workers and police share responsibilities in Eugene, Oregon.* https://www.npr.org/2020/06/10/874339977/cahoots-how-social-workers-and-police-share-responsibilities-in-eugene-oregon

Norcross, J. C. (Ed.). (2011). *Psychotherapy relationships that work* (2nd ed.). Oxford University Press.

Osher, F. C., D'Amora, D. A., Plotkin, M., Jarrett, N., & Eggleston, A. (2012). *Adults with behavioral health needs under correctional supervision: A shared framework for reducing recidivism and promoting recovery.* https://bja.ojp.gov/sites/g/files/xyckuh186/files/Publications/CSG_Behavioral_Framework.pdf

Ostermann, M., & Matejkowski, J. (2014). Exploring the intersection of mental health and release status with recidivism. *Justice Quarterly, 31*(4), 746–766. https://doi.org/10.1080/07418825.2012.677465

Pescosolido, B. A., Manago, B., & Monahan, J. (2019). Evolving public views on the likelihood of violence from people with mental illness: Stigma and its consequences. *Health Affairs, 38*(10), 1735–1743. https://doi.org/10.1377/hlthaff.2019.00702

Petersilia, J., & Turner, S. (1993). Intensive probation and parole. *Crime and Justice, 17*, 281–335.

Peterson, J., Skeem, J., Kennealy, P., Bray, B., & Zvonkovic, A. (2014). How often and how consistently do symptoms directly precede criminal behavior among offenders with mental illness? *Law and Human Behavior, 38*(5), 439–449. https://doi.org/10.1037/lhb0000075

Pew Center on the States. (2011). *State of recidivism: The revolving door of America's prisons.* https://www.pewtrusts.org/en/research-and-analysis/reports/0001/01/01/state-of-recidivism

Ray, B., & Dollar, C. B. (2013). Examining mental health court completion: A focal concerns perspective. *Sociological Quarterly, 54*(4), 647–669. https://doi.org/10.1111/tsq.12032

Redlich, A., & Han, W. (2014). Examining the links between therapeutic jurisprudence and mental health court completion. *Law and Human Behavior, 38*(2), 109–118. https://doi.org/10.1037/lhb0000041

Roberts, G., & Boardman, J. (2013). Understanding "recovery". *Advances in Psychiatric Treatment, 19*(6), 400–409.

Rogers, C. R. (1951). *Client-centered therapy.* Houghton Mifflin.

Rossler, M. T., & Terrill, W. (2017). Mental illness, police use of force, and citizen injury. *Police Quarterly, 20*(2), 189–212. https://doi.org/10.1177/1098611116681480

Rüsch, N., Angermeyer, M. C., & Corrigan, P. W. (2005). Mental illness stigma: Concepts, consequences, and initiatives to reduce stigma. *European Psychiatry, 20*(8), 529–539. https://doi.org/10.1016/j.eurpsy.2005.04.004

Skeem, J., Manchak, S., & Montoya, L. (2017). Comparing public safety outcomes for traditional probation vs specialty mental health probation. *JAMA Psychiatry, 74*(9), 942–948. https://doi.org/10.1001/jamapsychiatry.2017.1384

Skeem, J., Manchak, S., & Peterson, J. K. (2011). Correctional policy for offenders with mental illness: Creating a new paradigm for recidivism reduction. *Law and Human Behavior, 35*(2), 110–126. https://doi.org/10.1007/s10979-010-9223-7

Slate, R., & Johnson, W. (2009). Seeking alternatives to the criminalization of mental illness. *American Jails, 23*(1), 20–28.

Solomon, A., Kachnowski, V., & Bhati, A. (2005). *Does parole work: Analyzing the impact of postprison supervision on rearrest outcomes.* http://www.urban.org/UploadedPDF/311156_Does_Parole_Work.pdf

Solomon, P., Draine, J., & Marcus, S. C. (2002). Predicting incarceration of clients of a psychiatric probation and parole service. *Psychiatric Services, 53*(1), 50–56. https://doi.org/10.1176/appi.ps.53.1.50

Steadman, H. J., Deane, M. W., Borum, R., & Morrissey, J. P. (2000). Comparing outcomes of major models of police responses to mental health emergencies. *Psychiatric Services, 51,* 645–649. https://doi.org/10.1176/appi.ps.51.5.645

Steffensmeier, D., & Demuth, S. (2006). Does gender modify the effects of race–ethnicity on criminal sanctioning? Sentences for male and female white, black, and Hispanic defendants. *Journal of Quantitative Criminology, 22*(3), 241–261. doi:10.1007/s10940-006-9010-2

Steffensmeier, D., Ulmer, J., & Kramer, J. (1998). The interaction of race, gender, and age in criminal sentencing: The punishment cost of being young, black, and male. *Criminology, 36*(4), 763–798. https://doi.org/10.1111/j.1745-9125.1998.tb01265.x

Sung, H.-E., Belenko, S., & Feng, L. (2001). Treatment compliance in the trajectory of treatment progress among offenders. *Journal of Substance Abuse Treatment, 20*(2), 153–162.

Taxman, F. (2013). 7 keys to make EBPs stick: Lessons from the field. *Federal Probation, 77*(3), 76–86.

Thornicroft, G., Brohan, E., Rose, D., Sartorius, N., Leese, M., & Group, I. S. (2009). Global pattern of experienced and anticipated discrimination against people with schizophrenia: A cross-sectional survey. *The Lancet, 373*(9661), 408–415.

Tyler, T. R. (1988). What is procedural justice-criteria used by citizens to assess the fairness of legal procedures. *Law & Society Review, 22*(1), 103–136.

Van Deinse, T. B., Cuddeback, G. S., Wilson, A. B., & Burgin, S. E. (2018). Probation officers' perceptions of supervising probationers with mental illness in rural and urban settings. *American Journal of Criminal Justice, 43*(2), 267–277. https://doi.org/10.1007/s12103-017-9392-8

Van Voorhis, P., & Lester, D. (1997). Cognitive therapies. In P. Van Voorhis, M. Braswell, & D. Lester (Eds.), *Correctional counseling and rehabilitation* (pp. 183–206). Anderson.

Watson, A. C., Compton, M. T., & Draine, J. N. (2017). The crisis intervention team (CIT) model: An evidence-based policing practice? *Behavioral Sciences & the Law, 35*(5–6), 431–441. https://doi.org/10.1002/bsl.2304

Watson, A. C., Corrigan, P. W., & Ottati, V. (2004). Police officers' attitudes toward and decisions about persons with mental illness. *Psychiatric Services, 55*(1), 49–53. https://doi.org/10.1176/appi.ps.55.1.49

Watson, A. C., & Fulambarker, A. J. (2012). The crisis intervention team model of police response to mental health crises: A primer for mental health practitioners. *Best Practices in Mental Health, 8*(2), 71.

Watson, A. C., Ottati, V. C., Draine, J., & Morabito, M. (2011). CIT in context: The impact of mental health resource availability and district saturation on call dispositions. *International Journal of Law and Psychiatry, 34*(4), 287–294. https://doi.org/10.1016/j.ijlp.2011.07.008

Wilson, A. B., Farkas, K., Bonfine, N., & Duda-Banwar, J. (2018). Interventions that target criminogenic needs for justice-involved persons with serious mental illnesses: A targeted service delivery approach. *International Journal of Offender Therapy and Comparative Criminology, 62*(7), 1838–1853. https://doi.org/10.1177%2F0306624X17695588

Wilson, A. B., Ishler, K. J., Morgan, R., Phillips, J., Draine, J., & Farkas, K. J. (2020). Examining criminogenic risk levels among people with mental illness incarcerated in US jails and prisons. *The Journal of Behavioral Health Services & Research,* 1–16. https://doi.org/10.1007/s11414-020-09737-x

Zeng, Z. (2020). *Jail inmates in 2018.* https://www.bjs.gov/content/pub/pdf/ji18.pdf

11

History of Criminal Justice Theory

Constance L. Chapple and Matthew S. Lofflin

When tracing criminal justice theory development, it is wise to review its background in criminological thought. While criminal justice, as a separate academic discipline, emerged in the United States during Johnson's Great Society (Fernandes & Crutchfield, 2018), crime researchers and theorists have long been interested in the workings of the criminal justice system. The earliest writings in criminology by Beccaria, Bentham, and Hobbes (Roshier, 1989) address the criminal justice system's operation exclusively. As criminology developed as a scholarly discipline within the United States, criminal justice practitioners often borrowed heavily from prevailing research and theory to design effective crime prevention and management policies. Criminology has a long and respected history of ontological development into the causes of crime and why people behave the way they do. It is common practice to group criminological theories into three theoretical paradigms: classical paradigm, positivist paradigm, and postclassical paradigm. Grouping of theories within each paradigm is achieved by examining the theory's assumptions regarding human nature.

Theories within the classical paradigm assume that individuals have free will and are self-interested and rational decision makers (Roshier, 1989); many rational choice theories in criminology are included in this paradigm. The positivist paradigm assumes that internal or external forces determine individual actions and therefore offenders are different in their biology, psychology, or social experiences than nonoffenders. Crime is akin to disease and considered to be pathological; thus, social, psychological, or physical deficits lay at the root of crime and include learning, strain, and labeling theories. Theories within the postclassical paradigm combine elements from both the classical and positivist paradigms. According to human nature assumptions in the postclassical paradigm, individuals are neither wholly free in their choices nor wholly determined in their behaviors; instead, manipulability of action is highlighted. Understanding why an individual engages in crime and

Constance L. Chapple and Matthew S. Lofflin, *History of Criminal Justice Theory* In: *Handbook of Forensic Social Work*. Edited by: David Axlyn McLeod, Anthony P. Natale, and Kristin W. Mapson, Oxford University Press. © Oxford University Press 2024. DOI: 10.1093/oso/9780197694732.003.0011 the forces that allow or compel them into action underlay many criminal justice prevention and intervention efforts.

To better understand these theories and their applications in forensic social work practice, the chapter first reviews the history of criminological thought including the classical paradigm, positivist paradigm, and postclassical paradigm. Second, the chapter reviews past and current criminal justice policies and practices that use criminological theories as foundations. Finally, the chapter concludes with a review of today's most utilized theories in criminal justice that are applicable to forensic social work practice.

History of Criminological Theories

Classical Paradigm

Criminological theories have a long history in grounding criminal justice policy. Table 11.1 provides a summary of the human nature assumptions and an exemplar of policy for each paradigm. The earliest writing in criminology from the classical school specifically addresses criminal justice policies. For instance, Beccaria's (2009) emphasis that punishment should be "swift, certain and severe (proportional)" was designed to create policies that would deter crime among rational offenders. To that end, Bentham is renowned for describing thousands of calculations of the pleasure/pain ratio needed to deter a variety of criminal acts. The classical school in criminology has influenced modern criminal justice's emphasis on deterrence and "just deserts" in punishment (Braithwaite & Pettit, 1992) with the idea that if the costs or penalties associated with crime are high enough, they will outweigh the pleasure or self-interest to be gained. The influence of classical criminology's thesis of rationality, pleasure, and pain is apparent in modern rational choice theories in criminology (Cornish & Clarke, 2014) and the resulting contemporary criminal justice policy suggestions. Specifically, justice policies that focused on deterrence via increased penalties proliferated in the 1980s and 1990s as we saw growth in determinate sentencing (Zatz, 1984), three-strikes laws (Turner, Sundt, Applegate, & Cullen, 1995), and zero-tolerance policies at schools (Cullen et al., 2016). While many of these increasing-severity policies are ineffective (see death penalty research, Radelet & Akers, 1996) at curbing crime, advocates of harsher penalties remain.

Positivist Paradigm

At the turn of the 20th century in the United States, positivist criminology's paradigm took root and had wide-reaching criminal justice policy implications for decades. According

TABLE 11.1 Criminological Paradigms and Criminal Justice Policy

	Human Nature Assumptions	Exemplar Policy
Classical	Free will, rationality, self-interest	Deterrence, just deserts
Positivist	Determinism, difference, pathology	War on poverty
Postclassical	Soft-determinism, probability, manipulability	Situational crime prevention

to the positivist paradigm, the principles of crime causation include that behavior is determined by biological or social factors; that social, psychological, or biological pathology causes crime; and that offenders are either constitutionally or socially different from nonoffenders. The effects of biological positivism on criminal justice policy were marked, included recommendations ranging from medication to sterilization to death, and were embraced by the growing eugenics movement (Rafter, 2004). As such, we often view these practices as barbaric today. However, the effect of biological positivism on criminal justice policy lingers as we continue to see sanctions regarding chemical castration (Meyer & Cole, 1997) and seemingly benign requirements for adherence to prescribed psychoactive medication as a condition of an individual's release from supervision (Skeem et al., 2006). These conditions are particularly true in the subfield of drug courts and substance abuse treatments associated with criminal justice policies that often emphasize the heritability component of drug use and addiction (Gowan & Whetstone, 2012).

As the influence of biological positivism on criminological thought and policy began to wane in the United States after World War II, criminology emerged into a theoretical era of sociological positivism. Within sociological positivism, the causes of crime are social and point to deficits in social functioning and social structure. As such, theories and policies aligned with sociological positivism investigated the role of deviant peer groups (A. K. Cohen, 1955), poverty and structural inequality (Merton, 1938), educational inequality (Cloward & Ohlin, 2013), and social labeling (Lemert, 1999) on crime causation, prevention, and intervention. Many criminal justice programs of the 1950s through 1970s relied on social positivism principles and aimed to break up gangs, alleviate class inequality, and increase access to jobs. Much of Johnson's Great Society policies were firmly grounded in social positivist theory (Jencks, 1992) and included social programs such as Head Start and Job Corps. However, other darker agendas emerged during this time and as a result of the growing acceptance of the "culture of poverty" thesis (Lewis, 1966), which particularly targeted Black families for their "pathology" (Moynihan, 1965) and offered limited recognition to the influence of structural discrimination embedded in racialized outcomes. Finally, the deinstitutionalization and decriminalization movements within criminology (Jeffery, 1978) credit the pathological processes of label making and label applying to disadvantaged groups for their theoretical foundation.

Postclassical Paradigm

Finally, perhaps the most influential criminological theories on contemporary criminal justice policy in the United States are routine activities (L. E. Cohen & Felson, 1979) and situation prevention theories (Clarke, 1980). According to the theories, violent and property crimes are preventable if we intervene in three areas: motivation, guardianship, and target hardening. This is often referred to as the *calculus of crime* and has influenced many criminal justice policies. The rationale is that if a target's risk overwhelms the reward (i.e., the target is expensive but heavy or is encased in anti-theft devices), the potential offender will move on to an easier target. As such, we have seen the growth of locks, anti-theft devices, and alarms aimed at reducing the attractiveness of a potential crime target (Clarke, 2009). In a similar vein, policies aimed at increasing the supervision and visibility of places, things, and items have grown as well. These include redesigning commercial and private spaces to increase visibility, improving lighting on streets and around buildings, advising people to avoid spaces at night or when alone, and increasing foot patrols and neighborhood watches. Finally, to decrease target attractiveness and increase guardianship, well-known policies aimed at curbing "civil incivilities" (Salem & Lewis, 1986) and "broken windows" advocate for the increased policing of public order offenses like loitering, public drunkenness, and vandalism to keep potential offenders away (Kelling & Wilson, 1982). While the results of these "broken windows" policies are mixed, they have been responsible for the increase in the use of warrantless searches and criminal justice contact within poor, minority communities (Harcourt & Ludwig, 2007). Misdemeanor charges and their resultant fees and fines have proliferated within poor, minority communities across the United States (Harris et al., 2011).

While criminological theory has a storied history in criminal justice policies in the United States, we now turn our attention to the review of contemporary criminal justice theories. We review five of these theories: focal concerns, racial threat, restorative justice, cumulative disadvantage, and criminal justice systems theory. For each perspective, we review the existing literature and the theory's application to criminal justice policy.

Contemporary Criminal Justice Theories

Focal Concerns Theory

Focal concerns theory originated as an attempt to explain the decision-making processes for juvenile delinquents in their environments (Miller, 1958). It has since been integrated to explain the interaction between the criminal justice apparatus and society as a whole. From the criminal themselves to each of the criminal justice system actors, each actor has a different set of focal concerns that dictate how each case is ultimately processed. For instance, judges cite concern over public safety as a key "focal concern" in applying sentences (Steffensmeier et al., 1998). The actors in the criminal justice system, such as prosecutors, judges, and even parole officers, all work in an environment of uncertainty where they are expected to make decisions based on limited knowledge on offenders and their circumstances, which causes a reliance on cues to mitigate some of this uncertainty (Albonetti, 1991; Huebner & Bynum, 2006). These cues play a key role in how each criminal justice actor's focal concerns act when handling a case. We review research using focal concerns theory to explain the behavior of prosecutors and judges below. Table 11.2 provides a summary of how focal concerns theory operates in criminal justice decision-making.

TABLE 11.2 Focal Concerns Theory

Actor	Focal Concern	Problems Addressed
Prosecution	Bring offenders to adjudication for processing	Evaluate circumstances of each case and determine path forward
Judges	Assess blameworthiness or culpability of offenders	Judges enforce law or procedure
Sentencing	Through sentencing, judges incapacitate dangerous offenders to deter potential future offending	Judges represent their community's interests to keep communities safe

Prosecution

The focal concerns that guide prosecutors' decision-making reference the seriousness of the offense, the degree of harm to the victims, and the culpability of the suspects when determining how to handle each case (Holleran et al., 2010). On the one hand, convictions are seen as a measure of a prosecutor's effectiveness, while pleas are a method for obtaining more certain convictions, thus preventing trial (Ulmer et al., 2007). The public has little perception of prosecutors' roles and how they perform their duties, how powerful they are, and how misunderstood their role is to society (Forst, 2012). The bulk of crimes go unreported, and for those crimes that result in an arrest, mitigating circumstances such as lack of evidence could cause the case to be declined (Forst, 2012). Prosecutors need to evaluate each set of circumstances unique to each case in order to make a sound decision, which cannot be made with a formula, thus potentially opening the door for bias along each step of this process.

For every 15 defendants to be brought to a prosecutor by law enforcement, only one will go before a judge for trial (Forst, 2012). Prosecutors play substantial roles in helping judges recommend sentences, and they bargain with defendants with plea agreements that offer alternatives to trial, which can be risky and costly to courts (Forst, 2012). Many district attorneys are accountable to the public through voting; however, the true nature of their successes or failures is often shrouded in secrecy to protect the reputation of the office and to avoid public embarrassment (Forst, 2012).

Prosecutorial operations are not standardized, jurisdictions vary significantly by locale, and prosecutors could be selective of cases to pursue to maintain clearance rates. Accordingly, "the proactive approach thus results in selective patterns of enforcement and sanctioning, involving increased levels of intersystem coordination and exchanges that can combine increased enforcement with reduced sanctions for offenders" (Hagan, 1989, p. 127). This process places a considerable amount of power in the hands of prosecutors as they assess focal concerns and negotiate plea deals with offenders to gain the leverage needed for other cases (Bushway & Redlich, 2012). Also, this takes power out of the hands of judges and places discretion in the hands of the prosecutors (Hagan, Hewitt, & Alwin, 1979; Mauer, 2006). Add mandatory minimum prison sentences to the mix, and prosecutors are de facto granted further discretionary powers to charge a defendant in how they negotiate pleas or even in their sentencing recommendations made to judges (Mauer, 2006).

Judicial Decision-Making

From a judge's perspective, sentencing decisions reflect their focal concerns assessments of the blameworthiness or culpability of offenders, desire to protect the community by incapacitating dangerous offenders or deterring potential offending behavior, and concerns about the practical consequences, or social costs, of their decisions (Holleran et al., 2010). When using discretion, prosecutors still have to consider the strength of evidence and how they allocate resources, potentially opening the door for bias at every step (Forst, 2012). While prosecutors have immense power in determining which cases will be pled out versus which cases will be tried, judges have immense power in applying guidelines for sentencing even for cases that have been pled out. However, judges also have the power to allow or disallow evidence, they interpret procedure, they relay instructions to the jury, and they have discretion in handing down sentences.

While on one the hand judges have tremendous discretion if a case makes it to a trial, that power has been relatively neutralized through the mechanism of the plea bargain (Alexander, 2012; Bushway & Redlich, 2012; Ulmer et al., 2007). On the other hand, judicial decision-making can alter the entire course of a case, particularly concerning sentencing. Extra-legal circumstances, such as an offender's criminal history, financial support, social network, and pretrial detention status, are all factors related to sentence discrepancies (Wooldredge, 2011). Even when a judge grants bail as a condition of release or when they hand down a monetary sanction as punishment, a "punishment continuum" is then triggered for those who are in the custody of the criminal justice system (Harris, 2016). Through this continuum, judges hand down punishments such as jail time or legal financial obligations (LFOs) such as fines or restitution that are monitored by clerks (Harris, 2016). The clerks then report to the prosecutor who initially brought the charge if the offender has not made appropriate progress on their LFO (Harris, 2016). The prosecutor then has discretion on whether to prosecute the offender further if they neglected their obligation, creating additional exposure to additional LFOs or even incarceration (Harris, 2016). Each of these decisions can be examined through the focal concerns theory. This continuum opens yet another portal for discretion from all of the players in the criminal justice system, particularly judges, where the interpretation of local laws and each player's priorities in these jurisdictions further impact how laws and sentences are enforced (Harris, 2016).

Racial Threat Theory and Critical Criminology

The racial threat perspective suggests that as the relative size of a minority group increases, the majority group members perceive a growing threat to their positions and will take steps to reduce the competition (Blalock, 1967; Parker et al., 2005). Studies of racial threat theory focus on how people react to others from different races with social controls (Enos, 2016). Beginning with Key's (1949) study on the politics of White supremacy in the Jim Crow era of the Louisiana Democratic Party, racial threat studies have examined various aspects of social control such as the size of a police force, their arrest rates, and incarceration rates (Eitle et al., 2002). Within criminology, numerous studies have examined the various apparatuses that act as social control mechanisms (see Eitle et al., 2002; Enos, 2016; Parker et al., 2005 as examples).

Racial hostility and excessive discipline often led students to disengage from the classroom, with African American schoolchildren twice as likely to face discipline as White students (Rocque & Paternoster, 2011). However, racialized social control is not limited to schools. Municipalities, including progressive cities such as Seattle, have adopted anti-loitering ordinances for drug sales and prostitution in public parks and tourist areas that have similarities to vagrancy laws that were prevalent during the Jim Crow era (Beckett & Herbert, 2010). Serious reforms such as drug courts did not take shape for drug offenders until members of the White middle-class had accumulated records for nonviolent drug offenses (Quinones, 2015). African Americans are more likely to be the targets of a routine traffic stop, less likely to report that the police had a legitimate reason for the stop, and less likely to report that police acted appropriately (Lundman & Kaufman, 2006). The dramatic increase of legal financial obligations since the 1990s has added further surveillance for individuals convicted of minor offenses (Harris, 2016). Even the sanctions for cocaine (more popular with wealthier individuals) were much less severe compared to crack, which was a cheaper form of cocaine that was popular in the inner city, and open to much harsher mandatory minimum sentencing guidelines (Alexander, 2012, pp. 51–54; Mauer, 2006, p. 61). Racialized justice often utilizes various social control mechanisms to achieve its aims.

Restorative Justice

Restorative justice is a framework for healing the wounds caused by a crime rather than to impose a harsh sentence (Braithwaite, 2007). As a result, restorative justice places power in the hands of the people within a community by allowing the victim and the offender to discuss what can be done to repair the harm caused by the offense (Braithwaite, 2007). Crime tests our solidarity, so when codified norms are violated, the reaction to that violation is a characteristic societal reaction called "punishment," which can be an emotional reaction to an offense (Durkheim, 1972). Crime hurts, and therefore justice should heal society, and especially heal relationships (Braithwaite, 2007). Through restorative justice, the offenders and victims of a crime participate together and heal as a whole (Braithwaite, 2007).

Even though some societies, especially the United States, have extremely high incarceration rates, restorative justice is politically popular (Braithwaite, 2007). Minor nonviolent crimes such as drug possession and even loitering have caused individuals to incur long prison sentences or even large monetary fines. Several restorative justice initiatives, such as reformed sentencing guidelines for nonviolent crimes and the implementation of drug courts, have shown success in keeping individuals out of prison for minor crimes, and these programs have helped to limit the damage caused by crime. Once the opioid epidemic began sweeping through middle-class White communities, legislators began seeing first-hand the effects of the epidemic and how challenging a criminal record that reflected minor drug-related crimes such as possession or theft is to their constituents (Quinones, 2015). Rather than relying on incarceration that can cost a state tens of thousands of dollars per inmate per year, treatment has always been more effective and cheaper than prison (Quinones, 2015).

While restorative justice initiatives like drug courts have shown encouraging results, more restorative justice initiatives need to be considered related to reintegrative shaming, which offers forgiveness and a willingness to reintegrate an offender back into society (Braithwaite, 2007). As sentences for many gang-related or drug-related crimes began to carry hefty mandatory minimums, those who served long prison terms with little to no work experience were often unable to even qualify for jobs and were thus left behind (Bushway, 2011). Reforms include the removal of background checks and questions on prior criminal records for applicants, as well as pushes for increased vocational training for incarcerated inmates (Bushway, 2011). In addition to achieving job security, the use of monetary sanctions has increased from 25% of cases in 1991 to 66% of cases in 2004. These fees support court costs and victims' funds, surcharges that add interest to unpaid balances, the cost of public defenders, charges related to a stay in jail, victims' impact panels, and even judicial retirement funds (Harris, 2016). As a result, even when individuals are free from prison custody, legal financial obligations act as criminal justice custodians that serve as a punishment continuum (Harris, 2016).

Cumulative Disadvantage and Criminal Justice

Cumulative disadvantage theory emphasizes how early advantage or disadvantage is critical to how cohorts become differentiated over time (Ferraro & Kelly-Moore, 2003). Those without resources are caught up in a process that removes them from potential future success (Merton, 1988). With a lack of resources in a community comes a lack of economic opportunity, which leads to increased threats of crime within that community. Given this lack of opportunity, pervasive poverty distributed throughout entire neighborhoods, and increasing hopelessness of life in these disadvantaged neighborhoods, a social psychological dynamic is set in motion to produce a culture of class and racial segregation (Massey & Denton, 1993). In sum, as James Baldwin stated in *Nobody Knows My Name*: "Anyone who has ever struggled with poverty knows how extremely expensive it is to be poor" (Harris, 2016, p. 52).

The structural organization of society plays a profound role in shaping an individual's life chances (Massey & Denton, 1993). By removing poor Black people from job networks and limiting their exposure to people with stable histories of work and family formation, Black people became isolated from mainstream American society (Massey & Denton, 1993; Wilson, 1987). Further concentrating cumulative disadvantage was the War on Drugs, first declared by Nixon in 1973 but rapidly expanded by his successors (Alexander, 2012; Mauer, 2006). As a result of the War on Drugs, there was a 600% increase in the U.S. prison population between 1972 and 2004 (Mauer, 2006), largely due to roughly half of state and federal inmates serving time for nonviolent offenses (Mauer, 2006). Policies such as "broken windows" policing, which allocated law enforcement resources to disadvantaged communities; stop-and-frisk policies, which allow police to search anyone they deem as "suspicious"; and mandatory minimum sentencing for nonviolent drug crimes ushered in a new Jim Crow era that severely limited economic opportunities for minorities and forced already disadvantaged people into a perpetuating cycle of concentrated disadvantage (Alexander, 2012; Beckett & Herbert, 2010; Mauer, 2006; Rios et al., 2020).

Criminal Justice Systems Theory

Criminal justice systems theory outlines a process through which each criminal justice institution is regulated by the needs of the overall system (Bernard et al., 2015; Van Gigch, 1978). Much like an assembly line, this sequential system receives an input and prepares that item for the next stage of the process. However, in this system the "items" are people involved in the criminal justice system. Because of the vast array of components within the criminal justice system, research has produced relatively few specific theories to interpret the research that the field has produced (Bernard & Engel, 2001). In order to understand how criminal justice agencies act as a system, we have to understand how its components interact with individuals throughout the processing of a criminal case.

TABLE 11.3 General Systems Theory and Criminal Justice

Criminal Justice System Interactions	Case Processing Pressures
1. Criminal justice consists of multiple layers of systems in terms of input, output, and processing	Input is offender, who is processed, then placed back into society as output
2. Criminal justice system processes "cases"	System is funded by the public, who seeks vengeance
3. Offenders are the products of this system	Offenders deemed "defective" by society
4. Limited agreement on how to achieve the goals of this system	Priorities of police, prosecutors, judges, and jails could potentially be different
5. Lack of agreement between system actors because system lacks objective standards that predict future deviant acts	Each actor within the system has a degree of discretion
6. "Backward" pressure caused by backlog of cases	Pressure added to each additional stage to relieve pressure
7. Resulting pressure means cases are processed faster	Expedited processing means something might get missed
8. "Forward" pressure arises because of discretion	Infinite number of variations in uncontrolled environment makes predicting the future virtually impossible
9. Progressive narrowing of processing capacity within criminal justice system's hierarchy	Pressure to close cases that will stay closed

Source: Bernard et al. (2005).

Bernard and Engel (2001) suggest organizing theoretical research on individual criminal justice agents' behavior, then explaining the behavior of those agents through individual characteristics as well as the examination of the behavior of criminal justice organizations as functioning entities. This organizational scheme allows for comparisons of how society interacts within their respective environments (Bernard & Engel, 2001). Table 11.3 provides a summary of criminal justice systems theories. Feeley (2006) suggests two models that expand on Etzioni's *goal model,* focused on organizational effectiveness, and a *functional systems model,* focused on the system achieving a goal (see Etzioni, 1960). Hagan and colleagues (2007) view the criminal justice system as a "loosely coupled system" where each entity is responsive while still maintaining independent identities.

Bernard and colleagues (2005) offer nine points outlining each part of the criminal justice system and case processing pressures. Criminal justice consists of multiple layers of more encompassing systems in terms of input, processing, and output. First, the input is the offender, who is processed and placed back into society as output. Second, criminal justice processes "cases," which include offenders, victims, and the public. With the arrest of the individual and their adjudication, the criminal justice system, funded by the public, is tasked with seeking vengeance on behalf of the public through punishment while also deterring others who might consider committing a similar act (Durkheim, 1972). Third, the products of this system, the offenders, tend to return to society as "defective," as deemed by society. Through the lack of opportunity that a record of formal sanctions such as a conviction or incarceration can cause, the criminal justice system potentially produces too many defective products that potentially commit additional crimes (Bernard et al., 2005), thus entrapping these defective products into a perpetuating cycle of concentrated disadvantage (Alexander, 2012; Beckett & Herbert, 2010; Mauer, 2006; Rios et al., 2020). Fourth, there is a limited argument on how to achieve the goals of criminal justice processing. Given that there are many different layers in the criminal justice system that are tasked with different aspects of processing an offender, there may be different ideas in how to process that offender; however, the goal of protecting the general public from future criminal activity remains the same. Fifth, the lack of agreement between the system actors arises because the system lacks objective standards that predict future deviant acts. A police officer can decide if an arrest is warranted for a crime, a prosecutor can pursue the maximum penalty allowed even for a first-time offender if they feel that this act could be repeated, or a judge could elect to "throw the book" at the convicted person or show mercy through leniency (Bernard et al., 2005). Sixth, if the system is unable to process cases in a timely manner, "backward pressure" builds up, resulting in each additional stage being pressured to increase output to relieve pressure, meaning a prosecutor or a judge could have too big a caseload or a prison could be overcrowded (Bernard et al., 2005). Seventh, that backward pressure means that it becomes faster and easier to decide that processing is complete. The system is motivated to process input as quickly and as easily as possible. Eighth, forward pressure could arise because of discretion, meaning that we cannot accurately predict whether an offender who is not arrested for an act will commit that act in the future. Lastly, the progressive narrowing of processing capacity within the criminal justice system's hierarchy means that criminal justice agents must be able to "close cases that will stay closed" (Bernard et al., 2005, p. 208).

In essence, the criminal justice system causes an offender to interact with a unique system at each criminal justice process step. The initial interaction with a police officer means you are interacting with a single actor within the large apparatus that is a modern police department. Prosecutors work on behalf of an elected official within a large apparatus or they are the elected official themself and are responsible to the electorate. Even a defense attorney is accountable to the firm that employs them. A defendant's case is adjudicated by an appointed or elected official, who works on behalf of the people but is chosen to do so by those in elite circles of power. If the offender is fined as their punishment, a court clerk employed by the public then surveils the offender. If the offender is sentenced to prison, that system further processes the offender through many subsystems within that particular system once the offender first walks through the prison's doors.

Summary

The workings of the criminal justice system are complicated and sometimes contradictory. The system spans the state and federal agencies and nonprofit and for-profit organizations that service and supplement the legal system. While theorizing in criminal justice is not new and is at the heart of criminological theory, recent developments in criminal justice theory are noteworthy. We have theories that explain judicial and prosecutorial discretion (focal concerns theory), disproportionate minority contact (racial threat theory), reentry and reintegration (reintegrative shaming theory), and why people exiting the criminal justice system are often worse off than when they entered (cumulative disadvantage theory). These criminal justice theories were developed through criminological theorizing and borrowed heavily from criminology in terms of their assumptions about human nature. We encourage readers to think creatively about criminal justice theorizing so that they can help design future theories to explain and predict the workings of the criminal justice system.

References

Albonetti, C. A. An integration of theories to explain judicial discretion. *Social Problems, 38*(2), 247–266. https://psycnet.apa.org/doi/10.1525/sp.1991.38.2.03a00090

Alexander, M. (2012). *The New Jim Crow: Mass incarceration in the age of colorblindness.* New Press. https://www.google.com/books/edition/The_New_Jim_Crow/_SKbzXqmawoC?hl=en

Beccaria, C. (2009). *On crimes and punishments and other writings.* University of Toronto Press. https://www.google.com/books/edition/Beccaria_On_Crimes_and_Punishments_and_O/HwbvF8ymZawC?hl=en

Beckett, K., & Herbert, S. (2010). *Banished: The new social control in urban America.* Oxford University Press. https://oxford.universitypressscholarship.com/view/10.1093/acprof:oso/9780195395174.001.0001/acprof-9780195395174

Bernard, T. J., & Engel, R. S. (2001). Conceptualizing criminal justice theory. *Justice Quarterly, 18*(1), 1–30. https://doi.org/10.1080/07418820100094801

Bernard, T. J., Paoline, E. A., & Pare, P. (2015). General systems theory and criminal justice. *Journal of Criminal Justice, 33*(3), 203–211. https://doi.org/10.1016/j.jcrimjus.2005.02.001

Blalock, H. M. (1967). *Toward a theory of minority group relations.* John Wiley & Sons.

Braithwaite, J. (2007). Encourage restorative justice. *Criminology & Public Policy, 6*(4), 689–696. https://www.ojp.gov/ncjrs/virtual-library/abstracts/encourage-restorative-justice

Braithwaite, J., & Pettit, P. (1992). *Not just deserts: A republican theory of criminal justice.* https://www.google.com/books/edition/Not_Just_Deserts/d5faAAAAMAAJ?hl=en&gbpv=1&bsq=Not+just+deserts:+A+republican+theory+of+criminal+justice&dq=Not+just+deserts:+A+republican+theory+of+criminal+justice&printsec=frontcover

Bushway, S. B. (2011). Labor markets and crime. In J. Q. Wilson & J. Petersilia (Eds.), *Crime and public policy* (pp. 183–209). Oxford University Press. https://www.google.com/books/edition/Crime_and_Public_Policy/C3Gi1ob0W4oC?hl=en

Bushway, S. D., & Redlich, A. D. (2012). Is plea bargaining in the "shadow of the trial" a mirage? *Quantitative Criminology, 28*(3), 437–454. https://psycnet.apa.org/doi/10.1007/s10940-011-9147-5

Clarke, R. V. (1980). Situational crime prevention: Theory and practice. *British Journal of Criminology, 20*(2), 136–147. http://www.jstor.org/stable/23636692

Clarke, R. V. (2009). Situational crime prevention: Theoretical background and current practice. In M. D. Krohn, A. J. Lizotte, & G. P. Hall (Eds.), *Handbook on crime and deviance* (pp. 259-276). New York: Springer Science + Business Media.

Cloward, R. A., & Ohlin, L. E. (2013). *Delinquency and opportunity: A study of delinquent gangs.* Routledge. https://www.google.com/books/edition/Delinquency_and_Opportunity/Cb2AAAAAQBAJ?hl=en&gbpv=1&printsec=frontcover

Cohen, A. K. (1955). *Delinquent boys; The culture of the gang.* US Department of Justice. https://www.ojp.gov/ncjrs/virtual-library/abstracts/delinquent-boys-culture-gang

Cohen, L. E., & Felson, M. (1979). Social change and crime rate trends: A routine activity approach. *American Sociological Review,* 588–608. https://www.ojp.gov/ncjrs/virtual-library/abstracts/social-change-and-crime-rate-trends-routine-activity-approach

Cornish, D. B., & Clarke, R. V. (Eds.). (2014). *The reasoning criminal: Rational choice perspectives on offending* (1st ed.). Routledge. https://doi.org/10.4324/9781315134482

Cullen, F. T., Pratt, T. C., & Turanovic, J. J. (2016). It's hopeless: Beyond zero-tolerance supervision. *Criminology & Pubic Policy, 15*, 1215. https://doi.org/10.1111/1745-9133.12260

Durkheim, E. (1972). Forms of social solidarity. In A. Giddens (Ed.), *Emile Durkheim: Selected writings* (pp. 123–140). Cambridge University Press. https://doi.org/10.1017/CBO9780511628085.007

Eitle, D., D'Alessio, S. D., & Stolzenberg, L. (2002). Racial threat and social control: A test of the political, economic, and threat of black crime hypotheses. *Social Forces, 81*(2), 557–576. http://www.jstor.org/stable/3086482

Enos, R. D. (2016). What the demolition of public housing teaches us about the impact of racial threat on political behavior. *American Journal of Political Science, 60*(1), 123–143. https://doi.org/10.1111/ajps.12156

Etzioni, A. (1960). Two approaches to organizational analysis: A critique and a suggestion. *Administrative Science Quarterly, 5*(2), 257–278. https://doi.org/10.2307/2390780

Fernandes, A. D., & Crutchfield, R. D. (2018). Race, crime, and criminal justice: Fifty years since The Challenge of Crime in a Free Society. *Criminology & Public Policy, 17*(2), 397–417. https://doi.org/10.1111/1745-9133.12361

Ferraro, K. F., & Kelly-Moore, J. A. (2003). Cumulative disadvantage and health: Long-term consequences of obesity? *American Sociological Review, 68*(5), 707–729. https://www.ncbi.nlm.nih.gov/pmc/articles/PMC3348542/

Forst, B. (2012). Prosecution. In J. Q. Wilson & J. Petersilia (Eds.), *Crime and public policy* (pp. 437–466). Oxford University Press. https://books.google.com/books?id=C3Gi1ob0W4oC&newbks=0&hl=en

Gowan, T., & Whetstone, S. (2012). Making the criminal addict: Subjectivity and social control in a strong-arm rehab. *Punishment & Society, 14*(1), 69–93. https://doi.org/10.1177/1462474511424684

Hagan, J. (1989). Why is there so little criminal justice theory? Neglected macro- and micro-level links between organization and power. *Journal of Research in Crime and Delinquency, 26*(2), 116–135. https://doi.org/10.1177%2F0022427889026002002

Hagan, J., Hewitt, J. D., & Alwin, D. F. (1979). Ceremonial justice-crime and punishment in a loosely coupled system. *Social Forces, 58*(2), 506–527. https://www.ojp.gov/ncjrs/virtual-library/abstracts/ceremonial-justice-crime-and-punishment-loosely-coupled-system

Harcourt, B. E., & Ludwig, J. (2007). Reefer madness: Broken windows policing and misdemeanor marijuana arrests in New York City, 1989–2000. *Criminology & Public Policy, 6*, 165. https://doi.org/10.1111/j.1745-9133.2007.00427.x

Harris, A. (2016). *A pound of flesh: Monetary sanctions as punishment for the poor.* Russell Sage Foundation. http://www.jstor.org/stable/10.7758/9781610448550

Harris, A., Evans, H., & Beckett, K. (2011). Courtesy stigma and monetary sanctions: Toward a socio-cultural theory of punishment. *American Sociological Review, 76*(2), 234–264. https://doi.org/10.1177%2F0003122411400054

Holleran, D., Beichner, D., & Spohn, C. (2010). Examining charging agreement between police and prosecutors in rape cases. *Crime & Delinquency, 56*(3), 385–413. https://doi.org/10.1177%2F1362480617693706

Huebner, B. M., & Bynum, T. S. (2006). An analysis of parole decision making using a sample of sex offenders: A focal concerns perspective. *Criminology, 44*(4), 961–992. https://doi.org/10.1111/j.1745-9125.2006.00069.x

Jeffery, C. R. (1978). Criminology as an interdisciplinary behavioral science. *Criminology, 16*(2), 149–169. https://doi.org/10.1111/j.1745-9125.1978.tb00085.x

Jencks, C. (1992). *Rethinking social policy: Race, poverty, and the underclass.* https://www.ojp.gov/ncjrs/virtual-library/abstracts/rethinking-social-policy-race-poverty-and-underclass

Kelling, G. L., & Wilson, J. Q. (1982). Broken windows. *Atlantic Monthly, 249*(3), 29–36, 38. https://www.ojp.gov/ncjrs/virtual-library/abstracts/broken-windows

Key, V. O. (1949). *Southern politics in state and nation.* A. A. Knopf.

Lemert, E. M. (1999). Primary and secondary deviance. In S. H. Traub & C. B. Little (Eds.), *Theories of deviance* (pp. 385–390). Itasca, IL: Peacock Publications.

Lewis, O. (1966). The culture of poverty. *Scientific American, 215*(4), 19–25. http://www.jstor.org/stable/24931078

Lundman, R. J., & Kaufman, R. L. (2006). Driving while black: Effects of race, ethnicity, and gender on citizen self-reports of traffic stops and police actions. *Criminology, 41*(1), 195–220. https://doi.org/10.1111/j.1745-9125.2003.tb00986.x

Massey, D. J., & Denton, N. A. (1993). *American Apartheid: Segregation and the making of the underclass.* Harvard University Press.

Mauer, M. (2006). *Race to incarcerate.* New Press. https://www.google.com/books/edition/Race_to_Incarcerate/gTFVSw8Ip94C?hl=en&gbpv=1&dq=Race+to+Incarcerate&printsec=frontcover

Merton, R. K. (1938). Social structure and anomie. *American Sociological Review*, 3(5), 672–682. https://doi.org/10.2307/2084686

Merton, R. K. (1988). The Matthew Effect in science, II: Cumulative advantage and the symbolism of intellectual property. *Isis*, 79(4), 606–623. http://www.jstor.org/stable/234750

Meyer, W. J., & Cole, C. M. (1997). Physical and chemical castration of sex offenders: A review. *Journal of Offender Rehabilitation*, 25(3–4), 1–18. https://doi.org/10.1300/J076v25n03_01

Miller, W. B. (1958, Summer). Lower class culture as a generating milieu of gang delinquency. *Journal of Social Issues*, 14(3), 5–19. https://www.ojp.gov/ncjrs/virtual-library/abstracts/lower-class-culture-generating-milieu-gang-delinquency

Moynihan, D. P. (1965, March). *The Negro family: The case for national action*. US Department of Labor. https://www.dol.gov/general/aboutdol/history/webid-moynihan

Parker, K. F., Stults, B. J., & Rice, S. K. (2005). Racial threat, concentrated disadvantage and social control: Considering the macro-level sources of variation in arrests. *Criminology*, 43(4), 1111–1134. https://www.ojp.gov/ncjrs/virtual-library/abstracts/racial-threat-concentrated-disadvantage-and-social-control

Quinones, S. (2015). *Dreamland: The true tale of America's opiate epidemic*. Bloomsbury Press. https://www.google.com/books/edition/Dreamland/S9fVBgAAQBAJ?hl=en&gbpv=1&dq=Dreamland:+The+True+Tale+of+America's+Opiate+Epidemic&printsec=frontcover

Radelet, M. L., & Akers, R. L. (1996). Deterrence and the death penalty: The views of the experts. *Journal of Criminal Law and Criminology (1973-)*, 87(1), 1–16. https://doi.org/10.2307/1143970

Rafter, N. (2004). Earnest A. Hooton and the biological tradition in American criminology. *Criminology*, 42(3), 735–772. https://doi.org/10.1111/j.1745-9125.2004.tb00535.x

Rios, V. M., Prieto, G., & Ibarra, J. M. (2020). *Mano suave-mano dura*: Legitimacy policing and Latino stop-and-frisk. *American Sociological Review*, 85(1), 58–75. https://journals.sagepub.com/doi/pdf/10.1177/0003122419897348

Rocque, M., & Paternoster, R. (2011). Understanding the antecedents of the "school to jail" link. *Journal of Criminal Law and Criminology*, 101(2), 633–665. https://www.researchgate.net/publication/257942409_Understanding_the_antecedents_of_the_School-to-Jail_Link_The_relationship_between_race_and_school_discipline

Roshier, B. (1989). *Controlling crime: The classical perspective in criminology*. Lyceum Books. https://www.ojp.gov/ncjrs/virtual-library/abstracts/controlling-crime-classical-perspective-criminology

Salem, G. W., & Lewis, D. A. (1986). *Fear of crime: Incivility and the production of a social problem* [Report]. Transaction Publishers. https://www.ojp.gov/ncjrs/virtual-library/abstracts/fear-crime-incivility-and-production-social-problem

Skeem, J. L., Emke-Francis, P., & Louden, J. E. (2006). Probation, mental health, and mandated treatment: A national survey. *Criminal Justice and Behavior*, 33(2), 158–184. https://doi.org/10.1177%2F0093854805284420

Steffensmeier, D., Ulmer, J., & Kramer, J. (1998). Interaction of race, gender, and age in criminal sentencing: The punishment cost of being young, black, and male. *Criminology*, 36(4), 763–798 https://www.ojp.gov/ncjrs/virtual-library/abstracts/interaction-race-gender-and-age-criminal-sentencing-punishment-cost

Turner, M. G., Sundt, J. L., Applegate, B. K., & Cullen, F. T. (1995). Three strikes and you're out legislation: A national assessment. *Federal Probation*, 59, 16. https://mobile.heinonline.org/HOL/LandingPage?handle=hein.journals/fedpro59&div=44&id=

Ulmer, J. T., Kurlychek, M. C., & Kramer, J. H. (2007). Prosecutorial discretion and the imposition of mandatory minimum sentences. *Journal of Research in Crime and Delinquency*, 44(4), 427–458. https://doi.org/10.1177%2F0022427807305853

Van Gigch, J. P. (1978). *Applied general systems theory*. Harper and Row Publishers.

Wilson, W. J. (1987). *The truly disadvantaged: Inner city, the underclass, and public policy*. University of Chicago Press. https://doi.org/10.1111/j.1467-9906.1989.tb00195.x

Wooldredge, J. (2011). Distinguishing race effects on pre-trial release and sentencing decisions. *Justice Quarterly*, 29(1), 41–75. https://doi.org/10.1080/07418825.2011.559480

Zatz, M. S. (1984). Race, ethnicity, and determinate sentencing: New dimension to an old controversy. *Criminology*, 22(2), 147–171. https://doi.org/10.1111/j.1745-9125.1984.tb00294.x

12

Trauma-Informed Theory in Criminal Justice

Constance L. Chapple and Erin J. Maher

Many children, youth, and adults involved with the criminal justice system have long histories of emotional, psychological, and physical traumas, often stemming from child abuse and neglect (Baglivio et al., 2014; Jones, Worthen, Sharp, & McLeod, 2018). Estimates suggest that upwards of 80% of justice-involved youth report at least one adverse childhood experience (ACE), with parental violence and divorce being the most common and parental mental illness being the least common (Baglivio et al., 2014). This finding is echoed within a sample of justice-involved women, with nearly 90% indicating a history of emotional, physical, or sexual abuse (Pollock, 2002). Children and youth in juvenile justice disproportionately are maltreated (Baglivio et al., 2016), have a criminally involved parent (Rodriguez et al., 2009), have been in foster care (Turney & Wildeman, 2017), and have witnessed violence in their home or on the street (Chauhan & Reppucci, 2009). These youth then become justice-involved adults with trauma histories that are often exacerbated as they age through ongoing victimization (Ford, Grasso, Hawke, & Chapman, 2013), substance abuse (Boppre & Boyer, 2019), and associated financial adversity. Often, youth and adults who have been involved in the criminal justice system have extensive legal and financial obligations, which create additional stress on individuals and families (Link, 2019; Harris, 2016). As such, criminal justice populations often have multiple therapeutic service needs (Green, Miranda, Daroowalla, & Siddique, 2005). In this chapter, the authors review the ACEs and trauma research as it applies to criminal justice involvement. In particular, we examine how trauma such as child maltreatment and exposure to violence is represented in criminological theories such as general strain theory and the gendered pathways perspective and how criminal justice programs integrate trauma-informed responses into treatment, training, and education.

Constance L. Chapple and Erin J. Maher, *Trauma-Informed Theory in Criminal Justice* In: *Handbook of Forensic Social Work.* Edited by: David Axlyn McLeod, Anthony P. Natale, and Kristin W. Mapson, Oxford University Press. © Oxford University Press 2024. DOI: 10.1093/oso/9780197694732.003.0012

Adverse Childhood Experiences and Trauma

For over two decades, our understanding of trauma from both a scientific and practical standpoint has ballooned. It is now understood that our trauma experiences, particularly those that occur in early childhood, have significant and lasting impacts on our development, life course trajectories, and health. A landmark study on ACEs conducted by the Centers for Disease Control and Prevention and Kaiser Permanente from 1995 to 1997 on more than 17,000 members of the health maintenance organization transformed what was known about trauma's impacts on childhood development (Felitti et al., 1998). Figure 12.1 describes the original ACEs, their prevalence in the general population, and the risk behaviors and health conditions that have been shown to be associated with them.

Today, understanding of environmental influences has become embedded in best practices within criminal justice and other human service systems in the United States. In the ACEs study, patients were asked about childhood experiences and current health behaviors and health status. This original study's childhood experiences included 10 items focused on child maltreatment and "family dysfunction." Figure 12.1 presents a visual of the original ACEs, which include experiences with abuse and neglect, parental loss, and other family "dysfunction." The landmark ACEs study found that ACEs are common, with the majority of the sample reporting one or more ACEs. The number of ACEs has a graded dose-response relationship with risky health behaviors in adulthood and, ultimately, morbidity and early mortality (Felitti et al., 1998). This means that as the number of ACEs increases, so does lifetime risk of risky health behaviors.

The pathway by which ACEs affect health is shown in Figure 12.2 and describes a theory of change—how one set of circumstances can lead to another set of circumstances. This information is often shown as a pyramid with historical intergenerational trauma and social conditions at the bottom. These conditions affect neurological development, which can lead to impairment in executive function and decision-making. The link between ACEs and disrupted neurodevelopment occurs based on the brain and body's response to toxic stress. Thus, individuals are more likely to engage in unhealthy behaviors that can lead to disease, disability, and early death. Similarly, the relationship between impaired executive function and criminal behavior has been established, working through the mechanism of low self-control (Altikriti, 2021).

As illustrated in Figure 12.3, toxic stress is distinguished from positive and tolerable stress by prolonged activation and the absence of protective and nurturing relationships that help individuals cope with and end the stress response. ACEs, especially those enduring in their impact, cause toxic stress, which leads to biobehavioral adaptations. Toxic stress results in a fear response that overstimulates neural connections in the brain and leads to instigation of the stress response even in situations where there is little threat. These impulsive responses have negative behavioral consequences that can affect health and mental health in the long term. The overproduction of adrenaline and cortisol implicated in reactions to toxic stress impacts immune function, memory, metabolism, and other physiological responses associated with poor health (National Scientific Council on the Developing Child, 2005/2014). Often the biobehavioral consequences of toxic stress can

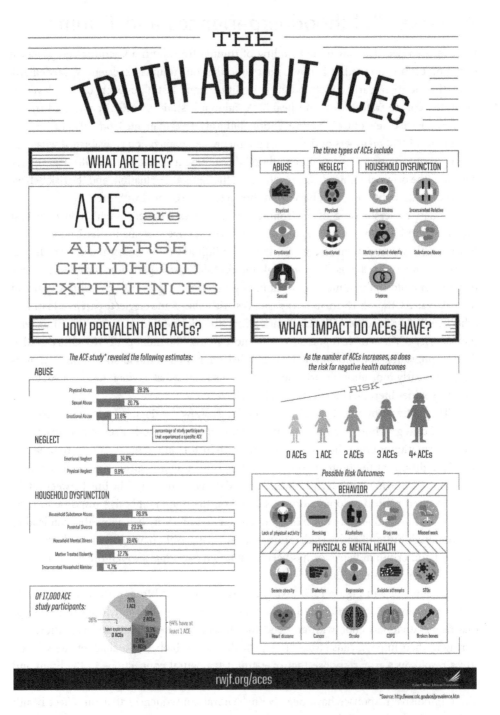

FIGURE 12.1 Overview of Adverse Childhood Experiences Copyright 2013. Robert Wood Johnson Foundation. Used with permission from the Robert Wood Johnson Foundation.

FIGURE 12.2 Pathway by Which ACEs Impact Undesirable Well-Being Outcomes Adapted from Centers for Disease Control and Prevention. (2020). The ACE pyramid [Infographic]. In *About the CDC-Kaiser ACE Study.* https://www.cdc.gov/violenceprevention/childabuseandneglect/acestudy/about.html

be buffered by nurturing and supportive relationships with adults, but the unique nature of ACEs is that the stress occurs within a family dynamic that is often the cause of the stress in the first place. In early childhood, the family is the source of most adult relationships.

Before the ACEs study, social stress theory (Pearlin, 1989) posited a similar relationship between stress and disease. Rather than focusing on traumatic events as the source of stress, this theory emphasizes the role that social disadvantage plays in leading to stress and, ultimately, disease (Pearlin, 1989). Social stress theory views underlying social stratification and inequalities as fundamental to the stressors people experience and their access to buffering resources or mediators, such as social support or coping skills (Pearlin & Aneshensel, 1986). Given the relationship between trauma and social disadvantage, discussed later, as well as the limited number and scope of the original ACEs, this theory complements our understanding of the relationship between experiences, trauma, social positions in society, and outcomes like health, well-being, and criminal justice involvement. Similarly, community psychologists have also recognized the impact of community-level conditions and experiences on individual well-being and how these are not independent of individual experiences and can lead to the same negative health outcomes (Biglan & Hinds, 2009; Coulton, Crampton, Irwin, Spilsbury, & Korbin, 2007). For example, adolescents and young adults who have experienced maltreatment in their families are also more likely to be exposed to violence in the community. Both experiences have a direct negative impact on their mental health (Cecil, Viding, Barker, Guiney, & McCrory, 2014).

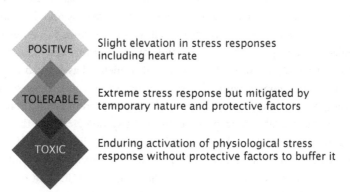

FIGURE 12.3 Types of Stress Adapted from the Center on the Developing Child. Accessed 2023. Toxic stress [Infographic]. In *A guide to toxic stress.* Harvard University. https://developingchild.harvard.edu/science/key-concepts/toxic-stress/

Since this original ACEs study, hundreds of subsequent studies have examined the impact of ACEs on physical, behavioral, and other health outcomes. General population studies have revealed that low-income and non-White populations have a significantly higher number of ACEs (Merrick, Ford, Ports, & Guinn, 2018). Analysis of the National Survey of Children's Health has shown that 13% of children in poverty experience three or more ACEs, compared to only 5% of children in households whose income is at least two times above the federal poverty line. This combined exposure of ACEs and poverty has a compounding and cumulative negative effect on child and adult health as they are also experiencing the stressors associated with poverty (Dong et al., 2004). In other words, social disadvantage and childhood trauma are interrelated, and both the ACEs framework and social stress theory contribute to our understanding of the causal mechanisms between trauma, stress, and disease and death. As mentioned previously, toxic stress stemming from chronic, enduring, or significant trauma can change the "architecture" of the brain in ways that negatively impact executive functioning, which can lead to low self-control, impaired judgement, and poor health decisions (National Scientific Council on the Developing Child, 2005/2014).

Many critiques of the measurement, theory, or application of research using ACEs exist (e.g., Edwards et al., 2019; Finkelhor, 2018; Taylor-Robinson et al., 2018). Given the clustering of ACEs for children in poverty and poor communities, it can be argued that the original ACEs are too limited. As some have done, the universe of adversity in childhood should be expanded to include poverty, parental separation due to immigration policies, historical trauma, genocide, witnessing community violence, and structural racism, to name a few. As described earlier, the mechanisms in the ACEs pyramid, or theory of change, acknowledge these conditions, but the standard measure of individual ACEs does not include them.

An additional critique of the ACEs research framework is that it does not include as much focus on protective factors, resiliency, or social psychological personality traits, such as hope or grit. Thus, a line of research has emerged that includes both ACEs and positive childhood experiences (Morris, Ratliff, & Hays-Grudo, 2020; Sege & Browne, 2017), the latter of which are viewed as playing a moderating or buffering role. Emerging theoretical frameworks incorporate protective relationships and contextual resources as mitigating forces to maladaptive responses to trauma and toxic stress that can impair child development (Hays-Grudo et al., 2021). The concept of resilience has a much longer research tradition for its role in coping with adversity but has some controversy surrounding its definition, components, and roots (Luthar et al., 2000). More recently, hope has gained some traction as an accessible concept representing a psychological trait that mitigates the impact of trauma (Munoz et al., 2020). This body of work alerts the field of the importance of understanding the situational, environmental, and psychological contexts in which childhood adversity occurs that may mitigate the impact of ACEs and other trauma on well-being. This understanding should inform both research and interventions. This advancement to examine the role of protective factors, psychological traits, and positive life experiences combined with ACEs is underutilized but important. Nonetheless, the influence of ACEs research on human service systems, including the criminal justice system, has been significant and paved the way toward trauma-informed approaches that justify this high-level overview of the original study and related theories.

Adverse Childhood Experiences and Criminal Justice Involvement

ACEs and criminal justice involvement interact in several ways. From the child's perspective, the loss of a primary caregiver to incarceration is one of the 10 original ACEs. Researchers have shown that having a parent incarcerated during childhood, even after controlling for demographic and other ACEs, is associated with higher smoking and heavy drinking, particularly among White and Hispanic youth (Gjelsvik et al., 2013). Adolescents who have experienced parental incarceration report significantly higher rates of depression, anxiety, and posttraumatic stress (Heard-Garris et al., 2019; Lee et al., 2013). Children of incarcerated parents are also more likely to engage in risky health behaviors, including having more sexual partners and illicit and prescription drug abuse (Heard-Garris et al., 2018). These impacts are particularly relevant to the United States, which has the highest incarceration rate in the world (Sawyer & Wagner, 2020). In fact, given the prevalence of incarceration in the United States, a national study found that 9% of adolescents have experienced parental incarceration (Heard-Garris et al., 2019).

Researchers have also found that ACEs, particularly child maltreatment, are associated with later criminal justice involvement (Asberg & Renk, 2013; Roos et al., 2016) and criminal behavior (Elklit, Karasoft, Armour, Feddern, & Christoffersen, 2013; Mersky et al., 2012). The association between ACEs and criminal justice involvement also has been documented among specific vulnerable populations such as veterans (Ross, Waterhouse-Bradley, Contractor, & Armour, 2018) and homeless people with mental illness (Edalati et al., 2017). In other words, ACEs are not simply associated with morbidity and mortality but also crime and the criminal justice system.

Adverse Childhood Experiences and Theories of Crime

Ellis and Dietz's (2017) PAIR of ACEs framework highlights the relationship between ACEs and crime when complementary theoretical frameworks are introduced. The tree roots reflect systemic inequalities, which lead to the negative life experiences theorized in both social stress theory described above and social disorganization theory. Social disorganization theory posits that social, economic, and cultural conditions of inequality within society or neighborhoods weaken social bonds and make criminal behavior more likely. Adverse social conditions lead to weakened social ties, increased residential instability, and social community isolation, which in turn lead to a breakdown in pro-social norms and proliferation of neighborhood crime and criminal behavior (Faris, 1955; Sampson, 1993; Sampson & Groves, 1989; Sampson & Wilson, 1995). Thus, experiences of trauma and adversity operate on the macro or structural scale, influencing individual behaviors.

One of the most robust, individual-level predictors of criminal offending and criminal justice contact is self-control (Gottfredson & Hirschi, 1990). Self-control is defined as the ability to control impulses, empathize with others, and develop persistence. Individuals with higher levels of self-control are more likely to see the costs of criminal behavior in terms of financial, emotional, physical, and social penalties and, as such, refrain from engaging in crime. Gottfredson and Hirschi (1990) suggest that self-control develops by age 10 through sustained parental attachment, supervision, and reasoned punishment and is stable throughout life. However, not all parenting is positive, and researchers indicate that negative parental behaviors like criminal offending (Boutwell & Beaver, 2010), child abuse (Bunch et al., 2018; Chapple, Hope, & Whiteford, 2005), and substance abuse (Chapple, Hope, et al., 2005; Nofziger, 2008) inhibit the development of self-control in childhood. Each of these negative parental behaviors can be subsumed under the ACEs construct.

To assess the causal effect of ACEs on the development of self-control, Meldrum et al. (2020) found that ACEs are tied to significantly lower levels of childhood self-control. Physical or emotional abuse (Bunch et al., 2018; Henschel et al., 2014; Kort-Butler et al., 2011), child neglect (Chapple, Hope, et al., 2005), and negative discipline (Hay, 2001; Vaughn, DeLisi, Beaver, & Wright, 2009) all inhibit the development of children's self-control. Also, the absence of positive parenting in early childhood, as measured by physical and emotional neglect, significantly predicted lower self-control levels in older children (Chapple, Hope, et al., 2005). Victimization and its adverse effect on self-control are not limited to experiences with child maltreatment. Researchers have found that victims of violence (Agnew et al., 2011; Davis et al., 2017) and even those who simply witness violence (Monahan, King, Shulman, Cauffan, & Chassin, 2015) report significantly lower levels of self-control. These findings persist net of controls for children's strain and stress reactions (Agnew et al., 2011; Bunch et al., 2018).

Finally, researchers find a notable intergenerational effect of self-control, with children whose parents exhibit low self-control reporting significantly lower levels of self-control themselves (Nofziger, 2008). The previous literature points to the reality for many children that often, family life is chaotic and riddled with multiple domains of adversity. Each of these experiences, and the timing in which they occur, can have substantial, independent effects on inhibiting the development of self-control for children.

Strain Theories: Anomie and Psychological Strain

Other theories in criminology also point to the criminogenic effects that adversity and trauma have on individuals. Beginning with Merton's anomie theory (Merton, 1938), social inequality creates an unequal playing field resulting in blocked access to conventional routes (education and work) to achieve financial goals. Blocked access creates strain and *anomie*, or a feeling of normlessness and social isolation, which is then relieved by substance use (*retreat*) or criminal behavior (*innovation*). Cohen (1955) writes at length about how failure at "middle class measuring rods" via educational success creates boys who are likely to alleviate these educational and social class strains through criminal behavior. Additionally, Cloward and Ohlin (2013) suggest that boys' stress at blocked conventional and criminal opportunities facilitates gangs' formation. Boys who experience strain when both conventional and criminal opportunities are blocked are likely to alleviate that strain by forming their conflict-ridden subcultures.

In a more recent iteration of strain theory, Agnew's general strain theory (1992) expands the scope of stressors beyond academic or financial challenges. It includes stressors emerging from "(1) strain as the actual or anticipated failure to achieve positively valued goals, (2) strain as the actual or anticipated removal of positively valued stimuli, and (3) strain as the actual or anticipated presentation of negatively valued stimuli" (Agnew, 1992, p. 47). As such, stressors in general strain theory include adverse experiences with child maltreatment, victimization, bullying, parental death and divorce, and witnessing violence. It is a far more comprehensive theory of toxic stressors than earlier criminological strain theories and highlights the influence of stressors on youth offending, running away, and substance use. According to Agnew, youth have a "fight or flight" response to cumulative or toxic stress and either confront the stressor in an aggressive way or retreat and manage negative emotions such as fear, loneliness, or sadness through retreat into substance use or fleeing a noxious situation (Agnew & White, 1992). Agnew's general strain theory is similar to the ACEs perspective as he suggests that delinquent responses are dependent on the accumulation and intensity of stressors (Botchkovar & Broidy, 2013) and the absence of healthy coping mechanisms, known as resilience factors in social stress theory (Patterson, 2002).

Gendered Pathways Perspective

Coming on the heels of general strain theory was an understanding that strains and stressors vary by individuals and, at times, by gender (Daly, 1992; Steffensmeier & Allen, 1996). The gendered pathways to crime perspective emerged from this idea that etiological pathways to crime differ for men and women and boys and girls (Heimer & DeCoster, 1999). According to this perspective, women and girls commit crimes for different reasons and often with male, intimate co-offenders (Sommers & Baskin, 1993) through different mechanisms such as reactions to intimate victimization and sexual assault (Belknap & Holsinger, 2006). According to the gendered pathways perspective, women and girls require different programs and treatments (Salisbury & Van Voorhis, 2009).

The gendered pathways framework suggests that female trauma is complex, is often sexually related (DeHart & Moran, 2015), and can involve leaving abusive living arrangements (Burgess-Proctor et al., 2016), which often differentiates it from male offending. Also, the gendered pathways perspective integrates macro-social mechanisms of sexual inequality by suggesting that girls' and women's disempowered social status increases their gendered victimization risk in public and private settings (J. Miller, 1998). The gendered risk factors that girls and women face are both individual and structural. The gendered pathways perspective is built on the idea that female offenders often have extensive histories of trauma both inside and outside of their families, including victimization by intimates and strangers and across multiple settings (Daly, 1992). The trauma experienced by women and girls often precedes or coincides with criminal behavior and involvement in the criminal justice system. Therefore, it is important to contextualize criminal offending within the scope of early and ongoing trauma.

Unlike the ACEs framework, the gendered pathways perspective suggests that trauma often extends beyond childhood and adolescence. For these reasons, there has been a rise in gender-responsive correctional programming for female offenders in the last 20 years

(Van Voorhis, Wright, Salisbury, & Bauman, 2010). Addressing past and current trauma (Wright, Van Voorhis, Salisbury, & Bauman, 2012) is often a hallmark of these programs. They aim to help women change negative, trauma-related behavior and improve their chance for success after their criminal justice involvement. Gender-responsive programming has opened the door for trauma-informed criminal justice programs and responses. Trauma-informed care for women involved with the criminal justice system often addresses co-occurring substance abuse disorders and the emotional and behavioral aftermath of childhood and adult victimization through counseling and drug treatment.

Trauma-Informed Programs

Criminal Justice Trauma-Informed Programs

Much of the current trauma-informed programs in criminal justice began in the gender-responsive criminal justice movement (Wright et al., 2012). King (2017) reviewed the results of five trauma-informed correctional programs for women (Seeking Safety, Helping Women Recover, Beyond Trauma, Esuba, and Beyond Violence) and found significant improvement in depression, anxiety, and posttraumatic stress disorder (p. 685) when compared to control groups. However, the growth of trauma-informed programming has not been limited to women, and girls' programming has been applied across criminal justice populations and institutions. Growth in trauma-informed programs and training relevant to policing (Bateson et al., 2020), corrections (Levenson & Willis, 2019), and courts (Buffington et al., 2010) is noteworthy.

These programs and training pieces are designed to inform criminal justice practitioners about how childhood and adult trauma manifest in socially undesirable ways that make compliance to institutional rules and reentry from incarceration challenging. As such, trauma-informed criminal justice policy and practice advises officials and practitioners to take a more holistic approach that includes investigations into early and ongoing traumatic experiences both within and outside of the criminal justice system when examining the reasons behind misconduct and noncompliance (Ko et al., 2008). Adoption of trauma-informed programs makes sense from both treatment and public safety perspectives, according to recent research on administering trauma-informed care in correctional settings (Leitch, 2017; N. A. Miller & Najavitz, 2012) as these programs have been found to reduce institutional misconduct and recidivism.

Trauma-Informed Juvenile Justice Programs

Trauma-informed programs in juvenile justice are important to help youth learn coping skills to navigate life challenges and avoid criminal justice involvement. The National Child Traumatic Stress Network (NCTSN, 2021) outlines a wealth of trauma-informed programs and resources in juvenile justice that range from trauma-informed courts to probation and residential placement. These programs and resources highlight the importance of recognizing complex trauma in children who have experience poly-victimization and early adversity and how this trauma may manifest itself in negative, risk-seeking, or delinquent behavior. Children who have experienced trauma manifest trauma differently from adults, such as behavioral regression, defiance, and somatic complaints (Oh et al., 2018). Juvenile justice agencies that have introduced trauma-informed practices have seen reductions in excessive juvenile punishments at adjudication (Benekos & Merlo, 2019), increased referrals for counseling by probation officers (Schwalbe & Maschi, 2012), and reduction in reports of posttraumatic stress among youth in residential facilities (Ford & Blaustein, 2013).

Starting earlier in the criminal justice process with trauma-informed policy and practice by designing juvenile interventions is critical to help young offenders reform, mature, and establish healthier lives. One such approach is "systemic self-regulation" (Ford & Blaustein, 2013) to mitigate posttraumatic stress behavior in adolescents involved in juvenile justice or the TARGET (Trauma Affect Regulation: Guide for Education and Therapy; Marrow, Knudsen, Olafson, & Bucher, 2012) program to reduce depression and improve pro-social outcomes. Additionally, many police agencies nationwide have adopted a trauma-informed approach when encountering a situation in which a child has directly witnessed or experienced trauma (Webb, 2016). This program is aimed to reduce both subsequent police contact and negative behavior by identifying children in need of mental or behavioral health services, which may prevent school discipline issues or criminal justice contact. While much of the trauma-informed juvenile justice practices are institutionally or agency based (e.g., within the juvenile court or in juvenile corrections; see Benekos & Merlo, 2019), many worthwhile trauma-informed policies and practices occur within traditional school settings (Ko et al., 2008). These policies are often aimed to reduce in-school disciplinary infractions (Dorado, Martinez, McArthur, & Leibovitz, 2016), truancy (Ko et al., 2008), and suspensions/expulsions (Jackson & Testa, 2020) and to interrupt the school-to-prison pipeline for traumatized youth (Dutil, 2020). These measures are even more necessary in minority-serving and socioeconomically disadvantaged schools that contribute disproportionately to the school-to-prison pipeline (Joseph, Wilcox, Hnilica, & Hansen, 2020).

Conclusion

There has been tremendous growth in trauma-informed research and practice since the landmark ACEs study was published in the late 1990s. Scholars and practitioners better understand how ACEs disrupt healthy brain development, which can manifest in poor problem-solving and result in negative behavioral choices. When children experience parental incarceration, a parent's death or divorce, a parent's mental health or substance use challenges, or child maltreatment or witness intimate violence, it disrupts healthy bonding and can create toxic stress. That stress is often alleviated in unhealthy ways, one of which is delinquent and criminal behavior. As such, people who have experienced four or more ACEs in their childhood are disproportionately more likely to engage in crime and, therefore, often contact the criminal justice system. Researchers have found that both juveniles and adults involved with the criminal justice system have extensive histories of adversity and trauma stemming from dysfunctional family environments, historical trauma, and socioeconomic inequality.

While childhood and adult trauma is often complex, its presence within criminal justice populations is common. Therefore, criminological theory and programming need to be trauma responsive to address how childhood adversity influences criminal behavior. Criminological theory has long utilized concepts of stress and strain to explain crime caused by stressors that range from the interpersonal to financial. This is evident in the four-strain theories reviewed earlier and is most fully developed in Robert Agnew's general strain theory. However, theorists have suggested that some strains are gendered and more attention needs to be paid to girls' and women's pathways to crime and criminal justice. In particular, the development of gender-specific theorizing on the gendered nature of victimization and pathways from trauma to crime has added substantially to the literature. We also know that childhood adversity overlaps and that it also crosses generations. This is particularly evident in the research that links childhood trauma to the inhibition in self-control development; parents who have not developed self-control are unlikely to nurture its growth in their children. Understanding how trauma impairs healthy emotional and behavioral regulation may help policymakers unpack individual-level causes of intergenerational crime and help social workers as they assist system-involved clients.

Finally, multiple institutions within the criminal justice system, from the police to corrections, have adopted trauma-informed policies grounded in trauma theory to decrease institutional misconduct and aid in the successful treatment of justice system–involved people. Police officers now have training on how to spot traumatized children and how trauma manifests itself in criminal behavior (Bateson et al., 2020). Judges now recognize the importance of understanding how early childhood adversity affects the behavioral histories of people in their court (McKenna & Holfreter, 2021). Finally, correctional officers and correctional programming have incorporated trauma-informed policies that show promise in reducing institutional misconduct (N. A. Miller & Najavits, 2012). Using a trauma-informed lens to understand the effect that early adversity has on negative behavior is key to criminological theorizing and criminal justice policy to increase public safety and hasten successful outcomes for justice-involved youth and adults.

References

Agnew, R. (1992). Foundation for a general strain theory of crime and delinquency. *Criminology, 30*(1), 47–88. https://doi.org/10.1111/j.1745-9125.1992.tb01093.x

Agnew, R., Scheuerman, H., Grosholz, J., Isom, D., Watson, L., & Thaxton, S. (2011). Does victimization reduce self-control? A longitudinal analysis. *Journal of Criminal Justice, 39*(2), 169–174. https://www.ojp.gov/ncjrs/virtual-library/abstracts/does-victimization-reduce-self-control-longitudinal-analysis

Agnew, R., & White, H. R. (1992). An empirical test of general strain theory. *Criminology, 30*(4), 475–500. https://doi.org/10.1111/j.1745-9125.1992.tb01113.x

Altikriti, S. (2021). Toward integrated processual theories of crime: Assessing the developmental effects of executive function, self-control, and decision-making on offending. *Criminal Justice and Behavior, 48*(2), 215–233. https://doi.org/10.1177%2F0093854820942280

Asberg, K., & Renk, K. (2013). Comparing incarcerated and college student women with histories of childhood sexual abuse: The roles of abuse severity, support, and substance use. *Psychological Trauma: Theory, Research, Practice, and Policy, 5*(2), 167–175. https://psycnet.apa.org/doi/10.1037/a0027162

Baglivio, M. T., et al. (2014). The prevalence of adverse childhood experiences (ACE) in the lives of juvenile offenders. *Journal of Juvenile Justice*, 3(2), 1–17. https://www.prisonpolicy.org/scans/Prevalence_of_ACE.pdf

Baglivio, M. T., Wolff, K. T., Piquero, A. R., Bilchik, S., Jackowski, K., Greenwald, M. A., & Epps, N. (2016). Maltreatment, child welfare, and recidivism in a sample of deep-end crossover youth. *Journal of Youth and Adolescence*, 45(4), 625–654. https://doi.org/10.1007/s10964-015-0407-9

Bateson, K., McManus, M., & Johnson, G. (2020). Understanding the use, and misuse, of Adverse Childhood Experiences (ACEs) in trauma-informed policing. *Police Journal*, 93(2), 131–145. https://doi.org/10.1177%2F0032258X19841409

Belknap, J., & Holsinger, K. (2006). The gendered nature of risk factors for delinquency. *Feminist Criminology*, 1(1), 48–71. https://doi.org/10.1177%2F1557085105282897

Benekos, P. J., & Merlo, A. V. (2019). A decade of change: Roper v. Simmons, defending childhood, and juvenile justice policy. *Criminal Justice Policy Review*, 30(1), 102–127. https://doi.org/10.1177%2F0887403416648734

Biglan, A., & Hinds, E. (2009). Evolving prosocial and sustainable neighborhoods and communities. *Annual Review of Clinical Psychology*, 5, 169–196. https://doi.org/10.1146/annurev.clinpsy.032408.153526

Boppre, B., & Boyer, C. (2019). "The traps started during my childhood": The role of substance abuse in women's responses to Adverse Childhood Experiences (ACEs). *Journal of Aggression, Maltreatment & Trauma*, 30(4), 429–449. https://doi.org/10.1080/10926771.2019.1651808

Botchkovar, E., & Broidy, L. (2013). Accumulated strain, negative emotions, and crime: A test of general strain theory in Russia. *Crime & Delinquency*, 59(6), 837–860. https://doi.org/10.1177%2F0011128711 0382346

Boutwell, B. B., & Beaver, K. M. (2010). The intergenerational transmission of low self-control. *Journal of Research in Crime and Delinquency*, 47(2), 174–209. https://doi.org/10.1177%2F0022427809357715

Buffington, K., Dierkhising, C. B., & Marsh, S. C. (2010). Ten things every juvenile court judge should know about trauma and delinquency. *Juvenile and Family Court Journal*, 61(3), 13–23. https://doi.org/10.1111/j.1755-6988.2010.01044.x

Bunch, J. M., Iratzoqui, A., & Watts, S. J. (2018). Child abuse, self-control, and delinquency: A general strain perspective. *Journal of Criminal Justice*, 56, 20–28. https://doi.org/10.1016/j.jcrimjus.2017.09.009

Burgess-Proctor, A., Huebner, B. M., & Durso, J. M. (2016). Comparing the effects of maternal and paternal incarceration on adult daughters' and sons' criminal justice system involvement: A gendered pathways analysis. *Criminal Justice and Behavior*, 43(8), 1034–1055. https://doi.org/10.1177%2F0093854816643122

Cecil, C. A. M., Viding, E., Barker, E. D., Guiney, J., & McCrory, E. J. (2014). Double disadvantage: The influence of childhood maltreatment and community violence exposure on adolescent mental health. *Journal of Child Psychology and Psychiatry*, 55(7), 839–848. https://doi.org/10.1111/jcpp.12213

Chapple, C. L., Hope, T. L., & Whiteford, S. W. (2005). The direct and indirect effects of parental bonds, parental drug use, and self-control on adolescent substance use. *Journal of Child & Adolescent Substance Abuse*, 14(3), 17–38. https://doi.org/10.1300/J029v14n03_02

Chapple, C. L., Tyler, K. A., & Bersani, B. E. (2005). Child neglect and adolescent violence: Examining the effects of self-control and peer rejection. *Violence and Victims*, 20(1), 39–53. https://connect.springerpub.com/content/sgrvv/20/1/39

Chauhan, P., & Reppucci, N. D. (2009). The impact of neighborhood disadvantage and exposure to violence on self-report of antisocial behavior among girls in the juvenile justice system. *Journal of Youth and Adolescence*, 38(3), 401–416. https://psycnet.apa.org/doi/10.1007/s10964-008-9326-3

Cloward, R. A., & Ohlin, L. E. (2013). *Delinquency and opportunity: A study of delinquent gangs*. Routledge. https://www.google.com/books/edition/Delinquency_and_Opportunity/Cb2AAAAAQBAJ?hl=en&gbpv=1&dq=Delinquency+and+opportunity:+A+study+of+delinquent+gangs&printsec=frontcover

Cohen, A. K. (1955). *Delinquent boys; The culture of the gang*. Free Press. https://www.google.com/books/edition/Delinquent_Boys/nlsVAAAAIAAJ?hl=en

Coulton, C. J., Crampton, D. S., Irwin, M., Spilsbury, J. C., & Korbin, J. E. (2007). How neighborhoods influence child maltreatment: A review of the literature and alternative pathways. *Child Abuse & Neglect*, 31(11–12), 1117–1142. https://doi.org/10.1016/j.chiabu.2007.03.023

Daly, K. (1992). Women's pathways to felony court: Feminist theories of lawbreaking and problems of representation. *Southern California Review of Law and Women's Studies, 2*, 11. https://www.researchgate.net/profile/Kathleen-Daly-2/publication/284292910_Women's_pathways_to_felony_court_Feminist_theories_of_lawbreaking_and_problems_of_representation/links/5721345708ae5454b2310228/Womens-pathways-to-felony-court-Feminist-theories-of-lawbreaking-and-problems-of-representation.pdf

Davis, J. P., Dumas, T. M., Berey, B. L., Merrin, G. J., Cimplan, J. R., & Roberts, B. W. (2017). Effect of victimization on impulse control and binge drinking among serious juvenile offenders from adolescence to young adulthood. *Journal of Youth and Adolescence, 46*(7), 1515–1532. https://psycnet.apa.org/doi/10.1007/s10964-017-0676-6

DeHart, D. D., & Moran, R. (2015). Poly-victimization among girls in the justice system: Trajectories of risk and associations to juvenile offending. *Violence Against Women, 21*(3), 291–312. https://doi.org/10.1177%2F1077801214568355

Dong, M., Anda, R. F., Felitti, V. J., Dube, S. R., Williamson, D. F., Thompson, T. J., Loo, C. M., & Giles, W. H. (2004). The interrelatedness of multiple forms of childhood abuse, neglect, and household dysfunction. *Child Abuse & Neglect, 28*(7), 771–784. https://doi.org/10.1016/j.chiabu.2004.01.008

Dorado, J. S., Martinez, M., McArthur, L. E., & Leibovitz, T. (2016). Healthy Environments and Response to Trauma in Schools (HEARTS): A whole-school, multi-level, prevention and intervention program for creating trauma-informed, safe and supportive schools. *School Mental Health, 8*(1), 163–176. https://psycnet.apa.org/doi/10.1007/s12310-016-9177-0

Dutil, S. (2020). Dismantling the school-to-prison pipeline: A trauma-informed, critical race perspective on school discipline. *Children & Schools, 42*(3), 171–178. https://doi.org/10.1093/cs/cdaa016

Edalati, H., Nicholls, T. L., Crocker, A. G., Roy, L., Somers, J. M., & Patterson, M. L. (2017). Adverse childhood experiences and the risk of criminal justice involvement and victimization among homeless adults with mental illness. *Psychiatric Services, 68*(12), 1288–1295. https://europepmc.org/article/med/28859582

Edwards, R., Gillies, V., & White, S. (2019). Introduction: Adverse Childhood Experiences (ACES)—Implications and challenges. *Social Policy and Society, 18*(3), 411–414. https://doi.org/10.1017/S1474746419000137

Elklit, A., Karasoft, K., Armour, C., Feddern, D., & Christoffersen, M. (2013). Predicting criminality from child maltreatment typologies and posttraumatic stress symptoms. *European Journal of Psychotraumatology, 4*(1), 19825. https://doi.org/10.3402/ejpt.v4i0.19825

Ellis, W. R., & Dietz, W. H. (2017). A new framework for addressing adverse childhood and community experiences: The Building Community Resilience model. *Academic Pediatrics, 17*(7S), S86–S93. https://doi.org/10.1016/j.acap.2016.12.011

Faris, R. E. L. (1955). *Social disorganization* (2nd ed.). Ronald Press Company. https://www.google.com/books/edition/Social_Disorganization/l8YMAQAAIAAJ?hl=en&gbpv=1&bsq=Social+Disorganization&dq=Social+Disorganization&printsec=frontcover

Felitti, V. J., Anda, R. F., Nordenberg, D., Williamson, D. F., Spitz, A. M., Edwards, V., Koss, M. P., & Marks, J. S. (1998). Relationship of childhood abuse and household dysfunction to many of the leading causes of death in adults: The Adverse Childhood Experiences (ACE) study. *American Journal of Preventive Medicine, 14*(4), 245–258. https://doi.org/10.1016/S0749-3797(98)00017-8

Finkelhor, D. (2018). Screening for adverse childhood experiences (ACEs): Cautions and suggestions. *Child Abuse & Neglect, 85*, 174–179. https://doi.org/10.1016/j.chiabu.2017.07.016

Ford, J. D., & Blaustein, M. E. (2013). Systemic self-regulation: A framework for trauma-informed services in residential juvenile justice programs. *Journal of Family Violence, 28*(7), 665–677. https://psycnet.apa.org/doi/10.1007/s10896-013-9538-5

Ford, J. D., Grasso, D. J., Hawke, J., & Chapman, J. F. (2013). Poly-victimization among juvenile justice-involved youths. *Child Abuse & Neglect, 37*(10), 788–800. https://doi.org/10.1016/j.chiabu.2013.01.005

Gjelsvik, A., Dumont, D. M., & Nunn, A. (2013). Incarceration of a household member and Hispanic health disparities: Childhood exposure and adult chronic disease risk behaviors. *Preventing Chronic Disease, 10*, E69. https://doi.org/10.5888/pcd10.120281

Gottfredson, M. R., & Hirschi, T. (1990). *A general theory of crime.* Stanford University Press. https://www.ojp.gov/ncjrs/virtual-library/abstracts/general-theory-crime

Green, B. L., Miranda, J., Daroowalla, A., & Siddique, J. (2005). Trauma exposure, mental health functioning, and program needs of women in jail. *Crime & Delinquency*, *51*(1), 133–151. https://doi.org/10.1177%2F0011128704267477

Harris, A. (2016). *A pound of flesh: Monetary sanctions as punishment for the poor*. Russell Sage Foundation. https://www.google.com/books/edition/A_Pound_of_Flesh/c3MADAAAQBAJ?hl=en&gbpv=1&dq=A+pound+of+flesh:+Monetary+sanctions+as+punishment+for+the+poor&printsec=frontcover

Hay, C. (2001). Parenting, self control, and delinquency: A test of self control theory. *Criminology*, *39*(3), 707–736. https://www.ojp.gov/ncjrs/virtual-library/abstracts/parenting-self-control-and-delinquency-test-self-control-theory

Hays-Grudo, J., Morris, A. S., Beasley, L., Ciciolla, L., Shrefflet, K., & Cross, J. (2021). Integrating and synthesizing adversity and resilience knowledge and action: The ICARE model. *American Psychologist*, *76*(2), 203. https://psycnet.apa.org/doi/10.1037/amp0000766

Heard-Garris, N., Winkelman, T. N. A., Choi, H., Miller, A. K., Kan, K., Shlafer, R., & Davis, M. M. (2018). Health care use and health behaviors among young adults with history of parental incarceration. *Pediatrics*, *142*(3). https://doi.org/10.1542/peds.2017-4314

Heard-Garris, N., Sarcotte, K. A., Winkelman, T. N. A., Cohen, A., Ekqueme, P. A., Barnert, E., Carnethon, M., & Davis, M. M. (2019). Association of childhood history of parental incarceration and juvenile justice involvement with mental health in early adulthood. *JAMA Network Open*, *2*(9), e1910465–e1910465. https://jamanetwork.com/journals/jamanetworkopen/fullarticle/2749232

Heimer, K., & Coster, S. D. (1999). The gendering of violent delinquency. *Criminology*, *37*(2), 277–318. https://doi.org/10.1111/j.1745-9125.1999.tb00487.x

Henschel, S., de Bruin, M., & Möhler, E. (2014). Self-control and child abuse potential in mothers with an abuse history and their preschool children. *Journal of Child and Family Studies*, *23*(5), 824–836. https://psycnet.apa.org/doi/10.1007/s10826-013-9735-0

Jackson, D. B., & Testa, A. (2020). Household food insecurity and preschool suspension/expulsion in the United States. *Preventive Medicine*, *141*, 106283. https://doi.org/10.1016/j.ypmed.2020.106283

Jones, M. S., Worthen, M. G. F., Sharp, S. F., & McLeod, D. A. (2018). Life as she knows it: The effects of adverse childhood experiences on intimate partner violence among women prisoners. *Child Abuse & Neglect*, *85*, 68–79. https://doi.org/10.1016/j.chiabu.2018.08.005

Joseph, A. A., Wilcox, S. M., Hnilica, R., & Hansen, M. (2020). Keeping race at the center of school discipline practices and trauma-informed care: An interprofessional framework. *Children & Schools*, *42*(3), 161–170. https://doi.org/10.1093/cs/cdaa013

King, E. A. (2017). Outcomes of trauma-informed interventions for incarcerated women: A review. *International Journal of Offender Therapy and Comparative Criminology*, *61*(6), 667–688. https://doi.org/10.1177%2F0306624X15603082

Ko, S. J., Ford, J. D., Kassam-Adams, N., Berkowitz, S. J., Wilson, C., Wong, M., Brymer, M. J., & Layne, C. M. (2008). Creating trauma-informed systems: Child welfare, education, first responders, health care, juvenile justice. *Professional Psychology: Research and Practice*, *39*(4), 396. https://psycnet.apa.org/doi/10.1037/0735-7028.39.4.396

Kort-Butler, L. A., Tyler, K. A., & Melander, L. A. (2011). Childhood maltreatment, parental monitoring, and self-control among homeless young adults: Consequences for negative social outcomes. *Criminal Justice and Behavior*, *38*(12), 1244–1264. https://doi.org/10.1177%2F0093854811423480

Lee, R. D., Fang, X., & Luo, F. (2013). The impact of parental incarceration on the physical and mental health of young adults. *Pediatrics*, *131*(4), e1188–e1195. https://doi.org/10.1542/peds.2012-0627

Leitch, L. (2017). Action steps using ACEs and trauma-informed care: A resilience model. *Health & Justice*, *5*(1), 1–10. https://www.ncbi.nlm.nih.gov/pmc/articles/PMC5409906/

Levenson, J. S., & Willis, G. M. (2019). Implementing trauma-informed care in correctional treatment and supervision. *Journal of Aggression, Maltreatment & Trauma*, *28*(4), 481–501. https://doi.org/10.1080/10926771.2018.1531959

Link, N. W. (2019). Criminal justice debt during the prisoner reintegration process: Who has it and how much? *Criminal Justice and Behavior*, *46*(1), 154–172. https://doi.org/10.1177%2F0093854818790291

Luthar, S. S., Cicchetti, D., & Becker, B. (2000). The construct of resilience: A critical evaluation and guidelines for future work. *Child Development*, *71*(3), 543–562. https://psycnet.apa.org/doi/10.1111/1467-8624.00164

Marrow, M. T., Knudsen, K. J., Olafson, E., & Bucher, S. E. (2012). The value of implementing TARGET within a trauma-informed juvenile justice setting. *Journal of Child & Adolescent Trauma*, 5(3), 257–270. https://doi.org/10.1080/19361521.2012.697105

McKenna, N. C., & Holtfreter, K. (2021). Trauma-informed courts: A review and integration of justice perspectives and gender responsiveness. *Journal of Aggression, Maltreatment & Trauma*, 30(4), 450–470. https://doi.org/10.1080/10926771.2020.1747128

Meldrum, R. C., Young, B. C., Soor, S., Hay, C., Copp, J. E., Trace, M., Smith-Darden, J. P., & Kernsmith, P. D. (2020). Are adverse childhood experiences associated with deficits in self-control? A test among two independent samples of youth. *Criminal Justice and Behavior*, 47(2), 166–186. https://doi.org/10.1177%2F0093854819879741

Merrick, M. T., Ford, D. C., Ports, K. A., & Guinn, A. S. (2018). Prevalence of Adverse Childhood Experiences from the 2011–2014 Behavioral Risk Factor Surveillance system in 23 states. *JAMA Pediatrics*, 172(11), 1038–1044. https://jamanetwork.com/journals/jamapediatrics/fullarticle/2702204

Mersky, J. P., Topitzes, J., & Reynolds, A. J. (2012). Unsafe at any age: Linking childhood and adolescent maltreatment to delinquency and crime. *Journal of Research in Crime and Delinquency*, 49(2), 295–318. https://doi.org/10.1177%2F0022427811415284

Merton, R. K. (1938). Social structure and anomie. *American Sociological Review*, 3(5), 672–682. https://doi.org/10.2307/2084686

Miller, J. (1998). Gender and victimization risk among young women in gangs. *Journal of Research in Crime and Delinquency*, 35(4), 429–453. https://doi.org/10.1177%2F0022427898035004004

Miller, N. A., & Najavits, L. M. (2012). Creating trauma-informed correctional care: A balance of goals and environment. *European Journal of Psychotraumatology*, 3(1), 17246. https://doi.org/10.3402/ejpt.v3i0.17246

Monahan, K. C., King, K. M., Shulman, E. P., Cauffan, E., & Chassin, L. (2015). The effects of violence exposure on the development of impulse control and future orientation across adolescence and early adulthood: Time-specific and generalized effects in a sample of juvenile offenders. *Development and Psychopathology*, 27(4, Pt1), 1267–1283. http://doi.org/10.1017/S0954579414001394

Morris, A. S., Ratliff, E., & Hays-Grudo, J. (2020). *Assessing resilience using the protective and compensatory experiences survey (PACES)* [Paper presentation]. Society for Research in Child Development, Philadelphia, PA. https://extension.okstate.edu/fact-sheets/paces-for-children-overcoming-adversity-and-building-resilience.html

Munoz, R. T., Hanks, H., & Hellman, C. M. (2020). Hope and resilience as distinct contributors to psychological flourishing among childhood trauma survivors. *Traumatology*, 26(2), 177. https://psycnet.apa.org/doi/10.1037/trm0000224

National Child Traumatic Stress Network. (2021). *NTCSN resources*. https://www.nctsn.org

National Scientific Council on the Developing Child. (2005/2014). *Excessive stress disrupts the architecture of the developing brain*. Working Paper No. 3. Updated Edition. www.developingchild.harvard.edu https://edn.ne.gov/cms/sites/default/files/u1/pdf/04SE2%20Stress%20Disrupts%20Architecture%20Dev%20Brain%203.pdf

Nofziger, S. (2008). The "cause" of low self-control: The influence of maternal self-control. *Journal of Research in Crime and Delinquency*, 45(2), 191–224. https://doi.org/10.1177%2F0022427807313708

Oh, D. L., Jerman, P., Marques, S. S., Koita, K., Boparai, S. K. P., Harris, N. B., & Bucci, M. (2018). Systematic review of pediatric health outcomes associated with childhood adversity. *BMC Pediatrics*, 18(1), 83. https://pubmed.ncbi.nlm.nih.gov/29475430/ https://www.ncbi.nlm.nih.gov/pmc/articles/PMC5824569/

Patterson, J. M. (2002). Integrating family resilience and family stress theory. *Journal of Marriage and Family*, 64(2), 349–360. https://doi.org/10.1111/j.1741-3737.2002.00349.x

Pearlin, L. I. (1989). The sociological study of stress. *Journal of Health and Social Behavior*, 20(3), 241–256. https://doi.org/10.2307/2136956

Pearlin, L. I., & Aneshensel, C. S. (1986). Coping and social supports: Their functions and applications. In L. H. Aiken & D. Mechanic (Eds.), *Applications of social science to clinical medicine and health policy* (pp. 417–437). Rutgers University Press. https://onesearch.nihlibrary.ors.nih.gov/discovery/fulldisplay?docid=alma991000004309704686&context=L&vid=01NIH_INST:NIH&lang=en&adaptor=Local%20Search%20Engine&tab=NIHCampus&query=mesh,exact,Cultural%20Competency,AND&mode=advanced

Pollock J. (2002). *Women, prison, and crime* (2nd ed.). Wadsworth Thomson Learning. https://www.ojp.gov/ncjrs/virtual-library/abstracts/women-prison-and-crime

Robert Wood Johnson Foundation. (2013). The truth about ACEs [Infographic]. In *Adverse childhood experiences.* https://www.rwjf.org/en/library/infographics/the-truth-about-aces.html#/download

Rodriguez, N., Smith, H., & Zatz, M. S. (2009). "Youth is enmeshed in a highly dysfunctional family system": Exploring the relationship among dysfunctional families, parental incarceration, and juvenile court decision making. *Criminology, 47*(1), 177–208. https://doi.org/10.1111/j.1745-9125.2009.00142.x

Roos, L. E., Afifi, T. O., Martin, C. G., Pietrzak, R. H., Tsai, J., & Sareen, J. (2016). Linking typologies of childhood adversity to adult incarceration: Findings from a nationally representative sample. *American Journal of Orthopsychiatry, 86*(5), 584. https://doi.org/10.1037/ort0000144

Ross, J., Waterhouse-Bradley, B., Contractor, A. A., & Armour, C. (2018). Typologies of adverse childhood experiences and their relationship to incarceration in US military veterans. *Child Abuse & Neglect, 79*, 74–84. https://psycnet.apa.org/doi/10.1016/j.chiabu.2018.01.023

Salisbury, E. J., & Van Voorhis, P. (2009). Gendered pathways: A quantitative investigation of women probationers' paths to incarceration. *Criminal Justice and Behavior, 36*(6), 541–566. https://doi.org/10.1177%2F0093854809334076

Sampson, R. J. (1993). The community context of violent crime. In W. J. Wilson (Ed.), *Sociology and the public agenda* (pp. 267–274). Sage Publications. https://www.google.com/books/edition/Sociology_and_the_Public_Agenda/CxN1AwAAQBAJ?hl=en&gbpv=1&dq=Sociology+and+the+public+agenda&printsec=frontcover

Sampson, R. J., & Groves, W. B. (1989). Community structure and crime: Testing social-disorganization theory. *American Journal of Sociology, 94*(4), 774–802. https://psycnet.apa.org/doi/10.1086/229068

Sampson, R. J., & Wilson, W. J. (1995). Toward a theory of race, crime, and urban inequality. In J. Hagan & R. D. Peterson (Eds.), *Crime and inequality.* (pp. 37–54) Stanford University Press. https://www.ojp.gov/ncjrs/virtual-library/abstracts/toward-theory-race-crime-and-urban-inequality-crime-and-inequality

Sawyer, W., & Wagner, P. (2020). *Mass incarceration: The whole pie 2020.* Prison Policy Initiative. https://www.prisonpolicy.org/reports/pie2022.html

Schwalbe, C. S., & Maschi, T. (2012). Unraveling probation officers' practices with youths with histories of trauma and stressful life events. *Social Work Research, 36*(1), 21–30. https://doi.org/10.1093/swr/svs007

Sege, R. D., & Browne, C. H. (2017). Responding to ACEs with HOPE: Health outcomes from positive experiences. *Academic Pediatrics, 17*(7), S79–S85. https://doi.org/10.1016/j.acap.2017.03.007

Sommers, I., & Baskin, D. R. (1993). The situational context of violent female offending. *Journal of Research in Crime and Delinquency, 30*(2), 136–162.

Steffensmeier, D., & Allan, E. (1996). Gender and crime: Toward a gendered theory of female offending. *Annual Review of Sociology, 22*(1), 459–487. https://www.ojp.gov/ncjrs/virtual-library/abstracts/situational-context-violent-female-offending

Taylor-Robinson, D. C., Straatmann, V. S., & Whitehead, M. (2018). Adverse childhood experiences or adverse childhood socioeconomic conditions? *Lancet Public Health, 3*(6), e262–e263. https://doi.org/10.1016/S2468-2667(18)30094-X

Turney, K., & Wildeman, C. (2017). Adverse childhood experiences among children placed in and adopted from foster care: Evidence from a nationally representative survey. *Child Abuse & Neglect, 64*, 117–129. https://doi.org/10.1016/j.chiabu.2016.12.009

Van Voorhis, P., Wright, E. M., Salisbury, E., & Bauman, A. (2010). Women's risk factors and their contributions to existing risk/needs assessment: The current status of a gender-responsive supplement. *Criminal Justice and Behavior, 37*(3), 261–288. https://doi.org/10.1177%2F0093854809357442

Vaughn, M. G., DeLisi, M., Beaver, K. M., & Wright, J. P. (2009). Identifying latent classes of behavioral risk based on early childhood: Manifestations of self-control. *Youth Violence and Juvenile Justice, 7*(1), 16–31. https://doi.org/10.1177%2F1541204008324911

Webb, T. (2016). Children exposed to violence: A developmental trauma informed response for the criminal justice system. *Journal of Child & Adolescent Trauma, 9*(3), 183–189. https://psycnet.apa.org/doi/10.1007/s40653-015-0069-5

Wright, E. M., Van Voorhis, P., Salisbury, E. J., & Bauman, A. (2012). Gender-responsive lessons learned and policy implications for women in prison: A review. *Criminal Justice and Behavior, 39*(12), 1612–1632. https://psycnet.apa.org/doi/10.1177/0093854812451088

13

Major Policies Impacting Child Welfare

Angela B. Pharris and Angelique Day

Major Policies in Practice

Perhaps no other system has more systematic and intentional integration of policy, law, and practice than public child welfare in the United States. This chapter defines public child welfare as a public system (state, county, tribe, or territory) with statutory oversight to protect and prevent child maltreatment and the affiliated court systems mandated to provide legal oversight and decision-making. While many significant public policies and laws shape public child welfare, we have elected to provide a critical overview of five important policies that describe the relationship between the public child welfare agency and the court in child welfare policy and practice implementation. A discussion of each policy and its primary goals, along with a critical review of each's policy's strengths and unintended consequences, is provided. Finally, the chapter will examine our perspective on the future directions of child welfare policy. The five selected policies highlight essential shifts in public child welfare practice over time.

Preventing child maltreatment and providing protection for children deemed unsafe are common goals of policymakers and citizens alike. But the pathways selected to pursue those goals are shaped by many different and influential forces. The number of children reported as victims of child abuse and neglect in the United States is large. Numerous stakeholder groups influence child welfare policy, including elected officials, presidential and governor appointees, policy advocacy organizations, researchers, think tanks, and experts in child welfare practice. Experts in more recent times have increasingly included those with lived experience (i.e., foster youth, foster and adoptive parents, kinship caregivers, and biological parents). Child welfare practice has also been shaped mainly by the courts themselves through class action litigation and judicial oversight of legal challenges to child

Angela B. Pharris and Angelique Day, *Major Policies Impacting Child Welfare* In: *Handbook of Forensic Social Work.* Edited by: David Axlyn McLeod, Anthony P. Natale, and Kristin W. Mapson, Oxford University Press. © Oxford University Press 2024. DOI: 10.1093/oso/9780197694732.003.0013 welfare policy and practice. Additionally, child welfare policy is a result of research analysis of state and tribal administrative data. Each of the policies described in this chapter provides a glimpse into the priorities that shaped child welfare practice, not only at the time of passage but also well beyond.

Child Abuse Prevention and Treatment Act

The Child Abuse Prevention and Treatment Act (CAPTA), initially authorized in 1974, provided the nation's first statutory opportunity for federal oversight of matters related to child abuse and neglect in the United States. Since its inception, it has had multiple reauthorizations, most recently amended on January 7, 2019, in the Victims of Child Abuse Act Reauthorization Act of 2018 (PL 115-424). This federal law provides formula-based funding and demonstration grants to states, tribes, and territories to support the prevention, assessment, investigation, prosecution, and treatment of child maltreatment (Child Welfare Information Gateway [CWIG], 2019). In addition, the law sets a minimum standard for a legal definition for child abuse and neglect and sexual abuse and requires states to adopt laws for maltreatment. At a minimum, states are required to define abuse and neglect as "any recent act or failure to act on the part of a parent or caretaker which results in death, serious physical or emotional harm, sexual abuse, or exploitation; or an act or failure to act, which presents an imminent risk of serious harm" (USCA § 5106g). As a result of CAPTA, states are also required to identify and assess all reports of child abuse and neglect, including information involving children known or suspected to be victims of sex trafficking.

The primary function of CAPTA is to ensure that states have a mechanism for individuals to report concerns for abuse and neglect, maintain adequate resources for investigation, and have the ability to handle an allegation of abuse and neglect in the courts, law enforcement, and child protection services. CAPTA also requires participation in a systematic effort to report state-level data archived annually in the National Data Archive for Child Abuse and Neglect. To qualify for funding, states submit a plan to the Department of Health and Human Services to ensure that states have laws, policies, and programs to provide organized child protection systems. Thus, CAPTA has provided the pathway and resources for states to build and maintain the child welfare systems and codify courts' and legal systems' explicit role as the central mechanism to intervene and oversee child maltreatment cases.

Within the provisions of CAPTA are the Children's Justice Act Grants, which provide funding and oversight for programs to employ interdisciplinary investigative practices in partnership with child welfare, law enforcement, and the courts, specifically through Child Advocacy Centers. Child Advocacy Centers provide a safe, child-friendly environment to conduct investigations into sexual abuse or, in cases of severe physical abuse, with a multidisciplinary team including law enforcement, attorneys, social workers, and other mental health professionals to coordinate forensic-focused investigative services. The funding also provides the resources to develop child and infant fatality review teams and other data reporting systems that improve law enforcement response systems (Child Welfare Information Gateway, 2019).

Legal Representation

High-quality legal representation for all parents, children, and youth should be provided in all stages of child welfare proceedings and is a mandate of courts in CAPTA. CAPTA requires that "in every case involving abused and neglected child, results in a judicial proceeding guardian ad litem shall be appointed to represent children in such proceedings" (42 USC §5106). The policy's original intent was to provide legal representation to both parents and children, but a 1996 amendment allowed nonlawyer advocates to represent the "best interest of the child." As a result, the guardian ad litem is often a trained citizen volunteer who advocates for a child in the case. There have been mixed evaluations on the effectiveness of the use of citizen volunteers. Very few studies examine different outcomes for children assigned a court-appointed special advocate volunteer and those without (Collins-Camargo et al., 2009). Competent legal representation, protection of legal rights, and due process are necessary because these are court cases in which parties may be required to testify under oath, be cross-examined, and be subject to court orders. The stakes are exceptionally high for parents, as their parental rights may be temporarily or permanently severed. Despite the significance of legal proceedings, not all states provide legal representation to parents and children. Some states fail to appoint legal representation early in the case or adequately trained in family law. Additionally, the description of what constitutes the "best interest of the child" is unclear and lacks a clear legal definition to guide the role (Glynn, 2007).

Mandatory Reporting

CAPTA also directed the adoption of state laws to outline and define mandatory reporting for suspected or known child abuse and neglect. Mandatory reporting is the set of U.S. federal and state laws that require specific individuals to report actual or suspected abuse to the legal or child welfare system. Although there is variation between state laws, almost all states require individual professionals (educators, social workers, law enforcement, health care) to report. In addition, several states have extended mandatory reporting laws to include all adults, leading to a significant increase in child maltreatment reporting to the child welfare agency. While reporting suspected child abuse has some benefits, the increase in compulsory reporting laws lacks evidence of being effective in improving the accurate detection of at-risk children (Raz, 2017).

On the contrary, evidence suggests that increased mandatory reporting laws have stressed the system with the reports of nonprofessionals (such as family, friends, and neighbors) and have decreased substantiation rates (Raz, 2017). Secondly, there is growing evidence to support racial and socioeconomic bias in reporting child abuse and neglect (Chibnall et al., 2003). A final alarming concern is evidence that mandatory reporting laws are significant deterrents for help-seeking adults in intimate partner violence. A recent study shows that mandatory reporting laws reduce help seeking in over one-third of survivors. Moreover, when mandatory reporting laws are triggered during the accessing of intimate partner violence services, mandatory reporting is more likely to worsen most survivors' situations (Lippy et al., 2020).

Unintended Consequences of CAPTA

Establishing robust justice system responses to address child maltreatment has also resulted in some problematic outcomes that require ongoing advocacy and reforms. A staggering 4.4 million cases were referred for investigation of abuse in 2019, and approximately 656,000 were substantiated cases of abuse or neglect, accounting for only 22% of the reported cases (HHS, 2021). The volume of overreporting issues that are often not at all linked to child abuse has resulted in a substantial allocation of resources into a vast system of employees and processes for reporting child abuse and neglect. Those funds could be much better spent on direct services and prevention of child abuse if accurate reporting improved. There is a lack of knowledge, even among professionals, to accurately identify and report child maltreatment. Professionals are often hesitant to make a report due to a perception that reporting a child or family for maltreatment does more harm than good (Gilbert et al., 2009). Professionals need more useful training to accurately recognize signs of abuse and distinguish between statutory neglect and scarcity conditions resulting from poverty.

Almost all states had child protection systems in place before the passage of CAPTA, but CAPTA set a precedent for the role of federal policy to direct priorities for states, and the goal was clear: Child safety is paramount. Child welfare professionals, advocates, and researchers have devoted decades to designing assessment tools that assess current and future risk, which have been adopted in most state child welfare agencies, by law enforcement, and in health care settings. However, a systematic review of the published empirical research on screening and other identification tools concluded that there is no gold standard for systematically identifying child maltreatment, despite the continued use of the assessment tools. Some of the risk assessment tools have low certainty. High numbers of false positives suggest that the risk assessment tools may create additional risks by engaging children and families in a child welfare investigation process that can be traumatizing (McTavish et al., 2020). Additionally, there is mounting evidence that most states' primary assessment tools are vulnerable to bias, contributing to persistent disparity and disproportionality in child welfare case decisions (removal, placement, reunification, etc.), which we will reflect on later in this chapter. In total, CAPTA's major unintended consequence is the creation of the child welfare system as a carceral system of surveillance.

Adoption and Safe Families Act

In the 1990s, the increase of strict criminal punishments for drug offenses from criminal justice reforms in the United States contributed to the number of children in foster care reaching an all-time high. The drastically high incarceration rates of mothers, coupled with the implementation of welfare reforms that reduced cash welfare benefits, contributed to a significant increase in the number of children placed in foster care (Zavez, 2008). Additionally, courts were remarkably slow in ensuring that children could be returned home or that another type of legal permanency could be established. Therefore, policy shifted to a focus on foster care and adoption reform. To address permanency and the time frames in which courts and child welfare systems respond to the child's and family's needs, the Adoption and Safe Families Act (ASFA; PL 105-89) was signed into law by President

Bill Clinton on November 19, 1997 (Phillips & Mann, 2013). This bipartisan bill focused on the relationship between the courts and child welfare agencies and included three primary goals: ensuring and overseeing the child's safety, permanency, and well-being. The law's primary focus was to promote permanency strategies to ensure timely reunification services for children in out-of-home care and services to encourage adoption if legal reunification is not possible.

The primary measures of ASFA focused attention on ensuring that foster care is a temporary system of care. Child welfare systems must respect a child's developmental needs and respond with a sense of urgency for children to reside with a permanent family (Congressional Research Service, 2004). ASFA directs states and courts to immediately plan for the child's permanency, including concurrent planning for adoption or another permanent living arrangement, when children cannot return home. Prior legislation, the Adoption Assistance and Child Welfare Act (1980), had mandated that "reasonable efforts" be made to support families and to find permanent adoptive homes for children who could not be reunified (Carolina & Virginia, 2020; Hort, 2001). The "reasonable efforts" language did not have enough guidance and significantly altered how the law was applied in states. ASFA still lacks guidelines on what is a reasonable effort. Still, it did make an important distinction: Reasonable efforts were determined with respect to the child and not focused on parental rights (Hort, 2001). ASFA gives the presiding courts the responsibility of ensuring reasonable efforts to reunification by ensuring the child welfare system has met the statutory requirements. The lack of guidance and oversight makes the reasonable mandate a concerning area of child welfare policy, as the law assumes that child welfare agencies can pursue all reasonable efforts to achieve reunification by providing resources to families (i.e., childcare, housing, vocational counseling, mental health treatment, etc.) that may not be readily available to the family.

When the child welfare agency has met those reasonable efforts to provide services to families and the family has not taken the necessary steps determined by the court presiding over the case, ASFA directs the courts to initiate a hearing for the termination of parental rights. In doing so, the law gives courts a specific timeline for the child welfare agency to take action, resulting in one of the more controversial rules in ASFA, the 15/22 rule. If a child has been in foster care for 15 of the last 22 months, attorneys and the state must compel the courts to move to terminate parental rights to make a child "legally free" for adoption. By building specific time limits and requiring states to pursue all reasonable efforts to ensure family reunification, the law authorized the use of funds to increase access to prevention services. These included substance abuse, mental health, counseling, employment, and family violence services that could reduce the risk of maltreatment for the child and maximize the likelihood of a safe reunification. States may add additional laws to guide the conditions of the 15/22 rule. Some offer more individual flexibility to extend the timeline, and others are adopting laws that give courts the authority to terminate parental rights before the timeline under certain conditions (Hort, 2001). As a result, there is still significant variation between states. These laws may prevent foster care "drift," where children stay in foster care too long. Still, it may also accelerate the termination of parental rights in situations when reunification is possible (Hort, 2001).

Attention to permanency has effectively reduced the number of children who spend a significant amount of time in out-of-home care. Before ASFA's authorization, an astonishing one-third of all the children placed in foster care stayed for 3 years or longer. In the two decades following, there has been a dramatic decrease in the average length of stay in foster care to an average of 17 months (HHS, 2020c). There have also been increases in the number of children adopted after the termination of parental rights since the passage of the law, most likely from adoption reforms in ASFA that authorized incentive payments to states that increase adoptions from foster care above a baseline number of adoptions. States were eligible to receive $4,000 for each child adopted from foster care above the foster care adoption baseline and $6,000 for children who have specialized care needs for each child adopted above the special needs adoption baseline (Golden & Macomber, 2009).

Challenges to ASFA Implementation

ASFA allows funds to be used for family support and family reunification services such as childcare, substance use, counseling, health, and behavioral health services (CWIG, 2020). However, adequate investments in community-based services and supports for struggling families are missing. ASFA has primarily addressed the operations of a child welfare system and does not provide specific guidance or mandates to ensure that services and supports of other public systems are delivered promptly and are readily accessible to children and families. As a result, there has not been sufficient attention to either the federal or the state levels to develop strategies that ensure cross-system collaboration. Targeted investments in these areas would help families overcome the issues that brought the family to the court's attention in the first place.

ASFA has increased the number of children who exit from the foster care system through adoption and guardianship, yet many youth exit foster care through emancipation and many without connections to a family. While permanency is generally considered essential for childhood, ASFA's emphasis on legal permanency has left gaps and undervalued other significant types of permanent children and youth connections. Under ASFA, permanency is defined as a legal permanent relationship resulting from reunification to family, permanent legal adoption, or legal guardianship. Relational permanency is a child's or youth's sense of belonging through enduring lifelong connections to caring adults (Louisell, 2008). Young people in foster care have reported that they feel they have little influence over their ability to maintain meaningful connections and relationships in their lives (Samuels & Pryce, 2008) but are likely to seek out important people in their lives after leaving foster care (Geenen & Powers, 2007; Samuels & Pryce, 2008), suggesting planned activities of the courts and child welfare agencies to establish and sustain relational permanence is important. Courts and child welfare professionals hold the primary responsibility to determine the child's best interest for permanency, and the courts have rarely provided youth with alternative options to legal permanency. Perhaps children perceive permanency differently from the courts and policy? Future policy efforts will need to evaluate the multiple paths to permanency and ensure that children and youth are given opportunities to identify and maintain relationships with adults and that the importance of community and familial relationships is emphasized. ASFA recognized, but did not sufficiently support, relative placement options, and some provisions of ASFA created challenges for a child to be placed with a fit and willing relative. Specifically, ASFA regulations require that relative foster homes be licensed in the same way as foster homes for children in nonrelative placements, with only limited case-specific expectations. In addition, ASFA provides financial incentives for states to place children with adoptive families. Still, no similar incentive for supporting children in exiting foster care for permanent legal guardianship (including relative/kinship guardianship) exists.

Finally, child welfare practice does not adequately focus on the well-being goals of ASFA. Implementation has focused almost exclusively on the two goals of safety and permanence. Once children are removed from unsafe or high-risk situations, the resources that accompany the law do not provide clear expectations regarding the system's obligations to children's development and emotional needs. Specifically, workers are often ill-equipped to address the trauma of abuse or neglect, the impact of removal and multiple placements, attachment and separation anxiety, and other needs of children involved in the child welfare system. Additionally, child well-being is multiple systems' responsibility, including education, juvenile justice, mental health, etc. Children involved in foster care frequently experience inadequate service coordination and delivery due to a lack of role clarification, conflicting case plans, and insufficient teaming and practice by interdisciplinary/interagency professionals responsible for their care and well-being (Wesley et al., 2020).

Multiethnic Placement Act/Interethnic Placement Act

Finding adoptive families for children is a complex challenge faced by child welfare agencies. In the 1990s the prevailing child placement practice allowed for consideration of the child's cultural, ethnic, or racial background during the placement process and assessment of prospective parents' capacity to provide the foster and adoptive child with cultural continuity. However, there was concern that this placement preference was causing Black and Indigenous children to languish in foster care. African American, Black, Indigenous, and Latinx children remained in foster care at a rate that exceeded White children (Brooks et al., 1999). The Multiethnic Placement Act (MEPA; PL 108-382), amended as the Interethnic Adoption Provisions Act of 1996 (IEPA; 42 U.S. Code § 1996b), mandated a colorblind approach to foster and adoptive placements that prioritized placement of children in homes without consideration for the race of the child or prospective adoptive parent(s). MEPA/IEPA explicitly prohibits states from denying any individual an opportunity to become a foster or adoptive parent based on race, ethnicity, or national origin. The law ensures that children, primarily Black and African American children, could be placed in White families' homes if they meet parenting criteria. Also, the law does not allow child welfare recruiters to ask questions about race and ethnicity during the screening process, nor are prospective parents required to take any additional steps in the recruitment and application process from any other foster or adoptive family race, ethnicity, or national origin. As a result, child welfare agencies were prohibited from requiring White parents to complete additional training or answer screening questions to assess transracial parenting readiness. To balance the need for more racial and ethnic diversity in foster and adoptive parents, MEPA requires the state to use diligent efforts to expand the recruitment of racially and ethnically diverse foster and adoptive parent candidates. States, or the organization that acts on behalf of states to recruit potential foster and adoptive families, are required to submit plans to the federal government with a description of their diligent recruitment plan. The recruitment plan should match a specific plan to recruit parents who match the characteristics of children who need homes and outline strategies to reach individuals and communities who match their characteristics.

Challenges With MEPA/IEPA Implementation

Despite its passage nearly three decades ago, the over-representation of Black, Indigenous, and people of color (BIPOC) children and youth placed in foster care has remained (HHS, 2020a). MEPA instructs the courts to consider the child's best interest by prioritizing transracial foster and adoptive placements over a child's cultural continuity. Is transracial adoption in the best interest of a child? Critics argue that the adoption process under MEPA benefits adopters who already have power and privilege in society and thus experience few barriers to adoption—namely White, heterosexual, middle-class couples—over services designed to meet the racial, cultural, and ethnic needs of the children in care (Jennings, 2006). Assimilation or being expected to adopt the dominant culture's norms or values can have negative psychological impacts on children (LaFomboise et al., 1993). For example, children may grow up feeling they need to reject their cultural communities to be successful.

Additionally, White parents may not be prepared to help BIPOC children navigate racism in a White-dominated society (Jennings, 2006). Today, most practitioners, researchers, and advocates agree that race should not be ignored when making placement decisions. The system should move from a legal permanency-focused approach to one that implements a multidimensional definition of permanency and considers relational and cultural permanency in addition to legal permanency.

Perhaps the most robust critique of MEPA/IEPA is states' requirement to provide diligent efforts to recruit families that match children's characteristics (Administration for Children and Families, 1995). There is an overwhelming lack of emphasis and accountability on states to ensure they follow diligent recruitment efforts. There is an absence of rigorous training for child welfare staff and courts to develop and implement inclusive plans (Kalisher, Spielfogel, Shenk, & Eduoard, 2020). A recent survey of child and family service review plans submitted every 5 years by states to the Administration for Children and Families found that 34 states' diligent recruitment plans were "needing improvement" to meet the minimum standard (Kalisher et al., 2020). The review only assesses the states' submitted plan, not the extent to which the plan is used or their actual efforts, making it unclear if those states' success meets expectations. MEPA has, in effect, lacked meaningful federal and state investment into programs, resulting in less support (training, funding) to states to build programs to recruit and retain foster and adoptive parents who represent children's characteristics, such as Black, African American, Latinx, and American Indian families.

MEPA specifically prohibits discrimination based on race, ethnicity, and national origin, and any abuse is a violation of the Civil Rights Act and Title IV. But the Civil Rights

Act explicitly identifies other protected classes, including religion, sex, physical and mental disability, and sexual orientation. At this time, many states do not have specific laws to guarantee explicit protection of LGBTQ individuals who are interested in foster care and adoption from discrimination (CWIG, 2016b). After the 2015 Supreme Court decision for marriage equality, states removed the explicit language that banned same-sex couples from adopting children. Still, they lack an affirmative statement and the implementation of inclusive protections. Studies have found that qualified gay and lesbian applicants report many obstacles in their efforts to become adoptive and foster parents (Brooks & Goldberg, 2001; Clarie & Moore, 2015). In recent legislative action, several conservative states have allowed state-funded child-placing agencies to refuse qualified candidates services and discriminate in the provision of adoption services due to religious beliefs. Limiting the number of qualified candidates for foster care and adoption is not in the child's or courts' and child welfare system's best interest. Future policy and law will need to advance sexual orientation and gender identity protections to prevent discrimination.

Indian Child Welfare Act

Similar to African American children, American Indian and Alaskan Native (AIAN) children also enter foster care at disproportionate rates. As of 2018, AIAN youth represented only 1% of the general population but 2.6% of foster youth (Puzzanchera & Taylor, 2020). AIAN children are less likely to be adopted than their White counterparts (Cross, 2011). Of the AIAN children who do get adopted, 56% are adopted to individuals outside of their community and family of origin (National Indian Child Welfare Association, n.d.).

To address historical and current-day traumas tribes have suffered as a result of government policies that forcibly removed large numbers of AIAN children from their families and placed them in government-sponsored boarding schools and/or foster/adoptive placements far away from their tribal lands (Day et al., 2020), the Indian Child Welfare Act (ICWA) was established in 1978. AIAN children are a unique child welfare subpopulation. Being AIAN is not only a cultural distinction but also a political one. Specifically, tribes have a right to govern their members from the sovereignty that predates European arrival and has been documented through treaties entered into by tribes and the U.S. government (Tribal Star, 2015). Tribes exercise their sovereignty in many ways, including designating ICWA representatives to receive notice from state child welfare agencies and state courts when a tribal citizen child comes to the attention of the state because of an allegation of abuse and neglect, defining expert witness criteria, and recommending tribal customary adoption as a permanency option for children. An expert witness is required in an ICWA case when making decisions on foster care placement and actions involving termination of parental rights. Specifically, when a state or tribe attempts a foster care placement, it must prove by clear and convincing evidence, including testimony by a qualified expert witness, that continued custody by a parent or other custodian of an AIAN child will result in severe emotional or physical damage (National Indian Law Library, n.d.). The focus of ICWA is twofold: the protection of Indian children against unnecessary removals from their families and tribes and the protection of tribes and tribal authority from encroachment by state or federal authorities (Atwood, 2008). Through ICWA, Congress attempted to restore judicial power to tribes over child welfare matters involving AIAN children, and it erected barriers to the removal of AIAN children from their homes. ICWA has been largely recognized as the "gold standard" of foster care practice and is a prime example of the importance of keeping children connected to their culture. It requires that diligent efforts be made to keep tribal youth within their culture of origin (Burge, 2020).

Challenges and Promising Practices Related to ICWA Implementation

For all its laudable goals, ICWA depends entirely on the willingness of states and tribes to work together to understand the law and incorporate its directives into everyday practice. Common obstacles to routine ICWA compliance include lack of knowledge regarding requirements, confusion regarding the impact of subsequent federal legislation, and difficulty identifying those children eligible for ICWA protection (Center for Court Innovation, 2011). First, there is no national consistency regarding ICWA compliance. For example, the identification of AIAN heritage is not easy. It cannot be presumed that a child's appearance, name, or domicile indicates AIAN heritage.

Furthermore, determining eligibility for membership in a tribe, the primary trigger for ICWA protections, can only be made by a tribe itself. There is a widespread erroneous belief that blood quantum, contact with the tribe, or other criteria are necessary for tribal enrollment. ICWA training for child welfare workers and courts is often not mandated by states, and when it is, the nuances are often lost in the vast amount of information that is communicated.

ICWA does not explicitly address the concept of permanency in child welfare placements and does not mandate permanency plans for AIAN children in foster care. As a result, tribes and states follow AFSA timelines in permanency planning. ASFA's emphasis on timely permanency moves away from the ICWA ideal of reunifying children with their parents unless all other options are exhausted. When considering both pieces of legislation, it has been the standard legal practice that when two statutes potentially conflict, the more specific statute controls; in this instance, ICWA has the more precise language (Center for Court Innovation, 2011).

Although AIAN children who are members of federally recognized tribes are eligible for protections under ICWA, AIAN children who are not eligible for enrollment, including those who are members of historic state tribes, and U.S. citizens who are members of Canadian First Nation tribes, are not eligible for protections under ICWA. For this subgroup of AIAN children, cultural continuity has been dependent on state expansions of implementation of ICWA. Specifically, six states have expanded definitions of children eligible to be served under ICWA (Washington, Nebraska, Minnesota, Michigan, Iowa, and Oklahoma).

Families First Prevention Services Act

The policies presented in the proceeding sections highlight the unique and often complex relationship in public policy and law between the child welfare system and the courts. All the rules described have been in use, with updates, for many years and reflect the legislative and administration's ongoing effort to improve safety, permanency, and well-being out-comes. Historically, child welfare policy and laws establish a set of values and ideology, establish rules and provide instructions for states and courts, establish mechanisms for ac-countability for child outcomes, and allocate funding to states to manage cases of child maltreatment while in out-of-home care. In effect, services, funding, and oversight from the federal government have been directed mainly after the maltreatment has occurred. Prior policy reforms have improved the overall reduction in foster care placements. Still, advocates believe that many of these cases could be resolved if the parent and family system had access to quality intervention services to prevent the need for a child's removal from the family into out-of-home care in the first place.

To address this gap in public policy and practice, Congress passed the Family First Prevention Services Act (FFPSA) in 2018 (PL 115-123). The FFPSA is one of the most ex-tensive policy reforms in the recent history of child welfare, allowing states to transform their child welfare systems and follow public health models that seek to reduce or eliminate the conditions that pose a significant risk for out-of-home placement. Primarily a budget and finance reform initiative, the FFPSA expands the use of Title IV-E funds for in-home parent skills training, substance abuse, mental health, and kinship navigation services for any caregiver or child who is designated as a potential "candidate for foster care" to allow them to stay with that parent or caregiver (HHS, 2019). The FFPSA shifts resources into programming expected to keep families together to avoid trauma from family separation. This policy emphasizes the importance of children growing up with their own families and aims to provide child welfare agencies resources to engage families in services designed to increase safety and support children and youth. When removal can't be avoided, the FFPSA promotes the practice of placing children in the least restrictive and most home-like envir-onments, including expanded supports and opportunities for placement with kin and re-ducing the use of congregate care such as group homes, emergency shelters, or other types of institutional settings (HHS, 2019).

Challenges to the FFPSA

While writing this chapter, the FFPSA is in a policy implementation phase across the United States. Many states are currently outlining their implementation strategies for the policy. To date, only 18 states, the District of Columbia, and two tribes have submitted their FFPSA plans to the Administration for Children and Families for review and approval (HHS, 2020d). While the FFPSA is mainly supported, policy advocates are concerned with some specific mandates that may pose a significant challenge to quality implementation by child welfare agencies and the courts. Of central concern is the directive that appro-priated funds can only be used for approved evidence-based programs. Researchers and professionals in practice generally agree on the value of evidence-informed programs to guide service delivery and interventions. However, many of the models and programs ap-proved for child maltreatment prevention were not developed, tested, and evaluated with child welfare populations. Agencies and courts may direct families to services that are not approved but require a rigorous evaluation of their effectiveness to qualify for federal re-imbursement. Many child welfare organizations and providers may not have the funding or expertise to execute this type of rigorous evaluation, potentially stifling innovation, inclusivity, and adapted practices, narrowing the options of services that states utilize to help families.[1]

There are also concerns about the ability to develop and implement evidence-based interventions in rural and tribal communities. The vision to provide prevention-type services requires a system of care that can meet the family's needs for mental health, substance abuse, and in-home parenting skills services that do not exist in many rural and tribal communities (Belanger et al., 2008). Empirical studies have consistently found that rural and tribal communities are significantly more likely to have low accessibility to social services and are more likely to experience unemployment, poverty, educational disparities, and substance use (Children's Bureau, 2018; Clary, Ribar, & Weigensberg, 2020). This lack of access to resources makes children and families more likely to experience child welfare system involvement and less likely to access prevention services. Rural and tribal communities have rich assets and strengths. Therefore, the FFPSA should provide additional policy adaptations for building the evidence for service delivery innovations to ensure children in rural and tribal communities have access to Title IV-E reimbursable prevention services (Clary et al., 2020).

The Future of Child Welfare Policy

In our final section, we wish to offer a perspective on the future of child welfare policy. The future landscape of child welfare policy and practice will need to tackle some of our nation's and communities' most prominent issues. In our view, the future of child welfare policy will need to address three distinct and essential areas: issues of disproportionality and disparity, resource allocation and funding for child welfare and court services, and ensuring the sovereignty and resources for tribal child welfare.

Racial Disparity and Disproportionality

Child welfare policy and practice cannot turn away from decades of evidence of a disparity in outcomes for Black, African American, and AIAN children and families. A significant amount of research and repeated national data trends have documented the overrepresentation of BIPOC children in child welfare service systems (Putnam-Hornstein et al., 2013; Summers & Darnell, 2015). Disparities are evident at each of the critical decision points that occur in the courts, including the decision to investigate, the decision to remove, the decision to place in out-of-home care, the decision to reunify or terminate parental rights, and the decision on who can adopt and access postpermanency services across the child welfare continuum (Dettlaff & Rycraft, 2010; Putnam-Hornstein et al., 2013). Addressing this disparity necessitates solutions centered around parent and youth voices and experiences as a critical program development strategy. Researchers and advocates argue two contributors to these outcomes: poverty and racism, and bias. Those who claim that poverty is the significant contributor for child welfare involvement cite the overrepresentation of children of color who experience poverty in the United States. If poverty is the contributor

---

1. For a list of programs approved for use under the FFPSA, visit the Title IV-E Prevention Services Clearinghouse at http://www.preventionservices.com.

to disproportionality, then future policy must directly address poverty reduction and economic security, community development, and programing with aggressive policies to prevent out-of-home placement for children. The other compelling argument is that child welfare is a carceral system designed to provide investigation and family surveillance. Like all the other carceral systems, there is an institutional and structural bias within the system that has been persistent and pervasive (Detlaff et al., 2020). Future policy must directly address this by holding the child welfare and court system accountable for deconstructing those systems and building an equitable and fair system. Future policy in child welfare will need to be deliberately anti-racist to eliminate bias and racism for meaningful reforms.

Resource Allocation in Child Welfare

Another challenge for future child welfare policy is the allocation and distribution of resources to ensure children's and families' safety, permanency, and well-being. Child welfare services are funded from braided and integrated sources, including Titles IV-E and IV-B of the Social Security Act, Medicaid funds, and Temporary Assistance to Needy Families (TANF) funds. Federal funding only provides a portion of the costs. Child welfare agencies require state funding to meet the total costs of agency services, resulting in a variation of resources allocated to provide needed services across the United States. Child welfare services are vulnerable to the ebb and flow of state economic turns and victims to budget cuts to funded services. The funding formulas used to support child welfare programming are complex, and each policy outlines specific requirements for states to draw funding from federal sources. Eligibility requirements attached to funding sources are not always driven by what children and families need. The complex funding process may guide programs and services to the funding source and not be driven by children and families.

Territory, Tribal Control, and Resource Allocation

Since the passage of ICWA, funding and allocation of resources have been primarily influenced by the tribe's relationship with the state. It was not until the passage of the Fostering Connections to Success Act (FCSA) of 2008 that tribes had the opportunity to work directly with the federal government to draw the resources they are eligible to receive. Of the 650 federally recognized tribes and native villages that exist in the United States today, only 17 have an approved IV-E plan to operate a foster care, adoption assistance, and guardianship assistance program directly with the federal government, and only 148 have approved IV-B plans (HHS, 2019). All other tribes rely exclusively on tribal-state agreements for the provision of child welfare services. Only about half of tribes with tribal-state agreements in place believe their agreements with states are consistently honored and believe that the tribe and state work collaboratively to serve AIAN children and families in culturally appropriate ways (National Resource Center for Tribes, 2011). Although the federal FCSA and other federal child welfare policies have allocated funds specifically to tribes, the amounts have been small and difficult to access. Resources are usually only accessible if the tribe adopts colonized child welfare practice standards that do not align with Indigenous traditions, families, and parenting practices. Child welfare policy of the future will need to ensure that tribal sovereignty is a priority and that Indigenous ways of parenting, child

TABLE 13.1 Key Terms and Descriptions for Child Welfare

Key Terms	Description
Another Planned Permanent Living Arrangement	A permanency option that can be used by the courts when other permanency options have been ruled out. The state must present compelling reasons that are case specific, demonstrating that this option is in the youth's best interest and cannot be used until a youth is age 16 or older (Capacity Building Center for States & Center for Courts, 2016).
Candidate for Foster Care	A child identified by the child welfare agency or courts to be at imminent risk of entering foster care but who can remain safely in the child's home or kinship placement as long as services needed to prevent the entry of the child into foster care are provided. http://lawfilesext.leg.wa.gov/biennium/2019-20/Pdf/Bills/Session%20Laws/House/1900.SL.pdf?q=20201207144044
Child Maltreatment	A generalized term used to describe any abuse or neglect to a person under the age of 18.
Concurrent Planning	An approach to planning designed to reduce the time in foster care by using a parallel pursuit of an alternate family goal (e.g., adoption) while also pursuing a plan for family reunification (CWIG, 2018).
Cultural Permanency	Ensuring the children and youth have long-term and meaningful connections in order to have knowledge of and maintain customs, traditions, ceremonies, or other vital aspects of their culture (Bennett, 2015).
Customary Adoption	A traditional alternative to standard adoption practice and considered a more appropriate permanency placement for AIAN children. Customary adoption allows children to be adopted without requiring termination of parental rights. This practice exercises tribal sovereignty and helps to maintain family connections.
Guardian Ad Litem (GAL)	A person appointed by the courts to represent the child's best interest in judicial proceedings. The GAL may be an attorney or a court-appointed special advocate (CASA), a trained community volunteer (CWIG, 2017).
Kinship Care/Relative Caregiver	The full-time care and protection of a child by relatives, members of their tribe or clan, godparents, stepparents, or other adults who have a family relationship to a child. These can be informal and private arrangements or formal custody arrangements by the courts (CWIG, 2016c).
Legal Permanency	A legal status such as adoption, legal guardianship, or reunification with one's biological family. Also can be called formal permanency. This often signals a discharge of the case from the child welfare system (Salazar et al., 2018).
Reasonable Effort	Refers to the state social service agencies' activities to provide assistance and services to preserve and reunify families (CWIG, 2020).
Relational Permanency	Semanchin-Jones and LaLiberte (2013) define relational permanency as "youth experiencing a sense of belonging through enduring, life-long connections to parents, extended family, or other caring adults, including at least one adult who will provide a permanent, parentlike connection for that youth" (p. 509). In other words, permanency is subjectively defined by the youth irrespective of a legal status.
Termination of Parental Rights	A court decision to end the legal parent-child relationship. This can be voluntary or involuntary. Once a relationship is terminated, a child is legally free to be placed for adoption (CWIG, 2016a).

caregiving, protection, and other practices are acknowledged and supported in funding sources and additional resource allocation (National Indian Child Welfare Association, 2018).

Conclusion

Ultimately, child welfare policy should focus on ending child maltreatment and neglect, taking a public health approach to preventing problems that contribute to child maltreatment and neglect by targeting policies and interventions via known risk indicators. Public health models use prevention strategies and primary interventions to prevent child maltreatment from occurring. In contrast, the current child welfare system and court systems are predominantly tertiary prevention services, providing services to prevent the reoccurrence of maltreatment. Ensuring economic security and universal access to mental health care, building comprehensive programs to prevent substance use and promote recovery, and focusing on whole-family well-being are the strategies to reduce or eliminate the risk of child maltreatment (Vieth, 2007). Advocates, researchers, social work professionals, and the legal system will need to work collaboratively to extend critical safety net programs to ensure our children's protection for the future.

References

Administration for Children and Families. (1995). *Program instruction*. U.S. Department of Health and Human Services. https://www.acf.hhs.gov/sites/default/files/cb/pi9523.pdf

Atwood, B. A. (2008). Wells conference on adoption law: Achieving permanency for American Indian and Alaska Native children—Lessons from tribal traditions. *Capitol University Law Review, 37*(2), 239–292.

Belanger, K., Price-Mayo, B., & Espinosa, D. (2008). The plight of rural child welfare: Meeting standards without services. *Journal of Public Child Welfare, 1*(4), 1–19. https://doi-org.10.1080/15548730902118181

Bennett, K. (2015). Cultural permanence for Indigenous children and youth: Reflections from a delegated Aboriginal agency in British Columbia. *First Peoples Child & Family Review, 10*(1), 99–115.

Brooks, D., Barth, R. P., Bussiere, A., & Patterson, G. (1999). Adoption and race: Implementing the multiethnic placement act and the interethnic adoption provisions. *Social Work, 44*(2), 167–178.

Brooks, D., & Goldberg, S. (2001). Gay and lesbian adoptive and foster care placements: Can they meet the needs of waiting children? *Social Work, 46*(2), 147–157. https://doi-org/10.1093/sw/46.2.147

Burge, P. (2020). Attempting to operationalize multi-dimensional definition of permanency in child welfare practice: Results from a demonstration project. *Journal of Public Child Welfare*. https://www.doi.10.1080/11548732.2020.1835784

Carolina, N., & Virginia, W. (2020). *Reasonable efforts to preserve or reunify families and achieve permanency for children*. U.S. Department of Health and Human Services, Administration for Children and Families, Children's Bureau.

Center for Court Innovation. (2011). *The Indian Child Welfare Act: Improving compliance through state-tribal coordination*. https://www.courtinnovation.org/sites/default/files/documents/ICWA.pdf

Chibnall, S., Dutch, N. M., Jones-Harden, B., Brown, A. Gourdine, R., Smith, J., Boone, A., & Snyder, S. (2003). *Children of color in the child welfare system: Perspectives from the child welfare community*. U.S. Department of Health and Human Services, Children's Bureau, Administration for Children and Families. https://www.childwelfare.gov/pubPDFs/children.pdf

Child Welfare Information Gateway (CWIG). (2016a). *Grounds for involuntary termination of parental rights*. U.S. Department of Health and Human Services, Children's Bureau. https://www.childwelfare.gov/pubPDFs/groundtermin.pdf

Child Welfare Information Gateway (CWIG). (2016b). *Frequently asked questions from lesbian, gay, bisexual, transgender and questioning (LGBTQ) prospective foster and adoptive parents*. U.S. Department of Health and Human Services, Children's Bureau.

Child Welfare Information Gateway (CWIG). (2016c). *Kinship caregivers and the child welfare system*. U.S. Department of Health and Human Services, Children's Bureau. https://www.childwelfare.gov/pubPDFs/f_kinshi.pdf

Child Welfare Information Gateway (CWIG). (2019). *About CAPTA: A legislative history*. U.S. Department of Health and Human Services, Children's Bureau. https://www.childwelfare.gov/pubs/factsheets/about/

Child Welfare Information Gateway (CWIG). (2020). *Reasonable efforts to preserve or reunify families and achieve permanency for children*. U.S. Department of Health and Human Services, Administration for Children and Families, Children's Bureau.

Clarie, K., & Moore, A. (2015). Attitudes to practice: National survey of adoption obstacles faced by gay and lesbian prospective parents. *Journal of Gay & Lesbian Social Services, 27*(4), 436–456. https://doi-org.ezproxy.lib.ou.edu/10.1080/10538720.2015.1085347

Clary, E., Ribar, C., & Weigensberg, E. (2020). *Challenges in providing substance use disorder treatment to child welfare clients in rural communities*. United States Department of Health and Human Services, Office of the Assistant Secretary for Planning and Evaluation. https://aspe.hhs.gov/reports/challenges-providing-substance-use-disorder-treatment-child-welfare-clients-rural-communities

Collins-Camargo, C., Jones, B. L., & Krusich, S. (2009). What do we know about strategies for involving citizens in public child welfare: A review of recent literature and implications for policy, practice, and future research? *Journal of Public Child Welfare, 3*, 287–304. htt:p://doi.org.10.1080/15548730903129954

Congressional Research Service. (2004, November 8). *Child welfare: Implementation of the Adoption and Safe Families Act (P.L. 105-89)*. https://www.everycrsreport.com/files/20041108_RL30759_96784ee8d3d99882a9c887e9da08de67ee99e872.pdf

Cross, T. (2011, July 18). *A "mission not impossible." Understanding and reducing disparities and disproportionality*. Tribal and Urban Indian Systems of Care Grantee Meeting. https://www.nicwa.org/wp-content/uploads/2016/11/MissionNotImpossible_DisparitiesDisproportionality.pdf

Day, A., Murphy, K. S., & Whitekiller, V. D. (2020). Characteristics and competencies of successful resource parents working in Indian Country: A systematic review of the research. *Children and Youth Services Review, 121*, 105834.

Dettlaff, A. J., & Rycraft, J. R. (2010). Factors contributing to disproportionality in the child welfare system: Views from the legal community. *Social Work, 55*(3), 213–224. https://doi.org/10.1093/sw/55.3.213

Detlaff, A. J., Weber, K., Pendleton, M., Boyd, R., Bettencourt, B., & Burton, L. (2020). It is not a broken system, it is a system that needs to be broken: The upEND movement to abolish the child welfare system. *Journal of Public Child Welfare, 14*(5), 500–517. ttps://doi.org/10.1080/15548732.2020.1814542

Geenen, S., & Powers, L. E. (2007). "Tomorrow is another problem": The experiences of youth in foster care during their transition into adulthood. *Children and Youth Services Review, 29*(8), 1085–1101. https://doi.org/10.1016/j.childyouth.2007.04.008

Gilbert, R., Kemp, A., Thoburn, J., Sidebotham, P., Radford, L., Glaser, D., & MacMillan, H. L. (2009). Recognizing and responding to child maltreatment. *The Lancet, 373*(9658), 167–180.

Glynn, G. F. (2007). The Child Abuse Prevention and Treatment Act—Promoting the unauthorized practice of law. *Journal of Law & Family Studies, 9*(1), 53–78. https://heinonline.org/HOL/P?h=hein.journals/jlfst9&i=62

Golden, O., & Macomber, J. (2009). *Intentions and results: A look back at the Adoption and Safe Families Act*. Urban Institute. https://affcny.org/wp-content/uploads/IntentionsandResults.pdf

Hort, K. A. (2001). Is twenty-two months beyond the best interest of the child? ASFA's guidelines for the termination of parental rights. *Fordham Urban Law Journal, 28*(6), 1879–1921.

Jennings, P. K. (2006). The trouble with the Multiethnic Placement Act: An empirical look at transracial adoption. *Sociological Perspectives, 49*(4), 559–581.

Kalisher, A., Spielfogel, J., Shenk, M., & Eduoard, K. (2020). *The Multiethnic Placement Act 25 years later: Diligent recruitment plans*. Washington, DC: Office of the Assistant Secretary for Planning and Evaluation. https://aspe.hhs.gov/system/files/pdf/264526/MEPA-Diligent-recruitment-report.pdf

LaFomboise, T., Coleman, L. K., & Gerton, J. (1993). Psychological impact of biculturalism. *Psychological Bulletin, 114*(3), 395–412.

Lippy, C., Jumarali, S. N., Nnawulezi, N. A., Williams, E. P., & Burk, C. (2020). The impact of mandatory reporting laws on survivors of intimate partner violence: Intersectionality, help-seeking and the need for change. *Journal of Family Violence, 35*(3), 255–267. https://doi.org/10.1007/s10896-019-00103-w

Louisell, M. J. (2008). *Six steps to find a family: A practice guide to family search and engagement (FSE)*. National Resource Center for Family-Centered Practice and Permanency Planning, Hunter College &

California Permanency for Youth Project. http://www.hunter.cuny.edu/socwork/nrcfcpp/downloads/SixSteps.pdf

McTavish, J. R., Gonzalez, A., Santesso, N., MacGregor, J. C. D., McKee, C., & MacMillan, H. L. (2020). Identifying children exposed to maltreatment: A systematic review update. *BMC Pediatrics, 20*(113), 1–14. https://doi.org/10.1186/s12887-020-2015-4

National Indian Child Welfare Association. (2018). *Tribal leadership series: Funding child welfare services, First Kids First.*

National Indian Law Library. (n.d.). *Topic 14. Expert witness.* https://narf.org/nill/documents/icwa/faq/expert.html

Phillips, C. M., & Mann, A. (2013). Historical analysis of the Adoption and Safe Families Act of 1997. *Journal of Human Behavior in the Social Environment, 23*(7), 862–868. https://doi.org/10.1080/10911359.2012.809290

Putnam-Hornstein, E., Needell, B., King, B., & Johnson-Motoyama, M. (2013). Racial and ethnic disparities: A population-based examination of risk factors for involvement with child protective services. *Child Abuse & Neglect, 37*(1), 33–46. https://doi.org/10.1016/j.chiabu.2012.08.005

Puzzanchera, C., & Taylor, M. (2020). *Disproportionality rates for children of color in Foster Care Dashboard.* National Council of Juvenile and Family Court Judges.

Raz, M. (2017). Unintended consequences of expanded mandatory reporting laws. *Pediatrics, 139*(4).

Salazar, A. M., Jones, K. R., Amemiya, J., Cherry, A., Brown, E. C., Catalano, R. F., & Monahan, K. C. (2018). Defining and achieving permanency among older youth in foster care. *Children and Youth Services Review, 87*, 9–16. https://doi.org.10.1016/j.childyouth.2018.02.006

Samuels, G. M., & Pryce, J. M. (2008). "What doesn't kill you makes you stronger": Survivalist self-reliance as resilience and risk among young adults aging out of foster care. *Children and Youth Services Review, 30*(10), 1198–1210.

Semanchin-Jones, A., & LaLiberte, T. L. (2013). Measuring youth connections: A component of relational permanence for foster youth. *Children and Youth Services Review, 35*(3), 509–517. https://doi.org/10.1016/j.childyouth.2012.12.006

Summers, A., & Darnell, A. (2015). What does court observation tell us about judicial practice and the courts in child welfare? *Journal of Public Child Welfare, 9*(4), 341–361. https://doi.org/10.1080/15548732.2015.1061467

Tribal Star. (2015). *Tribal sovereignty and child welfare: Practice tips for social workers to understand government-to-government relations in ICWA cases.* https://theacademy.sdsu.edu/wp-content/uploads/2016/03/tribal-sovereignty-rev-2015.pdf

Wesley, B. C., Pryce, J., & Samuels, G. M. (2020). Meaning and essence of child well-being according to child welfare professionals. *Child and Adolescent Social Work Journal, 37*, 425–441.

U.S. Department of Health and Human Services (HHS). (2019). *ACF-CB-IM-19-01.* Administration on Children, Youth, and Families. Available at https://fosteringchamps.org/wp-content/uploads/2019/02/Final-HHS-foster-family-model-licensing-standards.pdf

U.S. Department of Health and Human Services (HHS). (2020a). *ASPE research summary: The Multiethnic Placement Act 25 years later.* https://aspe.hhs.gov/system/files/pdf/264526/MEPA-Research-summary.pdf

U.S. Department of Health and Human Services (HHS). (2020b). *ACYF-CB-0IM-17-02,* Administration for Children and Families, Children's Bureau. https://www.acf.hhs.gov/sites/default/files/documents/cb/im1702.pdf

U.S. Department of Health and Human Services (HHS). (2020c). *The AFCARS report: Preliminary F.Y. 2019 estimates as of June 23.2020, No. 27.* Administration for Children and Families, Children's Bureau.

U.S. Department of Health and Human Services (HHS). (2020d). *Status of submitted Title IV-E prevention program five-year plans.* Administration for Children and Families, Children's Bureau. https://www.acf.hhs.gov/cb/data/status-submitted-title-iv-e-prevention-program-five-year-plans

U.S. Department of Health and Human Services (HHS). (2021). *Child maltreatment, 2019.* Administration for Children and Families, Children's Bureau. https://www.acf.hhs.gov/cb/report/child-maltreatment-2019

Vieth, V. I. (2007). Unto the third generation: A call to end child abuse in the United States within 120 years (revised and expanded). *Hamline Journal of Public Law & Policy, 28*(1), 1–74. https://www.actx.edu/cj/files/filecabinet/folder2/Handout_Unto_a_Third_Generation_revised_version_Vieth.pdf

Zavez, M. (2008). Use of the Adoption and Safe Families Act at 15/22 months for incarcerated parents. *Vermont Law Review, 33*(2), 187–199. https://lawreview-vermontlaw-edu.ezproxy.lib.ou.edu/wp-content/uploads/2012/02/11-Zavez-Book-2-Vol-33.pdf

14

Mass Incarceration and For-Profit Prisons

John Carl

At the time of the development of this text, the United States was once again facing a major threat from disease: A small virus that cannot be seen, known as COVID-19, was killing millions of people worldwide and was a threat not just to this country but to humanity. Of course, this is not the first challenge to confront this nation, and it most certainly won't be the last. Everyone can parrot the phrase "an ounce of prevention is worth a pound of cure," but that doesn't necessarily mean that a society is ready or willing to actually abide by this. As we can see with this example and prior health crises, the debate is consistent: What is the role of government in the example this epidemic, and what can be done? As we saw with the Spanish influenza of 1918, mishandling of a pandemic can result in millions of deaths. Whether or not COVID-19 will result in the same outcome is unknown at this time, but one thing is clear: Earlier public crises led to increasing roles of government in trying to curb social problems, be they pandemics or crime (Martini et al., 2019).

In times like this, those involved in the helping professions, including but not limited to social workers, are faced with challenging questions: How do you hold to the core values of your profession in times of great turmoil? The values of service, social justice, and dignity and worth of persons become challenging in an environment where personal safety can be jeopardized by an unsafe interaction. The same is true for those who work in prisons. My first experience in working in a prison came while I was still a master's of social work student doing a practicum. One of the first documents I was required to sign by the prison was a form that stated that they would not negotiate for my life in the event of a prison riot. Nothing will challenge your dedication to these values like determining whether or not you're willing to die on the job. These and many other challenges face the practitioner considering working in the prison system (National Association of Social Workers, 2017). This is a system with many different parts and a variety of justifications for why it exists as

John Carl, *Mass Incarceration and For-Profit Prisons* In: *Handbook of Forensic Social Work*. Edited by: David Axlyn McLeod, Anthony P. Natale, and Kristin W. Mapson, Oxford University Press. © Oxford University Press 2024. DOI: 10.1093/oso/9780197694732.003.0014 it does and the exact extent of its use. As a social worker and a criminologist, it seems self-evident that few who have studied our current system would label it as "ideal." Of course, finding an "ideal" way to lock people in small rooms against their will is a challenge that would seem obvious. The challenge of respecting the dignity and worth of a person can be particularly difficult especially when that person has committed some unspeakable act against an innocent person. My first experience was to do group therapy with convicted sex offenders inside a medium-security prison, and since that time I have taught classes inside with college students, both those incarcerated and those who are not. The problem for those who will work in this setting is always balancing the boundary between justice and service while acknowledging the real dilemma of personal security.

In this chapter we will look into the justification of punishment as well as the history of prisons in the United States, culminating in what most criminologists call the incarceration boom (Clear, 2007) of the 1980s, and the subsequent challenges to funding a prison system that, when compared to other democratic nations, is significantly larger. One thing is abundantly clear about the United States. When comparing it to other democratic and developed countries, it uses the prison system significantly more than do other similar nations. Table 14.1 shows the rate of incarceration in selected countries. Those chosen were selected by their strong record keeping and their similarity to the U.S. governmental structure. The nation with the highest incarceration rate in Europe is the United Kingdom and ranks 114th in the world. However, you'll notice that its crime index ranking is actually quite close to that of the United States. The same is true with France. In fact, the incarceration rate differences cannot be easily explained by crime rates. Why? Because the decision to use prisons and how to use them is a social decision. While it does seem true that the United States has more crime than many of these nations, the differences between the crime rates and the prison population rate are not proportional (World Prison Brief, 2020; World Population Review, 2020). Why? Because in general, the United States uses prison more frequently than do other nations. The criminal justice system has many options of what to do with miscreants, including fines, community service, warnings, house arrest,

TABLE 14.1 Rates of Incarceration in Different Countries

Title	Global Rank: Prison Rate	Prison Population per 100,000	Global Rank: Crime Index	Crime Index per 100,000
United States	1	639	50	47.7
United Kingdom	114	132	64	44.54
Portugal	138	109	102	29.83
Canada	141	107	78	40.64
France	156	87	52	47.37
Germany	174	69	90	35.14
Netherlands	183	63	109	27.15
Norway	202	49	91	34.62
Japan	206	39	122	21.67

Source: Compiled by the author (World Prison Brief, 2020; World Population Review, 2020).

and imprisonment. The United States uses imprisonment in almost 70% of criminal cases, while the United Kingdom uses it in only 33% of the cases and Germany in only 7.5% of cases (Justice Policy, 2011). So why do we use prisons so much, and how did we get to this point? To answer that we will turn our attention to a brief history of punishment and what has justified incarceration in the United States.

Societies have always had to deal with crime problems and in general have settled on the idea of punishment as the solution. The justifications of these punishments have been varied over time, and before we look deeply into the past and present of prisons in the United States, we should familiarize ourselves with some of the justifications for punishing our fellow citizens for doing things that we don't like.

Early societies in Greece and Rome served as the foundation for most of the legal systems of the West. Criminal punishments were variable but frequently included death, slavery, or banishment. At that time, banishment could be a serious punishment as the banished person would be left outside the protection of the group and have to fend for themselves in the wild.

The punishment systems found in Europe were quite similar to those of early Greece and Rome. Death and banishment were particularly severe punishments, but hard labor, such as working in forced labor camps and being forced to row war ships as galley slaves, was also used. In parts of Europe, mutilation by having the hands or feet cut off was akin to a death sentence and used throughout the Middle Ages. With the age of enlightenment and colonialism a new form of banishment came into vogue, known as transportation: Criminals were sent to "penal colonies" across the globe and left there to inhabit and create a new society still beholden to the imperial power that sent them there. While these represent only a few of the ways that the law tried to control behavior, it is important to note that no society of any size seems to have been able to eradicate crime from within its borders.

The thinking behind these forms of punishment is key to understanding them. The theory of *retribution or retaliation* is as ancient as human beings. This theory gives the wronged party a chance to impose a suitable punishment on the person who hurt them. It is essentially the justification for getting even. When you were a toddler and someone hit you on the playground for taking their swing, they were retaliating against you. Biblical references such as "an eye for an eye" are often quoted as the serene song of retribution theorists.

However, contrary to what many people may believe, the "eye for an eye" standard was actually intended to prevent people from taking excessive private vengeance for wrongs committed against them. Under this standard, while you may expect to be paid back by a thief who stole from you, you are not allowed to kill their entire family. One of the earliest legal codes known to humanity dates to 1770 BCE and is known as the Code of Hammurabi (n.d.). Named after the Babylonian king Hammurabi, this legal code provides clear laws for a number of matters including issues of inheritance, divorce, contracts, and, of course, crime and punishment. Legal codes describe both crimes and punishments, and in this code you can see the "eye for an eye" standard being applied.

While the idea of "eye for an eye" justice may appeal to us in its simplicity, in practice it can be exceptionally hard to apply, particularly in modern, complex societies. Stealing from thieves is hard to do, especially when they don't have the means to repay the owner for what they stole. Determining how to punish a rapist or a child predator who themself has no children can become exceptionally difficult using this standard. In the United States today, some suggest that this standard justifies the use of the death penalty for murder; however, not all murderers are charged with the death penalty, and many who take a life accidentally via some neglectful behavior are never themselves killed.

Expiation as justification for punishment looks at crime as the result of poor morality. Crimes are moral wrongs and so the purpose of doing something to the criminal is to allow them opportunity to atone for their "sins." Atonement can lead to expiation when the person who commits the moral wrong tries to make it right. If, for example, you realize that some gossipy lie you told is having long-term negative effects against another person, you might go to the person you told the lie to in the first place and admit your "sin."

Historically, particularly in the Christian West, criminality and "immoral behaviors" were linked. In the colonies in what would become the United States, punishments were frequently public and meant to embarrass the offender and shame them into no longer committing the wrong. For example, in *The Scarlet Letter* by Nathanial Hawthorne, the adulterous woman is required to wear a scarlet "A" on her clothing to show everyone in the community that she was an adulterer.

While today adultery is no longer seen as a crime, moral sentencing still may occur. Frequently petty or first-time offenders receive some type of community service to avoid jail time. When they are picking up trash in a park or volunteering at some approved setting, everyone knows the offender is a wrongdoer and the public humiliation and service are felt to teach them to avoid this wrong in the future.

The notion of *deterrence* is another justification of punishment built on a simple premise. Deterrence is rooted in a belief that people are self-interested and want to achieve pleasure and avoid pain. If we suffer for an action, we'll be deterred from doing it again. The justification is commonplace in parenting. Parents may try to socialize their children by placing them in "timeout" when they do something they're not supposed to do. The assumption is that having them sit in a corner for a few minutes will teach them not to do that act again. Deterrence holds with an assumption that people will avoid that which is painful, and so "learn" from their mistakes.

The application of deterrence theory is the basis for most of the U.S. criminal justice system. Punishments are supposed to be painful enough to deter future criminal actions, and in that vein there are two types of deterrence discussed by criminologists, general and specific.

General deterrence suggests that people will learn from the pain of another. If your 3-year-old sees his 5-year-old older brother get punished, he won't do the offending act because he saw the punishment received by his brother. The entire notion that society could lock you in prison is designed to serve as a general deterrent against criminal behavior. Most people have never even been inside a prison, and yet the fear that they might have to go there will generally deter them from breaking the law.

Specific deterrence happens to the person who was punished. When a person is sent to prison, the punishment is supposed to be sufficiently painful that they would not want to return. For deterrence to "work," people must experience some level of "pain," and so the 5-year-old who receives the punishment decides that timeout is terrible and so he won't engage in cookie theft again. In other words, proponents of specific deterrence believe that people can learn not to make the same mistake twice.

Jeremy Bentham (1789/1970), a British philosopher who died in the 1830s, suggests that deterrence should work, but in order for it to work three criteria must be met. The punishment must be swift, certain, and severe enough to deter the person from doing the act again, but not so severe that the punisher loses heart.

When the mother sees the little boy reaching for the cookie jar after he's been told he may not have a cookie, she must act then. Waiting a few hours and then punishing the child will not deter the behavior. The most important criterion required for deterrence to work is certainty. If you know you are going to get caught, you will most likely not commit the act. If the mother stands by the cookie jar, the little boy is unlikely to try to get inside of it. If you see a police officer on the side of the road, you will probably slow down your car. Finally, Bentham suggests says that the type of punishment itself will have some effect on its efficacy. Punishments that are too severe will not "work" to deter future acts because the individual will see the punishment as torture and not justified. If your mother slaps your hand for reaching into the cookie jar, that may make some sense; if she sends you to timeout for an hour, that may not. Bentham warns that punishment in and of itself is "evil" because it inflicts harm on another person, but it is a "necessary evil" that should be used carefully and cautiously.

In practice, punishment rarely meets these criteria, particularly when it is applied in a modern sense. For example, clearance rates of crimes in the United States show that very few crimes are actually solved. Table 14.2 shows the rate at which certain types of crimes are solved by arrest or for which a known criminal is believed to be guilty. Most crimes in the United States have low likelihoods of the offender getting caught, at least the first time they do it, with the notable exceptions of murder and assault. Since certainty is almost always on the side of the criminal, the odds of deterrence working are challenging. That doesn't mean it cannot work.

Criminologist Marcus Felson (1998) has suggested that many crimes can be "structured" out of society. For example, think about the tags that clothing stores put on their products and thus decrease the odds that people might try to steal them. Automobiles that

TABLE 14.2 Clearance Rates Compared to Crimes Committed

Crime	Clearance Rate
Murder/Homicide/Manslaughter	61.6%
Rape	34.5%
Robbery	29.7%
Aggravated Assault	53.3%
Burglary	13.5%
Larceny Theft	19.2%
Motor Vehicle Theft	13.7%

Source: Uniform Crime Reports Clearances (2017).

use electronic keys have made car theft less attractive and can decrease the ability of joy riders to simply "hot-wire" your car. This type of deterrence is not necessarily certain all the time, but Felson does argue that we can design out many crimes from society.

William Chambliss (1966) suggests that deterrence is more likely to be effective in certain types of crimes. For example, if you're thinking of robbing a convenience store and you walk in only to discover three police officers standing in the store talking, you're probably going to turn around and leave. Certainty will deter you from actions. However, if you are angry with your partner who works at the store and you've decided to shoot them over it, you're unlikely to care if police witness this crime or not. Crimes of passion, which are often violent offenses, are harder to deter because the actor is usually not thinking clearly. In order for deterrence to work well, criminals need to be thinking, and the certainty of being caught must be apparent.

Another justification for punishment that is close to atonement but slightly different is known as *rehabilitation*, or *moral reformation*. Here, instead of trying to "right a wrong," the wrongdoer is being "taught" that their actions were wrong and then trained to avoid them. Criminals end up in prison because they lacked the skills to make it on the outside. Therefore, the purpose of prison is to give them the skills to avoid making poor choices in the future. The job, then, of the corrections system is to "correct" the behavior. Thus, the purpose of locking someone in prison is to give them the skills and training to avoid those problematic actions in the future. Sometimes this involves teaching them job skills; other times it involves teaching them an entire new set of behaviors.

In the present day, so-called boot camp prisons strive to instill military-style discipline in inmates. Being incarcerated in a prison like this will likely lead you to have an extended boot-camp-like experience where exercise and hard work coupled with iron discipline are demanded. Inmates are immersed in a world that demands obedience to authority and will therefore learn new paths of behavior. Of course, these types of prisons may be popular with the public, but they have not shown much effect in curbing the behaviors of the people placed in them (Austin, 2000; Parent, 2003). We will look more deeply into the rehabilitation movement's rise and fall in the United States later in the chapter.

Perhaps the most central and agreed-upon purpose for punishment is to protect society from wrongdoers. When a serial killer or serial rapist is locked away, everyone is safer. The justification for punishing wrongdoers is to thus incapacitate them from being able to commit further acts against society and against innocent victims. While very few people in prison are serial killers, the justification for locking up drug dealers or credit card thieves is the same. The idea here is that simply locking away people who create problems will make the entire population safer.

The History and Role of Prisons in the United States

If you consider a brief history of punishment in the United States, you can see every one of these types of justifications for punishment applied. Throughout the history of the

United States, we have always had a "crime" problem, but that certainly is not unique to this country alone.

Almost immediately upon landing on the shores of the New World, landowners quickly discovered that not everyone coming to the New World was playing by the same rules. Many of the early colonists to the United States were actually sentenced to come to the New World through transportation. An estimated 50,000 British "criminals" were transported to the New World from 1717 to 1775 alone. Many of these were convicted of minor crimes including unpaid debts. At the time of the revolution there were 2.5 million residents in the United States, and around 50,000 of these were transported workers.

For many of the transported, the cities became the place to find work. Recall that at this time much of what we now see as the East Coast was actually unknown and unsettled. Cities were growing and of course the problems associated with all cities emerged. Issues related to vagrancy and theft were so common that jails were often the first public building built in a new town. In fact, at the time of the revolution, jails were more prevalent than schools or hospitals in most areas. Since the formation of the United States we've followed the punishment model, trying to extricate ourselves from miscreant behavior by inflicting some type of pain on criminals, be that through imprisonment, public shaming, or death (Christian, 1998).

At this time of our history the concept of a "prison" as we know it today didn't really exist. Early prisons were little more than large group holding cells where the people who were awaiting trial were housed along with those who had already had their punishment decided. But not long after the revolution the first "modern" prisons started to be built. By the early 1800s prisons were being built in 11 states and most were labeled penitentiaries.

The first was in Quaker Pennsylvania in 1790 and was named a penitentiary primarily because policymakers thought it should be a place where criminals could reflect upon their crimes, read the scriptures, and repent of their sinfulness. The structure of these buildings was designed to be an almost monastic-like building where the convicted lived in their "cells" and ideally spent time in prayer and reflection seeking God's forgiveness for whatever wrong they had committed. These buildings were intended to be a more humane way to deal with convicted offenders and frequently allowed them solitude so that they might have time to reflect upon their misdeeds.

Prisons sprung up across the new country in every state, creating a state penitentiary system in each of the former colonies. States each had their own rules and systems, but generally the idea behind most prisons was that crime was akin to a disease, and so like we do in a pandemic, we need to isolate and separate the criminal from society, but also from each other to stop the spread of the disease. Individual cells were common and they were "plush" compared to the dungeon-like group holding pens of earlier times. While many saw these as more humane, they did little more than house and incapacitate individuals.

While new states were being added to the Union, the business community decided that incarceration was a potential profit center. Today many might think that private prisons are a new creation started in the 1980s to house the incarceration boom. But the facts are clear: Private prisons have been around a long time. Prior to the Civil

War, states and territories were allowing industry to create and run prisons. The famous California prison, San Quinton, was originally run by private contractors after the inmates finished building it in 1852. Louisiana had private prisons dating back as far as 1844. Private prisons were generally run like the workhouses once so prevalent in Great Britain. Inmates worked in whatever the industry was of that particular prison. The inmate labor was free, and profit was the motive. Because these were private institutions, public authorities were rarely involved in overseeing what happened. Reports of torture and abuse of inmates were rampant. Following the Civil War, private prisons, particularly in the South, often incarcerated former slaves who were for all intents and purposes living in forced-labor camps that were not that much different than where they lived as slaves. Private prisons were most common in the South, but their history in the United States is a long one (Bauer, 2018).

This early background of jails and prisons began to change following the Civil War. The United States entered what is known as the Progressive Era at the end of the 19th century and into the 20th. Social welfare programs began to emerge, and social workers will note that during this time period Jane Addams built Hull House in Chicago, ushering in a systemic perspective of poverty and the problems associated with it. Instead of seeing poverty, addiction, and dysfunction as a sign of moral failure, Addams took the bold step of seeing it as the consequence of social conditions. She and others of her day were on the ground floor of the professional social work profession in the United States, and her ideas would find their way into many various social settings, including prisons (Addams & Case, 1923/1928).

Logically, if social structures can create problems, changing social structures can fix them. The writings of Emile Durkheim (1893/1933) called on thinkers of this time to ask what the proper functions of society were, and the role of law in society. In complex societies repressive law dominates. The punishment of the offender is not necessarily related to the damage to the victim, but the damage to society. If you are found to have robbed someone, the state will punish you. This is because law is created to create social order, and therefore violation of the social order should be punished by the society itself. His thinking is much in line with the thinking of Italian criminal justice scholar Cesare Beccaria, whose ideas, published more than 100 years earlier, would serve as the basis of modern justice systems throughout the world. In essence, Beccaria (1764/1995) points out that violations of the law are violations against the state, and therefore should be punished by the state. He argues that punishment must fit the crime, and that if applied properly, punishment can decrease criminality.

The second type of law Durkheim (1893/1933) discusses is known as restitutive law and focuses on the wrong inflicted on the victim. You might think of this as trying to right the wrong. If your car is damaged in an accident you didn't cause, you expect the person who hit you to fix the car. Lawsuits and damages directly applied to the perpetrator are the hallmarks of restitutive law. While both forms of law are present in modern society, the primary way in which law is applied against criminal action became repressive, or punishment. Durkheim (1893/1933) argues that this is expected since the society becomes so complex that offenders and victims frequently are not connected in any way, and so punishment is the only meaningful way that human behavior can be controlled and ensure society functions properly. What is important here to note is that criminals can be transformed and become functioning members of society once again.

These ideas supported the reform school movement of the early 1900s and later the rehabilitation movement in prisons. As the population was growing and cities were getting larger, bands of young men were increasingly creating problems in American cities. The first youth gangs started in the late 1800s and early 1900s, and states began to ask what could be done to change the problematic behaviors of these young people, almost exclusively young men. States began to increase their use of "reform schools," which were places where young men who had been in trouble with the law could be trained and treated and released to become contributing members of society. Like the ideas proposed by Jane Addams, the problem was seen as more structural than individual and so these individuals could be changed. Of course, many of these schools were rather inhumane, frequently beating the children housed in them, but the theory behind them was built on the idea that transformation was possible (Pisciotta, 1994).

During this time the government began to involve itself in deliberate policies to create a more just society. Laws against monopolies and child labor emerged at this time, as did the passage of the 19th Amendment to the Constitution in 1919, which prohibited the sale of alcohol in the United States. This was a clear effort to rebuild the values and practices of the nation through the passage of law and the enforcement of it. Social reformers saw alcohol as the primary cause of many social problems and so eliminating it from society would purge the nation of these problems. Of course, this same logic would be revisited in the 1970s and 1980s as the country ramped up its War on Drugs. While it took 15 years to repeal the 19th Amendment, the War on Drugs continues to this day and seems unlikely to end. It is a war that has been ongoing since 1971 when President Richard Nixon first coined the phrase and can be considered America's longest war. The logic of this war is consistent with the thinking of earlier social reformers: First, we can diminish or eliminate social problems from society through application of law. Second, if the law doesn't work, punishment will.

As this thinking relates to prisons in the early 20th century, states began to increase their efforts in rehabilitation. Offenders were considered to be "sick" or "feeble minded," and so prisons were set up to house and care for those who were "sick." Henry Goddard (1912) argued that prisoners were "feeble minded" and could not be helped by much of anything, but others disagreed. While this did not support the idea of rehabilitation, it is important because seeing offenders as "sick" emphasized a more scientific perspective. Goddard and others were soon out of vogue and by the 1930s helping the sick get well increasingly became the model that dominated incarceration in the United States. This was seen as a "win-win" solution to the crime problem. Reform is good for both the offender and the society because both benefit. The offender no longer needs to be locked up, while the society enjoys less crime (Christian, 1998).

Prisons soon became charged with a host of tasks that previously they had not experienced. Trade schools and specific training programs were established. Addams's ideas that education and knowledge would lead to reform seemed to win the day. Prisons, while still imperfect, became structures that were charged with changing the individuals who entered them. This model would reach its peak in the 1950s and continue to be applied through the 1980s, when the deinstitutionalization of psychiatric facilities and the War on Drugs would place new challenges on the U.S. prison system (Testa & West, 2010).

Prior to the 1950s the United States had essentially two separate systems for people who struggled with acceptable behavior. Individuals could be forced into prisons or committed to asylums. Asylums were found in the United States dating back to the early 1800s and were frequently filled with patients who suffered from dementia, seizure disorders, and even the psychological issues associated with syphilis. Asylums were generally little more than human warehouses where patients were placed, frequently for life. One brief episode of depression and a suicide attempt could lead to a lifetime of restraint and sedation. By the 1950s asylums in the United States had almost a half-million residents. The logic behind separating these people from society was at best to protect the vulnerable person. However, because many psychiatric hospitals were private, families with means could confine relatives against their will in what was often considered an "out of sight, out of mind" type of situation. Because these people lacked the capacity to make decisions, decisions were made for them. In some cases husbands used asylums to control their wives and families would simply move a troubled person into a mental hospital.

By the 1950s and 1960s many saw the civil commitment laws of the United States as too liberal. At the same time new psychiatric medications were being introduced, which was a hopeful sign in the treatment of mental health issues. Meanwhile talk therapy was moving past the Freudian couch and into the realm of existential therapists such as Rollo May, Gestalt therapists such as Fritz Pearls, and person-centered practitioners such as Carl Rogers and Virginia Satir, who were all making headlines for their interventions with people who at one time may have been considered candidates for commitment but now were living and functioning in society.

These innovations increased the number of people who were questioning lifetime commitments for individuals suffering from mental health problems. Through a long series of legal battles, long-term commitment laws slowly were challenged and changed, leading to the present day where lifetime commitment in a mental health hospital is highly unlikely regardless of the status of the person.

As Christopher Jencks argues, it was a perfect storm between civil liberals, who want to free individuals from needless restrictions, and fiscal conservatives, who saw mental health asylums as expensive and no longer necessary. Both groups began to work together to move mental health treatments to the community, arguing that it would be better for all concerned. The deinstitutionalization process took almost 20 years to be fully completed (Jencks, 1994).

In 1963 President Kennedy signed the Community Mental Health Centers Act, which was designed to help move patients from lockdown asylums back into their local communities and to pay for and provide the care they needed there. Deinstitutionalization began over the next 2 years, and as a result the amount of mental health hospitals in the United States decreased. This shifted the responsibility of care for the mentally ill from the institutional facility to the local community. The rapid decline in long-term psychiatric commitments followed and eventually we adopted the public policy that exists today. Only those who are deemed to be a "danger to self or others" may be considered for long- or short-term civil commitment (Testa & West, 2010).

As the asylums emptied the prisons began to fill, and by the 1980s we began to see increases in people with mental health problems being incarcerated. Prisons quickly became the institution in society that could not say no to anyone and so began to replace the asylums as the place of last resort. Many of the previously institutionalized individuals were released to cities where in a short time they would end up living in homeless shelters and committing petty crimes. Frequently these individuals struggled to find the public resources promised and so began to self-medicate through drugs and/or alcohol. Along the way many would break the law and end up in the new asylum, commonly called "prison" (Jencks, 1994).

Many criminological studies show that in fact the deinstitutionalization of psychiatric facilities has become nothing more than changing one institution for another. In what is sometimes referred to as "transinstitutionalization," the reality for many who suffer from persistent psychiatric disorders is that they find themselves inside once again. While prison can provide the structured environments once provided by asylums, they are not treatment centers. They are places where security demands must always be placed above the needs for treatment (Lamb & Weinberger, 2005; Prins, 2011).

The challenges of treating the mentally ill inside a prison are only exacerbated by the sheer number of the prison population. Definitional issues are always a part of deciding what percentage of inmates in the United States are mentally ill. Findings from the Bureau of Justice Statistics show that between 14% and 26% of inmates showed signs of serious psychological distress in the last 30 days. Twenty-four percent of inmates had been told they had some type of mental disorder in the past versus 5% in the general population. The transinstitutionalization process has made prisons a major player in dealing with the mentally ill population in the United States (Bronson & Berzofsky, 2017; Prins, 2014.).

Setting aside the issue of the mentally ill in U.S. prisons, the incarceration boom in this country can be traced to two individuals: President Ronald Reagan and sociologist Robert Martinson. These two individuals cannot be blamed for the entirety of our current situation, but both helped create the fertile ground for the mass incarceration movement in the United States. What does this mean, specifically? From 1980, the year Reagan was elected president, through the first year of the Clinton administration in 1996, the prison population of the United States grew by over 200%. However, that number continued to grow, and a recent study by the Sentencing Project shows that in the 40-year period since, incarceration has gone up over 500%, while at the same time, sentences have gotten longer and longer (Sentencing Project, 2020). So, who were these men and what did they do to open to door to mass incarceration?

Robert Martinson was what some today might consider a prison abolitionist. He had been involved in social activism most of his life and as a sociologist was interested in prisons in the United States. Looking into recidivism data and program efficacy, Martinson (1974) published an article entitled "What Works? Questions and Answers About Prison Reform." In that article Martinson argued that efforts at rehabilitation were not successful in curbing criminality, and soon thereafter he started appearing on television and in news articles proposing that "nothing worked" (Lipton et al., 1975).

This simple study published in a rather obscure journal would be cited over and over by policymakers looking to cut taxes by cutting money spent on social programs such as rehabilitation efforts in prisons. If "nothing works," then there is no point in doing anything. One can see how this could lead to mass incapacitation of offenders and essentially the warehousing of them, providing them few services and opportunities for rehabilitation.

Simple incapacitation quickly became the model for prisons. In effect, the goal was to separate miscreants from society and thus eliminate crime. Warehousing prisoners meant that you simply needed to keep them inside the fences, and since they were "bad people" anyway, there was no reason to waste money on programs that wouldn't work. Policymakers had "research" to support tax cuts and less spending (Cullen, 2013).

Subsequent research supporting rehabilitation efforts, using updated statistical processes not available to Martinson at the time, and Martinson himself suggesting his original research was flawed. By this time it was the late 1980s and politicians had quickly learned that no voter actually wanted to spend money on felons.

It was during this time that I was working as a social worker in a sex offender treatment program inside a medium-security prison. The constant defense of the efficacy of the program, which had as its goal "no more victims," eventually fell on deaf ears as budgets became tighter and tighter and services that were perceived as "soft on crime" fell out of favor.

This reality, however, should not infer to the reader that prison programs don't work. In fact, programs that include family therapy and cogitative problem-solving show great promise. Teaching offenders interpersonal skills and modeling appropriate conflict resolution both "work." Additionally, education and training as well as intense residential treatment of violent offenders have yielded positive effects on the long-term outcomes related to decreasing the likelihood of reoffense. However, once the horse is out of the barn and running down the road, it is hard to stop it (Gendreau & Ross, 1987).

Shortly after Martinson's article was published, President Reagan took office in 1980. He entered the political realm riding a sentiment that proposed that government was "too big" and spent too much. Conservativism prided itself on "cutting government waste," and one place where spending could be cut was prisons. Few if any were concerned about the ethical treatment of felons and so politicians both Republican and Democrat frequently ran on "get tough" policies.

During the Reagan years, the United States was flooded with a "new drug," cocaine, and its cheap derivative, crack cocaine. Cocaine and crack cocaine had found their way to the United States from Columbia and were in part responsible for a violent crime wave that gripped the country in the 1980s. Gangs and smugglers fought over turf to sell the drugs, and this led to even more concerns from the public.

Reagan and First Lady Nancy picked up Nixon's mantle of the War on Drugs and ran with it. They increased government spending on trying to stop drugs from coming into the country and punishing those buying the drugs. Throughout his presidency Reagan made it one of his goals to stamp out addiction and clearly seemed to think that locking people in prison was the way to do it. It would be unfair to suggest Reagan was the only president to support the War on Drugs. In fact, every president since his time, regardless of political party, has supported the effort to punish away addiction. The response by states was similar as "get tough" legislation became more and more common. The criminal justice system was flooded with offenders.

Laws such as "three strikes and you're out" were passed in many states under a simple idea that there were a small number of criminals creating the lion's share of crimes. Fueled by research by Albert Blumstein and colleagues (1986), the term "career criminal" became part of the popular culture. Blumstein had studied crime rates and concluded that most crime was committed by a small number of people. Policymakers decided that if we could just find those "bad seeds," we could decrease criminality across the country and so quickly passed laws that would extend the time in prison for repeat offenders. As was the case with Martinson, the research by Blumstein was widely debated in the literature and resulted in a number of studies, none of which seemed to support precisely the initial claims of the research.

From 1980 to 1998, the number of people incarcerated in the United States rose by over 200%, and of those incarcerated, less than 20% were incarcerated for some type of serious or "violent offense." What would emerge fairly quickly was that drug users were quite easy to catch, while drug dealers were not. The mountain of what Austin and Irwin (2001) termed "petty criminals" began to grow, and 20 years after Reagan was first elected, more than half of the U.S. prison population was incarcerated for nonviolent or petty crimes such as drug possession. In 10 more years the incarceration rate in the United States would continue to rise so high that one out of every 48 working-age adults in the country was in prison (Austin & Irwin, 2001). Contrary to hopes by Blumstein et al. (1986) and others, incarcerating this mountain of humanity seemed to have little effect on crime (Schmitt, 2010).

One thing about incarcerating large numbers of people is simply this. You take people off the street and transform them from being taxpayers to tax users. Prison budgets continued to climb on both the state and federal levels to the point that the United States was spending more on prisons than almost anything else (Schmitt, 2010).

The Pew Charitable Trusts reports on prisons show that from 1977 to 2003, expenditures on prisons increased by over 1,100%. At the same time spending on health and education grew by less than 600%. Spending on public welfare increased by 766%. If you judge a society by where it spends its money, it is pretty clear that the United States is spending a great deal of its resources on locking up its own citizens (Pew Charitable Trusts, 2007, 2013).

Of course, spending is not the only unseen effect of the decision to incarcerate large numbers of people. The U.S. system locks up about three-quarters of a million parents at any given time. Removal of a parent from a child's life will without a doubt disrupt family life but also can have serious detrimental effects on the children left behind. Data show that more than half the offenders incarcerated in the United States are parents. When we incarcerate the parent, the children are often pushed into new living situations with relatives or foster parents. Programs throughout the country grew to deal with this reality. While these are noble efforts, the evidence is clear that children whose parents are incarcerated have more than a 25% increased likelihood of going to prison than their counterparts whose parents have not been incarcerated. In short, many children of the incarcerated are merely waiting for their time in prison (Travis, 2005; Wakefield & Wildeman, 2014). Since more than half of all offenders are in fact parents, this trend has created new challenges for schools, as well as foster care and adoption agencies. Programs sprouted up throughout the country to attempt to heal the wounds of incarceration felt by the children of these offenders, and yet what we know is that incarcerating a parent dramatically increases the odds that the child will follow in the footsteps of that parent (Travis, 2005; Wakefield & Wildeman, 2014).

The social costs of mass incarceration were not uniformly distributed among the population. Mass incarceration was largely felt by poor people of color, who were caught committing nonviolent offenses, frequently related to drug addiction and distribution (Reiman, 1979).

Related to the issue of race, Blacks have made up a historically high percentage of the prison population of the United States. Alexander and West (2012) suggest that prisons in the United States have become a place where Blacks can once again become an income source for affluent investors. In their award-winning book *The New Jim Crow: Mass Incarceration in the Age of Colorblindness*, they point out that approximately 30% of all Black males either have been or will be incarcerated in their lifetime. At the same time, only 5.1% of the population as a whole will be incarcerated. Men are about eight times more likely than women to be incarcerated, but that rate is narrowing as more and more women are being incarcerated. Data suggest that Blacks are more likely than Hispanics or Whites to go to prison (Bonczarand & Beck, 1997). These and other data led Alexander and West (2012) to call for prison reforms related to drug laws that disproportionally applied harsher sentences to drugs frequently used by Blacks.

When the federal schedule of punishments was established in 1986, it contained a number of sentencing guidelines for a variety of illegal drugs based on how much of the drug was found on the offender. The idea was that large amounts of a drug should lead to a harsher punishment than smaller amounts so that traffickers would be more harshly punished than users. However, the law did not provide uniformity between various drugs. So, for example, the punishment discrepancy between crack cocaine and powder cocaine was 100 to 1: An individual could have 100 grams of power cocaine or 1 gram of crack cocaine and receive the exact same sentence. Since these two drugs are essentially the exact same substance, many pointed to the racial disparity of users as the reason for this discrepancy. It would take until 2010 for this law to be overturned, but by then, the damage was done (Alexander & West, 2012; Dvorak, 2000).

However, new analyses of data show that the gap between Blacks and Whites in prison is narrowing. While in raw numbers Whites have always outnumbered minorities in prison, their percentage has always been disproportionately low. However, between 2007 and 2017 there was a 20% decrease in the number of Black inmates, which was larger than the decrease in White inmates, decreasing the prison gap. Table 14.3 shows data from 2017 related to race and the prison population of the United States (Gramlich, 2019).

In 1983 the Corrections Corporation of America was formed and became one of the largest and most aggressive private prison companies in the United States. They claimed

TABLE 14.3 Comparing Race, the Rate of Incarceration, and the Percentage of the Prison Population

Race—Percentage of Population in the United States	Rate of Incarceration per 100,000	Percentage of Prison Population
Whites—64%	272	30%
Blacks—12%	1549	33%
Hispanics—16%	823	23%
Other—8%		14%

Source: Gramlich (2019).

to be able to build and operate prisons of the same quality as publicly owned prisons but at a much lower cost to the taxpayer (Gotsch & Basti, 2018). At the same time that states were expanding sentence lengths, cutting prison programs, and filling up their own bed spaces, prison corporations were able to step in and fill the need for prison bed space across the country (Looman & Carl, 2015). From 2000 to 2017 private prison populations grew by more than 70,000 residents (Table 14.4). For the 34 states that contracted with private prison corporations, private prisons seemed to be an answer to the question, how can you lock up more and more people at lower and lower costs?

The ethics of turning the incarcerated into a profit center for stock holders seemed to have little effect on the general public. Much like the privatization of child welfare services, profiting off of locking people away did not seem to influence voters to contact their polit-ical leaders and ask them to stop this. While some states like Arkansas completely elimin-ated their use of private prisons, others more than made up for these losses. Arizona, for example, increased its use of private prisons 479% in that 17-year period of time (Gotsch & Basti, 2018).

While the number of private prison beds grew, the public was in general supportive of politicians who used the "tough on crime" mantra as their rallying cry to voters (Looman & Carl, 2015). Few considered the growing expense and social costs of these decisions to the public. It quickly became what criminologist Jeffrey Reiman (1979) called a "Pyrrhic theory," one where those with the ability to change the system are unlikely to do so because it works to the benefit of those involved. Who would want their job to decrease in value? No one, and so once a society starts down a road it becomes particularly challenging to change its course.

While few believed that the corrections system was actually likely to "correct" any-thing, that didn't change the reality that it was popular to politicians seeking re-election, stock holders who saw private prisons as a great investment, and state and local leaders who observed their budgets getting larger and larger every year (Looman & Carl, 2015; Reiman, 1979).

Following the election of Donald Trump, share prices in private prison corporations doubled. The previous Obama administration had ordered the federal system to cease using private facilities, but President Trump announced a return to the use of private vendors to house federal inmates. Stock prices for the two largest corporations, CoreCivic, which was

TABLE 14.4 Private Prisons: A New Profit Center

Jurisdiction	% Change 2000–2017
Arkansas	–100
Kentucky	–100
Louisiana	–100
Maine	–100
Michigan	–100
North Dakota	–100
Utah	–100
Wisconsin	–100
North Carolina	–90.9
Alaska	–82.1
Maryland	–74.8
Idaho	–62.8
South Dakota	–24.4
Wyoming	–13.8
Texas	–9
Mississippi	–3.4
Virginia	–1.1
Oklahoma	6.1
New Jersey	6.4
Nevada	13.2
Hawaii	35
California	39.9
Montana	42.9
New Mexico	72.3
Federal System	77.6
Colorado	79.1
Georgia	110.4
Tennessee	116.8
Florida	198.5
Ohio	276.6
Indiana	309.8
Arizona	479.2

Source: Gotsch and Basti (2018).

originally known as Corrections Corp., and Geo Group, rose 140% and 98% respectively (Long, 2017). To put this into context, your savings account at the local bank probably pays you a return of between 0.5% and 1.5%.

As Alexander and West (2012) suggest, it seems apparent that incarceration is a good investment, and particularly one that the public feels is worth the money spent. However, like many investments with tax dollars, incarceration yields many problematic issues, from child poverty to socialization into the prison system from which the next generation of inmates is likely to come (Looman, 2015).

At the same time, almost all players in the criminal justice system benefit from the current system, with the notable exception of the inmates and their families. Both public and private prisons become job sources for local communities, replacing industries that long ago fled the United States for the cheaper labor and greener pastures of overseas manufacturing (Wilson, 1996).

In the United States, we seem to have a collective attraction to crime that is self-evident when you look at our movies or television shows. But the key players in the criminal justice system all benefit from mass incarceration. District attorneys benefit from mass incarceration because they can run for re-election on the grounds that they are "tough on crime" and claim that they are "making the streets safer." Lawmakers benefit for the same reason. Prison systems, whether public or private, gain increases in budgets and employees, which usually brings with it increased prestige and power in the system. This system, like many, seems built to make itself bigger, and when the prison system fails, it is rewarded with even more inmates who upon their return to prison bring with them bigger budgets and increased growth of the system (Looman, 2015).

Imagine any social work program where this were true, for example, a medical center failing to cure more than 50% of its patients but being rewarded with even more patients. Evidence-based social work practice is built on showing the efficacy of the intervention. When it comes to the prison system, it seems that it fails more people than it helps (Durose et al., 2014).

Studies of the rate of recidivism, returning to prison after incarceration, show about two-thirds of those released from prison return to it within a 3-year period, and 75% return in a 5-year period (Durose et al., 2014). Studies of this population show that about 20% of those who enter prison in any given year enter with a "parole revocation," meaning that they failed to do some condition of their parole but did not commit a new crime. This reality is increasingly supported by research showing that significant numbers of those who return to prison are linked not to new crimes but to violations of parole conditions (Burke & Tonry, 2006; Grattet et al., 2008, 2009; Petersilia et al., 2007).

In the face of all these issues, what is the role of the social worker? Looking at the core values of the profession, it becomes clear that both those working inside and outside the system are called to work for social justice. While this can certainly be related to ascertaining justice for victims of crime, it also includes working toward just sentencing guidelines and arrest practices while at the same time considering the dignity and worth of all people, including those who are being punished for whatever reason. If as social workers we truly believe in the importance of human relationships, then we believe in the possibility of change. The idea of "bad seeds" who must be locked away without any attempt to help them violates many of the ethical principles of the social work profession. Punishment for retaliation is in no way consistent with the values of the profession and places social workers who work within the system in the precarious position of constantly being called to make this system more humane.

References

Addams, J., & Case, E. W. (1923/1928). *Twenty years at Hull-House: With autobiographical notes*. Macmillan Company.

Alexander, M., & West, C. (2012). *New Jim Crow: Mass incarceration in the age of colorblindness*. New Press.Austin, J. (2000). *Multisite evaluation of boot camp programs: Final report*. George Washington University, Institute on Crime, Justice, and Corrections.

Austin, J., & Irwin, J. (2001). *It's about time: America's imprisonment binge*. Wadsworth/Thomson Learning.

Bauer, S. (2018). *American prison: A reporter's journey into the business of punishment*. New York.

Beccaria, C. (1764/1995). An essay on crimes and punishments. In I. Kramnick (Ed.), *The portable enlightenment reader* (p. 9). Penguin Books.

Bentham, J. (1789/1970). *An introduction to the principles of morals and legislation* (J. Burns & H. Hart, Eds.). Athlone Publishing.

Blumstein, A., Cohen, J., Roth, J. A., & Visher, C. A. (1986). *Criminal careers and "career criminals."* National Academy Press.

Bonczarand, T. P., & Beck, A. J. (1997). *Lifetime likelihood of going to state or federal prison*. Bureau of Justice Statistics Special Report, NCJ-160092. https://www.bjs.gov/content/pub/pdf/Llgsfp.pdf

Bronson, J., & Berzofsky, M. (2017, June 22). *Indicators of mental health problems reported by prisoners and jail inmates, 2011–2012*. NCJ 250612. https://www.bjs.gov/index.cfm?ty=pbdetail&iid=5946

Burke, P., & Tonry, M. (2006). *Successful transition and reentry for safe communities: A call to action for parole*. Center for Effective Public Policy.

Chambliss, W. J. (1966). The deterrent influence of punishment. *Crime & Delinquency, 12*(1), 70–75. https://doi.org/10.1177/001112876601200110

Christian, S. (1998). *With liberty for some: 500 years of imprisonment in America*. Northeastern University Press.

Clear, T. (2007). *Imprisoning communities: How mass incarceration makes disadvantaged neighborhoods worse*. Oxford University Press.

Code of Hammurabi. (n.d.). http://eawc.evansville.edu/anthology/hammurabi.htm

Cullen, F. T. (2013). Rehabilitation: Beyond nothing works. *Crime and Justice, 42*(1), 299–376.

Durkheim, E. (1893/1933). *On the division of labor in society* (G. Simpson, Trans.). MacMillan Company.

Durose, M., Copper, A., & Snyder, H. (2014). *Recidivism of prisoners released in 30 states in 2005: Patterns from 2005 to 2010—Update*. Bureau of Justice Statistics. https://www.bjs.gov/index.cfm?ty=pbdetail&iid=4986

Dvorak, R. (2000). Cracking the code: De-coding colorblind slurs during the congressional crack cocaine debates. *Michigan Journal of Race and Law, 5*(2), 611.

Felson, M. (1998). *Crime and everyday life*. Pine-Forge Press.

Gendreau, P., & Ross, R. (1987, September). Revivification of rehabilitation: Evidence from the 1980s. *Justice Quarterly, 4*(3), 349–407.

Goddard, H. H. (1912). *The Kallikak family: A study in the heredity of feeble mindedness*. MacMillan.

Gotsch, K., & Basti, V. (2018). *Capitalizing on mass incarceration: U.S. growth in private prisons*. https://www.sentencingproject.org/publications/capitalizing-on-mass-incarceration-u-s-growth-in-private-prisons/

Gramlich, J. (2019). *The gap between the number of blacks and whites in prison is shrinking*. Pew Research Center. https://www.pewresearch.org/fact-tank/2019/04/30/shrinking-gap-between-number-of-blacks-and-whites-in-prison/

Grattet, R., Petersilia, J., & Lin, J. (2008). *Parole violations and revocations in California*. U.S. Department of Justice.

Grattet, R., Petersilia, J., Lin, J., & Beckman, M. (2009). Parole violations and revocations in California: Analysis and suggestions for action. *Federal Probation, 73*(1), 2–11.

Jencks, C. (1994). *The homeless*. Harvard University Press.

Justice Policy. (2011). *Finding direction: Expanding criminal justice options by considering policies of other nations*. http://www.justicepolicy.org/uploads/justicepolicy/documents/sentencing.pdf

Lamb, H., & Weinberger, L. (2005). The shift of psychiatric inpatient care from hospitals to jails and prisons. *Journal of the American Academic Psychiatry Law, 33*, 529–534.

Lipton, D., Martinson, R., & Woks, J. (1975). *The effectiveness of correctional treatment: A survey of treatment valuation studies*. Praeger Press.

Long, H. (2017). *Private prison stocks up 100% since Trump's win*. https://money.cnn.com/2017/02/24/invest ing/private-prison-stocks-soar-trump/index.html

Looman, M. D., & Carl, J. D. (2015). *A country called prison: Mass incarceration and the making of a new nation*. Oxford University Press.

Martini, M., Gazzaniga, V., Bragazzi, N. L., & Barberis, I. (2019). The Spanish influenza pandemic: A lesson from history 100 years after 1918. *Journal of Preventive Medicine and Hygiene, 60*(1), E64–E67. https://doi.org/10.15167/2421-4248/jpmh2019.60.1.1205

Martinson, R. (1974). What works? Questions and answers about prison reform. *Public Interest*, Spring, 22–54.

National Association of Social Workers. (2017). *Code of ethics*. https://www.socialworkers.org/About/Eth ics/Code-of-Ethics/Code-of-Ethics-English

Parent, D. G., (2003). *Research for practice correctional boot camps: Lessons from a decade of research.*

Petersilia, J., Rosenfeld, R., Bonnie, R. J., Crutchfield, R. D., Kleiman, M. A. R., Laub, J. H., & Visher, C. A. (2007). *Parole, desistance from crime, and community integration*. National Research Council.

Pew Charitable Trusts. (2007). *When offenders break the rules: Smart responses to parole and probation violations*. http://www.pewtrusts.org/uploadedFiles/wwwpewtrustorg/Reports/sentencing_and_corrections/Condition-Violators-Briefing.pdf

Pew Charitable Trusts. (2013). *Sentencing and corrections: Condition violators briefing*. http://www.pewtru sts.org/uploadedFiles/wwwpewtrustsorg/Reports/sentencing_and_corrections/Condition-Violators-Briefing.pdf

Pisciotta, A. W. (1994). *Benevolent repression: social control and the American reformatory-prison movement*. New York University Press.

Prins, S. J. (2011). Does transinstitutionalization explain the overrepresentation of people with serious mental illnesses in the criminal justice system? *Community Mental Health Journal, 47*, 716–722.

Prins, S. J. (2014). Prevalence of mental illnesses in US state prisons: A systematic review. *Psychiatric Services (Washington, D.C.), 65*(7), 862–872. https://doi.org/10.1176/appi.ps.201300166

Reiman, J. (1979). Criminal justice through the looking glass. In D. Repetto (Ed.), *The rich get richer and the poor get prison*. John Wiley & Sons.

Schmitt, J. W. (2010). *The high budgetary cost of incarceration*. Center for Economic Policy and Research.

Testa, M., & West, S. G. (2010). Civil commitment in the United States. *Psychiatry, 7*(10), 30–40.

Travis, J. M. (2005). *Families left behind: The hidden costs of incarceration and reentry*. Urban Institute, Justice Policy Center.

Uniform Crime Reports Clearances. (2017). *Crime in the United States*. https://ucr.fbi.gov/crime-in-the-u.s/2017/crime-in-the-u.s.-2017/topic-pages/clearances

Wakefield, S., & Wildeman, C. (2014). *Children of the prison boom: Mass incarceration and the future of the American dream*. Oxford University Press.

Wilson, W. J. (1996). *When work disappears: The world of the new urban poor*. Vintage Books.

World Population Review. (2020). *Crime rate by country*. https://worldpopulationreview.com/country-rankings/crime-rate-by-country

World Prison Brief. (2020). *Highest to lowest—Prison population rate*. https://www.prisonstudies.org/high est-to-lowest/prison_population_rate?field_region_taxonomy_tid=All

15

Immigration Policy

Carmen Monico, Oscar A. Chacon,
Neema Olagbemiro, and Soonok An

Introduction

Immigration has been a controversial issue since the United States was established as a nation. In the 2020s, immigration has been on the top of the policy agenda. Forced cross-border migration has increased due to endemic national and regional social conflicts and a greater frequency of natural disasters related to climate change. The nation is divided on how to proceed with the large influx of asylum seekers at the U.S.-Mexico border, particularly during the most recent global health pandemic. Meanwhile, immigrants in the United States continue to serve on the frontlines of the health care system, food production, and other essential services. The Zero-Tolerance Policy and the 400-plus immigration-related executive orders introduced during the administration of President Donald Trump transformed the immigration system, all without legislation. The demographic changes occurring along the U.S. borders puts pressure on President Joe Biden's administration to engage in immigration reform to create a system that is not restrictive but welcoming of immigrants—authorized (nonexpired visas, temporary status, with asylum application pending, and others) or not (unauthorized entry, to work or travel).

This chapter explores how immigrants have historically been discriminated against despite being an integral part of society from the establishment of the United States until today. We discuss how immigration policies in the past have failed to meet the needs of this growing population, in great part due to persistent public anti-immigrant sentiments and the corporate-driven orientation of the U.S. immigration system. We also discuss how new immigration policies have been crafted during the last few administrations. We examine the many challenges the Biden administration faces in dismantling failed policies and adopting more humane approaches to immigration. We enunciate the concerns that

Carmen Monico, Oscar A. Chacon, Neema Olagbemiro, and Soonok An, *Immigration Policy* In: *Handbook of Forensic Social Work.* Edited by: David Axlyn McLeod, Anthony P. Natale, and Kristin W. Mapson, Oxford University Press. © Oxford University Press 2024. DOI: 10.1093/oso/9780197694732.003.0015 immigration advocates have regarding the ability of existing institutions to enact and implement new policies, and the impact of policies on immigrants and their communities at large. We call for the integration of immigration issues in social work practice, education, and research so that future generations may become more competent while working with immigrants and refugees alike.

Theoretical Perspective and Methodological Approach

Historically, immigration policy has been studied from a wide range of perspectives, as migration studies is not only an interdisciplinary field but also a contested field relevant to forensic social work. Most accepted analytical frameworks include push factors (encouraging outflows) and pull factors (encouraging inflows) of immigration and subsequent chain migration, which is widely utilized; transnationalism, which establishes and maintains multiple strands of social relations between the country of origin and the country of destination; and "convergence" and "gap" hypotheses, which predict the nature of the trend of migration policies (Rosenblum & Tichenor, 2012). Long-established perspectives focus on the structural factors influencing international migration and social networks (Rosenblum & Brick, 2011). Recent changes in international migration reflect a global change, and migration theories have been developed to explain this evolution via dimensions of space (geographically defined), time (permanent, temporary, circulatory), or volition (motives or conditions; Rosenblum & Tichenor, 2012).

A classical typology of international migration explaining movement from the Old to the New World recognizes four categories: "primitive, forced or impelled, free[,] and mass, caused respectively by ecological pushes, migration policies, migrants' aspirations, and collective behavior" (Petersen, 1958, as cited in Rosenblum & Tichenor, 2012, p. 39). In a careful examination of migration studies since the beginning of modern globalization (1990s) and the civil rights movement in the United States (1954–1968), "immigration [studies] have now formulated new analyses of race, social exclusion, and social inequality, [but] research . . . remains confined to . . . assimilation, acculturation, generational conflict, and social mobility" (Romero, 2008, p. 23). We consider these commonly used perspectives but primarily adopt a critical lens.

We consider that the push-pull factors framework is outdated in terms of the traditional factors and the type of social networks established between the countries of origin and destination. Theories of assimilation and acculturation are limited in explaining the immigrant experiences of biracial and multiracial identities. Those theories had better explain well-documented intergenerational conflicts, although they do not account for the social cohesion immigrant communities tend to sustain across generations via social networks, particularly during times of distress, such as the COVID-19 pandemic. Models of social mobility are insufficient because the dynamics of accumulating wealth and income, as well the institutionalization of social exclusion and social inequality, undermine such mobility.

To carry out the study presented in this chapter, we anchored ourselves around critical race theory (CRT) in migration studies. By definition, CRT examines "racial profiling, antiimmigration sentiment, the increased militarization of the US–Mexico border, and the high number of immigrant deaths on the border" (Romero, 2008, p. 23). CRT has become more accepted since police brutality and anti-immigrant hate crimes are now a key security concern, and during a period of history in which interpersonal, institutional, and structural racism (practices and policies that negatively affect a group of people based on their race or ethnicity) and White supremacy (the belief that White people are superior to other races, and the dominance of this group over other races and ethnic groups) are more openly discussed.

To develop this chapter, two academic migration scholars with an extensive background in immigration practice and an immigrant doctoral student, all from a historically Black university, joined with a leader of immigrant-led and immigrant-serving organizations in the United States with years of policy and direct practice experience. We used a set of questions to guide the interpretive, heuristic dialogue held concurrently with text analysis. This methodological approach is commonly used in hermeneutic phenomenology for the interpretive interaction between historically produced texts and the readers, who are not passive in the co-constructed analytical work of a phenomenon (e.g., immigration policy).

As per Pitard (2019), we used autoethnography as a tool of phenomenology to link the authors' personal knowledge with the specific cultural dynamics of race, ethnicity, and class in which the immigration policy of the United States has evolved in various geopolitical contexts throughout history. By examining the literature through text analysis, the authors-as-researchers engage in a process in which we are "carefully monitoring he impact of [our] biases, beliefs, and personal experiences" (Pitard, 2019, p. 1829) with respect to our personal immigration experiences and experiences with immigration policy in the United States.

We draw on our combined academic training and practice of more than 50 years, and the interdisciplinary perspectives of social work, public health, management studies, and economics. We met weekly via Zoom for 4 months (recording the conversations), critically discussing a set of policy milestones and inferring lessons learned from immigrant resistance to an unjust system. Between meetings and while writing this narrative, we compared and contrasted the major dialogue themes from our conversations with the immigration policy literature.

Forensic social work is concerned with the micro, mezzo, and macro levels of social work practice relevant to the criminal justice and legal systems. For this chapter, we examined key structural and institutional dimensions shaping immigration policy in the United States. These dimensions include history, demographics, racial-ethnic and gender dynamics, and political, socioeconomic, and ecological factors, as well as the multiple impacts of immigration policies on individuals and communities within the U.S. borders. Next, we offer a historical analysis, followed by a discussion of contemporary policy and its future direction. We also examine the values and roles of social workers and make recommendations about how to better serve the immigrant and refugee community.

Immigration Policy in Retrospective

Historical Overview of Immigration Policies in the United States

From a critical perspective, since the founding of the nation, the United States has a long history of rejection and abuse of the native cultures existing prior to the conquest in this hemisphere and the subsequent rejection of non-White immigrants. As the newly established sovereign nation struggled to separate from the economic and political dominance of colonial European countries, the first immigration waves from Europe to the United States during the 19th century were mostly White immigrants. During the age of colonization, with the first settlements of English pilgrims, Africans were exploited to work as indentured servants through a "global network of suffering" that ensured the transatlantic slave trafficking of 15 million to 20 million previously free Africans, destroying entire tribes and villages (U.S. Library of Congress, 2021). As Republican values prevailed, "Congress did provide for the counting of newcomers beginning in 1819, but the legislators were content to have the states deal with immigrants. States varied in their responses to immigration" (Rosenblum & Tichenor, 2012, p. 276). In fact, there was no federal-level immigration policy, and states were given the power to set policy at the local level.

With the mass arrival of Irish and German immigrants during the 1830s, economic deterioration, and social inequality, immigration exclusions were implemented. Both groups "faced massive discrimination by nativists; cultural barriers propagated negative stereotyping, which in turn created a nativist environment that excluded anyone of foreign nationality" (Tagore, 2014, p. 1). Without federal rules, race and ethnicity, socioeconomic status, and religion played a critical role in shaping immigration practices at the state and local levels. At first Irish newcomers were not welcomed and anti-immigrant sentiments resulted in the restriction of Catholic immigration. White Catholic, Anglophone, and wealthy immigrants were preferred during the early influx of immigrants (Rosenblum & Tichenor, 2012), while immigrants of color were excluded from the so-called "American Dream" through immigration policy.

For example, the United States enticed Chinese immigrants to come and work as gold miners, farmers, or railroad workers, aiding in the western expansion of the United States (Office of the Historian, n.d.). These Chinese immigrants played a vital role in not only building railroad tracks but also providing food and basic assistance, like laundry services. Yet, their low wages induced complaints from other immigrant workers who had to compete with the Chinese immigrants for jobs, although such low wages underscore how the Chinese migrants were exploited by the economic systems. In addition, Chinese migrants dealt with rumors of an inferior culture, such as stereotypes of prostitution and drug use. The Chinese Exclusion Act of 1882 was the result of growing tensions of social and cultural resentments toward Chinese immigrants. The act limited the number of Chinese migrants in any vessel traveling to the United States and implemented travel restrictions of all Chinese laborers, including scholars and diplomats. In 1886, the exclusion of Chinese immigrants was strengthened, and the reentry of Chinese immigrants to the United States, regardless of their legal status, was banned once they visited China. The Chinese Exclusion

Act of 1882 was the first anti-immigration policy in the history of the United States (Office of the Historian, n.d.).

Before the early 1900s, the United States was expanding economically and geographically, and more people were needed to fulfill jobs during a time of prosperity; consequently, there was not significant debate about foreign nationals immigrating to the United States. Businesses in the southern part of the country favored the short-term, seasonal immigration of Mexicans, which at the turn of the 20th century numbered about 60,000 per year. Immigration restrictions on Asian and European immigrants were adopted between the 1880s and the 1920s, and the anti-immigration backlash against Mexican migrants became acute during the Great Depression. Soon after the expiration of the Bracero Program in 1964, the Immigration and Nationality Act (INA) was enacted in 1965, which intended to eliminate the existing race-based national origins system by creating a seven-tier preference system that provided family- and employment-based visas to 29,000 applicants per year (Rosenblum & Brick, 2011). The visa quota system created a backlog in applications from countries that were seeking greater immigration (those producing immigrants who were historically unwelcome), while the anti-immigrant narratives expanded, accompanied by greater punishment, tighter restrictions, and further exclusion of mostly immigrants of color.

To address irregular immigration resulting from the bottlenecks that the preference system created, under President Ronald Reagan the Immigration Reform and Control Act (IRCA) was adopted in 1986, creating a path to citizenship to those who had entered prior to 1982. IRCA established a new set of border enforcement mechanisms and set criminal and civil penalties to employers who hired those without legal status. Although the United States later adopted the Immigration Act of 1990, which increased employment-based visas and increased border controls, the Illegal Immigration Reform and Immigration Responsibility Act of 1996 (IIRIRA) passed under President Bill Clinton further expanded enforcement measures (Rosenblum & Brick, 2011).

By the turn of the 20th century, immigration flows from Mexico grew during the beginning of the implementation of the North American Free Trade Agreement (NAFTA), adopted by President George H. W. Bush, followed by a large influx of Central Americans escaping from internal wars and regional natural disasters. The IIRIRA was not an "amnesty" program for the vast immigrant population; in fact, many immigrants were excluded based on its cutoff date and stringent requirements. Instead, the IIRIRA created a new counterfeit industry for fake licenses, passports, social security cards, and other identity documents. While border controls were heightened, those seeking asylum or other reliefs were choosing more dangerous routes, resulting in more people dying while attempting to cross the Mexico-U.S. border.

The so-called nation of immigrants that enslaved Africans until the Emancipation Proclamation of 1863 continues to exploit immigrant labor even after attempting to modernize the immigration system. Economic utility and political interests, not humanitarian pursuits (nor racially and ethnically inclusive policies), have been the driving force of immigration policy. Immigration policies and practices in the United States have been characterized by exclusion and inequality, which were necessary to build a nation where Whiteness (the social construction of White dominance in society) prevails. During the periods examined in this section, the immigrant population was increasing, establishing themselves in their communities, and making substantial contributions in all aspects of societal life. By 2019, the estimated total immigrant population was 44.9 million people, representing 13.7% of the U.S. population, compared to 4.7% in 1970 and 14.8% in 1890. Importantly, 57% of the total foreign-national population in 2019 was from 10 countries: Mexico (24%); India and China (each 6%); the Philippines (5%); El Salvador, Vietnam, Cuba, and the Dominican Republic (each accounting for 3%); and Guatemala and Korea (each 2%; Batalova et al., 2021). Yet, through history, citizens, mostly from nonimmigrant families, became fearful of immigrants and politicians used those fears to create a more restrictive immigration system. As discussed next, immigration policies prior to the 21st century failed to anticipate immigration trends that accompanied globalization.

Globalization and Immigration in the United States During the Obama Administrations

Globalization is associated with important technological advances and financial expansion, as well as stimulated transnational migration. At the heart of globalization are the structural adjustment programs the United States promoted during the 1980s and 1990s worldwide that have been linked to poverty, inequality, and environmental degradation around the world (Oringer & Welsh, 1998). These programs, in combination with a rise in natural disasters resulting from drastic climate change, resulted in exponential growth of forced migration in all regions of the world, including immigration to the United States. Critically examining these programs in Central and South America, we can see their contributions to the demographic changes occurring within U.S. borders. For instance, by 2020, 32 million people of Latin American heritage/origin became eligible to vote, counting for 13.3% of all eligible voters (Noe-Bustamante et al., 2021). These changes exerted pressure toward new immigration reform because most voters of Latin American heritage have made immigrant legalization a policy priority.

The Obama administration promised, since their first campaign, to carry out comprehensive reform yet did it mostly through executive action because legislative action was blocked by Congress after the 1986 IRCA failed to prevent further immigration; that is, after the legalization of 3 million undocumented immigrants based on the IRCA, illegal immigration continued (Skrentny & Lopez, 2013). This legislative failure was the case with the DREAM Act, which intended to benefit those who entered the United States at an early age, had not been arrested, and met educational and military requirements. The legislation passed the Democratic House in 2010 but failed to reach the Senate floor for debate (as of submission of this chapter).

While distinguishing between "criminal" immigrants (undeserving of legalization) and noncriminal immigrants (deserving of legal status), President Obama claimed to have deported 70% of "criminal" immigrants; in fact, yearly removal of immigrants through various enforcement actions had reached nearly 400,000 by 2011, an eightfold increase since 1991 and close to fourfold since 2000 (Skrentny & Lopez, 2013). President Obama adopted several executive actions, such as the provisional unlawful presence waivers granted to family members of U.S. citizens with pending petitions. The motive was to reduce the separation time involved to obtain a lawful visa to enter as a permanent resident. This and other policies were aimed at creating an image of an "immigrant friendly" administration (Skrentny & Lopez, 2013).

During the two Obama administrations (2009–2017), the most important programs introduced were those granting a temporary status with work permit eligibility to certain foreign nationals. The Deferred Action for Childhood Arrivals (DACA) favored those immigrants entering by their 16th birthday and under the age of 31 as of June 15, 2012, who had no prior criminal conviction and were attending school, had graduated from high school or had obtained a GED, or had been an honorably discharged veteran of the Coast Guard or Armed Forces. The Temporary Protected Status (TPS) was granted to foreigners from countries with "ongoing armed conflict, natural disasters (including epidemics), or other extraordinary and temporary conditions in the country that temporarily prevent its nationals from returning safely. . . . The president may authorize Deferred Enforced Departure (DED) in his discretion and as part of his constitutional power to conduct foreign relations" (U.S. Citizenship and Immigration Services [USCIS], 2021, p. 1). These programs have granted temporary relief from deportation actions (ordinarily 6 to 18 months with the possibility of similar extensions) and benefited over a million unauthorized immigrants. Another million and a half immigrants are potential beneficiaries eligible for DACA under the new TPS designations by President Biden.

As of December 31, 2020, there were 636,390 active DACA recipients with the potential for program eligibility by 1,331,000 (Migration Policy Institute, 2021). As of March 11, 2021, there are about 320,000 TPS recipients residing in the United States from El Salvador, Haiti, Honduras, Nepal, Nicaragua, Somalia, South Sudan, Sudan, Syria, and Yemen. President Biden recently granted TPS designations to Venezuela and Burma, with an estimated 323,000 Venezuelans and 1,600 Burmese beneficiaries (Congressional Research Service, 2021a). The USCIS does not keep records of the DED beneficiaries designated to foreign nationals from a small set of countries, including certain nationals from Liberia and Venezuela now granted this temporary status.

A few immigration laws adopted or issued during the two Obama administrations have provided foreign nationals an opportunity to adjust their immigration status and created for them a path to legal permanency. The Nicaraguan Adjustment and Central American Relief Act of 1997 (NACARA) provided deportation stay to certain individuals and nationalities (now mostly from El Salvador, Guatemala, some Eastern Europe countries, and previously Nicaragua). It benefited those who entered the United States before the 1990s, had no aggravated felony conviction, and were subjected to extreme cruelty or were battered in their home countries (USCIS, 2017a).

Individuals meeting the latter criterion may qualify for the Special Rule Cancellation of Removal for Battered Spouses and Children under Section 240A(b)(2) of the INA, which is affirmed in the Violence Against Women Act (VAWA; U.S. Department of Justice, 2009). The Haitian Refugee Immigration Fairness Act (HRIFA) of 1998 granted permanent residency to Haitian refugees who have resided in the United States since December 31, 1995, and meet other requirements (USCIS, 2017b). Since 1998, at least 1,000 Haitians have benefited from the HRIFA. The Legal Immigration Family Equity (LIFE) Act of 2000 of Public Law 553 is a status adjustment program available to immigrants with employment-based visas (U.S. Government Printing Office, 2000).

Immigration System Changes Under the Trump Administration

Like President Obama, President Trump used executive action to change immigration policy. The most significant changes introduced during the Trump administration were the Zero-Tolerance Policy and more than 400 other executive orders. The Department of Justice announced the Zero-Tolerance Policy on May 7, 2018, but it was halted via another executive order after a judicial order challenged its implementation, which had resulted in widespread child-family separation at the southern U.S. border. Prior to this policy, the apprehension of minors was mostly regulated by the Flores Settlement Agreement (FSA), the Homeland Security Act of 2002, and the Trafficking Victims Protection Reauthorization Act (TVPRA) of 2008. That is, children were detained for no more than 20 days and were placed as unaccompanied minors under the care of the Office of Refugee Resettlement (ORR) in the least restrictive facilities until released to proper guardians (families, relatives, or foster families). The minors are often screened for possible trafficking (for consideration of special visas) and were considered for other types of legal relief (Congressional Research Service, 2021b). However, under the Zero-Tolerance Policy, children and parents were placed in different facilities, their cases considered separately and in many cases without the proper records needed for reunification. Child-family separation became the major consequence of this policy, and its adverse impact on the safety, permanency, and well-being of children and their families has been well-documented (Monico & Méndez-Sandoval, 2019; Monico, Rotabi, & Lee, 2019; Monico, Rotabi, Vissing, & Lee, 2019). Furthermore, by July 2018, the ORR had received a total of 4,556 allegations of sexual abuse or sexual harassment of unaccompanied minors in U.S detention facilities (Folley, 2018).

Various executive orders introduced during the Trump administration transformed the immigration system while disregarding the United Nations High Commission for Refugees (UNHCR) guidelines regarding harsh and penitentiary policies. With little to no support among Republicans or Congress, the Trump administration enacted more than 400 executive actions, drastically changing immigration laws and practices at the border and within the United States (Pierce & Botler, 2020). At points of entry, border patrols assessed immigrants for inadmissibility: severe health conditions, having committed a crime, considered a national security threat or a potential public charge, lacking a labor certification, having committed a prior fraud or misrepresentation, and having an unlawful presence in the United States. The Migration Protection Protocols (MPPs) required returning to Mexico any recent arrival considered inadmissible, assuming that Mexico would provide them with protection when indeed asylum seekers have been sent back to dangerous conditions without assessing the merits of their asylum claims (Monico et al., under review).

The introduction of these interlocking policies limited the rights of immigrants to seek asylum at the border, increased immigration enforcement at the southern border, raised apprehensions and internal enforcement, and heightened family separations, stress, and mental health concerns. The increasing apprehension of nonviolent immigrants has contributed to overcrowding in detention facilities and poses an economic burden to taxpayers. The misplaced messages that immigrants are a threat to the U.S. economy, bring crime, and take jobs from Americans were particularly reinforced during the Trump administration. Yet, efforts to reduce authorized immigrant entries at the southern border failed notwithstanding Trump administration policies (Pierce & Bolter, 2020).

Immigration Policy During the COVID-19 Pandemic

Recently, COVID-19 has severely affected Brazil and South America, European Union countries, and India, in addition to over half a million deaths in the United States (New York Times, 2020). Yet, overt and covert forms of exclusions were levied on immigration in the United States since the start of the pandemic (Libal et al., 2021). Immigrants, particularly those in low-skilled labor and held in detention facilities, have been disproportionately affected by the COVID-19 pandemic. The Marshall Project, tasked to monitor conditions in the U.S. prison system, reported that "at least 249,883 people tested positive" for COVID-19 in detention facilities in December 2020 (New York Times, 2020). A fragmented health care system, accompanied by poor living conditions in detention facilities, contributes to an increase in COVID-19 infection (Bick, 2007).

The Department of Health and Human Services Section 265 of the U.S. Code of Title 42 authorizes the Centers for Disease Control and Prevention (CDC) to prevent entry to the United States by individuals suspected of posing a danger of spreading communicable diseases (American Immigration Council, 2021). The Trump administration conveniently utilized this code to mandate the closure of the U.S border effective March 20, 2020. This affected asylum seekers' ability to apply for asylum at the border and violated their civil and human rights. In the midst of the COVID-19 pandemic the Trump administration failed to meet basic immigrant human rights. As the Trump administration attempted to stop the inflow of immigrants to the United States, internal border policing was increased, which was observed in the increase in rates of arrests and incarceration of adult immigrants. Apprehensions of accompanied minors, individuals in a family unit, single adults, and unaccompanied children were 180,034 in May 2021, significantly higher from 23,237 in May 2020 (U.S. Customs and Border Protection, 2021). The mass incarceration among adult immigrants has fragmented family unity and left families vulnerable economically and physically and with adverse mental health impacts (Monico et al., under review).

During the first quarter of 2021, 33,000 unaccompanied minors arrived at the southern U.S. border; they were detained in temporary facilities in military bases and convention centers (Anthropologist Action Network for Immigrants and Refugees [AANIR], 2021). This environment does not facilitate quarantining measures for COVID-19. Children and unaccompanied minors held in temporary processing facilities and placed in ORR secure facilities are exposed to neglect and abuse. Some of these facilities were reported as unsafe to accommodate social distance measures for COVID-19, and medical care is often late or inadequate (Monico et al., under review). The influx of guards and detainees fostered transmission of COVID-19, and the regular transfer of detainees from one institution to another aided in disease transmission (Monico et al., under review).

Travel bans as a result of newly enacted policies prohibited movement of people into the United States and resulted in a larger number of restrictions of permanent immigrants from entering the United States (Chishti & Pierce, 2020). Visa processing services were temporarily suspended, making it impossible for people from areas with high rates of COVID-19 to enter the country. Even though these regulations impacted U.S. citizens as well, they were particularly detrimental to immigrants. The policies made it difficult for immigrants to access asylum-seeking services, putting them in dangerous and violent living conditions.

Border security measures were a major part of Trump's immigration reform, which increased southern border security, interior enforcement, and apprehensions of nonviolent immigrants (Pierce & Bolter, 2020). The closure of the southern U.S. border shifted resources to additional internal forces where the U.S. Immigration and Customs Enforcement (ICE) could collaborate with local police enforcement to arrest and detain migrants. The increase in arrests and detainments of immigrants further contributed to overcrowding in detention facilities and heightened the risk of COVID-19 transmission. The deportation of immigrants without due process delayed legal counsel, and family separation became a reality to most immigrants.

Debate and Perspectives About the Future of Immigration

The Shaping of a New Immigration Policy Agenda Under the Biden Administration

President Biden ranked immigration issues as a top priority, and efforts have been underway to reverse Trump's more than 400 executive actions (American Immigration Lawyers Association [AILA], 2021); however, Biden's efforts have been confronted with harsh realities of the difficulties in undoing the previous administration's immigration policies, which have proven costly both economically and politically. The Biden administration promised new immigration policies compared to those implemented through Trump's executive orders, and Biden has issued 45 as of May 21, 2021 (U.S. Federal Register, 2021a). Given their importance, we summarize five of those orders directly addressing immigration:

(1) The establishment of the Interagency Task Force on the Reunification of Families (Executive Order 14011). This orders the reunification of families separated under the Zero-Tolerance Policy between January 20, 2017, and January 20, 2021. It mandates the establishment of an Interagency Task Force on the Reunification of Families from the Departments of State, Justice, Health and Human Services, and Homeland Security to issue parole (temporary release for a special purpose). It considers other reliefs to ensure provision of services to address the trauma children and their families have experienced and to reunite the entire family unit for humanitarian reasons (U.S. Federal Register, 2021b).

(2) The establishment of the Restoring Faith in Our Legal Immigration Systems and Strengthening Integration and Inclusion Efforts for New Americans (Executive Order

14012). This mandates the establishment of the Domestic Policy Council (DPC), which will oversee federal government efforts in the establishment of policies and procedures that welcome diversity and give fair opportunity for immigrants and refugees to become part of American life and society. It mandates immigration procedures that are free of bias, are accessible to all, and provide pathways to citizenship for immigrants and refugees. Within 3 months of this order issuance, the federal government will submit to the president a strategy and steps toward naturalization (U.S. Federal Register, 2021c).

(3) The establishment of the Creating a Comprehensive Framework to Address the Causes of Migration, to Manage Migration Throughout North and Central America, and to Provide Safe and Orderly Processing of Asylum Seekers at the United States Border (Executive Order 14010). The task force is asked to collaborate with countries such as El Salvador, Guatemala, and Honduras in developing strategies that are humane, alleviate human suffering, and increase opportunities for vulnerable groups. Other procedures include ending efforts that created fear and bias among immigrants and refugees such as the "catch and release" program. Cases of those placed in the expedited removal process will be reviewed to ensure the fairness and transparency of the process (U.S. Federal Register, 2021d).

(4) The establishment of Reforming Our Incarceration System to Eliminate the Use of Privately Operated Criminal Detention Facilities (Executive Order 14006). This orders the reduction of mass incarceration linked to private and for-profit detention facilities. The attorney general is tasked with discontinuing contracts with private operated criminal detention facilities and emphasizing correctional facilities that are cost effective, rehabilitate, and aim to improve the lives of minorities, particularly people of color (U.S. Federal Register, 2021e).

(5) The revision of Civil Immigration Enforcement Policies and Priorities (Executive Order 139903). This mandates the secretary of state, the attorney general, the secretary of Homeland Security, the directors of the Offices of Management and Budget and Personnel Management, and the heads of other executive departments and agencies to review and prioritize immigration laws securing the border. The intention is to respect human dignity via due process (U.S. Federal Register, 2021f).

Although these executive orders have direct relevance to immigration policy, other executive orders also influence the well-being of immigrants. They include those affirming the federal government's commitment to racial equity and underserved communities and those committed to addressing the COVID-19 pandemic. The combination of these executive orders is the beginning of policy changes, but they are insufficient to overhaul the immigration system. For instance, families have been given options to either reunite in the United States or their country of origin (Kabot, 2021); however, fear and uncertainty among immigrant families still persists, as shelters holding children remain open (Ordoñez, 2021). The trauma experienced through migration, deportation, and family separation has lasting physical and mental health consequences, and resources to address these needs are imperative for the well-being of this population. As the future of U.S. immigration policies and practices remains in limbo, immigrant communities are left to endure the long-term implications of past immigration reform.

The Biden administration faces many challenges requiring the adoption of more humane approaches to immigration. By the end of the first 100 days of the Biden administration, four major promises are yet to be fulfilled: (a) suspend the detention of immigrant families seeking asylum and while waiting for the consideration of their cases; (b) increase the cap on the number of refugees resettled annually in the United States, including considering those that are affected by climate change; (c) suspend border wall construction and further inquire into diverted funding for this purpose; and (d) reunite all families affected by family separation from the Zero-Tolerance Policy (Ainsley, 2021). In order to advance a new policy agenda, government checks and balances are essential, such as holding accountable those responsible for the harm done to immigrants, developing a transparent process in detention and justice procedures, and promoting more favorable public perceptions about immigrants.

Concerns Over Future Immigration Policies and the Institutional Capacity to Implement Them

Immigration advocates have expressed concerns about the ability of existing public and private institutions to implement a new set of policies aimed at creating a massive path to citizenship, in particular, the implementation of the new executive orders and proposed paths to legalization of Dreamers, and other temporary statutes (TPS and DED beneficiaries). This is because one of the failures of the IIRIRA implementation was the reduced capacity to assist people in their legalization process. Under the IIRICA, eligible immigrants became victims of individuals and firms offering easy solutions, and the same could happen under a mass legalization process. In 2019, 23.2 million immigrants were naturalized (i.e., became U.S. citizens), "accounting for approximately 52% of the total foreign-born population (44.9 million) and 7% of the U.S. population (328.2 million)" (Batalova et al., 2021, p. 1). As a nation, the United States needs to figure out how to increase the number and capacity of organizations providing services to a larger population seeking legalization. With a divided Congress, legislative changes are not likely to happen very soon; thus, incremental policies may be more viable to move forward.

Nonattorney "accredited representatives" of "recognized organizations" are required to be accredited and then reaccredited every 3 years through the Recognition and Accreditation (R&A) Program of the Board of Immigration Appeals (BIA) "to represent aliens before the Department of Homeland Security (DHS) and the Executive Office for Immigration Review (EOIR), which includes the immigration courts and the Board of Immigration Appeals (BIA)" (U.S. Department of Justice, 2021, p. 1). The AILA has called for the supervision of certified immigration service providers; most importantly, the AILA is calling for provision of legal status to unauthorized immigrants, as part of a roadmap for becoming a welcoming nation (AILA, 2021). In the context of massive immigration reform, the lack of institutional capacity within government and civil society creates opportunities for providers of legal services to take advantage of those who are seeking services by charging high processing fees, for example. Training, resources, and oversight are necessary to increase the overall capacity to address the legalization needs proposed by immigrant advocates.

Immigrants themselves could lead the proposed reforms not only by articulating proposals but also by engaging in policy implementation, especially because the immigration system has become more complicated, including the naturalization process. There are organizations led by Mexicans and Central Americans, such as the League of United Latin American Citizens (LULAC) founded in 1929, the Central American Resource Center (CARECEN) founded in 1983, Hermandad Mexicana established in 1951 in California, and Centro Presente established in 1981 in Boston.

Many immigrant groups have expressed concerns regarding the proposed immigration policy changes; however, many of them will continue to engage in immigrant assistance as immigration reforms are implemented. For example, Alianza America, created in 2004, has focused on advocacy, but with the pandemic it began capturing resources. It now focuses on health education with funding from the CDC, of which 21 member organizations are participating (Alianza America, 2021). Alianza America is a national association of immigrant-led organizations with 55 members, 25 of them providing legal services. It is serving as an intermediary to strengthen and scale up institutional capacity with grant funding from the Latino Commission on AIDS, where 19 smaller partners are involved in health education.

Immigration and Social Work
Influence of Immigration Policy on Social Work
Social workers have confronted challenges to serve clients of immigrants, refugees, and asylum seekers due to the influence of anti-immigration policies, especially in the era of the COVID-19 pandemic. Although infectious disease is a borderless phenomenon, the United States closed its physical and humanitarian borders at the beginning of the pandemic. We have witnessed the suffering of immigrant children, families, and workers due to travel restrictions, deportation, detentions, and disproportional infections and mortality rates of COVID-19. Many immigrants have lost jobs and insurance and delayed testing for and treating COVID-19 (Clark et al., 2020; Macias Gil et al., 2020). Immigrant communities have been inevitably isolated. Social workers have also experienced restrictions to assist immigrants based on our limited capacity, compliance with preventive measures of COVID-19, and conflicts between immigration policies and our jobs.

The long history of anti-immigration policies has deprived immigrant individuals and families of essential resources they desperately need. For example, food security was deprived when supplementary food benefits and other public assistance programs were no longer available to immigrants as of 1996. The COVID-19 pandemic and the associated Zero-Tolerance Policy and other Trump executive orders have threatened immigrants' psychological and physical safety based on encouraged discrimination, and have prevented employment and acquisition or maintenance of legal status. For example, hate crimes and discrimination toward Asian Americans and Pacific Islanders exploded during the COVID-19 pandemic, and 3,800 hate crimes toward the population were reported be-tween March 19, 2020, and February 29, 2021 (S.937-COVID-19 Hate Crimes Act, 2021). Constant attempts to implement wage discriminations toward H1 visa applicants in 2020 was another example (Anderson, 2021). The political notion of "immigrants are taking our jobs" was augmented during the Trump administration surrounding the pandemic (Waslin & Witte, 2020), which led to threats to the legal status of the educated, immigrant work-force. Overall, the exclusion of immigrants from various legal, social, economic, cultural, and health resources is very concerning. These concerns call for social workers' action and solidarity to support immigrants who have experienced human rights issues and to explic-itly oppose racial/ethnic tensions and discrimination.

Relevance to Social Work Ethics, Education, and Practice

Social workers need to engage in a better understanding of why humane immigration pol-icies are aligned with the values of social work. Social workers constantly pursue social changes on behalf of vulnerable and oppressed individuals and groups of people regarding issues such as poverty, unemployment, discrimination, and other forms of social justice (National Association of Social Workers [NASW], 2017). We serve individuals in meeting their needs and assist them to improve their capacities and opportunities by being mindful of their differences and self-determination (NASW, 2017). The values of social justice and dignity and worth of the person are intrinsically aligned with humanitarian perspectives of immigration policy; they underscore the inclusion of global citizens and their needs in our society.

Many forced migrants and their families are enduring deportation, loss of employ-ment, loss of legal status, separation from family, and the related health, violence, and pov-erty issues, which have been accelerated by the pandemic as global mobilization has been restricted (Libal et al., 2021). Forced migration is not solely a U.S. issue: It is a global con-cern because climate change has a global impact. "Climate change is a public health issue because it affects the quality of our water, air, food supplies, and living spaces in a multitude of key ways" (Jackson, 2017, p. 1). It also has long-term effects such as mental health is-sues, as we have witnessed from the example of Hurricane Katrina. Unfortunately, climate change puts the most vulnerable at greater risk. Immigrants and refugees, including chil-dren, women, older adults, and the poor, are harder hit and slower to recover (Jackson, 2017). Water pollution at the U.S.-Mexico border has influenced residents in both nations (Carruthers, 2008). Immigration policy in the United States has been unresponsive to the heightened needs of shared global responsibility to combat climate change and embrace climate refugees.

Social workers have received increasing pressure to critically appraise the effects of climate change on global communities and its impact on migration. Social workers must address forced migration as a matter of environmental justice (Powers, 2019). The Council on Social Work Education (2015) urged that environmental justice aims to help "everyone, regardless of race, color, national origin, or income, enjoy the same degree of protection from environmental and health hazards and equal access to the decision-making process to have a healthy environment in which to live, learn, and work" (p. 1). The international social work perspective includes improving skills such as advocacy, education, community organizing, and research, which are critical to facilitate solidarity among global communities and support climate refugees.

Interdisciplinary approaches and collective responses at the local, national, and international levels must emphasize environmental justice (Jackson, 2017). At the micro, mezzo, and macro levels, there are three prominent and broad areas of social work practice: (a) mitigation of environmental changes, (b) adoption of environmental changes by developing coping capacity and resilience, and (c) secondary and tertiary interventions toward physical and mental health and other impacts on well-being due to environmental changes (Jackson, 2017). The American Academy of Social Work and Social Welfare's Grand Challenges encourages responses to environmental challenges at the national level but also apply to the global level. Social workers must acknowledge the role of anti-immigration sentiments in perpetuating the adverse effects of environmental changes, especially toward vulnerable groups, which deprives them of opportunities to access a healthy environment.

Together with social work ethics and values, nine standards of cultural competency (NASW, 2003) help highlight potential roles of social workers in serving immigrants and their needs. Social workers "[must] examin[e] their own cultural backgrounds and identities while seeking out the necessary knowledge, skills, and values that can enhance the delivery of services to people with varying cultural experiences associated with their race, ethnicity, gender, class, or other cultural factors" (p. 65). Self -awareness (Standard 2) of the privileges of social workers in service delivery is pivotal. From an intersectionality perspective, the power of those delivering services can become a form of oppression in the intersection of different identities (Crenshaw, 1991). When social workers serve immigrants, refugees, and asylum seekers, we must reflect on our privileges and be aware that our inherited backgrounds, such as U.S. citizenship, language proficiency, education, and professional position, can interfere with truly listening to and understanding the needs of immigrants. We need to be learners and check our own biases because we have been exposed to many false political messages that accuse immigrants of unemployment and violence in the United States. We need to educate ourselves and learn from the unique stories of our clients who left their countries of origin in search of safety and a better life and resettled themselves in the United States. Immigrants can benefit from the support of social workers who are immigrants themselves and have similar backgrounds.

Developing a diverse workforce (Standard 7) within the social work profession is another way to enhance the quality of cultural competency in serving immigrants from diverse backgrounds (NASW, 2003). Social work education will benefit from training social workers of immigrant heritage/origin to empower and advocate for immigrant communities, especially those sharing their language and culture (Standard 6). Language and communication play a key role in engaging with clients and lead to effective service delivery and outcomes (Standard 9). Promoting cultural competence by various routes will potentially enhance immigrants' psychosocial adjustment to the United States and help them develop their full potential.

Conclusion

Although immigration has been on the top of the policy agenda in the United States prior to and during the 21st century, immigration policy continues to be restrictive instead of welcoming. Provisional 2020 data on births was just over 3.6 million, which was 4% down from 2019 (Hamilton et al., 2021), which may be indicative of the need to rethink whether the contributions of immigrants to the labor market are not needed. Endemic national and regional conflicts, corrupt governments in countries of origin, international organized crime, and the growing number of natural disasters will continue to propel forced immigration, creating more crises at the border and within our executive, legislative, and judicial systems.

COVID-19 forced policymakers and practitioners to rethink how to address communicative diseases, which have no borders. The United States is divided on how to proceed with the large influx of asylum seekers along the U.S.-Mexico border, particularly during the recent pandemic. COVID-19 has aggravated the global financial outlook in this century and is increasing inequality and threatening the advances achieved in terms of human development (Stiglitz, 2020). The welfare of migrants worldwide has deteriorated (Lee & Monico, 2022). Because immigrants have been on the frontlines of our health care system, food production, and other essential services, the pandemic has adversely impacted this essential population. The United States must be strategic about its future immigration policy and view it not in isolation but in the context of the current socioeconomic, demographic, geopolitical, and climate change trends.

Establishing a more humane immigration system includes (a) restoring the right to apply for asylum when seeking protection along the U.S.-Mexico border while ensuring COVID-19 testing and vaccination, as necessary; (b) compliance with the FSA to ensure that children are not held in custody for more than 20 days and are placed in appropriate facilities; (c) suspending the deportation of immigrants seeking asylum and other reliefs, and ensuring that they have access to legal representation and adequate interpretation in court hearings; and (d) ending the mass incarceration of immigrants during the pandemic and afterward, as other alternatives to detention are less costly (Monico, Rotabi, & Lee, 2019a; Monico, Rotabi, Vissing, & Lee, 2019b). Besides dismantling the mass incarceration system (Sawyer & Wagner, 2020), Section 287(g) of the Immigration and Nationality Act (ICE, 2020), which delegates enforcement authority to localities, must be eliminated, and ICE and other enforcement agencies must be reoriented toward the implementation of more immigrant-friendly policies and more culturally sensitive practices. Immigrants themselves must be involved in service delivery; with the proper training, they can be best suited to implement immigration policies for which they inform and advocate.

The causes and consequences of emigration from developing countries are gaining importance in the literature (Hatton, 2014). Although the United States continues to face border challenges, very few empirical studies have been conducted among deportees from the United States to any country in the world, including the Central America Northern Triangle (Denny et al., 2021). A combined perspective on migration and development is appropriate in this era of globalization to ensure "integrating and amending insights from the new economics of labor migration, livelihood perspectives in development studies and transnational perspectives in migration studies" (de Hass, 2018, p. 227). To inform U.S. immigration policy, contemporary migration studies must examine the critical factors triggering immigration and deepen the understanding of emigration from those deported from the United States. For instance, with respect to the Northern Triangle, the Biden administration must address the border crisis promptly while orienting humanitarian aid to address root migration causes and also combat corruption and improve governance and transparency for long-term solutions.

Forensic social work considers the multidimensional levels (micro, mezzo, macro) of our criminal justice and legal systems. As professionals involved in migration-related practices and forensic social work, we must be concerned with the personal safety and well-being of immigrants and ensure their access to civil and legal rights to which they are entitled. That includes humane treatment while in detention, language interpretation and legal representation when seeking asylum or other forms of relief, and making sure that families are kept together as they interface with the immigration system.

We need to pay attention to the dominant and exploitative relationships between social groups and across borders within the Americas and globally. We must recognize the influential role of nationalism and Whiteness within our criminal and justice systems and their pervasiveness in transracial relations within the United States. We need to examine the role of transnational organized crime and climate change in creating the large waves of immigration at the Mexico-U.S. border. We must also account for the contributions that international social networks and transnational families and communities can make in a global society. Greater integration of immigration issues in social work practice, education, and research is necessary so that future professionals become competent in working with the immigrants, as well as refugees, in our midst.

References

Ainsley, J. (2021, April 21). *Five major immigration promises Biden has yet to keep.* NBC News. https://www.nbcnews.com/politics/immigration/five-major-immigration-promises-biden-has-yet-keep-n1264836

Alianza America. (2021, April 30). *#SomosSalud: Immigrant communities lead local health initiatives to keep families safe during COVID-19 pandemic.* https://www.alianzaamericas.org/press-release/somossalud-immigrant-communities-lead-local-health-initiatives-to-keep-families-safe-during-covid-19-pandemic/?lang=en

American Immigration Council. (2021, March 29). *A guide to Title 42 expulsions at the border.* https://www.americanimmigrationcouncil.org/research/guide-title-42-expulsions-border

American Immigration Lawyers Association (AILA). (2021, April 14). *America as a welcoming nation: A roadmap.* https://www.aila.org/advo-media/tools/ailastandswithdreamers-week-of-action/american-as-a-welcoming-nation-a-roadmap

Anderson, S. (2021, February 1). *The story of how Trump officials tried to end H1-B visas.* https://www.forbes.com/sites/stuartanderson/2021/02/01/the-story-of-how-trump-officials-tried-to-end-h-1b-visas/?sh=6596734f173f

Anthropologist Action Network for Immigrants and Refugees (AANIR). (2021, May 14). *AANIR calls on Biden administration to cease the separation of im/migrant families and the detention of children.* http://www.anthropologistactionnetwork.org/statement-on-ceasing-separation-of-families-may-2021.html

Batalova, J., Hanna, M., & Levesque, C. (2021, February 11). *Frequently requested statistics on immigrants and immigration in the United States.* Migration Policy Institute. https://www.migrationpolicy.org/article/frequently-requested-statistics-immigrants-and-immigration-united-states-2020

Bick, J. A. (2007). Infection control in jails and prisons. *Clinical Infectious Diseases: An Official Publication of the Infectious Diseases Society of America, 45*(8), 1047–1055. https://doi.org/10.1086/521910

Carruthers, D. (2008). The globalization of environmental justice: Lessons from the US-Mexico border. *Society and Natural Resources, 21*, 556–568. https://doi.org/10.1080/08941920701648812

Chishti, M., & Pierce, S. (2020, July 22). *The U.S. stands alone in explicitly basing coronavirus-linked immigration restrictions on economic grounds.* https://www.migrationpolicy.org/article/us-alone-basing-immigration-restrictions-economic-concerns-not-public-health

Clark, E., Fredricks, K., Woc-Colburn, L., Bottazzi, M. E., & Weatherhead, J. (2020). Disproportionate impact of the COVID 19 pandemic on immigrant communities in the United States. *PLoS Neglected Tropical Diseases, 14*(7), e0008484. https://doi.org/10.1371/journal.pntd.0008484

Congressional Research Service. (2021a, May 12). *Temporary protected status and deferred enforced departure.* https://fas.org/sgp/crs/homesec/RS20844.pdf

Congressional Research Service. (2021b, February 2). *The Trump administration's "Zero Tolerance" immigration enforcement policy.* https://fas.org/sgp/crs/homesec/R45266.pdfCouncil on Social Work Education. (2015). *Educational policy and accreditation standards for baccalaureate and master's social work programs.* https://www.cswe.org/getattachment/Accreditation/Standards-and-Policies/2015-EPAS/2015EPASandGlossary.pdf.aspx

Crenshaw, K. (1991). Mapping the margins: Intersectionality, identity politics, and violence against women of color. *Stanford Law Review, 43*(6), 1241–1299. https://doi.org/10.2307/1229039

de Hass, H. (2018). Migration and development: A theoretical perspective. *International Migration Review, 44*(1), 227–264. https://doi.org/10.1111/j.1747-7379.2009.00804.x

Denny, E., Dow, D., Ordoñez, J., Pitts, W., Romero, D., Tellez, J., Villamizar Chaparro, M., Wibbels, E., & Zabala, P. (2021, April 2). *4 things the Biden administration should pay attention to with the border crisis.* Future Development. Brookings Institute. https://www.brookings.edu/blog/future-development/2021/04/02/4-things-the-biden-administration-should-pay-attention-to-with-the-border-crisis/

Folley, A. (2018, July 17). *Migrant women describe sexual assault in ICE detention facilities: Report.* The Hill. https://thehill.com/blogs/blog-briefing-room/news/397382-migrant-women-describe-being-sexually-assaulted-in-ice

Hamilton, B. E., Martin, J. A., & Osterman, M. J. K. (2021, May). *Births: Provisional data for 2020.* Vital Statistics Rapid Release, no. 12. U.S. National Health Statistics Center. https://www.cdc.gov/nchs/data/vsrr/vsrr012-508.pdf

Hatton, T. J. (2014). The economics of international migration: A short history of the debate. *Labour Economics, 30*, 43–50. https://doi.org/10.1016/j.labeco.2014.06.006

Jackson, K. (2017). Climate change and public health: How social workers can advocate for environmental justice. *Social Work Today, 17*(6), 10. https://www.socialworktoday.com/archive/ND17p10.shtml

Kabot, C. (2021). Setting the wrong standard. A review of *Separated: Inside an American Tragedy. Georgetown Journal of International Affairs, 22*(1), 138–143. https://doi.org/10.1353/gia.2021.0005

Lee, J., & Monico, C. (2022). Impacts of global pandemics on people on the move. In P. Fronek & K. Smith Rotabi (Eds.), *Social work in health emergencies: A global perspective.* Routledge. https://www.routledge.com/Social-Work-in-Health-Emergencies-Global-Perspectives/Fronek-Rotabi-Casares/p/book/9780367628734

Libal, K., Harding, S., Popescu, M., Berthold, S. M., & Felten, G. (2021). Human rights of forced migrants during the COVID-19 pandemic: An opportunity for mobilization and solidarity. *Journal of Human Rights and Social Work, 6*(2), 148–160. Online First Article. https://doi.org/10.1007/s41134-021-00162-4

Macias Gil, R., Marcelin, J. R., Zuniga-Blanco, B., Marquez, C., Mathew, T., & Piggott, D. A. (2020). COVID-19 pandemic: Disparate health impact on the Hispanic/Latinx population in the United States. *Journal of Infectious Diseases, 222*(10), 1592–1595, https://doi.org/10.1093/infdis/jiaa474

Migration Policy Institute. (2021). *Deferred Action for Childhood Arrivals (DACA) data tools.* https://www.migrationpolicy.org/programs/data-hub/deferred-action-childhood-arrivals-daca-profiles

Monico, C., & Méndez-Sandoval, J. (2019). Group and child–family migration from Central America to the United States: Forced child–family separation, reunification, and pseudo adoption in the era of globalization. *Genealogy, 3*(4), 68. https://doi.org/10.3390/genealogy3040068

Monico, C., Méndez-Sandoval, J., & Olagbemiro, N. (under review). Migrants and mass incarceration of immigrant children and their families in the United States: The human and civil rights violations of immigrant detention during COVID-19. *Journal of Human Rights and Social Work*.

Monico, C., Rotabi, K. S., & Lee, J. S. (2019a). Forced child–family separations on the southwestern U.S. border under the "zero-tolerance" policy: Preventing human rights violations and child abduction into adoption (Part 1). *Journal of Human Rights and Social Work*, 4, 164–179. https://doi.org/10.1007/s41 134-019-0089-4

Monico, C., Rotabi, K. S., Vissing, Y. M., & Lee, J. S. (2019b). Forced child–family separations in the southwestern U.S. border under the "zero-tolerance" policy: The adverse impact on well–being of migrant children (Part 2). *Journal of Human Rights and Social Work*, 4, 180–191. https://doi.org/10.1007/s41 134-019-00095-z

National Association of Social Workers (NASW). (2003). *Standards and indicators for cultural competence in social work practice.* https://www.socialserviceworkforce.org/resources/standards-and-indicators-cultu ral-competence-social-work-practice

National Association of Social Workers (NASW). (2017). *Code of ethics.* https://www.socialworkers.org/ About/Ethics/Code-of-Ethics/Code-of-Ethics-English

New York Times. (2020, December 15). *Coronavirus in the U.S.: Latest Map and case count.* https://www.nyti mes.com/interactive/2021/us/covid-cases.html

Noe-Bustamante, L., Budiman, A., & Hugo Lopez, M. (2021, January 31). *Where Latinos have the most eligible voters in the 2020 election.* Pew Research Center. https://www.pewresearch.org/fact-tank/2020/01/ 31/where-latinos-have-the-most-eligible-voters-in-the-2020-election/

Office of the Historian. (n.d.). *Chinese immigration and the Chinese Exclusion Acts.* https://history.state.gov/ milestones/1866-1898/chinese-immigration

Ordóñez, F. (2021, April 1). *Biden administration considers overhaul of asylum system at southern border.* NPR. https://www.npr.org/2021/04/01/982795844/biden-

Oringer, J., & Welch, C. (1998, April 1). *Structural adjustment programs.* Institute for Policy Studies. https:// ips-dc.org/structural_adjustment_programs/

Pierce, S., & Bolter, J. (2020, July). *Dismantling and reconstructing the U.S. immigration system: A catalog of changes under the Trump presidency.* Migration Policy Institute. https://www.migrationpolicy.org/resea rch/us-immigration-system-changes-trump-presidency

Pitard, J. (2019). Autoethnography as a phenomenological tool: Connecting the personal to the cultural. In P. Liamputtong (Ed.), *Handbook of research methods in health social sciences* (pp. 1829–1845). Springer. https://doi.org/10.1007/978-981-10-5251-4_48

Powers, M. C. (2019, Spring). Seeing the connections: Climate change and migration. *NASW-NC Newsletter*, 12. https://www.naswnc.org/page/Newsletter

Romero, M. (2008). Crossing the immigration and race border: A critical race theory approach to immigration studies. *Contemporary Justice Review*, 11(1), 23–37. https://doi.org/10.1080/10282580701850371

Rosenblum, M. R., & Brick, K. (2011, August). *U.S. immigration policy and Mexican/Central American migration flows: Then and now.* Migration Policy Institute. https://www.migrationpolicy.org/sites/default/ files/publications/RMSG-regionalflows.pdf

Rosenblum, M. R., & Tichenor, D. J. (Eds.). (2012). *The Oxford handbook of the politics of international migration.* Oxford University Press.

S.937-COVID-19 Hate Crimes Act, Publ. L. No. 117-113. (2021). https://www.congress.gov/bill/117th-congress/senate-bill/937/text

Sawyer, W., & Wagner, P. (2020, March 24). *Mass incarceration: The whole pie 2020.* Prison Policy Initiative. https://www.prisonpolicy.org/reports/pie2020.html

Skrentny, J. D., & Lopez, J. L. (2013). Obama's immigration reform: The triumph of executive action. *Indiana Journal of Law and Social Equality*, 2(1), 3. http://www.repository.law.indiana.edu/ijlse/vol2/iss1/3

Stiglitz, J. (2020, Fall). *The pandemic has laid bare deep divisions, but it's not too late to change course.* Finance & Development. International Monetary Fund. https://www.imf.org/external/pubs/ft/fandd/2020/09/ COVID19-and-global-inequality-joseph-stiglitz.htm

Tagore, A. A. (2014). *Irish and German immigrants of the nineteenth century: Hardships, improvements, and success* [Unpublished honors thesis]. Pace University Honors College, 136. https://digitalcommons.pace.edu/honorscollege_theses/136

U.S. Citizenship and Immigration Services (USCIS). (2017a). *Nicaraguan Adjustment and Central American Relief Act (NACARA) 203: Eligibility to apply with USCIS.* https://www.uscis.gov/humanitarian/refugees-and-asylum/asylum/nicaraguan-adjustment-and-central-american-relief-act-nacara-203-eligibility-to-apply-with-uscis

U.S. Citizenship and Immigration Services (USCIS). (2017b). *Green card for a Haitian refugee.* https://www.uscis.gov/green-card/green-card-eligibility/green-card-for-a-haitian-refugee

U.S. Citizenship and Immigration Services (USCIS). (2021, May 24). *Temporary Protected Status and Deferred Enforced Departure.* https://www.uscis.gov/i-9-central/complete-correct-form-i-9/temporary-protected-status-and-deferred-enforced-departure

U.S. Customs and Border Protection. (2021, June 9). *Southwest land border encounters.* https://www.cbp.gov/newsroom/stats/southwest-land-border-encounters

U.S. Department of Justice. (2009). *25 I&N Dec. 66 (BIA 2009), Interim Decision #365366. Matter of A-M-, Respondent.* https://www.justice.gov/sites/default/files/eoir/legacy/2014/07/25/3653.pdf

U.S. Department of Justice. (2021, April 14). *Recognition & accreditation (R&A) program.* https://www.justice.gov/eoir/recognition-and-accreditation-program

U.S. Federal Register. (2021a). *2021 Joe Biden executive orders.* Retrieved June 23, 2021, from https://www.federalregister.gov/presidential-documents/executive-orders/joe-biden/2021

U.S. Federal Register. (2021b, February 5). *Establishment of interagency task force on the reunification of families. Executive Order 14011 of February 2, 2021.* Executive Office of the President. https://www.govinfo.gov/content/pkg/FR-2021-02-05/pdf/2021-02562.pdf

U.S. Federal Register. (2021c, February 5). *Restoring faith in our legal immigration systems and strengthening integration and inclusion efforts for new Americans. Executive Order 14012 of February 2, 2021.* Executive Office of the President. https://www.govinfo.gov/content/pkg/FR-2021-02-05/pdf/2021-02563.pdf

U.S. Federal Register. (2021d, February 5). *Creating a comprehensive regional framework to address the causes of migration, to manage migration throughout North and Central America, and to provide safe and orderly processing of asylum seekers at the United States border. Executive Order 14010 of February 2, 2021.* Executive Office of the President. https://www.govinfo.gov/content/pkg/FR-2021-02-05/pdf/2021-02561.pdf

U.S. Federal Register. (2021e, January 29). *Reforming our incarceration system to eliminate the use of privately operated criminal detention facilities. Executive Order 14006 of January 26, 2021.* Executive Office of the President. https://www.govinfo.gov/content/pkg/FR-2021-01-29/pdf/2021-02070.pdf

U.S. Federal Register. (2021f, January 25). *Revision of civil immigration enforcement policies and priorities. Executive Order 13993 of January 20, 2021.* Executive Office of the President. https://www.govinfo.gov/content/pkg/FR-2021-01-25/pdf/2021-01768.pdf

U.S. Government Printing Office. (2000). *Public Law 106-553.* https://www.govinfo.gov/content/pkg/PLAW-106publ553/html/PLAW-106publ553.htm

U.S. Immigration and Customs Enforcement. (2020, November 24). *Immigration enforcement: Delegation of immigration authority Section 287(g) Immigration and Nationality Act.* https://www.ice.gov/287g

U.S. Library of Congress. (n.d.). *Immigration and relocation in U.S. history.* https://www.loc.gov/classroom-materials/immigration/african/beginnings/

Waslin, M., & Witte, J. (2020, July 21). *Guiding principles for immigration policy in a post-pandemic world.* https://www.thecgo.org/research/guiding-principles-for-immigration-policy-in-a-post-pandemic-world/

16

Drug Policy

Mark Plassmeyer

Impact of Drug Policy

Over the past 40 years, the number of people incarcerated in the United States has increased by over 500%, resulting in more than 2 million people incarcerated daily in federal and state prisons (Bureau of Justice Statistics [BJS], 2015; Sentencing Project, 2020). Still, this fails to account for the nearly 24 million people cycling through local jails each year and the 7 million others under state supervision via probation or parole (Glaze et al., 2010).

Although not solely responsible, this increase in prison and jail populations is largely due to punitive approaches to drug use, possession, manufacture, and distribution stemming from legislation passed beginning in the 1970s (Alexander, 2012; Cowles, 2019; Hari, 2015; Hinton, 2016). In 1980, about 40,000 people spent time in jail or prison nationwide for drug offenses. By 2013, that number rose to upwards of 500,000, which represented nearly 25% of all people incarcerated in the United States and 50% of those federally incarcerated (Sentencing Project, 2015).

Arrests for drug crimes had also skyrocketed since 1980, when close to 600,000 people were arrested. By 1995, over 1.5 million people were arrested for drug crimes each year. Drug arrests peaked in 2006 at nearly 1.9 million. Although annual drug arrests have declined since then, they have remained steady at around 1.5 million per year and recently peaked at over 1.65 million in 2018 (Drug War Facts [DWF], 2020). Furthermore, these arrests are overwhelmingly for simple possession. Of the 14.1 million drug arrests made from 2010 through 2019, over 11.8 million (84%) were for simple drug possession, while around 2.2 million (16%) were for drug manufacture or sales (DWF, 2020). Among these 11.8 million possession arrests from 2010 to 2019, cannabis (marijuana) makes up the lion's share, accounting for nearly 5.6 million (47.2%) arrests compared to about

Mark Plassmeyer, *Drug Policy* In: *Handbook of Forensic Social Work*. Edited by: David Axlyn McLeod, Anthony P. Natale, and Kristin W. Mapson, Oxford University Press. © Oxford University Press 2024. DOI: 10.1093/oso/9780197694732.003.0016

2.5 million (21.7%) for cocaine and heroin, about 650,000 (5.4%) arrests for synthetic or manufactured drugs, and a little over 3 million (25.7%) arrests for what the Federal Bureau of Investigation (FBI) refers to as "other dangerous drugs" (DFW, 2020). Although cannabis arrests do not make up the majority of drug arrests in the United States, they still constitute the single largest category for drug possession arrests—his despite cannabis being legal for recreational adult consumption in 18 states and Washington, DC and for medical use for people over the age of 18 in 36 states and Washington, DC (as of writing in June 2021; Marijuana Policy Project [MPP], 2021).

Over 95% of those who enter jails and prisons are eventually released (Pettus-Davis, 2014). As early as 1999, people with drug offenses began to make up the largest percentage (33%) of incarcerated people released each year (Roman & Travis, 2004). Given that nearly 700,000 people are released from state and federal prisons each year (Carson, 2015), at least 230,000 people return from incarceration with a drug conviction each year, along with millions of others with drug arrests on their record. Overall, more than 32.5 million people have been arrested for a drug offense in the United States since 1996, suggesting that large swaths of the population have criminal drug records (DWF, 2020). This fact is problematic when considering the significant legal challenges, referred to as collateral consequences, that people with criminal histories face when trying to secure or maintain housing, employment, education, and public benefits.

While some struggle to reintegrate into society or deal with the loss of necessary aspects of life like employment and housing, others struggle with addiction and lack adequate access to effective treatment largely due to the focus on punitive drug policies in the United States (Cowles, 2019; Macy, 2018; Szalavitz, 2016; Westhoff, 2019). Still, despite all the negative consequences that can accompany drug use in the United States, use and addiction continue to flourish unabated. Take the current drug overdose epidemic, which has taken the lives of upwards of 70,000 people a year for the last half-decade while exposing millions of others to the criminal legal system and its collateral consequences (Cowles, 2019; Scholl et al., 2019; Westhoff, 2019).

So how did the United States get to this point? And how can we serve people who use substances and those whose lives have been damaged by current (and past) drug policies more effectively? The current system of prohibition, where some substances are deemed illegal to manufacture, distribute, or possess, is not the only possible policy framework available to address those substances. To provide readers with a better understanding of how the United States came to criminalize some substances and the people who use them, this chapter begins with descriptions of the major historical policies in the United States that led to our current drug control framework, along with some current efforts at reform. Next, readers are exposed to alternative approaches to drug policy by exploring the practices and policies geared at treating drug use as a public health issue, reducing the harm of drug use, and moving away from punitive approaches. The conclusion briefly discusses the drug policies and practices most in line with social work values and the need for social work to engage in shaping drug policy moving forward.

The Criminalization of Substances, Substance Use, and Substance Users

Although drug prohibition seems as if it is the way that policymakers have always responded to drug use, most prohibitions are less than 100 years old. Much of the policy was built piecemeal during the first half of the 1900s before a more cohesive set of policies was introduced in the 1970s and '80s. At the turn of the 20th century, there were no federal laws regarding which substances could or could not be consumed, manufactured, distributed, or possessed. Many medicines available over the counter at the time included opiates and other narcotics such as cocaine, and traveling salesmen frequently sold patent medicines that included a mix of opiates and other unknown ingredients (Hari, 2015; Westhoff, 2019).

Early Drug Control Policy

Pure Food and Drug Act of 1906

In 1906, the federal government passed the Pure Food and Drug Act, which required that all ingredients and their amounts be made explicit on product labels. Warning labels were placed on products such as marijuana tincture and other medicines containing narcotics that were deemed addictive or dangerous (Hari, 2015; Redford & Powell, 2016). Although not overt drug control, consumers were now aware if the products they purchased contained any narcotics or other addictive ingredients (Hari, 2015; Redford & Powell, 2016).

Smoking Opium Exclusion Act of 1909

Up until 1909, there was no federal policy that specifically barred the import or consumption of narcotics in the United States. Smoking opium was targeted because it was the preferred method of opium consumption of Chinese immigrants, and building public consensus for banning smoking opium was made easier given the overtly racist and hostile attitudes toward Chinese immigrants common at the time (Gieringer, 2009; Redford & Powell, 2016). This is evidenced by the lack of tariffs and import restrictions applying to crude forms of opium at the time or other derivatives such as morphine. Also, native-born people of Chinese descent and other U.S. citizens did not face restrictions on their ability to import smoking opium, making it as readily available as it was before tariffs and treaties, but at higher costs to consumers (Gieringer, 2009; Redford & Powell, 2016). To remedy this glaring loophole, Congress ultimately passed the Smoking Opium Exclusion Act of 1909, which banned the importation of smoking opium regardless of who imported the drug (Gieringer, 2009; Redford & Powell, 2016). Redford and Powell (2016) note that the law did have its intended effect as the number of people smoking opium decreased in the United States. However, people simply changed their preferred method of consumption in response to the new law. More people turned to heroin and morphine, which are both stronger and more addictive forms of opiates. Ultimately, this led to the call for more intervention (Redford & Powell, 2016; Westhoff, 2019).

Harrison Narcotics Act of 1914

By 1914, the Harrison Narcotics Act was passed, bringing about the first time that multiple substances were made illegal for nonmedical consumption federally in the United States. This bill placed a hefty tax on prescriptions for narcotics that were once available over the counter, including opiates and cocaine. It made the use of narcotics illegal without a prescription, and the tax served as a further impediment for use and distribution (Hari, 2015; Redford & Powell, 2016).

Prohibition

Five years later, the prohibition of alcohol began in the United States with the passage of the Volstead Act and the 18th Amendment. While prohibition and the Harrison Narcotics Act did produce some initial decreases in drinking and narcotic use, they also had the unintended consequence of creating a bourgeoning black market of unregulated (and unlabeled) narcotics and alcohol along with a new category of criminal: drug offender (Bishop-Stall, 2018; Bonnie & Whitebread, 1999; Hari, 2015). Ultimately, the prohibition of alcohol would be repealed in 1933; it was deemed a failure, and the black market it produced led to increased violence and organized crime in the United States (Bishop-Stall, 2018; Hari, 2015).

The Marihuana Tax Act of 1937

Narcotics remained illegal, and cannabis would soon be added to the list of illegal drugs. In 1937, Congress passed the Marihuana Tax Act, which required people growing or selling cannabis or cannabis products to apply for a tax stamp by providing authorities with detailed accounts of how they produced the product. The catch was that the law also made marijuana production illegal in the United States, and applying for the stamp would amount to admitting guilt and facing fines or jail. The name of the legislation is telling as well. Cannabis was purposely referred to as marihuana in the law as part of a campaign to sway public opinion against cannabis use by associating it with Mexican immigrants, who were often depicted as inherently criminal and dangerous (Bonnie & Whitebread, 1999; Hari, 2015). Again, this speaks to the racist roots of many U.S. drug policies and their lasting racialized impact on the criminal legal system (Alexander, 2012). Ultimately, the law would be deemed unconstitutional for violating the Fifth Amendment at the beginning of the 1970s (Gill, 2008; Hari, 2015).

Mandatory Minimum Sentencing

In 1951, Congress enacted the Boggs Act (Bonnie & Whitebread, 1999; Gill, 2008). This produced the first use of mandatory minimum sentences to deter drug use, distribution, and manufacturing in the United States. The law mandated at least 2 to 5 years for a drug offense and did not stipulate any differences in sentencing between possession, distribution, or manufacturing (Gill, 2008). The Narcotics Control Act of 1956 removed discretionary power for judges and increased mandatory minimums from 2 to 5 years for a first offense and 10 years for any future offenses (Bonnie & Whitebread, 1999; Gill, 2008).

Controlled Substances Act of 1970

During the Nixon administration, Congress passed the Controlled Substances Act, which prioritized federal drug enforcement through the creation of the Drug Enforcement Agency (DEA). At the same time, Congress repealed the Boggs Act, ending mandatory minimum sentences, which had been deemed ineffective (Bonnie & Whitebread, 1999; Gill, 2008). This legislation also created a five-tiered system known as scheduling to classify substances and detail whether they are available for legal use. Schedule I is the most restrictive, where substances are deemed to have a high potential for abuse, no medical use, and a lack of acceptable safety and are not legally available. This schedule includes drugs like heroin, cocaine, cannabis, LSD, and MDMA (ecstasy). The schedules decrease in the severity of the potential abuse and dependence, ending with schedule V, which contains drugs that are considered to have the lowest potential for abuse and dependence and are available with a prescription. In recent years, and even at the onset of the schedules, the categorization of some substances has been controversial and debated. The Nixon administration's own Schaffer Commission on drugs recommended that cannabis not even be scheduled, but they proceeded anyway (Bonnie & Whitebread, 1999; Westhoff, 2019; Table 16.1). Requests to schedule/reschedule or de-schedule can come from the DEA, the Department of Health and Human Services (HHS), or any concerned third party such as advocacy organizations. If accepted, the DEA initiates the request, and then the HHS researches the request and offers recommendations. Ultimately, the director of the DEA makes the final decision regarding scheduling requests (DEA, n.d.). This decision structure promotes a conservative approach as the DEA's longevity depends on the existence of illegal substances for them to police.

Comprehensive Crime Control Act of 1984

This legislation was introduced in the Senate in August of 1984. The law incentivized the use of civil asset forfeiture as a deterrent to engaging in criminal activity, particularly drug trafficking (Dunn, 2000). Civil forfeiture is when the state seizes someone's property when

TABLE 16.1 DEA Drug Schedules

Schedule	Justification	Example Substances	Prescription
I	No currently accepted medical use and a high potential for abuse	Heroin, LSD, cannabis, ecstasy, peyote	No
II	High potential for abuse and severe physical or psychological dependence	Vicodin, cocaine, methamphetamine, methadone, oxycodone, fentanyl, Adderall/Ritalin	Yes
III	Moderate to low potential for physical or psychological dependence	Tylenol with codeine, ketamine, anabolic steroids, testosterone	Yes
IV	Low potential for abuse or dependence	Xanax, Soma, Valium, Ativan, Ambien, tramadol	Yes
V	Lower potential for abuse than schedule IV	Robitussin AC, Lomotil, Motofen, Lyrica	Yes

Source: DEA (n.d.).

they suspect that it either has been used in criminal activity or is a product of criminal activity, effectively suggesting the property in question is involved in a crime. This differs from criminal asset forfeiture, which requires a conviction before asset seizure. Dunn (2000) notes that access to seized property was extended to local and state law enforcement by the law, ultimately resulting in forfeitures worth 20 times more in 1991 than had been seized in 1985. In 1997, $700 million of forfeitures from drug-related assets were recouped by state and local law enforcement agencies, helping to keep them operational, while it is estimated that up to 80% of people who have their property seized were never charged with a crime (Dunn, 2000).

The Anti-Drug Abuse Acts of 1986 and 1988

The Anti-Drug Abuse Act of 1986 reinstituted mandatory minimums for drug offenses (Alexander, 2012; Gill, 2008). It was intended to reinstate mandatory minimums only for those involved in drug distribution and trafficking. However, the Anti-Drug Abuse Act of 1988 established mandatory minimums for possession of crack cocaine (Alexander, 2012; Hinton, 2016). Also, weights triggering a trafficking charge fluctuated from drug to drug. Disproportionately small weights of crack cocaine as opposed to powder cocaine resulted in mandatory minimums for trafficking. Due to its affordability, crack was disproportionately used by poor Americans in the 1980s and '90s, particularly Black Americans living in areas of concentrated poverty. The punitive and highly racialized response to crack cocaine use would result in the disproportionate increases in incarceration for Black Americans and other people of color in the United States over the next 30 years (Alexander, 2012; Gill, 2008; Hinton, 2016).

Illicit Drug Anti-Proliferation Act of 2003

This law amended legislation from the 1980s known as the Crack House Statute that was intended to rein in the abuse of crack cocaine and was part of the Anti-Drug Abuse Act of 1986. In the original law, knowingly operating or owning any sort of property or place intended to be used for the manufacture, distribution, or consumption of controlled substances was made illegal. Similarly, the original legislation made it illegal for anyone to knowingly rent or lease any property or space of any kind for the purpose of the manufacture, storage, distribution, or consumption of controlled substances (Rayfield, 2008; Sachdev, 2004). The 2003 Illicit Drug Anti-Proliferation Act amended the original legislation by adding temporary accommodations (Sachdev, 2004). The law was passed largely in response to electronic dance music parties known as raves, where the use of synthetic substances like ecstasy (MDMA), LSD, and GHB were popular. These events were often one-night parties taking place in warehouses and other temporary venues. The idea is that the DEA would be able to raid these parties or threaten promoters with prosecution if they could show that they knew there would be drug use and dealing at these events (Sachdev, 2004). Although it is fair to assume that rave promoters and music promoters more generally may assume that drugs might be consumed at their events, it is more difficult to prove that their main purpose in holding an event is to provide a place to distribute and consume controlled substances as opposed to providing people with access to live music and a shared experience (Rayfield, 2008). Regardless, the DEA has taken a more liberal approach to enforcement, or at least the threat of enforcement.

Collateral Consequences

By 2019 researchers had identified more than 40,000 restrictive statutes nationwide for people with criminal records and nearly 6,500 that specifically target those with drug crimes on their records (National Inventory of Collateral Consequences of Conviction [NICCC], 2019). Over 30 million people have been arrested for a drug crime in the last 25 years, indicating that tens of millions of people are subject to collateral consequences specific to drug offenses. Although collateral consequences for people with criminal drug records (PCDR) had existed before the 1990s, Congress's efforts to reform welfare in that decade expanded and enhanced many collateral consequences for PCDR.

The difficulties faced by PCDR in finding employment are well documented (Pager et al., 2009). Public and private employers can rely solely on arrests in 38 states when deciding whether to hire PCDR. Private-sector employers can deny employment or terminate PCDR without considering personal history or any other circumstances in all but eight states. Public sector employers have this freedom in 34 states. And in 26 states, all state licensure agencies can revoke or deny licenses without considering any other information besides a drug arrest or conviction (Legal Action Center [LAC], 2009; Pager et al., 2009).

In nine states, PCDR face lifetime bans from public benefits such as the Supplemental Nutrition Assistance Program (SNAP), Temporary Assistance to Needy Families (TANF), and any cash assistance. In 33 other states, PCDR are eligible only if they complete substance use rehabilitation and have only possession charges or convictions (LAC, 2009). PCDR are also ineligible to live with relatives or friends who receive public benefits. Those receiving benefits face the loss of these resources and their housing if they allow PCDR to live with them while they are subject to a ban or any restrictions, a policy included in the Personal Responsibility and Work Opportunity Reconciliation Act (PRWORA, or "welfare reform") of 1996 (Hinton, 2016; Tran-Leung, 2015). Only nine states do not specifically restrict benefits for PCDR (LAC, 2009).

PCDR face housing bans ranging from 3 years, as mandated by federal law, to a lifetime ban in New Mexico. These bans limit eligibility for publicly subsidized housing in projects or through housing choice vouchers (Tran-Leung, 2015). In 48 states, Public Housing Authorities offer some leeway—such as completing substance use rehab and the time since the last drug offense—to determine lengths of public housing bans for PCDR. Only New Mexico and Ohio have automatic bans for any drug arrest or conviction. Thirty states use drug arrests without convictions to help determine public housing ban lengths (LAC, 2009).

The Higher Education Act of 1998 established barriers to higher education for PCDR by making them ineligible for any form of federal student aid. However, it was amended in 2005 to include only drug offenses occurring while one is receiving financial aid. The lengths of bans for federal loans and other aid vary with the weight and type of drug (Alexander, 2012; Gill, 2008; Hari, 2015; Hinton, 2016). Still, much like the overarching theme for many welfare reform policies from the 1990s, this policy aims to limit and reduce access to an essential aspect for full participation in society in hopes to deter drug use, distribution, and manufacture.

Recent Efforts at Reform

Currently, drug control policy in the United States includes mandatory minimums for those caught with drugs and collateral sanctions for those attempting to either reenter or fully participate in society (Alexander, 2012; LAC, 2009; Radice, 2012; Roman & Travis, 2004). If these tactics intended to suppress drug use, production, and distribution were effective, there should have been a reduction in some of these indicators since the mid-1990s. That simply is not the case (Alexander, 2012; Hari, 2015; Hinton, 2016). Over 1.65 million people were arrested for a drug crime in 2018—the highest number since 2010—and recidivism rates for PCDR are higher than 75% (Durose, et al, 2014; DWF, 2020). Further, from 2013 to 2017, drug use and overdose deaths increased significantly in 35 out of 50 states (Scholl et al., 2019).

Given these outcomes, it is not surprising that policymakers are starting to push for reforms in both the front end (criminality, sentencing) and back end (collateral sanctions, reentry) criminal justice and drug policy. For example, in 2010, Congress passed the Fair Sentencing Act, increasing the amount of crack cocaine needed to trigger the "intent to sell" part of the law, which induces mandatory minimums for drug trafficking and distribution. The law also jettisoned mandatory minimum sentences for simple possession of crack cocaine (Love & Schlussel, 2019). In 2018, Congress passed the First Step Act, which made the Fair Sentencing Act retroactive and gives judges more discretion regarding sentencing for drug offenses. However, these policies do not address collateral consequences for drug offenses. Overall, Congress has failed to address federal collateral consequences in over a decade (Love & Schlussel, 2019).

Fair Chance Legislation

With no federal action, states have begun to address collateral consequences on their own. Every state has passed some form of legislation since 2012 that specifically deals with the reintegration of people with criminal records. Known as fair chance legislation, these reforms tend to either restore rights or reduce barriers. In 2018, 32 states, DC, and the Virgin Islands passed 62 pieces of legislation addressing collateral consequences (Love & Schlussel, 2019).

Restoring Rights. A good example of restoring rights was seen in Florida in 2018, when residents voted to restore voting rights to over 1 million people with felony convictions. This repealed an 1880s law restricting voting rights for poor (primarily Black) people receiving felony charges from laws criminalizing aspects of poverty such as vagrancy (Love & Schlussel, 2019).

Another method states use to restore rights to PCDR and others with criminal histories is a certificate of relief/rehabilitation. These take different forms and apply to different offenses state to state, but generally, they provide legal relief from the collateral consequences associated with a given offense and are granted by the courts. These documents can also provide employers and landlords with protection from litigation for knowingly hiring or providing housing to someone with a criminal history (Ehman & Reosti, 2015; Love & Schlussel, 2019).

Reducing Barriers. The most common method that states have implemented to reduce barriers is through clearing criminal records. This process typically uses expungement or sealing of records, which legally makes them disappear from background searches. These methods vary from state to state, with some offenses being ineligible. There are also issues with access, given that in many places, the process involves hiring a lawyer and filing a petition with the court. However, some states are making efforts to reduce barriers to clearing a record for eligible people through automation and other innovations (Love & Schlussel, 2019).

Another common tactic to reduce barriers to employment is to focus on occupational licensure. Typically, these are incremental reforms that reduce the types of offenses that can trigger bans for various occupational licenses, thus expanding access to employment for people with criminal histories to more fields like counseling and law (Love & Schlussel, 2019).

One of the more well-known ways that states and municipalities have tried to reduce barriers for PCDR and other people with criminal histories is through restricting when or if employers or landlords can even inquire about criminal histories. This type of legislation is often referred to as "ban the box" but takes many forms from location to location. Some policies only restrict inquiries about criminal histories to initial screening, whereas others have gone so far as considering the denial of housing or employment based on criminal history (for certain offenses) as discrimination punishable by fines or even jail (Love & Schlussel, 2019). It should be noted that some policies that reduce barriers still leave people vulnerable to records searches due to the existence of for-profit companies that make criminal histories readily available online. In some jurisdictions, these organizations are under no specific obligation to ensure the accuracy of the information they make available, oftentimes rendering expungement moot (Radice, 2012).

Cannabis Reform and Expungement. Another interesting policy innovation that some states have incorporated into cannabis legalization frameworks is the sealing or expungement of current and old cannabis offenses that would no longer be illegal under new laws (Berman, 2018; Rosen, 2019). This is not without precedent. Franklin Roosevelt pardoned thousands of alcohol offenders when prohibition ended and cleared their records of any alcohol offenses (Bishop-Stall, 2018). Still, there is a lack of uniformity in cannabis legalization and decriminalization frameworks across the states implementing these reforms, and some of these policy frameworks do not address those with past offenses or those currently serving time for a cannabis offense. Also, most of the expungement policies related to cannabis policy reforms are in their infancy. Little is known about whether they will be particularly beneficial to PCDR or if expungement will be included in new legalization frameworks moving forward (Berman, 2018).

Research on Fair Chance Policy. The research on policies that aim to mitigate the impact of collateral consequences is sparse given that these policies are new developments across the United States. However, two recent studies evaluated programs or policies that addressed collateral sanctions, and both offer positive results. The Vera Institute evaluated a

New York City Public Housing Authority program that let some people being released from prison move into public housing if family members occupied a unit. In 2 years only one out of 85 participants had been convicted of a new crime (Bae et al., 2016).

Researchers in Michigan found that those taking advantage of Michigan's new expungement law had low rates of recidivism and that their subsequent crime rates were on par with that of the general population. Participants also had significant increases in employment rates and significant increases in wages. However, they did find that only 6.5% of eligible people took advantage of the law and point to lack of information about the law, costs, and the administrative process/time as significant barriers to participation (Prescott & Starr, 2019).

Both studies provide preliminary evidence that when given access to important resources or removing the evidence of prior criminal behavior, people with criminal histories can successfully reintegrate into and participate fully in society as law-abiding citizens. They also point to the need for more research on the impact of similar policies being implemented across the country.

REDEEM and MORE

REDEEM. The Record Expungement Designed to Enhance Employment (REDEEM) Act (2015) was first introduced in the U.S. Senate in 2015. REDEEM directly addresses many collateral consequences that are detrimental for full participation in society for PCDR (Whittle, 2016). The act provides an avenue for sealing or expunging criminal records for nonviolent offenses and amends PRWORA by removing the bans for drug offenders from TANF-funded programs and the SNAP program. This is important because it allows PCDR to live with people receiving SNAP, along with other federal benefits. Furthermore, denial of these benefits to PCDR would be prohibited if they have completed or agree to complete a substance abuse treatment program, are a parent with custody, have a serious illness, are pregnant, or complied with the terms of their sentence (REDEEM, 2015). The law would also require that the Department of Justice establish a protocol for quick release of accurate criminal records through the FBI's background check system for employment purposes, while at the same time requiring consent for release of these records from any person having their criminal history checked for reasons of employment, housing, and credit. It also codifies the right of people to challenge the completeness and accuracy of their records (REEDEM, 2015). REDEEM (2015) prohibits access to records for arrests over 2 years old, nonserious offenses such as drunkenness and loitering, or anything that is not clearly an arrest. The last stipulations in this law are particularly important given the current readily accessible nature of criminal histories online (Radice, 2012). REDEEM will likely be reintroduced in the 117th (2021–2022) Congress and has enjoyed bipartisan support, yet its fate remains uncertain given that it died in committee the last time it was introduced.

MORE. In December of 2020, the House of Representatives passed the Marijuana Opportunity Reinvestment and Expungement (MORE) Act of 2019, sending it to the Senate, where it did not receive a vote by the end of the 116th Congress (MORE, 2019). Still, MORE's passage in the House does reflect a significant shift in the willingness of mainstream politicians to embrace the legalization, or at least the decriminalization of cannabis in the United States. It also suggests that many politicians are on board with the notion that individuals and communities negatively impacted by cannabis prohibition over the last 80 years deserve some compensation (DeCiccio, 2020). The main goal of the MORE Act is to end the prohibition of cannabis by removing it from the list of scheduled substances (like alcohol) in the Controlled Substances Act and eliminating criminal sanctions for those possessing, distributing, or growing cannabis. Some other aspects of the bill intended to help end prohibition and redress the harms caused by it include (a) creating a trust fund to provide resources and services to people and communities negatively impacted by prohibition, (b) implementing a 5% tax on cannabis products to help build and maintain the value of the trust fund, (c) prohibiting denial of public benefits for people with cannabis convictions or arrests, (d) developing an expungement process and sentencing review guidelines for those with convictions for federal cannabis crimes, and (e) requiring research into the effects of legalizing cannabis at the federal level (MORE, 2019). Again, the passage of this legislation through the House has not changed the legal status of cannabis at the federal level, yet it is indicative of a growing consensus that cannabis prohibition does more harm than it prevents and is likely short-lived in the United States (DeCiccio, 2020).

Drug Courts

Drug courts are specialized courts that offer alternatives to sentencing and incarceration for justice-involved people that have issues with problematic substance use and substance dependency. These courts can serve a range of target populations from juveniles and adults to specific groups of people such as veterans and people exiting prison but generally employ similar tactics to reduce drug use, relapses, and recidivism. Most courts use assessments; treatment (often mandatory); case management or supervision from judges, social workers, or other court-appointed officers (e.g., probation, specialty police officers, etc.); drug testing; and sanctions—such as short jail stints—that become increasingly severe if participants relapse or fail to comply with the stipulations of their given program (Mitchell et al., 2012). Successful participants no longer serve lengthy jail or prison sentences, and, in some models, convictions are rescinded, effectively clearing one's criminal record. Research indicates that models that defer convictions are more effective. In a systematic review of 152 drug courts nationwide, Mitchell et al. (2012) found that the use of a deferred conviction or dropped charges upon completion of drug court was a significant predictor of reduced recidivism. Dechenes et al. (2009) also found that offering education and vocation services significantly increased graduation rates from drug court programs, with 57% of participants reporting gains in employment graduating as opposed to just 20% graduating who did not. This is important as many drug court programs have graduation rates under 50% (Mitchell et al., 2012). Francis and Able (2014) note that low completion rates are often due to failed drug tests or participants' difficulties paying for frequent drug tests. So, although drug courts can be an effective tool for reducing drug use and recidivism, they do not always shield participants from collateral consequences and often have low success rates. They also still criminalize drug use at a time when the public and decision makers are shifting toward looking at drug use as a public health issue (DeCiccio, 2020).

The Overdose Epidemic and Harm Reduction

The COVID-19 pandemic could not have come at a worse time for people who use drugs, particularly for those who use drugs deemed dangerous, addictive, and with little medical use, according to the Controlled Substances Act. Upwards of 70,000 people were dying of drug overdoses annually in the years leading up to the pandemic, and 2020 will likely see the highest death totals during the overdose epidemic (Cowles, 2019; Macy, 2018; Westhoff, 2019). The pandemic has contributed to the existing epidemic by forcing many people into isolation, which can be deadly for people using opioids or other substances that may be adulterated with stronger opioids such as fentanyl. If a user overdoses alone, no one is there to try to reverse the overdose with an opioid antagonist like naloxone or call for emergency medical assistance. Moreover, more and more drugs have been adulterated with fentanyl and other agents over the course of the past 10 years, putting a more diverse group of drug users in harm's way, not just those who use opioids (Westhoff, 2019). Ultimately, this raises the stakes even further as substance use evolves toward more novel/synthetic drugs during the pandemic, and substance users are found to be more susceptible to severe cases of COVID-19 (Zaami et al., 2020). Still, even before the pandemic hit, lawmakers around the country were trying to figure out policy solutions to help stem the overdose epidemic. Some have gone with a punitive approach exemplified by the resurgence of drug-induced homicide laws, while others have tried approaches based on the principles of harm reduction as exemplified by good Samaritan laws. In some jurisdictions, both approaches are being incorporated, bringing into question whether there is a coherent strategy or philosophy guiding policy decisions in those areas.

Drug-Induced Homicide Laws

When I lived in western Pennsylvania around 2018, there was a troubling bumper sticker that became popular. It read, "Kill your local heroin dealer." It is certainly understandable why this bumper sticker became so popular in western Pennsylvania, eastern Ohio, and northwest West Virginia. The overdose epidemic was and is hitting these areas hard, and many people lost and continue to lose friends, family members, and other loved ones, which produces justifiable anger at the people providing the drugs resulting in those deaths (Cowles, 2019; Macy, 2018). This same anger and desire to punish or hold someone accountable for an accidental death is often the impetus behind many of the new laws charging people with homicide when they either sold to or used drugs with someone who dies of an overdose (Cowles, 2019; Westhoff, 2019). However, what these laws fail to grapple with is the incredibly blurry line between user and dealer when it comes to drug use, particularly for those with substance use disorders or full-blown substance dependency (Szalavitz, 2016). These "dealers" are often themselves users and, especially when they are small-time "dealers" selling primarily to friends or close acquaintances, are just as susceptible to overdose or death given their limited knowledge of drug purity (Cowles, 2019; Macy, 2018). Regardless, these laws continue to proliferate with active laws in 25 states and at the federal level (Prescription Drug Abuse Policy System [PDAPS], 2020a).

Good Samaritan Laws

In a converse approach to drug-induced homicide laws, many states and localities have passed good Samaritan laws to encourage people to call emergency medical services when someone experiences an overdose. These laws tend to shield people from criminal charges or prosecution for small amounts of drugs and drug paraphernalia if they call 911 when someone they are using drugs with experiences an overdose. Interestingly, there are only five states that do not have a good Samaritan law (PDAPS, 2020b). In total, there are 20 states that have both good Samaritan laws and drug-induced homicide laws (PDAPS 2020a, 2020b). These contradicting policies make the decision to call authorities during an overdose tricky as fellow users may be unsure if they are susceptible to criminal charges, not just for drugs but possibly even for homicide or murder.

Harm Reduction

Harm reduction is a concept that has been gaining traction over the course of the overdose epidemic but that has been a part of U.S. policy for decades. Harm reduction is an approach to inherently dangerous activities or behaviors that finds methods to do them as safely as possible. Some well-known examples are the use of condoms during sex, seat belts while driving, and designated drivers to stem drunk driving (Cowles, 2019; Westhoff, 2019). In the case of illicit drug use, harm reduction accepts that people will use drugs regardless of negative outcomes and looks to make the harm caused by drug use as minimal as possible (Szalavitz, 2016). The following are some approaches that those practicing harm reduction for drug users employ to help ensure they are as safe as possible when engaging in inherently risky behavior.

Naloxone

Naloxone is an opioid antagonist that has been available for decades but has recently garnered attention for its role in the overdose epidemic. Opioid antagonists impede the effects of opioids by connecting to opioid receptors in the body and blocking the receptors opioids connect to in the brain. If someone is experiencing an overdose, administering a dose of naloxone basically ends the high for a brief period, allowing time for proper medical care to be administered, likely at an emergency room (Health Care Resources Center, 2020). Given that it reverses the effects of opioids, those administering naloxone should be prepared for a less than enthusiastic response from the recipient. It should also be noted that naloxone does not guarantee that someone experiencing an overdose will not slip back into that state as it has a limited window of effectiveness. Still, carrying naloxone and knowing how to administer it can help save lives (Cowles, 2019; Westhoff, 2019).

Test Strips

When people think of drug testing, they often think of checking to see if people have drugs in their system or peeing in a cup. But there is another kind of drug testing much more in line with the values of harm reduction. This version allows users to test the drugs they are about to ingest to check for impurities or dangerous substances such as fentanyl. Even if one finds evidence of fentanyl or other adulterants, they might still decide to take those drugs but may do so in a smaller quantity, or they may decide not to take them at all. But at least testing drugs before using them allows for some idea of what is about to be ingested and whether the substance is safe (Palamar et al., 2019). Interestingly, many music festivals of various genres do not allow organizations that conduct drug testing to operate at their events, at least openly. This relates back to the Illicit Drug Anti-Proliferation Act of 2003 because allowing drug testing indicates that promoters know that there is drug use taking place at their events and puts them in danger of criminal liability. This likely unintended consequence often puts people who use drugs at these events at a higher risk of preventable overdoses (Palamar et al., 2019; Westhoff, 2019).

Syringe Exchange

These programs are one type of harm reduction service available in the United States. They offer people who inject drugs (PWID) the opportunity to trade used syringes for new ones to reduce the transmission of blood-borne illnesses like HIV and hepatitis C. Using new syringes also cuts down on wounds, abscesses, and other injuries common when using dull and dirty syringes to inject drugs or other substances like steroids or hormones. Laws vary regarding the number of new syringes participants can receive when turning in old ones, but the most restrictive laws require a one-to-one ration. Some more liberal laws simply re-quire that participants bring in used syringes and are given back what they deem necessary (Fernandez-Vina et al., 2020). Many providers also make efforts to do periodic cleanups in their neighborhoods to show that they are as committed to providing clean syringes to PWID as they are to keeping used syringes out of public spaces. As of mid-2019, syringe exchange programs were operating in 41 states and Washington, DC, while only 32 states explicitly allowed them by law. However, in some states, participants can still face parapher-nalia fines and charges if caught with syringes regardless of whether they have drug residue on them or are unused/clean (Fernandez-Vina et al., 2020).

Safe Consumption Centers

Much like syringe exchange programs, safe consumption centers aim to reduce the inherent harms of illicit drug use while also reducing harm to the community at large. These sites offer users of various drugs a place to consume their drugs in a sterile setting under the su-pervision of medical professionals trained to intervene in the case of overdose or any other medical issues that might arise. The benefit to the community is that some illicit drug use is moved out of public spaces such as parks and public restrooms into places where parapher-nalia is disposed of hygienically and out of view of the public (Cowles, 2019; Davidson et al., 2020). There are currently no sanctioned safe consumption centers operating in the United States. However, much like before syringe exchanges became legal in the United States, unsanctioned safe consumption centers are known to be operating in an underground ca-pacity (Davidson et al., 2020).

In other countries in Europe, as well as Canada, safe consumption centers have been operating for years. Research shows that there has never been an overdose death at any of these facilities and that crime rates in the areas where they are built have no significant change (Cowles, 2019; Davidson et al., 2020; Westhoff, 2019). Efforts to establish safe consumption centers in multiple major U.S. cities have been underway for years in places like Denver, San Francisco, and Philadelphia. Philadelphia was set to open the first site in the United States but was taken to court by the federal prosecutor for the area on the grounds that it would violate crack house statutes (Westhoff, 2019). It remains to be seen if a new presidential administration will be less hostile to such programs.

Medication-Assisted Treatment

Medication-assisted treatment (MAT) is most often used in cases where people have developed a physical dependency to opioids. MAT offers replacement substances that fend off the effects of opioid withdrawal while allowing patients to operate in society without concerns about finding their next hit of illicit opioids. MAT has been proven effective and remains a viable option for treating opioid addiction in many countries outside the United States (Blanken et al., 2010). To be fair, there are MAT programs available in the United States, with most of them using methadone or suboxone as their main alternatives to opioids secured on the street. However, these programs often have waitlists and limited availability and often subject participants to surveillance mechanisms similar to those imposed by the criminal legal system, such as drug testing, which can be counterproductive (Cowles, 2019; Macy, 2018; Westhoff, 2019).

Decriminalization and Legalization

Decriminalization and legalization are similar strategies that have been used within the United States and in other countries as efforts at reforming drug control policy. Both offer a form of harm reduction, as one of the greatest harms that comes from drug use is involvement in the criminal legal system and incarceration. These reforms have mostly concentrated on cannabis policy in the United States. As of June 2021, 18 states and Washington, DC have legalized recreational use of cannabis for adults over the age of 21. Not all these states have frameworks for the legal distribution of cannabis, but most allow for heavily regulated grow operations and dispensaries to sell cannabis to eligible citizens, much akin to alcohol sales, although subject to higher taxes (MPP, 2021). Decriminalization has been more widespread and has extended to all illicit drugs in places like Portugal and, most recently, the state of Oregon. It has also been applied to psilocybin mushrooms in places like Denver, Colorado, with Oakland, California, likely to follow in those footsteps (Hughes & Stevens, 2010; MPP, 2021). So, what are the differences between decriminalization and legalization for using, possessing, distributing, and manufacturing illicit substances?

Decriminalization

Decriminalization removes criminal penalties, typically for possession of relatively small amounts of drugs or amounts deemed small enough for personal use. However, distribution and manufacturing/growing of illicit substances remain illegal. This brings some interesting legal gray area into the issue, given that it is impossible for one to possess illicit substances if someone else did not manufacture or distribute them to begin with. Regardless, this approach has been shown to be a viable alternative to pure criminalization of drug use and has had some positive outcomes for people who use drugs where it has been implemented in places such as Portugal (Cowles, 2019; Hughes & Stevens, 2010; Westhoff, 2019).

Legalization

The legalization of substances completely removes criminal penalties for possession, distribution, and manufacturing/growing of illicit substances. This approach has only been applied to cannabis so far in 18 U.S. states and the countries of Canada and Uruguay (MPP, 2021; Rosen, 2019). Although it can take many forms, legalization generally means that a substance (again, only cannabis so far) is removed from scheduling according to the Controlled Substances Act and is available for sale in regulated markets, like alcohol or cigarettes. This is not always the case, as Washington, DC has legalized adult use and personal growing of cannabis but does not currently have a regulated market or stores where people can purchase cannabis legally (MPP, 2021).

Room for Improvement

Both approaches have their flaws. With decriminalization, people still face fines and other punitive actions, such as mandatory rehab, while they are spared the struggles that come along with a criminal record. Also, decriminalization does not address the issue of adulterated or unsafe drug supplies, given that illicit drugs continue to be unregulated and imported/exported by "criminal" organizations not subjugated to a given country's standards for drug purity (Westhoff, 2019). Furthermore, decriminalization does not address the thin line between users and dealers so prevalent among users of various drugs. The amount of weight of a given substance that it takes to trigger trafficking or distribution charges varies from state to state and even city to city, often rendering decriminalization useless except for those caught with minuscule amounts of illicit substances. Also, drug use or possession can remain criminalized through other means. For instance, if possession and use are decriminalized but it remains illegal to use in public, drug use will still be criminalized for the most vulnerable people who use drugs (i.e., people experiencing homelessness or other forms of housing instability; Cowles, 2019; Hughes & Stevens, 2010).

With legalization, the main concerns early on are equity and redressing the impact of previous punitive drug legislation. Since the first legal cannabis markets opened in Colorado, there has been an abundance of people with access to capital, profiting immensely on the newly legal industry, while those with criminal histories for drug crimes have been shut out of the burgeoning industry, much like they are shut out of other economic, political, and social opportunities due to their past drug offenses. Because the criminal legal system disproportionately criminalizes people of color and low- or no-income people for drug crimes in the United States, these policies serve as mechanisms to exclude those groups from this new legitimate economic opportunity (Berman, 2018; Caulkins et al., 2015; Rosen, 2019). As such, more recent cannabis legalization frameworks in the United States have included provisions that make amends to individuals and communities that have borne the weight of most negative aspects of prohibition.

Many of the new frameworks include language setting up expungement of cannabis offenses, release for people currently serving cannabis sentences, and reinvestment in the communities disproportionately impacted by prohibition (Berman, 2018; Rosen, 2019). Also, the current shift toward commercialized recreational cannabis does not necessarily need to be implemented the way most states are choosing. Expensive fees and costly regulations regarding the security of stores and growing operations make entry into the new cannabis industry often something accessible only to those who already have access to capital or the connections necessary to raise it (Caulkins et al., 2015). Caulkins et al. (2015) note that there are many ways to implement a legal system of cannabis distribution that are not necessarily solely motivated by profit. Just because profit-driven frameworks are currently the norm does not mean that future legalization strategies for cannabis and other illicit substances will or should follow suit, especially when it comes to substances that are riskier to consume. Lastly, even if every state were to decriminalize drug use and possession or legalize cannabis and other drugs, drugs remain illegal federally. Currently, owners and employees of cannabis operations in states that have legalized it are still in violation of federal law and could be arrested and prosecuted by federal agents and prosecutors if a presidential administration felt so inclined. Although such actions would likely produce public and political backlash, it speaks to the necessity for federal decriminalization and legalization policies to achieve comprehensive versions of either type of policy framework in the United States.

Conclusion

Some scholars suggest that the original basis for many of the punitive drug laws discussed in this chapter had little to do with any available evidence regarding the positive or negative impacts of drug use or the ability of these policies to deter drug use or distribution. They argue that many of the policies passed in the 1910s and 1930s, which first made substances such as heroin, cocaine, and cannabis illegal, were based on commonly held and overtly racist fears of sexual integration between races, along with myths of hypercriminality among people of color (Bonnie & Whitebread, 1999; Hari; 2015; Szalavitz, 2016). Ultimately, the contention is that these attitudes contributed to the disproportionate enforcement of drug laws in communities of color. These disparities in enforcement then lead to disparities in incarceration, which would then be exacerbated by the War on Drugs, leading to the current state of mass incarceration that has been so destructive to poor communities of color in the United States (Alexander, 2012; Bonnie & Whitebread, 1999; Hari, 2015; Hinton, 2016; Szalavitz, 2016).

This chapter provides an abridged history of the major pieces of drug policy that helped shape current drug policy in the United States. It also offers an overview of current efforts at policy reform and explores practices intended to improve the quality of life for people who currently use illicit drugs. Social workers are challenged by our code of ethics to work to enhance well-being and meet basic needs for all while focusing our efforts on vulnerable groups of people experiencing oppression and poverty (National Association of Social Workers [NASW], 2017). As such, the policy reforms discussed in this chapter, along with harm reduction approaches outlined, fall in line with our mission and core values. People who use drugs are a heavily marginalized group in this country, often due to criminal histories for drug offenses. They face extreme difficulty procuring stabilizing mechanisms like employment, housing, education, and public benefits. It is imperative that we work to implement policies that improve the lives of people who use drugs and those with criminal drug records instead of further isolating them from society. Still, we cannot deny that drug use can be problematic or that addiction can destroy lives and communities, but we must keep in mind the harms that punitive policies have done to these same people and communities without making a dent in drug use or curbing addiction in the United States.

Politicians, at least some, no longer seem scared to question whether current drug policies in the United States are effective or useful, and many are calling for widescale systemic change. Portugal decriminalized drug use and possession 20 years ago, and although drug use has not disappeared and many still struggle with addiction, drug use has not gone up, drug users no longer fill the prisons, and more people are able to access the treatment they need (Hari, 2015; Hughes & Stevens, 2010; Westhoff, 2019). In the U.S. states that have legalized recreational cannabis, fears about increased use among youth have not come to fruition (Cowles, 2019), suggesting that it is possible to effectively regulate drugs like cannabis without putting youth at increased risk.

Cannabis legalization also provides examples of how drug policy reform can perpetuate existing inequalities if specific mechanisms are not put in place to ensure that those who already have resources do not benefit the most, both financially and politically, from current and future legalization frameworks. Social workers need to be more involved in the formation of legalization frameworks moving forward to help ensure they allocate resources in a way that rights past wrongs as opposed to being used simply to stabilize state budgets. How can social work say it cares about impoverished people if we are not advocating for some sort of reparations for people and communities caught up in the ongoing drug war? We need to push for policies that make amends for past harms and the harms currently taking place. This does not just apply to cannabis prohibition but to the prohibition of all illicit substances. The most glaring contradiction that politicians seem unable to fathom is that the legalization of cannabis alone is hardly a cure-all for the damages wrought on people and communities by punitive drug policy. Also, although certainly an appreciable gesture, using only cannabis money to redress the wrongs done by the War on Drugs seems mind-bogglingly simplistic. If the War on Drugs is a great failure, as many politicians now claim it to be, why are they not also calling for the legalization and regulation of all drugs in some form, or at least decriminalization? At the same time, why are they not calling for the diversion of existing resources used for the enforcement of ineffective policies with clearly racist roots to the very communities that have borne the brunt of 50+ years of increasingly punitive drug policy? Social work can help hold these politicians accountable and strive to have them live up to their rhetoric by advocating for coherent, evidence-based policies. We must also ensure that these new policies and reforms represent ideas coming from the people and communities that have suffered the most from our previous drug policies, including people who use drugs themselves.

References

Alexander, M. (2012). *The new Jim Crow: Mass incarceration in the age of colorblindness*. (rev. ed.). New Press.

Bae, J., diZerega, M., Kang-Brown, J., Shanahan, R., & Subramanian, R. (2016). *Coming home: An evaluation of the New York City Housing Authority's Family Reentry Pilot Program*. Vera Institute of Justice.

Berman, D. A. (2018). Leveraging marijuana reform to enhance expungement practices: Ohio State public law working paper no. 444. *Federal Sentencing Reporter, 30*(4), 305–317. https://dx.doi.org/10.2139/ssrn.3165001

Bishop-Stall, S. (2018). *Hungover: The morning after and one man's quest for the cure*. Penguin Books.

Blanken, P., Hendriks, V. M., Van Rae, J. M., & Van Den Brink, W. (2010). Outcome of long-term heroin-assisted treatment offered to chronic, treatment-resistant heroin addicts in the Netherlands. *Addiction, 105*(2), 300–308. https://doi.org/10.1111/j.1360-0443.2009.02754.x

Bonnie, R. J., & Whitebread, C. J., II. (1999). *The marijuana conviction: A history of marijuana prohibition in the United States*. Lindesmith Center.

Bureau of Justice Statistics. (2015). *Estimated number of persons under correctional supervision in the U.S., 1980–2013*. http://www.bjs.gov/index.cfm?ty=kfdetail&iid=487

Carson, A. E. (2015). *Prisoners in 2014*. https://bjs.ojp.gov/library/publications/prisoners-2014

Caulkins, J. P., Kleiman, M. A., MacCoun, R. J., Midgett, G., Oglesby, P., Pacula, R. L., & Reuter, P. H. (2015). *Considering marijuana legalization: Insights for Vermont and other jurisdictions*. RAND.

Cowles, C. (2019). *War on us: How the war on drugs & myths about addiction have created a war on all of us*. Fidalgo Press.

Davidson, P. J., Kral, A. H., Lambdin, B. H., & Wenger, L. D. (2020). Evaluation of an unsanctioned safe consumption site in the United States. *New England Journal of Medicine, 383*(6), 589–590. https://www.nejm.org/doi/full/10.1056/NEJMc2015435

Dechenes, E. P., Ireland, C., & Kleinpeter, C. B. (2009). Enhancing drug court success. *Journal of Offender Rehabilitation, 48*(1), 19–36. 10.1080/10509670802577473

DeCiccio, E. (2020, December 5). *Bill decriminalizing marijuana "great step" but "largely symbolic," says cannabis COO*. CNBC. https://www.cnbc.com/2020/12/05/bill-decriminalizing-marijuana-great-step-but-largely-symbolic.html

Drug Enforcement Administration. (n.d.). *Drug scheduling*. https://www.dea.gov/drug-information/drug-scheduling

Drug War Facts. (2020). *Total number of arrests by year and type of offense*. https://www.drugpolicyfacts.org/node/235#overlay=table/total_arrests

Dunn, K. (2000). Reining in forfeiture: Common sense reform in the war on drugs. *Frontline*. https://www.pbs.org/wgbh/pages/frontline/shows/drugs/special/forfeiture.html

Durose, M. R., Cooper, A. D., & Snyder, H. N. (2014). *Recidivism of prisoners released from 30 states in 2005: Patterns from 2005 to 2010*. http://www.bjs.gov/content/pub/pdf/rprts05p0510.pdf

Ehman, M., & Reosti, A. (2015). Tenant screening in an era of mass incarceration: A criminal record is no crystal ball. *New York University Journal of Legislation & Public Policy Quorum, 1*, 1–28.

Fernandez-Vina, M. H., Prood, N. E., Herpolsheimer, A., Waimberg, J., & Burris, S. (2020). State laws governing syringe exchange services programs and participant syringe possession 2014–2019. *Public Health Reports, 135*(1), 128S–137S. https://doi.org/10.1177/0033354920921817

Francis, T. R., & Able, E. M. (2014). Redefining success: A qualitative investigation of therapeutic outcomes for non-completing drug court clients. *Journal of Social Service Research, 40*(3), 325–338. https://doi.org/10.1080/01488376.2013.875094

Gieringer, D. (2009, February 6). *The opium exclusion act of 1909*. Counter Punch. https://www.counterpunch.org/2009/02/06/the-opium-exclusion-act-of-1909/

Gill, M. M. (2008). Correcting course: Lessons from the 1970 repeal of mandatory minimums. *Federal Sentence Reporter, 21*(1), 55–68.

Glaze, L. E., Bonczar, T. P., & Zhang, F. (2010). *Probation and parole in the United States, 2009*. U.S. Department of Justice.

Hari, J. (2015). *Chasing the scream: The first and last days of the war on drugs*. Bloomsbury.

Health Care Resources Center. (2020). *What is an opioid antagonist?* https://www.hcrcenters.com/blog/what-is-an-opioid-antagonist/

Hinton, E. (2016). *From the war on poverty to the war on crime: The making of mass incarceration in America.* Harvard University Press.

Hughes, C. A., & Stevens, A. (2010). What can we learn from the Portuguese decriminalization of illicit drugs? *British Journal of Criminology, 50*(6), 999–1022. https://doi.org/10.1093/bjc/azq038

Legal Action Center. (2009). *After prison: Roadblocks to reentry. A report on state legal barriers facing people with criminal records. 2009 update.* http://www.lac.org/roadblocks-to-reentry/upload/lacreport/Roadblocks-to-Reentry-2009.pdf

Love, M., & Schlussel, D. (2019). *Reducing barriers to reintegration: Fair chance and expungement reforms in 2018.* https://ccresourcecenter.org/2019/03/28/updated-report-on-2018-fair-chance-and-expungement-reforms/#more-19033

Macy, B. (2018). *Dopesick: Dealers, doctors, and the drug company that addicted America.* Little, Brown and Company.

Marijuana Opportunity and Reinvestment Act of 2019. (2019). H.R.3884, 116th Congress. https://www.congress.gov/bill/116th-congress/house-bill/3884

Marijuana Policy Project. (2021). *State policy.* https://www.mpp.org/states/

Mitchell, O., Wilson, D., Eggers, A., & MacKenzie D. (2012). Drug courts' effects on criminal offending for juveniles and adults. *Campbell Systematic Reviews, 4*, i–87. https://doi.org/10.4073/csr.2012.4

National Association of Social Workers. (2017). *NASW code of ethics.* https://www.socialworkers.org/About/Ethics/Code-of-Ethics

National Inventory of Collateral Consequences of Conviction. (2019). *National inventory of collateral consequences of conviction.* https://niccc.csgjusticecenter.org/

Pager, D., Western, B., & Sugie, N. (2009). Sequencing disadvantage: Barriers to employment facing young black and white men with criminal records. *Annals of the American Academy of Political and Social Science, 623*, 195–213.

Palamar, J. J., Acosta, P., Sutherland, R., Shedlin, M. G., & Barratt, M. J. (2019). Adulterants and altruism: A qualitative investigation of "drug checkers" in North America. *International Journal of Drug Policy, 74*, 169–169. https://doi.org/10.1016/j.drugpo.2019.09.017

Pettus-Davis, C. (2014). Social support among releasing men prisoners with lifetime trauma experiences. *International Journal of Law and Psychiatry, 37*, 512–523. http://dx.doi.org/10.1016/j.ijlp.2014.02.024

Prescott, J. J., & Starr, S. B. (2019). Expungement of criminal convictions: An empirical study. *Harvard Law Review,* Forthcoming; University of Michigan Law & Economic Research Paper No. 19–001. https://dx.doi.org/10.2139/ssrn.3353620

Prescription Drug Abuse Policy System (PDAPS). (2020a). *Drug inducted homicide laws.* http://www.pdaps.org/datasets/drug-induced-homicide-1529945480-1549313265-1559075032.

Prescription Drug Abuse Policy System (PDAPS). (2020b). *Good Samaritan overdose prevention laws.* http://pdaps.org/datasets/good-samaritan-overdose-laws-1501695153

Radice, J. (2012). Administering justice: Removing statutory barriers to reentry. *University of Colorado Law Review, 83*, 715–779.

Rayfield, M. E. (2008). Pure consumption cases under the federal "crackhouse" statute. *University of Chicago Law Review, 75*(4), 1805–1832.

Record Expungement Designed to Enhance Employment Act of 2015. (2015). S. 675, 114th Congress. https://www.congress.gov/bill/114th-congress/senate-bill/675

Redford, A., & Powell, B. (2016). Dynamics of intervention in the war on drugs: The buildup to the Harrison Act of 1914. *Independent Review, 20*(4), 509–530.

Roman, C. G., & Travis, J. (2004). *Taking stock: Housing, homelessness and prisoner reentry.* https://www.urban.org/research/publication/taking-stock

Rosen, A. (2019). *High time for criminal justice reform: Marijuana expungement statutes in states with legalized or decriminalized marijuana laws.* https://dx.doi.org/10.2139/ssrn.3327533

Sachdev, M. V. (2004). The party's over: Why the illicit drug anti-proliferation act abridges economic liberties. *Columbia Journal of Law and Social Problems, 37*(4), 585–626.

Scholl, L., Seth, P., Kariisa, M., Wilson, N., & Bladwin, G. (2019). Drug and opioid-involved overdose deaths—United States, 2013–2017. *MMWR Morbidity and Mortality Weekly Report, 67*, 1419–1427. http://dx.doi.org/10.15585/mmwr.mm675152e1

Sentencing Project. (2015). *Drug policy*. http://www.sentencingproject.org/template/page.cfm?id=128

Sentencing Project. (2020). *Criminal justice facts*. https://www.sentencingproject.org/criminal-justice-facts/

Szalavitz, M. (2016). *Unbroken brain: A revolutionary new way of understanding addiction*. St. Martin's Press.

Tran-Leung, M. C. (2015). *When discretion meets denial: A national perspective on criminal records barriers to federally subsidized housing*. http://povertylaw.org/sites/default/files/images/publications/WDMD-final.pdf

Westhoff, B. (2019). *Fentanyl, Inc. How rogue chemists created the deadliest wave of the opioid epidemic*. Grove Press

Whittle, T. N. (2016). Felony collateral sanctions effects on recidivism: A literature review. *Criminal Justice Policy Review, 29*(5), 505–524. https://doi.org/10.1177%2F0887403415623328

Zaami, S., Mainelli, E., & Vari, M. R. (2020). New trends of substance abuse during COVID-19 pandemic: An international perspective. *Frontiers in Psychiatry, 11*, 1–3. https://doi.org/10.3389/fpsyt.2020.00700

17

Capital Punishment

Trina L. Hope, Heather M. Lepper-Pappan,
and Anthony P. Natale

The System

Most Americans are at least vaguely aware of the existence of the system of capital punishment. However, most don't give it much thought—until they see news coverage of a "news-
worthy" murder or end up among the unlucky few Americans who have direct experience
with it. Most are unaware of America's history and unique relationship with capital punishment, how it works in practice, or its enduring connection to racial oppression. A journey
into the past and current system of capital punishment in the United States speaks to many
issues at the heart of social work practice, including racial and class inequality, trauma,
equal protection under the law, and fundamental human dignity questions.

This chapter will explore the history and current practice of capital punishment in the
United States, followed by an evaluation of capital punishment as a criminal justice policy.
Next, we will discuss the collateral damage associated with capital punishment, including
the families of both victims and offenders, as well as those who work in the system. Finally,
we will discuss the implications for social workers.

A Brief History of Capital Punishment in the United States

The Colonial Era

The history of capital punishment in the United States is inexorably linked to its colonial
roots. Used extensively in 17th-century England, capital punishment continued in the New
World, with the first documented execution in 1608 in Virginia's Jamestown settlement.
Captain George Kendall was executed for spying on behalf of Spain (Bohm, 2017). While

Trina L. Hope, Heather M. Lepper-Pappan, and Anthony P. Natale, *Capital Punishment* In: *Handbook of Forensic Social Work*. Edited
by: David Axlyn McLeod, Anthony P. Natale, and Kristin W. Mapson, Oxford University Press. © Oxford University Press 2024.
DOI: 10.1093/oso/9780197694732.003.0017

common in both the Northern and Southern colonies, capital punishment's underlying purposes differed by region.

Among the Northern colonies, particularly those founded by Puritans, capital punishment enforced religious purity. Steiker and Steiker (2016) describe the execution of Mary Dyer on June 1, 1660. Dyer was a Quaker who refused to accept her banishment from the Massachusetts Bay Colony. They point out that while Dyer is now viewed as a symbol of religious freedom, at the time, she was a stark warning of the dangers of challenging the authority of religious leaders. Other examples of executions from this period include Mary Lathan, who was hung for adultery in 1644, and Thomas Granger, a teenaged servant hung in 1642 for bestiality with livestock (the livestock were also executed, according to biblical principles). The Massachusetts Bay Colony's list of 12 death-eligible crimes included idolatry, witchcraft, blasphemy, murder, manslaughter, poisoning, bestiality, sodomy, adultery, man stealing, false witness in capital cases, and conspiracy and rebellion, most accompanied by a biblical quote (Bohm, 2017).

Among the Southern colonies, the primary purpose of capital punishment was to protect the system of slavery. Fear of slave rebellions and a desire to preserve the tobacco trade resulted in a long list of specific death-eligible crimes. Executions of slaves were extremely violent and brutal, including burning at the stake and breaking on the wheel (Steiker & Steiker, 2016). The Virginia Dade Code described 25 specific capital offenses, including stealing grapes or ears of corn, killing a chicken, or trading with Native Americans (Bohm, 2017; see also Bessler, 2012, 2014). Since the 18th century, the South has carried out the most executions of any region, with African Americans making up the majority of those executed (Steiker & Steiker, 2016).

As the regional differences described above indicate, capital punishment during colonial times was viewed as a local affair, "primarily a tool of local criminal justice, invoked by local officials to address distinctively local concerns" (Steiker & Steiker, 2016, pp. 6–7). Additionally, while most statutes mandated a death sentence for individuals convicted of death-eligible crimes, local control persevered via mitigating mechanisms allowing officials to bypass mandated death sentences when deemed necessary. Jury nullification (where juries refuse to convict because they disagree with the mandatory sentence), judicial pardons from judges, and clemency from colonial governors were used extensively during this time—particularly as a way to protect White southerners from harsh mandatory sentences (Bohm, 2017).

The Postcolonial Era

One hundred sixty-two executions occurred in the 17th century, 1,391 in the 18th century, 6,000 in the 19th century, and more than 7,000 in the 20th century before the 1972 capital punishment moratorium resulting from the Supreme Court's *Furman* decision. Since the reinstatement of the death penalty in 1976, 1,521 executions have taken place (for comprehensive statistics on U.S. executions, see the "Espy File," a database of executions in the United States and the earlier colonies from 1608 to 2002, as well as the (Espy & Smykla, 2016). While these statistics show a dramatic increase in the number of executions over time, the long-term trend in the rates of executions over the centuries is downward when considering changes in the population. Although capital punishment was common in the early years of the republic, there were always those who pushed for reform/abolition, and as Steiker and Steiker (2016) point out, from the colonial era to the late 20th century, at least four waves of locally driven death penalty reforms occurred, including (a) a narrowing of the range of death-eligible crimes, (b) a shift from mandatory to discretionary sentencing, (c) executions occurring in private rather than public, and (d) a shift in methods of execution to more humane practices.

Serious federal intervention into the practice of capital punishment did not begin in earnest until the 1960s. One of the seminal moments came in 1963 when Supreme Court Justice Arthur Goldberg challenged the death penalty's constitutionality in a dissent written in response to the court's refusal to hear two cases where the defendants received the death penalty (*Rudolph v. Alabama* and *Snider v. Cunningham*). While this dissent had no legal effect, it did inspire members of the NAACP's Legal Defense and Educational Fund (LDF) to take on the death penalty issue. The LDF had traditionally focused on civil rights, but as mentioned above, the death penalty has long been, and continues to be, disproportionality applied to African Americans, and the overwhelming majority of those executed for the crime of rape were Black (for more detail on the role of race in the death penalty and rape, see the amicus brief filed by the American Civil Liberties Union et al. [2008] in *Kennedy v. Louisiana*). The LDF lawyers, working with other prominent civil rights lawyers such as Anthony Amsterdam, represented more than 300 death row inmates between 1965 and 1972 (Bohm, 2017). Their efforts culminated in the 1972 *Furman* case.

In *Furman*, lawyers argued to the Supreme Court that allowing judges/juries "unbridled discretion" when sentencing defendants to death resulted in extreme arbitrariness in applying death penalty statutes. This arbitrariness violates both the Eighth Amendment's prohibition against cruel and unusual punishment and the 14th Amendment's guarantees of equal protection under the law (Bohm, 2017). All three defendants were Black—two sentenced to death for the rapes of White women, the third (Furman) for the murder of a White man. Mandery (2013) describes one of the exchanges between the court and the lawyers. Arguing on behalf of Furman, Amsterdam was asked by Justice Douglas about the "kinds of people on which the death penalty is imposed" and what kind of standards exist "for the exercise of discretion by the judge or jury" (p. 148). In response, Amsterdam noted:

> The problem in a democracy is that legislation can be arbitrarily, selectively, and spottily applied to a few outcast pariahs, whose political position is so weak, and whose personal situation is so unpopular, and who are so ugly, that public revulsion which would follow the uniform application of the penalties doesn't follow. (p. 149)

At the end of Amsterdam's allotted time, Justice Douglas came back to this issue, asking again, "Is there anything in the record that indicates what kind of people Georgia executes?" Amsterdam's response: "Georgia executes black people" (p. 159).

Amsterdam's more cautious approach focused on the *application* of capital punishment rather than the constitutionality of the punishment itself and turned out to be a compelling argument. In its 5–4 decision, the majority concluded that "The Court holds that the imposition and carrying out of the death penalty in these cases constitute cruel and un- usual punishment in violation of the Eighth Amendment" (Mandery, 2013, p. 235). While many assumed that the *Furman* decision would be the end of capital punishment in the United States, as Bohm (2017) notes, "The Court seemed to be implying that if the process of applying the death penalty could be changed to eliminate the problems cited in *Furman*, then it would pass constitutional muster" (p. 86). And in response to the court's decision, 35 states wrote new capital punishment statutes. The court addressed these statutes' consti- tutionality in its 1976 review of five carefully selected test cases, collectively known as the *Gregg* decision. As Bohm (2017) notes, "All five cases involved a white defendant; felony murders, none of which was especially brutal; and perhaps most important, each case was selected from a state that had one of the five different types of new death penalty laws" (p. 89). With few exceptions, the court accepted the newly written statutes and ruled that capital punishment was no longer unconstitutional in its application (for a detailed discus- sion of the legal, political, and social reasons for the court's reversal of itself between the *Furman* and *Gregg* decisions, see Steiker & Steiker, 2016, and Mandery, 2013).

Steiker and Steiker (2016) argue that the *Furman* and *Gregg* decisions heralded a new era of "constitutional regulation" of capital punishment, whose administration the federal government was no longer willing to leave to the states. Capital punishment went from being virtually unregulated by the federal government to the most commonly heard cate- gory of cases on the Supreme Court's docket. They note that "the court embraced at least four principles that would guide its extensive constitutional doctrine going forward:

(1) States must guide sentencing discretion and narrow the class of offenders subject to the punishment.
(2) The death penalty must be proportionate to the offense triggering the punishment.
(3) Defendants must receive an individualized assessment of the appropriateness of the death penalty that includes consideration of their character, background, and the cir- cumstances of the offense.
(4) The categorical difference between death and all other punishments ("death is dif- ferent") requires that capital proceedings be especially fair and reliable" (p. 71).

These constitutional doctrines mean that the entire process—from how charges are filed, to the trial and sentencing, to postsentencing appeals—is significantly different in the cap- ital and noncapital system. Together these rules surrounding the application of the death penalty are referred to as "super due process" and include the following (Bohm, 2013, p. 5):

- Bifurcated trials. The first phase determines guilt. If the accused is found guilty, the second phase determines the penalty. Evidence and witnesses are presented in both stages of the trial. Unless a defendant specifically requests a bench rather than a jury trial, the jury determines the sentence.
- Sentencing guidelines require jurors to weigh aggravating and mitigating factors. Aggravating factors are "facts or situations that increase the blameworthiness of a crim- inal act." They can focus on offender characteristics (e.g., prior criminal history), the

circumstances of the murder (premeditation or torture), or victim characteristics (e.g., the murder of a police officer). Jurors are required to find at least one aggravating factor to impose a sentence of death. Aggravating factors are intended to narrow the range of death-eligible murders (to the "worst of the worst"). Suppose jurors find one or more aggravating factors. In that case, they must then weigh them against any mitigating factors, which are "facts or situations that do not justify or excuse a capital crime but reduce the degree of a defendant's blameworthiness and thus may reduce his punishment." Examples of mitigating factors include immaturity, no prior criminal record, or "being under the influence of another person." If the aggravating factors outweigh the mitigating factors, then the sentence is death. If the mitigators outweigh the aggravators, the penalty is life without parole. If the two are equal, then a death sentence may be imposed.

- Automatic appellate review. Although not constitutionally required, almost all capital punishment jurisdictions require an automatic review of the state supreme court's conviction and sentence.
- Proportionality reviews. These also are not mandated by the court, but some states are required to compare the sentence being reviewed to those imposed in similar cases in the state to identify disparities in sentencing.

Under "super due process," the court's requirements promised a new and improved capital punishment system—free from the arbitrary and discriminatory system of the past. The reality, however, fell far short of the hopeful assumptions of the court.

The Current State of Capital Punishment in the United States

Among industrialized, democratic nations of the world, the United States stands almost alone in its continued use of capital punishment. Japan is the only other democracy that still imposes and carries out death sentences, and these are rarely used, and almost exclusively for those who commit mass murder. Currently, 27 states, the U.S. government, and the U.S. military retain capital punishment (Death Penalty Information Center, 2021). While just a handful of executions were carried out in the years immediately following the *Gregg* decision, beginning in the mid-1980s, states began carrying out executions with regularity. The number of executions increased steadily, peaking at 98 in 1999. There has been a steady decline in executions since then, with only 15 carried out in 2020. It is important to note, however, that 10 of the 15 executions in 2020 were carried out by the U.S. government, which had not executed anyone since 2003 (three of the 2020 executions, and three more in 2021, were carried out after Trump lost his re-election bid, which is unprecedented; Davidson, 2021).

A review of the current statistics on the capital punishment system illustrates the continuing legacy of slavery and Jim Crow, which were state and local statutes that legalized racial segregation. African Americans are disproportionately represented among those executed, and over 80% of all post-*Furman* executions have taken place in the South (Death Penalty Information Center, 2021). Zimring (2003) indicates that adherence to "vigilante values" drives enthusiasm for capital punishment in the South. Rather than viewing capital punishment as a troubling display of governmental power, executions, like lynchings of the past, are viewed as being carried out on behalf of the community to defend its values and as essential to the maintenance of social order. In his analyses of lynchings between 1889 and 1918 and executions between 1977 and 2000, Zimring (2003) demonstrates the continuing legacy of slavery and Jim Crow on the modern system of capital punishment. Accounting for less than 35% of the population, the 14 states identified as "high lynching" carried out 85% of modern executions, compared to the 14 "low lynching" states, which accounted for only 3.2% of executions. As Bohm (2017) points out, lynchings outnumbered executions 82 to six in the 1870s and 92 to 40 in the 1890s (p. 14). In a related argument, Garland (2010) asserts that the system of Jim Crow and capital punishment in many ways replaced what he refers to as "spectacle" or "public torture" lynchings, in a kind of "negative symmetry," stating that "for all the inversion of form, the social forces and political processes that enabled lynchings, mobilized lynch mobs, and made lynchings useful for political actors have somehow persisted and continue to structure the modern death penalty's deployment and utility" (pp. 34–35; see also Jacobs et al., 2005). As Zimring notes, America's relationship with capital punishment is one of contradiction. Our federalism system means we don't have *one* criminal justice system, but 52 (counting the U.S. government and the military). These contradictions are further illustrated by the partisan nature of public opinion regarding capital punishment.

Gallup regularly includes questions about capital punishment in its national opinion polls. Support for capital punishment between 1936 and 2019 varied from a low of 42% in 1967 (the only year in the poll's history where the percent opposed to the death penalty was greater than the percent in favor) to a high of 80% in 1995. The latest poll, conducted in September/October of 2019, found that 55% of Americans favor the death penalty, 43% are not in favor, and 2% have no opinion. When life without the possibility of parole (LWOP) is included as an option, support for the death penalty declines significantly, and in 2019, for the first time since the question was introduced in 1985, a greater percentage of respondents chose LWOP (60%) over the death penalty (26%). Both Democrats (79%) and Independents (60%) are more likely to choose imprisonment, compared to only 38% of Republicans. These partisan differences line up with the broader research on predictors of support for the death penalty, which shows that Whites, males, conservatives, southerners, those with less than a college education, and those over the age of 50 are the most supportive of capital punishment. The effects of religion vary by race—White evangelical protestants are the strongest supporters of capital punishment, while Black and Hispanic protestants are the least supportive (Bohm, 2017).

Opposition to capital punishment is most vigorous among Black Americans, who are most likely to view capital punishment as inhumane, discriminatory, and disproportionally affecting the poor and minorities (Baker et al., 2005). Research on personality traits associated with stronger support for the death penalty shows that those who score higher on measures of right-wing authoritarianism (McKelvie, 2013), anti-Black bias/racial resentment (Aguirre & Baker, 1993; Soss et al., 2003; Unnever et al. 2005), "myth adherence" (Cedric & Cochran et al., 2011), sexism and homophobia (Bohm, 2017), Christian nationalism (Davis, 2018), and belief in a "masculine" God (Baker & Whitehead, 2020) are more supportive of capital punishment.

Finally, declining public support for capital punishment since the 1990s tracks with an increasing number of states moving toward abolition, as well as Supreme Court decisions that have limited the scope of death-eligible crimes. States that have abolished the death penalty in the past 10 years include Colorado (2020), Connecticut (2012), Delaware (2016), Illinois (2011), Maryland (2013), New Hampshire (2019), Virginia (2021), and Washington (2018). California (2019), Oregon (2011), and Pennsylvania (2015) are operating under gubernatorial moratoriums. In *Atkins v. Virginia* (2002), the Supreme Court ruled that the execution of persons with "mental retardation" violates the Eighth Amendment; *Roper v. Simmons* (2005) prohibits the execution of individuals who were under 18 at the time of the offense; and in *Kennedy v. Louisiana* (2008), the court ruled that a Louisiana statute that allowed the death penalty for child rape was unconstitutional. Despite the appearance of a highly regulated practice, the court has done little to address the same issues brought to its attention in the 1970s. As Steiker and Steiker (2016) note in their chapter entitled "The Failures of Regulation":

> The resulting complexity conveys the impression that the current system errs, if at all, on the side of heightened reliability and fairness. And the fact of minimal regulation, which invites if not guarantees the same kinds of inequality as the pre-*Furman* regime, is filtered through time-consuming, expensive proceedings that ultimately do little to satisfy the concerns that led the Court to regulate this country's death penalty practices in the first place. In short, the last four decades have produced a complicated regulatory apparatus that achieves extremely modest goals while maximizing political and legal discomfort. (p. 176)

Studies of the reversal rates of death sentences confirm Steiker and Steiker's conclusions, showing a highly inefficient system riddled with error. In their study of error rates in capital punishment cases between 1973 and 1995, Liebman et al. (2000) found that 68% of cases were reversed 9 years postsentencing due to serious error, leaving only 32% eligible for execution.

The Effectiveness of Capital Punishment as Criminal Justice Policy

Capital punishment is deeply entrenched in the history of the United States, with criminal justice policies being created and modified based on public support and factors such as the deterrent effects of capital punishment, the arbitrariness of its implementation, incapacitation as a goal for policy, cost, wrongful convictions, and racial discrimination (Acker, 2009). Deterrence is an important consideration for policymakers, with research focusing on the specific deterrence of individual actors and general deterrence focusing on legal implications for the general public (Stafford & Warr, 2016). Arbitrariness is a particular focus for advocates against capital punishment, with research looking at how state policies vary regarding post-*Furman* statutes and execution rates (Arkin, 1980). Incapacitation, cost, and wrongful convictions have policy implications for state and federal budgets, sentencing guidelines, and due process laws (Amsterdam & Mahoney, 1987). The role of racial discrimination has been apparent in multiple studies of the capital punishment system, showing the need for policy reform (Aguirre & Baker, 1993; Baker et al., 2005; Baldus et al., 1998). These factors are not exhaustive but provide an overview of capital punishment policy's effectiveness in the United States.

Deterrence

Deterrence was traditionally the most common argument for capital punishment, with supporters claiming that the threat of execution prevents crime, specifically homicide. Before 1975, research examining the deterrent effect of capital punishment focused on homicide rates in states with and without the death penalty, murder rates before and after the abolition of the death penalty, and short-term murder trends before and after highly publicized executions (Bohm, 2017; Sellin, 1959, 1967;). These studies all showed no deterrent effect of capital punishment on homicide rates, including police killings and prison murders.

Economist Isaac Ehrlich (1975) was among the first researchers to apply multivariate regression analyses to the death penalty and claimed that each execution prevented/deterred seven to eight homicides. Ehrlich's findings were criticized due to severe flaws in the study's methodology. Continued research on the topic has shown that significant results from this type of research rely on imperfect models with a high likelihood of error. Researchers caution that the results should not be a basis for policy implications (Barnett, 1981). Studies have shown that statistical support for deterrence is based on what specific models are used to find such an effect (Durlauf et al., 2013).

Post-Ehrlich studies conducted by researchers such as William Bailey, Frank Zimring, and others continue to find no deterrent effect of capital punishment on crime or homicide rates, adding to the research invalidating the deterrence hypothesis (Archer et al., 1983; Bailey, 1977, 1978, 1983; Zimring et al., 2010). Some research has found a counter-deterrent or "brutalizing" effect, showing that one execution *adds* roughly three more homicides the following year (Bowers & Pierce, 1980). Further research has supported this "brutalization effect," with studies designed to show a deterrent effect instead finding increased homicide rates in the months after an execution (Land et al., 2012). In 2012, the National Academy of Sciences issued a report stating research on the deterrent effect of capital punishment "is not likely to produce findings that will or should have much influence on policymakers" (Bohm, 2017, p. 243).

Arbitrariness

Arbitrariness is embedded in the administration of capital punishment and its policies. Since *Furman v. Georgia* (1972), few death-eligible offenders have been executed (approximately 1% to 2% of those on death row; Bohm, 2017). There is stark variation in capital punishment practices across states, regions, jurisdictions, and time. As of 2013, only 15%

of U.S. counties accounted for all executions occurring since 1977, and only 2% of counties accounted for 52% of those executions (Dieter, 2013; for a detailed discussion of the drastic differences in how the system of capital punishment varies across states, see Steiker and Steiker's [2016] discussion of "de facto abolitionist," "symbolic," and "executing" states).

While *Furman v. Georgia* was supposed to have set the groundwork for eliminating racial discrimination and arbitrariness in the imposition of capital punishment, research has shown that death penalty statutes have not resolved the issue of arbitrariness (Arkin, 1980). Ironically, post-Furman regulations seem to *justify* arbitrariness by including explicitly enumerating aggravating factors, allowing for jurors to misunderstand or underestimate their sentencing obligations, following inconsistent rule changes by the Supreme Court, failing to determine murderous intent accurately, and choosing the availability and use of plea bargaining (Bohm, 2017). As a result of the way death penalty statutes are written, rather than being applied to the "worst of the worst," which is how most assume the system functions, imposition of the death penalty remains as the court described it in 1976—"inflicted arbitrarily and capriciously" (Breyer, 2016).

In his dissent in *Glossip v. Gross*, Supreme Court Justice Breyer described a study (Donohue, 2014) of death penalty sentences between 1973 and 2007 in Connecticut (before abolition in 2012). The study examined 205 statutorily death-eligible homicide cases, 12 of which resulted in a death sentence, nine of which were sustained on appeal. Using a measure of the "egregiousness" of the murders, Donohue compared the nine cases that ended in a death sentence to the 196 cases where the defendant was convicted but not sentenced to death. Justice Breyer notes: "Application of the studies' metrics made clear that only 1 of those nine defendants was indeed the 'worst of the worst' (or was, at least, within the 15% considered most 'egregious'). The remaining eight were not. Their behavior was no worse than the behavior of at least 33 and as many as 170 other defendants who had not been sentenced to death" (Breyer, 2016, p. 77).

Rick Unklesbay (2019), who worked as a prosecutor in Arizona for almost 40 years and tried multiple capital cases, describes cases that seem to be textbook examples of the most egregious murders imaginable resulting in life in prison rather than death sentences; in other cases, the more culpable of codefendants is given life in prison, while the less culpable ends up on death row. He concludes: "Who dies and who lives is a decision that becomes the arbitrary application of convoluted statutes and conflicting and inconsistent court decisions, as one of my judges announced. I think he was right" (p. 132).

Finally, appellate courts perpetuate arbitrariness in the capital punishment system as well. As mentioned above, it is assumed that the law gives special consideration to the rights of the condemned in capital punishment cases. However, case rulings at the appellate level and the Supreme Court show there is still little consideration for capital offenders. Appeals for capital punishment are legally and practically a "mixed bag," with the courts ruling on cases quickly rather than fairly (Amsterdam & Mahoney, 1987). Delays in decisions and appeals also undermine the capital punishment system and public opinion of its efficiency. Given that the death penalty is irrevocable and there is inevitably human error in the decision-making process, this is concerning. As researchers continue to show that capital punishment is applied inconsistently and often based on race, geography, and poverty rather than on facts or evidence, it is not surprising that abolishment of capital punishment by state supreme courts has become increasingly common.

Incapacitation

When capital trial juries begin deliberating whether a death sentence is appropriate, research from the Capital Jury Project (Bohm, 2017, p. 263) finds that the issue of incapacitation based on future dangerousness is a critical determinate. Opponents of the death penalty look to sentencing alternatives such as LWOP as viable incapacitation methods. At the same time, supporters of capital punishment argue that the possibility of escape by inmates, costs associated with LWOP, and the potential for offenders to kill again are too great to consider LWOP, let alone any alternative other than death. Future dangerousness is regarded as a special sentencing issue in Texas and Oregon and an aggravating factor in Idaho, Wyoming, Virginia, and Oklahoma (Bohm, 2017).

The assumption that death row defendants are, by definition, so dangerous that even a life sentence in a maximum-security facility will not prevent future violence fits with our earlier discussion of the false assumption that capital murder charges are reserved for the "worst of the worst." Because of these assumptions, jurors rely on predictors of future dangerousness when making sentencing decisions. However, research on predictions of future dangerousness shows that they are incredibly inaccurate, whether such predictions are made by jurors or "experts" (for a damning illustration of the fallibility of the predictions of "experts" in death row trials, see the 95% error rate from the Texas Defender Services' 2004 Death Row Inmate Study). Studies on death row inmates who were mainstreamed into the general prison population (Cunningham et al., 2008) or those who had their sentences commuted to LWOP show that former death row inmates are no more violent than other inmates convicted of serious crimes (Sellin & American Law Institute, 1959). Additionally, prison conditions on death row are harsher. Most inmates spend the remainder of their life in solitary confinement, leading to additional financial costs and collateral damage from the system of capital punishment (Johnson, 2016).

Cost

Central to the debate surrounding capital punishment is the cost of the death penalty versus LWOP. The assumption that capital punishment is cheaper than LWOP is widespread, and for capital cases in the pre-*Furman* era, this was accurate. Trials were disposed of quickly, no extraordinary due process procedures were followed, reversals were relatively rare, executions were carried out within months of sentencing, and costs associated with execution methods were minimal. However, in the post-*Furman* era, the average cost to execute an offender for a capital offense is estimated to range from $1.4 million to $7 million. On average, it is as much as five times more expensive than a plea-bargained LWOP sentence (Bohm, 2017).

Execution is an expensive practice due to additional costs for capital cases at every stage of the process: pretrial, trial, posttrial, imprisonment, and execution. Investigations are conducted more thoroughly and for more extended periods at the pretrial stage. Capital cases are much more likely to go to trial rather than be plea bargained. Hiring expert witnesses, sequestering jurors, and defense costs, including having two attorneys present for the defense at a capital trial, are just some examples of the higher costs of maintaining capital punishment (Douglas & Stockstill, 2008). These costs impact local budgets by spurring tax increases, freezing employee raises, and cutting programs such as highway appropriations, libraries, and even police budgets (Bohm, 2017).

Posttrial, automatic appellate review, attorney costs, and filing motions for postconviction relief add to the cost of maintaining the death penalty. In terms of imprisonment, the average length of time from sentencing to execution (20 years) has increased, the rate of executions per year has decreased, death row inmates are being housed longer, and time served on death row is more expensive (Death Penalty Information Center, 2020). The actual execution is the least costly part of the capital punishment system. While streamlining the appellate and postconviction process would eliminate some additional costs, most of the system's costs are frontloaded and have to be paid for regardless of whether defendants are convicted, sentenced to death, or executed. Using LWOP as an alternative to the death penalty would considerably cut taxpayers' costs without contributing to prison overcrowding. Finally, the prohibitive costs of capital punishment add to the arbitrariness of capital punishment—the difference between a capital and noncapital murder charge often comes down to whether the county can afford it rather than whether the crime warrants it (Bohm, 2017; Douglas & Stockstill, 2008).

Wrongful Conviction

For capital punishment opponents, the single biggest concern is miscarriages of justice resulting in the innocent's conviction or execution. Separate from the overall reversal rate of 68% quoted above, it is estimated that the wrongful conviction rate is about 4% (Gross et al., 2014). While there are various definitions of "innocence," the criteria in the legal realm include the following: a government official has admitted error, the defendant was wholly uninvolved or convicted of a crime that did not occur, or a case is dismissed or found not guilty at retrial (Bohm, 2017). Another concept is "innocent of death," which occurs when an offender has been correctly convicted of the crime but should not have been charged with a capital crime or sentenced to death based on state death penalty statutes (Kreitzberg, 2006).

It was assumed that post-*Furman* miscarriages of justice were rare. However, researchers Hugo Bedau and Michael Radelet studied cases where miscarriages of justice were present and found that since 1973 it is estimated there is one wrongful conviction for every nine inmates executed for a crime. This rate is increasing into the early 21st century (Bedau & Radelet, 1987). Mass media reporting of capital punishment has shifted considerably since the 1970s, and stories about the miscarriages of justice by the current death penalty system have increased rapidly since 2000. The effect of this shift in media framing has impacted public opinion of the death penalty, such that media stories focusing on the exoneration of death row inmates have challenged the views of capital punishment supporters (Dardis et al., 2008).

Bohm (2017) notes that errors can either be "harmless" and not affect a case or severe or prejudicial, where they actually influence the outcome. *Chapman v. California* (386 U.S.

18 [1967]) states that remedies are not required for a violation of a defendant's rights unless the error or errors are serious or prejudicial. Errors also become more restrictive and preserved at each stage of an appeal. The primary sources of error in capital cases are flawed investigation or misconduct by police, eyewitness misidentification and perjury by prosecution witnesses, false confessions, guilty pleas by innocent defendants to avoid a possible death sentence, prosecutorial misconduct, inadequate DNA testing requirements, judicial misconduct or error, ineffective or counterproductive defense lawyers, or problems with the jury (Death Penalty Information Center, 2020).

Potential changes to the system to decrease or eliminate miscarriages of justice could include reforming assistance of counsel for defendants; improving investigations, interrogations, and the handling of evidence; improving eyewitness identification techniques and procedures; ensuring the credibility of crime lab technicians and DNA testing requirements; and increasing police training. Setting standards for jailhouse informants; punishing misconduct by defense attorneys, prosecutors, and police; allowing for better movement of trial judges; and guiding prosecutors' decision to seek the death penalty are also steps to reform. In 2004, the Innocence Protection Act was passed to increase DNA testing funding postconviction, improve legal representation, and compensate inmates who were unjustly convicted (Bohm, 2017).

Racial Discrimination

Discrimination remains evident under the post-*Furman* system of capital punishment, resulting in racial disparity in the number of African Americans sentenced to death and executed. Other types of discrimination exist in the administration of capital punishment—for example, there has never been the execution of an affluent member of society; only 17 women have been executed post-*Furman*; and while the execution of juvenile offenders is no longer allowed, younger defendants are less likely to be charged and sentenced to death (Bohm, 2017). However, race remains a significant and consistent factor in capital punishment sentencing. Studies show that even when controlling for aggravating and mitigating factors, prosecutors are more likely to seek the death penalty for Black defendants (Baldus et al., 1998), juries are more likely to sentence Black defendants to death than non-Black defendants (Phillips, 2008), and Black defendants are twice as likely to be wrongfully convicted of murder compared to non-Black defendants and spend more years imprisoned than non-Black exonerees (Gross et al., 2017). A study on implicit anti-Black bias found that Black men who looked more "highly stereotypically" Black were significantly more likely to be sentenced to death than Black men rated low on stereotypical Black features (Eberhardt, 2019). Furthermore, the death penalty is more likely to be sought when the crime victim is White (Baldus et al., 1998; Boger & Unah, 2001).

Cases with the combination of a White victim and a Black defendant are most likely to result in capital charges (Paternoster & Brame, 2008), are less likely to result in a plea bargain (Vito, Higgins, & Vito, 2014), and are "most likely to be upgraded and least likely to be downgraded" (Radelet & Pierce, 1985, p. 601, in Bohm, 2017, p. 392). As the Death Penalty Information Center (2021) notes, "In 96% of states where there have been reviews of race and the death penalty, there was a pattern of either race-of-victim or race-of-defendant discrimination, or both" (p. 2). Bohm (2017) states there are three theories regarding racial discrimination in the administration of capital punishment: judicial actors intentionally discriminate, judicial actors believe they are not racially prejudiced or are not conscious they are, or racial disparities are the results of institutional racism that has been embedded into the criminal justice system since its inception. All three of these are persistent problems in the capital punishment system.

As Steiker and Steiker (2016) note, despite overwhelming evidence of racial bias in the system of capital punishment, it has been rendered nearly "invisible" by the Supreme Court. Despite hearing case after case presenting statistical evidence of systemic racial discrimination in the system of capital punishment, the court has avoided addressing the issue head-on: "One can read the entire canon of the Court's path-breaking cases on capital punishment during the 1960s and 1970s without getting the impression that the death penalty was an issue of major racial significance in American society" (p. 79). This pattern has continued and is especially obvious in the *McCleskey* (1987) decision, where the Supreme Court ruled that statistical proof of racial discrimination is not relevant—only direct proof of individual discrimination. "Thus the Court avoided the enormity of the remedy sought for systemic discrimination while still maintaining, albeit disingenuously, that the Constitution prohibited racial discrimination in individual cases" (Steiker & Steiker, 2016, p. 109). Legislation has been proposed to address racial discrimination found by the General Accounting Office in the Racial Justice Act (1994) and the Fairness in Death Sentencing Act (1994), but both were rejected in the House and Senate. While social justice movements such as Black Lives Matter continue to bring awareness to racial discrimination and institutional racism in the criminal justice system, it is unclear how policy reform will address this ongoing issue, particularly in the states where capital punishment is most utilized.

As our review of the empirical evidence clearly shows, the system of capital punishment in the United States "is simply bad policy" (Steiker & Steiker, 2016, p. 321). It does not deter potential murderers, is both arbitrary and discriminatory, and is unnecessary for incapacitation. It costs significantly more than LWOP and is riddled with errors. Not surprisingly, the continued use of capital punishment comes with tremendous collateral damage— to the families of both victims and offenders, as well as those who work in the system.

Collateral Damage of the System of Capital Punishment

The Families of Victims

Experiencing the murder of a loved one is, by definition, an event of acute and long-lasting trauma. In his book *Capital Punishment's Collateral Damage* (2013), Bohm points out that families of murder victims experience "secondary victimization" at the hands of the criminal justice system—and that often their experiences with the system are as traumatic as, if not more traumatic than, the murder itself. Many of these experiences would still occur outside the capital punishment system, but it adds additional trauma layers when a murder is deemed death eligible. First, whether a prosecutor deems the murder "worthy" of a capital charge is tainted by bias. The families of poor and Black murder victims, who already feel disrespected by the system, are reminded of their marginalized status when they discover that those who murder White victims are significantly more likely to be charged with capital murder than those whose victims are Black. Because of the virtually unbridled discretion the system gives to prosecutors, decisions about who is charged with capital murder become another reminder of how the criminal justice system deems the lives of some victims more "valuable" than others.

Second, when the death penalty is sought, the cases are significantly more likely to go to trial than are noncapital cases. Murder trials are always hard on family members, but the extra publicity that death penalty cases garner makes all aspects of the process more stressful. Some family members are not allowed in court because they will be called as witnesses, while those in court must listen to the gruesome details of their loved one's murder while sitting a few feet away from the accused. Without the death penalty, many more cases would be resolved via plea bargains, sparing the families the trial trauma. Finally, while some families support the prosecutor's decision to seek the death penalty, many do not. Not only do prosecutors regularly seek the death penalty despite families' objections, but also some families also being criticized by criminal justice officials, or even being denied victim support resources, because they refuse to support death penalty charges (Sharp, 2005).

For those families whose loved one's murderer is convicted and sentenced to death, the process is far from over. The appeals process takes years, and given high reversal rates, exonerations, and multiple stages of appeals, the defendant's execution is an unlikely outcome. For those death sentences that result in execution, the average time between sentencing and execution is over 20 years (Death Penalty Information Center, n.d.). More prisoners have died of natural causes in states such as California than have been executed in the post-*Furman* era (Kaufman, 2015). These statistics are particularly relevant in light of one of the claims of pro–capital punishment groups—that capital punishment provides "closure" to the families of murder victims.

Zimring (2003) discusses the concept of closure. In the post-*Furman* era, proponents of capital punishment looked to "repackage" the death penalty in a more palatable way. As mentioned earlier, part of the role of vigilante values in support of capital punishment stems from executions being characterized not as government overreach but as reflections of local values. The idea of providing closure to the families of murder victims reinforces this idea—that is, the government is providing a *service* to the victims' families. Zimring refers to the concept of closure as a "public relations godsend" (pp. 51–52). Considering that less than 2% of all murderers end up executed for their crimes (Bohm, 2017), closure is only granted to a tiny number of families, and the families of White victims murdered by Black offenders are most likely to be the recipients of this "public service." Despite its usefulness as a public relations strategy, there is little evidence that executions bring closure to the families of murder victims. As Bohm notes, while some families feel a sense of relief following the execution of their loved one's murderer, many are offended by the very idea of closure. Bohm (2013) quotes the parents of a murdered son and daughter-in-law. While they hope to perhaps one day get to acceptance or finality, they have little use for the idea of closure: "Does anyone know or care to know that the favored term 'closure' is so wrong and so offensive, even though it's most often used when talking about victims' families? There is no closure, nor can there ever be any" (p. 68).

Arizona prosecutor Rick Unklesbay's (2019) experiences reinforce the feelings expressed by the family quoted above. When discussing the immediate aftermath of executions, he argues that the "ending is anticlimactic." The execution does not bring the victim back and, "with few exceptions, has not brought anyone any satisfaction. Families continue to try to survive their loss, but I'm yet to be told that an execution has brought closure" (p. 132). Unfortunately, the trauma experienced by the families of victims in the capital punishment system is shared by another set of traumatized people—the offenders' families.

The Families of the Accused

While victims' families receive a great deal of attention—from the media, researchers, social services, and the criminal justice system—offenders' families are mostly ignored. Sharp (2005) conducted in-depth interviews with 58 individuals, all of whom faced the reality of a family member ending up on death row. Their experiences ran the gamut—some had loved ones who came close to being charged with capital murder; others witnessed their loved one's journey through the whole process, culminating in an execution. Sharp discovered that the accused's families share many experiences with the families of victims—psychological trauma, the decline of mental and physical health, the breakup of families, financial devastation, social isolation, unwanted media attention, and feeling abused by the system.

While the families of victims are often referred to as "secondary victims," families of the accused are often treated as "vicarious offenders" (Sharp, 2005, p. 7). The shame of having a family member charged with capital murder is devastating to families. They almost universally reported experiencing social isolation; harsh judgment from friends, coworkers, or religious congregations; and public hostility from the media, the criminal justice system, and the families of victims. Like the families of murder victims, they face losing a loved one, but their bereavement process is stretched across years or even decades. "Like the families of victims, the families of those sentenced to death must live with the loss of a relative. However, they must also live with the humiliation and stigma of being related to a person deemed so vile that he had to be exterminated" (Sharp, 2005, p. 7).

While the families of the accused in the capital punishment system experience similar challenges to victims' families, they don't have the support provided to victims' families—whether formally through the system or informally through social networks. They experience the horror of the system mostly ignored. When they are recognized, it is likely to be in negative ways, from news stories to how they are portrayed in the trial's sentencing phase to treatment when they visit death row and when their loved ones are executed. Like the families of victims, the accused's families are traumatized by lengthy appeals, overturned verdicts and retrials, the possibility of commutations, last-minute reprieves, exoneration, and execution.

The loss of a child by execution at the hands of the state is as traumatic for the mother of a condemned man as the trauma experienced by the mother whose child was murdered. Sharp (2005) pointed her readers to a National Public Radio special, *Witness to an Execution*, where a journalist who witnessed a number of executions in Texas noted that "You'll never hear another sound like a mother wailing whenever she is watching her son be executed. There's no other sound like it. It is just this horrendous wail. You can't get away from it. That wail surrounds the room. It's something you won't ever forget" (Sharp, 2005, p. 89). Several of Sharp's interview subjects continue to experience trauma relating to their loved one's execution, even decades later. Sharp notes that "Contrary to media descriptions of executions, many of these people did not view the execution as peaceful, with the offender going to sleep. Instead, it was a painful and traumatic experience" (Sharp, 2005, p. 101), and "several of my interview subjects talked about replaying the execution in their minds daily" (Sharp, 2005, p. 100). The capital punishment system exacts an immense toll on the families unlucky enough to experience it. The final group of people who share capital punishment's collateral damage are those who work within the criminal justice system.

Participants in the Capital Punishment System

Bohm (2013) notes that those who participate in the formal capital punishment process do so, for the most part, voluntarily. While it's often part of the job description, there are generally ways to minimize contact if one wishes. This means that, for the most part, the people who keep the system running are there voluntarily. But this does not mean that they don't experience collateral damage as a result of their participation. From police officers to jurors to prison wardens, individuals pay the price for their involvement in each step in the process.

Police officers are the first group of participants in the system of capital punishment— particularly homicide detectives and other investigative personnel. As Justice Breyer noted in his dissent in *Glossip v. Gross* (2016), cases that end up being charged as capital murders are often those that garner the most attention (when a young White woman is the victim, for instance), and therefore police, prosecutors, and jurors are under intense community pressure to secure a conviction. Breyer argues that death penalty cases may be *more* likely than noncapital cases to produce wrongful convictions because of this pressure. Bohm (2013) notes that detectives feel acute pressure to "not screw up!" (p. 23). They put this pressure on themselves and feel pressure from the families of victims, their superiors, and the community. As Bohm notes, even if the death penalty were to be abolished, detectives would still face the pressures of investigating and solving high-profile murders. Still, if they get it wrong, "the consequences of their mistakes would not be fatal—innocent people would not be executed—and the vast resources expended on capital punishment could be used for other policy priorities, especially more effective methods of reducing violent crime" (p. 40). Once law enforcement completes its investigation of the crime and makes an arrest, the prosecutor takes over the case.

Prosecutors are the single most powerful actors in the capital punishment system. They act as the "gatekeepers" for the system. Due to the broad wording of statutes regarding aggravating circumstances, they have virtually unchecked discretion when deciding who will be charged with a capital offense. Not surprising, prosecutorial misconduct is one of the most common sources of arbitrariness and discrimination in the system (and prosecutors who engage in misconduct are rarely punished, even when their behavior results in a death sentence and decades served on death row before exoneration). As elected officials who fear accusations of being "soft on crime," prosecutors often decide about charges based on political reasons rather than the details of the case. Capital trials are significantly longer than noncapital cases, even before the sentencing stage, and prosecutors report significant physical and emotional toll from these trials. While most prosecutors continue to support the death penalty, some do not. Bohm (2013) quotes Ray Markey, a Florida prosecutor known for his dogged pursuit of the death penalty, who came to see the system in a different light over time.

> If we had deliberately set out to create a chaotic system, we couldn't have come up with anything worse. It's a merry-go-round; it's ridiculous; it's so clogged up only an arbitrary few ever get it. I don't get any damn pleasure out of the death penalty, and I never have. . . . And frankly, if they abolished it tomorrow, I'd get drunk in celebration. (p. 65)

While prosecuting attorneys report feeling pressure while trying capital cases, defense attorneys feel even more at both the trial and postconviction stages, since they are literally tasked with saving their clients' lives. Judged by broader society for defending "the worst of the worst," defense attorneys focus not so much on guilt or innocence but on protecting the rights of defendants and the integrity of the process. The overwhelming majority of death penalty defendants are disadvantaged, which means they are being defended by either over-worked and underpaid public defenders (if they are lucky) or court-appointed attorneys (who often have little trial experience at all, let alone capital trial experience).

Defense attorneys have access to significantly fewer resources compared to prosecutors. While it's often said that no competent defense attorney should have a trial that ends in a death sentence for their client, there is much more to the idea of "capable" than one would assume. As Bohm (2013) notes, "Most capital defendants are represented by defense attorneys who are inexperienced, untrained in life and death cases, unskilled, over-worked, understaffed, unprepared, less resourceful, and less independent; who too often have been reprimanded, disciplined, or subsequently disbarred; and who frequently lose capital cases" (p. 88).

Public defenders report working long hours; physical, psychological, and emotional stress; weight loss; sleep issues; etc. They must have a strategy for the trial's guilt/innocence phase and a second strategy for the penalty phase. Mitigating circumstances are critical to a successful penalty phase, but defendants can resist allowing testimony showing child-hood abuse, mental illness, etc. As one former public defender notes, they live with the "huge, looming fear" of losing and their client being executed—"The fear that someone is sitting on death row with your name on him" (Bohm, 2013, p. 103). Postconviction attorneys spend years, if not decades, trying to save their clients' lives and feel even more pressure to prevent their executions.

Judges and juries also experience tremendous pressure during capital trials. While juries make sentencing decisions in most cases, judges have to sign off on the sentences, and in some cases (when defendants request bench rather than jury trials) impose the penalty. Judges worry about mistakes during the trial and express concerns about the system's flaws, and appeals court judges are faced with requests for stays or reversals hours before executions are scheduled to be carried out. Capital jurors face a complicated system that they do not understand. Research from the Capital Jury Project reveals that jurors who don't understand sentencing guidelines are often not advised by judges even when they seek guidance, and therefore end up "erring on the side of caution" by imposing death sentences, often because they incorrectly believe that a sentence of LWOP will result in the defendant eventually being released. Some report fearing reprisal from victims' families if they do not vote for a death sentence or from the accused's families if they do.

When a capital trial results in a death sentence, defendants are sent to death row, where they are watched over by prison staff as they await their execution date, and where some are put to death by an execution "team." Wardens, corrections officers, execution team members, and clergy all play a part in the death row system. All report the stress of working on death row. Wardens are significantly less supportive of the death penalty than most might assume. They get to know death row inmates over decades, and therefore, unlike police, prosecutors, or jurors, come to see them as actual people rather than just murderers. They worry that they may be presiding over the execution of an innocent person and express frustration at the exorbitant costs of maintaining the system. Bohm (2013) provides quotes from in-depth interviews with prison wardens who've presided over multiple executions. One interview was with Ron McAndrew, a retired warden and 23-year veteran of the Florida corrections system. He began to feel guilt for his part in a system that he increasingly viewed with "disgust" (p. 123). Following one execution, McAndrew described "begin[ning] to feel as a pawn for the filthy chest-pounding politicians who had asked me to do this dirty work. I began [to] question why anyone would hide out in the governor's office with a speakerphone waiting to hear that the killing they'd ordered had been carried out. [Following his execution] [t]here was a serious psychological emptiness in my stomach. I began to go home, shower for a long time, change clothing, and try to send the guilt down the drain" (p. 215). The officers who guard death row inmates, while recognizing that the job is safer than working the yard, wall, or perimeter, prefer not to be on death row due to the stress. Members of the execution team are commonly former military. While they describe the emotional rollercoaster of last-minute stays and rescheduled executions, most report feeling at peace with their role. Still, some members suffer long-term psychological damage from their experiences. Finally, the prison chaplains who minister to the inmates and their families avoid thinking of the politics surrounding the death penalty and instead focus on their ministerial duties, doing what they can to "meet their needs, whatever I can do to make their last hours meaningful and productive, and easy for everyone" (p. 242).

Another group of participants in the capital punishment system is execution witnesses. In most states, both the victim's and offender's families are allowed to be present, along with lawyers from both sides. Some states do not allow any additional witnesses, but in 16 states, a minimum number of "official witnesses" must attend. Some are ordinary citizens who volunteer to be witnesses, but most are members of the press. Journalists report feeling several dissociative symptoms (feeling detached from other people or their own emotions, feeling that things around them are unreal or dreamlike, trying to avoid thoughts or feelings about the execution, etc.) during the process. Most are not supporters of the death penalty but feel an obligation to "hold up a mirror to the people of what their world is" (Bohm, 2013, p. 250).

The final group of participants in the system is governors. Executive power gives governors (and presidents in the federal system) the ability to "exercise leniency or mercy" (Bohm, 2013, p. 257) via reprieves (temporary stays of execution pending appeals or additional investigation), commutations (where the sentence is commuted from death to imprisonment), or pardons (when there are severe doubts about guilt). Supreme Court Chief Justice William Rehnquist referred to clemency as the "fail-safe of the criminal justice system" (Bohm, 2013, p. 258), but governors in the post-*Furman* era rarely grant clemency. As Bohm notes, before the 1970s, governors in death penalty states routinely commuted up to one-third of all reviewed death sentences. But in the modern age of capital punishment, clemency is seen as "akin to political suicide" (p. 258). While governors claim that clemency decisions are among the most difficult they face, political concerns outweigh leniency or mercy concerns. "In today's political climate, a governor's decision about granting clemency is a highly charged political action that could jeopardize his or her political career. That is why so few commutations and pardons are granted in capital punishment cases" (p. 262).

At the end of his exploration of the collateral damage of capital punishment, Bohm (2013) notes that if the system produced some net social good, perhaps we could accept the collateral damage as part of the price we pay for achieving a greater good. As we have illustrated in this chapter, however, the system of capital punishment fails to live up to its purpose across every dimension that can be empirically evaluated. He thus concludes that "capital punishment is unnecessary to accomplish any utilitarian or moral goals, which begs the question: Why incur capital punishments' collateral damage?" (p. 266).

Conclusion

It would be logical to assume that based on the lack of empirical evidence supporting the death penalty as an effective criminal justice policy, the myriad ways it harms society, and declining public support for death sentences, the abolition of capital punishment in the United States is inevitable. Unfortunately, this assumption is likely wrong. While more states than ever have abolished capital punishment, rarely use it, or are under moratoriums, the reality is that the vast majority of executions occur in a small number of southern states, which are unlikely to abolish the death penalty—via legislation or state court decisions. Before the election of Donald Trump, many saw a chance for a change in the Supreme Court's makeup that seemed likely to declare capital punishment unconstitutional. But with the appointments of Neil Gorsuch, Brett Kavanaugh, and Amy Coney Barrett, the court's current composition is unlikely to make such a declaration. And while some research suggests that exposure to facts about capital punishment reduces support (referred to as the "Marshall Hypothesis," after Supreme Court Justice Thurgood Marshall), most Americans' support of the death penalty is driven not by a careful review of the empirical evidence, but by a desire for retribution (Swift, 2014). And for those whose support is rooted in retribution, the Marshall Hypothesis does not apply (Vollum et al., 2009). All the evidence suggests that the United States' unique relationship with capital punishment is likely to continue.

Social Work Ethical Considerations

There is no greater punishment for crimes committed than termination of an individual life. This is likely why advanced democratic societies, as they have evolved, have grappled with and generally moved away from capital punishment as a form of punishment, leaving the United States among only a few developed nations to utilize this barbaric retributive practice disguised as justice. In the National Association of Social Workers' (NASW's) *Social Work Speaks, Policy Statements by the National Association of Social Work* (2020), on the topic of the death penalty, the policy statement is clear that capital punishment is antithetical to two core social work values and points to the NASW Code of Ethics (2017) for support of that claim. Termination of human lives stands in stark contrast to valuing individuals' dignity and inherent worth, a core social work value. Also, the profession disputes the notion that the death penalty provides justice, as its champions purport.

Social Work Ethical Value: Dignity and Worth of the Person

The social work ethical value of dignity and worth of a person is operationalized as the ethical principle that social workers respect the inherent dignity and worth of a person (NASW, 2017). Put simply, state-sponsored executions limit human value and continue cycles of violence rather than ending them. As long as violence is the supported solution to violence, social workers believe that the possibility of ending societal violence will remain elusive. Embedded in the principle that social workers respect individuals and their inherent dignity is the notion that humans have a capacity for growth and change. Capital punishment ends the individual's opportunity to change or to address their needs to fit within the broader society.

Both deterrence and incapacitation are commonly espoused as reasons to support capital punishment. However, as was presented earlier in this chapter, the evidence does not support that assertion (Archer et al., 1983; Bailey, 1977, 1978, 1983; Zimring et al., 2010). Worse still, as Land et al. (2012) noted, there are findings of increased homicide rates in the presence of capital punishment policies. The social work profession advocates for the replacement of capital punishment with life in prison. Both professional and lay future predictions of danger used for incapacitation are notoriously inaccurate (Cunningham, Sorensen, & Reidy, 2005), thereby undermining the support of capital punishment.

Social Work Ethical Value: Social Justice

The social work value of social justice is operationalized as social workers challenging social injustice (NASW, 2017). While there may be several social injustices to choose from, capital punishment may present the most significant challenge to fulfilling the social work professional code. Several portions of the social work code of ethics under the value of social justice stand in opposition to capital punishment. Among them are parts of the code that prohibit condoning, facilitating, collaborating, or practicing discrimination in all forms, and the portion of the code that holds responsible social workers engaging and taking action to eliminate domination, exploitation, and discrimination of vulnerable groups. It is clear from recent studies that racial and ethnic minority communities are more often selected for capital punishment and more often executed. This trend is troubling enough, but in recent years, the addition of people with limited intellectual capacity and individuals who are gravely impoverished have become increasingly represented among those executed.

The arbitrary application, cost, wrongful conviction rates, and racial discrimination patterns are all social justice challenges. While *Furman v. Georgia* was intended to eliminate arbitrariness in applying capital punishment, its promise has not been realized. As long as the variations in practices across states, regions, and jurisdictions exist, capital punishment cannot achieve any modicum of social justice. Bohm (2017) empirically disposes of the myth that capital punishment is a cost-effective option by revealing that due to modern-day trial costs (expert witnesses, sequestering jurors, defense costs, two attorneys present), it is actually five times more expensive than a plea-bargained LWOP sentence.

Given that capital punishment cannot be reversed, wrongful convictions remain a powerful challenge to social justice. Given the demonstrated rates of errors, big and small (one in nine in 1973, and increasing), found in the processing of cases, miscarriages of justice through wrongful conviction will remain a significant challenge to achieving social justice. Social workers' final challenge to social justice is that the death penalty is applied in a racially disparate way. In ways that we have expounded on previously, in case after case, race is a factor in the application of capital punishment (Baldus et al., 1998; Boger & Unah, 2001; Bohm, 2017; Eberhardt, 2019; Gross et al., 2017; Phillips, 2008; Pierce & Radelet, 2005). So long as the state continues to use its executive powers against racial minority communities in disproportionate ways while using the same power with White communities in dispassionate ways, capital punishment will remain a significant challenge to realizing social justice.

In Summary

Our exploration of the history and current practice of capital punishment in the United States revealed distinct time periods in which the policy and practice would be reformed to the system's current iteration. We then followed this review with an evaluation of capital punishment as a criminal justice policy and determined that the empirical evidence does not support its continuation. The evidence is clear that capital punishment is arbitrary, is costly, does not act as a deterrent, produces wrongful convictions, and is littered with a history of racial discrimination. Perhaps even worse than capital punishment missing the mark in terms of its intended effects is the collateral damage associated with capital punishment, including the families of both victims and offenders, as well as those who work in the system. We closed the chapter with an application of the social work code of ethics to the issue of capital punishment and concluded that the practice of the death penalty is antithetical to the aims of social work.

References

Acker, J. R. (2009). *The flow and ebb of American capital punishment*. Springer New York.

Aguirre, A., & Baker, D. V. (1993). Racial prejudice and the death penalty: A research note. *Social Justice*, *20*(1–2), 150.

American Civil Liberties Union, the ACLU of Louisiana, & the NAACP Legal Defense and Educational Fund, Inc. (2008). *Amicus brief in support of petitioner, Kennedy v. Louisiana*.

Amsterdam, A. G., & Mahoney, M. (1987). In favorem mortis: The Supreme Court and capital punishment. *Human Rights*, *14*(1), 14–60.

Archer, D., Gartner, R., & Beittel, M. (1983). Homicide and the death penalty: A cross-national test of a deterrence hypothesis. *Journal of Criminal Law and Criminology (1973-)*, *74*(3), 991–1013.

Arkin, S. D. (1980). Discrimination and arbitrariness in capital punishment: An analysis of post-*Furman* murder cases in Dade County, Florida, 1973–1976. *Stanford Law Review*, *33*(1), 75–101.

Bailey, W. C. (1977). Imprisonment v. the death penalty as a deterrent to murder. *Law and Human Behavior*, *1*(3), 239–260.

Bailey, W. C. (1978). *Deterrence and the celerity of the death penalty: A neglected question in deterrence research*. Institute for Research on Poverty, University of Wisconsin–Madison.

Bailey, W. C. (1983). Disaggregation in deterrence and death penalty research: The case of murder in Chicago. *Journal of Criminal Law & Criminology*, *74*(3), 827–859.

Baker, D. N., Lambert, E. G., & Jenkins, M. (2005). Racial differences in death penalty support and opposition: A preliminary study of White and Black college students. *Journal of Black Studies*, *35*(4), 201–224.

Baker, J. O., & Whitehead, A. L. (2020). God's penology: Belief in a masculine God predicts support for harsh criminal punishment and militarism. *Punishment and Society*, *22*(2), 135–160.

Baldus, D. C., Woodworth, G., Zuckerman, D., Weiner, N. A., & Broffitt, B. (1998). Racial discrimination and the death penalty in the post-*Furman* era: An empirical and legal overview, with recent findings from Philadelphia. *Cornell Law Review*, *83*(6), 1638.

Barnett, A. (1981). The deterrent effect of capital punishment: A test of some recent studies. *Operations Research*, *29*(2), 346–370.

Bedau, H. A., & Radelet, M. L. (1987). Miscarriages of justice in potentially capital cases. *Stanford Law Review*, *40*(1), 21–179.

Bessler, J. D. (2012). *Cruel and unusual: The American death penalty and the founders' Eighth Amendment*. Northeastern University Press.

Bohm, R. M. (2013). *Capital punishment's collateral damage*. Carolina Academic Press.

Bohm, R. M. (2017). *Deathquest: An introduction to the theory and practice of capital punishment in the United States* (5th ed.). Routledge.

Bowers, W. J., & Pierce, G. L. (1980). Deterrence or brutalization: What is the effect of executions? *Crime & Delinquency*, *26*(4), 453–484.

Breyer, S. (2016). *Against the death penalty* (J. Bessler, Ed.). Brookings Institution Press.

Cedric, M., & Cochran, J. (2011). The effects of information change in death penalty support: Race- and gender-specific extensions of the Marshall Hypotheses. *Journal of Ethnicity in Criminal Justice*, *9*, 291–313.

Cunningham, M., Reidy, T., & Sorenson, J. (2008). Assertions of "future dangerousness" at federal capital sentencing: Rates and correlates of subsequent prison misconduct and violence. *Law and Human Behavior*, *32*, 46–63.

Cunningham, M. D., Sorensen, J. R., & Reidy, T. J. (2005). An actuarial model for assessment of prison violence risk among maximum security inmates. *Assessment*, *12*(1), 40–49.

Dardis, F. E., Baumgartner, F. R., Boydstun, A. E., De Boef, S., & Shen, F. (2008). Media framing of capital punishment and its impact on individuals' cognitive responses. *Mass Communication & Society*, *11*(2), 115–140.

Davidson, J. (2021, January 9). President Trump's expensive death penalty binge could continue next week. *Washington Post*.

Davis, J. (2018). Enforcing Christian nationalism: Examining the link between group identity and punitive attitudes in the United States. *Journal for the Scientific Study of Religion*, *57*(2), 300–317.

Death Penalty Information Center. (2020). *Death Penalty Information Center report*.

Death Penalty Information Center. (2021). *Facts about the death penalty*.

Dieter, R. (2013). *The 2% death penalty: How a minority of counties produce the most death cases at enormous costs to us all*. Death Penalty Information Center.

Donohue, J. J. (2014). An empirical evaluation of the Connecticut death penalty system since 1973: Are there unlawful racial, gender, and geographic disparities? *Journal of Empirical Legal Studies, 11*, 637–696.

Douglas, J. W., & Stockstill, H. K. (2008). Starving the death penalty: Do financial considerations limit its use? *Justice System Journal, 29*(3), 326–337.

Durlauf, S. N., Chao, F., & Salvador, N. (2013). Capital punishment and deterrence: Understanding disparate results. *Journal of Quantitative Criminology, 29*(1), 103–121.

Eberhardt, J. L. (2019). *Biased: Uncovering the hidden prejudice that shapes what we see, think, and do*. Viking, an imprint of Penguin Random House LLC.

Ehrlich, I. (1975). Deterrence: evidence and inference. *Yale Law Journal, 85*, 209.

Espy, M. W., & Smykla, J. O. (2016). *Executions in the United States, 1608–2002: The Espy File (ICPSR 8451)*.

Garland, D. (2010). *Peculiar institution: America's death penalty in an age of abolition*. Belknap Press.

Gross, S. R., O'Brien, B., Hu, C., & Kennedy, E. H. (2014). Rate of false conviction of criminal defendants who are sentenced to death. *Proceedings of the National Academy of Sciences of the United States of America, 111*(20), 7230–7235.

Gross, S. R., Possley, M., & Stephens, K. (2017). *Race and wrongful convictions in the United States*. National Registry of Exonerations, Newkirk Center for Science and Society, University of California, Irvine.

Jacobs, D., Carmichael, J., & Kent, S. (2005). Vigilantism, current racial threat, and death sentences. *American Sociological Review, 70*, 656–677.

Johnson, R. W. (2016). Solitary confinement until death by state-sponsored homicide: An Eighth Amendment assessment of the modern execution process. *Washington and Lee Law Review, 73*(3), 1213.

Kaufman, S. (2015, September 4). Here's how many death row inmates dies while waiting to die. *The Week*.

Kreitzberg, E. (2006). Innocent of a capital crime: Parallels between innocence of a crime and innocence of the death penalty. *Tulsa Law Review, 42*(2), 437.

Land, K. C., Teske, R. H. C., & Zheng, H. (2012). The differential short-term impacts of executions on felony and non-felony homicides. *Criminology & Public Policy, 11*(3), 541–563.

Liebman, J. S., Fagan, J., & West, V. (2000). *A broken system: Error rates in capital punishment cases, 1973–1995*. Columbia University School of Law.

Mandery, E. J. (2013). *A wild justice: The death and resurrection of capital punishment in America*. W. W. Norton & Company.

McKelvie, S. J. (2013). Are attitude towards capital punishment and right-wing authoritarianism related to capital and non-capital sentencing? *Journal of Scientific Psychology, 1*, 1–13.

National Association of Social Workers. (2017). *Code of ethics of the National Association of Social Workers*. NASW Press.

Paternoster, R., & Brame, R. (2008). Reassessing race disparities in Maryland capital cases. *Criminology, 46*(4), 971–1008.

Phillips, S. (2008). Racial disparities in the capital of capital punishment. *Houston Law Review, 45*, 807–840.

Radelet, M. L., & Pierce, G. L. (1985). Race and prosecutorial discretion in homicide cases. *Law & Society Review, 19*, 587.

Sellin, J. T. (1959). *The death penalty*. American Law Institute.

Sellin, J. T. (Ed.). (1967). *Capital punishment*. Harper & Row.

Sellin, J. T., & American Law Institute. (1959). *The death penalty: A report for the model penal code project of the American Law Institute: Executive office*. American Law Institute.

Sharp, S. F. (2005). *Hidden victims: The effects of the death penalty on families of the accused*. Rutgers University Press.

Soss, J., Langbein, L., & Metelko, A. R. (2003). Why do white Americans support the death penalty? *Journal of Politics, 65*(2), 397–421.

Stafford, M. C., & Warr, M. (2016). A reconceptualization of general and specific deterrence. *Journal of Research in Crime and Delinquency, 30*(2), 123–135.

Steiker, C. S., & Steiker, J. M. (2016). *Courting death: The Supreme Court and capital punishment.* Belknap Press of Harvard University.

Swift, A. (2014, October 23). *Americans: "Eye for an eye" top reason for death penalty.* Gallup.com.

Unklesbay, R. (2019). *Arbitrary death: A prosecutor's perspective on the death penalty.* Wheatmark.

Unnever, J. D., Cullen, F. T., & Roberts, J. V. (2005). Not everyone strongly supports the death penalty: Assessing weakly-held attitudes about capital punishment. *American Journal of Criminal Justice, 29*(2), 187–216.

Vito, G. F., Higgins, G. E., & Vito, A. G. (2014). Tracking capital homicide cases in Jefferson County, KY 2000–2010. *American Journal of Criminal Justice, 39*, 331–340.

Vollum, S., Mallicoat, S., & Buffington-Vollum, J. (2009). Death penalty attitudes in an increasingly critical climate: Value-expressive support and attitude mutability. *Southwestern Journal of Criminal Justice, 5*, 221–242.

Zimring, F. E. (2003). *The contradictions of American capital punishment.* Oxford University Press.

Zimring, F. E., Fagan, J., & Johnson, D. T. (2010). Executions, deterrence, and homicide: A tale of two cities. *Journal of Empirical Legal Studies, 7*(1), 1–29.

18

Mental Health Policies

Anna M. Scheyett and Margaret B. Leonard

Introduction

One of the most influential mental health social reformers of the 19th century was Dorothea Dix. A schoolteacher in New England in 1841, Dix volunteered to teach Sunday school classes to women inmates at the East Cambridge Jail. When she visited, she was horrified to see prisoners with mental illness treated inhumanely. They were often without heat, painfully restrained, and regularly abused. This discovery galvanized Dix, who began to investigate the treatment of individuals with mental illness in jails, prisons, poorhouses, and asylums. She used her findings to encourage state legislatures to change policies to improve mental illness treatment. She ultimately persuaded Congress to appropriate public land in each state for hospitals to treat mental illness—a bill later vetoed by President Franklin Pierce. Undeterred, she continued her campaign to improve the conditions for individuals with mental illness and ultimately founded or significantly expanded hospitals for the mentally ill in 14 states (Parry, 2006; Quam, 2013).

This story of the reformer Dix highlights three key points, which are woven throughout this chapter. First, individuals with mental illness are often tangled within the criminal justice system and are particularly vulnerable to abuse. Second, identifying problems and making policy-level changes to address these problems is essential if individuals with mental illness are to receive just and humane treatment in the justice system. Finally, the problems of those with mental illness in the justice system are long-standing and recalcitrant—Dix's story could be the story of any social worker today going into a prison for the first time.

Individuals With Mental Illness in the Criminal Justice System

Individuals with mental illness are particularly vulnerable populations in the criminal justice system. Mental illnesses may in and of themselves factor into behaviors that result in

Anna M. Scheyett and Margaret B. Leonard, *Mental Health Policies* In: *Handbook of Forensic Social Work*. Edited by: David Axlyn McLeod, Anthony P. Natale, and Kristin W. Mapson, Oxford University Press. © Oxford University Press 2024. DOI: 10.1093/oso/9780197694732.003.0018 criminal justice involvement, sometimes raising the question of culpability and responsibility. Once in the system, individuals with mental illness may have difficulty understanding the complex processes and rules of the criminal justice system and may struggle to participate in their own defense or experience longer times of incarceration because they are held for pretrial assessment or restoration of competency to stand trial (Fuller et al., 2016). Stigma and stereotypes about mental illness and violence may result in harsher sentences, decrease the likelihood of parole, and increase incarceration and length of sentence (Council of State Governments, 2012).

Prisons and jails in the United States house a disproportionate number of individuals with mental illness. They are often called "the new asylums," and it has been estimated that there are nearly three times the number of individuals with a serious mental illness in prisons and jails as there are in state psychiatric hospitals (Torrey et al., 2014). Bronson and Berzofsky (2017) found that 14% of prison inmates and 26% of jail inmates reported severe psychological distress in the previous 30 days. Nearly 37% of prison and 44% of jail inmates had been told at some point by a mental health provider that they had a mental health disorder. By comparison, only 5% of nonincarcerated adults met the criteria for serious psychological distress.

While incarcerated, individuals with mental illness are very unlikely to stabilize or become less symptomatic. Between two-thirds and three-quarters of jail inmates with severe psychological distress received no treatment while incarcerated; the same is seen in between two-thirds and one-half of prison inmates (Bronson & Berzofsky, 2017; James & Glaze, 2006). In addition, the conditions of incarceration, including a loud, crowded, and often violent environment, can of themselves exacerbate symptoms of mental illness (Houser et al., 2019).

Individuals with mental illness are particularly vulnerable while incarcerated. They often struggle to meet the jail or prison environment's demands; there is a strong association between psychiatric disorders and infractions while incarcerated (Matejkowski, 2017). Because of the elevated infractions rate, individuals with mental illness are more likely to serve their maximum sentence and less likely to be released to community supervision (Sarteschi, 2013). They are also more likely to spend time in solitary confinement, a form of punishment known to produce psychiatric impairment and increase self-harm risk (Wilson, 2016). Besides the stigma of mental illness, symptoms also make individuals with mental illness easy targets for other inmates (Blitz et al., 2008). Compared with the general inmate population, individuals with mental illness are at elevated risk of suicide while incarcerated (Hayes, 2010).

As is seen from the discussion above, individuals with mental illness are a particularly vulnerable group in the justice system, with tremendous unmet needs. Because of the paucity of mental health services in the United States, the de facto policy in this country is that the criminal justice system is the primary locus of care for individuals with mental illness (Lamb & Weinberger, 2017). However, the justice system, grounded in constructs of punishment and public safety, is an unacceptable and inadequate setting to address mental health treatment needs. Structural changes are required to adequately and fairly address the needs of those with mental illness who are justice involved. Therefore, well-researched, tenacious, and intentional long-term social work advocacy for policy change is essential. Social workers must understand both mental health policy and justice system policy to navigate the two spheres and their intersection where change is needed. It is with this basic assumption that we write this chapter.

A comprehensive discussion of forensic mental health policy in one chapter is a daunting task; entire books have been written discussing this wide-ranging topic. To be able to explore topics in some depth, we have decided to take a narrower focus. One could argue that individuals with mental illness are most vulnerable to abuse and harm during times they are physically removed from society—when they are incarcerated. Therefore, we focus this chapter on policies regarding the process wherein an individual is sentenced to be incarcerated and the time of incarceration in jail or prison. During these times of vulnerability, and in many ways of invisibility, people with mental illness need social work advocates to address their individual situations and work for change in unjust policies.

In the Courtroom

Mental Health Policy, Definitions, and the Courts

One of the most challenging aspects of social work with justice-involved individuals with mental illness is the differences between legal and mental health meanings of specific terms (Torry & Billick, 2010). Social workers, particularly those who do not regularly work in forensic settings, need to understand these differences. A diagnosis of a *mental illness* is usually given based on meeting a specific set of criteria that include disturbances in thought or affect and reduced functioning. However, in a courtroom, having a diagnosis of a mental illness is not sufficient to be determined to be incompetent to stand trial or insane and thus not guilty by reason of insanity (NGRI). These legal terms require that additional criteria be met. For *competence to stand trial,* the criteria include the ability to understand the proceedings and participate in the process.

To be determined *NGRI,* the criteria include not merely the presence of a mental illness but also the inability to know that the criminal act in which they engaged while mentally ill was wrong and/or the inability to control their behavior regarding the criminal act. To make things more confusing, these criteria will vary from state to state, which will vary from the federal definitions (Torry & Billick, 2010). If social workers are to be effective advocates for justice-involved clients, they must understand these specific legal definitions, both federal and within their state, as well as the flaws within these definitions.

Competence to Stand Trial

Individuals with a mental illness are particularly vulnerable when caught in the court system's complexities. Their rights can be at risk as they stand trial. Like all individuals in the United States who have been charged with a crime, they have the right to *due process.* The 14th Amendment of the Constitution guarantees this by stating, "nor shall any State deprive any person of life, liberty, or property, without due process of law; nor deny to any person within its jurisdiction the equal protection of the laws" (U.S. Const. amend. XIV,

§1). Due process includes notification of the legal process, an opportunity to be heard, and an impartial tribunal (*Mullane v. Central Hanover Bank & Trust Co.*, 1950). For an individual with a mental illness facing trial, due process may be compromised by symptoms of the illness. Symptoms can prevent the individual from understanding the legal process, and thus they are not truly "notified." The symptoms can also interfere with the individual's ability to effectively present their case and have an "opportunity to be heard."

To protect the rights of those with a mental illness who face trial, it is essential to ensure that the individual is competent to understand and participate in the process. This determination is often referred to as *competence to stand trial*. Here the individual is evaluated by a mental health professional (which can be a social worker), and based on evaluation(s) and other information, the court makes a decision regarding competency. If the individual is found incompetent, they are provided with a process to restore their competency, usually treatment within an inpatient setting. Once competence has been restored, the individual returns to court for trial (Schwermer, 2020). To be effective advocates, social workers need to understand the definition and process of determining competence, both in general and for their specific jurisdiction. They also need to understand what happens to individuals deemed incompetent and the potential risks to rights during this time.

The requirement for competence was established in the case *Dusky v. U.S.* (1960), which held that a defendant must have "sufficient present ability to consult with his lawyer with a reasonable degree of understanding" and "a rational as well as factual understanding of the proceedings" (362 U.S. 402). Incompetence differs from simply having a psychiatric diagnosis, focusing on understanding and ability rather than symptoms. The statutory definitions of incompetence vary somewhat from state to state and may or may not even require a psychiatric diagnosis (Reisner & Peil, 2018).

When advocating for an individual with a mental illness, social workers must ensure that someone who is not competent to stand trial is identified and provided with treatment (referred to as restoration) before moving forward with the case. However, it is also essential for the social worker to understand that individuals have the right to refuse psychotropic medication during restoration, though this right is not absolute. In *Sell v. United States* (2003), the Supreme Court determined that to override an individual's refusal of medication while in restoration, four criteria must be met: (a) important governmental interests are at stake in bringing the individual to trial, (b) the medication will be substantially likely to render the individual competent to stand trial and substantially unlikely to have side effects that will interfere with the individual's ability to assist the defense, (c) less invasive alternative treatments are unlikely to be effective, and (d) administering the drug is medically appropriate (Cochrane et al., 2013).

When the individual is referred for an evaluation to determine competence, they are at risk of discrimination and other rights violations. Pirelli et al. (2011) completed a meta-analysis of research on competency to stand trial and found that non-White defendants were significantly more likely to be found incompetent than White defendants. The lack of reliability in competency determinations was also highlighted by Guarnera and Murrie (2017), who found low agreement (kappa = 0.49) between evaluators in their determinations. Upon determination of incompetence, the evaluator must next determine the likelihood of restoration to competence and the ability to stand trial. Here we also see significant bias, with men, older individuals, and those whose prior criminal records were known to the evaluator significantly less likely to be identified as "restorable" (Warren et al., 2013). Those deemed unrestorable are at risk of being referred to open-ended forensic treatment or incarceration, which may result in a much longer loss of freedom than if the individual had simply served their sentence (Wik et al., 2017).

Time in custody is one of the most disturbing aspects of the determination-of-competence process. Despite the right to a speedy trial guaranteed in the Constitution's Sixth Amendment and the Supreme Court decisions *Jackson v. Indiana* (1972), which stated that "a defendant cannot be held more than the reasonable period of time necessary to determine whether there is substantial probability that he will attain competency in the foreseeable future" (406 U.A. 738), the process for restoration can be horrifically slow. Gowensmith (2019) reports the following harrowing case:

> Mr. Jamycheal Mitchell was a 24-year-old man charged with misdemeanors of petty larceny and trespassing after allegedly stealing a bottle of Mountain Dew, a Snickers bar, and a snack cake from a convenience store in April 2015 (Harki, 2018; Swaine, 2015). He was then booked into a Virginia county jail. After more than one month and one transfer to another regional county jail, he was adjudicated as incompetent to stand trial due to symptoms of psychosis. Mr. Mitchell was ordered to competency restoration in a nearby forensic hospital; however, after more than 2 months he had still not been transferred. At his next court hearing, 71 days after the original competency hearing, the court reinstated the order as he continued to be held in the county jail. Sadly, while awaiting his transfer, Mr. Mitchell's mental status deteriorated significantly. Relatives assert that he refused to take antipsychotic medication, was not coherent enough to contact relatives, and began refusing to eat. On August 19, 2015, Mr. Mitchell was found dead, alone in a cell covered with urine and feces and having lost 46 pounds, still awaiting transfer for competency restoration services. (p. 1)

While not the norm, Mr. Mitchell's case is not unique. Several states have faced lawsuits contending that defendants experienced unconstitutional delays in waiting for restoration services (Heilbrum et al., 2019). A study by the National Association of State Mental Health Program Directors (Wik et al., 2017) found that 25% of states reported waiting times for restoration services of between 181 and 365 days. Often restoration services have no specific end date, and states can hold an individual in custody for long periods. The same study found that 22% of states could hold an individual for an unlimited period of time.

Given these rights violations and abuses with tragic consequences, social workers should be galvanized to action. Advocacy is needed for reform at every step of the process. Unbiased evaluation processes are needed, as are adequate, evidence-based restoration services. Throughout the process, lack of service capacity and dehumanizing treatment must be addressed.

Not Guilty by Reason of Insanity

While often found in the plots of made-for-TV movies, the defense of *NGRI* is used in about 1% of criminal cases. It is successful in only 10% to 25% of those (Smith, 2012). NGRI is grounded in the concepts of responsibility and culpability—*mens rea* and *actus reus*. It is not enough that an individual engaged in a "guilty act" (*actus reus*) for there to be culpability. The idea that it is unjust to punish for an act engaged in without *mens rea* (guilty mind) has been recognized since the time of Aristotle (Torry & Billick, 2010).

The most widely known criteria for an insanity defense were developed in 1843 with the case of Daniel M'Naghten. M'Naghten assassinated the assistant to the prime minister while under a persecutory delusion. The M'Naghten test required the accused to clearly prove that at the time of committing the crime, they were "operating under such a defect of reason, from a disease of the mind, as to not know the nature and quality of the act he was doing, or if he did know it, that he did not know it was wrong" (p. 257). This remains the standard for insanity in nearly half of the states today (Torry & Billick, 2010). Other standards for NGRI exist, including acquittal if the criminal conduct was a product of mental illness (*Durham v. United States*, 1954) or if the individual "lacked substantial capacity either to appreciate the criminality of the conduct or conform his conduct to the requirements of the law" (American Law Institute, 1985, Section 401(1)). All NGRI standards have three requirements: mental disorder, impaired functioning, and causal link between disorder and functional impairment. All are difficult to apply (Smith, 2012).

At a trial when the defendant is seeking a verdict of NGRI, the jury is provided with instructions about the meaning and criteria for the verdict. During the trial, evidence based on psychiatric evaluation is provided. Significant risks of bias and injustice are present throughout this process. Jurors may not fully understand NGRI instructions—one study found that jurors understood less than 30% of the judge's instructions (Ghandi & Prabhu, 2017). Research has also shown juror bias grounded in media misportrayal of NGRI, emotional and political considerations, lack of understanding of mental illness, and racial bias (Kapoor et al., 2020; Maeder et al., 2020; Shneiderman, 2014).

If found NGRI, an individual is committed to a psychiatric hospital for treatment until the individual can prove, by a preponderance of the evidence, that they no longer have a mental illness and are no longer dangerous. This is determined through regular review hearings. It has been demonstrated that insanity acquittees spend more time institutionalized than defendants convicted on equivalent charges (Ghandi & Prabhu, 2017). Again, bias plays a role in decision-making; minority status and the nature of the crime have both been shown to predict failure in release decisions (Monson et al., 2001).

Incarceration

Assessment

Upon incarceration, individuals with mental illness need to be identified and assessed to provide appropriate treatment and ensure the application of relevant policies and protections. The majority of correctional facilities report providing mental health screening. In

2000, 78% of state prisons reported that they screened inmates for mental illness at intake (Beck & Maruschak, 2001). Intake assessments administered to inmates vary significantly between jurisdictions in terms of the screening tool, consistency of delivery, and structure, breadth, and depth of the screening (Beck & Maruschak, 2001; Gebbie et al., 2008; Steadman et al., 2005). Consequently, the mental health needs of inmates may not be quickly and comprehensively understood by the institutions responsible for caring for their well-being. Al-Rousan and colleagues (2017) found that after initial intake in the Iowa Department of Corrections, it took an average of 11 months to get diagnosed with substance use disorder, 14 months for bipolar disorder, 21 months for posttraumatic stress disorder, 24 months for anxiety, 26 months for depression, 29 months for personality disorders, 45 months for persistent depressive disorder, and 52 months for schizophrenia.

Factors other than screening inconsistencies may impact whether or not an inmate is correctly diagnosed with mental illness. While individuals must be screened for mental illness within the first week of incarceration, identifying mental illness in this setting should be understood to be a continuous process. Some experts argue that diagnosing mental illnesses might be more accurately determined after the individual has had time to acculturate to their new surroundings (Martin et al., 2016; Steadman et al., 2005). Training correctional staff to identify and engage with mental illness could help clinical staff to decrease diagnostic error and help inmates to receive diagnoses more quickly (Comartin, Milanovic, et al., 2021; Martin et al., 2016).

The consensus among experts is that a two-part screening strategy would improve correctional facilities' ability to identify inmate mental health needs (Livingston, 2009). The first part would consist of a brief standardized screening, including a suicide assessment, documented at intake, administered by trained correctional staff. A mental health professional would conduct a second more comprehensive screening within 2 weeks of admittance (Hill et al, 2004; Livingston, 2009). Oregon's Department of Corrections has enacted these guidelines; with this structure, 60% of incarcerated individuals with mental illness were identified and treated, a rate that far exceeds national averages (Hill et al., 2004; James & Glaze, 2006).

Research has shown that assessing inmates for mental health issues, particularly suicide risk, can mean life or death. The National Commission for Correctional Health Care (NCCHC), an accreditation body for correctional health services, requires facilities to have a suicide prevention program to meet their standards (Hanson, 2010). While most jails indicate that they give staff suicide prevention training, most of these opportunities are 2 hours or less in length (Hayes, 2010). The NCCHC recommends that correctional staff receive 8 hours of initial suicide prevention training, with 2 hours of refresher training every year after (Dlugacz, 2014; Hanson, 2010).

Since facilities are not required to adhere to these recommendations, the unfortunate reality is that most individuals who complete suicide were not screened for suicidality when they arrived at their correctional facility (Lamberti & Weisman, 2004). According to the National Study of Jail Suicide, the majority of individuals who completed suicide did not receive a suicide assessment by a qualified mental health professional (Hayes, 2010). Suicide rates in jails are higher than in prisons, 48% of which occur within the first week of admittance (Mumola, 2005; Patterson & Hughes, 2008). There is strong evidence that instituting more robust screening guidelines and engaging screening as a continuous process can improve suicide prevention outcomes (Dlugacz, 2014). After New York implemented a system-wide suicide prevention program in which all staff received 8 hours of screening and intervention training, suicide rates dropped significantly in jails and prisons (Lamberti & Weisman, 2004).

Treatment While Incarcerated

When screening procedures correctly identify inmates with mental illness, the individual becomes entitled to appropriate and adequate care. Many court cases have shaped and defined the medical treatment to which inmates have a right, as inmates have sued the government to protect their health and mental health. In 1976 (*Estelle v Gamble*), the U.S. Supreme Court determined that correctional facilities violate the Eighth Amendment, submitting prisoners to cruel or unusual punishment if they acted with deliberate indifference to the prisoners' medical needs (Cohen & Dvoskin, 1992; Daniel, 2009). The U.S. Court of Appeals established no significant difference between the right to receive physical or mental health care in the 1977 case *Bowring v. Godwin* (Cohen & Dvoskin, 1992). In the class-action lawsuit *Ruiz vs. Estelle* (1980), the U.S. Supreme Court outlined minimum requirements for mental health services in correctional facilities (Daniel, 2007). These included "trained mental health professionals, systematic screening and evaluation, treatment, appropriate use of behavior-altering medications, accurate recording, and suicide-prevention programs" (Daigle et al., 2007, p. 128).

Although courts have defended inmates' rights to receive mental health services, and most correctional facilities have access to some form of mental health services, only about one-third of state prisoners who have mental health problems receive treatment after admission. The rate is even lower for inmates in federal prisons (24%) or local jails (17%; James & Glaze, 2006). Untreated individuals with mental illness have a high risk of increased symptoms, including psychosis, behavioral issues, and suicide (Lamberti & Weisman, 2004).

Because correctional facilities were not designed in either environment or staffing to be treatment facilities, the needs of individuals with mental illness can be overwhelming (Scheyett et al., 2009). Availability of specialized mental health services varies widely from facility to facility and is seldom adequate. Several barriers to treatment in correctional facilities include (a) overcrowding; (b) rapid turnover of inmates, particularly in jails; (c) staff culture that stresses punishment over care; (d) limited staff, training, resources, and money; and (e) communication breakdown among treatment staff (Gonzalez & Connell, 2014). An interesting strategy to increase access to mental health services, particularly in remote facilities, is telemedicine, now seen in multiple states (Chari et al., 2016).

Historically, correctional facilities hired their mental health staff, but this is changing, and privatization is more common as facilities and jurisdictions try to meet inmates' growing mental health needs. Some states contract with medical schools to deliver medical care to inmates; others have used a combination of private vendors and medical schools. Twenty-four states have contracted with private vendors to provide medical care (Daniel, 2007). There is some evidence that for-profit facilities may provide less mental health care than nonprofit facilities (Comartin, Nelson, et al., 2021). Because of this, and because of the general lack of mental health services in corrections, monitoring of the adequacy and quality of mental health care in correctional facilities should be an area of advocacy and research in social work.

Psychiatric medication is the most common form of mental health treatment offered to incarcerated individuals (James & Glaze, 2006; Shelton et al., 2010), sometimes as a continuation of treatment received in the community. Upon admission, it is not uncommon for staff to change or discontinue an inmate's medication, risking destabilization and decompensation. Changes in psychiatric medications may occur due to inadequate screening, misdiagnosis, or restricted formulary lists (Daniel, 2009; James & Glaze, 2006).

Correctional facilities, particularly for-profit ones, have an interest in keeping overhead costs down per inmate. A cost-saving measure often implemented is restricting the psychotropic medication list to generic and older formularies (Daniel, 2007). Restricted formulary lists may limit a clinician's ability to prescribe effective medications. Responses to psychotropic medication are idiosyncratic. Medications that are not in the formulary may improve the symptoms and quality of life of individuals with mental illness more than those available in the formulary.

Some correctional facilities offer inmates mental health treatment other than psychotropic medication. Approximately 13% of state prison inmates received mental health therapy after admission, 3% had an overnight hospital stay, and 2% had other mental health treatments (James & Glaze, 2006). Research shows that mental health interventions with offenders can "reduce symptoms of distress, improved their ability to cope with problems, and resulted in improved behavioral markers including institutional adjustment and behavioral functioning" (Morgan et al., 2012, pp. 45–46). Specific evidence-based treatment outcomes of incarcerated individuals with mental illness are insufficient. The absence of research makes it challenging to develop system-wide policies for mental health care in jails and prisons (Fontanarosa et al., 2013).

Forced Medication

Consistent adherence to psychotropic medication regimes can be challenging, even under ideal conditions. As previously discussed, correctional facilities have a constitutional duty to treat individuals with mental illness properly. The question then arises, what are the correctional facilities' obligations when an individual refuses needed psychotropic medication?

Whether individuals in state facilities have the right to refuse medication was decided in *Washington v. Harper* (1990). The Supreme Court acknowledged that an incarcerated individual has a constitutional right to refuse treatment according to the 14th Amendment (due process; Martwick, 1991; Torrey et al., 2014). However, they ruled that Washington state's procedures, consisting of an administrative hearing involving prison officials and mental health professionals, provided adequate due process (Floyd, 1990; Torrey et al., 2014). It is important to note that this due process required neither a judicial hearing nor an independent medical review panel to override the patient's treatment request. Critics of the *Harper* decision disagree with the court's decision, citing the inmate's right to refuse medication based on the First Amendment (right to privacy) or Eighth Amendment (protection from cruel and unusual punishment; Floyd, 1990).

States have dealt with the application of *Washington v. Harper* differently in their prison systems. While 31 states have followed the precedent of this case and require only administrative hearings to determine whether a facility can administer medication against objection, 13 states require a full judicial hearing. Five states and the federal district require inmates to be sent to a state psychiatric hospital instead of administering nonemergency medication against objection (Torrey et al., 2014). The majority of states require that the inmate be found to be "gravely disabled" and have a "likelihood of serious harm" to be given medication against objection. Six states require the inmate to be unable to give informed consent before involuntary medication may be given. New Mexico requires the court to appoint a guardian to make mental health treatment decisions (Torrey et al., 2014).

Despite the consistent support of a patient's right to refuse medication and the general ethical call to respect one's patients' autonomy, clinicians face additional ethical pressure to treat individuals forcibly. A clinician may be held liable if they do not seek involuntary treatment when a client may pose harm to another individual. In *Petersen v. State of Washington* (1983), the Washington Supreme Court ruled that a psychiatrist could be held responsible for failing to confine patients who unintentionally injure another individual (Brofsky, 1984; Wortzel, 2006). Similarly, in *Lipari v. Sears, Roebuck & Co.* (1980), the U.S. District Court in Nebraska held a psychiatrist liable for failing to confine a patient who later fired a gun into a nightclub (Glassberg, 1983). While these cases have not been specifically applied to the jail and prison setting, Wortzel (2006) suggests that this line of reasoning could be applied to the mental health clinician's duty to protect the well-being of other inmates and correctional staff.

Some correctional facilities find ways to circumvent their inability to medicate against objection. State prisons in Maryland can only medicate against wishes in emergencies. However, they can transfer the incarcerated individual to a state hospital and administer the medication over objection in that setting (Johnston, 2011). In Massachusetts, if an inmate refuses medication, the prison can request the court, without a hearing, to transfer the individual to a state hospital for 30 days (Prisoners' Legal Services of Massachusetts, 2020). The hospital can administer medication against objection if the individual is a risk to themselves or others.

Discipline During Incarceration

Incarcerated individuals who have mental illness are more likely than those without to be charged with violating facility rules, whether minor infractions or verbally or physically assaulting facility staff or another inmate (Hill et al., 2004; James & Glaze, 2006; Matejkowski, 2017). As a result, they will likely face disciplinary repercussions that may result in more extended imprisonment (Hill et al., 2004). Incarcerated individuals with mental illness remain in state prisons on average 4 months longer than those without mental illness (James & Glaze, 2006). Inmates with mental illness may be denied conditional release because of parole board bias, justified by misconduct violations. Inmates in federal prisons can earn "good time credit" for good behavior, reducing their sentence (18 U.S.C. § 3624), an opportunity less available to inmates with mental illness, and resultant conduct violations.

Some protections against disciplinary actions for inmates with mental illness do exist. The Federal Bureau of Prisons does not allow its institutions to take disciplinary action against inmates determined to be incompetent or not responsible for personal conduct by mental health staff (28 C.F.R. § 541.6). Though not as common, several states also protect mentally ill individuals from punishment following correctional facility rule violations (Krelstein, 2002). Mental health professionals' involvement in these disciplinary hearings varies from state to state. Some states argue that excluding the clinician from disciplinary hearings helps individuals maintain a trusting relationship with their client, the inmate in question. Other states allow mental health clinicians to provide relevant clinical data about disciplinary actions but may not allow them to give an opinion about the inmate's disciplinary responsibility (Krelstein, 2002).

More than 200 years ago, reforms sought to incorporate ideas of the Enlightenment into criminal justice and explored shifting the U.S. system away from corporal punishment and toward solitude (Cloud et al., 2015). They believed that silence would help incarcerated individuals live more pious and socially responsible lives. Today, practices of isolating individuals are used primarily as a punitive measure. Individuals may be placed in "solitary confinement" or "single cell" where they are separated from others; an entire wing or building for solitary confinement is called an "isolation unit" or "administrative segregation." Secure housing units or entire facilities that confine inmates in solitary confinement are referred to as "supermax" prisons (Patterson & Hughes, 2008). These institutions were first developed in the 1980s and are designed to restrict all human contact—visual and physical. By the turn of the century, hundreds of facilities contained segregation units, and 40 states operated supermax facilities (Cloud et al., 2015).

Individuals with serious mental illness are more likely to be placed in solitary confinement while incarcerated than those without mental illness. This is true for several reasons: The individuals may have difficulty understanding and complying with facility rules, staff may misinterpret distress or psychosis symptoms for willful noncompliance, and individuals with mental illness are more likely to need protection from being victimized by other inmates. Research estimates that around 33% of those in segregation units suffer from a mental illness (Cloud et al., 2015).

Living conditions under these circumstances are quite harsh. These individuals are placed by themselves in a small room, usually for 23 hours a day (Dlugacz, 2014; Patterson & Hughes, 2008), and do not have access to support programs or group mental health treatment. Since these individuals often pose a risk, the rooms contain little that could be used to harm oneself or others. Often they have a few pieces of furniture in the room—a bed, desk, toilet, and sink—that have been bolted to the floor and walls (Cloud et al., 2015). If they pose a suicidal risk, they may not be allowed sheets or cloth uniforms; even with these restrictions, suicide is not uncommon in solitary confinement. Patterson and Hughes (2008) found that 73% of completed suicides occurred in single cells over 6 years in California.

In *Madrid v. Gomez* (1995), it was found that all mentally ill prisoners should be moved out of security housing units. The judge wrote that being in a supermax facility "may press the outer borders of what most humans can psychologically tolerate . . . [and] cause mentally ill inmates to seriously deteriorate" (Toch, 2001, pp. 378–379). However, this case did not ultimately rule on the constitutionality of all long-term isolation of mentally ill individuals or incarcerated individuals, so supermax facilities remain an integral part of the U.S. correctional system.

Solitary confinement is an important area for social work advocacy. The National Association of Social Workers has identified solitary confinement and its adverse impacts on individuals with mental illness as a priority for policy reform (Wilson, 2016). Their social justice brief, *Solitary Confinement: A Clinical Social Work Perspective*, calls on social workers to advocate for increased mental health treatment in jails and prisons and eliminate abusive uses of solitary confinement.

Preparation for Release From Incarceration

For an individual with mental illness, resumption of mental health treatment upon release from incarceration is imperative, and the ability to access care should be a part of release preparation. However, a significant barrier to accessing care is cost. Approximately 80% of incarcerated individuals, before 2014, lacked resources to pay for either health insurance or the health care they received with it (Bandara et al., 2015). While Medicare and Medicaid are available to formerly incarcerated individuals, Medicaid coverage is suspended when individuals are in custody (Regenstein & Rosenbaum, 2014). One policy that has been of some help in this area is the Affordable Care Act (ACA). With the ACA's implementation, Cuellar and Cheema (2012) estimated that 33.6% of released inmates would be eligible to enroll in Medicaid upon release. However, after the U.S. Supreme Court ruled against mandatory Medicaid expansion, Regenstein and Rosenbaum (2014) estimated that only about 20% of individuals released from jail in states without Medicaid expansion would be able to apply for coverage.

Reentry plans in jails and prisons are rarely comprehensive and vary significantly by the facility. However, on average, inmates are released with no more than a 2-week supply of medication and no follow-up plans with a medical professional (Rich et al., 2011). Research has shown that individuals with severe mental illness released from jail with Medicaid are more likely to access community health services and receive treatment more quickly than those without Medicaid (Morrissey et al., 2006).

Despite barriers to this process, policy changes can help make the reentry process easier for incarcerated individuals. For example, in New York before 2007, inmates' Medicaid benefits were terminated upon incarceration (Bandara et al., 2015). In 2007 legislation changed so that benefits were no longer terminated but instead suspended and immediately reinstated upon release. Other states use presumptive eligibility (a process that assumes a person is eligible for Medicaid before completing the application and offers short-term coverage so that providers can deliver services) to help former inmates receive Medicaid benefits more quickly after release. Other states allow inmates to apply for Medicaid benefits before being released from a correctional facility (Bandara et al., 2015).

When helping individuals with mental illness reintegrate into society, social workers must help their clients resume, re-enroll, or enroll in Medicaid coverage, when applicable, to help avoid treatment disruption. Social workers should also advocate for policies that will increase access to health care coverage, such as ACA and Medicaid expansion; reduce barriers to access such as the need for specific identification documents; and require that jails and prisons ensure that inmates have a way to access and afford mental health care before their release.

Conclusions and Recommendations

Mental health policies in courtrooms, jails, and prisons are in tremendous need of social work action. With a person-in-environment lens and robust set of ethical principles, social workers can contribute in unique and valuable ways to criminal justice reform. However, in order to be maximally effective in moving forensic mental health policies toward social justice, social workers must work within four action fields: (a) gaining a deep understanding of the complexities of policies, (b) identifying and acting to change unjust policies, (c) engaging in research to inform policies, and (d) grounding the problems of forensic mental health policies within the larger systemic challenges to social justice in our society.

Complexities

As illustrated throughout this chapter, the laws and policies governing the treatment of people with mental illness in the courtroom, jail, and prison are complex. They are an amalgam of legislation, case law, and institutional policy. They vary from state to state, from institution to institution, and can be both difficult to interpret and challenging to enforce. Since any practicing social worker may have a client who becomes justice involved, all social workers must have a thorough understanding of the policies in their state that determine how an individual with mental illness will move through the justice system as well as the policies that protect their rights while within the justice system.

Social workers need to know that this understanding of policy must be grounded in the realization that the justice system's conceptualization of mental illness is very different from that of social work. Criminal justice policies are based on the concept of insanity, a state where one cannot understand or control actions, and on resultant culpability, with the goals of public protection and punishment of the guilty. Social work, by comparison, is based on a biopsychosocial understanding of behavior, with the goals of supporting recovery, autonomy, and respect for the inherent worth of the individual. If a social worker does not understand these two different worldviews and languages, they will be unable to communicate with the justice system in ways that can be understood. Without this understanding, social workers will be unable to influence outcomes for individual clients, nor will they be able to effect policy change.

An additional area of complexity to which social workers must attend is that of the inherent ethical complexities of work within forensic mental health policies. Social workers must engage in thoughtful and professional self-reflection about the ethical dilemmas they may face with justice-involved clients. How will they navigate the tensions between self-determination and client well-being in a situation where a client wishes to refuse medication and may thus be held in involuntary commitment restoration for an indefinite period of time—perhaps for decades? What will they decide to do if an incarcerated client asks them not to identify them as mentally ill because of the resultant bias, stigma, and abusive treatment in jail, but not identifying them as such precludes their ability to receive needed treatment? These are only a few of the ethical dilemmas social workers will face within the tangle of forensic mental health policy, and within which they will need to be prepared to act.

Policy Changes

Throughout this chapter, we have identified numerous problematic policies, or lack of policies, that harm individuals with mental illness. Social workers must advocate for policy change to protect the rights and ensure the fair treatment of people with mental illness. They must also ensure that existing policies for people with mental illness are applied fairly and consistently.

The potential targets for change are multiple: changes to the definition of *incapable* and *insane* to ground them in a science-based understanding of individuals whose mental health symptoms shape their behavior; establishment of policies to ensure that individuals with mental illness do not languish in jails or hospitals for extended periods of time awaiting trial; policies to mandate effective identification and treatment of those with mental illness who are in jails or prisons; policies to require effective linkage to treatment upon release from prison or jail. The list of needed policy changes is extensive. All social workers must engage in advocacy efforts and partner with other advocacy groups who care about those who are justice involved and work together for more effective and just policies.

Research

One of the more striking observations in the literature on forensic mental illness policies is the paucity of research in the field. A great deal of energy is expended on studying rates and prevalence of mental illness in the criminal justice population. Less research is found on evidence-based practices for those with mental illnesses in the justice system, even though this research is desperately needed to inform policy. Evidence-based screening tools exist but are not plentiful and are used inconsistently. Research is needed to develop valid and reliable tools and also needed to increase the use of these tools in the justice system. Similarly, more research on effective interventions for justice-involved people with mental illnesses is needed. Little is known about the most effective ways to restore someone to competency to stand trial; there is also a tremendous need for better models of care within jails and prisons.

The lack of rigorous policy analysis research should be shocking and concerning to social workers. Throughout this chapter, we have discussed the wide variation in policies from state to state. Evaluation of these various policies to identify the most effective policies is needed; current policy decisions sometimes seem to be made in an informational vacuum, shaped by stereotypes, anecdotes, and biases. Evidence-informed policy is essential for justice. With our ability to see the interconnections between direct practice and policy, and with an understanding of the importance of using evidence for ethical practice, social workers can provide essential contributions as researchers in this field.

Systemic Challenges to Social Justice

Social workers know that it is essential to see the challenges in forensic mental health policies as woven with and embedded within larger systemic challenges. As discussed above, research has shown that juries demonstrate bias with regard to race and make decisions without fully understanding mental illness (Kapoor et al., 2020; Maeder et al., 2020; Shneiderman, 2014). Discipline in jails and prisons is often grounded in a lack of understanding and bias against mental illness (Krelstein, 2002).

The criminal justice system itself is steeped in bias and racism. The disproportionate number of Black individuals incarcerated in the United States is horrifying (James & Glaze, 2006). The long history of racism in this institution cannot be ignored (Alexander, 2010). Similarly, poverty has always been intertwined with the justice system; debtors' prison was an early form of incarceration, and currently, those who are incarcerated are overwhelmingly poor (Brookings Institute, 2018). Individuals with mental illness can be caught in the frightening intersectionality of multiple oppressed identities, simultaneously experiencing discrimination and unjust treatment due to the stigma of mental illness (Scheyett, 2005), racism, poverty, and other vulnerable aspects of their selves.

The fact that mental health policies for those who are justice involved are grounded in the more significant social justice issues of our time means that this is an action area for all social workers. We have a responsibility to understand these policies' complexities, advocate for change, engage in research to inform improved policies, and work together to ensure that not simply the law but true justice is served for individuals with mental illness in the justice system.

References

18 U.S. Code § 3624. (2014). Release of a prisoner.

28 C.F.R. § 541.6. (2011). Mentally ill inmates.

Alexander, M. (2010). *The new Jim Crow: Mass incarceration in the age of colorblindness.* New Press.

Al-Rousan, T., Rubenstein, L. M., Sieleni, B., Deol, H., & Wallace, R. B. (2017). Inside the nation's largest mental health institution: A prevalence study in a state prison system. *BMC Public Health, 17,* 342–350. doi:10.1186/s12889-017-4257-0

American Law Institute. (1985). Model Penal Code, section 401.

Bandara, S. N., Huskamp, H. A., Riedel, L. E., McGinty, E. E., Webster, D., Toone, R. E., & Barry, C. L. (2015). Leveraging the Affordable Care Act to enroll justice-involved populations in Medicaid: State and local efforts. *Health Affairs, 34*(12), 2044–2051. doi:10.1377/hlthaff.2015.0668

Beck, A. J., & Maruschak, L. M. (2001). *Mental health treatment in state prisons, 2000.* Bureau of Justice Statistics, U.S. Department of Justice. https://bjs.ojp.gov/content/pub/pdf/mhtsp00.pdf

Blitz, C., Wolff, N., & Shi, J. (2008). Physical victimization in prison: The role of mental illness. *International Journal of Law and Psychiatry, 31*(5), 385–393. doi.org/10.1016/j.ijlp.2008.08.005

Brofsky, M. A. (1984). Tort law—Psychiatrists' duty to protect foreseeably endangered third parties. *Suffolk University Law Review, 18*(4), 879–886.

Bronson, J., & Berzofsky, M. (2017). *Indicators of mental health problems reported by prisoners and jail inmates, 2011–12.* Bureau of Justice Statistics, U.S. Department of Justice. https://bjs.ojp.gov/content/pub/pdf/imhprpji1112.pdf

Brookings Institution. (2018). *Work and opportunity before and after incarceration*. Economic Studies at Brookings. https://www.brookings.edu/research/work-and-opportunity-before-and-after-incarceration

Chari, K., Simon, A., DeFrances, C., & Maruschak L. (2016). National Survey of Prison Health Care: Selected findings. *National Health Statistics Reports,* no 96. National Center for Health Statistics. https://bjs.ojp.gov/content/pub/pdf/nsphcsf.pdf

Cloud, D. H., Drucker, E., Browne, A., & Parsons, J. (2015). Public health and solitary confinement in the United States. *American Journal of Public Health, 105*(1), 18–26. doi:10.2105/AJPH.2014.302205

Cochrane, R., Herbel, B., Reardon, M., & Lloyd, K. (2013). The *Sell* effect: Involuntary medication treatment is a "clear and convincing" success. *Law and Human Behavior, 37,* 107–116. doi.org/10.1016/j.ijlp.2008.08.005

Cohen, F., & Dvoskin, J. (1992). Inmates with mental disorders: A guide to law and practice. *Mental and Physical Disability Law Reporter, 16*(4), 462–471.

Comartin, E. B., Milanovic, E., Nelson, V., & Kubiak, S. (2021), Mental health identification practices of jails: The unmet needs of the "silent" population. *American Journal of Community Psychology, 67,* 7–20. doi.org/10.1002/ajcp.12466

Comartin, E., Nelson, V., Hambrick, N., Kubiak, S., Sightes, E., & Ray, B. (2021). Comparing for-profit and nonprofit mental health services in county jails. *Journal of Behavioral Health Services and Research, 48,* 320–392. doi.org/10.1007/s11414-020-09733-1

Council of State Governments. (2012). *Improving outcomes for people with mental illnesses involved with New York City's criminal court and correction system.* Council of State Governments Justice Center. https://csgjusticecenter.org/publications/improving-outcomes-for-people-with-mental-illnesses-involved-with-new-york-citys-criminal-court-and-correction-systems/

Cuellar, A. E., & Cheema, J. (2012). As roughly 700,000 prisoners are released annually, about half will gain health coverage and care under federal laws. *Health Affairs, 31*(5), 931–938. doi:10.1377/hlthaff.2011.0501

Daigle, M. S., Daniel, A. E., Dear, G. E., Frottier, P., Hayes, L. M., Kerkhof, A., Konrad, N., Liebling, A., & Sarchiapone, M. (2007). Preventing suicide in prisons, part II: International comparisons of suicide prevention services in correctional facilities. *Crisis, 28*(3), 122–130. doi:10.1027/0227-5910.28.3.122

Daniel, A. E. (2007). Care of the mentally ill in prisons: Challenges and solutions. *Journal of the American Academy of Psychiatry and the Law, 35*(4), 406–410.

Daniel, A. E. (2009). Suicide-related litigation in jails and prisons: Risk management strategies. *Journal of Correctional Health Care, 15*(1), 19–27. doi:10.1177/1078345808326618

Dlugacz, H. A. (2014). Correctional mental health in the USA. *International Journal of Prisoner Health, 10*(1), 3–26. doi:10.1108/IJPH-06-2013-0028

Durham v. United States 214 F.2d 862 D.C. Cir (1954).

Dusky v. United States, 362 U.S. 402 (1960).

Estelle v. Gamble, 429 U.S. 97 (1976).

Floyd, J. (1990). The administration of psychotropic drugs to prisoners: State of the law and beyond. *California Law Review, 78*(5), 1243–1285. doi.org/10.2307/3480747

Fontanarosa, J., Uhl, S., Oyesanmi, O., & Schoelles, K. (2013, August). *Interventions for adult offenders with serious mental illness.* Report No.: 13-EHC107-EF. Agency for Healthcare Research and Quality. PMID: 24049841. https://effectivehealthcare.ahrq.gov/sites/default/files/pdf/mental-illness-adults-prisons_research.pdf

Fuller, D. A., Sinclair, E., Geller, J., Quanbeck, C., & Snook, J. (2016). *Going, going, gone: Trends and consequences of eliminating state psychiatric beds, 2016.* Treatment Advocacy Center. https://www.treatmentadvocacycenter.org/storage/documents/going-going-gone.pdf

Gebbie, K. M., Larkin, R. M., Klein, S. J., Wright, L., Satriano, J., Culkin, J. J., & Devore, B. S. (2008). Improving access to mental health services for New York State prison inmates. *Journal of Correctional Health Care, 14*(2), 122–135. doi:10.1177/1078345807313875

Ghandi, T., & Prabhu, M. (2012). Jury instructions on the consequences of an insanity verdict. *Legal Digest, 45,* 121–122.

Glassberg, T. A. (1983). Psychiatrists are subject to tort liability for failing to protect the public from their patients' unintentional acts: Petersen v. State, 100 Wash. 2d 421, 671 P.2d 230. *Washington Law Review, 63*(2), 315–324.

Gonzalez, J., & Connell, N. (2014). Mental health of prisoners: Identifying barriers to mental health treatment and medication continuity. *American Journal of Public Health, 104,* 2328–2333. doi:10.2105/AJPH.2014.302043

Gowensmith, W. (2019). Resolution of resignation: The role of forensic mental health professionals amidst the competency services crisis. *Psychology, Public Policy, and the Law, 25,* 1–14. doi.org/10.1037/law0000190

Guarnera, L., & Murrie, D. (2017). Field reliability of competency and sanity options: A systematic review and meta-analysis. *Psychological Assessment, 29,* 795–818. doi.org/10.1037/pas0000388

Hanson, A. (2010). Correctional suicide: Has progress ended? *Journal of the American Academy of Psychiatry and the Law, 38*(1), 6–10.

Harki, G. A. (2018, August 23). Horrific deaths, brutal treatment: Mental illness in America's jails. *Virginian-Pilot.* Retrieved from https://pilotonline.com/news/local/projects/jail-crisis/article_5ba8a112-974e-11e8-ba17-734814f14db.html

Hayes, L. M. (2010). *National study of jail suicide: 20 years later.* National Institute of Corrections, U.S. Department of Justice. https://s3.amazonaws.com/static.nicic.gov/Library/024308.pdf

Heilbrum, K., Giallella, C., Wright, J., DeMatteo, D., Griffin, P., Locklair, B., & Desai, A. (2019). Treatment for restoration of competence to stand trial: Critical analysis and policy recommendations. *Psychology, Public Policy, and Law, 25,* 266–283. doi.org/10.1037/law0000210

Hill, H., Siegfried, C., & Ickowitz, A. (2004) *Effective prison mental health services: Guidelines to expand and improve treatment.* National Institute of Corrections. https://info.nicic.gov/nicrp/system/files/018604.pdf

Houser, K., Vilcica, E., Saum, C., & Hiller, M. (2019). Mental health risk factors and parole decisions: Does inmate mental health status affect who gets released. *International Journal of Environmental Research and Public Health, 16,* 2950–2969. doi:10.3390/ijerph16162950

Jackson v. Indiana, 406 U.S. 738 (1972).

James, D. J., & Glaze, L.E. (2006). *Mental health problems of prison and jail inmates.* Bureau of Justice Statistics, U.S. Department of Justice. https://bjs.ojp.gov/content/pub/pdf/mhppji.pdf

Johnston, J. A. (2011). Mental health and Maryland's prisons. *Maryland Bar Journal, 6,* 28–33.

Kapoor, R., Wasser, T., Funaro, M., & Norko, M. (2020). Hospital treatment of persons found not guilty by reason of insanity. *Behavioral Science and the Law, 38,* 426–440. doi:10.1002/bsl.2484

Krelstein, M. S. (2002). Role of mental health in the inmate disciplinary process: A national survey. *Journal of the American Academy of Psychiatry and the Law, 30*(4), 488–496.

Lamb, H., & Weinberger, L. (2017). Understanding and treating offenders with serious mental illness in public sector mental health. *Behavioral Sciences & the Law, 35*(4), 303–318. doi.org/10.1002/bsl.2292

Lamberti, J. S., & Weisman, R. L. (2004). Persons with severe mental disorders in the criminal justice system: Challenges and opportunities. *Psychiatric Quarterly, 75*(2), 151–164. doi:10.1023/b:psaq.0000019756.34713.c3

Lipari v. Sears, Roebuck & Co., 497 F. Supp. 185 (1980).

Livingston, J. D. (2009). *Mental health and substance use services in correctional settings: A review of minimum standards and best practices.* International Centre for Criminal Law Reform and Criminal Justice Policy. https://icclr.org/publications/mental-health-and-substance-use-services-in-correctional-settings-a-review-of-minimum-standards-and-best-practices/

Madrid v. Gomez, 889 F. Supp. 1146 (1995).

Maeder, E., Yamamoto, S., & McLaughlin, K. (2020). The influence of defendant race and mental disorder type on mock juror decision-making in insanity trials. *International Journal of Law and Psychiatry, 68,* 1–7. doi.org/10.1016/j.ijlp.2019.101536

Martin, M. S., Hynes, K., Hatcher, S., & Colman, I. (2016). Diagnostic error in correctional mental health: Prevalence, causes, and consequences. *Journal of Correctional Health Care, 22*(2), 109–117. doi:10.1177/1078345816634327

Martwick, C. R. (1991). Washington v. Harper: The Supreme Court defines procedural due process in the prison. *Loyola University Chicago Law Journal, 22*(2), 517–538.

Matejkowski, J. (2017). The moderating effects of antisocial personality disorder on the relationship between serious mental illness and types of prison infractions. *Prison Journal, 97*, 202–223. doi:10.1177/0032885517692804

Monson, C., Gunnin, D., Fogel, M., & Kyle, L. (2001). Stopping (or slowing) the revolving door: Factors related to NGRI acquittees maintenance of a conditional release. *Law and Human Behavior, 25*, 257–267. doi.org/10.1023/A:1010745927735

Morgan, R. D., Flora, D. B., Kroner, D. G., Mills, J. F., Varghese, F., & Steffan, J. S. (2012). Treating offenders with mental illness: A research synthesis. *Law and Human Behavior, 36*(1), 37–50. doi:10.1037/h0093964

Morrissey, J. P., Steadman, H. J., Dalton, K. M., Cuellar, A. E., Stiles, P., & Cuddeback, G. S. (2006). Medicaid enrollment and mental health service use following release of jail detainees with severe mental illness. *Psychiatric Services, 57*(6), 809–815. doi.org/10.1176/ps.2006.57.6.809

Mullane v. Central Hanover Bank & Trust Co., 339 U.S. 306 (1950).

Mumola, C. J. (2005). *Suicide and homicide in state prisons and local jails.* Bureau of Justice Statistics, U.S. Department of Justice. https://bjs.ojp.gov/content/pub/pdf/shsplj.pdf

Parry, M. (2006). Dorothea Dix. *American Journal of Public Health, 96*(4), 624–625. doi.org/10.2105/AJPH.2005.079152

Patterson, R. F., & Hughes, K. (2008) Review of completed suicides in the California department of corrections and rehabilitation, 1999 to 2004. *Psychiatric Services, 59*(6), 676–682. doi.org/10.1176/ps.2008.59.6.676

Petersen v. State, 100 Wash. 2d 421, 671 P.2d 230 (1983).

Pirelli, G., Gottdiener, W., & Zapf, P. (2011). A meta-analytic review of competency to stand trial research. *Psychology, Public Policy, and Law, 17*, 1–53. doi:10.1037/a0021713

Prisoners' Legal Services of Massachusetts. (2020). *Right to refuse treatment.* https://plsma.org/prisoner-self-help/pro-se-materials/medical-mental-health/right-to-refuse-treatment/

Quam, J. (2013). Dix, Dorothea Lynde. In T. Mizrahi (Ed.), *Encyclopedia of social work.* NASW Press. https://doi.org/10.1093/acrefore/9780199975839.013.676

Regenstein, M., & Rosenbaum, S. (2014). What the Affordable Care Act means for people with jail stays. *Health Affairs, 33*(3), 448–454. doi:10.1377/hlthaff.2013.1119

Reisner, A., & Piel, J. (2018). Mental condition requirement in competency to stand trial assessments. *Journal of the American Academy of Psychiatry and Law, 46*, 86–92.

Rich, J. D., Wakeman, S. E., & Dickman, S. L. (2011). Medicine and the epidemic of incarceration in the United States. *New England Journal of Medicine, 364*(22), 2081–2083. doi:10.1056/NEJMp1102385

Ruiz v. Estelle. 503 F. Supp. 1265, S.D. Tex. (1980).

Sarteschi, C. (2013). *Mentally ill offenders involved with the US criminal justice system: A synthesis.* Sage.

Scheyett, A. (2005). The mark of madness: Stigma, serious mental illness, and social work. *Social Work in Mental Health, 3*, 79–97. doi.org/10.1300/J200v03n04_05

Scheyett, A., Vaughn, J., & Taylor, M. (2009). Screening and access to services for individuals with serious mental illness in jails. *Community Mental Health Journal, 45*, 439–451. doi.org/10.1007/s10597-009-9204-9

Schwermer, R. (2020). *Improving the justice system response to mental illness: Interim report.* State Justice Institute. https://www.ncsc.org/__data/assets/pdf_file/0025/38680/Competence_to_Stand_Trial_Interim_Final.pdf

Sell v. United States 539 U.S. 166 (2003).

Shelton, D., Ehret, M. J., Wakai, S., Kapetanovic, T., & Moran, M. (2010). Psychotropic medication adherence in correctional facilities: A review of the literature. *Journal of Psychiatric and Mental Health Nursing, 17*(7), 603–613. doi:10.1111/j.1365-2850.2010.01587.x

Shneiderman, A. (2014). No such thing as a sure thing. *Jury Expert, 26*, 11–12.

Smith, S. (2012). Neuroscience, ethics, and legal responsibility: The problem of the insanity defense. *Science and Engineering Ethics, 18*, 475–481. doi:10.1007/s11948-012-9390-7

Steadman, H. J., Scott, J. E., Osher, F., Agnese, T. K., & Robbins, P.C. (2005). Validation of the brief jail mental health screen. *Psychiatric Services, 56*(7), 816–822. doi:10.1176/appi.ps.56.7.816

Swaine, J. (2015, August 25). Young black man jailed since April for alleged $5 theft found dead in cell. *The Guardian.* Retrieved from https://www.theguardian.com/us-news/2015/aug/28/jamycheal-mitchell-virginia-jail-founddead

Toch, H. (2001). The future of supermax confinement. *Prison Journal, 81*(3), 376–388. doi:10.1177/0032885501081003005

Torrey, E. F., Zdanowicz, M. T., Kennard, A. D., Lamb, H. R., Eslinger, D. F., Biasotti, M. I., & Fuller, D. A. (2014). *The treatment of persons with mental illness in prisons and jails: A state survey.* Treatment Advocacy Center. https://www.treatmentadvocacycenter.org/storage/documents/backgrounders/smi-in-jails-and-prisons.pdf

Torry, Z., & Billick, S. (2010). Overlapping universe: Understanding legal insanity and psychosis. *Psychiatric Quarterly, 81*, 253–262. doi:10.1007/s11126-010-9134-2

U.S. Const. amend. (1868). XIV, §1.

Warren, J., Chauhan, P., Kois, L., Dibble, A., & Knighton, J. (2013). Factors influencing 2,260 opinions of defendants' restorability to adjudicative competency. *Psychology, Public Policy, and Law, 19*, 495–508. doi:10.1037/a0034740

Washington v. Harper, 494 U.S. 210 (1990).

Wik, A., Hollen, V., & Fisher, W. (2017). *Forensic patients in state psychiatric hospitals: 1999–2016.* National Association of State Mental Health Program Directors. https://nasmhpd.org/sites/default/files/TACPaper.10.Forensic-Patients-in-State-Hospitals_508C_v2.pdf

Wilson, M. (2016). *Solitary confinement: A clinical social work perspective.* NASW Press. http://www.socialworkblog.org/wp-content/uploads/Solitary-Confinement.pdf

Wortzel, H. S. (2006). The right to refuse treatment. *Psychiatric Times, 23*(14). https://www.psychiatrictimes.com/view/right-refuse-treatment

19

Juvenile Justice Policy

Susan McCarter, Vanessa Drew, Saliseah Scales, and Keshawn Mathews

An Overview of Juvenile Justice Policy in the United States

Before the first juvenile court was created in 1899, with significant support from the forensic social workers of the time, all youthful offenders were treated the same as adults without considering what was developmentally appropriate. This chapter provides a historical overview of juvenile justice policy in the United States, including the debate about the knowledge and evidence base, value, and impact of each policy from the colonial period through today. The chapter then concludes with an examination of how policies influence current social work practice using a critical lens of social work values and ethics.

Colonial Period (1636–1823)

Adolescence is a relatively new phenomenon (McCarter, 2018). Prior to the 19th century, children were the responsibility of their parents, and in instances where parents could not discipline their children, the youthful offenders received the same punishment as adults of the time—being whipped, flogged, sent to the stocks, or even executed (Bartollas, 2006). The American colonists brought justice ideals from England's chancery courts designed to handle matters considered outside of typical legal actions. These courts followed the philosophy of *parens patriae*, which granted the state power to protect and care for a child—acting in the stead of the child's parents (Siegel & Welsh, 2009).

Susan McCarter, Vanessa Drew, Saliseah Scales, and Keshawn Mathews, *Juvenile Justice Policy* In: *Handbook of Forensic Social Work*. Edited by: David Axlyn McLeod, Anthony P. Natale, and Kristin W. Mapson, Oxford University Press. © Oxford University Press 2024. DOI: 10.1093/oso/9780197694732.003.0019

Houses of Refuge Period (1824–1899)

As the U.S. population grew in the mid-1800s, individuals and families began moving toward cities with commercial centers and manufacturing jobs. Children in some low-income families were left to fend for themselves. Once the communities could no longer shoulder the burden of these youth by offering them apprenticeships or servanthood, they built poorhouses/almshouses, workhouses, and orphanages. In 1825, the first house of refuge was established in New York City. Similar facilities followed in Boston and Philadelphia, followed by New Orleans, Cincinnati, Chicago, and St. Louis, with houses in most U.S. cities by 1850 (Siegel & Welsh, 2009). It was believed that these houses would offer wayward children the structure, religion, and discipline they needed. The family's will was superseded by the state's, and these facilities were designed to reform juvenile delinquency. Wealthy social activists of the time advocated to extend the state's control over drinking, vagrancy, and delinquency, which had been the family's responsibility. These activists were called "child savers." They included many of the same individuals involved in the Society for the Prevention of Cruelty to Children (1874), National Conference on Charities and Correction (1879, precursor to the National Conference of Social Welfare), Juvenile Psychopathic Institute (1909), and Los Angeles Coordinating Councils (1932) and numerous early forensic social workers (Popple & Leighninger, 1996). Yet despite their intentions and the structure they provided, houses of refuge were soon overcrowded, deteriorated, and disordered, and despite the intention of saving children, some realized that these youthful offenders were denied the constitutional rights afforded to adults. Then, the child savers advocated for the passage of the Illinois Juvenile Court Act of 1899, which established the first independent court in the United States designated for those younger than 16 who were deemed "delinquent."

The Juvenile Court Period (1899–1960)

This first juvenile court was founded in Cook County, Illinois, with support from Jane Addams, Julia Lathrop, Ellen Henrotin, and Louise Bowen (Roberts & Brownell, 1999). The court was established for those younger than 16 years old who were neglected as well as those committing delinquent acts, created more informal procedures to adjudicate children instead of criminalizing them, separated children from adults in proceedings and programs, prohibited the detention of those younger than 12 in a police station or jail, and developed probation programs designed in the best interests of the state and the child. The philosophy of the new juvenile justice system was that (a) children are still developing and thus are less culpable than adults, (b) the juvenile system should treat and rehabilitate versus punish, (c) disposition should be determined based on the child's circumstances and needs, and (d) the system flow and procedures should be less complicated than the criminal justice system (Siegel & Welsh, 2009). By 1925, juvenile courts were established in every state and most local jurisdictions.

The Juvenile Rights Period (1960–1980)

This period in the history of juvenile justice was typified by five significant court cases (1966–1975) plus the Juvenile Justice and Delinquency Prevention Act of 1974. All of this legislation sought to bring more structure to the system and protections to juveniles than had been previously provided by the philosophy of *parens patriae*.

Kent v. United States, 383 U.S. 541 (1966)

Morris Kent Jr. was arrested for housebreaking, robbery, and rape at the age of 16. Kent admitted to the charges. Kent was held in detention, and the judge transferred his case to adult criminal court. But Kent never received a hearing. The Kent decision challenged the juvenile court's lack of procedural and evidentiary standards and is credited with providing children due process rights, such as having an attorney present during transfer hearings (*Kent v. United States*, 1966; Ketcham, 1996).

In re Gault, 387 U.S. 1 (1967)

Fifteen-year-old Gerald Gault was taken into police custody for allegedly making a lewd telephone call to a neighbor. The hearing took place in the judge's chambers without the accuser present, without any attorneys present, without any record of the proceedings, and without having sworn anyone in for the process. The judge committed Gault to the state industrial school until he turned 21 years old. Gault filed for a writ of habeas corpus to challenge the juvenile court's constitutionality on the grounds of denial of procedural due process rights. The Supreme Court overruled Gault's conviction, deciding that juveniles have due process rights, including notice of the charges, right to counsel, right to confrontation and cross-examination, the privilege against self-incrimination, right to a transcript of the trial record, and right to appellate review (*In re Gault*, Oyez, 1966).

In re Winship, 397 U.S. 358 (1970)

Samuel Winship was arrested and charged for going into a women's locker and stealing $112 from her pocketbook at the age of 12. Based on a preponderance of the evidence, Winship was adjudicated "delinquent." He was committed to a training school for 18 months with a possible extension until he turned 18. The Supreme Court determined that the 14th Amendment due process clause protects the accused against conviction except upon proof beyond a reasonable doubt (Oyez, 1969).

McKeiver v. Pennsylvania, 403 U.S. 528 (1971)

Joseph McKeiver, 15, and Edward Terry, 16, were charged with robbery, larceny, assault, and escape. In the juvenile court of Pennsylvania, these charges are all felonies, and both McKeiver and Terry were denied the right to a jury trial. McKeiver challenged the right to a jury trial as a juvenile using the 14th Amendment due process clause. The Supreme Court upheld the decision that juveniles do not have the right to a jury trial, stating that jury trials would cause delays and would be public and that juvenile proceedings should instead emphasize fact-finding (Oyez, 1970).

Breed v. Jones, 421 U.S. 519 (1975)

A juvenile court adjudicated 17-year-old Gary Jones delinquent for acts that would be considered robbery if he was tried as an adult. Following the hearing, the courts decided that Jones should be tried as an adult. Jones filed a habeas corpus on the grounds that the criminal trial would be double jeopardy, or prosecuting a person more than once for the same offense. The trial court, court of appeal, and Supreme Court of California denied the writ. The case went to trial, and the court found Jones guilty of robbery in the first degree.

Jones again filed for a writ of habeas corpus asserting double jeopardy. The federal district court denied the petition, stating that the juvenile and criminal court trials are different, so double jeopardy does not apply. The U.S. Court of Appeals court reversed the decision, suggesting that it is double jeopardy even if juvenile and criminal proceedings are different. The Supreme Court upheld the decision, stating that the juvenile court has the chance to determine if a juvenile should be tried as an adult in the preliminary hearing (Oyez, 1974).

The Juvenile Justice and Delinquency Prevention Act of 1974

In 1974, Congress enacted the Juvenile Justice and Delinquency Prevention Act (JJDPA; Pub. L. No. 93-415, 42 U.S.C. § 5601 et seq.). The JJDPA of 1974 legislated two core requirements: deinstitutionalization of status offenders and "sight and sound" separation. Status offenses are unique to the juvenile justice system because if adults committed these offenses, they would not be considered crimes—examples including truancy, running away, etc. The "sight and sound" separation requirement is designed to keep youthful offenders separated from adults in detention, jails, and lock-ups such that they cannot be seen or heard by one another. The JJDPA also created the Formula Grants program and eliminated the Youth Development and Delinquency Prevention Administration, replacing it with the federal Office of Juvenile Justice and Delinquency Prevention (OJJDP) designed to support local and state efforts to prevent delinquency and improve the juvenile justice system. This act guides national juvenile justice planning and allocates federal funding for delinquency prevention and juvenile justice reform.

The JJDPA was amended and reauthorized in 1976, 1977, 1980, and 1988. In 1977, the JJDPA further emphasized prevention and treatment versus detention and incarceration for youth, and it strengthened and expanded the deinstitutionalize status offenders (DSO) "sight and sound" separation requirements. The 1980 reauthorization added the valid court order exception to the DSO requirement and implemented the jail removal requirement (mainly in response to research on high suicide rates; frequent physical, mental, and sexual assault by adult inmates and staff; inadequate educational, recreation, and vocational programming; negative labeling and self-images; and contact with serious offenders or inmates with severe mental health challenges for youth incarcerated in adult facilities). (See the next section for a discussion of the JJDPA after 1980.)

The Crime Control Period (1980–2000)

Toward the end of the 1970s, Americans began to criticize the effectiveness of the juvenile justice system and feared a rise in juvenile crime. According to Hess and Drowns (2004, pp. 32–33):

> Citizens and lawmakers, amid mounting skepticism of the principles established by the JJDP Act, began calling for more punitive measures against juvenile offenders, especially those who committed serious or violent felonies. The result was a much harsher attitude toward youth crime and a call to "get tough" with youthful lawbreakers, philosophies characteristic of the crime control period.

The Reagan administration vowed to crack down on juvenile delinquency, drug and alcohol abuse, teenage pregnancy, and youth suicide. The five foci of the Reagan administration's juvenile crime control policies were preventative detention, transfer of violent juveniles to adult court, mandatory and determinate sentencing for violent juveniles, increased confinement of juveniles, and enforcement of the death penalty for juveniles who commit brutal and senseless murders (Bartollas, 2006).

During this period, in 1988, the JJDPA was amended again to include attention to the overrepresentation of youth of color in the juvenile justice system (McCarter, 2011). The Disproportionate Minority Confinement (DMC) stipulation required states to assess and address the number of children of color in secure juvenile confinement. In 1992, the DMC was elevated to a core requirement of the JJDPA, meaning that 25% of each state's Formula Grant allocation could be withheld if efforts were not taken to address and reduce disproportionate minority confinement.

Current Period (2000–Today)

There is no consensus among juvenile justice scholars or forensic social work practitioners regarding whether the United States has transitioned from the crime control period or not. Yet, there is recognition within social work that when the pendulum swung away from rehabilitation and more toward punishment in the 1980s, the profession largely left juvenile justice work (Scheyett et al., 2012). Scholars attribute this shift to three primary reasons: (a) a dearth of effective practice techniques and rehabilitation for offenders, (b) philosophical differences between social work and law enforcement/corrections, and (c) few juvenile and/or criminal justice training opportunities and field placements provided in schools of social work (Ivanoff et al., 1993). Those who suggest that the United States has moved beyond the crime control period essentially suggest that the new era is more aligned with social work values and is responsible for increasing interest in the field of forensic social work (Scheyett et al., 2012).

In 2002, the JJDPA was reauthorized in 2002 as the Juvenile Justice and Delinquency Prevention Act of 2002, enacted as Title II, Subtitle B, of the 21st Century Department of Justice Appropriations Authorization Act (Pub. L. 107-273). The 2002 reauthorization included a third amendment that changed DMC language from "disproportionate minority confinement" to "disproportionate minority contact." This change in vernacular acknowledged the overrepresentation of youth of color in stages before incarceration and recognized that systemic influences might also need to be examined to reduce disproportionality in the system (McCarter, 2011). This legislation also applied to JJDPA grant programs through fiscal year 2007 or 2008, but unbeknownst to legislators at the time; this would be the last reauthorization of the JJDPA until 2018.

On December 21, 2018, the JJDPA was reauthorized for 5 years through the Juvenile Justice Reform Act of 2018. Because the act had not been reauthorized since 2002, forensic social workers across the country viewed the 2018 legislative action as potential for justice reform (Coalition for Juvenile Justice, n.d.). The latest reauthorization includes several specific policy changes: (a) strengthens the decarceration of status offenders, (b) extends sight and sound separation to juveniles tried as adults, and (c) revises DMC (disproportionate minority contact) to racial and ethnic disparities (RED) in juvenile justice. The intent of this change is not documented, but "racial and ethnic disparities" is a more precise terminology since there are jurisdictions in which youth of color make up the statistical majority, the term "minority" indicates a less powerful or "less than" position, and stating "ethnicity" elevates the experiences of additional groups including Latinx youth.

The Juvenile Justice Reform Act of 2018 also includes new requirements for states. The act mandates states to reduce the overrepresentation of youth of color in the juvenile justice system, requires states to submit a 3-year plan that explains how their juvenile justice practices are guided by neuroscience and research on adolescent brain development and behavior, and includes additional stipulations for states' Formula Grant funding. Moreover, the act eliminates particular restraints on pregnant juvenile inmates, imposes other valid court order exceptions for status offenders, supports the educational progress of youthful offenders by requiring compliance with Part A of Title I of the Elementary and Secondary Education Act of 1965, and implements systems to screen for, identify, and document domestic human trafficking.

Finally, the act also includes elements of the Youth PROMISE Act (the Youth Prison Reduction Through Opportunities, Mentoring, Intervention, Support, and Education Act), first proposed in 2009. The 2018 reauthorization also requires that states' advisory group (SAG) members have specific expertise (e.g., in adolescent development) and qualifications (e.g., mental health or substance abuse state licenses). As amended, Section 223(a)(3) of the 1974 JJDPA designates group representation—for example, members of victims' or witness-advocacy groups, tribal representation, and members of the impacted group (such as those who are or have been under the jurisdiction of the juvenile justice system or a parent or guardian; codified as amended at 34 U.S.C. § 11133 (a)(3) (2018)). The SAG provisions also note the importance of cross-sector collaboration, including more formalized school-justice partnerships and community-based prevention and treatment services.

The **Comprehensive Youth Justice Amendment Act** (DC Law 21-0238, 2016) was passed unanimously by the DC Council in fall 2016 and became law in April 2017. This act is a true paradigm shift in juvenile justice reform. It strives to decriminalize juveniles and instead focus on ways to rehabilitate youth and help them be productive members of society. The Comprehensive Youth Justice Amendment has five active foci: (a) preventing children from entering the juvenile or criminal justice systems, (b) reducing current overincarceration rates, (c) providing age-appropriate sentences for youth, (d) improving confinement conditions (for those who need out-of-home placements), and (f) expanding the oversight of services.

Finally, the **Juvenile Incarceration Reduction Act** (H.R. 7644, 2020) was introduced to the U.S. House by John Lewis the day before he died. The act highlights the bias of risk and needs assessments. The Juvenile Incarceration Reduction Act would ban or limit risk and needs assessments in federal cases with minors to (a) decide whether a child should be tried as an adult, (b) determine one's likelihood of recidivism, (c) decide whether a child should be held in detention during the trial or before the adjudication of guilty or not guilty, and (d) determine eligibility for a recidivism reduction program. Since being introduced on July 16, 2020, the act has not been cosponsored by any other House member, nor has it been voted on by the House Judiciary Committee.

Intersection of Forensic Social Work and Juvenile Justice Policy

Historically, social work was very involved in juvenile/criminal justice. But during the crime control period, when the nature of justice became more punitive and less rehabilitative, instead of challenging this shift, social work largely left forensic, juvenile, and criminal justice settings (Scheyett et al., 2012). As the War on Drugs and mass incarceration have proven to be epic failures, social workers' interest and critical involvement in forensic social work, and juvenile justice specifically, has burgeoned. Forensic social workers often bridge transdisciplinary collaborations in juvenile justice as well, often including partners from child welfare, health/mental health/substance use, juvenile courts, and education systems, and from law enforcement (e.g., police officers, school resource officers, probation officers), the courts (e.g., defense attorneys, prosecutors, judges), and other service providers (e.g., teachers, counselors, social workers, health care providers; McCarter et al., 2017).

Applying a Critical Lens to Forensic Social Work in Juvenile Justice Policy

Critical race theory (CRT) can be used to assess the juvenile justice system as an examination of the social construction of race in this system. CRT has been used to evaluate and challenge how race and racial power are constructed and embodied in the U.S. legal culture

(Delgado & Stefancic, 2017). Critical race theorists suggest that legal scholarship must include discussions of how racial power is constructed and exercised legally and ideologically (Crenshaw et al., 1996). This discourse provides insight into the disparate racial/ethnic data within each level of the juvenile justice system and between systems, such as in the cases of the school-to-prison pipeline (education and justice systems; McCarter, 2017), crossover youth (child welfare and justice systems; Ryan et al., 2008), and justice-involved youth with mental health challenges (Liebenberg & Ungar, 2014).

CRT suggests that "race-neutral" policies keep Black, Indigenous, and other people of color (BIPOC) youth trapped in a lower caste that increases their disproportionate involvement with the juvenile justice system while advantaging youth who identify as White (Crenshaw et al., 1996). Racism and the racialized power within the juvenile justice system wrongfully convict youths of color at higher rates (Birckhead, 2017). CRT asserts that even the data disseminated and the stories being told about BIPOC youth and their juvenile justice involvement are conveyed through the lens of White supremacy. CRT questions who controls the narratives and imagery about youth of color and their involvement with juvenile justice. Applying a critical lens to the juvenile justice system should be conducted at the micro, mezzo, and macro levels.

A micro-level example is the emotional impact on juveniles housed in youth detention centers. Incarceration can increase misbehavior from youth trying to manage the emotional impact of detention and their mental, educational, and behavioral problems (Crosby, 2016). The internalizing and externalizing behaviors that youth experience while in youth detention centers could be addressed by mental health professionals/forensic social workers within the facilities.

A mezzo-level example is school discipline. A study of Missouri schools found that African American students experienced higher rates of juvenile court referrals than White students (Nicholson-Crotty et al., 2009). Additionally, "although their behaviors are no more problematic than their peers, children of color and children of color with disabilities are punished at higher rates" than their White counterparts (Hughes et al., 2020, p. 72). School social workers and forensic social workers with a critical race lens should help create and revise discipline policies within schools.

A macro-level example is the criminalization of young children and the overrepresentation of Black youth in the juvenile justice system (Abrams et al., 2021). This mixed-method study from California suggests that discretion in school-based discipline and arrests contributes to the disparities. Forensic social work macro practitioners could work toward two macro-level solutions—increasing alternatives to formal juvenile justice processing and raising the minimum age of justice involvement.

Grand Challenge Juvenile Justice Policy Recommendations

In 2013, the American Academy of Social Work and Social Welfare identified the grand challenges for social work (https://grandchallengesforsocialwork.org/). These challenges represent a professional initiative to champion social progress powered by science. In June 2020, a working paper to address juvenile justice was added to the social work grand challenge to Achieve Equal Opportunity and Justice. This working paper identifies the following five actionable and measurable goals to improve the equality and justice of the U.S. juvenile system in the next 5 to 10 years.

Assess Relative Rate Indices Across All Nine Contact Points for All Vulnerable Populations

Data collection requirements for the OJJDP changed in 2019 to lower the required number of contact points from nine to five. The required contact points now include (a) arrest, (b) diversion/not approved for court, (c) detention, (d) placement, and (e) transfer to adult/criminal justice. The OJJDP's website indicates that this updated the data collection process by utilizing the most important contact points supported by research. However, juvenile justice researchers contend that narrowing the data collection points is due to the notable federal funding cuts made to the OJJDP and that collecting data at all nine contact points is the best strategy to address disparities within juvenile justice (Tamilin et al., 2019). These disparities also require context for the data collected, and scholars recommend using relative rate indices. Finally, the 2018 reauthorization of the JJDPA replaced the term "disproportionate minority contact" with "racial and ethnic disparities." This is important because mathematical majorities vary by jurisdiction, the term "minority" suggests "less than," and racial equity advocates are striving not simply for proportionality but also equity (McCarter et al., 2017). This advocacy also extends to other marginalized groups in juvenile justice (e.g., students with disabilities; lesbian, gay, bisexual, and transgender youth; students from households with low socioeconomic status) such that their outcomes in juvenile justice are also evaluated (Kim et al., 2020).

Increase Positive Discipline Options to Dismantle the School-to-Prison Pipeline and Decriminalize Nonviolent School Behaviors and Status Offenses

A single suspension increases the likelihood that students may drop out, repeat a grade, and enter the juvenile justice system (Fabelo et al., 2011; Losen et al., 2014). And youth who contact the juvenile justice system are at a higher risk of depression and suicide, have lower educational attainment, and have fewer employment opportunities (Holman & Ziedenberg, 2013; Robinson & Kurlychek, 2019; Sharlein, 2018). Therefore, the goal should be to prevent children from justice system contact. School discipline is currently meted out by school resource officers (SROs) who focus more on a law enforcement approach to school discipline (McCarter, 2016). Approaching school discipline from this perspective without a thorough education in child and adolescent development puts youth at risk of contacting the juvenile justice system. Instead, positive discipline options for nonviolent school behaviors and status offenses would decriminalize youth and dismantle the school-to-prison pipeline. Providing educators with positive discipline keeps students engaged, increases educational outcomes, and leads to higher graduation rates (Kim et al., 2020). Therefore, the following three goals are suggested: (a) establish official school-justice partnerships in various states, (b) decrease the use of zero-tolerance policies in various states and increase the use of positive discipline strategies and strategies, and (c) reduce in-school arrests for nonviolent behaviors (Kim et al., 2020).

Offer Diversion Alternatives for First-Time and Low-Risk Offenders

Diversion keeps youth from being formally processed through the court system while also holding them accountable for their behaviors. Diversion programs are designed to reduce the impact of labeling, redirect developing offending patterns (Sullivan et al., 2007), connect youth with relevant services, and lessen the chances of youth socializing with other offenders and learning disorderly attitudes (Loeb et al., 2015). And diversion is very effective for first-time and/or low-risk offenders (H. A. Wilson & Hoge, 2012). Forensic social worker practitioners recommend incorporating diversion into 25% of the school-justice partnerships and increasing the number of low-risk and first-time offenders diverted by 50% (Kim et al., 2020).

Implement a Consistent Age of Criminal Responsibility at 21 Years, Keeping Youth in the Juvenile Justice System Through the Age of 20 Years

The age at which offenders are considered adults varies by state in the United States (Menon & McCarter, 2021). This lack of a consistent age of majority for criminal responsibility advantages some while disadvantaging others. In 2017, two states defined the age of criminal responsibility or considered individuals as adults at 16 years old and older, and six states considered those 17 years old and older as adults (Hockenberry & Puzzanchera, 2019). Finally, five out of every 1,000 juvenile cases (1%) were transferred to criminal court (Hockenberry, 2021).

Whether a young person is served by the juvenile or adult court varies by age, offense, and geography. Since 2007, 11 states have enacted legislation to raise the age of criminal responsibility to 18 years old: Connecticut (2007), Illinois (2010), Mississippi (2010), Massachusetts (2013), New Hampshire (2014), Louisiana (2016), South Carolina (2016), New York (2017), North Carolina (2017), Missouri (2018), and Michigan (2019; Justice Policy Institute, 2017). There are currently three states whose upper age of juvenile jurisdiction is set at 17 years old: Georgia, Texas, and Wisconsin (Campaign for Youth Justice, 2019; Justice Policy Institute, 2017; Puzzanchera, 2018). Vermont is the first state in the United States whose upper age of the juvenile is raised to 20 years old (Vastine & Chester, 2019).

Raising the age is congruent with the social work value of social justice and the grand challenge to Achieve Equal Opportunity and Justice (Kim et al., 2020; Menon & McCarter, 2021). Keeping youth in the juvenile justice system improves their community and institutional safety outcomes and educational outcomes, lessens the impact of a criminal record, lowers recidivism rates, increases parent and family involvement as well as cost-effectiveness for states, and delivers more developmentally appropriate services (Kim et al.,

2020). Therefore, most practitioners and scholars recommend setting the age of criminal responsibility to at least 21 years (Farrington et al., 2017). Moreover, given the reauthorization of the JJDPA and a new federal administration that supports improving equity in justice systems, there is currently strong bipartisan support for this particular juvenile justice reform. Forensic social workers are specifically suited to change policy to improve equity and the lives of youth, their families, and communities by raising the national age in juvenile justice to 20 years old.

Employ a Rigorous Wraparound Model to Improve Reentry Success for Youth Transitioning From Justice Systems Back Into Their Communities

The wraparound model has been successful with justice-involved youth and offers interrelated services that engage youth, peer support/community systems, and families (Howell et al., 2004). The wraparound model was developed in the 1980s and provides a collaborative and coordinated response of practitioners designed to streamline service delivery. The model is strengths based, family centered, and culturally sensitive, and flexible enough to individualize each service plan to the young person's needs, values, and talents (Snyder et al., 2012). Finally, wraparound services require a team-based approach with the child, family, and service practitioners in developing, implementing, and evaluating each part of the service plan (Carney & Buttell, 2003; K. J. Wilson, 2008). This fosters positive youth, cost, and system outcomes (Bruns et al., 2004). Probation reform is also required to help youth return to their homes/communities and not return to justice facilities. Technical or probation violations were the most serious offenses for 23% of detained youth in 2015 (Hockenberry & Puzzanchera, 2018). Furthermore, significant racial disparities continue: Youth of color account for nearly 70% of youth committed to a residential facility for a technical violation (Hockenberry & Puzzanchera, 2018). The Urban Institute reported that wraparound services could lessen the number of youth in violation of their probation conditions (Esthappan et al., 2019).

References

Abrams, L. S., Mizel, M. L., & Barnert, E. S. (2021). The criminalization of young children and overrepresentation of Black youth in the juvenile justice system. *Race and Social Problems, 13*(1), 73–84. https://doi.org/10.1007/s12552-021-09314-7

Bartollas, C. (2006). *Juvenile delinquency* (7th ed.). Allyn & Bacon.

Birckhead, T. R. (2017). The racialization of juvenile justice and the role of the defense attorney. *Boston College Law Review, 58*(2), 379.

Bruns, E. J., Walker, J. S., Adams, J., Miles, P., Osher, T. W., Rast, J., VanDenBerg, J. D., & Campaign for Youth Justice. (2019). *2019 Legislation on youth prosecuted as adults in the states.* http://campaignforyouthjustice.org/2019/item/2019-legislation-on-youth-prosecuted-as-adults-in-the-states

Carney, M. M., & Buttell, F. (2003). Reducing juvenile recidivism: Evaluating the wraparound services model. *Research on Social Work Practice, 13*(5), 551–568. https://doi.org/10.1177/1049731503253364

Coalition for Juvenile Justice. (n.d.) https://www.juvjustice.org/

Comprehensive Youth Justice Amendment Act of 2016. https://code.dccouncil.us/dc/council/laws/21-238.html

Crenshaw, K., Gotanda, N., Peller, G., & Thomas, K. (1996). *Critical race theory: The key writings that formed the movement.* New Press.

Crosby, S. (2016). Trauma-informed approaches to juvenile justice: A critical race perspective. *Juvenile and Family Court Journal, 67*(1), 5–18. https://doi.org/10.1111/jfcj.12052.

Delgado, R., & Stefancic, J. (2017). *Critical race theory: An introduction* (3rd ed.). New York University Press.

Esthappan, S., Lacoe, J., & Young, D. (2019). *Juvenile probation transformation: Applying the approach in Lucas County, OH, and Pierce County, WA.* Urban Institute. https://www.urban.org/research/publication/juvenile-probation-transformation

Fabelo, T., Thompson, M. D., Plotkin, M., Carmichael, D., Marchbanks, M. P., III, & Booth, E. A. (2011). *Breaking schools' rules: A statewide study of how school discipline relates to students' success and juvenile justice involvement.* Council of State Governments Justice Center and Public Policy Research Institute. https://ppri.tamu.edu/files/Breaking_Schools_Rules.pdf

Farrington, D. P., Loeber, R., & Howell, J. C. (2017). Increasing the minimum age for adult court: Is it desirable, and what are the effects? *Criminology & Public Policy, 16*(1), 83–92. doi:10.1111/1745-9133.12259

Hess, K. M., & Drowns, R. W. (2004). *Juvenile justice* (4th ed.). Wadsworth/Thomson Learning.

Hockenberry, S. (2021). *Delinquency cases waived to criminal court, 2018.* Office of Juvenile Justice and Delinquency Prevention. https://ojjdp.ojp.gov/publications/delinquency-cases-waived-2018.pdfHockenberry, S., & Puzzanchera, C. (2018). *Juvenile court statistics 2016.* Office of Juvenile Justice and Delinquency Prevention. https://www.ojjdp.gov/ojstatbb/njcda/pdf/jcs2016.pdf

Hockenberry, S., & Puzzanchera, C. (2019). *Juvenile court statistics 2017.* Office of Juvenile Justice and Delinquency Prevention. http://www.ncjj.org/pdf/jcsreports/jcs2017report.pdf

Holman, B., & Ziedenberg, J. (2013). *The dangers of detention: The impact of incarcerating youth in detention and other secure facilities.* Justice Policy Institute. http://www.justicepolicy.org/images/upload/06-11_rep_dangersofdetention_jj.pdf

Howell, J. C., Kelly, M. R., Palmer, J., & Mangum, R. L. (2004). Integrating child welfare, juvenile justice, and other agencies in a continuum of care. *Child Welfare, 83*(2), 143–156.

Ivanoff, A., Smyth, N., & Finnegan, D. (1993). Social work behind bars: Preparation for fieldwork in correctional institutions. *Journal of Teaching in Social Work, 7,* 137–147. doi:10.1300/J067v07n01_11

Justice Policy Institute. (2017). *Raise the age: Shifting to a safer and more effective juvenile justice system.* http://www.justicepolicy.org/uploads/ justicepolicy/documents/raisetheage.fullreport.pdf

Juvenile Incarceration Reduction Act of 2020. https://www.congress.gov/bill/116th-congress/house-bill/7644/text?r=1&s=1

Kent v. United States, 383 U.S. 541. (1966). https://njdc.info/wp-content/uploads/2013/11/Kent-v-United-States-slip-opinion.pdf

Ketcham, O. W. (1996, June/July). *Kent revised.* Office of Justice Program. https://www.ojp.gov/library/abstracts/kent-revisited

Kim, B. E., McCarter, S., & Logan-Greene, P. (2020). *Achieving equal opportunity and justice in juvenile justice* (Grand Challenges for Social Work Initiative Working Paper No. 25). Grand Challenges for Social Work. https://grandchallengesforsocialwork.org/wp-content/uploads/2020/06/Achieving-Equal-Opportunity-and-Justice-in-Juvenile-Justice-3.pdf

Liebenberg, L., & Ungar, M. (2014). A comparison of service use among youth involved with juvenile justice and mental health. *Children and Youth Services Review, 39,* 117–122. doi:10.1016/j.childyouth.2014.02.007

Loeb, R. C., Waung, M., & Sheeran, M. (2015). Individual and familial variables for predicting successful completion of a juvenile justice diversion program. *Journal of Offender Rehabilitation, 54*(3), 212–237. doi:10.1080/10509674.2015.1023482

Losen, D., Hewitt, D., & Toldson, I. (2014). *Eliminating excessive and unfair exclusionary discipline in schools: Policy recommendations for reducing.* National Juvenile Justice Network. http://www.njjn.org/uploads/digital-library/OSF_Discipline-Disparities_Disparity_Policy_3.18.14.pdf

Hughes, T., Raines, T., & Malone, C. (2020). School pathways to the juvenile justice system. *Policy Insights from the Behavioral and Brain Sciences, 7*(1), 72–79. https://doi.org/10.1177/2372732219897093

McCarter, S. A. (2011). Disproportionate minority contact in the American juvenile justice system: Where are we after 20 years, a philosophy shift, and three amendments? *Journal of Forensic Social Work, 1*(1), 96–107. https://doi.org/10.1080/1936928X.2011.541217

McCarter, S. A. (2017). The school-to-prison pipeline: A primer for social workers. *Social Work, 62*(1), 53–61. https://doi.org/10.1093/sw/sww078

McCarter, S. A. (2018). Adolescence. In E. D. Hutchison (Ed.), *Dimensions of human behavior: The changing life course* (6th ed., pp. 189–230). Sage.

McCarter, S. A., Chinn-Gary, E., Trosch, L. A., Jr., Toure, A., Alsaeedi, A., & Harrington, J. (2017). Bringing racial justice to the courtroom and community: Race Matters for Juvenile Justice and the Charlotte Model. *Washington and Lee Law Review, 73*(2), 641–686. https://scholarlycommons.law.wlu.edu/wlulr-online/vol73/iss2/6/

Menon, S. E., & McCarter, S. A. (2021). Make juvenile justice more just: Raise-the-age to 20 years old. *Journal of Policy Practice and Research, 2*, 119–139. https://doi.org/10.1007/s42972-021-00030-5

Nicholson-Crotty, S., Birchmeier, Z., & Valentine, D. (2009). Exploring the impact of school discipline on racial disproportion in the juvenile justice system. *Social Science Quarterly, 90*(4), 1003–1018. https://doi.org/10.1111/j.1540-6237.2009.00674.x

Office of Juvenile Justice and Delinquency Prevention (OJJDP). (2022). https://ojjdp.ojp.gov/about/legislation

Oyez. (1966). *In re Gault.* https://www.oyez.org/cases/1966/116

Oyez. (1969). *In re Winship.* https://www.oyez.org/cases/1969/778

Oyez. (1970). *McKeiver v. Pennsylvania.* https://www.oyez.org/cases/1970/322

Oyez. (1974). *Breed v. Jones.* https://www.oyez.org/cases/1974/73-1995

Popple, P. R., & Leighninger, L. L. (1996). *Social work, social welfare, and American society* (3rd ed.). Allyn & Bacon.

Puzzanchera, C. (2018). *Juvenile arrests 2016.* Office of Juvenile Justice and Delinquency Prevention. https://www.ojjdp.gov/pubs/251861.pdf

Roberts, A. R., & Brownell, P. (1999). A century of forensic social work: Bridging the past to the present. *Social Work, 44*(4), 359–356. https://doi.org/10.1093/sw/44.4.359

Robinson, K., & Kurlychek, M. (2019). Differences in justice, differences in outcomes: A DID approach to studying outcomes in juvenile and adult court processing. *Justice Evaluation Journal, 2*(1), 35–49. doi:10.1080/24751979.2019.1585927

Ryan, J. P., Testa, M. F., & Zhai, F. (2008). African American males in foster care and the risk of delinquency: The values of social bonds and permanence. *Child Welfare, 87*(1), 115–140.

Scheyett, A., Pettus-Davis, C., McCarter, S., & Brigham, R. (2012). Social work and criminal justice: Are we meeting in the field? *Journal of Teaching in Social Work, 32*(4), 438–450. https://doi.org/10.1080/08841233.2012.705241

Sharlein, J. (2018). Beyond recidivism: Investigating comparative educational and employment outcomes for adolescents in the juvenile and criminal justice systems. *Crime & Delinquency, 64*(1), 26–52. doi:10.1177/0011128716678193

Siegel, L. J., & Welsh, B. C. (2009). *Juvenile delinquency: Theory, practice, and law* (10th ed.). Wadsworth.

Snyder, E. H., Lawrence, C. N., & Dodge, K. A. (2012). The impact of system of care support in adherence to wraparound principles in Child and Family Teams in child welfare in North Carolina. *Children and Youth Services Review, 34*, 639–647. doi:10.1016/j.childyouth.2011.12.010

Sullivan, C. J., Veysey, B. M., Hamilton, Z. K., & Grillo, M. (2007). Reducing out-of-community placement and recidivism: Diversion of delinquent youth with mental health and substance use problems from the justice system. *International Journal of Offender Therapy and Comparative Criminology, 51*(5), 555–577. doi:10.1177/0306624X06296237

Tamilin, E., Behrendt-Mihalski, J., McCarter, S., Daroowalla, P., Sekle, S., & Cumby, H. (2019, October). *Juvenile justice in Mecklenburg County: National Juvenile Justice Awareness Month.* Race Matters for Juvenile Justice and the Council for Children's Rights. https://rmjj.org/wp-content/uploads/2019/11/2019JuvenileJusticeAwarenessMonth-FINALREPORT.pdf

Vastine, K., & Chester, L. (2019, November 13). *Act 201 implementation: Vermont's Raise the Age Initiative* [Presentation]. https://legislature.vermont.gov/Documents/2020/WorkGroups/Justice%20Oversight/ Juvenile%20Justice/W~Karen%20Vastine~Act%20201%20Implementation-%20Vermont%27s%20 Raise%20the%20Age%20Initiative%20~11-13 -2019.pdf

Wilson, H. A., & Hoge, R. D. (2012). The effect of youth diversion programs on recidivism: A meta-analytic review. *Criminal Justice and Behavior, 40*(5), 497–518. doi:10.1177/00938548 12451089

Wilson, K. J. (2008). *Literature review: Wraparound services for juvenile and adult offender populations.* Center for Public Policy Research.

20

Civil Commitment Policies

Anthony P. Natale

Involuntary Civil Commitment Policies: Implications for Social Workers

Abridging the civil rights of another is perhaps the gravest decision a social worker can make in practice. The decisions involved often have implications that have life and death in the balance. As such, social workers are advantaged by knowledge of civil commitment policies. This chapter will provide the overarching goals for civil commitment policies and review different types of civil commitment. Next, the emergency detention policies that regulate detention are reviewed, including variations between states. A detailed overview of civil commitment policy development, which underscores important implications for social work practice, is provided. The next section of the chapter focuses on vulnerable populations implicated in the application of civil commitment policies. The chapter closes with a review of the knowledge base, values, and ethics of social work involved in civil commitment policies.

Involuntary Civil Commitment Background and Context

Involuntary civil commitment is a legal process that generally refers to an individual's involuntary commitment to a psychiatric institution, either inpatient or outpatient, for further evaluation, treatment, and stabilization. Civil commitment policies exist in all 50 states and Washington, DC. However, Hedman et al. (2016) highlight differences between state laws in hold duration, who can initiate an emergency hold, judicial oversight, and clients' rights during a hold. A civil commitment provides for assessment and treatment of mental illness, chemical dependency, and harmful behaviors among those with developmental disabilities, when an individual is unable or unwilling to seek evaluation or treatment on their own, to protect themselves or others from severe harm due to the illness or disability (Hedman et al., 2016).

Several conditions are required to meet the standards for civil commitment: (a) the dangerous behaviors present a clear and present danger to the individual or someone else; (b) the

Anthony P. Natale, *Civil Commitment Policies* In: *Handbook of Forensic Social Work*. Edited by: David Axlyn McLeod, Anthony P. Natale, and Kristin W. Mapson, Oxford University Press. © Oxford University Press 2024. DOI: 10.1093/oso/9780197694732.003.0020 dangerous behaviors clearly stem from a mental illness, chemical dependency, or developmental disability; (c) the behaviors exhibited through mental illness, chemical dependency, or developmental disability are amenable to treatment; and (d) the individual is not consenting, or cannot consent, to treatment. The U.S. Supreme Court characterizes involuntary civil commitment as a massive curtailment of liberty against those who have committed no crime (Substance Abuse and Mental Health Services Administration [SAHMSA], 2019).

Tracking the number of Americans impacted by involuntary civil commitment policies is difficult. SAMSHA (2019) indicates that for 2015, on average, across the states, evaluators for civil commitment detain an estimated nine out of every 1,000 persons with a serious mental illness. Each state varies in its estimated annual commitment rate, from a low of 0.23 per 1,000 persons with serious mental illness in Hawaii to 43.8 per 1,000 persons with serious mental illness in Wisconsin. Swanson et al. (2003) found lifetime civil commitment rates variable by state, perhaps impacted by the state laws themselves, with a higher commitment rate of 12.8% in Florida than a low of 4.7% in Connecticut.

Civil Commitment Types

A civil commitment can lead to three distinct types of involuntary treatment (Figure 20.1). The first type is emergency hospitalization for evaluation, which is the assessment for emergency detention that 31 states have given social workers the right to initiate by law. Time limits vary by state, although in general, this evaluation period lasts for up to 72 hours for evaluation and stabilization. The second type of inpatient civil commitment occurs if the behaviors persist that warranted the emergency evaluation. A judge assesses if the individual behaviors continue to meet the state's civil commitment criteria. Social workers can

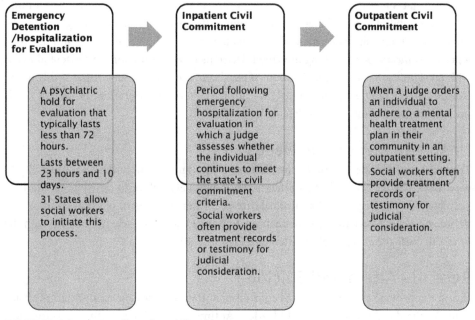

FIGURE 20.1 Involuntary Commitment Types

provide treatment notes and testimony to assist the court in its assessment. The final type of involuntary treatment under civil commitment exists in 46 states: Outpatient civil commitment occurs when individuals are mandated to adhere to a mental health treatment plan in their community (SAHMSA, 2019).

Involuntary Civil Commitment Criteria

Dangerous Due to Mental Illness

The Treatment Advocacy Center (TAC) provides a state-level guide for examining civil commitment laws' differences. The dangerousness standard exists in all 50 states, although four do not require that the dangerousness is due to mental illness. The dangerousness standard includes both danger to oneself (suicide) and danger to others (assault, homicide). States such as Hawaii and Washington also include danger to property under the dangerousness criteria when an individual with a mental illness inflicts or threatens to inflict damage to any property in a manner that constitutes a crime (TAC, 2020).

While dangerousness remains a category in all 50 states, the criteria for establishing it varies by state. In most states, dangerousness infers the likelihood of risk to violent physical behavior. But in states like Iowa, persons may be committed because of inflicting serious emotional injury on another person. Also, over time, the criteria for dangerousness have changed. Initially, dangerousness required an assessment of imminent dangerousness linked to a recent overt act. Now the risk presented no longer needs to be imminent or immediate for dangerousness criteria to be met (TAC, 2020).

Gravely Disabled

Nineteen states provide criteria for civil commitment due to grave disability. The framings of grave disability across the states hold some differences in wording but generally the same intent. Grave disability generally means that as a result of a mental health disorder, a person is incapable of making informed decisions or providing for their essential needs without significant supervision. Without supervision, their risk of substantial bodily harm, worsening concomitant condition, significant psychiatric deterioration, or critical needs mismanagement results in considerable harm (TAC, 2020).

Unable to Meet Basic Needs

Ten states provide the criteria for involuntary civil commitment based on an inability to meet basic needs. Generally, this refers to an individual's failure to satisfy their need for nourishment, clothing, essential medical care, or shelter resulting in physical injury, debilitation, or death. States that use the inability to self-care standards do not overlap with the others that use the grave disability standard (TAC, 2020).

Recently Attempted Suicide

Five states provide criteria for a civil commitment that includes a recently attempted suicide, despite the absence of present ideation. At times it is included in the dangerousness provision, as is the case in Missouri, while in North Carolina, the criteria stand alone (TAC, 2020).

Civil Commitment Initiation

All 50 states permit police or peace officers the authority to initiate emergency holds. In contrast, only 31 states provide criteria that include mental health practitioners (social workers, psychologists, counselors), and 22 states allow medical personnel (physicians and nurses) to initiate an emergency hold. In comparison, in 22 states, any interested person (family, guardian, or friend) can begin an emergency hold. Eight states (Connecticut, Georgia, Illinois, Hawaii, Massachusetts, Minnesota, New Jersey, Rhode Island) expressly mentioned social workers as those who initiate emergency commitments. State statutes in Colorado, Florida, and New York specify that social workers can participate in a free detention emergency hearing, while state statutes in North Dakota, Nevada, and Wyoming include social workers in postdetention emergency hearings (TAC, 2020).

Emergency Detention for Evaluation Process and Applicable Policy

Several steps to the emergency detention for an evaluation process are shaped over time by state statute and judicial decisions. Figure 20.2 presents a model that depicts the general steps involved in the process.

The first stage of the civil commitment process involves a prepetition screening and interview. During this personal interview with the individual, the social worker must first notify the individual of their rights per applicable state law, which usually includes revealing that the information they share informs initial involuntary detention that can last up to 72 hours. Next, the social worker investigates the alleged behaviors that meet the threshold of requiring commitment while also exploring the least restrictive options available rather than

TABLE 20.1 Emergency Commitment Criteria by State

Emergency Commitment Criteria	States
Danger to self due to mental illness	AK, AL, AZ, CA, CO, CT, DE, FL, GA,* IA, ID, IN, KS, KY, LA, MA, ME, MI, MN, MO, MS, MT, NC, ND, NE, NH, NJ, NM, NV, OK, OR, PA, RI, SC, SD, TN, TX, UT, VA, VT, WA, WV, WY
Danger to self	AR, HI, IL, MD, NY
Danger to others due to mental illness	AK, AL, AR, AZ, CA, CO, CT, DE, FL, GA, HI, IA, ID, IL, IN, KS, KY, LA, MA, MD, ME, MI, MN, MO, MS, MT, NC, ND, NE, NH, NJ, NM, NV, NY, OK, OR, PA, RI, SC, SD, TN, TX, UT, VA, VT, WA, WV, WY
Danger to others	AR, HI, IL, MD, NY
Recently attempted suicide	MO, MT, NE, NM, PA
Gravely disabled or unable to meet basic needs	AK, CA, CO, CT, FL, ID, KS, LA, MI, MN, MO, MT, NC, ND, NH, VA, WI

* GA criteria are having a mental illness and being in need of treatment.

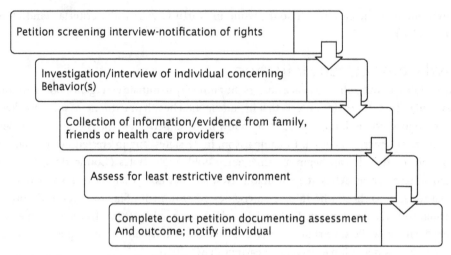

FIGURE 20.2 Emergency Detention for Evaluation Process

commitment. The social worker then gathers information from others (e.g., family, partners, case managers, therapists, prescribers), including the need for medications and willingness to participate in treatment. Next, the social worker assesses the presenting problems, social and psychological supports, and available treatments to determine the least restrictive environment appropriate for the individual. The least restrictive option is to discharge to the community, and the most restrictive option is involuntary inpatient psychiatric treatment. In that range, the other options to rule out include voluntary inpatient hospitalization, outpatient crisis management, day treatment, medication management, and outpatient therapy. The final stage consists of completing the petition paperwork for civil commitment, carefully documenting the assessment process and outcome required by law.

Before a typically 72-hour hold expires, a judge, with the assistance of a physician, will determine if the behaviors remain present that require a continued civil commitment hold of varying lengths, extendable for up to 6 months. Suppose an individual is refusing medications and cannot decipher for themselves the appropriate level of treatment. In that case, a court can hold a medication hearing review to examine how the medicine might impact the individual's ability to consent to treatment. If necessary, the court can order individuals to receive medication against their will. After the initial civil commitment period expires, courts are bound to provide a review that usually occurs semiannually for persons with mental illness and chemical dependency and intermittently for persons with developmental disabilities. These reviews focus on the presence of the behaviors that warranted civil commitment and an assessment for continued commitment.

The emergency detention leading to civil commitment is an important intervention point for social workers. During the emergency detention, individuals detained receive treatment, and those who improve significantly may no longer need involuntary inpatient treatment. An evaluator can then explore other options such as voluntary inpatient treatment or community-based outpatient treatment. The social worker must remain aware of the patients' rights during the emergency detention process, as reviewed in Table 20.2.

TABLE 20.2 Patient Rights in Civil Commitment

Patient Rights in Civil Commitment				
Notice of hearing, if hearing is required by state statute	Assistance of counsel	Appear, testify, and present witnesses and other evidence	Question witnesses appearing in support of their commitment	Jury trial, if allowed by state statute

History of Civil Commitment Policy

The Time of Limited Regulation (1800–1899)

For most of the country's history, jails or almshouses provided mental health institutional care (Testa & West, 2010). Hospitals intended to maintain people with mental illness did not emerge in the United States until the early 1830s. Mental health care in hospitals first occurred with a few private hospitals that tended to serve wealthy families. As a result, the family often had a disproportional influence on care. State-run institutional care began to develop due to the critique of Dorothea Dix of mental health institutional care (Modak et al., 2016). Her efforts would lead to state-run mental health institutions in New Jersey, North Carolina, and Illinois. Soon, these state-run asylums became models for providing institutional care across the American South.

During this period, admission to an institution was always considered involuntary, and the admission criteria were that someone needed or would benefit from treatment (Appelbaum, 1994). The societal zeitgeist of the time was that mentally ill people were hindered from making their own decisions. Common ailments for admission included dementia, seizures, and advanced neurosyphilis, for which there were no treatments. As a result, these asylums became long-term care facilities for individuals without much hope for treatment beyond restraint and sedation and no hope for improvement (Testa & West, 2010).

Expansion of Civil Commitment Patient Rights and Treatments (1900–1950s)

By the turn of the 20th century, several cases that established wrongful commitment made their way through the courts, resulting in many transformations to civil commitment policy (Slobogin, 2015). Among these were judicial certification requirements, access to an attorney before hospitalization, and the right to a jury trial. These efforts intended to install legal protections ensuring the constitutional right to liberty of the person hospitalized (Testa & West, 2010).

The growth of American asylums continued into the early 1950s, with a peak of 559,000 inpatient psychiatric patients in 1953 (Testa & West, 2010). By this point, courts were unable to deal with certification for the number of new cases, thereby resulting in treatment delays. The convergence of these two factors led the National Institute of Mental

Health (NIMH) to call for commitment decision-making to return to medical professionals (SAMHSA, 2019). The states took this guidance and moved to make the judicial certification required after admission.

The 1950s would mark a great leap forward in the treatment of psychiatric mental illness. The development of antipsychotic medications such as Thorazine allowed for the effective treatment of psychosis for the first time. These medications were so effective that community-based rather than institutional-based treatment questions began to emerge, particularly given the number of disruptive community relationships resulting from involuntary institutional treatment.

Deinstitutionalization and the Rise of Community Mental Health (1960s–1970s)

By the 1960s, critique of government institutions was commonplace (Harcourt, 2011). The commentary also applied to mental health institutions given overcrowding, concerns about care, and the emergence of effective treatments. In response to this critique, Congress passed the Community Mental Health Centers Act of 1963 to facilitate individuals' transition from inpatient care to community-based care. Later passed in 1965, Medicare and Medicaid were the policy response to address the health care access for people suffering from mental disorders. The process of deinstitutionalization was quite effective in reducing the number of people receiving psychiatric inpatient care, from a peak in 1953 of over 550,000 to a low in the 1990s of 30,000 individuals (Testa & West, 2010).

The promise that supported deinstitutionalization—that community mental health centers would be equipped and staffed with cutting-edge best practices to help individuals with mental health challenges—never materialized. Instead, community mental health centers were immediately overwhelmed with the influx of individuals with persistent mental illness into their communities (Harcourt, 2011; Novella, 2010). The treatments were only useful for some, leaving some with thought disorders, for example, surviving untreated in the community. The convergence of these factors would lead to a revolving door between inpatient psychiatric care and community health centers for those who were most vulnerable, including those unable or unwilling to consent to voluntary treatment, such as those with anosognosia, which is when an individual is unaware of their mental health condition. Deinstitutionalization impacts would not surface for at least another decade. Still, by the end of the 1970s, it became clear to mental health advocates that the movement fell well short of its intended promise (Novella, 2010).

It is also during the 1960s that civil commitment moved from a need for treatment and moved to behavior(s) resulting from mental illness that posed an imminent threat(s) to themselves (suicide) or others (assault or homicide). This reform established the dangerousness standard (Harcourt, 2011; Novella, 2010). The criteria for grave disability also emerged, generally referring to an individual's inability to manage basic survival conditions due to mental illness.

Simultaneously, while deinstitutionalization was reforming mental health care, the courts were also reforming civil commitment law. Several judicial decisions that impact social workers would refine civil commitment policy. In 1966, in *Lake v. Cameron*, the U.S.

Supreme Court established the least restrictive environment consideration (Canady, 2019). Essentially, this decision required civil commitment initiators to review all settings before determining the least restrictive location based on the presenting behaviors. All civil commitments today must include consideration of the least restrictive environment as a result.

In the 1971 case of *Lessard v. Schmidt*, the U.S. Supreme Court supported the dangerousness standard. It indicated that to establish dangerousness, the danger must be imminent, with recent evidence to support the conclusion of substantial harm to oneself or another. In the 1975 case of *O'Connor v. Donaldson*, the U.S. Supreme Court ruled that institutions could not detain individuals indefinitely without providing them treatment (Canady, 2019). This decision was significant because, before it, psychiatric institutions were serving as de facto correctional institutions. In 1979, in *Addington v. Texas*, the U.S. Supreme Court reset the burden of proof standard for an involuntary commitment by establishing that the burden of proof required is clear and convincing evidence, not just a preponderance of the evidence. This standard for burden of proof is more significant than a preponderance of the evidence but not as high as the highest standard of evidence, beyond a reasonable doubt, which was the standard argued for in the *Addington* case (Canady, 2019).

Rise of Assisted Outpatient Programs (1980s–Present)

By the 1980s, a new wave of programming emerged to address the revolving-door problem that deinstitutionalization had borne out. The revolving door's financial costs to inpatient care gave rise to a new conceptualization of committing the patient to a treatment plan in their community. As a way of diverting these utilizers of inpatient hospitalization services, assertive community treatment (ACT) programs supported these individuals with intensive case management, supportive housing, medication management, therapy, and access to auxiliary services such as education or employment (Canady, 2019). As the number of ACT programs grew across the nation, it became more common for high utilizers of inpatient psychiatric care to receive assisted outpatient program commitments rather than inpatient commitments (Canady, 2019).

The development of mental health courts during the 1980s also impacted civil commitments. Mental health courts seek to address the underlying mental health issue that contributed to criminal behavior. Those involved with mental health courts agreed to individualized treatment plans and ongoing monitoring to remain out of the traditional court system or jail. Mental health courts differ from traditional courts, given their problem-solving approach for defendants with mental illness. During involvement with the court, the defendant undergoes periodic reviews to meet the conditions of participation.

With the passage of the 21st Century Cures Act of 2016, the most remarkable reforms in two generations occurred to civil commitment laws. The Cures Act reformed SAMHSA to focus on science- and evidence-based solutions for mental health and substance abuse (Kesselheim & Avorn, 2017). The act also strengthened outpatient treatment programs for people with severe mental illness by providing competitive grant funding to increase residential treatment facilities in crisis stabilization units. Further, the act included provisions for decriminalizing mental illness, including offering assertive outpatient treatment opportunities rather than incarceration and initiating a federal mental health court. Another provision of the act reformed the data collection mechanisms that report on psychiatric beds, crisis stabilization units, and residential treatment facilities that serve individuals with severe mental illness. Other provisions in the act focused on clarifying Health Insurance Portability and Accountability Act (HIPAA) regulations, increasing accountability for protection advocacy, and Medicaid mental health parity in establishing federal-level adult assessments and programs (Kesselheim & Avom, 2017).

Civil Commitment and Vulnerable Populations

Civil commitment generally impacts several vulnerable populations in unique ways. Among them are people with substance abuse or chemical dependency disorders, people with mental health diagnoses such as schizophrenia, people with developmental disabilities, individuals who have committed sex offenses, and individuals who were found not guilty of crimes because of insanity.

People With Substance Abuse/Chemical Dependency

For people with chemical dependency or substance abuse disorders, the civil commitment threshold involves the substance posing a clear and present threat of mortality to the individual. The civil commitment criterion of grave disability applies to individuals at risk of death from substance use. Grave disability is generally defined as an inability to complete essential care and daily living tasks, including eating, bathing, toileting, and taking necessary medications, though not limited to these criteria alone. The Narcotic Addiction Rehabilitation Act (NARA) allows for the commitment of persons with addictions to narcotics where chemical dependency is presently lethal (Linddblad, 1988).

Findings from the 2016 National Survey on Drug Use and Health revealed that only 10% of American adults meeting the criteria for substance use treatment were currently receiving it (Park-Lee et al., 2017). Nearly 90%, the vast majority, of people who met the criteria did not think they needed substance use treatment. This gap is stunning and used as the rationale for civil commitment due to substance abuse (Christie et al., 2017).

Jian, Christopher, and Appelbaum (2018) describe many challenges to involuntary treatment for substance use disorders, including variability of access to treatment and the impact on mandatory inpatient or outpatient treatment paths. States vary in the length of civil commitment periods for substance use disorders and variations for the substances included. In some states there are even different civil commitment periods for various substances.

People With Certain Mental Health Diagnoses

For people with persistent mental illness, the categories most often used for civil commitment are danger to self (generally defined as suicidal ideation with intent and viable plan), danger to others (generally defined as homicidal ideation with intent and viable plan), and grave disability or inability to complete basic tasks (generally defined as an inability to complete essential care tasks of daily living including eating, bathing, toileting, and taking necessary medications; Canady, 2019).

Separate from substance use, specific mental health diagnoses presents particular challenges to civil commitment law. Several diagnoses consistently appear in civil commitments, including antisocial personality disorder, which tends to be associated with higher levels of dangerousness to others, and borderline personality disorder, which tends to be associated with higher levels of dangerousness to self. Also, eating disorders and thought orders such as schizophrenia tend to be associated with higher levels of grave disability, particularly when accompanied by anosognosia, a lack of awareness of one's mental illness. Anorexia too might be accompanied by anosognosia (Appelbaum & Rumpf, 1998). For people with persistent mental illness, the categories most often used for civil commitment are a danger to self (generally defined as suicidal ideation with intent and viable plan), danger to others (generally defined as homicidal ideation with intent and viable plan), and grave disability or inability to complete basic tasks (generally defined as an inability to complete essential care tasks of daily living including eating, bathing, toileting, and taking necessary medications).

For those with developmental and intellectual disabilities, the civil commitment criterion of grave disability or inability to meet basic needs is most often used (generally defined as an inability to complete essential care and daily living tasks, including eating, bathing, toileting, and taking necessary medications). Still, it is not limited to this domain alone. It is often the case that people with disabilities are committed to long-term state care facilities instead of acute or medium-term hospital care (Slobogin, 2015).

The civil commitment of people with developmental and intellectual disabilities presents another distinct set of challenges. A civil commitment of these individuals removes decision-making authority from themselves and their families, relegating that instead to judicial review (Slobogin, 2015). Advocates have called for an end to the civil commitment of people with developmental and intellectual disabilities, pointing out that when the state enacts care decisions on their behalf instead of themselves of family members, these individuals are commonly moved to institutions far from their homes, restricting family and community access (Lee, 2010).

People Who Have Committed Sex Offenses

For people who have committed a sex offense, the most often used category for civil commitment is a danger to others (generally defined as a threat of sexual assault). Twenty states have passed statutes for civil commitment laws that focus on sexually violent predators. The civil commitment criteria are being diagnosed with a mental illness and presenting a risk because of that diagnosis. Legal challenges to the civil commitment of individuals who have committed sex offenses but have completed their sentences have arisen under the double jeopardy guarantee of the U.S. Constitution (Deming, 2008). Judicial decisions have come down on both sides: those supporting the right of individuals from double jeopardy and those supporting civil commitment due to present and ongoing danger (Miller, 2010).

People Who Have Been Found Not Guilty by Reason of Insanity

Despite public perception that being found not guilty by reason of insanity is getting off without consequence, that is far from reality. Those acquitted of crimes by reason of insanity enter the inpatient mental health system. They remain under civil commitment until they can prove that they no longer pose a risk to society. This commitment entails detailed assessments of treatment progress and challenging-to-measure discharge criteria, if there's even a discharge setting available (Silver et al., 1994). Disposable commitment has received critique by Monson et al. (2001), who point out that civil commitment length of stay has exceeded the same length of stay for the original crime committed.

Knowledge Base, Value, and Impacts of Civil Commitment Policies

An essential task for a social worker is to consider the knowledge base, values, and impacts of any policy regulating the civil commitment practice. The knowledge base for civil commitment policies has changed drastically over time. After settling on the dangerousness standard, the value for civil commitment policies often utilizes that frame. Without a doubt, civil commitment policies have impacts on the individual that often go unconsidered.

Knowledge Base

It seems apparent that the policies used for a civil commitment have changed significantly over time. Those policies were no longer palatable when individuals went untreated for their mental health disorders in jails and almshouses. In turn, this led to the growth of institutions intended to provide standardized inpatient care based on cutting-edge knowledge that would inform psychiatric treatments. As it turned out, this standardization wasn't so standard, which led to a critique of these policies as having failed to deliver. Thus, policy and practice moved toward deinstitutionalization with services provided in local communities, which was cutting-edge best practice at the time. The establishment of community mental health centers and new pharmaceutical treatments was not the panacea promised, thereby giving rise to a new era of civil commitment and a host of reforms that advanced criteria clarity and patients' rights. Given the need for continued inpatient care despite the decreasing number of inpatient beds and exceeding costs of hospitalization, outpatient civil commitment in the form of assisted outpatient treatment has emerged as the most recent best practice relative to civil commitment.

Value of Civil Commitment Policy

It is nearly impossible to weigh the value of civil commitment policies given the tradeoffs between individuals under commitment and society in maintaining safety. Civil commitment policy intends to prevent harm (suicide, homicide, property destruction) by its nature. Like any prevention policy, it's difficult to fully understand its value—how many times enforcement of the policy prevented harm. On the other hand, civil commitment policy allows society to uphold the social contract in which safety is expected.

Evidence and literature uphold that intensive community treatment for at least 6 months is associated with improved quality of life and reduced hospitalization incidents among mentally ill people (Swartz & Swanson, 2020). However, there are significant variations among ACT programs that make determining their overall efficacy difficult. Critical differences between programs include what the program provides, who qualifies for the program, and how it is implemented and enforced. As Lamberti, Weisman, and Faden (2004) conclude, these programs are only as effective as the available resources.

Impacts of Civil Commitment Policy

There are several consequences significant for consideration relative to social work practice in civil commitment. Individuals involuntarily committed to state treatment facilities receive a bill for all or part of their costs of care. The billing will continue over the individual's lifetime, according to the ability to pay. At the time of that person's death, the state has the right to file a claim against their estate for the total cost of care.

Also, states have commonly enacted state-level policies that are additional effects of civil commitment. For example, in Minnesota, any person civilly committed as chemically dependent, mentally ill, or developmentally disabled may not possess any firearm unless they have undergone a legal procedure before the court for restoring their ability to maintain a firearm. Civil commitment can also impact professional or personal licenses with the agency or board issuing the licenses holding those detailed provisions. It is also important to note that court records are public information and that while portions of the record are sealed, the civil commitment itself is public information.

Social Work Ethical Considerations

Nothing should give a social worker more professional pause than considering abridging an individual's civil rights through a civil commitment. The National Association of Social Workers (NASW) Code of Ethics (NASW, 2017) is a crucial tool to consider civil commitment through the profession's ethical lens. This lens is critical because social workers will often make civil commitment decisions within practice contexts where they may be the only professional social worker or by far the minority profession. Each profession represented has complementary and yet distinct values and professional ethics, so it is essential to the session worker tick around their decisions and the NASW Code.

Personal Autonomy—Social Work Value: Dignity and Worth of Person

Given the limitations on liberty that a civil commitment poses, social workers must consider personal autonomy questions. For the social worker, this is often manifested in the value of dignity and worth of the person and through the ethical principle of social workers respecting the person's inherent dignity and worth. Mandated inpatient treatment is coercive; there is no doubt, although justifiable given the alternatives—danger to self, others, or risks from grave disability. If the dangerousness standard goes away, what is the reason for the mandated outpatient treatment of a civil commitment? Although it may be gently informed by considerations of the least restrictive environment and competence in making decisions about mental health treatment, the answer remains elusive.

Nonmaleficence—Social Work Value: Service

The "do no harm" principle that transcends medicine to all helping disciplines holds that interventions should not cause harm. The complementary question is, do no harm to who, the individual or society? The answer to that question isn't always the same relative to interventions. For the social worker, nonmaleficence is reflected in the value of service and manifested in the ethical principle that the social worker's primary goal is to help people in need to address social problems (NASW, 2017).

As a result of being civilly committed to an inpatient facility, many unintentional harms have come to individuals, including loss of employment, loss of parental rights (temporary or permanent), loss of animal ownership rights, homelessness, and loss of familial and other supportive relationships (Zervakis et al., 2007). The question that is always present is whether the benefits presented to the individual by a civil commitment outweigh the potential risks of harming themselves and others in its absence.

Beneficence—Social Work Values: Integrity and Competence

Questions of beneficence for social workers applying civil commitment policy are usually concerned with what is good for the individual and others and prevents harm. Beneficence often means assessing self-determination and social responsibility simultaneously. For the social worker and efficiency is reflected in two values. The first is integrity, which manifests by the social worker behaving in a trustworthy manner. The second is competence, made manifest by the ethical principle that social workers practice within their competence areas and develop and enhance their professional expertise (NASW, 2017).

Civil commitment is ethically justifiable after careful assessment and conclusion that the individual cannot consider their psychiatric symptoms, safety, or proper course of treatment to mitigate their and other risks. It is also essential for the social worker to view beneficence questions along the time continuum: what is good for self and others and prevents harm in both the long and short term. This assessment may lead the social worker to a more in-depth analysis of involuntary inpatient versus outpatient treatment.

Equitable Treatment—Social Work Value: Social Justice

Social justice issues involved in civil commitment appear straightforward but are very complicated upon a longer view. Civil commitment policy requires social justice consideration. In these deliberations, social workers should center on the value of social justice, made manifest by the ethical principle of social workers challenging social injustice. One glaring social justice issue revealed in this chapter is the differences in state statutes regulating criteria for commitment, length of stay, and treatment criteria. A civil commitment stay and measures should not be dependent on the state of your commitment. Another social justice issue is clear considerations of the special populations entangled under civil commitment policies. While institutional care has undoubtedly improved over the last 200 years, that shouldn't be considered a rationale for the continued civil commitment of individuals who are not likely to benefit from that level of treatment.

Swanson and colleagues (2009) reveal troubling disparities in outpatient civil commitment among African Americans in New York State. In the United States, African Americans are overrepresented in almost all institutions. Their civil liberties are bridged, including in foster care, aging care, criminal justice systems, health care systems, and mental health systems where civil commitment is allowed. These institutions feature discriminatory policies and practices that, when linked across institutions, foster structural inequality for African Americans, thereby, directly and indirectly, leading to them being disproportionally represented among those civilly committed.

In Summary

This chapter began by reviewing the overarching goals for civil commitment policies, essentially protecting oneself, others, and property from harm. This overview formed the foundation for discussing the types of civil commitment and their criteria across the United States. Next, the chapter discussed emergency detention policies that regulate the civil commitment process while highlighting variations between states. This provided the foundation for a detailed overview of civil commitment policy development with important implications for social work. The chapter closed with a review of the knowledge base, values, and ethics of social work involved in civil commitment policies.

References

Appelbaum, P. S. (1994). *Almost a revolution*. Oxford University Press.

Appelbaum, P. S., & Rumpf, T. (1998). Civil commitment of the anorexic patient. *General Hospital Psychiatry*, *20*(4), 225–230.

Canady, V. A. (2019). SAMHSA document outlines historical references, updates to civil commitment. *Mental Health Weekly*, *29*(16), 1–6.

Christie, C., Baker, C., Cooper, R., Kennedy, P. J., Madras, B., & Bondi, P. (2017, November 1). *The president's commission on combating drug addiction and the opioid crisis*. U.S. Government Printing Office.

Deming, A. (2008). Sex offender civil commitment programs: Current practices, characteristics, and resident demographics. *Journal of Psychiatry & Law*, *36*(3), 439–461.

Harcourt, B. E. (2011). Reducing mass incarceration: Lessons from the deinstitutionalization of mental hospitals in the 1960s. *Ohio State Journal of Criminal Law*, *9*, 53.

Hedman, L. C., Petrila, J., Fisher, W. H., Swanson, J. W., Dingman, D. A., & Burris, S. (2016). State laws on emergency hold for mental health stabilization. *Psychiatric Services*, *67*, 529–535.

Jain, A., Christopher, P., & Appelbaum, P. S. (2018). Civil commitment for opioid and other substance use disorders: Does it work? *Psychiatric Services*, *69*(4), 374–376.

Kesselheim, A. S., & Avorn, J. (2017). New "21st Century Cures" legislation: Speed and ease vs science. *Jama*, *317*(6), 581–582.

Lamberti, J. S., Weisman, R., & Faden, D. I. (2004). Forensic assertive community treatment: Preventing incarceration of adults with severe mental illness. *Psychiatric Services*, *55*(11), 1285–1293.

Lee, B. Y. (2010). The U.N. Convention on the Rights of Persons with Disabilities and its impact upon involuntary civil commitment of individuals with developmental disabilities. *Columbia Journal of Law & Social Problems*, *44*, 393.

Lindblad, R. (1988). Civil commitment under the federal narcotic addict rehabilitation act. *Journal of Drug Issues, 18*(4), 595–624.

Miller, J. A. (2010). Sex offender civil commitment: The treatment paradox. *California Law Review, 98*(6), 2093–2128.

Modak, T., Sarkar, S., & Sagar, R. (2016). Dorothea Dix: A proponent of humane treatment of mentally ill. *Journal of Mental Health and Human Behaviour, 21*(1), 69.

Monson, C. M., Gunnin, D. D., Fogel, M. H., & Kyle, L. L. (2001). Stopping (or slowing) the revolving door: Factors related to NGRI acquittees' maintenance of a conditional release. *Law and Human Behavior, 25*(3), 257–267.

National Association of Social Workers. (2017). *Code of ethics.* https://www.socialworkers.org/About/Eth ics/Code-of-Ethics/Code-of-Ethics-English

Novella, E. J. (2010). Mental health care in the aftermath of deinstitutionalization: A retrospective and prospective view. *Health Care Analysis, 18*(3), 222–238.

Park-Lee, E., Lipari, R. N., Hedden, S. L., Kroutil, L. A., & Porter, J. D. (2017). Receipt of services for substance use and mental health issues among adults: Results from the 2016 National Survey on Drug Use and Health. In *CBHSQ data review* (pp. 1–35). Substance Abuse and Mental Health Services Administration.

Silver, E., Cirincione, C., & Steadman, H. J. (1994). Demythologizing inaccurate perceptions of the insanity defense. *Law and Human Behavior, 18*(1), 63–70.

Slobogin, C. (2015). Eliminating mental disability as a legal criterion in deprivation of liberty cases: The impact of the Convention on the Rights of Persons With Disabilities on the insanity defense, civil commitment, and competency law. *International Journal of Law, 40*(2015), 36–42.

Substance Abuse and Mental Health Services Administration. (2019). Civil Commitment and the Mental Health Care Continuum: Historical Trends and Principles for Law and Practice. https://www.samhsa. gov/sites/default/files/civil-commitment-continuum-of-care.pdf

Swanson, J., Swartz, M. S., Elbogen, E., Wagner, H. R., & Burns, B. J. (2003). Effects of involuntary outpatient commitment on subjective quality of life in persons with severe mental illness. *Behavioral Sciences and the Law, 21*, 473–491.

Swanson, J., Swartz, M., Van Dorn, R., Monahan, J., McGuire, T., Steadman, H., & Robbins, P. (2009). Racial disparities in involuntary outpatient commitment: Are they real? *Health Affairs, 28*(3), 816–826.

Swartz, M. S., & Swanson, J. W. (2020). Mandated community treatment in services for persons with mental illness. In *The Palgrave handbook of American mental health policy* (pp. 171–196). Palgrave Macmillan.

Testa, M., & West, S. G. (2010). Civil commitment in the United States. *Psychiatry (Edgmont), 7*(10), 30.

Treatment Advocacy Center. (2020). State Standards for Civil Commitment. https://www.treatmentadvocacy center.org/storage/documents/state-standards/state-standards-for-civil-commitment.pdf

Zervakis, J., Stechuchak, K., Olsen, M., Swanson, J., Oddone, E., Weinberger, M., Bryce, E. R., Butterfield, M. I., Swartz, M. S., & Strauss, J. L. (2007). Previous involuntary commitment is associated with current perceptions of coercion in voluntarily hospitalized patients. *International Journal of Forensic Mental Health, 6*(2), 105–112.

21

Intimate Partner Violence Policies

Leah E. Gatlin and Anthony P. Natale

Background and Context

On average, in the United States, 20 people are physically abused by an intimate partner every minute, equaling more than 10 million women and men across the span of one year (National Coalition Against Domestic Violence, 2020), with one in four women and one in seven men falling victim to serious physical violence in their lifetime. The National Center for Injury Prevention and Control (NCIPC) at the Centers for Disease Control and Prevention (CDC) defines intimate partner violence (IPV) as "abuse or aggression that occurs in a romantic relationship" (NCIPC, 2020). While victims of IPV are represented along the gender continuum, it is clear that women are the targets more often and bear the disproportionate impacts of IPV. More than one in every three (36.4%, or 43.6 million) women in the United States have reported experiencing IPV during their lifetime (S. G. Smith et al., 2018). Of these women, 6.6 million (about one in 18, or 5.5%) were exposed to IPV in the 12 months prior in 2014. From 2003 to 2012, IPV accounted for 15% of all nonfatal violent crimes (Truman & Morgan, 2014). Both current and former intimate partners count in IPV statistics. Statistics include both single incidents and repeated incidents.

Definitions and legal terms for IPV vary by state and jurisdiction and are distinct from domestic violence. IPV can occur between romantic partners who *do not live in the same household*. In contrast, domestic violence occurs between two people *who live in the same household* (National Network to End Domestic Violence, n.d.). Depending on the state or agency defining IPV, there are many types of IPV: physical violence, sexual violence, threats of physical or sexual violence, psychological/emotional violence, stalking, financial abuse, psychological aggression, and controlling behaviors (NCIPC, 2020;

Leah E. Gatlin and Anthony P. Natale, *Intimate Partner Violence Policies* In: *Handbook of Forensic Social Work*. Edited by: David Axlyn McLeod, Anthony P. Natale, and Kristin W. Mapson, Oxford University Press. © Oxford University Press 2024. DOI: 10.1093/oso/9780197694732.003.0021

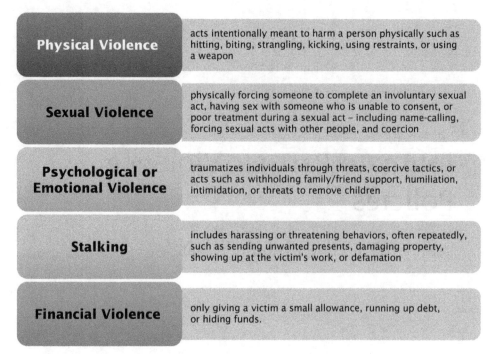

FIGURE 21.1 Types of Intimate Partner Violence

National Institute of Justice, 2007; National Network to End Domestic Violence, n.d.; World Health Organization, 2012). Figure 21.1 presents the types of IPV along with examples of each type.

IPV cases generally are heard in one of three courts: criminal, civil, or divorce/family (Table 21.1; American Bar Association, 2000). In divorce/family courts, IPV is particularly salient in determining custody and visitation schedules—a less direct link to instances of IPV. Criminal courts that can prosecute the offender and civil courts are more straightforward, which determine orders of protection or allow for offenders to be sued. IPV cases may be heard in one or all three courts. The National Conference of State Legislatures (NSCL) notes that 38 states' criminal codes include specific IPV definitions and penalties. In contrast, almost every state has a definition in their social service or domestic relations codes. The definitions vary broadly in what states consider to be IPV (NSCL, 2019).

TABLE 21.1 Intimate Partner Violence and the Courts

Criminal Courts	Civil Courts	Family Courts
Handle cases of criminal law violations (harassment, assault, murder)	Handle cases involving civil domestic violence actions that seek protection from another	Handle cases involving domestic cases such as divorce and child custody
The prosecutor brings the case against the abuser (at times against the wishes of the survivor, who may be called to testify)	The survivor brings the case against the abuser	Salient in determining custody and visitation schedules where IPV has been implicated

Intimate Partner Violence Policies

Policy Goals

The National Council of Juvenile and Family Court Judges (NCJFCJ, 1994) notes the importance of policy in preventing and reducing the number of IPV cases each year. Because policy, including legislation, was such a priority and the group asserted the importance of coordination among different parts of government and those who provide services to victims of IPV, the NCJFCJ developed a model code for family violence that states could adopt themselves. This model code includes general provisions for definitions, criminal penalties and procedures (e.g., mandatory arrest, the role of police, conditions for release, spousal privilege, and requirements for diversion or deferment), civil orders of protection, topics related to families and children (such as visitation), and prevention and treatment. In addition, other governmental entities, such as the CDC, recognize the importance of prevention and have offered to fund grants or pilot programs to study best practices (Estefan et al., 2019).

Harm Prevention and Crime Deterrent

The overall goal of IPV policies is to prevent harm in the first place. The 1984 U.S. Attorney General's Task Force on Family Violence (TFFV) noted that the primary goal in IPV policy is "to break the cycle and to prevent family violence from occurring" (p. 3). The authors claim that legal sanctions, such as prosecution, should have the most significant deterrent effects in cases of IPV because the victim knows the perpetrator, unlike many crimes where the victim does not know the perpetrator. They state, "If family violence were always reported and if the legal system always acted based on its knowledge, the deterrent effects of swift and certain legal penalties would be great" (p. 5). The authors point out that one of the significant problems in IPV is that the perpetrator does not realize the behavior is abuse.

Researchers from the World Health Organization highlighted the importance of primary prevention—attempting to decrease or stop new instances of IPV altogether (Harvey et al., 2007). This is different from, though often in conjunction with, other prevention types that seek to reduce the adverse effects of intimate partner violence in victims' lives. The authors highlight that IPV rates might decrease through policies targeting other areas, such as alcohol-related harm or child abuse. Estefan and colleagues (2019) point to the absence of information about IPV prevention. Several issues make it difficult for primary prevention research in IPV, such as the numerous and varied causes, existing knowledge base, and how many practitioners have been trained (Martin et al., 2009). Since each of these issues is complex, no one strategy would lead to violence prevention.

Armstead and colleagues (2018) highlight the few IPV primary prevention programs that have been evaluated. Through its NCIPC, the CDC funded the Domestic Violence Prevention Enhancement and Leadership Through Alliances (DELTA) program from 2002 to 2013 (NCIPC, 2018). The DELTA Program endeavored to reduce the incidence of first-time IPV events (Armstead et al., 2017; NCIPC, 2018). The program utilized state domestic violence agencies and local coordinated community response (CCR) teams to develop prevention resources, train practitioners, and research best practices to prevent IPV.

The project considered individual, relational, community, and societal influences to create comprehensive plans to reduce IPV. The DELTA Project addressed individuals and groups throughout the life cycle, including teens, to reduce IPV incidence. This aligns with several authors who have pointed out that longitudinal studies show that future IPV can be predicted during the teen years (Ehrensaft & Cohen, 2012; Moffitt et al., 2001; McNaughton Reyes et al., 2012). Participants in the DELTA FOCUS program believed their work added to the national dialogue on prevention, especially in creating awareness and catalyzing action (Estefan et al., 2019). Recipients were also able to effect change through training based on the most current research, including lessons learned in the DELTA FOCUS program. The 19 participating state coalitions continued almost all of their prevention activities (Freire et al., 2015).

Services to Victims

The three foundational federal laws regarding IPV are the Family Violence Prevention and Services Act (FVPSA), the Victims of Crime Act (VOCA), and the Violence Against Women Act (VAWA; Figure 21.2). Each piece of legislation is distinctive and discussed more throughout the chapter; all three include services for victims (Family and Youth Services Bureau, 2020; Office for Victims of Crime, 1996; Sacco, 2019). Martin and colleagues (2009) highlight that practitioners in IPV and sexual violence fields are generally more concerned with providing services to victims than primary prevention efforts. Both FVPSA and VAWA provide resources for prevention, but VOCA does not.

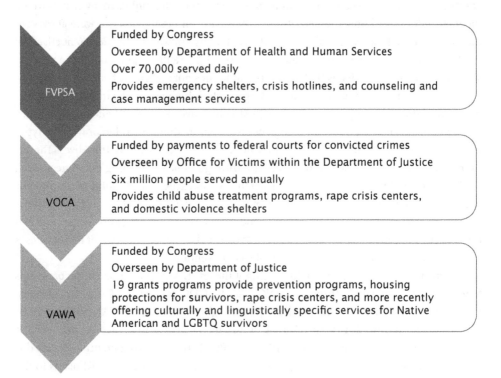

FIGURE 21.2 Intimate Partner Violence Foundational Policies' Key Features

The TFFV (1984) highlights that victim services must be innovative and malleable since victims may often feel ashamed and fearful about what happened. In general, victims' services try to increase self-efficacy and hope for the future and provide access to community resources, support, and opportunities (Sullivan, 2018). Ultimately, the goal is to enhance victims' and their children's social and emotional well-being. Victims' needs are often multifaceted and include employment assistance, housing, childcare, and daily demands on top of treatment for mental and physical injuries (TFFV, 1984). Victims' services also education about survivors' rights, safety planning, skill-building, emotional support, and increasing connections with the community (Sullivan, 2018).

Additionally, victims' services organizations support victims by advocating for community and system changes in IPV. The entry point for many of these services is emergency shelters (Messing et al., 2015). On one day in 2020, 76,525 adults and children received shelter services or other housing options provided by local IPV organizations, and domestic violence hotlines received 21,321 contacts (National Network to End Domestic Violence, 2021). Of all the requests received, 11,407 went unmet due to service providers lacking resources to meet those requests; 57% of the unmet demands were for emergency shelter and housing.

Coordinated Response

After observing the effects of a fragmented system response to IPV, including how a lack of coordinated policies endangered victims, leaders in the field realized the best response was coordination among the various systems intervening in IPV cases (American Prosecutors Research Institute [APRI] & NCJFCJ, 1998; Shorey et al., 2014). These coordinated efforts are sometimes called coordinating councils or CCRs. These groups improve communication among organizations, establish protocols for responding to IPV, and educate the community on the complex issues involved in IPV.

In 1981, the Duluth (Minnesota) Abuse Intervention Project (DAIP) expanded previous work. It became a national model on CCRs for IPV by bringing nine city, county, and private agencies together to coordinate their responses to IPV and family violence cases (APRI & NCJFCJ, 1998; Domestic Abuse Intervention Programs [DAIP], n.d.). The DAIP developed protocols and procedures for agencies with protecting victims in mind. Though not the first model, it became one of the most commonly used models in the United States. In 1994, the Bureau of Justice Affairs, as part of VAWA, awarded the APRI and NCJFCJ (1998) a grant to provide technical assistance to three jurisdictions with CCRs on how to implement new programs or augment existing ones. After this, the number of CCRs in the United States continued to grow. CCRs became so common that the second iteration of the DELTA grant, DELTA FOCUS, included having each state coalition support one or two CCRs (Estefan et al., 2019). Recent years have also shifted from coordinating agencies to coordinating communities, including adding community-based organizations such as religious organizations and schools (Klevens & Cox, 2008).

CCRs include police, the legal system, service providers, government, health care, educational and vocational programs, and IPV advocates (Klevens & Cox, 2008; Shorey et al., 2014). The goal is a more comprehensive system where one part of the system (such as shelters) can help victims obtain services from other parts of the system (such as filing a police report or protective order). CCRs help victims learn about benefits and access them in a way that provides less frustration or burden to them. Available research has inconsistent results in examining the effectiveness of CCRs (Klevens & Cox, 2008). Nearly all studies show some benefit in communities that have CCRs versus those that do not. Other studies have shown benefits in coordinated criminal justice responses, though they lacked a control group of a community without a coordinated criminal justice response. A more recent systematic review of the literature explained that the wide variety in terms, types of cases included, nature of CCRs, and outcomes used for research make it difficult for researchers to form broader conclusions about how effective CCRs are (Johnson & Stylianou, 2020).

Policy Types

Mandatory Reporting Laws

Mandatory reporting laws are designed to protect public safety and those unable to defend themselves (Jordan & Pritchard, 2021). To accomplish this, states have generally adopted mandatory reporting in four areas: (a) injuries indicative of a crime or resulting from certain weapons; (b) neglect, abuse, or exploitation of children; (c) neglect, abuse, or exploitation of vulnerable adults; and (d) sexual assault or domestic violence. Laws vary widely by state as to who are mandatory reporters and what circumstances require a report (Lippy et al., 2020). Estefan and colleagues (2019) point to the absence of information about IPV prevention. IPV survivors may encounter mandatory reporting laws in their state due to direct compulsory IPV-related reporting guidelines, having injuries consistent with compulsory crime-related reporting laws (such as being shot), having children who witnessed the domestic violence, or encountering other mandatory reporters (such as domestic violence advocates).

The literature shows that mandatory reporting laws often adversely affect IPV victims' help-seeking behaviors (Bledsoe et al., 2004; Jordan & Pritchard, 2021; Lippy et al., 2020). One reason is that victims fear mandatory reporting will lead to court involvement or having their children removed, an outcome well documented in the literature. Lippy and colleagues (2000) highlight the heterogeneity of victims' opinions about the helpfulness of mandatory reporting laws—ranging from thinking laws might be helpful to decreasing the likelihood of seeking support. Bledsoe and colleagues (2004) highlight objections to IPV mandatory reporting laws due to concerns about victim autonomy, fear of increased risk to victims, and confidentiality in the doctor-patient relationship.

Civil Protection (Restraining) Orders

Since the mid-1990s, every state has had a statute related to civil protection (Benitez et al., 2010; Fagan, 1996; Sack, 2004). Protection orders function to reduce the threat of harm (Benitez et al., 2010). The criteria are different in each state and jurisdiction. They can come from criminal court when the perpetrator is accused of misdemeanors and felonies, such as assault. Family courts can issue them in cases like divorce proceedings. Civil courts offer protection orders after hearing victims' evidence concerning violence, stalking, or harassment and the victim asks the court to intervene to stop the behavior(s). All are designed to protect victim safety. The Interstate Stalking Punishment and Prevention Act of 1996 also mandated that a protection order filed in one state must be followed in every other state, and as a result crossing state lines to violate a protection order became a federal crime. Protection orders are also commonly called restraining orders, anti-harassment orders, civil protection orders, and other terms. States also enacted separate laws making violating protection orders either a crime or contempt of court (Sack, 2004). Breaking protection orders is one of the ways to measure how effective protection orders are. A review of articles about protection orders found that a range of 7.1% to 81.3% of perpetrators violate protection orders.

One of the better articles in the study, which included larger samples and had control groups with no protection orders, found that victims with protection orders were less likely to be physically abused over the next 12 months. Another larger-scale study with a control group in the same review compared women who had reported domestic violence and either filed for a protection order or did not; the results showed the women were less likely to experience contact, threat, sustained psychological abuse, and physical abuse than women who did not ask for a protective order. Likewise, McFarlane and colleagues (2004) found that women who asked for a 2-year order of protection, regardless of whether or not that order was granted, later reported less abuse. Cordier and colleagues (2021) conducted a meta-analysis of studies exploring the impact that protection orders have on recidivism. They found that reports of perpetrators violating their protection orders were highest when the victims reported police reports, which makes sense knowing that not all victims report abuse to the police. Violation rates decreased when protection orders were used in conjunction with arrests. The rates also decreased when perpetrators had no prior history of arrest for violence, perpetrators did not stalk, and couples had medium to high incomes.

Holt and colleagues (2002) found among women in Seattle ($n = 2,691$) that having a temporary order of protection increased the risk of psychological abuse, while having a permanent protection order reduced risk compared to the control group (no protection order). In general, the available literature demonstrates that protection orders, especially long-term or permanent ones, increase victim safety, even if results are mixed about how effective they are in reducing offender recidivism.

One downside to the high availability of civil protection orders is IPV perpetrators also seeking these orders to encourage judges to deny both orders, manipulate victims, or benefit their criminal cases (Sack, 2004). Victims may agree to mutual protection orders in some cases, especially to end the relationship or gain something else in divorce proceedings (Topliffe, 1992). Since there does not need to be a complaining party asking for protection, judges can issue mutual protection orders without hearing any evidence (Sack, 2004; Topliffe, 1992). Topliffe (1992) raises concerns about the messaging that mutual protection orders send perpetrators about their violence and the ability to hold them accountable. Perhaps most disturbingly, police have less clear guidelines when responding to a violation of a mutual order of protection, leading to either no arrest or both parties being arrested. Orders of protection can also be used against victims later, including in decisions about child custody (Sack, 2004; Topliffe, 1992).

Another downside to mutual protection orders is victims facing charges for aiding and abetting the violation of a civil protection order (a crime in many states) if they allow the perpetrator near them, even if the victim is coerced (Jeske, 2017; Sack, 2004). Some states distinguish between cases where the victim willingly let the perpetrator and subject of the order of protection near the victim and cases where the victim was coerced, surprised, or otherwise an unwilling participant (Jeske, 2017). Jeske (2017) highlights the Ohio Supreme Court decision that a victim was "immune" to being charged with aiding and abetting her abuser. The Ohio Supreme Court noted that charging victims with aiding and abetting would also likely lead to a decrease in reporting protective order violations. Jeske (2017) also discusses the complex reasons a victim might contact their abuser.

Arrest Laws

Before the early 1980s, arrests in IPV cases were low (Sack, 2004). This began to change after a study of mandatory arrest in IPV cases in Minneapolis. The study compared arrest, mediation, and making the offender leave the house for 8 hours and found that arrest had a significant impact on reducing later recidivism for IPV (Fagan, 1996; Sack, 2004). The U.S. Attorney General used the study results in 1984 to advocate for arrest in IPV, which became the standard law enforcement response (U.S. Attorney General's Task Force on Family Violence, 1984). These policies were designed to remove less effective options and subvert police officers' resistance to arresting IPV perpetrators (Sack, 2004). Advocates also pushed for these laws to remove pressure on victims to cooperate with police to make cases and signal to communities that IPV was no longer a tolerated crime (Fagan, 1996; Sack, 2004). The arrest policy also ensured victim safety while looking for safer alternatives and made it easier for social service providers to interact with victims. Mandatory arrest policies have dramatically increased the number of arrests for IPV, although the research about whether mandatory arrests lead to less recidivism is mixed.

One unintended consequence of mandatory arrest laws was the rise of dual arrest laws (Dichter et al., 2007; Hirschel & Deveau, 2017). When police are unsure who the victim is in an IPV call, they sometimes arrest both the perpetrator and aggressor. Critics point to the unfairness of this to victims. Some states instituted primary aggressor laws to lower mutual arrest rates, which force police officers to label a primary aggressor at the incident. Several authors found primary aggressor policies to decrease the number of mutual arrests (Dichter et al., 2011; Hirschel & Deveau, 2017; Hirschel et al., 2007, 2021; McMahon & Pence, 2003).

In addition to mandatory arrest and primary aggressor laws, several jurisdictions have instituted "no-drop policies" or evidence-based prosecution in response to the high number of dismissed IPV cases, often due to uncooperative victims or inability to locate victims (B. E. Smith & Davis, 2004). Instead of depending on a victim being willing to press charges or testify, prosecutors utilize other types of evidence to bring charges against perpetrators (Messing et al., 2015; B. E. Smith & Davis, 2004). These alternative types of evidence include 911 tapes, police testimony and reports, emergency room reports, physical evidence collected from the scene, and testimony from other witnesses. IPV advocates are mixed in their support of this form of prosecution. Some argue that it takes the pressure off the victim, while others point out that it takes power away from the victim while assuming the state's interests are greater than those of the victim. It is unclear whether these policies are effective in lowering risk. Some authors have found that mandatory arrest or no-drop-type policies can increase perpetrators' risk of retaliating against victims (Barner & Carney, 2011). In their seminal work on no-drop policies, Ford and Regoli (n.d.) found that having the ability to choose to drop the prosecution, either by the victim or prosecutor, decreased the likelihood that the victim would experience future violence. That being said, victims who decided to drop prosecution were more likely to experience future violence.

History of IPV Policy in the United States

1640: The Beginning of IPV Policies

From 1640 to 1680, Puritans in the United States enacted the first laws in the world against wife abuse and child abuse (Fagan, 1996; Pleck, 1989). The Puritans used community, church, and state to decrease IPV; in fact, it was common for neighbors to check for signs of abuse and report any to the local minister or police officer (Pleck, 1989). In 1639 the New Haven Colony enacted the first law addressing family violence (incest, mainly) in the United States, though this law was never applied to any individual. In 1649 the first law against wife abuse in the United States and Western world was passed in the Massachusetts Bay Colony. Although the laws were written, there is limited evidence that offenders were ever prosecuted.

From 1672 to 1850, no new laws were written relating to family violence (Pleck, 1989). In 1850, Tennessee passed a law making it illegal for husbands to beat their wives (Fagan, 1996; Pleck, 1989). While courts were close to tenements and women could easily access them, they could not count on charges against their husbands. Wives were sometimes sent to jail after their husbands were fined for beating them. Although these laws existed at the state level, there were also at least three state court cases that found that husbands could *reasonably* discipline their wives physically, leading some historians to say there were no laws on family violence at the time. By the 1870s, though, judges no longer supported the idea of husbands being able to discipline their wives, instead choosing to let criminal courts handle cases of abuse (Schneider, 2000). Several states passed laws prohibiting husbands from beating their wives.

From 1874 to 1890, spousal abuse and incest victims received some small efforts while the Societies for the Prevention of Cruelty to Children (SPCC) were being formed (Pleck, 1989; Schneider, 2000). This was partially due to an uptick in crime in the post–Civil War United States, a revitalized desire to institute Protestant morality, and the middle class's fear of crime (Pleck, 1989). From 1900 to 1920, family court judges and those heading SPCCs thought the state's role was to control family privacy more than police and prosecute family violence (Fagan, 1996; Pleck, 1989). These individuals believed social casework to be more efficient, humane, and better at rehabilitating these families. From 1900 to the 1950s, social agencies encountered family violence but attributed them to causes such as economic hardship, family problems, and psychiatric difficulties.

1960s: The Feminist Movement Urges Action

In the 1960s, feminist advocates and lawyers became more public in highlighting the problem of abuse against women, especially after a group of doctors founded the term "battered child syndrome" (Kempe et al., 1962; Schneider, 2000). While awareness about child abuse was increasing and states were passing mandatory reporting laws related to child abuse, the battered women's movement was campaigning for laws that increased protections for women who were being abused and made it easier for them to file complaints (Pleck, 1989). During this time, battered women's shelters were being founded, and feminist advocacy groups encouraged women to file police reports so their abusers would be punished. In the mid- to late 1970s, funding decreased for domestic violence programs to protect the family and their privacy. Police were taught to tell husbands to take a walk or cool off during IPV calls (Fagan, 1996; Hirschel & Deveau, 2017; Sack, 2004). Mediation between the parties was also typical (Hirschel & Deveau, 2017). Police were also instructed not to make arrests because the prevailing belief was that IPV was a family issue, not a criminal issue (Fagan, 1996; Sack, 2004). If a police officer did arrest husbands, the cases were rarely prosecuted (Sack, 2004). Prosecutors generally would not continue with charges if the victim did not want to press charges. While the prosecution was scarce, states did start to pass legislation related to protection orders for victims. In fact, until the late 1970s, women were unable to apply for restraining orders against their husbands unless they also applied for a divorce at the same time (Fagan, 1996).

1980s: Arrest Law Reforms and Development of Victims Support Programs

By the 1980s, several police departments across the nation started changing their IPV arrest laws after both civil lawsuits and pressure from battered women advocates (Dichter et al., 2007; Fagan, 1996; Sack, 2004). This included making it possible to arrest batterers and charge them with misdemeanors. The U.S. Congress passed the FVPSA in 1984, under the Child Abuse Prevention and Treatment Act revisions (Family and Youth Services Bureau, 2020). At its core, the act recognized domestic violence as a public health issue. The act created a 24-hour hotline for domestic violence, funded grants to communities to help survivors of domestic violence, and increased culturally sensitive training and research in domestic violence. The act also increased training, research, and collaboration around domestic violence and its relationship to homelessness and housing. Congress also passed VOCA in 1984 (Office for Victims of Crime, 1996). VOCA's main policy goals were to expand services to victims of crime, expand direct and comprehensive services, encourage victim cooperation, and help victims obtain benefits. VOCA has a special section focusing on victims of domestic violence, sexual assault, and child abuse. Finally, in 1984, the U.S. Attorney General's Task Force on Family Violence recommended that states legislate mandatory arrest policies in IPV cases (U.S. Attorney General's Task Force on Family Violence, 1984).

In 1992, the U.S. Supreme Court first acknowledged how widespread and severe IPV had become in its opinion on *Planned Parenthood of Southeastern Pennsylvania v. Casey*, a case regarding a Pennsylvania statute requiring a pregnant woman to notify her spouse before seeking an abortion (*Planned Parenthood of Southeastern Pennsylvania v. Casey*, 1992;

Schneider, 2000). The court sided with Planned Parenthood, which expressed concerns about women utilizing all reproductive choices when afraid to tell their husbands they were pregnant. By the mid-1990s, every state also had some level of civil protection (restraining order) statutes (Sack, 2004). Several also added mandatory arrest laws, databases of domestic violence incidents in local precincts, and policies on documenting all domestic violence calls—even if no arrests were made. VAWA was passed in 1994 (Sacco, 2021).

2000 to Present: Emphasis on Support to Indigenous Tribes

VAWA and its subsequent reauthorizations in 2000, 2005, 2013, and 2021 specifically targeted violence against women at federal, state, local, and tribal levels (Sacco, 2019). Federally, VAWA made victim restitution for certain federal sex offenses mandatory and added enhanced sentencing guidelines for repeat sex offenders at the federal level. For states, tribes, and local entities, VAWA authorized grant funds to help both investigate and prosecute violence against women. In addition, VAWA addressed research, victim services, governmental collaboration, and public attitudes concerning domestic violence, sexual violence, stalking, and dating violence. FVPSA, VOCA, and VAWA are the three major pieces of federal legislation regarding domestic violence.

IPV and Vulnerable Populations

IPV impacts several vulnerable populations in unique ways. Without a doubt, women are uniquely vulnerable to IPV across the world when cultures are embedded in sexism that denies the value and autonomy of women. Unfortunately, the pervasiveness of these cultures has increased the vulnerability to IPV in both shared and distinctive ways among different populations of women.

Women

The World Health Organization (2012) indicates that IPV results from individual, family, community, and societal variables that merge to enhance the conditions of risk and protective factors that beget IPV. Known IPV risk factors for women include lower levels of education, a history of child maltreatment, witnessing family violence, harmful alcohol use, low levels of gender equality in law, and weak legal sanctions for sexual violence. Each of these risk factors singly or compounded together raises the risk of IPV in a woman's life. In addition, while the shared risk factors are present in most women's lives, there are distinctive risk factors for women who hold identities that are also marginalized, such as having a disability or being elderly, an immigrant, or transgender, thus layering on additional risks.

Women With Disabilities

Muster (2021) asserts that without a doubt, women with disabilities are among the most vulnerable populations globally, and this pattern carries over for IPV. Sasseville and colleagues (2020) underscore the reality that vulnerability to IPV for women with disabilities is rarely centered in the IPV conversation. This is despite the findings of Barrett et al. (2009), who revealed that women with disabilities are significantly more vulnerable to IPV when compared to women without disabilities (33.2% vs. 21.2%, respectively). One unique vulnerability of women with disabilities is described by Alhusen et al. (2020), who indicate that reproductive coercion is associated with an increased risk of unintended pregnancy. Women with disabilities already encounter significant barriers to health and health care. IPV in their lives tends to exacerbate existing challenges, thereby diminishing already poor health outcomes (Barrett et al., 2009).

Older Women

The lifetime prevalence of IPV experienced by older women is estimated at between 16.5% and 54.5%, reflecting the variability in defining IPV in older adults (Pathak et al., 2019). Both age and life transitions lead to different experiences with IPV among older adults compared to their younger counterparts. In addition, older women who are dependent on their partners face unique barriers to accessing help. For example, Beaulaurier and colleagues (2007) identified response a family, responsive clergy, response of the justice system, and responsiveness and community resources as unique barriers among older adult women in accessing supports for their IPV situations.

Immigrant and Refugee Women

Prevalence rates for IPV among immigrant and refugee women are as high as 41% (Park et al., 2021). Language difficulties, confusion over legal rights, cultural acceptance of violence against women, and stress adaptation to new cultural and social structures are palpable barriers for immigrant and refugee women who experience IPV (Runner et al., 2009). Poverty present in the lives of immigrant and refugee women is a consistent theme in IPV vulnerability; marriage and relationships bound by uneven social and economic resources make foreign-born women especially vulnerable to control by their partners. Social isolation is a common experience for immigrant and refugee women, leaving them with virtually no social support, financial assistance, or ways to gain knowledge of their rights. Immigration status is a unique risk factor present in the lives of immigrant and refugee women as abusers can threaten deportation (Runner et al., 2009).

Transgender Women

In a meta-analysis of IPV prevalence and correlates in transgender populations, Peitzmeier et al. (2020) established the median lifetime prevalence of physical IPV at 37.5% and sexual IPV at 25% for transgender individuals. That makes transgender women 1.7 times more likely to experience IPV compared to cisgender women. There are many unique risk factors present in the lives of transgender women that make them uniquely vulnerable to IPV, including denial of access to services such as shelters and a history of poor experiences with both police and health service organizations when reporting IPV (Valentine et al., 2017). For parents who are transgender women, the risk of losing custody of their child can influence decisions about reporting IPV. Also, threatening to reveal their partner's transgender status is a unique risk factor that only women who are transgender will experience (Cook-Daniels, 2015). Accessing health and mental health providers who are transgender affirming and inclusive is a unique treatment challenge for transgender women (Saad et al., 2020).

Lesbian, Gay, and Bisexual People

The CDC's National Intimate Partner and Sexual Violence Survey revealed that bisexual women are 1.8 times more likely to report lifetime IPV than heterosexual women (Walters et al., 2013). Messinger (2011) estimated that 3.6% of lesbians had experienced lifetime IPV. Using a representative sample, Goldberg and Meyer (2013) estimated that 26.9% of gay and bisexual men had experienced IPV in their lifetimes. Several risk factors are present in the lives of gay and bisexual men that increase the risk of IPV, including legal definitions or practices that exclude same-sex couples, low levels of confidence in law enforcement or the courts actually helping, homophobia, and discrimination from health and mental health providers (Mustanski et al., 2007). In addition, lesbian, gay, and bisexual people face the unique risk of having their sexual orientation revealed to friends, family, people in the workplace, and society (Edwards et al., 2015). Accessing health and mental health providers who affirm and are inclusive of lesbian, gay, and bisexual people remains a unique treatment challenge (Martos et al., 2018).

Social Work Ethical Implications

Social workers have an ethical responsibility to address IPV through prevention, intervention, and treatment, as well as helping to advance legislation that improves IPV policies and practices. Wilson and Webb (2018) provide a vital reminder that IPV impacts mostly women, regardless of race, ethnicity, or socioeconomic status. Trauma resulting from IPV is lifelong and multidimensional (physical, sexual, psychological). IPV impacts are not individual—criminal justice, public health, and child welfare systems are also overwhelmed by IPV (Wilson & Webb, 2018). While a number of social work ethical values are implicated in IPV practice, two are featured here as they relate to foundational IPV policies (the FVPSA, VOCA, and VAWA).

Ethical Value: Dignity and Worth of the Person

The social work ethical value of dignity and worth of the person are made manifest as the ethical principle that social workers respect a person's inherent dignity and worth (National Association of Social Workers [NASW], 2017). Without a doubt, IPV is a fundamental betrayal of the dignity and worth of the person that annually over 10 million Americans encounter. The sobering reality is that some will not survive (Black et al., 2011). Forensic social workers in IPV practice may find themselves engaging with some of the 1,500-plus programs funded through the FVPSA, including emergency shelters, crisis hotlines, and counseling and case management services.

For decades the gap between need and available resources has grown, while the budget of the FVPSA has not. While this is true for most social safety net programs, the nature of IPV presents unique challenges to survivors to rely on these supports for their very survival. Over 70,000 people are served by FVPSA funding daily, while nearly 12,000 requests for services go unmet (Congressional Research Service, 2022). In light of their ethical responsibility within the IPV field of practice, social workers can manifest the value of dignity and worth of the person by sustained advocacy for federal funding to close the FVPSA service gap requests.

Social Work Value: Social Justice

The social work value of social justice is made manifest as social workers challenge social injustice (NASW, 2017). Survivors of IPV often lose a sense of physical, psychological, and sexual safety (Wilson & Webb, 2018). Each of these diminishes personal agency and autonomy (Edwards et al., 2008), thereby complicating the task of recovering from IPV. Being an IPV survivor can also come with unexpected financial costs over the life course to address physical and psychological trauma (Peterson et al., 2018).

VOCA provides 6 million IPV survivors with support services annually through funds paid by convicted criminals to federal courts, including child abuse treatment programs, rape crisis centers, and domestic violence shelters. Starting in 2018, the fund began markedly shrinking, setting off a series of cuts to essential support services. This trend cannot continue. In light of their ethical responsibility, social workers can manifest the value of social justice through advocacy for reforms to VOCA that amend the law to allow for penalties and fines from nonprosecution and deferred prosecution to be deposited into the Crime Victims Fund. Additionally, social workers should advocate for protections for VOCA that disallow VOCA funds from being redirected to other Department of Justice programs.

VAWA has improved federal, tribal, state, and local responses to IPV crimes by providing prevention programs, housing protections for survivors, rape crisis centers, and, more recently, culturally and linguistically specific services for Native American and LGBTQ survivors. Unfortunately, VAWA expired in February 2019. Although its current programs will remain in effect for particular populations and victim service categories, it cannot receive funding expansion or address emerging service needs until reauthorized by Congress. Social workers can manifest the value of social justice through advocacy for the reauthorization of VAWA that closes critical funding gaps while expanding to include LGBTQ+ people (Wilson & Webb, 2018).

In Summary

IPV survivors face several immediate and long-term challenges. IPV policies are intended to prevent this public health crisis while also providing essential supports. Forensic social workers engaged in IPV as a field of practice must know the three foundational policies intended to address this societal scourge. Knowledge of each of these policies, how they are developed, who they serve, and how they are funded can aid the social worker in direct client support and legislative advocacy. The gap between need and funding has never been more significant, and social workers need to be engaged at macro levels in lobbying to ensure passage of needed reforms.

References

Alhusen, J. L., Bloom, T., Anderson, J., & Hughes, R. B. (2020). Intimate partner violence, reproductive coercion, and unintended pregnancy in women with disabilities. *Disability and Health Journal, 13*(2), 100849.

American Bar Association. (2020, December 3). *Domestic violence basics.* https://www.americanbar.org/groups/legal_services/milvets/aba_home_front/information_center/family_law/domestic_violence/domestic_violence_basics/

American Prosecutors Research Institute & National Council of Juvenile and Family Court Judges. (1998). *Confronting violence against women: A community action approach.*

Armstead, T. L., Kearns, M., Rambo, K., Estefan, L. F., Dills, J., Rivera, M. S., & El-Beshti, R. (2018). The Use of the Data-to-Action Framework in the evaluation of CDC's DELTA FOCUS program. *Journal of Public Health Management and Practice, 24*(Suppl 1), S51–S58. https://doi.org/10.1097/PHH.0000000000000677

Armstead, T. L., Rambo, K., Kearns, M., Jones, K. M., Dills, J., & Brown, P. (2017). CDC's DELTA FOCUS Program: Identifying promising primary prevention strategies for intimate partner violence. *Journal of Women's Health, 26*(1), 9–12. https://doi.org/10.1089/jwh.2016.6251

Barner, J. R., & Carney, M. M. (2011). Interventions for intimate partner violence: A historical review. *Journal of Family Violence, 26*(3), 235–244. https://doi.org/10.1007/s10896-011-9359-3

Barrett, K. A., O'Day, B., Roche, A., & Carlson, B. L. (2009). Intimate partner violence, health status, and health care access among women with disabilities. *Women's Health Issues, 19*(2), 94–100.

Beaulaurier, R. L., Seff, L. R., Newman, F. L., & Dunlop, B. (2007). External barriers to help-seeking for older women who experience intimate partner violence. *Journal of Family Violence, 22*(8), 747–755.

Benitez, C. T., McNiel, D. E., & Binder, R. L. (2010). Do protection orders protect? *Journal of the American Academy of Psychiatry and the Law Online, 38*(3), 376.

Black, M., Basile, K., Brieding, M., Smith, S., Walters, M., Merrick, M., Stevens, M., & Chen, J. (2011). National Intimate Partner and Sexual Violence Survey: 2010 summary report.

Bledsoe, L. K., Yankeelov, P. A., Barbee, A. P., & Antle, B. F. (2004). Understanding the impact of intimate partner violence mandatory reporting law. *Violence Against Women, 10*(5), 534–560. https://doi.org/10.1177/1077801204264354

Congressional Research Service. (2022). Family Violence Prevention and Service (FVSPA): Background and Funding. https://sgp.fas.org/crs/misc/R42838.pdf

Cook-Daniels, L. (2015). Intimate partner violence in transgender couples: "Power and control" in a specific cultural context. *Partner Abuse, 6*(1), 126–140.

Cordier, R., Chung, D., Wilkes-Gillan, S., & Speyer, R. (2021). The effectiveness of protection orders in reducing recidivism in domestic violence: A systematic review and meta-analysis. *Trauma, Violence, & Abuse, 22*(4), 804–828. https://doi.org/10.1177/1524838019882361

Dichter, M. E., Marcus, S. C., Morabito, M. S., & Rhodes, K. V. (2011). Explaining the IPV arrest decision: Incident, agency, and community factors. *Criminal Justice Review, 36*(1), 22–39. https://doi.org/10.1177/0734016810383333

Domestic Abuse Intervention Programs. (n.d.). *Coordinated community response.* https://www.theduluthmodel.org/about-us/coordinated-community-response/

Edwards, K. M., Merrill, J. C., Desai, A. D., & McNamara, J. R. (2008). Ethical dilemmas in the treatment of battered women in individual psychotherapy: Analysis of the beneficence versus autonomy polemic. *Journal of Psychological Trauma, 7*(1), 1–20.

Edwards, K. M., Sylaska, K. M., & Neal, A. M. (2015). Intimate partner violence among sexual minority populations: A critical review of the literature and agenda for future research. *Psychology of Violence, 5*(2), 112–121.

Ehrensaft, M. K., & Cohen, P. (2012). Contribution of family violence to the intergenerational transmission of externalizing behavior. *Prevention Science, 13*(4), 370–383. https://doi.org/10.1007/s11121-011-0223-8

Estefan, L. F., Armstead, T. L., Rivera, M. S., Kearns, M. C., Carter, D., Crowell, J., El-Beshti, R., & Daniels, B. (2019). Enhancing the national dialogue on the prevention of intimate partner violence. *American Journal of Community Psychology, 63*(1–2), 153–167. https://doi.org/10.1002/ajcp.12318

Fagan, J. (1996). *The criminalization of domestic violence: Promises and limits.* National Institute of Justice. https://www.ojp.gov/pdffiles/crimdom.pdf

Family and Youth Services Bureau. (2020). *Family Violence Prevention and Services program* [Fact sheet]. U.S. Department of Health and Human Services. https://www.acf.hhs.gov/sites/default/files/documents/fysb/fysb_fvpsa_factsheet_oct_2020_508.pdf

Ford, D., & Regoli, M. (1993). The criminal prosecution of wife assaulter: Process, problems, and effects. In N. Z. Hilton (Ed.), *Legal responses to wife assault: Current trends and evaluation* (pp. 127–164). Sage Publications.

Freire, K. E., Zakocs, R., Le, B., Hill, J. A., Brown, P., & Wheaton, J. (2015). Evaluation of DELTA PREP: A project aimed at integrating primary prevention of intimate partner violence within state domestic violence coalitions. *Health Education & Behavior, 42*(4), 436–448. https://doi.org/10.1177/1090198115579413

Goldberg, N., & Meyer, I. (2013). Sexual orientation disparities in history of intimate partner violence: Results from the California Health Interview Survey. *Journal of Interpersonal Violence, 28*(5), 1109–1118.

Harvey, A., Garcia-Moreno, C., & Butchart, A. (2007). *Primary prevention of intimate-partner violence and sexual violence* [Background paper]. WHO expert meeting. World Health Organization. https://www.who.int/violence_injury_prevention/publications/violence/IPV-SV.pdfHirschel, D., Buzawa, E., Pattavina, A., Faggiani, D., & Reuland, M. (2007). *Explaining the prevalence, context, and consequences of dual arrest in intimate partner cases* (Final report NIJ 2001-WT-BX-0501). Department of Justice.

Hirschel, D., & Deveau, L. (2017). The impact of primary aggressor laws on single versus dual arrest in incidents of intimate partner violence. *Violence Against Women, 23*(10), 1155–1176. https://doi.org/10.1177/1077801216657898

Hirschel, D., McCormack, P. D., & Buzawa, E. (2021). A 10-year study of the impact of intimate partner violence primary aggressor laws on single and dual arrest. *Journal of Interpersonal Violence, 36*(3–4), 1356–1390. https://doi.org/10.1177/0886260517739290

Holt, V. L., Kernic, M. A., Lumley, T., Wolf, M. E., & Rivara, F. P. (2002). Civil protection orders and risk of subsequent police-reported violence. *JAMA, 288*(5), 589–594. https://doi.org/10.1001/jama.288.5.589

Jeske, E. C. (2017). Punishing victims for being victims: Aiding and abetting violations of protective orders. *Wake Forest Journal of Law and Policy, 7*(1), 275–293.

Johnson, L., & Stylianou, A. M. (2020). Coordinated community responses to domestic violence: A systematic review of the literature. *Trauma, Violence & Abuse, 1.*

Jordan, C. E., & Pritchard, A. J. (2021). Mandatory reporting of domestic violence: What do abuse survivors think and what variables influence those opinions? *Journal of Interpersonal Violence, 36*(7–8), NP4170–NP4190. https://doi.org/10.1177/0886260518787206

Kempe, C. H., Silverman, F. N., Steele, B. F., Droegemueller, W., & Silver, H. K. (1962). The battered-child syndrome. *Journal of the American Medical Association, 181*(1), 17–24. https://doi.org/10.1001/jama.1962.03050270019004

Klevens, J., & Cox, P. (2008). Coordinated community responses to intimate partner violence: Where do we go from here? *Criminology and Public Policy, 7*(4), 547–556. https://doi.org/10.1111/j.1745-9133.2008.00527.x

Lippy, C., Jumarali, S. N., Nnawulezi, N. A., Williams, E. P., & Burk, C. (2020). The impact of mandatory reporting laws on survivors of intimate partner violence: Intersectionality, help-seeking and the need for change. *Journal of Family Violence, 35*(3), 255–267.

Martin, S. L., Coyne-Beasley, T., Hoehn, M., Mathew, M., Runyan, C. W., Orton, S., & Royster, L.-A. (2009). Primary prevention of violence against women: Training needs of violence practitioners. *Violence Against Women, 15*(1), 44–56. https://doi.org/10.1177/1077801208327483

Martos, A. J., Wilson, P. A., Gordon, A. R., Lightfoot, M., & Meyer, I. H. (2018). "Like finding a unicorn": Healthcare preferences among lesbian, gay, and bisexual people in the United States. *Social Science & Medicine, 208,* 126–133.

McFarlane, J., Malecha, A., Gist, J., Watson, K., Batten, E., Hall, I., & Smith, S. (2004). Protection orders and intimate partner violence: An 18-month study of 150 black, Hispanic, and white women. *American Journal of Public Health, 94*(4), 613–618. https://doi.org/10.2105/ajph.94.4.613

McMahon, M., & Pence, E. (2003). Making social change: Reflections on individual and institutional advocacy with women arrested for domestic violence. *Violence Against Women, 9*(1), 47–74. https://doi.org/10.1177/1077801202238430

McNaughton Reyes, H. L., Foshee, V. A., Bauer, D. J., & Ennett, S. T. (2012). Heavy alcohol use and dating violence perpetration during adolescence: Family, peer and neighborhood violence as moderators. *Prevention Science, 13*(4), 340–349. https://doi.org/10.1007/s11121-011-0215-8

Messing, J. T., Ward-Lasher, A., Thaller, J., & Bagwell-Gray, M. E. (2015). The state of intimate partner violence intervention: Progress and continuing challenges. *Social Work, 60*(4), 305–313.

Messinger, A. (2011). Invisible victims: Same-sex IPV in the National Violence against Women Survey. *Journal of Interpersonal Violence, 26*(11), 2228–2243.

Moffitt, T. E., Caspi, A., Rutter, M., & Silva, P. A. (2001). *Sex differences in antisocial behavior: Conduct disorder, delinquency, and violence in the Dunedin longitudinal study.* Cambridge University Press.

Mustanski, B., Garofalo, R., Herrick, A., & Donenberg, G. (2007). Psychosocial health problems increase risk for HIV among urban young men who have sex with men: Preliminary evidence of a syndemic in need of attention. *Annals of Behavioral Medicine, 34*(1), 37–45.

Muster, C. L. (2021). The silenced voices of hidden survivors: Addressing intimate partner violence among women with disabilities through a combined theoretical approach. *Affilia, 36*(2), 156–166.National Center for Injury Prevention and Control. (2018). *Domestic Violence Prevention Enhancement and Leadership Through Alliances (DELTA).* https://www.cdc.gov/violenceprevention/intimatepartnerviolence/delta/index.html

National Center for Injury Prevention and Control, Centers for Disease Control and Prevention. (2020). *Preventing intimate partner violence.* https://www.cdc.gov/violenceprevention/pdf/ipv/IPV-factsheet_2020_508.pdf

National Coalition Against Domestic Violence. (2020). *Domestic violence.* https://assets.speakcdn.com/assets/2497/domestic_violence-2020080709350855.pdf?1596811079991

National Conference of State Legislatures. (2019). *Domestic violence/domestic abuse definitions and relationships.* https://www.ncsl.org/research/human-services/domestic-violence-domestic-abuse-definitions-and-relationships.aspx

National Council of Juvenile and Family Court Judges. (1994). *Family violence: A model state code.* https://www.ncjfcj.org/wp-content/uploads/2012/03/modecode_fin_printable.pdf

National Institute of Justice. (2007). *Overview of intimate partner violence.* https://nij.ojp.gov/topics/articles/overview-intimate-partner-violence

National Network to End Domestic Violence. (n.d.). *Forms of abuse.* https://nnedv.org/content/forms-of-abuse/

National Network to End Domestic Violence. (2021). *15th annual domestic violence counts report.* https://nnedv.org/wp-content/uploads/2021/05/15th-Annual-DV-Counts-Report-National-Summary.pdfOffice for Victims of Crime. (1996). *Report to Congress: July 1996.* U.S. Department of Justice. https://www.ncjrs.gov/ovc_archives/repcong/welcome.html

Park, T., Mullins, A., Zahir, N., Salami, B., Lasiuk, G., & Hegadoren, K. (2021). Domestic violence and immigrant women: A glimpse behind a veiled door. *Violence Against Women, 27*(15–16), 2910–2926.

Pathak, N., Dhairyawan, R., & Tariq, S. (2019). The experience of intimate partner violence among older women: A narrative review. *Maturitas, 121,* 63–75.

Peitzmeier, S. M., Malik, M., Kattari, S. K., Marrow, E., Stephenson, R., Agénor, M., & Reisner, S. L. (2020). Intimate partner violence in transgender populations: Systematic review and meta-analysis of prevalence and correlates. *American Journal of Public Health, 110*(9), e1–e14.

Peterson, C., Kearns, M. C., McIntosh, W. L., Estefan, L. F., Nicolaidis, C., McCollister, K. E., . . . Florence, C. (2018). Lifetime economic burden of intimate partner violence among U.S. adults. *American Journal of Preventive Medicine, 55*(4), 433–444.

Planned Parenthood of Southeastern Pennsylvania v. Casey, 505 U.S. 833 ___. (1992). https://www.loc.gov/item/usrep505833/

Pleck, E. (1989). Criminal approaches to family violence, 1640–1980. *Crime and Justice, 11*, 19–57.

Saad, M., Burley, J. F., Miljanovski, M., Macdonald, S., Bradley, C., & Du Mont, J. (2020, March). Planning an intersectoral network of healthcare and community leaders to advance trans-affirming care for sexual assault survivors. In *Healthcare management forum* (Vol. 33, No. 2, pp. 65–69). SAGE Publications.

Sacco, L. N. (2019). *The Violence Against Women Act (VAWA): Historical overview, funding, and reauthorization* (No. R45410). Congressional Research Service. https://sgp.fas.org/crs/misc/R45410.pdf

Sacco, L. N. (2021). *The Violence Against Women Act (VAWA): Reauthorization: Issues for Congress* (No. R46742). Congressional Research Service. https://crsreports.congress.gov/product/pdf/R/R46742

Sack, E. J. (2004). Battered women and the state: The struggle for the future of domestic violence policy. *Wisconsin Law Review, 2004*(6), 1657–1740.

Sasseville, N., Maurice, P., Montminy, L., Hassan, G., & St-Pierre, É. (2022). Cumulative contexts of vulnerability to intimate partner violence among women with disabilities, elderly women, and immigrant women: Prevalence, risk factors, explanatory theories, and prevention. *Trauma, Violence, & Abuse, 23*(1), 88–100.

Sasseville, N., Maurice, P., Montminy, L., Hassan, G., & St-Pierre, É. (2020). Cumulative contexts of vulnerability to intimate partner violence among women with disabilities, older women, and immigrant women: Prevalence, risk factors, explanatory theories, and prevention. *Trauma, Violence, & Abuse*, 1524838020925773.

Schneider, E. M. (2000). Introduction: Battered women, feminist lawmaking, and equality. In *Battered women and feminist law-making* (pp. 3–10). Yale University Press.

Shorey, R. C., Tirone, V., & Stuart, G. L. (2014). Coordinated community response components for victims of intimate partner violence: A review of the literature. *Aggression and Violent Behavior, 19*(4), 363–371. https://doi.org/10.1016/j.avb.2014.06.001

Smith, B. E., & Davis, R. C. (2004). *An evaluation of efforts to implement no drop policies: Two central values in conflict* (NCJ 199719). National Institute of Justice. https://www.ojp.gov/pdffiles1/nij/199719.pdf

Smith, S. G., Zhang, X., Basile, K. C., Merrick, M. T., Wang, J., Kresnow, M., & Chen, J. (2018). *The National Intimate Partner and Sexual Violence Survey (NISVS): 2015 data brief—Updated release*. National Center for Injury Prevention and Control, Centers for Disease Control and Prevention. https://www.cdc.gov/violenceprevention/pdf/2015data-brief508.pdf

Sullivan, C. M. (2018). Understanding how domestic violence support services promote survivor well-being: A conceptual model. *Journal of Family Violence, 33*(2), 123–131.

Topliffe, E. (1992). Why civil protection orders are effective remedies for domestic violence but mutual protective orders are not. *Indiana Law Journal, 67*(4), 1039–1046.

Truman, J. L., & Morgan, R. E. (2014). *Non-fatal domestic violence, 2003–2012*. Bureau of Justice Statistics. https://bjs.ojp.gov/content/pub/pdf/ndv0312.pdf

U.S. Attorney General's Task Force on Family Violence. (1984). *Final report*. U.S. Government Printing Office. https://files.eric.ed.gov/fulltext/ED251762.pdf

Valentine, S. E., Peitzmeier, S. M., King, D. S., O'Cleirigh, C., Marquez, S. M., Presley, C., & Potter, J. (2017). Disparities in exposure to intimate partner violence among transgender/gender nonconforming and sexual minority primary care patients. *LGBT Health, 4*(4), 260–267.

Walters, M. L., Chen, J., & Breiding, M. J. (2013). *The National Intimate Partner and Sexual Violence Survey (NISVS): 2010 findings on victimization by sexual orientation*. Atlanta, GA: National Center for Injury Prevention and Control.

Wilson, M. H., & Webb, R. (2018). Social work's role in responding to intimate partner violence. *Social Justice Brief*, 1–11. https://www.socialworkers.org/LinkClick.aspx?fileticket=WTrDbQ6CHxI%3D&portalid=0

World Health Organization. (2012). *Intimate partner violence (understanding and addressing violence against women)*. https://apps.who.int/iris/bitstream/handle/10665/77432/WHO_RHR_12.36_eng.pdf

22

Reentry

Challenges, Collateral Consequences, and Advocacy for Returning Community Members

Carly Sommers, Elizabeth A. Justesen, and George S. Leibowitz

Introduction

Over 600,000 people return from prison each year, not including the millions revolving through jails from shorter, local sentences referred to as the "jail churn" (Bureau of Justice Statistics [BJS], 2018; Sawyer & Wagner, 2019). "Reentry" is a broad term with multiple definitions that typically describes the process by which previously court-involved people return to their community. Although the term was traditionally used to refer to individuals discharged from jails and prisons, in this chapter, we will define this term as inclusive of the time of arrest, referring to any persons who have spent even the most minimal time *in custody*. Even if they are eventually found innocent and subject to wrongful incarceration, those discharged from prison must reenter their communities and navigate a return to their lives, which is often fraught with significant challenges (e.g., Maschi et al., 2015). Additionally, the global impact of the COVID-19 pandemic resulted in barriers to successful reentry, including the need for mitigation efforts to prevent the spread of the virus among incarcerated individuals returning to the community, as well as co-occurring mental health issues and psychosocial stressors (Desai et al., 2021).

Bail involves releasing a person upon a promise to appear at a subsequent criminal proceeding, a system that often negatively impacts people of color and low-income communities (Page et al., 2019). Among states with aggressive and/or archaic bail structures, arrested individuals face many obstacles, including being detained before adjudication of

Carly Sommers, Elizabeth A. Justesen, and George S. Leibowitz, *Reentry* In: *Handbook of Forensic Social Work*. Edited by: David Axlyn McLeod, Anthony P. Natale, and Kristin W. Mapson, Oxford University Press. © Oxford University Press 2024. DOI: 10.1093/oso/9780197694732.003.0022 their case, despite the legal presumption of innocence. Detainment can encompass hours or days, and significant interpersonal disruptions and family stress often occur within the first 24 to 72 hours. One can imagine the process of being arrested, held on bail, and unable to call one's employer as problematic for job security. In addition to the cumulative disadvantage of populations living in poverty and facing homelessness becoming involved in the criminal justice system, the disproportionality of stigmatized subgroups is also reflected in marginalization based on age, health, gender, mental health, and legal status. Moreover, individuals impacted by social determinants of health, including traumatic stress, community violence, housing issues, unemployment, and food insecurity, are at risk for ongoing family court and child welfare system involvement. Huntington (2014) argues that regulations and criminal justice policies are often punitive and at odds with the needs of families to provide stable, positive, healthy relationships necessary for individuals and societies to flourish.

For individuals allowed to post bail while their case is pending, some pretrial consequences or arrests can be mitigated. Typically, reentry can prove challenging and traumatic and diminish dignity. For persons who are eventually convicted and sentenced, after "paying their debt to society" (in the context of a conviction and whether via the imposition of a fine, probation, jail, and/or prison sentence), the stigma and collateral consequences will persist, which in many cases constitutes lifelong punishment (Malcolm & Siebler, 2017). In this chapter, we will explore these ethical and legal challenges and provide social workers with the knowledge and frameworks to understand the barriers to reentry and the complexity of the problem. We will also offer alternative perspectives on community safety and guidance for policy and advocacy to help this diverse, underserved population.

Scope of the Issue

The steady increase in mass incarceration is well documented (Sawyer & Wagner, 2020). The United States incarcerates more people than any other country globally, with approximately 2.6 million people in custody in the United States. This accounts for 25% of the world's incarcerated population (BJS, 2018). There are also significantly more imprisoned women and children in the United States, by proportion, than in other countries. Following the civil rights movement in the United States in the 1960s, America embarked on numerous punitive policies, pieces of legislation, and programs, including, for example, the War on Drugs and mandatory sentencing laws (DuVernay 2016). Despite decreasing crime rates in the latter part of the 1990s, incarceration rates continued to increase. More money continues to be dedicated to building jails and prisons rather than schools (Ash, 2019).

According to the U.S. Department of Justice Office of Justice Programs, 641,100 people were released from state and federal prisons in 2015. Another 10.6 million cycle through local jails (BJS, 2018), including short remands and short-term sentences. Approximately 95% of incarcerated people will return home one day, and many from state or federal prisons are accountable for additional supervision or oversight. About 2 to 3 million individuals are currently under probation and parole services (Sawyer, 2019).

As the formerly incarcerated return home to their communities, the obstacles they encounter are vast, whatever the length of the sentence. According to the American Bar Association (2015), there are more than 45,000 collateral consequences for those who have criminal convictions. Collateral consequences are federal, state, and local laws and ordinances restricting people with criminal convictions from employment, educational license attainment, housing, benefits, and civic participation (see National Inventory of Collateral Consequences, https://niccc.nationalreentryresourcecenter.org/). For those with felony convictions, the future can be even more uncertain. The challenges they face exacerbate recidivism. One study of state prisoners found that an estimated 68% of released prisoners were rearrested within 3 years, 79% within 6 years, and 83% within 9 years, and recidivism rates were typically associated with increased psychosocial stress (Alper et al., 2018).

Other conditions that attenuate risk, and require evidence-based treatment, include a history of trauma (e.g., exposure to domestic violence), poverty, community violence, substance abuse issues, and untreated mental health disorders. One study found that 30% to 60% of men in state prisons had posttraumatic stress disorder (PTSD), compared to 3% to 6% of the general male population, requiring strategies for trauma-informed care (Wolff et al., 2014). According to the BJS (2018), 36.7% of women in state prisons experienced childhood abuse, compared to 12% to 17% of all adult women in the United States. At least half of incarcerated women identify at least one traumatic event in their lives (Green et al., 2016; Widra, 2020). These issues remain unaddressed in our current system of imprisonment, where people are subjected to further trauma by both other incarcerated individuals and prison staff (Wolff et al., 2013). The sequelae of traumatic stress manifest when individuals return to their families and communities of origin and are forced to navigate a postconviction landscape that does not provide support for success.

Overcoming Trauma

The prison experience can be traumatic, exposing detainees to further violence. Novisky and Peralta (2020) found that secondary violence was frequently experienced in prison, and prisoners often witnessed weaponized and nonweaponized assaults, multiperpetrator assaults, and homicide while incarcerated. Responses to witnessed violence behind bars can result in psychological distress and manifest as anxiety, depression, avoidance, hypersensitivity, hypervigilance, dissociation, suicidality, flashbacks, and difficulty with emotional regulation. Participants described experiencing significant current PTSD symptomatology after release (Green et al., 2016). The COVID-19 pandemic provided a new set of challenges for this population. As the calls for attention were paid to jails and prisons, relaxed responses resulted in many infections and needless deaths by June 2020. By May 2021, 397,965 cases of incarcerated people tested positive, and 32,683 lost their lives to the disease (Marshall Project, 2021). Personal protective equipment was scarce, with many imprisoned people using the same masks for weeks. Solitary confinement was used as a treatment measure, and the disbursement of vaccines was slow and deemed controversial, given public misinformation about its efficacy and the science.

Trauma while incarcerated is compounded by the punitive approaches to correctional management. After experiencing this trauma, returning people must acclimate to their new "free" life and engage in simple tasks such as grocery shopping, planning for a job interview, and adapting to a nonstructured routine. This can be overwhelming. One thing is sure: Our returning community members can benefit from counseling to address the multitude of issues that led them to the courthouse and those that persist upon their return.

Effective Treatment Modalities

The Substance Abuse and Mental Health Services Administration (SAMHSA), a subsidiary of the U.S. Department of Health and Human Services, provided treatment strategies for working with the justice-involved population. *Principles for Community-Based Behavioral Health Services for Justice-Involved Individuals: A Research-Based Guide* (2019) reviews evidence-based practices and recommends those listed in Tables 22.1 through 22.8. In addition to the therapeutic interventions, which may prove vital for returning community members' mental health and stability as they navigate the reentry landscape, social workers working with this population should be aware of the additional obstacles and challenges their clients will face.

TABLE 22.1 Evidence-Based Programs in Mental Health Treatment for Justice-Involved Individuals

Domains	Description
Assertive Community Treatment (ACT)	Treatment coordinated by a multidisciplinary team with high staff-to-client ratios that assumes around-the-clock responsibility for clients' case management and treatment needs
Critical Time Intervention	Nine-month, three-stage intervention that develops individualized linkages in the community and facilitates engagement with treatment, supports, and housing through building problem-solving skills, motivational coaching, and connections with community agencies
Integrated Mental Health and Substance Use Services	Treatment and service provision to support recovery from co-occurring mental and substance use disorders through a single agency or entity
Supported Employment	Matches and trains people with severe developmental, mental, and physical disabilities where their specific skills and abilities make them valuable assets to employers
Permanent Supportive Housing (PSH)	Combines permanent housing with a system of professional or peer supports or both that allows a person with mental illness to live independently in the community; supports may include regular staff contact and the availability of crisis services to prevent relapse, such as those focusing on mental health, substance use, and employment
Pharmacotherapy	Treatment that uses one or more medications as part of a comprehensive plan of psychosocial and behavioral interventions to reduce symptoms associated with mental illness or mental health issues

TABLE 22.2 Evidence-Based Practice in Mental Health Treatment for Justice-Involved Individuals

Domains	Description
Cognitive-Behavioral Therapy (CBT)	A therapeutic approach that attempts to solve problems resulting from dysfunctional thoughts, moods, or behaviors through brief, direct, and time-limited structured counseling; CBT for substance use disorders adds a component of coping strategies to stop substance use and address other co-occurring issues
Motivational	A "person-centered counseling style for addressing the common problem of ambivalence about change" (Miller & Rollnick, 2013)

TABLE 22.3 Promising Programs in Mental Health Treatment for Justice-Involved individuals

Domains	Description
Forensic Assertive Community Treatment (FACT)	FACT is an adaptation of ACT for individuals involved in the criminal justice system. FACT provides the same level and type of treatment services of ACT but also includes interventions targeted to criminogenic risk and need factors.
Forensic Intensive Case Management (FICM)	Like FACT, FICM involves the coordination of services to help individuals sustain recovery in the community and prevent further involvement with the criminal justice system. Unlike FACT, FICM uses case managers with individual caseloads as opposed to a self-contained team.
Assisted Outpatient Treatment (AOT)	AOT, also known as conditional release, outpatient commitment, involuntary outpatient commitment, or mandated outpatient treatment, is intended to facilitate the delivery of community-based outpatient mental health treatment services to individuals with serious mental illness who have refused psychiatric treatment in the past, are at risk for deterioration or harming themselves or others, and for whom hospitalization is unnecessarily restrictive.

TABLE 22.4 Promising Practices in Mental Health Treatment for Justice-Involved individuals

Domains	Description
Cognitive Behavioral Treatment Targeted to Criminogenic Risks	CBT interventions (e.g., Reasoning and Rehabilitation or Thinking for a Change) are designed to address criminogenic risks and may focus on anger management, problem-solving, and assuming personal responsibility for behavior.
Case Management	Case management is a coordinated approach to the delivery of physical health, substance use, mental health, and social services, linking individuals with appropriate services to address specific needs and achieve stated goals in a case management plan.
Forensic Peer Specialists	Formerly justice-involved individuals who are in recovery provide support to other individuals who are also involved, or at risk of becoming involved, in the criminal justice system.

TABLE 22.5 Evidence-Based Program for Treatment of Substance Use Disorders for Justice-Involved Individuals

Domains	Description
Modified Therapeutic Community (MTC)	MTCs alter the traditional therapeutic community approach in response to the psychiatric symptoms, cognitive impairments, and other impairments commonly found among individuals with co-occurring disorders. These modified programs typically have (a) increased flexibility, (b) decreased intensity, and (c) greater individualization.

TABLE 22.6 Promising Programs for Treatment of Substance Use Disorders for Justice-Involved Individuals

Domains	Description
12-Step or Other Mutual Aid Groups	Groups of nonprofessionals share a problem and support one another through the recovery process.
Peer-Based Recovery Support Programs	Formerly justice-involved individuals who are in recovery provide support to other individuals who are also involved, or at risk of becoming involved, in the criminal justice system.

TABLE 22.7 Evidence-Based Practices for Treatment of Substance Use Disorders for Justice-Involved Individuals

Domains	Description
Cognitive-Behavioral Therapy (CBT)	A therapeutic approach that attempts to solve a problem resulting from dysfunctional thoughts, moods, or behaviors through brief, direct, and time-limited structured counseling; helps individuals address problematic behaviors and develop effective coping strategies to stop substance use and address other co-occurring issues
Motivational Interviewing	A person-centered counseling style for addressing the common problem of ambivalence about change (Miller & Rollnick, 2013)
Contingency Management Interventions	Interventions that reinforce an individual's commitment to abstinence and to reduce their drug use using positive incentives (e.g., vouchers) and negative consequences (e.g., increased supervision) in response to desired and undesired behaviors
Pharmacotherapy (i.e., Medication-Assisted Treatment)	Treatment that uses one or more medications as part of a comprehensive plan of psychosocial and behavioral interventions to reduce symptoms associated with substance or alcohol use disorders
Relapse Prevention Therapy	A systematic treatment method of teaching recovering clients to recognize and manage relapse warning signs
Behavioral Couples Therapy (BCT)	A family treatment approach for couples that uses a "recovery contract" and behavioral principles to engage both people in treatment, achieve abstinence, enhance communication, and improve the relationship

TABLE 22.8 Promising Practice for Treatment of Substance Use Disorders for Justice-Involved Individuals

Domains	Description
Case management	A coordinated approach to the delivery of physical health, substance use, mental health, and social services, linking individuals with appropriate services to address specific needs and achieve stated goals in a case management plan.

Source: SAMHSA (2019, *permission to use and duplicate without permission within the report*).

The Basics: Identification, Food, Shelter, and Support

One of the essential things a returning community member needs after an extended period of incarceration is formal identification (ID). Although some states permit people to use their prison ID to get a driver's license or nondriver ID, that is not always the case. In addition to not being able to access personal documents needed to provide proof of identity, costs can become prohibitive for someone returning home with limited resources. Not having this government-issued identification will hinder one's ability to apply for benefits, housing, and employment (Wise, 2020).

When a person is incarcerated, their Supplemental Security Income (SSI) or Social Security benefits are suspended, and if they are detained for over a year, those benefits are terminated. For those with suspended benefits, reinstatement can be a reasonably straightforward process. Terminated benefits, however, can take months to resume. Some correctional facilities have prerelease agreements with the Social Security Administration to allow for applications to be reviewed before release. Regarding Medicare, Part A will continue while in prison, but Part B will terminate once monthly premiums are not paid. Medicaid is terminated upon admission into prison (see https://www.SocialSecurity.gov).

Homelessness

Transitioning "home" is another serious issue for those reentering communities postsentence. Many people entering the criminal justice system experienced housing instability before incarceration. People experiencing homelessness are 11 times more likely to face imprisonment than the general population, and formerly incarcerated individuals are almost 10 times more likely to be homeless than the general public (Texas Criminal Justice Coalition, 2019). According to the BJS, 15.3% of the U.S. jail population comprised individuals who had been homeless anytime in the year before arrest (BJS, 2018). Nearly 50,000 people per year enter homeless shelters directly following release from correctional facilities (U.S. Interagency Council on Homelessness, 2010).

Family Issues and Reunification

Most practitioners and researchers agree that family relationships are critical in helping individuals reintegrate successfully after incarceration (Bahr, 2015). Where a returning person will live, who they will live with, and which support services they receive can be crucial to their success. When people reenter, returning to their families can be a significant challenge. During their absence, the family dynamics may have changed; partners may have become estranged, and children are older. They may have become reliant on other people for guidance, and family members may be reluctant to believe the returning member is capable of change. A prisoner's family may not be willing to accept them back; old peer groups stand ready to support the resumption of criminal habits and drug and alcohol abuse, and mental and physical health issues may have been exacerbated in prison (Urban Institute, 2002).

In *Returning Home*, Bahr (2015) suggests there are four critical factors for the assessment of whether family relationships will promote or hinder the reintegration process: (a) preprison experiences, (b) family relationships during the incarceration, (c) family influences after release from prison, and (d) the person's ability to adapt in compliance with probation/parole and re-establishing ties with family and significant others. Within each factor are multiple layers of issues that can help or hinder a person's adaptability, including stability of housing, food security, financial stability, trauma experiences, community violence, exposure to illicit substances, and mental health status.

Another issue worth mentioning is parenting and the effects of parental incarceration on children. According to the BJS, in 2018, 684,500 state and federal prisoners were parents of at least one minor child. Prisoners reported having an estimated 1,473,700 minor children, 1.5 million aged 17 or younger (BJS, 2018). Parenting from prison has many challenges. In addition to the lack of ability to afford phone calls and visits, in-person time is restricted and rigid. One study of incarcerated parents identified five major themes of concern:

1. parental incarceration creates a significant hardship on most children and families,
2. there are many barriers for parents to communicate and maintain relationships with their children while incarcerated,
3. incarcerated parents experience many challenges understanding and navigating the criminal justice system,
4. the pervasive cycle of incarceration, and
5. the need for more programs and services (Correa et al., 2021).

When an incarcerated parent returns home, their children have grown and developed. The returning parent may have difficulty establishing their roles and responsibilities, mainly when a child has created new relationships and bonds with other caregivers, parents, and friends (Urban Institute, 2002).

Child Support

Historically, for purposes of the law court-ordered child support could continue to accrue during both short jail sentences and more extended imprisonment despite the small, if any, income a prisoner may have. Carceral confinement is considered, by the state, to be *voluntary*. The rationale is that incarcerated individuals engage of their own free will in the conduct causing that incarceration. In other words, parents are in prison because of their actions, so they are held responsible for not earning income to support their minor children. However, a new rule under the Obama administration changed this terminology from "voluntary impoverishment" to "involuntarily impoverishment." This allows incarcerated parents to stop or minimize child support orders while incarcerated. Child support debt is not dischargeable in bankruptcy. When an individual files for Chapter 7 bankruptcy, that prevent individuals from seeking new claims against the debtor. Since child support is usually an ongoing claim, this doesn't apply.

Public Benefits

Federal benefits are a highly politicized issue when it comes to reentry. Eligibility criteria for federal benefits (listed below) are based partly on a relatively small body of research that such benefits can reduce recidivism. However, reentry and recidivism research focuses on rates rather than the outcomes for success and well-being.

Unemployment

Unemployment benefits are only available to individuals who have a working history in the state. They must:

1. not have left their job voluntarily or have been fired,
2. have contributed to the unemployment system to receive benefits, and
3. be ready to work if work arises.

The purpose of unemployment is to assist individuals who have involuntarily left their job until they gain new employment. The federal government does not count work performed by a person in a penal institution as a working history (Internal Revenue Code, 2011). It is up to each state to determine if incarceration is considered voluntarily or involuntarily leaving a job. However, as discussed in the child support section, the federal government views incarceration as involuntary underresourced for accruing child support.

As a result, unemployment benefits are typically unavailable to returning citizens. To receive benefits, individuals need a working history and to have paid an unemployment tax in the position before their application. Because of this, if an individual is working for cash, they often cannot get unemployment benefits if they lose their job. Unemployment benefits are only available to individuals employed in the legal sector and are frequently unavailable to those returning from prison. To receive unemployment, individuals need to have consistently paid into the system and have lost their job through no fault.

Losing a job after being arrested is common, especially if the person cannot afford bail. If the person cannot afford bail, they are incarcerated as a pretrial detainee until their case is resolved. This can take months. Most employers will not hold a person's job with an unclear return date. If someone lost their job because they were arrested, they could qualify for unemployment if not currently incarcerated. This satisfies the "ready to work" requirement because they are not incarcerated. If they were detained, they could not be ready and available to work.

This is not to say that unemployment is never available for returning citizens. It is simply not available to those who have completed long prison sentences when they need the support. For example, if a citizen returned home in 2018, is employed until the 2020 COVID-19 pandemic, and is then laid off, that individual would be eligible for unemployment benefits given the significant work history. There is no absolute ban on reentering citizens receiving unemployment. However, it is limited to individuals with an immediate history of working in the legal sector.

Food Assistance

Previously known as food stamps, the Supplemental Nutrition Assistance Program (SNAP) helps individuals struggling to put food on the table. Individuals convicted under federal or state law of any crime with a controlled substance are ineligible for SNAP or assistance for any state program funded under Part a of Title IV of the Social Security Act. 21 (U.S. Drug Abuse Prevention and Control: Denial of Assistance and Benefits for Certain Drug-Related Convictions, 2016). However, a state can opt out of this requirement (U.S. Drug Abuse Prevention and Control: Denial of Assistance and Benefits for Certain Drug-Related Convictions, 2016), and many states have (see https://www.clasp.org/publications/report/brief/no-more-double-punishments). Interestingly, scholars have found that removing SNAP benefits can *increase* recidivism, and SNAP can mitigate the probability of recidivism among drug traffickers (Tuttle, 2019). In other words, if SNAP were provided to these individuals, they would be less likely to be reincarcerated.

Housing: Section 8

The U.S. Department of Housing and Urban Development Section 8 program provides housing vouchers for low-income Americans. The program enables low-income Americans to rent housing and have part of their rent covered by the program. The tenant is responsible for the remainder of the rent. There are two absolute bans on participating in the Section 8 program, both related to a criminal record. The first of these is related to *lifetime sex offenders*. The second is related to *methamphetamine convictions*, (U.S. Code: Housing and Urban Development: Denial of Admission and Termination of Assistance for Criminals and Alcohol Abusers, 2002).

Public housing authorities (PHAs) can prohibit the admission of a household to the program if the household member has engaged in (a) drug-related criminal activity; (b) violent criminal activity; (c) other criminal activity that may threaten the health, safety, or right to peaceful enjoyment of the premises by other residents or persons residing in the immediate vicinity; or (d) other criminal activity that may threaten the health or safety of the owner, property management staff, or persons performing a contract administration function or responsibility on behalf of the PHA, including a PHA employee or a PHA contractor, subcontractor, or agent (U.S. Code: Housing and Urban Development: Denial of Admission and Termination of Assistance for Criminals and Alcohol Abusers, 2002).

Exceptional Circumstances: Sex Offenders and Reentry

Across the nation, millions of people have been convicted of felony crimes, some categorized as violent. However, for one subgroup, the collateral consequences are more severe. Although those who commit murder, manslaughter, arson, armed robbery, child abuse, or other significant crimes are unknown to most of us, nationally and in almost every state those who committed sex offenses are required to register and their information is made available for the public. Additionally, many restrictions and rules about housing, internet access, and employment complicate the transition home for a person designated a sex offender.

The Adam Walsh Child Protection and Child Safety Act of 2006 created the Title 1 Sex Offender Registration and Notification Act (SORNA), which applies to states, territories, the District of Colombia, and Native American tribes. It establishes uniform and comprehensive sex offender registration and notification requirements. The act also gave guidance to states as to which offenses should be included, periods of registration, and other various rules (Snarr & Frederick, 2018). Forensic social workers should research their state guidelines and be proficient in the regulations and requirements that pertain to their clients who bear this label and consider the ethical and social justice implications of community notification policies that often have adverse, iatrogenic effects (Levinson et al., 2016).

A sex offender's release into the community can involve a high level of attention in the media, stigma, and a heightened state of community fear that prevents successful reentry into society. They can be driven underground, negatively impacting community safety (Levinson et al., 2016). Moreover, incarcerated populations with violent or sex offense histories experience significant challenges based on the stigma of their criminal convictions in being granted parole or obtaining access to services after prison release (Maschi, Viola, & Koskinen, 2015).

Community Safety and Restorative Approaches

Circles of Support and Accountability (COSAs) in high-risk sex offender cases have been enacted in many communities in the United States, Canada, the United Kingdom, and Australia as a community reintegration model following the United Nations Standards for the Treatment of Prisoners. It involves offender accountability and community safety protocols, acknowledging that traditional public safety measures and notification policies have been inadequate, as discussed previously. That accountability combined with support with community integration can prevent recidivism (Wilson et al., 2008).

COSAs are an example of a tested and research-based community reintegration program that can lead to desistance from offending and is designed for high-risk sex offenders based on principles of restorative justice aimed at increasing public safety and decreasing recidivism while involving victims, offenders, and the community (Duwe, 2013; Wilson et al., 2008). COSAs fill the gap between programming inside prison and compliance and supervision in the community through probation and parole by providing needed support and resources to reduce the likelihood of recidivism. In the Vermont COSA model (Fox, 2013), reentry coordinators help balance support and accountability and identify services (e.g., life skills training) offered by various agencies in the community. Policy and legislative responses to sex offenders in reentry have historically involved strict registration, residency restrictions, and community notification laws, which can have iatrogenic consequences (Levenson et al., 2016), and negative media coverage can make successful reentry very challenging.

Incarceration and Recidivism

There are approximately 4.5 million people under probation and parole each day in the United States (Jones, 2018). That number far exceeds the 600,000 returning from prison each year, which are usually subject to postsupervision release or parole. Many within that total represent people placed on probation due to their criminal conviction, which, though likely favorable to jail or prison, brings complicating factors that can lead to new arrests and incarceration. According to the BJS, 47% of people released in 2005 were rearrested within 3 years (BJS, 2018). The average person on probation must comply with approximately 18 requirements daily (Jones, 2018). Unemployment hovers around 27% for those released within the previous 2 years (Couloute & Kopf, 2018). The rates of homelessness, housing insecurity, and marginal housing (renting a room) are higher among those formerly incarcerated than in the general population (Couloute & Kopf, 2018).

There is no single factor that predicts recidivism. On an individual level, the person's age, family and community factors before and upon release, past criminal history (which will affect employment and their skills for the job market), substance use/abuse, and mental health all contribute. Interwoven in the individual factors are family factors, such as the need to provide for a family financially and reacclimate into the family system (Barrenger et al., 2017). The criminological literature has focused on *desistance* as a field of inquiry to investigate why some individuals persist in offending behavior while others desist from that behavior over life. Theories of desistance or refraining from crime have tended toward social structural explanations in which specific factors supportive of desistance were tested, such as the presence of social bonds and prosocial relationships (Laub & Sampson, 2001; Paternoster et al., 2016), as well as housing and employment. Desistance theorists incorporated both internal and cognitive factors as well as external factors. These include internal characteristics such as the offender's self-identity and positive sense of self (Maruna, 2016, 2017). Weaver (2015) reconceptualizes structure, agency, and identity in the desistance process by examining the central role of social relations and life narratives and the specific properties of social relations (e.g., friendships, intimate connections, and engagement in communities) that can sustain desistance from offending as individuals work to end the cycle of criminal justice involvement and reintegrate in their communities. Of relevance to drug-related offenses discussed later in this chapter, the interplay between individual and external factors can promote recovery and desistance from addictions and criminal behavior and create social capital (Best et al., 2017). Incorporating findings from the desistance literature can inform programs and agencies providing support to formerly incarcerated persons by addressing the structural, external, and internal factors that can lead to desistance.

To illustrate the importance of interventions that promote desistance, the utilization of surveillance and intense monitoring can have iatrogenic effects among individuals returning home under the supervision of probation or parole:

> Annually, nearly 350,000 people are shifted from community supervision to prison or jail. Supervision "failures" are the predictable result of probation and parole conditions. First, people under community supervision live under intense scrutiny, which often leads to the detection of low-level offending (such as drug use) or technical violations (such as breaking curfew). Normally, incarceration would not be appropriate for such low-level offenses; they would typically be addressed through fines, community service, drug treatment programs, or no criminal justice response. However, these minor offenses and technical violations can lead to incarceration for people under community supervision. This creates a "revolving door" between community supervision and incarceration, which can lead to job loss, housing instability, difficulty caring for children, interruptions in healthcare, and a host of other collateral consequences. (Jones, 2018)

Parolee Reform: Compassionate and Geriatric Release

Compassionate and geriatric release laws also have gained increased attention from scholars, policymakers, and the public. For example, Maschi et al. (2016) analyzed the compassionate and geriatric release laws in the United States using content analysis. Of the possible 52 federal and state corrections systems (50 states, Washington, DC, and federal corrections), 47 laws for incarcerated people, or their families, to petition for early release based on advanced age or health were found. Six major categories of these laws were identified: (a) physical/mental health, (b) age, (c) pathway to release decision, (d) postrelease support, (e) nature of the crime (personal and criminal justice history), and (f) stage of review. The federal government also has called for the reform of compassionate and geriatric release laws, given that many incarcerated people have not been released based on their current provisions. The Compassionate and Geriatric Release Checklist (CGR-C; Maschi, 2016) was created for social workers and allied professionals, policymakers, advocates, and other key stakeholders to use as an assessment tool to develop or amend existing compassionate and geriatric release laws. Social workers can also use this tool to prepare expert testimony for local, state, or federal hearings or as an educational or professional training exercise.

The Rise of E-Carceration

The expanding reliance on correctional surveillance technology as tools for decarceration at pretrial and postconviction hearings marks a quiet transformation within the criminal justice system (Arnett, 2020). The increased use of electronic monitoring (EM) in ankle bracelets is cause for concern. In addition to the ongoing costs of the monitoring, the stigma of having the device on one's leg can be crippling. EM occurs when an offender is under house arrest, requiring the person to ask permission to go anywhere. Although preferable for most over jail and prison, it is disproportionately problematic for low-income and minority populations (Kilgore, 2015).

Mandates, Fees, and Fines

Under some form of supervision, most people reentering are mandated to multiple programs and services that can hinder their scheduling availability and cost a lot of money. For many, these burdens can reduce their chances of successful employment and increase the likelihood of recidivism. In addition to curfews, driving restrictions or prohibitions, and geographic restrictions for travel (if allowed), probation and parole routinely require people to engage in substance abuse and mental health evaluations and follow treatment recommendations. They may also be referred for other programs, for example, anger management, domestic violence, and parenting skills training. In addition, employment options may be limited due to various considerations. For many who return home or are under supervision (even if never being incarcerated), the fines and fees associated with their criminal justice involvement can be unbearable. One research study found that the average amount of money spent on conviction-related costs, including restitution and attorney fees, was $13,607. Commissary or court-related programs were additional expenses (deVuono-Powell et al., 2015). While a person is incarcerated, their family may encounter food and housing insecurity, many with young children at home. One study found that two-thirds of families of an adult member incarcerated had difficulty meeting basic needs. Nearly one in five could not afford housing (deVuono-Powell et al., 2015). Therefore, when the person incarcerated comes home, the family is in turmoil, faced with hardships further compounded by their loved one's reentry struggles. Once a person returns home, the imposition of court fees continues. Restitution, fees for incarceration, court fines, surcharges, and the fees associated with supervision, EM, sex offender registration, and mandated programs can result in enormous burdens on people and their families (Evans, 2014).

Restitution

Restitution is a debt an individual must pay back for the crimes they have committed. This is separate and apart from the sentence the person serves. It is not uncommon for restitution to be tens or hundreds of thousands of dollars. If an individual has not paid restitution, most courts consider this individual not to have completed their sentence. In some states like Florida, these individuals are ineligible to vote. Criminal restitution is not discharge-able in bankruptcy (U.S. Code: Bankruptcy: Exceptions to Discharge, 2012). For those who do not pay in the designated time, the restitution can be converted into a money judgment, which will continue to collect interest until paid. In some states, these judgments can result in the seizure of any assets or wage garnishment. When judgments are entered, they can affect access to employment, loans, and housing, further delaying resolution. Unpaid fines and fees can also impair the ability to receive postconviction relief such as certificates of re-habilitation, sealing, and/or expungement.

Education, Employment, and Licensing

As part of the 1990s "tough on crime" agenda, Pell Grants for college education were taken away from prisoners. Research shows that those who receive a postsecondary education in prison reenter their communities with competitive skills and qualifications, leading to higher employment rates, increased earnings, and lower recidivism. By contrast, people who emerge ill-prepared to compete for a job often get stuck in a cycle of poverty and reinvolvement in the criminal justice system (Oakford et al., 2019). Below are some on-going postconviction issues that prove troubling for returning community members.

College and Trade School

In the hopes of creating a new life, many returning community members seek postsecondary education for a trade or profession. This can become complicated if the schools use crim-inal background checks in their admissions process. Three national surveys of institutional admissions practices, conducted in 2009, 2010, and 2014 by separate research teams, found that 60% to 80% of private institutions and 55% of public institutions require undergrad-uate applicants to answer criminal history questions as part of the admissions process. While the practice is more common at 4-year institutions, 40% of community colleges report collecting such information (Scott-Clayton, 2017).

Although trade school can offer excellent lifelong careers, those with criminal con-victions can still face challenges when trying to participate in this arena (see https://www.trade-schools.net/articles/jobs-for-felons). The U.S. Department of Labor and county-affiliated offices provide funding for vocational training. However, criminal background checks can prevent people from accessing these subsidies. Furthermore, although many trade unions do not bar those with criminal convictions, certain county, state, and federal worksites conduct criminal background screenings of the labor teams for special projects, resulting in exclusion and work furloughs for those with criminal convictions.

Student Loans

Federal student loans enable students who otherwise could not afford college the chance to afford a college education. The U.S. government takes seriously drug use, drug convictions, and sexual offenses. As a result, the Free Application for Federal Student Aid (FAFSA) asks questions about drug use and convictions. You will be banned from participating in the program if:

a. You were convicted as an adult for the possession or sale of illegal drugs while receiving federal student aid. (FAFSA, 1)
b. But, you can regain eligibility by successfully completing an *approved drug rehabilitation program*
   i. OR passing two unannounced drug tests administered by an approved drug rehabilitation program (FAFSA, 1; U.S. Code: Higher Education Resources and Student Assistance: Student Eligibility, 2012)
   ii. OR, if the conviction is reversed or set aside (U.S. Code: Higher Education Resources and Student Assistance: Student Eligibility, 2012)

Of note, controlled substances *include marijuana* (U.S. Code: Controlled Substances Act, 2012) (see table below).

Individuals in states where marijuana is legalized should see if they can get their convictions expunged, sealed, or otherwise removed. It is unknown at this time if expungement will permit students to access federal aid.

The *Possession* of a Controlled Substance	Ineligibility Period
First offense	1 year
Second offense	2 years
Third offense	*Indefinite*
The *Sale* of a Controlled Substance	**Ineligibility Period**
First offense	2 years
Second offense	*Indefinite*

The families of students with felony drug convictions are also affected. The American Opportunity Tax Credit allows families to get a tax credit for education expenses. However, this is denied to families if the student is convicted of a felony drug offense (U.S. Code: American Opportunity and Lifetime Learning Credits, 2020). They also do not limit this to the distribution or sale of drugs; it includes possession of a controlled substance (U.S. Code: American Opportunity and Lifetime Learning Credits, 2020). Marijuana is a federally controlled substance despite some states where it is legal. This could be problematic for a student charged with a misdemeanor or even a violation under state law but which would be a felony under federal law.

Employment Issues

Finding postconviction employment is another problem for returning community members. For those under parole supervision, restrictions on their ability to drive, geographic location, and curfew can impede their ability to gain meaningful employment. Due to the discrimination those with criminal convictions face, some states categorize criminal convictions under the larger umbrella of "disabilities" to provide protection. Despite this categorization, many people with criminal convictions remain unemployed and underemployed. Couloute and Kopf (2018) reported that formerly incarcerated people are unemployed at a rate of over 27%, mirroring the rates of the Great Depression. These rates are likely also influenced by racial and ethnic biases that further the inability of some to find full-time work capable of providing a living wage. Those entering prison generally have lower than average incomes, and the time spent in the system diminishes their ability to continue school and attain job skills to help them in their return (Lo & Akua, 2020).

Nine out of 10 employers use background checks as part of their applicant hiring process (Lo & Akua, 2020). The accessibility of criminal records, whether officially through the court or through myriad private agencies offering the service, makes job searching complex and demanding for these people. One major issue is related to the inaccuracies and inappropriate reporting that takes place. An applicant with a criminal record is 50% to 63% less likely to get called back or an actual offer as compared to those with no criminal record (Lo & Akua, 2020).

Government Employment Programs

Federal Bonding

The federal government recognizes the hardships returning citizens face in the job market. The Federal Bonding Program (FBP, 2016) was created in 1966 for at-risk or hard-to-place job seekers. The FBP reimburses employers for any loss they incur because of employee theft, forgery, larceny, and embezzlement. The program has a 99% success rate, with only 460 of 42,000 employees proving to be dishonest workers. The FPB is an often underused tool for individuals with a criminal record. FBP costs employers nothing. Employers are insured for potential employees up to $5,000 with a $0 cost for the first 6 months. The FBP is available for any employer hiring for any job in any state and for any work, part time or full time. Additionally, employers are only ensured up to $5,000; anything above that insurance coverage incurs additional costs, or the employer is responsible for the loss. This is a rare occurrence, given the high success rate.

Fair Credit Reporting Act

Almost all companies run background checks on potential employees. These background check companies are often not the official sources of case reports. Even when an individual gets the official disposition (result) from the court, the disposition could be wrong. Typos and common names are causes of inaccuracy. Errors frequently occur. However, individuals have rights under federal law against third-party reporting companies. The Fair Credit Reporting Act (FCRA) establishes minimum requirements for reporting accurate criminal histories (U.S. Consumer Credit Protection Act: Compliance Procedures, 2012). Known as an "EB" claim, these reporting companies must (a) follow reasonable procedures and (b) ensure *maximum* possible accuracy (U.S. Consumer Credit Protection Act: Compliance Procedures, 2012). EB claims arise when a company has failed to update its records with official reporting sources, or when a company has failed to use an individual's correct name. The standard is *maximum* possible accuracy, not minimum.

In May 2020, the Institute for Justice published a national study analyzing the effects that criminal convictions have on licensing. *Barred from Working: A National Study of Occupational Licensing Barriers for Ex-Offenders* is a comprehensive guide to how states address criminal convictions when addressing educational licenses and gives an overall grade on the legal protections for licensing applicants with criminal records (see https://ij.org/report/barred-from-working/)

The highlights from that report include the following:

- The average state grade is a C–.
- Licensing boards in nine states generally disqualify applicants based on any felony.
- In 21 states, boards are free to deny licenses without ever considering whether an applicant has been rehabilitated.
- Applicants in 34 states can be denied licenses based on an arrest that did not lead to a criminal conviction.
- In 12 states, applicants have no right to appeal board decisions.
- Eighteen states exempt entire categories of occupational license from their main laws providing protections for ex-offenders seeking licenses (predominantly in health-related fields; Sibilla, 2020)

Another report by the Justice Center, Council of State Governments, and the National Reentry Resource Center in January 2021 focused on the fields most affected by criminal convictions. Health care, public employment, education, and schools are at the top of the list. Nearly half of all employment-related collateral consequences are "mandatory," meaning they prohibit the employment, retention, or licensing of a person with a conviction for a specified offense regardless of evidence of rehabilitation, the relationship between the person's offense and the job, or other considerations. The remaining "discretionary" consequences allow employers, licensing entities, and other decision makers to impose a consequence but do not require it (Umez & Joshua, 2021).

A recent report by the Brennan Center for Justice focused on how involvement in the criminal justice system, even when a jail or prison sentence is not imposed, has a significant impact on lifetime earnings. Specifically, the report determined that conviction and imprisonment have a more severe effect than previously realized, impacting annual earnings, keeping people in poverty, and disproportionately affecting low-income and minority communities (Craigie et al., 2020). This report further estimates that total losses to the national economy in 1 year can be as high as $372.3 billion.

Policy Advocacy

Embedded in the mission of the National Association of Social Workers (NASW) Code of Ethics is the notion of enhancing human well-being to help meet basic human needs (NASW, 2021). Ethical Standard 6 reinforces social workers' ethical responsibility to the broader society. Specifically, Standard 6.04 states that social workers "ensure all have access to resources, employment, services, and opportunities." We uphold that advocacy for the populations in reentry and returning to their communities deserves our attention and efforts. We propose a critical analysis of the following legal issues related to the reentry population.

Parole

One issue that has significantly helped drive the numbers of incarcerated people over the years is lengthy sentences with limited to no parole opportunities. Advocates in all 50 states tried to advance legislation to address the inequities of parole release. In *Grading the Parole Release Systems of All 50 States*, Renaud (2019) examined factors such as discretionary parole and the transparency of the process to determine the effectiveness of the parole system, with findings that raised questions about inequity (https://www.prisonpolicy.org/reports/grading_parole.html). Recommendations for change included providing opportunities for discretionary parole, more significant preparation for people being released, more transparency in the process, yearly reviews after denials, and discharge planning for individuals to have structure upon their release.

Limiting the Use of Criminal Records and Inaccuracy Issues

Advocates for the reentry population strongly suggest that the issues of inaccuracy, prejudice, and reliance on criminal records must be addressed to better reduce stigma. Rap sheets (arrest and prosecution reports) can vary from state to state. Many are plagued with inaccurate dispositions, arrests that did not result in actual convictions, and clerical errors that allow reporting when cases are sealed or adjudicated in ways other than a conviction. Further, employers are not trained to read the criminal history checks and easily misinterpret them (see The Reintegration Agenda During Pandemic: Criminal Records Reforms in 2020: https://ccresourcecenter.org/wp-content/uploads/2021/01/CCRC_The-Reintegration-Agenda-During-Pandemic_2020-Reforms.pdf).

Ban the Box

"Ban the box" and "fair chance hiring" refer to employers not inquiring about criminal history before the opportunity to interview or before a formal offer of employment. Laws differ from state to state and within states themselves, as counties enact protective laws that vary. National initiatives by groups such as the NAACP would like to see fair chance hiring and ban the box throughout the country. Congress has banned the box, which means employers cannot ask potential employees about a criminal record before a conditional offer of employment is made (U.S. Code: Rights and Protections Relating to Criminal History Inquiries, 2019). In some states, banning the box is also referred to as the Fair Chance Act/Second Chance Act. There are three exceptions to this federal ban the box law:

a. When the job requires access to classified information, national security, service in the armed forces, or a position of public trust (U.S. Code: Access to Criminal History Records for National Security and Other Purposes, 2012)

b. As a federal law enforcement officer (U.S. Code: Fair Chance to Compete for Jobs Act, 2019)

c. Positions involving interaction with minors, access to sensitive information, or managing financial transactions (U.S. Code: Government Organizations and Employees, 2010)

Many states and localities have banned the box because marking a box tells an employer little about an individual's criminal record. There is a big difference between petty larceny and first-degree murder. However, the box "whether you have a criminal record" does not make this vital distinction. Also, some individuals will mistakenly believe they have a criminal record when the case could have been expunged, sealed, dismissed, or dismissed in their favor.

Clean Slate Legislation

Beyond banning the box, legislation that promotes automatic sealing and expungement of records after a certain period after the completion of a sentence can dramatically change the ability of those with criminal convictions and returning community members to get gainful employment. States and jurisdictions vary in the type of relief, eligible convictions, and waiting periods (see https://ccresourcecenter.org/2021/02/17/after-a-haul-of-record-relief-reforms-last-year-more-states-launch-clean-slate-campaigns/).

Voting

States vary on whether felons can vote and when. Social workers can advocate for policies that fully allow returning community members to participate in civic engagement (see https://www.ncsl.org/research/elections-and-campaigns/felon-voting-rights.aspx).

Jury Service

A fundamental constitutional right is that when we face criminal charges, we have those charges and the evidence considered by "a jury of our peers"; however, many states have bans on who can serve on a jury based on criminal convictions. An outright prohibition due to a criminal conviction denies all people an actual jury of peers. Social workers can help advocate for laws that permit full participation for all in the court system (see https://www.prisonpolicy.org/reports/juryexclusion.html).

Conclusion: Enhancing Community Resources for Successful Reentry

Research on health and justice disparities has demonstrated that minority groups had less access to quality care and justice and experience more health and justice disparities than Whites (Adler & Rehkopf, 2008). Criminal justice practices since the 1970s continue to exacerbate economic and racial inequality, which only increased during the COVID-19 pandemic. The 1990s "broken windows" policing policies resulted in an influx of people into the criminal justice system, primarily for misdemeanor charges, which resulted in millions of arrests and thus criminal records, leading to a system of perpetual punishment for citizens (Kohler-Hausman, 2018). This continued through the 2000s when crime rates were dropping.

The United States spends over $182 billion a year on policing and courts (Wagner & Rabuy, 2017). If a shift were made to invest in substance use disorder prevention and treatment, mental health disorder prevention and treatment for younger and older populations, community centers, education, employment development, gang reduction, and resources for families with incarcerated family members, stigma and disparity could be reduced, and reentry success could increase. Lessons from the desistance literature, restorative justice, and nonpunitive approaches can effectively address recidivism concerns and promote well-being among individuals returning to the community. Social workers can help advocate for these policy changes and utilize effective community-engaged models.

References

Adler, N. E., & Rehkopf, D. H. (2008). US disparities in health: Descriptions, causes, and mechanisms. *Annual Review of Public Health, 29*, 235–252. https://doi.org/10.1146/annurev.publhealth.29.020907.090852

Alper, M., Durose, M. R., & Markman, J. (2018). 2018 update on prisoner recidivism: A 9-year follow-up period (2005–2014). Washington, DC: US Department of Justice, Office of Justice Programs, Bureau of Justice Statistics.

American Bar Association. (2015). *National Summit on Collateral Consequences: Conference report.* https://www.americanbar.org/content/dam/aba/publications/criminaljustice/cc_national_summit_report.pdf

Arnett, C. (2019). From decarceration to E-carceration. *Cardozo Law Review, 41*, 641. https://ssrn.com/abstract=3388009

Ash, G. (2019, September 16). *More money goes to the US prison system than it does education.* Study International. https://www.studyinternational.com/news/education-spend-prison-system-us/

Bahr, S. J. (2015). *Returning Home: Reintegration After Prison or Jail.* Washington DC: NASW Press.

Barrenger, S. L., Draine, J., Angell, B., & Herman, D. (2017). Reincarceration risk among men with mental illnesses leaving prison: A risk environment analysis. *Community Mental Health Journal, 53*(8), 883–892. https://doi.org/10.1007/s10597-017-0113-z

Best, D., Irving, J., & Albertson, K. (2017). Recovery and desistance: What the emerging recovery movement in the alcohol and drug area can learn from models of desistance from offending. *Addiction Research & Theory, 25*(1), 1–10. https://doi.org/10.1080/16066359.2016.1185661

Bureau of Justice Statistics (BJS). (2018). *Prisoners in 2016 (updated in 2018).* https://bjs.ojp.gov/content/pub/pdf/p16.pdf

P. Correa, N., K. Hayes, A., M. Bhalakia, A., Lopez, K. K., Cupit, T., Kwarteng-Amaning, V., . . . Van Horne, B. S. (2021). Parents' perspectives on the impact of their incarceration on children and families. *Family Relations, 70*(1), 162–170.

Couloute, L. (2018). *Nowhere to go: Homelessness among formerly incarcerated people.* Prison Policy Initiative. https://www.prisonpolicy.org/reports/housing.html

Couloute, L., & Kopf, D. (2018). *Out of prison & out of work: Unemployment among formerly incarcerated people.* Prison Policy Initiative. https://www.prisonpolicy.org/reports/outofwork.html

Craigie, T., Grawert, A., & Kimble, C. (2020). *Conviction, imprisonment, and lost earnings: How involvement with the criminal justice system deepens inequality.* Brennan Center for Justice. https://www.brennancenter.org/our-work/research-reports/conviction-imprisonment-and-lost-earnings-how-involvement-criminal

Desai, A., Durham, K., Burke, S. C., NeMoyer, A., & Heilbrun, K. (2021). Releasing individuals from incarceration during COVID-19: Pandemic-related challenges and recommendations for promoting successful reentry. *Psychology, Public Policy, and Law, 27*(2), 245–255.

DuVernay, A. (2016). *The 13th* [Documentary movie]. Netflix. https://www.youtube.com/watch?v=krfcq5pF8u8

Duwe, G. (2013). Can Circles of Support and Accountability (COSA) work in the United States? Preliminary results from a randomized experiment in Minnesota. *Sexual Abuse, 25*(2), 143–165.

deVuono-Powell, S., Schweidler, C., Walters, A., & Zohrabi, A. (2015). *Who pays? The true cost of incarceration on families.* http://whopaysreport.org/

Evans, D. N. (2014). *The debt penalty: Exposing the financial barriers to offender reintegration.* https://jjrec.files.wordpress.com/2014/08/debtpenalty.pdf

Federal Bonding Program. (2016). *The Federal Bonding Program: What is it?* https://bonds4jobs.com/

Fox, K. J. (2013). *Circles of Support and Accountability: Qualitative evaluation. Final report prepared for the State of Vermont Department of Corrections.* University of Vermont.

Green, B. L., Dass-Brailsford, P., Hurtado de Mendoza, A., Mete, M., Lynch, S. M., DeHart, D. D., & Belknap, J. (2016). Trauma experiences and mental health among incarcerated women. *Psychological Trauma: Theory, Research, Practice, and Policy, 8*(4), 455–463. https://doi.org/10.1037/tra0000113

Huntington, C. (2014). *Failure to flourish: How law undermines family relationships.* Oxford University Press.

Interagency Council on Homelessness (U.S.). (2010). *Opening doors: Federal strategic plan to prevent and end homelessness.* U.S. Interagency Council on Homelessness.

Internal Revenue Code, 26 USCA § 3306. (2011). https://www.govinfo.gov/app/details/USCODE-2010-title26/USCODE-2010-title26-subtitleC-chap23-sec3306

Jones, A. (2018). *Correctional control 2018.* Prison Policy Initiative. https://www.prisonpolicy.org/reports/correctionalcontrol2018.html

Kilgore, J. (2015). *Electronic monitoring is not the answer.* Media Justice. https://mediajustice.org/resource/electronic-monitoring-is-not-the-answer-2015

Kohler-Hausmann, I. (2018). misdemeanorland: criminal courts and social control in an age of broken windows policing. New Jersey: Princeton UP.

Laub, J. H., & Sampson, R. J. (2001). Understanding desistance from crime. *Crime and Justice: A Review of Research, 28*(28), 1–69. http://www.press.uchicago.edu/presssite/metadata.epl?mode=synopsis&bookkey=34093

Levenson, J., Grady, M., & Leibowitz, G. S. (2016). Grand challenges: Social justice and the need for evidence-based sex offender registry reform. *Journal of Sociology and Social Welfare, 43*(2), 3–38. https://scholarworks.wmich.edu/jssw/vol43/iss2/2

Lo, K., & Akua, A. (2020*). Update to "News You Can Use: Research Roundup for Reentry Advocates."* Center for American Progress. https://www.americanprogress.org/issues/criminal-justice/news/2020/06/25/486864/update-news-can-use-research-roundup-re-entry-advocates/

Malcolm, J. G., & Siebler, J. M. (2017). *Collateral consequences: Protecting public safety or encountering recidivism?* Washington, DC: Heritage Foundation. https://www.heritage.org/crime-and-justice/report/collateral-consequences-protecting-public-safety-or-encouraging-recidivism

Marshall Project. (2021). *A state-by state look at coronavirus in prisons.* https://www.themarshallproject.org/2020/05/01/a-state-by-state-look-at-coronavirus-in-prisonsMaruna, S. (2016). Desistance and restorative justice: It's now or never. *Restorative Justice, 4*(3), 289–301. https://doi.org/10.1080/20504721.2016.1243853

Maruna, S. (2017). Desistance as a social movement. *Irish Probation Journal, 14,* 5–16. http://www.probation.ie/en/PB/Pages/WP17000058

Maschi, T. (2016). *Applying a Human Rights Approach to Social Work Research and Evaluation: A Rights Research Manifesto.* New York: Springer Publishing.

Maschi, T., Leibowitz, G., Rees, J., & Pappacena, L. (2016). Analysis of US compassionate and geriatric release laws: Applying a human rights framework to global prison health. *Journal of Human Rights and Social Work, 1*(4), 165–174. https://doi.org/10.1007/s41134-016-0021-0

Maschi, T., Viola, D., & Koskinen, L. (2015). Trauma, stress, and coping among older adults in prison: Towards a human rights and intergenerational family justice action agenda. *Traumatology, 21*(3), 188.

Maschi, T., Viola, D., Morgen, K., & Koskinen, L. (2015). Trauma, stress, grief, loss, and separation among older adults in prison: The protective role of coping resources on physical and mental well-being. *Journal of Crime and Justice, 38*(1), 113–136. https://doi.org/10.1080/0735648X.2013.808853

Miller, W. R., & Rollnick, S. (2013). *Motivational Interviewing: Helping People Change* (3rd ed.). New York: Guilford.

National Association of Social Workers. (2021). Preamble to the code of ethics. Retrieved May 4, 2022, from http://www.socialworkers.org/pubs/ Code/code.asp

Novisky, M. A., & Peralta, R. L. (2020). Gladiator school: Returning citizens' experiences with secondary violence exposure in prison. *Victims & Offenders, 15*(5), 594–618. https://doi.org/10.1080/15564886.2020.1721387

Oakford, P., Brumfield, C., Goldvale, C., diZerega, M., & Patrick, F. (2019*). Investing in futures: Economic and fiscal benefits of postsecondary education in prison.* Vera Institute of Justice. https://www.vera.org/publications/investing-in-futures-education-in-prison

Page, J., Piehowski, V., & Soss, J. (2019). A debt of care: Commercial bail and the gendered logic of criminal justice predation. *RSF: The Russell Sage Foundation Journal of the Social Sciences, 5*(1), 150–172. https://doi.org/10.7758/RSF.2019.5.1.07

Paternoster, R., Bachman, R., Kerrison, E., O'connell, D., & Smith, L. (2016). Desistance from crime and identity: An empirical test with survival time. *Criminal Justice and Behavior, 43*(9), 1204–1224.

Renaud, J. (2019). *Grading the parole systems of all 50 states.* Prison Policy Initiative. https://www.prisonpolicy.org/reports/grading_parole.html

Sawyer, W., & Wagner, P. (2019). *Mass incarceration: The whole pie 2019.* Prison Policy Initiative. https://www.prisonpolicy.org/reports/pie2020.html

Scott-Clayton, J. (2017). *Thinking "beyond the box": The use of criminal records in college admissions.* Brookings. https://www.brookings.edu/research/thinking-beyond-the-box-the-use-of-criminal-records-in-college-admissions/

Sibilla, N. (2020). *Barred from working: A nationwide study of occupational licensing barriers for ex-offenders.* Institute for Justice. https://ij.org/report/barred-from-working/

Snarr, H., & Frederick, S. P. (2018). *The complexities of sex offender registries.* National Conference of State Legislatures. https://www.ncsl.org/research/civil-and-criminal-justice/the-complexities-of-sex-offender-registries.aspx

Substance Abuse and Mental Health Services Administration (SAMSHA). (2019). *Principles of community-based behavioral health services for justice-involved individuals: A research-based guide.* https://store.samhsa.gov/product/Principles-of-Community-based-Behavioral-Health-Services-for-Justice-involved-Individuals-A-Research-based-Guide/SMA19-5097

Texas Criminal Justice Coalition. (2019). *Return to nowhere.* Texas Center for Justice & Equity. https://www.texascjc.org/return-nowhere

Tuttle, C. (2019). Snapping back: Food stamp bans and criminal recidivism. *American Economic Journal: Economic Policy, 11*(2), 301–327. https://www.aeaweb.org/articles?id=10.1257/pol.20170490

Umez, C., & Joshua, G. (2021). *After the sentence, more consequences: A national report of barriers to work.* Council of State Governments Justice Center. https://csgjusticecenter.org/publications/after-the-sentence-more-consequences/national-report/

U.S. Code: Access to Criminal History Records for National Security and Other Purposes, 5 U.S.C.A. § 910. (2012). https://www.govinfo.gov/app/details/USCODE-2011-title5/USCODE-2011-title5-partIII-subpartH-chap91-sec9101

U.S. Code: American Opportunity and Lifetime Learning Credits, 26 U.S.C.A. § 25A. (2020). https://www.govinfo.gov/content/pkg/USCODE-2020-title26/pdf/USCODE-2020-title26-subtitleA-chap1-subchapA-partIV-subpartA-sec25A.pdf

U.S. Code: Bankruptcy: Exceptions to Discharge, 11 U.S. Code § 523. (2012). https://www.govinfo.gov/app/details/USCODE-2011-title11/USCODE-2011-title11-chap5-subchapII-sec523

U.S. Code: Controlled Substances Act, 21 U.S.C.A. § 802. (2012). https://www.govinfo.gov/app/details/USCODE-2011-title21/USCODE-2011-title21-chap13-subchapI-partA-sec802

U.S. Code: Drug Abuse Prevention and Control: Denial of Assistance and Benefits for Certain Drug-Related Convictions. U.S.C.A. § 862a. (2016). https://www.govinfo.gov/app/details/USCODE-2015-title21/USCODE-2015-title21-chap13-subchapI-partD-sec862a

U.S. Code: Higher Education Resources and Student Assistance: Student Eligibility, 20 US C. 1091. (2012). https://www.govinfo.gov/app/details/USCODE-2011-title20/USCODE-2011-title20-chap28-subchapIV-partF-sec1091

U.S. Code: Housing and Urban Development: Denial of Admission and Termination of Assistance for Criminals and Alcohol Abusers, 24 CFR § 982.553. (2002). https://www.govinfo.gov/app/details/CFR-2002-title24-vol4/CFR-2002-title24-vol4-sec982-553

U.S. Code: Rights and Protections Relating to Criminal History Inquiries, 2 U.S.C.A. § 1316b. (2019). https://www.govregs.com/uscode/title2_chapter24_subchapterII_partA_section1316b_notes

U.S. Consumer Credit Protection Act: Compliance Procedures, 15 U.S.C.A. § 1681e. (2012). https://www.govinfo.gov/app/details/USCODE-2011-title15/USCODE-2011-title15-chap41-subchapIII-sec1681e

Wagner, P., & Rabuy, B. (2017). *Following the money of mass incarceration*. Prison Policy Initiative. https://www.prisonpolicy.org/reports/money.html

Weaver, B. (2015). *Offending and desistance: The importance of social relations*. Routledge.

Widra, E. (2020). *No escape: The trauma of witnessing violence in prison*. Prison Policy Initiative. https://www.prisonpolicy.org/blog/2020/12/02/witnessing-prison-violence/#:~:text=Even%20before%20entering%20a%20prison,of%20the%20general%20male%20population

Wilson, R. J., McWhinnie, A. J., & Wilson, C. (2008). Circles of Support and Accountability: An international partnership in reducing sexual offender recidivism. *Prison Service Journal*, *138*(178), 26–36.

Wise, C. (2020). *Leaving prison without a government ID can block access to housing, jobs and help*. PBS News Hour. https://www.pbs.org/newshour/nation/leaving-prison-without-a-government-id-can-block-access-to-housing-jobs-and-help

Wolff, N., Huening, J., Shi, J., & Frueh, B. C. (2013). Screening for and treating PTSD and substance use disorders among incarcerated men. Center for Behavioral Health Services & Criminal Justice Research. [Policy Brief]. New Brunswick, NJ: Rutgers. Retrieved from http://www. cbhs-cjr. rutgers. edu/pdfs/ Policy_Brief_Oct_2013. pdf

Wolff, N., Huening, J., Shi, J., & Frueh, B. C. (2014). Trauma exposure and posttraumatic stress disorder among incarcerated men. *Journal of Urban Health*, *91*(4), 707–719. https://pubmed.ncbi.nlm.nih.gov/24865800/

23

Child Welfare

Angela B. Pharris, Kirsten Havig, and
Bonni Goodwin

Fields of Practice in Criminal Justice: Child Welfare

The child welfare system in the United States is a complex network of tribal, state, and federal policies, laws, and practices that involve and intersect with forensic institutions. The child welfare system is distinct from but also intersects at several points with other forensic systems detailed in this text, including criminal justice, intimate partner violence, human trafficking, mental health, and substance abuse systems, to name a few. The courts have jurisdiction (the ability to make a decision) over many of the actions and decisions occurring during the process of a child abuse investigation, placement, reunification, or alternative permanency decisions. Therefore, the child welfare system is internally driven by the policies that govern criminal and civil procedures related to reporting, investigation, and the disposition of child maltreatment. The child welfare system and the courts work together to navigate a complex system of processes and responses, including reporting and identifying maltreatment, investigating and assessing the child's risk and safety, and various case disposition points.

While the intersection of court systems with child protection services is the primary focus of this chapter, the reader should keep in mind that multiple convening systems enhance primary and secondary prevention of child maltreatment. Social workers and other professionals often work in programs that provide parenting classes to improve parenting strategies that reduce the risk of harm and increase positive parenting capacity. Social workers also practice in therapeutic settings that improve family systems or prepare parents to manage and support their children's behavioral needs, or in mental health settings that promote positive adaptation and coping skills to handle adversity and stress among high-risk families. As a whole, the child welfare system is directed by evidence-based practices

Angela B. Pharris, Kirsten Havig, and Bonni Goodwin, *Child Welfare* In: *Handbook of Forensic Social Work*. Edited by: David Axlyn McLeod, Anthony P. Natale, and Kristin W. Mapson, Oxford University Press. © Oxford University Press 2024. DOI: 10.1093/oso/9780197694732.003.0023

with a drive toward prevention, using a strengths perspective and developmentally informed framework, trauma-informed care, active family involvement, child-centered
decision-making, and cultural literacy and sensitivity (DePanfilis, 2018).

The following chapter will focus on those processes that occur in child welfare
through formal court proceedings. To do so, we will focus on a set of decision points that
occur in the legal setting to determine the child's best interest. This includes decisions to
investigate, decisions to place a child in emergency out-of-home care, and decisions to reunify the family or pursue an alternative legal permanent family for the child. As a profession, social work is grounded in ethics and a system of values that at times are inherent in
the child protection and child welfare system. Likewise, the courts and legal processes are
guided and governed by laws, rules, and procedures. At times, the two systems can quickly
converge, and at other times there can be a test between the role of social work practice
and the court's role. But we believe there is no better place for social work practice relative
to legal issues that emerge in protecting children and the enhancement of family well-
being. The primary aims of the process between the courts and the child welfare system
are to ensure that children's safety, permanency, and well-being are at the forefront of all
decisions and actions (Adoption and Safe Families Act, PL 105-89). This is accomplished
using formal and informal structures and interventions with children, families, and communities to achieve these outcomes.

Child Maltreatment Reporting and Investigation

The entry point for child welfare and legal system involvement typically occurs at the
point of referral when someone suspects a child is experiencing abuse and/or neglect
from their primary or custodial caregivers. In 2019, nearly 4.5 million reports of suspected child maltreatment were made across the United States and included a total of
7.9 million children. Approximately 3.5 million (54%) of those reports were "screened in"
by the child welfare agency as meeting the criteria for investigation. In all, 656,000 children were determined to be victims of maltreatment (substantiated allegation), the majority of which were for cases of neglect (74.9%), followed by physical abuse (17.5%) and
sexual abuse (7%). Child abuse and neglect reporting show an upward trend for the first
time since 2015, with infants and young children at the highest risk (U.S. Department of
Health and Human Services, 2021).

Mandated Reporting and Screening

Almost all states, tribes, and territories have some law or regulation regarding reporting
any activity where abuse or neglect from the primary caregiver is reported. Although
any citizen may report maltreatment concerns, the majority (68%) of reporters come
into contact with children from professional settings such as educators, social workers,
health care professionals, and law enforcement officials. Family members, neighbors,
friends, and other relatives are also likely to report suspicion of child maltreatment and
account for 15.7% of those who report child maltreatment concerns. The remaining
15% of reports come from various others who may come into contact with children.
Generally, cases may be screened for further investigation if there is enough information

to believe that child abuse or neglect may have occurred under the statutory rule. Most cases are screened out at the time of reporting, often because they fail to meet the statutory limits of child maltreatment or the reporter cannot provide ample actionable or identifying information.

Risk assessment at this stage involves gathering information about the allegations themselves, the existence of any allegations involving other children in the home, exposure to drugs or violence in the home, ages of the involved children, relationship to and presence of the alleged perpetrator, and impacts to and current health and safety of the children. Some instances will require an immediate response from the child protection agency, such as cases of sexual abuse or a methamphetamine lab in the home, due to the level of danger and harm to the child, and reports of a shaken baby, due to the vulnerability and age of the child as well as potential harm. In contrast, others may be deemed lower risk with an allowable response time of days instead of hours, such as an allegation of educational neglect because a child has missed a lot of school.

Mandated reporters are those who, by statute, are required to report suspected child abuse or neglect to child protection authorities for investigation. The child maltreatment reporting system is shaped by structures and policies established in state law. Reporting systems may be centralized for the state or decentralized to the local government or involve a combination of the two. Each reporting system has benefits and drawbacks. Most states maintain a statewide hotline where calls are received by a central office, screened, and then directed to the appropriate next action step, whereas in some states the reporting system has remained local and exists on a city or county level. The clear benefit of the centralized hotline model is that one toll-free number is in place across the state and does not require the reporter to recognize maltreatment that may be occurring or discern who made or where to make a report. Of course, many report the maltreatment directly to law enforcement, especially where there is a concern of imminent risk, or to serve as a connector to the child welfare system. Generally, only law enforcement, a physician, or the court itself can take a child into emergency custody before a due process hearing to protect children from imminent harm (DePanfilis, 2018).

Trends over time indicate that a shift toward centralization has occurred. Still, none of the underlying assumptions that seem to guide these choices, such as the importance of local knowledge in decentralized models or the impact of easier access to reporting, have been tested empirically (Steen, 2011). Key policy-based factors impacting reporting include whether a state has a universal mandate for all citizens to report (versus certain identified groups), if there are consequences for not reporting, and the state's approach to categorizing whether substance exposure during pregnancy is considered reportable and actionable maltreatment. Little empirical evidence supports the conclusion that mandated reporting laws impact private citizens' decisions to report possible child maltreatment, but such evidence does exist about professionals as mandated reporters (Ashton, 2009; Bryant & Milsom, 2005; Hawkins & McCallum, 2001). In one of the few studies that has examined policies and outcomes associated with mandated reporting, Palusci et al. (2016) did find significantly increased total and confirmed case reporting rates in states with universal reporting laws and/or clergy reporting requirements. However, other research has contradicted these findings, pointing to a continuing uncertainty regarding empirically based policy in this area (Krase & DeLong-Hamilton, 2015). Overall, the data suggest that universal mandatory reporting laws have significantly increased the volume of calls (and therefore the burden of managing the reporting systems) without improving the frequency and quality of child maltreatment intervention.

Despite the fact that a large number of reports are made each year, child maltreatment remains significantly underreported. One reason for this is a failure to report concerns for child maltreatment by mandatory reporters. Concerns about the fairness of the child welfare and court systems and fear that child removal and placement into foster care may pose more harm in the long term lead many to delay or resist reporting. There is also some uncertainty by many on the signs of maltreatment and their responsibility for reporting. In response to many high-profile sexual abuse cases occurring within religious, youth, and educational institutions in recent years, many states have updated their statutes to include more groups as mandated reporters and to enhance penalties for adults who fail to report knowledge of abuse. Additional changes to state laws and statutes include special categories for those who abuse positions of power to perpetuate abuse on a child and eliminating the statute of limitations in recognition of the dynamics of trauma and the nature of abuse, especially sexual abuse, as a complex crime often existing for years within a family or community.

Child Maltreatment Investigations

Once reported, child welfare agencies or tribes then follow their statutory processes to initiate an investigation based on the allegation of maltreatment and assess the likelihood of ongoing future risk. Many of the reported and even investigated cases are not substantiated or are resolved with some prevention services and safety planning and do not require court intervention. However, parents cannot be labeled as abusive or neglectful or be ordered to go into any type of treatment without a court hearing. The purpose of a child abuse investigation is to determine if there has been a *willful act* resulting in physical, mental, sexual, or emotional injury to the child or sustained unwillingness to meet the child's primary care needs such as food, security, health care, or education. A parent's inability to meet some of the child's basic needs due to poverty or fleeing dangerous or violent settings should not be considered neglect by social workers or the courts.

If it is determined that harm to the child has occurred and is likely to continue without oversight and protection, the investigator will petition the courts for a civil protection order. The child welfare investigator or the state attorney will draft a petition describing the allegations and present evidence before a judge to demonstrate their case for maltreatment. For the most part, child welfare and family courts are civil court proceedings. Most cases that are substantiated, adjudicated, and even result in removing a child from the home do not result in a criminal case. A parallel criminal case may be pursued, but it is far less likely. The overlap between the two is most likely to occur when the maltreatment involves violent physical abuse or sexual abuse, because those are considered assaults, or when the maltreatment has led to death or serious bodily injury to a child in order to protect siblings.

Law Enforcement and Child Welfare Investigation of Maltreatment

Depending on how an allegation of child maltreatment is reported and the nature of the allegations, law enforcement may have varying levels of involvement in the actual investigation. If a child maltreatment case is first reported to or discovered by law enforcement, they can involve child protection authorities in order to prompt a child maltreatment investigation and connect the family with the system.

Case Disposition

Child maltreatment case disposition may follow one of several avenues. When necessary, child welfare investigators have the authority to take a child into custody on an emergency basis and place the child in out-of-home care. If not initially screened out, some cases are closed after investigation due to the lack of evidence necessary to substantiate the allegation of maltreatment. It is important to note that substantiation of a case in family court from the evidence presented by the child protection investigation requires a lower standard of proof than a criminal court would need for a conviction. When the judge hears the case and evidence and determines there is evidence to believe, the family cannot currently meet a sufficient standard for safety without court oversight. Judges have many choices once a case has been substantiated. The judge may mandate, along with the investigator's recommendation, that a family receive intensive in-home services that work with the family to prevent the removal of children from the home and resolve the pressing risks that brought the case before the courts. The judge may order temporary custody to the state and instruct them to place the children in out-of-home care as wards of the state, either with family members, with other kin, or in a state-supervised care setting. Because of the impact that each of these decisions has on the well-being of children and their families, evidence-driven tools to help the investigators and the courts make fair, unbiased assessments of future risk for maltreatment, along with an assessment of family strengths and resources, are crucial, as is the professional competence to perform high-level assessments and case decision-making. Tools to support the assessment of child and family risks and strengths should guide an appropriate differential response. Investigators may find evidence of child maltreatment or have concerns about family safety and well-being that do not rise to the level of court involvement to formalize oversight by the state. In these cases, services and resources should be provided without court oversight, such as parenting support, connection with public assistance, and safety assessment.

Forensic Interviewing and the Child Advocacy Center Model

Child advocacy centers (CACs) are multidisciplinary sites where investigatory functions like interviews with alleged child victims, interagency collaboration, and medical examinations are conducted using a child-centered approach. CACs were created in large part as a response to the negative impacts to children who are subject to a police or child protection agency investigation, as well as to tighten communication and collaboration within the child welfare multidisciplinary team of law enforcement, prosecutors and district attorneys, guardians ad litem, parent counsel, child welfare agency staff, and others (Child Welfare Information Gateway, 2017; Cross et al., 2007). CAC services include case review and tracking, victim advocacy, therapeutic intervention, and an essential specialty within the child welfare system, forensic interviewing. Forensic interviewing requires targeted special training on one of several models aimed at eliciting accurate information from child victims according to their developmental stage and recognizing the impact the experience will have on them.

The CAC aims to gather critical victim or witness evidence for use in a legal setting, in child welfare or family or criminal court proceedings (Child Welfare Information Gateway, 2017). Forensic interviewing is most frequently done by trained law enforcement, child protection, and therapeutic professionals, ideally in the CAC setting rather than at a police station. CACs meet the child-centered standard by putting into place policies, practices, settings, and other agency responses that place children's well-being at the forefront, even over the attainment of evidence toward a child abuse allegation substantiation or criminal charge. Cases referred to CACs are more likely to have law enforcement involvement and are generally reserved only for the most severe types of allegations, including sexual abuse, severe physical abuse, and when children witness a traumatic crime such as homicide (Cross et al., 2007). Additionally, forensic interviews in a CAC setting are often recommended to investigate offenses perpetrated on very young children, as they may require time and specialized interactions for the viable information necessary for evidence in criminal trials to be collected. While the CAC model is rooted in both an evidence-based framework and a child-centered philosophy, there remains a need for additional development of sound models and programs that work for children with disabilities, for instance, in order to bring that vision to realization for all (Olafson, 2012).

From there, attention turns from the child welfare and court systems to the oversight of the child during out-of-home care. Families may work within the family court system toward reunification, preserving the family, and exiting legal involvement in the system. Unfortunately, once removed from the home, too many children cannot be reunified with their parent(s) or other family caregiver and find themselves wards of the state until they are adopted or age out of the system. The importance of permanency and stability for children and youth cannot be overstated and is a guiding principle of the child welfare system. In our next section, we will examine how child welfare practice and the courts work together to ensure the child's permanency.

Child and Youth Permanency

There are approximately 400,000 children in out-of-home care within the United States, and about 250,000 children will exit the foster care system each year (U.S. Department of Health and Human Services, 2021). Throughout the entire child welfare case process, courts have an essential role in children and families' permanency decisions. Permanency is a legal concept in which the child's relationship to an adult is recognized by law, as in the child's birth, kin, or adoptive parent. Relational permanency is a term used to acknowledge that children may have long-term and essential relationships that help them belong and have permanency connections that exist beyond legal court processes. Social workers must understand how laws, policies, and practices work together to ensure a safe and stable placement during out-of-home care, as well as a safe return home. Decisions regarding reunification, adoption, or another legal permanent custody status are all legal decisions with significant consequences for the child and family. Ideally, the families, along with the judge, attorneys, advocates, and social workers, collaborate to make decisions regarding the placement of children into the least restrictive and most family-like setting and permanency goals and outcomes. The directive from public policy is to prioritize decisions that keep children with family members or other kinship relationships before placement into a foster home, group home, or shelter. The courts serve as gatekeepers to the placement and permanency process.

Permanency Decision Hearing

Foster care and other forms of out-of-home placement are meant to be temporary. Removal of children from their homes is disruptive and traumatic with long-term negative consequences. Research has demonstrated that stable attachments during childhood are critical for healthy development. The priority thought out the permanency process of child welfare is the resolution of cases for child maltreatment and an emphasis on moving quickly in the child's best interest. When reunification is not possible, another permanent legal arrangement is planned, including adoption or another permanent guardianship. Some older children at the time of foster care placement may plan for emancipation. Each year in the United States, nearly 91% of the children and youth who exit foster care do so to a permanent home. In 2019, 47% of children exited out-of-home placement for reunification with their parent(s) or primary caretaker(s), 7% exited custody to live with another relative, and 11% were placed into some permanent guardianship (U.S. Department of Health and Human Services, 2020).

Permanency hearings occur at routine intervals after the initial determination of removal. Permanency hearings should ensure that the child is safe in their out-of-home placement, the child's needs are addressed to ensure well-being, and permanency plans are in place. The permanency hearing also oversees visitation conditions to ensure families and siblings have adequate and appropriate family visitations, provide oversight to the case process, and ensure competent and adequate representation for all. Court proceedings monitor many aspects of the case, but the primary objective is to determine if *reasonable efforts* are being pursued in reunification. The court's decisions continue to be made months after the removal of a child for maltreatment. Still, an administrative review must occur at a minimum of every 6 months, although most courts will monitor the case more frequently (Title IV-E of the Social Security Act). This long time frame is problematic to the child's well-being and development. Therefore, the courts and all other contributors to the child and family case should act with urgency to resolve the safety issues contributing to the out-of-home placement. Each court hearing is focused on evaluating if progress is being made to correct the conditions that brought the child and family into the court and if the child welfare agency has made reasonable efforts to provide the services needed to meet the family and child's needs. The court monitors efforts to maintain contact and the placement of siblings together. It also monitors to ensure that youth who are nearing adulthood are provided with opportunities to plan and prepare for the transition. The permanency court hearings also monitor the quality of care and evaluate the ongoing appropriateness of out-of-home care placement.

Challenges to permanency in child welfare are well documented. Problems include recruitment and identification of permanent families, a lack of services necessary to achieve and support long-term permanency, uncertainty on the determination of reasonable efforts, and inadequate permanency planning. Public policymakers and child welfare advocates have long argued for practice and policy strategies that address permanency and the urgency necessary for the case to end and the child(ren) to grow in a permanent home.

Concurrent Planning

Concurrent planning is a permanency strategy that assumes a primary case goal of reunification and services for the child's family. Still, it moves strategically to develop and deploy a concurrent case plan to terminate parental rights and provide another legal permanency option if reunification efforts fail. Concurrent planning was designed to address the complexities of both types of case goal plans and expedite permanency outcomes for children. Research has found that when concurrent permanency planning is used, permanency is achieved in a shorter period and reduces the time children are in foster care (Child Welfare Information Gateway, 2018).

Concurrent planning for permanency by courts has both strengths and challenges because it pursues concurrent case plan goals, which are fundamentally competing approaches to the case, where the "rights" of the children are placed against the "rights" of the family (Child Welfare Information Gateway, 2018). Permanency goals are driven by the child's best interest and taken broadly to mean the quickest permanent outcome and case closure. However, parents on the path to reunification often face complex issues that lead to maltreatment and safety concerns, such as addiction, intimate partner violence, poverty, housing instability, and health problems that require time to resolve. Additionally, the path to completing reunification plans may require vital community resources to accomplish those goals that may be lacking, such as substance abuse recovery services, quality counseling services, and employment opportunities. There is little research on the impact of concurrent case planning on the parents. Advocates worry that when courts initiate a new case goal for termination of parental rights (TPR), it may functionally decrease parent motivation to continue pursuing the steps necessary to decrease the likelihood of reunification.

Termination of Parental Rights

The court's most consequential determination for families is legal TPR. TPR can be voluntary and can occur outside of the child welfare maltreatment context. Within the child protection system, TPR cases are often an involuntary process. When reunification cannot be achieved, the courts make a legal determination that all reasonable efforts for reunification have failed. The courts and the child welfare system both seek the necessary steps to help children achieve legal permanency by other means. TPR is such an extreme and final action that the Supreme Court referred to it as an "awesome authority of the State" (M.L.B. v. S.L.J, 519 U.W. 102, 128 [1996]), and other courts have equated the decision in family court to have the same levity as the death penalty in criminal court (*In re* Smith, 601 N.E.2d 45, 55

[Ohio Ct. App. 1991]; see also *In re* K.A.W., 133 S.W. 3di,12 [Mo. 2004]. TPR requires a higher standard of proof than previous court decisions in the child welfare case. To proceed with TPR, the courts must have "clear and convincing evidence" as well as consideration for what is in the best interest of the child after all possible services that could improve the conditions of the family that led to removal have been provided and reunification is no longer possible (Vesneski, 2011). TPR typically involves expert testimony and case evidence to the courts given the severity of the action. TPR orders sever the legal relationship between the parent and child and allow the child(ren) to become legally free for legal permanence, such as adopting another caretaker. The Adoption and Safe Families Act requires states to pursue TPR if a child has been in foster care for 15 of the most recent 22 months, although several states have provisions to accelerate TPR under certain conditions.

Research on permanency outcomes demonstrates that certain families are at greater risk of failed reunification and TPR. A recent estimate (2016) is that one in 100 American children will experience TPR, with younger children, American Indian/Alaska Native children, and African American children significantly more likely to experience it (Wildeman et al., 2020). Rural families suffering from poverty and where community resources are not adequate to resolve maltreatment issues and do not allow the parents to meet the child's needs are more likely to have parental rights terminated (Wallace & Pruitt, 2012). Also, families with intersectional issues of poverty, mental illness, and substance abuse are more likely to have parental rights terminated (Wallace & Pruitt, 2012).

Adoption and Other Planned Permanent Legal Relationship

The courts and child welfare system's efforts to promote family reunification in policy and practice have reduced the number of children in the foster care system and the length of time children spend in out-of-home care. However, the increase in adoption and other forms of legal permanence persist. In 2019, just over 71,000 children were adopted in the United States from the foster care system. Still, an additional 122,000 children were legally free for legal permanency and waiting for an adoptive family (U.S. Department of Health and Human Services, n.d., p. 27). Adoption is the legal process in which the parent's parental rights and responsibilities are acquired by another person (Acosta, 2013). State laws and state courts mostly govern adoption proceedings. The only consideration by law in an adoption is the child's best interest, rather than the birth parents' or adoptive parents' interest (Acosta, 2013). During the adoption process, it is the responsibility of a trained social worker, who often specializes in adoption practice, and the courts to provide a thorough assessment of compatibility with the adoptive family and their readiness to take permanent parental and family responsibility for the child. In most cases, the adoption proceedings will mark the end of monitoring the child's well-being by the courts.

With the increase in adoptions and other forms of legal permanency, little is known about the quality of adoption decisions and their impact on a child's overall well-being throughout the lifespan, the quality of the child's attachment postadoption, and the child's general sense of belonging, which may all be impacted by childhood trauma and the negative consequence of stress during out-of-home placement. Longitudinal studies have shown that 10% to 15% of children who achieved permanency experienced postadoption disruption (Rolock, 2015). There is also a considerable amount of evidence to be concerned about the practice of unregulated transfer of custody. According to the Center for States, unregulated transfer of custody is the practice of adoptive parents transferring custody to another adult or family without court involvement (Center for States, 2018). While some states have adopted legislation to address this practice and, in some cases, to criminalize unauthorized transfer of custody, it is apparent that postadoption services are needed. Researchers, practitioners, and policymakers agree that adoption is a time during which both children and adoptive families experience myriad emotions and experiences that include joy, excitement, and a sense of belonging but also feelings of loss, rejection, grief, identity loss, shame, and guilt (Barbee et al., 2011; Goodwin et al., 2020). These emotions can occur over time both before and after the finalization of the adoption, leading to a call by advocates for specialized adoption support services and specialized training in adoption for social workers and other counseling professionals who provide supportive services to children and families throughout the adoption process (Goodwin et al., 2020).

Adoption is the preferred outcome for all children and youth in the foster care system, but the decision is a mutual one between the child and adoptive family for older youth. The Adoption and Safe Families Act (1997) provides courts with the alternative to use Another Planned Permanent Living Arrangement (APPLA). APPLA is only available for youth aged 16 and older and can only be selected when other efforts to pursue permanency options are not available. While it is an option for case goals, it is the least preferred permanency option for children and young adults. If APPLA is selected, courts must document the intensive and ongoing unsuccessful efforts for a family placement, including efforts to find biological and other kinship connections. Additionally, the court and social workers much ensure youth are involved in their permanency outcomes and allow the young person opportunities to engage in age-appropriate activities at each permanency hearing (Center for States, 2018). Despite the alternative permanency options presented in APPLA, 8% of youth who exit custody each year will emancipate and transition to adulthood without a legal permanent family (U.S. Department of Health and Human Services, 2020).

Critical Review of Permanency Outcomes

Removal of a child from their home, even when maltreatment conditions are substantiated, is disruptive and traumatic and has long-term negative consequences. Research has demonstrated that stable attachments are essential for child development. While improvements have been observed over time, the average length of time for children in care remains at 19 months (U.S. Department of Health and Human Services, 2020). Permanency outcomes have gained significant policy and practice improvements over time, but critical problems persist. The emphasis on a timely permanency process and urgency for the child's benefit requires the legal system to move in a manner that is not common in other types of judicial proceedings.

Additionally, evidence-based approaches to child welfare and the courts have been prioritized in public policy. Evidence-based practice refers to the process of working with children and families to employ services and approaches to care that make use of the best available evidence to address the child and family's needs. The child welfare system and courts struggle to deliver high-quality and effective evidence-based services. There are few controlled studies and even less when given the contextual issues of race, ethnicity, gender, and known to have higher risk outcomes in child welfare.

Certain types of risk factors have been associated with poor permanency outcomes. These include specific child and parent characteristics and contextual issues. Courts and professionals must improve court practices to reduce permanency risks through continuous quality improvement or court improvement programs and ongoing training. Certain parent and child characteristics are risk factors for the achievement of permanency. One example is the age of the child. Younger children are more likely to achieve permanency than older children (Bass et al., 2004). Children who are part of larger sibling groups often struggle to find permanency (Gustavsson & MacEachron, 2010), despite public policy efforts to reinforce the importance of helping siblings remain together.

Additionally, children with emotional, cognitive, or social development issues are less likely to achieve permanency (Becker et al., 2007). Children with intellectual or cognitive disabilities are less likely to achieve permanency through reunification or adoption (Becker et al., 2007; McDonald et al., 2007). For the parents, frequent contact with the children is essential, and less regular contact between the parents and children is associated with more extended periods in foster care. Parents who have complex and intersecting issues that lead to removing children from their home for maltreatment, such as mental illness, substance abuse, and poverty, are less likely to achieve timely reunification and permanency (McDonald et al., 2007).

Other contextual issues may contribute to poor permanency outcomes. One example is geographic differences. In many states, the geographic location of the case is a strong predictor of successful permanency; some studies show that urban areas have the lowest rates of successful reunification (Becker et al., 2007), whereas other studies have found that urban areas have the highest probability of exiting state custody (Glisson et al., 2000). Parents in certain rural communities have been found more likely to have a TPR determination, because rural families are more likely to experience poverty and community resources are less likely to allow the parent to meet the child's needs, suggesting courts may struggle with stereotypes of poverty and a failure to account for the realities of rural communities (Wallace & Pruitt, 2012). Poverty is often a contextual issue that negatively impacts reunification and permanency outcomes. States, advocates, and policymakers all assert that poverty alone is not a legitimate reason for removing children, preventing the child's reunification with their family, or TPR.

Racial Disproportionality and Disparity

Each of the decision points in child welfare has evidence of disproportional outcomes for children, youth, and families of color in comparison to their White counterparts (Child Welfare Information Gateway, 2016. Research on racial disproportionality and disparity and theories for why they occur is, at the time, conflicting; however, a significant amount of research has documented the overrepresentation of certain racial and ethnic populations such as African Americans and Native Americans in the child welfare system. Conversely, Asian American and Hispanic children are underrepresented in child welfare based on national-level data, the former much more so (Child Welfare Information Gateway, 2016). Several challenges and potential explanations for disparities exist, including differing offense definitions and responses across states, a lack of training in culturally sensitive practices, racial bias, and the impact of distinct but related issues such as poverty that also disproportionately impact people of color. Prevention, early intervention, educational standards, and training for child welfare workers are among proposed remedies for race-based differences in child welfare system involvement.

As with all forensic systems, child welfare investigations and service provision are fraught with a history marked by racial inequity and disparities persisting into the 21st century. Historical policy practice of removal of the child from the home, TPR, and adoption out of nonoffending families for Indigenous children in the United States occurred through the 1970s, until the passage of the Indian Child Welfare Act (ICWA). The ICWA provides protections for citizens of tribal nations and prioritizes those sovereign nations' rights to make decisions for their members based on their cultural rights, needs, and strengths. When applied as intended, the ICWA effectively reduces bias and the disproportionate representation of Native children in child welfare systems; it should be noted here that this is not a racial issue but one of citizenship. While criticisms persist of the ICWA, mainly outside of researchers and advocates within the child welfare community, as providing unequal advantage based on race, these result from a lack of understanding of the policy and its purpose and intent. Race continues to be an area of disparity in child welfare that requires continued attention in research, policy advocacy, training, and decision-making practices.

Emerging Evidence

Specialized approaches to the court process are some of the most promising practices for permanency outcomes in child welfare. Treatment courts, such as the Family Dependency Treatment Court (FDTC), are a decades-old method for handling substance-using caregivers with families involved in child welfare. National data indicate that alcohol and other drug use is the second most frequent reason for a child maltreatment investigation and removal (U.S. Department of Health and Human Services, 2020). The FDTC uses intervention-based multidisciplinary teams that include the judge, child workers welfare, Court Appointed Special Advocates, and community treatment providers to oversee the substance abuse treatment process while also considering the permanency goals and timelines for child welfare (National Center for State Courts [NCSC], 2017). While there are multiple strategies across different court systems, they are all based on service provision models that have been able to show improved outcomes in child welfare over traditional dependency courts in supporting parents to enter substance abuse treatment earlier and complete treatment and reducing substance use, which are all necessary steps to reunification with their children (Chuang et al., 2012). To date, there are over 370 family drug court programs in 45 states and tribal courts (NCSC, 2017), but more courts are needed as this number only serves a small percentage of families who could benefit from the court model. Future evaluation of program outcomes, specifically across all groups and identities, is needed. Continued examination of which aspects of the model are critical to producing the best outcomes for child welfare goals is needed.

Nearly a third of children entering the child welfare system are aged 3 or younger. The Safe Babies Court Approach (SBCA) is an infant-toddler specialized court program that utilizes a trained, multidisciplinary team to strategically work with the families and child welfare system to prevent removal and placement into foster care and promote family re-unification. The program adopts an expedited approach designed with the child's urgency and critical tasks for healthy development during the early years in mind. In addition to child welfare programming, comprehensive services include carefully planned and frequent family time (often several times a week) for ongoing parent and child relationship building and sustaining (Zero to Three, 2020). There is promising research evidence that SBCA children exit the foster care system faster than other children in the same age group and are more likely to exit foster care through family reunification and with lower rates of abuse and neglect reoccurrence (Faria et al., 2020; McCombs-Thornton & Foster, 2012).

Intersection With the Courts and Other Forensic Systems

The relationship of child welfare agencies with courts is a complex one, and one that rests within a gap of empirical research aimed at understanding and improving that intersection. The primary function of family courts responding to child maltreatment is to ensure children's safety and help parents provide a safe environment (Child Welfare Information Gateway, 2016). Ellett and Steib (2005) mapped out several key characteristics of both effective and problematic court processes around child welfare cases. Their findings indicated several strengths and concerns about a court's ability to make decisions in the child's best interests. Lack of training and education about child development, family dynamics, environmental factors, and decision-making factors related to child placement on the part of attorneys, judges, and other case parties outside of the child welfare agency are detrimental to this aim. Factors that were found to be key to effective decision-making by courts to ensure that decisions are rooted in children's best interests included high communication and collaboration in the multidisciplinary team, mutual professional regard, organized and well-prepared hearings, and valuing the perspectives of all parties. Court improvement projects across the nation continue to study and develop best-practice guidance to align with the findings of this study and move toward more specialized court practice, such as integrating trauma-informed principles and utilizing evidence-based special court models. This would help align the courts' purpose with public policy and with social work values and ethics for practice. Both would likely improve outcomes for children and families who are involved in the child welfare system.

In many ways, the child welfare system is functionally a reflection of the shortcomings of the many other institutions that have failed to improve the conditions that lead to family distress. For almost all the families involved in the child welfare system, there may be a significant intersection with other forensic systems that lack a rehabilitative focus. For instance, according to Phillips et al. (2004), about one of every eight children who are the subject of maltreatment reports has a parent who had experienced a recent arrest. Approximately 11% of mothers and 2% of fathers serving time in prison have children in foster care (Glaze & Maruschak, 2008). This grim association has only worsened due to the opioid epidemic as addiction, incarceration, and death increase across communities. An increase in maltreatment reports and increased placement in out-of-home care result from parental opioid abuse and have placed a strain on an already overstressed system (Crowley et al., 2019). It is important to keep in mind that for a child, removal from the home is a traumatic experience and should be prevented, whether through safety and supportive interventions for a family or policies that take into consideration the impact of harsh drug-related sentencing. Parental incarceration is one of the adverse childhood experiences about which ample research has been conducted to show its far-reaching negative impacts (Dube et al., 2001 2003; Felitti et al., 1998; Hughes et al., 2017). The outcomes for children who have experienced child welfare system involvement are worse compared to those who have not according to a host of measures: juvenile and criminal justice system involvement, mental and physical health problems, trauma, homelessness, low educational attainment, unemployment, poverty, sexual exploitation, and more.

The Future of Social Work in Child Welfare Practice

The complexities of the child welfare system are the precise reasons social work professionals should engage in practice, leadership, policy advocacy, and the general advancement of professional child welfare practice. For social work professionals who do not plan to work directly within the child welfare system, you will likely interact as a supportive professional to an adult, child, or family caregiver who has current court and child welfare system involvement. In fact, we argue that there is no professional setting in which you will practice where some degree of involvement of the child welfare system is not likely. A social worker in clinical practice will have children and families who are under court supervision, a social worker in criminal justice settings will be supporting parents as they plan for community integration, and even a social worker in aging services will be supporting grandparents who often find themselves providing primary care for grandchildren. When examining current practice in child welfare, the current work of policy advocates, and the emerging evidence base, we believe the future of child welfare will be focused on improvements in three primary areas: providing secondary prevention services to reduce the number of children who are placed into out-of-home care; improving decision-making process to ensure assessments, case planning, and other determinations made by the courts and professionals are evidence driven and actively reduce systemic biases that exist; and ensuring workers in both child welfare and the courts are trained for best practices.

The prevention of child maltreatment and forensic system involvement has far-reaching positive impacts and must continue to receive focus as the federal, state, and tribal governments examine criminal justice and other reforms. Advocates will argue that that is not enough. In our best efforts, we should collectively be focused on ending child maltreatment and eliminating the need for a forensic setting response for the protection of children altogether. Despite the complexity of child welfare and its intersection with forensic systems, the simple vision is providing for the best interests of children, and this shared goal helps guide and direct the field of child welfare practice in the present and for the future.

Child Welfare Case Example: The Webber Family

Information/Case History

Parents Tisha (age 27) and Scott Webber (age 28) have been working with the child welfare system after their oldest child, Kennedy (age 8), was23 found outside of the family home by local law enforcement around 1:00 a.m. They also have a newborn child, Paris (8 weeks).

Child Welfare History

The Webbers have had two previous referrals to the child welfare system. The first occurred when Kennedy was 3 years old due to an unexplained bruise to his left ear and cheek. Kennedy was seen by a physician, who determined the bruise was consistent with the parent's account of the injury. At that time, no referral for services or safety planning occurred, and the case was closed. Two years later, at age 5, Kennedy was referred by the school after reoccurring head lice along with some concerns that Kennedy's parents may not be providing adequate food because he was often starving when arriving at school. Services for support and some help with eliminating the head lice were offered by community services, and a referral to food resources was completed. The case was then closed.

The most recent referral came after local law enforcement found Kennedy walking in the neighborhood at approximately 1:00 a.m. When asked why, Kennedy stated, "The baby was crying, and my parents told me to go outside." Upon returning Kennedy to the home, the officer on duty reported the event to Child Protection Services (CPS), resulting in an immediate investigation of the child's safety in the middle of the night.

The CPS social worker began the initial safety assessment during the follow-up home visit. During the investigation, the CPS worker interviewed and completed an assessment of the child(ren) and family's safety and well-being. Tisha reported she had directed Kennedy to "go back to bed" when the baby had started crying and believed that was where Kennedy had gone. Tisha thought that Kennedy may have been "sleepwalking" and that she did not notice him leave the house while tending to Paris's cries and middle-of-the-night feedings. Scott was sleeping the entire time. The parents explained to the CPS worker they were exhausted from caring for a newborn but insisted their home was safe. The family was doing well and assured the CPS investigator this was just a simple, one-time misunderstanding. The CPS investigator visually assessed Paris and found her in clean clothes, fed, diapered, and resting in a crib by her parents' bed.

The following morning, the CPS social worker met with Kennedy at school. Kennedy insisted that his mother "told me to go outside" and said she was angry and "yelling dirty words" at him. Earlier in the night, she said he "got too loud" and he was spanked with a bare hand on the bottom for waking up the baby. When the investigator asked Kennedy questions about how often this happens, Kennedy responded, "Momma hits me all the time, or she kicks me out of the house—unless she wants me to take care of Paris, especially if she is drinking."

Critical Thinking/Ethics
- *How does the history of reporting and investigation integrate into the current report by law enforcement? How could the frame of the professional limit or bias the assessment of the child's safety?*
- *Should a report of abuse by a law enforcement officer be considered more severe than those reported by other professionals or citizens?*
- *What additional information should the CPS social worker gather to decide and present evidence to the courts? What would the courts and social workers need to understand about this case to determine that a willful act of abuse and neglect has occurred, or could something else explain the events? How could issues of poverty or race be evaluated in this case?*

Case Disposition

After the meeting with Kennedy, the CPS investigator returned to the family home to continue an assessment focused on safety. It became clear that the parents were overwhelmed with the care of the new baby, and Tisha admitted she has been purchasing prescription medications from a friend and needs them to help her stay awake during the day. She also stated she occasionally would smoke pot and have a few beers at night to wind down. Tisha admitted that it is possible she did direct Kennedy to go outside, but she was not sure. It became clear during the follow-up meetings that Tisha was blacking out a few times a week from substance use and was not sure what the children were doing during that time. The CPS investigator provided the assessment information to the attorney representing the state. They agreed that a court order for temporary removal of Kennedy and Paris was in the family's best interest due to concerns for the parents' substance use and lack of appropriate supervision. At the same time, they referred the parents for substance abuse and newborn support services. In the court hearing, the judge agreed that the evidence presented provided enough information about the child's safety and well-being and ordered Kennedy to be placed with an aunt. Aunt Becky lives in the same community, has a great relationship with Kennedy, and provides care for both children.

Permanency

Shortly after the court hearing, the family met with the child welfare permanency social worker to develop a plan to address the child and family safety concerns and ensure the children and family have access to services and programs that will improve their well-being while sustaining their family bond. After working together to determine specific goals and strategies to accomplish those goals, the plan was presented to the courts in a permanency hearing. The judge agreed to the plan and cautioned the parents that they needed to "get moving and get all the work done" or the courts would have to consider a more permanent plan for Kennedy. Both Tisha and Scott quickly completed the newborn parenting classes, and Tisha indicated they have been beneficial and reduced her stress for providing newborn care. The permanency plan also included screening for substance abuse. Tisha completed the screening within weeks of the initial permanency hearing and began an outpatient treatment plan. But Scott was reluctant to complete the task and indicated that the only alcohol and drugs in the house were Tisha's. Scott is concerned that missing work for a drug screening would alert his boss to a problem and cost him a good job.

Kennedy and Paris are doing well at their aunt's home. Kennedy has not missed any school, is keeping up with his homework, and won his teacher's "star citizen" award last week. His mom has started regular visitation with both of them. During the visits, Kennedy plays with Paris and shares about school and what he does on the weekends with Aunt Becky. He was very excited to share with his mom about winning "star citizen." Kennedy said that he likes living with Aunt Becky because she plays Uno with him often and is always there to help him with his homework. She doesn't yell at him or say "dirty words." He also said that he misses his dad and wonders why he doesn't come to visit as often as his mom. In the last visit to the home, Kennedy asked the new social worker, "How long until I get to go home with mom again?" Scott cannot attend visitation because he cannot miss work for fear of not having enough income to pay for the household needs.

Critical Thinking/Ethics
- *What do you consider to be reasonable efforts in this case? Who is responsible for ensuring reasonable effort for reunification?*
- *How should the courts and child welfare system be held accountable for ensuring the family has every opportunity for visitation and successful and quick reunification?*
- *What are the conditions that you would look for to make a case for reunification?*
- *If Kennedy is doing well living with the aunt, should that be disrupted? Why?*

After 7 months, Tisha has completed the outpatient treatment program, is working with a sponsor in her local Alcoholics Anonymous group, and has met many of the requirements set by the courts. However, Scott has been unable to initiate the requirements of the permanency plan. The permanency child welfare social worker has been visiting the family biweekly and feels that returning Kennedy to live with his mother would be safe and is in Kennedy's best interest. But the worker is less confident in Scott's ability to provide safety in the home. Knowing the courts will need to consider reunification or concurrent planning soon, the social worker cautioned Tisha that she might have to make a difficult choice between Kennedy and Scott. This panicked Tisha, as she is financially dependent on Scott to provide for the household, and he is Paris's father. She does not want to choose between reunification with Kennedy and separation from Scott.

Critical Thinking/Ethics

- *What should the permanency worker do to help the family achieve permanency?*
- *What is the role of the courts? Whose "best interest" should be considered in this family?*
- *Discuss how each of the permanency options would create different outcomes for the family. What are the benefits and deficits of each of those options?*

References

Acosta, L. (2013, May). *Adoption law: United States*. Law Library of Congress. https://www.loc.gov/law/help/adoption-law/unitedstates

Ashton, V. (2009). The effect of statutory regulations on social workers' decisions to report child maltreatment. *Advances in Social Work, 10*, 128–143. https://doi.org/10.18060/255

Bryant, J., & Milsom, A. (2005). Child abuse reporting by school counselors. *Professional School Counseling, 9*, 63–71.

Barbee, A. P., Christensen, D., Antle, B., Wandersman, A., & Cahn, K. (2011). Successful adoption and implementation of a comprehensive casework practice model in a public child welfare agency: Application of the Getting to Outcomes (G.T.O) model. *Children and Youth Services Review, 33*(5), 622–633. https://doi.org/10.1016/j.childyouth.2010.11.008

Bass, S., Shields, M. K., & Behrman, R. E. (2004). Children, families, and foster care: Analysis and recommendation. *Future of Children, 14*(1), 5–29.

Becker, M. A., Jordan, N., & Larsen, R. (2007). Predictors of successful permanency planning and length of stay in foster care: The role of race, diagnosis and place of residence. *Children and Youth Services Review, 29*(8), 1102–1113.Capacity Building Center for States. (2018). *Child protective services: A guide for caseworkers*. Children's Bureau, Administration for Children and Families, U.S. Department of Health and Human Services. https://www.childwelfare.gov/

Chuang, E., Moore, K., Barrett, B., & Young, M. S. (2012). Effect of an integrated family dependency treatment court on child welfare reunification, time to permanency and reentry rates. *Children and Youth Services Review, 34*(9), 1896–1902. https://doi.org/10.1016/j.childyouth.2012.06.001

Child Welfare Information Gateway. (2016). *Understanding child welfare and the courts*. U.S. Department of Health and Human Services, Children's Bureau. https://www.childwelfare.gov/pubs/factsheets/cwandcourts/

Child Welfare Information Gateway. (2017). *Forensic interviewing: A primer for child welfare professionals.* U.S. Department of Health and Human Services, Children's Bureau. https://www.childwelfare.gov/pubs/factsheets/forensicinterviewing/

Child Welfare Information Gateway. (2018). *Concurrent planning for timely permanency.* U.S. Department of Health and Human Services, Children's Bureau. https://www.childwelfare.gov/pubs/concurrent-planning/

Cross, T. P., Jones, L. M., Walsh, W. A., Simone, M., & Kolko, D. (2017). Child forensic interviewing in Children's Advocacy Centers: Empirical data on a practice model. *Child Abuse & Neglect, 31*(10), 1031–1052. doi:10.1016/j.chiabu.2007.04.007. Epub 2007 Nov 8. PMID: 17996298.

Crowley, D. M., Connell, C. M., Jones, D., & Donovan, M. W. (2019). Considering the child welfare system burden from opioid misuse: Research priorities for estimating public costs. *American Journal of Managed Care, 25*(13), S256–S263.

DePanfilis, D. (2018). *Child protective services: A guide for caseworkers.* U.S. Department of Health and Human Services, Administration for Children and Families Administration on Children, Youth, and Families, Children's Bureau Office of Child Abuse and Neglect. https://www.childwelfare.gov/pubPDFs/cps2018.pdf

Dube, S. R., Anda, R. F., Felitti, V. J., Chapman, D. P., Williamson, D. F., & Giles, W. H. (2001). Childhood abuse, household dysfunction, and the risk of attempted suicide throughout the life span: Findings from the adverse childhood experiences study. *Journal of American Medical Association, 286*(24), 3089–3096. https://doi.org/10.1542/peds.111.3.564

Dube, S. R., Felitti, V. J., Dong, M., Chapman, D. P., Giles, W. H., & Anda, R. F. (2003). Childhood abuse, neglect, and household dysfunction and the risk of illicit drug use: The adverse childhood experiences study. *Pediatrics, 111*(3), 564–572. https://doi.org/10.1542/peds.111.3.564

Ellett, A. J., & Steib, S. D. (2005). Child welfare and the courts: A statewide study with implications for professional development, practice, and change. *Research on Social Work Practice, 15*(5), 339–352. https://doi.org/10.1177/1049731505276680

Faria, A. M., Bowdon, J., Conway-Turner, J., Pan, J., Ryznar, T., Michaelson, L., Derrington, T., & Walston, J. (2020). *The Safe Babies Court team evaluation: Changing the trajectories of children in foster care.* American Institutes for Research. https://www.air.org/sites/default/files/Safe-babies-court-team

Feletti, V. J., Anda, R. F., Nordenberg, D., Williamsons, D. F., Spitz, A. M., Edwards, V., Marks, J. S. (1998). Relationship of childhood abuse and household dysfunction to many of the leading causes of death in adults: The adverse childhood experiences (ACES) study. *American Journal of Preventative Medicine, 14*(4), 245–258. https://doi.org/10.1016/S0749-3797(98)00017-8

Fluke, J., Jones Harden, B., Jenkins, M., & Reuhrdanz, A. (2011). *Disparities and disproportionality in child welfare: Analysis of the research* [Paper presentation]. Research symposium convened by the Center for the Study of Social Policy and the Annie E. Casey Foundation on behalf of the Alliance for Racial Equity in Child Welfare. https://repositories.lib.utexas.edu/

Glaze, L., & Maruschak, L. (2008). Parents in prison and their minor children. In US Department of Justice Bureau of Justice Statistics Special Report 1–25.

Glaze, L. E., & Maruschak, L. M. (2010). *Bureau of Justice statistics special report: Parents in prison and their minor children.* U.S. Department of Justice, Office of Justice Programs. https://www.bjs.gov/content/pub/pdf/pptmc.pdf

Glisson, C., Bailey, J. W., & Post, J. A. (2000). Predicting the time children spend in state custody. *Social Services Review, 74*(2), 253–280. https://doi.org/10.1086/514479

Goodwin, B., Madden, E., Singletary, J., & Scales, L. T. (2020). Adoption workers perspectives of adoption adjustment and the honeymoon period. *Children and Youth Services Review, 119*, 105513. https://doi.org/10.1016/j.childyouth.2020.105513

Gustavsson, N. S., & MacEachron, A. E. (2010). Sibling connections and reasonable efforts in public child welfare. *Families in Society, 91*(1), 39–44. https://doi.org/10.1606/1044-3894.3956

Hawkins, R., & McCallum, C. (2001). Effects of mandatory notifications training on the tendency to report hypothetical cases of child abuse and neglect. *Child Abuse Review, 10*, 301–322.

Hughes, K., Bellis, M. A., Hardcastle, K. A., Sethi, D., Butchart, A., Mikton, C., & Dunne, M. P. (2017). The effect of multiple adverse childhood experiences on health: A systematic review and meta-analysis. *Lancet Public Health, 2*(8), e356–e366. https://doi.org/10.1016/S2468-2667(17)30118-4

Krase, K. S., & DeLong-Hamilton, T. A. (2015). Comparing reports of suspected child maltreatment in states with and without universal mandated reporting. *Children and Youth Services Review, 50*, 96–100. https://doi.org/10.1016/j.childyouth.2015.01.015

McCombs-Thornton, K. L., & Foster, E. M. (2012). The effect of the ZERO TO THREE Court Teams initiative on types of exits from the foster care system—A competing risks analysis. *Children and Youth Services Review, 34*(1), 169–178.

McDonald, T. P., Poertner, J., & Jennings, M. A. (2007). Permanency for children in foster care: A competing risks analysis. *Journal of Social Service Research, 33*(4), 45–56. https://doi.org/10.1300/J079v33n04_04

National Center for State Courts. (2017). *Plans of safe care: An issue brief for judicial officers.* Quality Improvement Center, Collaborative Community Court Teams, Administration on Children, Youth, and Families, Children's Bureau. https://ncsacw.acf.hhs.gov/topics/family-treatment-courts.aspx

Olafson, E. (2012). A call for field-relevant research and child forensic interviewing for child protection. *Journal of Child Sexual Abuse, 21*, 109–129. https://doi.org/10.1080/10538712.2012.642469

Palusci, V., Vandervort, F., & Lewis, J. M. (2016). Does changing mandated reporting laws improve child maltreatment reporting in large U.S. counties? *Children and Youth Services Review, 66*, 170–179. https://doi.org/10.1016/j.childyouth.2016.05.002

Phillips, S. D., Burns, B. J., Wagner, H. R., & Barth, R. P. (2004). Parental arrest and children involved with child welfare services agencies. *American Journal of Orthopsychiatry, 74*(2), 174–186.

Rolock, N. (2015). Post-permanency continuity: What happens after adoption and guardianship from foster care? *Journal of Public Child Welfare, 9*(2), 153–173. https://doi.org/10.1080/15548732.2015.1021986

Steen, J. A. (2011). Organizational configurations of American child maltreatment reporting systems. *Journal of Public Child Welfare, 5*, 471–480.

U.S. Department of Health and Human Services, Administration for Children and Families, Administration on Children, Youth, and Families, Children's Bureau. (2021). *Child maltreatment, 2019.* https://www.acf.hhs.gov/cb/research-data-technology/statistics-research/child-maltreatment

Vesneski, W. (2011). State law and the termination of parental rights. *Family Court Review, 49*(2), 364–378. https://doi.org/10.1111/j.1744-1617.2011.01377.x

Wallace, J. L., & Pruitt, L. R. (2012). Judging parents, judging place: Poverty, rurality, and termination of parental rights. *Missouri Law Review, 77*(1), 95–148. https://heinonline.org/HOL/P?h=hein.journals/molr77&i=98

Wildeman, C., Edwards, F. R., & Wakefield, S. (2020). The cumulative prevalence of termination of parental rights for US children, 2000–2016. *Child Maltreatment, 25*(1), 32–42.

Zero to Three. (2020). *The Safe Babies Court team approach: Core components and key activities.* Zero to Three National Resource Center. Https://www.zerotothree.org/resources/services/the-safe-babies-court-team-approach

24

Domestic & Relational Violence

David Axlyn McLeod and Burcu Ozturk

Introduction

The definition of domestic violence varies depending on the context in which the term is used; it is an umbrella term that encompasses intimate partner and family violence of multiple sorts. Domestic, family, and intimate partner violence (IPV) in this chapter will collectively be referred to as *relational violence*. This is done to incorporate the broad aspects of the phenomenon that move away from traditional conceptualizations of identity, heteronormativity, and gender. Domestic violence has been defined as "a pattern of assaultive and coercive behaviors, including physical, sexual, and psychological attacks, as well as coercion that adults or adolescents use against their intimate partners" (Ganley, 995, p. 16). Relational violence includes and builds on this to include manipulation along with any covert or explicit behavior intended to control or inhibit the autonomy and freedom of a partner or relative. Survivors can often experience multiple types of abuse in relationships. This is known as poly-victimization (Finkelhor et al., 2007).

Relational violence has been identified as a "three-pronged attack," which includes the use of control, threats, and violence (Hester, 2011), and the model of systemic relational violence outlined in this chapter further operationalizes the concept. Scholars have established the associations between coercive control and traditional interpersonal or domestic violence conceptualizations with this theoretical inclusion (McLeod et al., 2021). Coercive control is an act or pattern of acts of threats, humiliation, and intimidation to frighten or pressure a romantic partner or family member into a state of continuous behavioral compliance used to harm their victims (Stark & Hester, 2019). As a result, victims in the scenarios can face significant adverse mental health issues and threats to their immediate and long-term health, livelihood, and safety (K. L. Anderson, 2010). Relational violence exists for people in communities worldwide regardless of age, race, gender, sexual orientation, gender identity, faith, culture, or class. It is a physical and psychological assault on the autonomy

David Axlyn McLeod and Burcu Ozturk, *Domestic & Relational Violence* In: *Handbook of Forensic Social Work*. Edited by: David Axlyn McLeod, Anthony P. Natale, and Kristin W. Mapson, Oxford University Press. © Oxford University Press 2024. DOI: 10.1093/oso/9780197694732.003.0024 of the abused partner and can be apparent in various manipulative contexts. Developing a better understanding of the issue and advancing more successful interventions will increase safety, liberty, and autonomy for individuals, partnerships, family units, and communities.

Scope of Problem

Relational violence impacts men, women, children, and individuals in all types of relationships (McLeod et al., 2021). It is widespread, reaching people of all cultures, regions, and economic statuses. In the United States, about 20 people per minute are physically abused by an intimate partner (National Coalition Against Domestic Violence, 2020). Approximately one in 10 women have survived rape, and one in three women have endured physical violence in their lifetimes (Black et al., 2010; Breiding et al., 2014). The National Intimate Partner and Sexual Violence Survey (NISVS, 2010–2012) reported that approximately one in three women (37.3%) experienced sexual or physical violence and stalking abuse by their intimate partner at some point in their lives in the United States from 2010 to 2012 (Smith et al., 2017). There are roughly 10 million victims of relational violence each year in the United States (Truman & Morgan, 2014). But, despite these numbers, victims often hesitate to report this violence to the police, and only about half of the actual estimated cases are represented on the National Crime Victimization Survey (Truman & Morgan, 2014).

According to the NISVS, male victimization is a significant public health concern. Almost a quarter of men in the United States have reported experiencing relational violence (Centers for Disease Control and Prevention [CDC], 2020). Moreover, in one out of every 10 of those men, first-time victimization occurred before the age of 25, and many male victims first experienced relational violence before the age of 18 (CDC, 2020). Across the U.S. states, nearly one in 10 men have reported experiencing sexual violence, physical violence, and stalking by an intimate partner during their lifetime (CDC, 2020). However, there is very little research on this matter because men fear they will not be believed if they report the abuse. A study of male victims of relational violence was conducted in the Netherlands in 2013, and it was revealed that abuse is perpetrated by both men and women (Drijber et al., 2013). The study found that male victims are abused by their partners both mentally and physically, with 54% of survivors in these cases having been physically abused (Drijber et al., 2013). In addition, the study found that men were more likely to report to police if they were physically attacked and less likely to report other types of abuse (Drijber et al., 2013). Despite mythology to the contrary, this abuse is present in all kinds of relationships, including heterosexual ones.

The complexity of personal identity plays a role as well. Multiracial women experience relational violence more often throughout their lifetimes than other racial groups (Sugg, 2015), and the prevalence of relational violence is even higher among immigrants, ranging from 30% to 60% (Biafora & Warheit, 2007; Erez et al., 2009; Hazen & Soriano, 2005; Sabina et al., 2014). One study found that immigrant women were at higher risk of experiencing relational violence after migrating to the United States because of a lack of social support, limited English language ability, and vulnerability to the legal system (Erez et al., 2009).

A study among Filipina, Indian, and Pakistani women in the United States showed that 95% of the women had experienced physical abuse in their lifetime (Yoshihama et al., 2011). In addition, immigrant women who experience relational violence are more likely to experience mental health issues. For instance, Latina immigrants who experience relational violence are three times as likely to be diagnosed with posttraumatic stress disorder (PTSD) as Latina immigrants with no relational violence experiences (Fedovskiy et al., 2008).

Further, transgender survivors were two times more likely to report they had experienced violence by a former or ex-partner than survivors who were cisgender (National Coalition of Anti-Violence Programs [NCAVP], 2016). In 2015, the NCAVP published a report related to LGBTQ and HIV-affected IPV. They reported 13 homicides due to IPV; of the 13 homicides, six were transgender women, four were cisgender men, and three were cisgender women. All six transgender women were women of color, including four who were Black and two who were Latinx. In addition, they reported 1,976 survivors of relational violence, with the majority identifying as gay or lesbian (NCAVP, 2016).

Criminal justice systems are often tasked with addressing this social problem. Still, the limitations of these systems have been revealed due to their focus on acts of physical violence and their lack of ability to intervene in psychological and emotionally abusive situations, which often preclude physical violence (Hester, 2011). Forms of coercion and control, such as emotional, financial, social, and psychological abuses, can be devastating to survivors but are not typically part of the criminal justice system's responses for many reasons. These include the complicated nature of these interactions and difficulty obtaining evidence of harm. In addition, due to the often-complicated nature of relational violence, many professionals struggle with the nonphysical characteristics of the phenomenon. Professionals in various intersecting professional spaces such as social work, law enforcement, and the courts are working to address this, but much more is needed. This chapter will provide the historical and modern context and theoretical aspects of the phenomenon. We will detail the tools historically used in service provision and provide a new evidence-based method to understand this experience from the paradigm of those involved.

Impact of Violence in Relationships

Physical Impacts

Researchers have consistently demonstrated the lifelong physical health effects of relational violence. Violence can cause short-term and long-term damaging health and well-being problems for survivors (World Health Organization [WHO], 2012). The impact of relational violence can create issues with walking, dizziness, pain, memory loss, and difficulty carrying out daily activities (WHO, 2005). A study found women who had experienced relational violence had an increased risk of stroke, heart disease, and asthma (Houry et al., 2006). Furthermore, sexually and physically abused women reported 50% to 70% more central nervous system problems, stress-related problems, and gynecological difficulties (Campbell, 2002). Sexually transmitted infections, chronic pelvic pain, and urinary tract infections are also common among survivors of relational violence (Campbell, 2002).

A study revealed a significant association between HIV infection and experiences or histories of relational violence in women (Sareen, 2009). Therefore, the various physical health consequences that can occur are present at the time of the violence but might remain far beyond the period of abuse.

Mental Health Impacts

Although the physical effects of relational violence are often apparent, the psychological impacts are often less visible. Relational violence can cause various emotional and mental health disorders (De Mendonça & Ludermir, 2017). For instance, several studies were conducted to investigate the correlation between relational violence and its effects on mental health. Survivors have higher PTSD and depression rates than those who have not experienced relational violence (Black et al., 2011; Fedovskiy et al., 2008; Krause et al., 2008; J. Lee et al., 2007). Those who experience poly-victimization report even higher rates of PTSD and depression than those who do not (Black et al., 2011; Fedovskiy et al., 2008). Suicidal behaviors, depression, and emotional distress are common among women who have experienced relational violence (Kim & Lee, 2013), and men who experience it report higher rates of PTSD, depression, anxiety, insomnia, and social dysfunction than those who have not (Campbell, 2002).

One cross-cultural study revealed that female survivors of relational violence worldwide typically experienced higher stress and fatigue levels (WHO, 2005). Numerous studies conducted in Brazil, Ethiopia, Pakistan, the United States, and Vietnam confirmed a significant relationship between relational violence and psychological disorders such as anxiety, depression, and suicidal intention (Ali & Naylor, 2013; Bonomi et al., 2007; Deyessa et al., 2008; Ellsberg et al., 2008; Ludermir et al., 2008; Vung et al., 2009). One study conducted among Pakistani women in Karachi indicated a strong correlation between mental health symptoms and all types of violence exposure among survivors (Ali & Naylor, 2013).

Impact on Children and Families

Relational violence also has substantial negative consequences on the family unit, with one study reporting that 26% of U.S. children have been exposed to violence in the home (Child Welfare Information Gateway, 2014). In addition, research has shown how children exposed to family violence are also more likely to be the victims of simultaneous child abuse (K. L. Anderson, 2010). Moving this trajectory a step forward, researchers indicate that children who experienced poly-victimization were also at a greater risk of being victimized in adolescence and adulthood (Finkelhor et al., 2007).

By one measurement, over the course of a year in the United States, approximately 20,000 children received residential domestic violence services, and an additional 23,000 adults received advocacy and support (Child Welfare Information Gateway, 2014). Children are removed from their homes at alarming rates in the United States due to exposure to domestic violence. This is a complicating factor for relational violence intervention, considering that the risk of having children removed is often why survivors are hesitant to seek help. Furthermore, exposure to domestic violence is a commonly accepted predictor of life adversity as a recognized risk factor on the adverse childhood experiences questionnaire (Child Welfare Information Gateway, 2014). Studies have identified strong connections between poly-victimization and symptoms of psychological distress such as anxiety or depression (Finkelhor et al., 2007). Children who witness domestic violence are more likely to have behavioral and cognitive challenges and long-term mental health issues such as anxiety, depression, problems with peers and anger/aggression, and low self-esteem (Gilbert et al., 2015). In addition, children are more likely to be delayed in physical and cognitive skill development and have trouble concentrating. These effects are not limited to behavioral and mental challenges alone. Children who experience poly-victimization have a 3.7 times higher likelihood of suffering from chronic pain and developing gastrointestinal, respiratory, metabolic, or musculoskeletal disorders (Riedl et al., 2019).

Impact on Communities

The damage of relational violence not only affects individuals and families but also damages our broader society. One study found the estimated cost of medical, mental health services, and productivity loss due to relational violence to be about $5.8 billion each year in the United States (National Center for Injury Prevention and Control, 2003). Relational violence costs approximately $4.1 billion annually in medical and mental health services alone (National Center for Injury Prevention and Control, 2003). In addition, women who experience relational violence are nine times more likely to require higher levels of health care services and are more likely to require high-cost specialty care (Campbell, 2002; Sugg, 2015).

Convergence of Impact

The impacts of relational violence, as listed above, rarely happen in isolation. As Figure 24.1 demonstrates, physical, social, and mental damage often overlap, creating a complexity of lived experience. Historically, physical impacts have been more commonly associated with relational violence survivorship. This could be for various reasons mentioned throughout this chapter, the most of which are often related to the ease of identification of these

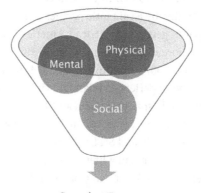

Complex Trauma

FIGURE 24.1 Convergence of Impact

phenomena. The mental (psychological and emotional) impacts can be more complex and range from distress to the development of disorders and a fundamental alteration of expectations for people and relationships in everyday life. Social impacts could be varied and could be connected to community interaction or family unit relationships. These could also be related to employment or other interactive spaces in the community. Whatever they may be, the impacts often overlap and create a type of complex trauma for the survivor, which often are added to by other external realities of lived experience in today's world. This complex trauma has a cumulative effect greater than the sum of its parts (Herman, 1992).

Race, Ethnicity, and Immigrant Populations

The immigrant population has grown steadily in the United States, increasing from 14.1 million in 1980 to 44.8 million by 2018 (Budiman et al., 2020; Singer, 2013). Because the immigrant population will continue to expand, we must raise awareness of relational violence within this group. In one survey of immigrant women, most who had experienced relational violence said violence in their homes escalated after moving to the United States (Erez et al., 2009). When people travel to other nations, they must adjust to a new way of life, which can be stressful (Bui & Morash, 1999). They face language barriers, social isolation from family and friends, immigration status concerns, and financial hardships (Menjívar & Salcido, 2002).

The American Indian and Alaskan Native (AIAN) population is a diversified ethnic minority group in the United States, with 566 federally recognized tribes spread across 33 states (U.S. Department of the Interior Indian Affairs, 2012). According to the 2010 NISVS, which included all AIAN women in one group, 46% of the collective population has been exposed to relational violence at some point in their lives (Black et al., 2011). Individual tribe surveys, on the other hand, have indicated percentages of up to 91% (Robin et al., 1998).

Over 20 countries of origin are represented within the Latino/Hispanic community in the United States, including Spain, Mexico, Cuba, Puerto Rico, and Central and South American countries. According to the 2010 NISVS, Hispanic women had a lifetime rate of IPV of 35% (Black et al. 2011), but rates vary substantially among studies of women from different places of origin (Hazen & Soriano 2007; Kantor et al. 1994).

Approximately 45% of Black women in the United States have experienced physical or sexual violence and/or stalking by a romantic partner during their lifetime (Smith et al., 2017). From there, the disparity gets worse. African American women between the ages of 25 and 29 are over 10 times more likely to be murdered while pregnant or in the first year of their child's life (Sharps et al., 2007). Breiding et al. (2014) found 41% of Black women in the sample of their study to have experienced relational violence in their lifetime, compared to 31% of White women, 30% of Hispanic women, and 15% of Asian women.

East, Central, and South Asian countries such as China, Japan, Korea, Mongolia, Vietnam, India, Pakistan, Bangladesh, and Sri Lanka are Asian American. According to the 2010 NISVS, Asian American women had a lifetime rate of IPV of 20% (Black et al. 2011). There have been few studies of Asian American women's relational violence experiences, so making comparisons between different populations is challenging (Abbey et al., 2010; Y. S. Lee & Hadeed, 2009).

Women's description and reporting of their experiences with violence may be influenced by their cultural origins (White et al., 2013). Furthermore, many women are impacted by more than one aspect of their minority status, and these aspects frequently interact. For example, immigration patterns connect with country of origin (e.g., Arab Americans may be Muslims, Christians, or Druze), and country of origin intersects with religion (e.g., Arab Americans may be Muslims, Christians, or Druze; White et al., 2013). As a result, focusing on just one aspect of minority status produces an incomplete picture of a person's identity (White et al., 2013). Relational violence instruments that are culturally acceptable must be sensitive to within-group differences while still being suitable for usage across subgroups of a population to make comparisons (White et al., 2013).

Issues of Economics

Poverty

People in low-income families are significantly more likely to experience relational violence and the accompanying stress. Some survivors lack financial independence and depend on their partners' income (Parenzee & Smythe, 2003). Whenever these people leave their homes, they can risk employment, housing, and income loss. Several empirical studies have shown that as a woman's income increases (either absolutely or in relative terms), domestic violence against her decreases (Aizer, 2011; Angelucci, 2009; Bobonis et al., 2009; Bowlus & Seitz, 2005, Farmer & Tiefenthaler, 1997). In essence, financial independence can be a protective factor for women in potentially abusive relationships.

Affluence

However, although poverty can put people at greater risk of becoming victims, highly educated, high-income individuals experience different types of barriers when seeking help for relational violence. Financial abuse is a common occurrence. Financial or economic abuse is described as using resources to threaten the economic security and potential for self-sufficiency of another (Adams et al., 2008). Thus, a financial abuse perpetrator controls what their victim can and cannot do. Survivors may be financially dependent on their abusive partner or work together in the same company. This finding was consistent with other studies that showed how a survivor's choices to stay with the abusive partner are often related to financial dependency (M. A. Anderson et al., 2003; Davis, 2002; Kim & Gray, 2008).

Some researchers have demonstrated how IPV occurs even among people with higher education and financial independence levels. For example, Midlarsky et al. (2006) conducted a study to explore relational violence among highly educated women. Their study revealed that women might be vulnerable to abuse even though they have a career life because of gender roles, lack of support, family values, and other stress factors. A qualitative study including women without financial dependency found that the sample remained reluctant to leave an abusive relationship because they did not want to leave their children (Ozturk, 2020). Among survivors, there is also often a great deal of self-judgment and self-blame for becoming victims, so many women can be reluctant to seek help out of embarrassment or shame. Therefore, when a partner is abusive and has power, influence, and the ability to threaten to keep the children away, the victim may feel powerless to seek help and hesitate to report abuse.

Theoretical Foundations of Service Delivery

Cycle Theory of Violence

Various theories are utilized to understand relational violence. One of the theories, the *cycle theory of violence*, was developed by Walker (1979). Walker's theory includes three phases in a battering relationship (Walker, 2016). The cycle theory of violence proposes that relational violence occurs predictably through three stages. These include tension building, acute-battering incidents, and loving contrition (Walker, 2006). The tension-building stage begins the cycle with increasing interpersonal stress and tension about domestic issues. This tension grows despite the survivor's attempts to appease the batterer. Nonphysical forms of abuse may also occur during this phase (Walker, 2006). Physical violence occurs during the acute-battering incident phase. In the third phase, the perpetrator feels ashamed of their behavior, apologizes to the survivor, and convinces the survivor the abuse will not happen again. Walker suggests that the final phase, loving contrition, consists of a "honeymoon" between the two parties. Walker (1979) describes this last phase as a "respite" from the suffering. This stage, along with Walker's learned helplessness, is often used to explain why survivors remain in violent relationships (Ehrensaft et al., 2003; Terrance et al., 2012).

Understanding different perspectives from scholars is essential to the awareness of why survivors may stay or leave their abusive relationships (Ozturk, 2020). The cycle theory of violence is one of the most widely used models when training professionals to respond to survivors exposed to violence in the home. However, this theory is viewed as problematic for many reasons. Survivors feel the near-constant presence of power and control in the relationship, and many survivors never describe a honeymoon phase (Rothenberg, 2003). In addition, the cycle theory of violence highlights a stable pattern where actions are repeated. Many survivors describe an escalating series of incidents where the violence becomes more and more life-threatening over time.

At times, suggesting a survivor was a passive or helpless victim did more harm than good, so many professionals began to distance themselves from this theory (Rothenberg, 2003). The cycle theory of violence does not explain the ongoing nature of violence and the many nonphysical forms of abuse in controlling relationships (Stark, 2007). The cycle theory of violence has undoubtedly made contributions to the field; however, there has been a need to develop a model that more closely resembles the experiences of those involved in relational violence. The learned helplessness that Walker (1979) describes as the force that keeps women in violent relationships has been criticized and disproved in numerous studies (Bowker, 1983; Pagelow, 1981). To address this, Gondolf and Fisher's *survivor theory* placed the foundation for challenging Walker's cycle of violence theory and the concepts of learned helplessness (Hayes, 2013). According to the survivor theory, victims actively seek help from various direct or indirect assistance sources (Gondolf & Fisher, 1988). Consequently, victims from this perspective are not passive.

The Duluth Power and Control Wheel

Another widely used model for explaining relational violence is the *power and control wheel* (Domestic Abuse Intervention Programs, 2011). Minnesota's original power and control wheel was developed in cooperation with domestic violence intervention programs. It was known as the *Duluth model,* developed in the 1990s in Minnesota (Domestic Abuse Intervention Project, ca. 1993). These materials are among some of the most widely used theoretical constructs in batterer intervention programs in the United States (Rizza, 2009). The wheel includes male privilege, coercion, threats, intimidation, emotional abuse, economic abuse, using children, isolation, minimizing, denying, and blaming, all-important constructs that further explore the experiences of survivors.

Even though the power and control wheel model is highly used in programs across the country, advocates and scientists have criticized it. One of the major criticisms is the assumption made in the model of a male abuser and a female victim (McLeod et al., 2021). The research highlights how both males and females can perpetuate relational violence against their partners in heterosexual and same-sex relationships (Rizza, 2009). One study revealed that women were just as likely to resort to violence during a conflict with intimate partners as men (Johnson, 2009). Although the Duluth model is utilized in most (male-centered) batterers' programs across the United States, the National Institute of Justice reports how multiple studies have not supported the utilization of the Duluth model in offender treatment since 2003 (Jackson et al., 2003). Advocates against using the power and control wheel essentially highlight misalignments in viewing the perpetrator as powerful and forceful and the victims as passive and helpless. This forced dichotomy assumes a two-dimensional perspective that fails to address the complexity of relationships and the potential for reciprocity in violent behavior. Johnson described three types of violence to standardize domestic violence statistics (Johnson, 2009). Two of those types have the central theme of power and control. The third type, called situational couple violence, occurs when a particular situation provokes violence between a couple when neither person is otherwise trying to exert power or authority in the relationship (Johnson, 2009). Situational couple violence is believed to be a common type of relational violence and cannot be described using the cycle theory of violence or the power and control wheel (Johnson, 2009).

Model of Systemic Relational Violence

A new model was developed to address the critiques of the above-listed models and educate individuals, the public, and service delivery professionals about the complicated nature of violent intimate relationships. In its construction, the new model represents the potential diversity of both perpetrators and victims and highlights the interconnections between interactive relationship behaviors, coercive control, and specific abusive events (McLeod et al., 2021). In addition, the new model displays the continuous and potentially escalating tendencies of control and violence in unhealthy relationships (McLeod et al., 2021). Most notably, the new model guides people to recognize the transition from normalized to unhealthy behavior patterns in relationships and can be used as a practical intervention for identifying and processing individualized experiences (McLeod et al., 2021).

The *model of systemic relational violence* (MSRV) was developed from multiple research studies and informed by survivors, service providers, and the literature exploring the connections between coercive control and domestic violence (McLeod et al., 2021). The model depicts how those experiencing relational violence often describe a constant state of control that the older models mentioned above do not explain. In the MSRV, particular attention was paid to the presence of emotional, psychological, and expressed coercion and control, conveyed through threats and demands (implied and overt) from an abusive partner. In the model of systemic relational violence, these threats and demands are placed on the marginalized partner to reduce their autonomy and control their behavior across multiple domains of their day-to-day lives. The threats and demands of the abusive partner can be incredibly subtle but still serve the function of psychological and emotional abuse. When more subtle tactics no longer allow the abusive partner to control the behavior of the abused partner, their demands are enforced through ever-increasing psychological, emotional, and social attacks, which can escalate to incidents of physical, sexual, and otherwise externally hurtful actions focused on returning the abused partner to a state of compliance.

This model illustrates a continuous expression of behavioral *rules* that can fluctuate and later be enforced through physical and nonphysical actions. In addition, the model demonstrates how the perpetrator repetitively maintains behavioral control in the relationship and acts in unique and discreet ways to enforce their authority. The model notes how all relationships have the potential for controlling behaviors, manipulation, and coercion; however, that movement away from balance and reciprocity in the relationships can evolve into abusive behavior. Data associated with the construction of the MSRV suggested that the honeymoon phase (as mentioned above) is a phenomenon viewed from an outsider's perspective rather than that of the person in the relationship. Therefore, the model demonstrates how the absence of physical violence or the external appearance of reconciliation can be part of the control system. Even though a partner might minimize enforcement techniques at certain times within the relationship, the control and threat of enforcement, through sentinel events, is ever-present.

Utilizing the Model

Figure 24.2 can be used to help practitioners, service providers, advocates, survivors, and those who have participated in abusive behaviors recognize how relationships can include systems of control and abuse between partners. It is important to note that this is not a model that suggests abuse is a cycle that goes on and off, but rather one that shows how traditional markers of domestic abuse are merely small parts of a more extensive relational system of control and interpersonal domination. All relationships fluctuate over time in a variety of ways. Healthy fluctuations are ever-present as individuals in relationships grow and evolve both individually and with each other and their environment. This evolution is typically healthy and appropriate, but when a power dynamic shifts so that one party in the relationship is controlling the behavior of another in that fluctuating cycle, the behavior becomes abusive and indicates the potential for more severe escalation of that abuse to maintain control. This most typically happens unidirectionally, but not always, as the exhibitions of power and struggle for control can be far more complicated and bilateral in relationships.

Model of Systemic Relational Violence
Conceptualizing IPV as a continuous system of domination

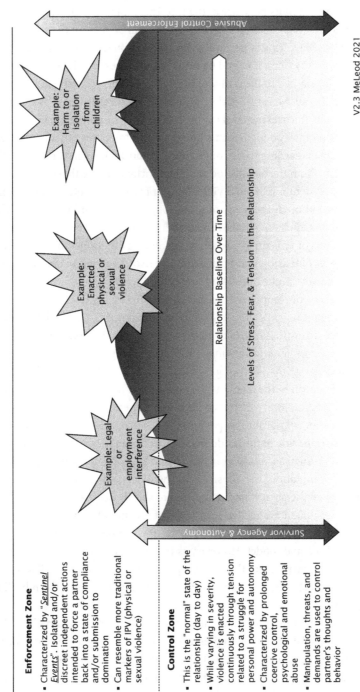

Abusive Control Enforcement

Example: Harm to or isolation from children

Example: Enacted physical or sexual violence

Example: Legal or employment interference

Relationship Baseline Over Time

Levels of Stress, Fear, & Tension in the Relationship

Survivor Agency & Autonomy

V2.3 MeLeod 2021

Enforcement Zone

- Characterized by "*Sentinel Events*". Isolated and/or discreet independent actions intended to force a partner back into a state of compliance and/or submission to domination
- Can resemble more traditional markers of IPV (physical or sexual violence)

Control Zone

- This is the "normal" state of the relationship (day to day)
- While varying in severity, violence is enacted continuously through tension related to a struggle for personal power and autonomy
- Characterized by prolonged coercive control, psychological and emotional abuse
- Manipulation, threats, and demands are used to control partner's thoughts and behavior

FIGURE 24.2 The Model of Systemic Relational Violence

The *levels of stress, fear, and tension in the relationship* are depicted by a wave that moves from left to right, fluctuates up and down, and appears in intensity from nonexistent at the bottom to bold in its presence at the top. This represents how relationships fluctuate over time and that levels of stress, fear, and tension can be present in varying degrees at any point in a relationship. This is not unlike fluctuations that occur in healthy relationships, although in unhealthy ones, it would be expected that these levels could be more severe or radical in their instability. In the center of the figure is an arrow that points from left to right and represents the *relationship baseline over time*. Each relationship is different, and this baseline represents the average level of stress, fear, or tension that a relationship may have. Those phenomena may be higher on some days and lower on others, but every relationship has a baseline regarding these components. Abnormalities in the relationship are seen when fluctuations from the baseline occur. It's important to note that these two components of the model of systemic relational violence are present in all types of relationships, both healthy and not, although the levels of these components would undoubtedly be different in a healthy relationship compared to an unhealthy one. It's also important to recognize that certain stress levels or tension in a relationship may be functional for some people. In contrast, similar levels of tension may be maladaptive in other relationships. In short, all people and relationships are unique but share these components.

The next series of components are not present in healthy relationships but do have the potential to manifest in controlling and abusive relationships. On the left side of the model is a double-sided arrow that moves from the lower part to the upper part of the figure. This represents *survivor agency and autonomy*. The essential representation depicted by this continuous arrow suggests that as the agency and autonomy of the abused party grow, so do stress, fear, and tension in the relationship. Likewise, as the survivor loses or forfeits control of their daily activities, levels of stress or fear may appear to decrease. This is primarily related to the behaviors of the abusive party in the relationship. A similar double-sided arrow exists on the far-right side of the model and moves from the bottom to the top of the figure. This represents *abusive control enforcement*. In unhealthy relationships that involve a system of control and domination, the abusive party will create or exhibit behaviors specifically intended to reduce the agency and autonomy of the abused partner. These behaviors can be very subtle and often are related to manipulation and what previous models may have considered behaviors exhibited in a honeymoon-type phase. These would be present in the lower parts of the visual model. However, as those types of manipulative behaviors fail to control the abused party (from the abuser's perspective), the abuser will escalate their behavioral control mechanisms to subdue the abused party and force them back into behavioral compliance.

There is a dotted line that runs through the middle of the figure. This dotted line is different for every relationship but represents a threshold that separates two primary zones. The lower zone is described on the left side of the page as the *control zone*. The control zone is unique to each relationship but represents a normal state of day-to-day operations. Specific behavioral controls are present, including prolonged coercive control and psychological and emotional abuse. Manipulation and threats from subtle to overt are used to control the abused party's behavior. At some point in the relationship, the abusive party determines that the autonomy and independence of the abused party can no longer be controlled through subtle acts of manipulation. At this point, the threshold is passed (represented by the dotted line) and behaviors from the abusive party enter what is characterized in the model as the *enforcement zone*. At this point in the relationship, the abusive party begins using externalized behaviors to force the abused party back into a state of daily control and compliance. This model recognizes those external phenomena as *sentinel events*. These are defined as isolated or discrete independent actions intended to force a partner back into a state of compliance or submission to domination. These can be traditional markers of domestic violence but often include other externally harmful behaviors such as actions that separate the abused partner from their children or behaviors that cause legal trouble for the partner. The sentinel acts are limitless in their definition and could include many hurtful behaviors. The ones most typically recognized by our existing criminal justice system are discrete physical or sexual violence acts.

When using this model to explore the components of any relationship, as related to control and domination, it is essential to recognize that each person will have different interpretations or experiences concerning each of the components. The components are made to help people understand the interactions between coercion and control and the actions used to maintain the behavioral compliance of a partner. The model also helps people understand how relationships fluctuate in and out of healthy or acceptable periods. These are all crucial aspects when explaining the phenomenon of relational violence across different service providers and intervention systems. This model also allows for application to various relationships due to its flexibility. One of the more diverse components of the model is that in its application, it can be helpful in different ways to everyone involved in the relationship. Perhaps both partners display some traits of coercion and control or dominance in the relationship. The mechanisms they use to enforce that control on the other party could be diverse and multifaceted. The model does not suggest that one type of abuse or the effects of a kind of abusive behavior equal parity or reciprocity compared to other types of abuse or control in the relationship. The impact of one sentinel event may be different from the impact of another, and each of these will be contextual, based on the people and circumstances of the people in the relationship.

Exploration of Service Delivery Applications of Theory

Different approaches and theories have been utilized to understand and develop comprehensive interventions (Figure 24.3). As we described above, Walker (1979) proposed the cycle of violence theory to demonstrate the patterns of violence. After this, Gondolf and Fisher's survivor theory placed the foundation for challenging Walker's cycle theory and learned helplessness (Hayes, 2013). According to survivor theory, the victims actively seek help from various direct or indirect assistance sources (Gondolf & Fisher, 1988). From this work, anti-oppressive, survivor-defined, trauma-informed practices have become the gold standard for domestic violence service programs (Glenn & Goodman, 2015; Goodman

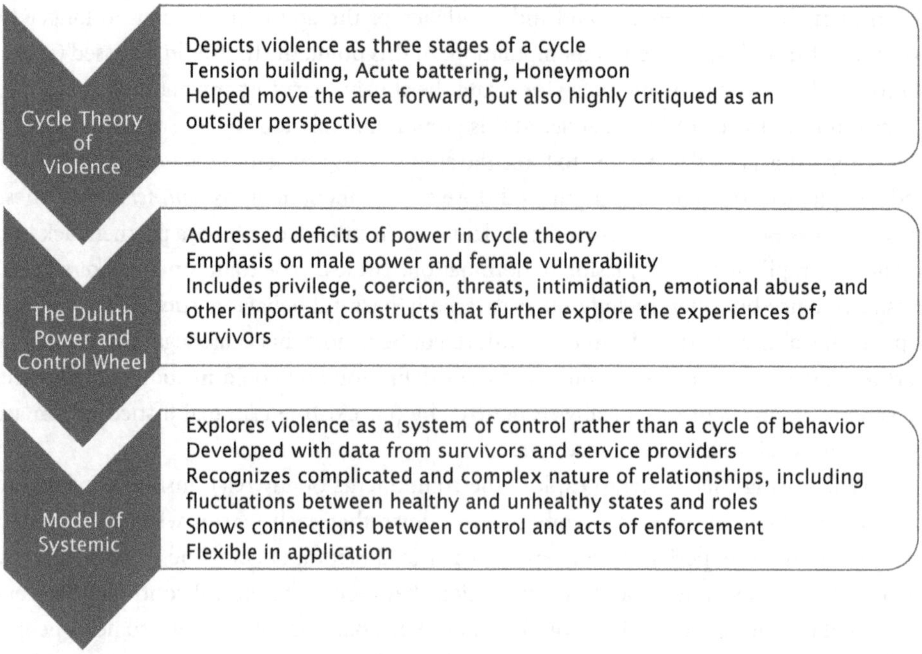

Cycle Theory of Violence	Depicts violence as three stages of a cycle Tension building, Acute battering, Honeymoon Helped move the area forward, but also highly critiqued as an outsider perspective
The Duluth Power and Control Wheel	Addressed deficits of power in cycle theory Emphasis on male power and female vulnerability Includes privilege, coercion, threats, intimidation, emotional abuse, and other important constructs that further explore the experiences of survivors
Model of Systemic	Explores violence as a system of control rather than a cycle of behavior Developed with data from survivors and service providers Recognizes complicated and complex nature of relationships, including fluctuations between healthy and unhealthy states and roles Shows connections between control and acts of enforcement Flexible in application

FIGURE 24.3 Evolution of Theoretical Foundations of Service Delivery

& Epstein, 2008). Anti-oppressive practices critically examine the use of power that can be "overtly, or indirectly racist, classist, sexist, and so on" (Clifford, 1995, p. 65) and actively work to dismantle structural oppression. Survivor-defined practices support survivor decision-making determined by their aims, priorities, and risks rather than through program requirements that tend to direct survivors toward determined consequences (Davies & Lyon, 2013; Goodman & Epstein, 2008). In addition, trauma-informed service models are utilized in the field. The trauma-informed perspective encourages domestic violence shelter services modified to ensure physical and emotional safety and maximize survivor choice and autonomy (Sullivan et al., 2018). As the social work profession prioritizes implementing anti-oppressive, survivor-defined, trauma-informed practices, many organizations are shifting direct service practices to better align with this paradigm (Wilson et al., 2015).

Moving Forward

Historically, different approaches and models have been utilized in the field and are often challenged by scholars. This chapter focuses on using the MSRV as an effective tool to address physical, sexual, social, and economic violence in relationships. This model identifies how the relationships and identities of both abusers and survivors can be intertwined. The model is also available for use in diverse relationship contexts. For example, in LGBTQIA+ relationships, controlling behaviors in daily life could be enforced by a threat of, or engagement in, "outing" as a sentinel event to impose compliance. In this context, the abuser could utilize societal heterosexism or internalized homophobia as tools in their control system over their partner. The MSRV demonstrated how these specific events occur in abusive or violent relationships, and while incredibly impactful in isolation, they are also markers of an underlying unhealthy system of control. This provides a more flexible tool for training and intervention and a broader application to diverse community experiences.

The MSRV also explores the relationship between the status of the perpetrator and victim for both physical and nonphysical forms of control that can be displayed, enforced, and reciprocated. Relational violence can cause significant mental and physical health as well as social, economic, developmental, and community problems. This model can expand existing training on the phenomenon to explain how the presence of coercion and control plays a role in domestic and interpersonal violence (McLeod et al., 2021). It can also inform policymakers and stakeholders on the nuances of relational violence beyond the discreet incidents of a physical engagement (McLeod et al., 2021). Forensic social workers can utilize the model in the clinical field to assist people in identifying their routines of behavior in relationships (McLeod et al., 2021). People in these relationships can explore how to manage and change behavior patterns and be empowered to make their own decision for their lives and relationships. Relationship-based violence is an epidemic and public health issue, and this model can assist service providers with an additional tool to explore these issues further in treatment and advocacy. The MSRV highlights that anyone can experience relational violence regardless of age, sex, gender, gender identity or expression, and sexual orientation. It provides opportunities to enhance the delivery of services to victims of relational violence. In addition, a significant contribution of this model lies in its person-centered perception. The model can be utilized in training to expand how interprofessional systems understand relationship violence and support people to live healthier, happier lives.

Conclusion

This chapter defined relational violence and more historical approaches used in the field. We proposed a new model that can be useful in relational violence settings to understand the experiences of survivors with complexity. Relational violence is an epidemic and public health issue in every society. We discussed the existing models explaining relational violence and identified how there is more to this phenomenon than meets the eye. We explored how different intervention and prevention programs have been utilized in the literature. We critiqued the cycle of violence and the Duluth power and control wheel and explored how the MSRV provides a potential extension for those theoretical models.

While some social workers have job titles associated explicitly with service delivery in relational violence–serving organizations, the truth is that all social workers will be involved in intervention and service to clients who are experiencing varying levels of these types of phenomena. Some social workers, like court advocates or victim service delivery specialists embedded in police departments, will serve to advocate in these roles with daily consistency. However, anyone who interacts with people in the field will find at some point in their career that they need to intervene regarding situations involving relational violence. From school social workers to gerontological social workers to different types of therapists or substance abuse treatment providers, everyone who works with people will have clients with complex, potentially violent, and hurtful relationships. Sometimes relational violence is easy to identify. Other times it is far more nuanced and hidden. At different times, violence in relationships flows in and out of what people may find healthy or acceptable. Sometimes controlling relationships are reciprocal in behavior even if differential in the outcome. Whatever the case, social workers are involved in helping people through the most challenging times of their lives and will inevitably be serving those impacted by relational violence.

While traditional tools, theories, and concepts have helped unpack these behaviors and serve individuals and families, newer models allow for and expand the ways social workers think about intervening. The data has shown how relational violence is often far more nuanced and complex than previously thought. Modern tools allow social workers to explore that complexity with confidence and support.

References

Abbey, A. D., Jacques-Tiura, A. J., & Parkhill, M. R. (2010). Sexual assault among diverse populations of women: Common ground, distinctive features, and unanswered questions. In H. Landrine & N. F. Russo (Eds.), *Handbook of diversity in feminist psychology* (pp. 391–425). Springer Publishing Co.

Adams, A. E., Sullivan, C. M., Bybee, D., & Greeson, M. R. (2008). Development of the scale of economic abuse. *Violence Against Women*, *14*(5), 563–588. https://doi.org/10.1177%2F1077801208315529

Aizer, A. (2011). Poverty, violence, and health the impact of domestic violence during pregnancy on newborn health. *Journal of Human Resources*, *46*(3), 518–538. https://dx.doi.org/10.1353%2Fjhr.2011.0024

Ali, P. A., & Naylor, P. B. (2013). Intimate partner violence: A narrative review of the feminist, social and ecological explanations for its causation. *Aggression and Violent Behavior*, *18*(6), 611–619. http://doi.org/10.1016/j.avb.2013.07.009

Anderson, K. L. (2010). Conflict, power, and violence in families. *Journal of Marriage and Family*, *72*(3), 726–742. https://doi.org/10.1111/j.1741-3737.2010.00727.x

Anderson, M. A., Gillig, P. M., Sitaker, M., McCloskey, K., Malloy, K., & Grigsby, N. (2003). "Why doesn't she leave?": A descriptive study of victim reported impediments to her safety. *Journal of Family Violence*, *18*(3), 151–155. https://doi.org/10.1023/A:1023564404773

Angelucci, M. (2008). Love on the rocks: Domestic violence and alcohol abuse in rural Mexico. *B.E. Journal of Economic Analysis & Policy*, *8*(1). https://doi.org/10.2202/1935-1682.1766

Biafora, F., & Warheit, G. (2007). Self-reported violent victimization among young adults in Miami, Florida: Immigration, race/ethnic and gender contrasts. *International Review of Victimology*, *14*(1), 29–55. https://doi.org/10.1177%2F026975800701400103

Black, M. C., Basile, K. C., Breiding, M. J., Smith, S. G., Walters, M. L., Merrick, M. T., & Stevens, M. R. (2011, November). The National Intimate Partner and Sexual Violence Survey (NISVS): 2010 summary report. National Center for Injury Prevention and Control, Centers for Disease Control and Prevention. https://cdc.gov/ViolencePrevention/pdf/NISVS_Report2010-a.pdf

Bobonis, G. J., González-Brenes, M., & Castro, R. (2013). Public transfers and domestic violence: The roles of private information and spousal control. *American Economic Journal: Economic Policy*, *5*(1), 179–205.

Bonomi, A. E., Anderson, M. L., Rivara, F. P., & Thompson, R. S. (2007). Health outcomes in women with physical and sexual intimate partner violence exposure. *Journal of Women's Health*, *16*(7), 987–997. https://doi.org/10.1089/jwh.2006.0239

Bowker, L. H. (1983). *Beating wife-beating*. Lexington Books.

Bowlus, A. J., & Seitz, S. (2006). Domestic violence, employment, and divorce. *International Economic Review*, *47*(4), 1113–1149. https://doi.org/10.1111/j.1468-2354.2006.00408.x

Breiding, M. J., Chen, J., & Black, M. C. (2014). *Intimate partner violence in the United States: 2010.* Centers for Disease Control and Prevention.

Budiman, A., Tamir, C., Mora, L., & Noe-Bustamante, L. (2020, October 1). *Facts on U.S. immigrants, 2018.* Pew Research Center. https://www.pewresearch.org/hispanic/2020/08/20/facts-on-u-s-immigrants/

Bui, H. N., & Morash, M. (1999). Domestic violence in the Vietnamese immigrant community: An exploratory study. *Violence Against Women, 5*(7), 769–795. https://doi.org/10.1177%2F10778019922181473

Campbell, J. C. (2002). Health consequences of intimate partner violence. *The Lancet, 359*(9314), 1331–1336. https://doi.org/10.1016/S0140-6736(02)08336-8

Centers for Disease Control and Prevention (CDC). (2020). *Intimate partner violence, sexual violence, and stalking among men.*

Child Welfare Information Gateway. (2014). *Domestic Violence and the Child Welfare System. Bulletin for professionals.* U.S. Department of Health and Human Services, Children's Bureau.

Clifford, D. (1995). Methods in oral history and social work. *Oral History, 23*(2), 65–70.

Davies, J., & Lyon, E. (2013). *Domestic violence advocacy: Complex lives/difficult choices.* Sage Publications.

Davis, R. E. (2002). Leave-taking experiences in the lives of abused women. *Clinical Nursing Research, 11*(3), 285–305. https://doi.org/10.1177%2F10573802011003005

De Mendonça, M. F. S., & Ludermir, A. B. (2017). Intimate partner violence and incidence of common mental disorder. *Revista de Saúde Pública, 51*, 32. http://doi.org/10.1590/S1518-8787.2017051006912

Deyessa, N., Berhane, Y., Alem, A., Ellsberg, M., Emmelin, M., Hogberg, U., & Kullgren, G. (2009). Intimate partner violence and depression among women in rural Ethiopia: A cross-sectional study. *Clinical Practice and Epidemiology in Mental Health, 5*(1), 8. https://doi.org/10.1186/1745-0179-5-8

Domestic Abuse Intervention Programs. (2011). *Home of the Duluth model: Social change to end violence against women.* https://www.theduluthmodel.org/

Domestic Abuse Intervention Project. (n.d., circa 1993). *Power and control wheel.* National Center on Domestic and Sexual Violence. http://www.ncdsv.org

Drijber, B. C., Reijnders, U. J., & Ceelen, M. (2013). Male victims of domestic violence. *Journal of Family Violence, 28*, 173–178.

Ehrensaft, M. K., Cohen, P., Brown, J., Smailes, E., Chen, H., & Johnson, J. G. (2003). Intergenerational transmission of partner violence: A 20-year prospective study. *Journal of Consulting and Clinical Psychology, 71*(4), 741. https://psycnet.apa.org/doi/10.1037/0022-006X.71.4.741

Ellsberg, M., Jansen, H. A., Heise, L., Watts, C. H., & Garcia-Moreno, C. (2008). Intimate partner violence and women's physical and mental health in the WHO multi-country study on women's health and domestic violence: An observational study. *The Lancet, 371*(9619), 1165–1172. https://doi.org/10.1016/S0140-6736(08)60522-X

Erez, E., Adelman, M., & Gregory, C. (2009). Intersections of immigration and domestic violence. *Voices of Battered Immigrant Women. Feminist Criminology, 4*(1), 32–59. https://doi.org/10.1177%2F1557085108325413

Farmer, A., & Tiefenthaler, J. (1997). An economic analysis of domestic violence. *Review of Social Economy, 55*(3), 337–358. https://doi.org/10.1080/00346769700000004

Fedovskiy, K., Higgins, S., & Paranjape, A. (2008). Intimate partner violence: How does it impact major depressive disorder and posttraumatic stress disorder among immigrant Latinas? *Journal of Immigrant and Minority Health, 10*(1), 45–51. https://doi.org/10.1007/s10903-007-9049-7

Feldhaus, K. M., Koziol-McLain, J., Amsbury, H. L., Norton, I. M., Lowenstein, S. R., & Abott, J. T. (1997). Accuracy of 3 brief screening questions for detecting partner violence in the emergency department. *Journal of the American Association, 277*, 1357–1361. https://doi.org/10.1016/S1075-4210%2897%2990044-4

Finkelhor, D., Ormrod, R. K., & Turner, H. A. (2007). Poly-victimization: A neglected component in child victimization. *Child Abuse & Neglect, 31*(1), 7–26. https://doi.org/10.1016/j.chiabu.2006.06.008

Ganley, A. L. (1995). *Understanding domestic violence: Improving the health care response to domestic violence: A resource manual for health care providers.* San Francisco: Family Violence Prevention Fund

Gilbert, L. K., Breiding, M. J., Merrick, M. T., Thompson, W. W., Ford, D. C., Dhingra, S. S., &Parks, S. E. (2015). Childhood adversity and adult chronic disease: An update from ten states and the District of

Columbia, 2010. *American Journal of Preventive Medicine, 48*(3), 345–349. https://doi.org/10.1016/j.ame pre.2014.09.006

Glenn, C., & Goodman, L. (2015). Living with and within the rules of domestic violence shelters: A qualitative exploration of residents' residents. *Violence Against Women, 21*(12), 1481–1506. https://doi.org/10.1177%2F1077801215596242

Gondolf, E. W., & Fisher, E. R. (1988). *Battered women as survivors: An alternative to treating learned helplessness.* Lexington Books/DC Heath and Com.

Goodman, L. A., & Epstein, D. (2008). *Listening to battered women: A survivor-centered approach to advocacy, mental health, and justice.* American Psychological Association.

Hayes, B. E. (2013). Women's resistance strategies in abusive relationships: An alternative framework. *Sage Open, 3*(3), 1–10. https://doi.org/10.1177%2F2158244013501154

Hazen, A. L., & Soriano, F. I. (2007). Experiences with intimate partner violence among Latina women. *Violence Against Women, 13*, 562–582. https://10.1177/1077801207301558.

Herman, J. L. (1992). *Complex PTSD: A syndrome in survivors of prolonged and repeated trauma.* http://www.onlinelibrary.wiley.com/doi/abs/10.1002/jts.2490050305

Hester, M. (2011). The three-planet model: Towards an understanding of contradictions in approaches to women and children's safety in contexts of domestic violence. *British Journal of Social Work, 41*(5), 837–853. https://doi.org/10.1093/bjsw/bcr095

Houry, D., Kemball, R., Rhodes, K. V., & Kaslow, N. J. (2006). Intimate partner violence and mental health symptoms in African American female E.D. patients. *American Journal of Emergency Medicine, 24*(4), 444–450. https://doi.org/10.1016/j.ajem.2005.12.026

Jackson, S., Feder, L., David, R. F., Davis, R. C., Maxwell, C. D., & Bruce, G. T. B. (2003). *Batterer intervention programs: Where do we go from here?* U.S. Department of Justice, Office of Justice Programs, National Institute of Justice.

Johnson, M. P. (2009). Where do "domestic violence" statistics come from and why do they vary so much? In *Toward a common understanding: Domestic violence typologies and implications for healthy marriage and domestic violence programs* (pp. 1–12). http://www.healthymarriageinfo.org/download.aspx?id=342

Kantor, G., Jasinski, J. L., & Aldarondo, E. (1994). Sociocultural status and incidence of marital violence in Hispanic families. *Violence and Victims, 9*, 207–222. https://doi.org/10.1891/0886-6708.9.3.207

Kim, J., & Gray, K. A. (2008). Leave or stay? Battered women's decision after intimate partner violence. *Journal of Interpersonal Violence, 23*(10), 1465–1482. https://doi.org/10.1177%2F0886260508314307

Kim, J., & Lee, J. (2013). Prospective study on the reciprocal relationship between intimate partner violence and depression among women in Korea. *Social Science & Medicine, 99*, 42–48. http://doi.org/10.1016/j.socscimed.2013.10.014

Krause, E. D., Kaltman, S., Goodman, L. A., & Dutton, M. A. (2008). Avoidant coping and PTSD symptoms related to domestic violence exposure: A longitudinal study. *Journal of Traumatic Stress, 21*(1), 83–90. https://doi.org/10.1002/jts.20288

Lee, J., Pomeroy, E. C., & Bohman, T. M. (2007). Intimate partner violence and psychological health in a sample of Asian and Caucasian women: The roles of social support and coping. *Journal of Family Violence, 22*(8), 709–720. https://doi.org/10.1007/s10896-007-9119-6

Lee, Y. S., & Hadeed, L. (2009). Intimate partner violence among Asian immigrant communities: Health/mental health consequences, help-seeking behaviors, and service utilization. *Trauma, Violence, & Abuse, 10*(2), 143–170. https://doi.org/10.1177%2F1524838009334130

Ludermir, A. B., Schraiber, L. B., D'Oliveira, A. F., França-Junior, I., & Jansen, H. A. (2008). Violence against women by their intimate partner and common mental disorders. *Social Science & Medicine, 66*(4), 1008–1018. https://doi.org/10.1016/j.socscimed.2007.10.021

McLeod, D. A., Pharris, A., Boyles, E., Winkles, R., & Stafford, W. (2021). The model of systemic relational violence: Conceptualizing IPV as a method of continual and enforced domination. *Trauma Care, 1*(2), 87–98. https://doi.org/10.3390/traumacare1020009

Menjívar, C., & Salcido, O. (2002). Immigrant women and domestic violence: Common experiences in different countries. *Gender & Society, 16*(6), 898–920. https://doi.org/10.1177/089124302237894

Midlarsky, E., Venkataramani-Kothari, A., & Plante, M. (2006). Domestic violence in Chinese and South Asian Immigrant Communities. *Annals of New York Academy of Sciences, 1087*(1), 279–300. https://doi.org/10.1196/annals.1385.003

National Center for Injury Prevention and Control. (2013). *Costs of intimate partner violence against women in the United States*. Department of Health and Human Services, Centers for Disease Control and Prevention, National Center for Injury Prevention and Control.

National Coalition Against Domestic Violence. (2020). *National statistics domestic violence fact sheet*.

National Coalition of Anti-Violence Programs (NCAVP). (2016). Lesbian, gay, bisexual, transgender, queer, and HIV-affected hate violence in 2016.

Ozturk, B. (2020). *Unheard stories from middle eastern immigrant women IPV survivors: A qualitative study* [Doctoral dissertation, University of Alabama]. http://ir.ua.edu/handle/123456789/7639

Pagelow, M. D. (1981). *Woman-battering: Victims and their experiences* (Vol. 129). Sage.

Parenzee, P., & Smythe, D. (2003). *Domestic violence and development: Looking at the farming context*. Institute of Criminology, University of Cape Town.

Riedl, D., Beck, T., Exenberger, S., Daniels, J., Dejaco, D., Unterberger, I., & Lampe, A. (2019). Violence from childhood to adulthood: The influence of child victimization and domestic violence on physical health in later life. *Journal of Psychosomatic Research, 116*, 68–74. https://doi.org/10.1016/j.jpsychores.2018.11.019

Rizza, J. (2009). Beyond Duluth: A broad spectrum of treatment for a broad spectrum of domestic violence. *Montana Law Review, 70*, 125. https://scholarworks.umt.edu/mlr/vol70/iss1/5

Robin, R. W., Chester, B., & Rasmussen, J. K. (1998). Intimate violence in a Southwestern American Indian tribal community. *Cultural Diversity and Mental Health, 4*, 335–344. https://psycnet.apa.org/doi/10.1037/1099-9809.4.4.335

Rothenberg, B. (2003). "We don't have to wait for social change": Cultural compromise and the battered woman syndrome. *Gender & Society, 17*(5), 771–787. https://doi.org/10.1177%2F0891243203255633

Sabina, C., Cuevas, C. A., & Lannen, E. (2014). The likelihood of Latino women to seek help in response to interpersonal victimization: An examination of individual, interpersonal and sociocultural influences. *Psychosocial Intervention, 23*(2), 95–103. https://doi.org/10.1016/j.psi.2014.07.005

Sareen, J., Pagura, J., & Grant, B. (2009). Is intimate partner violence associated with HIV infection among women in the United States? *General Hospital Psychiatry, 31*(3), 274–278. https://doi.org/10.1016/j.genhosppsych.2009.02.004

Sharps, P. W., Laughon, K., & Giangrande, S. K. (2007). Intimate partner violence and the childbearing year: Maternal and infant health consequences. *Trauma, Violence, & Abuse, 8*(2), 105–116. https://doi.org/10.1177/1524838007302594

Singer, A. (2013). Contemporary immigrant gateways in historical perspective. *Daedalus, 142*(3), 76–91. https://doi.org/10.1162/DAED_a_00220

Smith, S. G., Basile, K. C., Gilbert, L. K., Merrick, M. T., Patel, N., Welling, M., & Jain, A. (2017). *National intimate partner and sexual violence survey (NISVS): 2010–2012 state report*. Center for Disease Control.

Stark, E. (2009). *Coercive control: The entrapment of women in personal life*. Oxford University Press.

Stark, E., & Hester, M. (2019). Coercive control: Update and review. *Violence Against Women, 25*(1), 81–104. https://doi.org/10.1177%2F1077801218816191

Sugg, N. (2015). Intimate partner violence: Prevalence, health consequences, and intervention. *Medical Clinics, 99*(3), 629–649. https://doi.org/10.1016/j.mcna.2015.01.012

Sullivan, C. M., Goodman, L. A., Virden, T., Strom, J., & Ramirez, R. (2018). Evaluation of the effects of receiving trauma-informed practices on domestic violence shelter residents. *American Journal of Orthopsychiatry, 88*(5), 563. https://psycnet.apa.org/doi/10.1037/ort0000286

Terrance, C. A., Plumm, K. M., & Rhyner, K. J. (2012). Expert testimony in cases involving battered women who kill: Going beyond the Battered Woman Syndrome. *North Dakota Law Review, 88*, 921. Truman, J. L., & Morgan, R. E. (2014). *Nonfatal domestic violence*. U.S. Department of Justice, Bureau of Justice Statistics.

U.S. Department of the Interior Indian Affairs. (2012). *Who we are*. http://www.bia.gov/WhoWeAre/index.htm

Vung, N. D., Ostergren, P. O., & Krantz, G. (2009). Intimate partner violence against women, health effects and health care seeking in rural Vietnam. *European Journal of Public Health, 19*(2), 178–182. https://doi.org/10.1093/eurpub/ckn136

Walker, L. E. (1979). *The battered woman*. Harper & Row.

Walker, L. E. (2006). Battered woman syndrome: Empirical findings. *Annals of the New York Academy of Sciences, 1087*(1), 142–157. https://doi.org/10.1196/annals.1385.023

Walker, L. E. (2016). *The battered woman syndrome*. Springer.

White, J. W., Yuan, N. P., Cook, S. L., & Abbey, A. (2013). Ethnic minority women's experiences with intimate partner violence: Using community-based participatory research to ask the right questions. *Sex Roles, 69*(3), 226–236. https://doi.org/10.1007/s11199-012-0237-0

Wilson, J. M., Fauci, J. E., & Goodman, L. A. (2015). Bringing trauma-informed practice to domestic violence programs: A qualitative analysis of current approaches. *American Journal of Orthopsychiatry, 85*(6), 586. https://doi.org/10.1037/ort0000098

World Health Organization (WHO). (2005). *WHO multi-country study on women's health and domestic violence against women: Summary report of initial results on prevalence, health outcomes, and women's responses*.

World Health Organization (WHO). (2012). *Understanding and addressing violence against women*. http://apps.who.int/iris/bitstream/handle/10665/77432/WHO_RHR_12.36_eng.pdf?sequence=1

Yoshihama, M., Bybee, D., Dabby, C., & Blazevski, J. (2011). *Lifecourse experiences of intimate partner violence and help-seeking among Filipina, Indian, and Pakistani women: Implications for justice system responses*. National Institute of Justice. https://www.ncjrs.gov/pdffiles1/nij/grants/236174.pdf

25

Juvenile Justice

Susan McCarter, Sujeeta E. Menon, and Kris Taylor

Forensic Social Work Practice With Justice-Involved Youth

Forensic social workers who practice with youth also practice with systems since all youth are part of the education system (the vast majority learn in school settings), most youth are served by the health care system, and a smaller percentage interact with mental health providers, substance abuse treatment, the child welfare system, and the juvenile or criminal justice system. This chapter explores forensic social work practice with justice-involved youth (and the other systems they contact), their challenges to development including trauma and adverse childhood experiences (ACEs), and their relevant subpopulation groups including gender identity, LGBTQ+ identity, poverty, and race/ethnicity. The chapter presents theoretical foundations in juvenile justice services and current treatment strategies with a focus on youth development, wraparound service provision, reentry, trauma-informed care, culturally relevant interventions, and probation reform. The chapter concludes with an exploration of forensic social work settings and the role of social work with justice-involved youth along with a case study of Savan.

Child Welfare

Children growing up with neglect, maltreatment, and abuse are overrepresented in the juvenile justice system (Ryan et al., 2008). Ryan et al. (2008) attribute this to the notion that when children are removed from their homes, the likelihood of delinquency increases because youth have lower levels of investment from adults and weaker social bonds, including lack of permanency, commitment, and attachment. Youth in child welfare are exposed to multiple risks from their family of origin and the foster care system, which can lead to a hostile response in the form of externalizing behaviors such as running away, truancy, fighting, etc. (Crosland & Dunlap, 2015; Langton et al., 2012). Foster care placement increases a

Susan McCarter, Sujeeta E. Menon, and Kris Taylor, *Juvenile Justice* In: *Handbook of Forensic Social Work*. Edited by: David Axlyn McLeod, Anthony P. Natale, and Kristin W. Mapson, Oxford University Press. © Oxford University Press 2024. DOI: 10.1093/oso/9780197694732.003.0025 child's chances of being detained (Conger & Ross, 2001) and receiving a disposition for out-of-home placement (Tam, Abrams, Freisthler, & Ryan, 2016). Finally, research suggests that up to 60% of the youth committing serious offenses had been or were currently in the child welfare system (Zajac et al., 2015).

Trauma

Neuroscience research suggests that early ACEs, such as abuse and neglect, can negatively impact children's neurological development, impairing a child's emotional, social, and cognitive domains (Ford, 2009). Consistent across several studies, a large majority of justice-involved youth (75% to 93%) reported experiencing traumatic events in their lives compared to a quarter of the general youth population (Adams, 2010; Baglivio et al., 2014).

Youth who report traumatic experiences often experience extended lifetime exposure to abuse, neglect, and violence within their milieu, which includes their families, communities, and peer circles (Ford et al., 2012). Justice-involved youth experience additional trauma from their involvement in the juvenile justice system. This literature has recently expanded to examine the impact of ACEs for justice-involved youth. These unique traumatic experiences include rough contact with law enforcement through arrest or detainment; navigating the court system; out-of-home placements in residential, group home, or foster care; juvenile detention; seclusion; lack of privacy; and physical and sexual victimization in residential placements (Espinosa et al., 2019; Kerig, 2018).

Intersectionally, Black youth are often more disadvantaged by trauma as compared to White youth, based on environmental exposure to violence (Proctor et al., 2020), oppressive teaching practices (Coles & Powell, 2020), being overpoliced (Crenshaw et al., 2015; King & Bracy, 2019), and microaggressions (Pearce, 2019). These effects are exacerbated for justice-involved Black youth, where they face the systemic racism that is pervasive within the justice systems (Potter, 2015). Their trauma can be perpetuated by contact with law enforcement, the court system, detention, incarceration, or the reentry process (Kerig, 2018). Yet, children of color are far less likely to receive programs and services that address their mental, emotional, behavioral, physical, and educational needs when compared to similarly situated White youth (Liebenberg & Ungar, 2014).

Mental Health

Twenty-two percent of the general youth population (18 years old and younger) in the United States is estimated to experience psychiatric disorders, but that figure is approximately 70% for justice-involved youth (Cocozza & Shufelt, 2006; Teplin et al., 2012). Forensic estimates suggest that 30% of justice-involved youth have diagnosable learning disabilities and more than 50% experience mental, emotional, and behavioral health challenges (Sedlak & McPherson, 2010); 75% have experienced traumatic victimization; and 93% had ACEs, including domestic/community violence, child abuse, and exposure to substance abuse/mental illness (Baglivio et al., 2014; Logan-Greene et al., 2020). For youth between the ages of 10 and 19 in detention and correctional facilities, most were diagnosed with a conduct disorder (Fazel et al., 2008), and between 39% (Schubert et al., 2011) and 79% (Cocozza & Shufelt, 2006) had substance use issues with an additional mental health challenge. Additionally, these mental health challenges can include an increased risk of aggression or displays of anger, self-regulatory challenges, substance use, and trauma symptoms (Wasserman et al., 2002).

Black youth with mental health challenges are disproportionately represented in the juvenile justice system and have a higher likelihood of experiencing mental illnesses compared to other racial groups (Hicks, 2011; Office of Juvenile Justice and Delinquency Prevention [OJJDP], 2019). Justice-involved girls also experience higher levels of mental illness compared to justice-involved boys (Chesney-Lind et al., 2008).

Substance Use

Substance use is illegal for juveniles and thus certainly increases the likelihood that youth may come into contact with the justice system. Similarly, trauma, abuse, mental health, and exposure to violence are all correlated to substance use and justice involvement. Chassin (2008) estimates that up to half of justice-involved youth have been diagnosed with a substance use disorder. She further contends that justice-involved youth are disproportionately impacted as compared to their peers who are not involved with this system. One longitudinal study of youth serving detention in Chicago reports that 51% of their sample had a comorbid diagnosis of substance abuse plus anxiety, affective, or conduct disorder, and 73% of their sample had a drug dependence problem and a behavioral disorder, including either conduct or oppositional defiant disorder (Teplin et al., 2012).

Developmental Challenges

Adolescence includes distinctive developmental stages of profound biological, psychological, and social changes. During this period, many young people try out various risky behaviors, including substance use and delinquency (McCarter, 2018), but most youth typically grow out of these behaviors as they mature (Lambie & Randell, 2013). Most scholars conclude that 40% to 60% of adolescents who experiment with delinquency cease offending by early adulthood (Piquero et al., 2012). Meanwhile, youth who are committed to juvenile justice settings risk having their development further disrupted, being exposed to offending peers, and facing stigma connected to juvenile justice involvement (Dmitrieva et al., 2012). Altschuler and Brash (2004) propose three transitions faced by justice-involved youth at the same time: (a) transitioning developmentally from adolescence to young adulthood, where critical milestones are achieved; (b) transitioning biopsychosocially and cognitively; and (c) transitioning from the correctional institution to society. Moreover, traumatic experiences negatively impair emotional, cognitive, and biological functioning due to stunted neurobiological development, where one's neural pathways are altered (Ford, 2009).

Populations/Subgroups

Despite steadily declining juvenile justice system involvement, the U.S. juvenile justice custody rate remains the highest in the world at approximately 26.9 for every 1,000 persons younger than age 18. Yet several marginalized groups are overrepresented in juvenile justice: boys, LGBTQ+ and gender nonconforming youth, poor children, and children of color.

Gender Identity

The vast majority of juvenile justice service providers do not recognize juveniles' gender identity beyond a cisgender male/female binary, which can be problematic due to the lack of research on the unique needs of youth who do not identify within this binary (Irvine & Canfield, 2016). That said, since the inception of the juvenile court, rates of juvenile justice involvement have been higher among boys than among girls. Historically, girls in the juvenile justice system have been punished more often for subjective moral offenses (e.g., actual or suspected sexual behavior) or waywardness (Kim et al., 2020; MacDonald & Chesney-Lind, 2001) than for finite acts of delinquency. And currently, most girls who become involved in the juvenile justice system do so through nonviolent status offending, such as truancy or running away, conflictual family relationships, substance use, victimization, and technical probation violations (Zahn et al., 2010). In 2019, girls accounted for 31% of all juvenile crime (OJJDP, 2020), but rates of delinquency for girls are starting to rise. Despite increased attention to the needs of girls in the justice system (Leve & Chamberlain, 2004), much of the practice and policy are driven by evidence derived from male-dominated juvenile justice samples (Lipsey & Cullen, 2007). So, forensic social work practice recognizes that theories and programs previously developed for boys need to be revisited to be appropriate for girls (Chesney-Lind et al., 2008).

Justice-involved girls have higher rates of ACES, neglect, poly-victimization, being witness to violence, running away from home, domestic violence and family dysfunction, sexual abuse (including being trafficked and sex for survival), substance use, chronic mental health issues, poor health and sexual health, sexually transmitted infections (STIs), and educational challenges compared to boys (Abrams & Terry, 2017; Baglivio et al., 2014; Javdani & Allen, 2016; Kerig, 2018; Zahn et al., 2008). Additionally, high-sexual-risk behaviors such as unprotected sex render justice-involved girls more likely to be pregnant compared to their counterparts who are not sexually active (Crosby et al., 2004; OJJDP, 2019). Girls referred to the Texas state juvenile justice department were 3.5 times more likely to have a child as a teenager compared to their counterparts who were not involved in the justice system (Widom et al., 2018).

LGBTQ+ Identity

Estimating the number of lesbian, gay, bisexual, transgender, queer, and questioning (LGBTQ+) youth who come into contact with the juvenile justice system is difficult as few intake processes ask youth to identify their sexual orientation, gender identity, and expression (Irvine & Canfield, 2016). Yet, there is mounting evidence that LGBTQ+, non-cisgender, and gender-expansive youth are overrepresented in the juvenile justice system (Irvine & Canfield, 2016; Majd et al. 2009). Studies report that approximately 13% to 15% of youth in detention facilities identify as lesbian, gay, bisexual, and/or transgender (Majd et al., 2009). Irvine (2010) surveyed six jurisdictions across the United States and found that approximately 11% identified as lesbian, gay, or bisexual, including 19% of gender-conforming girls and 9% of gender-conforming boys. The 2012 National Survey of Youth in Custody, conducted by the Bureau of Justice Statistics, estimated that 12% of adjudicated youth placed in residential facilities identified as lesbian, gay, or bisexual (Beck et al., 2013).

As reported in *Pediatrics*, Himmelstein and Brückner (2011) conducted a nationally representative longitudinal study with over 15,000 youth and found that queer and gender-expansive students were more likely to be suspended, expelled, and arrested at school, without any evidence that they misbehaved more or committed more delinquent acts. Among queer youth in the juvenile justice system, queer-identifying girls are suggested to be overrepresented as a result of policing efforts against girls' sexuality and the response to girls with a more masculine or assertive gender identity expression by the media and juvenile justice system. Finally, additional research suggests that LGBTQ+ youth are at greater risk for victimization, including bullying and sexual/physical abuse, as well as for challenges such as substance use, depression, and suicide (Friedman et al., 2011; Himmelstein, & Brückner, 2011; Kann et al., 2016).

Poverty Status

Childhood poverty is associated with elevated later risks for self-directed and externalized violence (Mok et al, 2018). According to Bright and Johnson-Reid (2008), exposure to street violence and other structural factors closely related to poverty may normalize this behavior. Further, committing acts of criminality may serve as an opportunity to adapt and survive (Bright & Johnson-Reid, 2008). Youth with incarcerated parents are more likely to experience structural poverty (Kjellstrand & Eddy, 2011) as well as the lack of their parents' availability and presence in the home (Mears & Siennick, 2016).

Policing behavior is also a factor between the juvenile justice system and low-income neighborhoods. Those living in low-income neighborhoods are monitored and targeted differently than those individuals living in higher socioeconomic areas (Bright & Johnson-Reid, 2008). This phenomenon leads to more criminal charges being filed against youth living in poverty than their counterparts residing in areas of higher wealth (Birckhead, 2012).

Race and Ethnicity

In 2018, for every 1,000 American Indian youth in the United States, 22.8 had an active delinquency case; the delinquency rate was 4.4 for Asian youth, 55.5 for Black youth, 18.0 for Latinx youth, and 19.3 for White youth (Hockenberry & Puzzanchera, 2020). (The National Center for Juvenile Justice classifies American Indian and Alaska Native together; the Asian category includes Asian, Native Hawaiian, and Other Pacific Islander; and persons who identify as Hispanic/Latinx are treated as a distinct racial group; Hockenberry & Puzzanchera, 2020).

Youth of color are affected by systemic barriers such as harsher sentencing practices by the juvenile court as compared to Whites committing the same offenses (Cochran & Mears, 2014). Yet, a study conducted with institutions and stakeholders who encounter justice-involved youth revealed a general ignorance of racial and ethnic disparities (REDs) in the juvenile justice system. The interviews conducted with these stakeholders revealed that they are unaware of disproportionality and disparate outcomes, have preconceptions about justice-involved youth of color, and lack an appreciation of the impact of the system on Black, Indigenous, and people of color (BIPOC) youth (Dawson-Edwards et al., 2020).

Another study investigated disparities within program referrals and found a difference between the types of programs to which youth were referred (Fader et al., 2014). Youth of color had a higher probability of being referred to programs with a physical component such as boot camps or outdoor wilderness programs compared to their White peers, who were more likely to obtain therapy-based services such as substance abuse intervention and mental health services (Fader et al., 2014). Figure 25.1 depicts the complexity of potential interactions for system involved youth.

Fields of Practice/Treatment in Juvenile Justice

The juvenile justice system is the second-largest mental health provider to youth in the United States, behind the public school system (McCarter, 2019). The focus of the juvenile justice system is supporting and rehabilitating youth while maintaining public safety. Often, however, the evaluation metrics that are used focus more on the public safety than they do on supporting youth. For example, recidivism is the typical benchmark for juvenile justice/reentry success. Recidivism measures rely on official statistics from the system databases that indicate whether one has reoffended (yes or no) within the allotted amount of time (Butts & Schiraldi, 2018). This measure is often biased as it disguises the systemic and structural-level inequities that perpetuate racial, social, and economic marginalization built into the justice system processes (Zara & Farrington, 2016). Hence, the goal of correctional treatment within the juvenile justice system should be to support desistance (cessation from crime) rather than preventing or reducing recidivism (Kazemian, 2015). The former will eventually result in the latter. This shift in theoretical orientation requires different measurements of positive outcomes.

Theoretical Foundations

Two current theoretical frameworks guiding treatment in juvenile justice settings are desistance and the developmental approach of the positive youth justice model. The desistance framework is moving practitioners toward a paradigm shift in youth justice. The positive youth justice model builds upon the ideals of desistance in a strengths-based manner focused on prosocial and healthy relationships, activities, and opportunities versus reoffending for justice-involved youth.

McNeill and Maruna (2007) referred to desistance as a fundamental change in how people view themselves and their world. Desistance can be achieved when one moves toward a new identity without delinquency/criminality, a sense of personal agency and control, and a desire to be productive and contribute back to society (Maruna, 2001). A desistance-focused treatment and asset-based intervention for justice-involved youth can have a higher chance of reentry and well-being in the long run (Menon & Cheung, 2018).

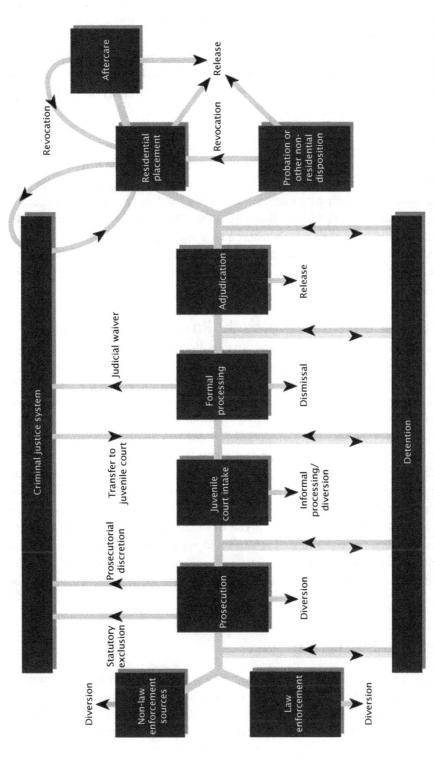

FIGURE 25.1 Case Flow Diagram for Juvenile Justice Source: The Office of Juvenile Justice and Delinquency Prevention, https://www.ojjdp.gov/ojstatbb/structure_process/case.html.

In a British study of desistance, the authors identified nine key factors central to desistance: (a) getting older and maturing, (b) family and relationships, (c) sobriety, (d) employment, (e) hope and motivation, (f) having something to give to others, (g) having a place within a social group, (h) not having a criminal identity, and (i) being "believed in" (Maruna, 2001). A consideration of these factors requires a shift from a deficit, risk-focused framework to a positive, asset-based framework, which is more closely aligned with social work and forensic social work values.

A deeper investigation into the environmental milieu of the young person such as the depth of relationships among their family, peers, and the community or the internal sense of self and identity is central to long-term change. These factors move beyond the "myopic" individual risk factors that have been addressed by "programs and pills" to include a consideration of environmental influences as well as how the milieu affects the young person in order to achieve desistance (Goshe, 2019, p. 560). The emphasis on these protective factors could challenge the status quo, where the current priority is more so on reducing risk factors and ensuring adherence to legal expectations and conditions. One of the ways to achieve these outcomes is to employ a developmental approach such as positive youth justice.

The Developmental Approach: Positive Youth Justice

Using a developmental approach, the positive youth justice model provides a more asset-based approach to supporting young people involved with the justice system. This approach also focuses on the desistance process including the building of prosocial and healthy relationships, activities, and opportunities versus recidivism as the sole outcome (National Research Council, 2013). These prosocial and positive experiences can produce a different trajectory for young people as they seek to utilize personal efficacy or agency and find their sense of belonging within the larger community (Butts et al., 2010). Research suggests that the positive development of a young person is dependent on a variety of opportunities, support systems, responsibilities, and relationships with others (Butts et al., 2010). The positive youth justice model includes 12 key components, depicted as a 2 × 6 matrix (Table 25.1). Each cell in the matrix represents the interaction of two core assets needed by all youth (learning/doing and attaching/belonging) with six different life areas (work, education, relationships, community, health, and creativity). These domains include measurable outcomes to evaluate the effectiveness of the model (Butts et al., 2010).

Program Evidence

The U.S. Department of Justice Office of Justice Programs actively evaluates programs with a rigorous methodology classifying programs as effective, promising, or with no effects, based on the outcomes of the programs for justice-involved youth (National Institute of Justice [NIJ], 2021). There are currently 92 effective and 365 promising programs that were evaluated and documented on http://www.crimesolutions.ojp.gov (as of February 10, 2021). This chapter will highlight reentry services, the general wraparound model, wraparound

TABLE 25.1 Positive Youth Justice Model

CORE ASSETS

PRACTICE DOMAINS	Learning/Doing			Attaching/Belonging	
	Domain-Specific Example[a]	Activity or Opportunity	Outcome Measures	Activity or Opportunity	Outcome Measures
Work	Job readiness	Resume writing workshop	Resume submitted to potential employer	Job seeker support group	Frequency or length of group participation
Education	Computer skills	One-on-one skill building in HTML or other language	Youth has an operating website	Youth-to-youth tutoring program	Number of successful tutoring matches
Relationships	Communication skills	Training in conflict management	Youth completes a training program	Youth-adult mentor program	Frequency and duration of mentoring relationship
Community	Youth-led civic improvement campaign	Prepare and present formal testimony	Youth speaks at a public hearing	Launch new advocacy organization	Number of meetings attended
Health	Physical fitness	Weight training	Number of training circuits completed	Team sports	Number of games played
Creativity	Self-expression	Mural art program	At least one mural designed or completed	Group performance, music, or theater	Number of performances in which youth participated

Source: Butts et al. (2010).

and probation reform, multilevel wraparound, trauma-informed care, healing-centered engagement, and culturally relevant interventions.

Reentry Services

Reentry services are critical for young people reentering society from correctional settings, especially to reduce reoffending rates (Cuevas et al., 2019). For example, lower recidivism rates were found for youth who participated in reentry services such as a correctional boot camp or intensive case management services as opposed to youth who did not receive these services (Bouffard & Bergseth, 2008). There is a distinction between reentry programs and the traditional juvenile justice model. Reentry programs offer youth transitional services and appropriate supervision in the community based on their level of need as they reenter society. However, in the traditional model, youth have time-restricted supervision and may not be provided with services in the community (Weaver & Campbell 2015).

Wraparound Model

Service needs across multiple public systems, including child welfare and mental health systems, schools, and social services, may either leave youth lingering in the juvenile justice system or increase the risk that they return to the system. Some studies estimate that as many as 55% of youth are rearrested within 1 year of release (Liebenberg & Ungar, 2014; Seigle et al., 2014). A successful reentry strategy entails coordinated services that engage youth, families, and community/peer support systems (Howell et al., 2004). Such a strategy is often termed the *wraparound model*. The 2018 Juvenile Justice and Delinquency Prevention Act reauthorization also includes this language:

> Reentry planning . . . for juveniles will include—
> (A) A written case plan based on an assessment of needs that includes—
>   (i)   the pre- and post-release plans for juveniles;
>   (ii) the living arrangement to which the juveniles are to be discharged; and
>   (iii) any other plans developed for the juveniles based on an individualized assessment. (codified as amended at 34 U.S.C. § 11133 (a)(31) (2018))

Thus, before a juvenile is released from an out-of-home placement, a final assessment must be conducted and a postrelease plan written. Yet, practitioners need to increase the integration of evidence-based practice into wraparound services. National research by the Council of State Governments suggests that successful reentry for youth is guided by four overall principles:

1. Base supervision, service, and resource-allocation decisions on the results of validated risk and needs assessments.
2. Adopt and effectively implement programs and services demonstrated to reduce recidivism and improve other youth outcomes, and use data to evaluate system performance and direct system improvements.
3. Employ a coordinated approach across service systems to address youths' needs.

4. Tailor system policies, programs, and supervision to reflect the distinct developmental needs of adolescents. (Seigle et al., 2014, pp. iii–iv)

A substantial evidence base indicates that a rigorous wraparound model meets these four principles. Such a model also provides a focus on family voice and choice, individualized services, team and community base, natural supports, collaboration, cultural competence, strengths, and persistence. These attributes foster positive youth, system, and cost outcomes (Bruns et al., 2004). There are 63 wraparound programs that were rated as effective and promising, which can be used as a point of reference for the development of reentry programs in the future (NIJ, 2021).

Wraparound and Probation Reform

Helping youth return to their communities and not revisit justice facilities also requires probation reform over the next decade. According to the National Center for Juvenile Justice (n.d.), in 2017, approximately 63% of juvenile court–involved youth had probation as part of their disposition. Conditions of probation range from approximately five to as many as 30 conditions, yet practitioners find that youth only remember about a third of their probation conditions (Peralta et al., 2012). In 2015, the most serious offense for 23% of all detained youth was a technical or probation violation, as it was for 15% of youth currently committed. Moreover, the significant disparities by race continue: Youth of color represent almost 70% of those committed to a residential facility for a technical violation (Hockenberry, 2018). In a comprehensive report on *Juvenile Probation Transformation*, the Urban Institute reports that wraparound services can reduce the number of youth who violate the conditions of their probation (Esthappan et al., 2019).

Multilevel Wraparound

The Change Happens VOICES program, an OJJDP-funded program, utilizes a wraparound model that includes three pillars: intensive case management, group services, and systems-level intervention. These three pillars deliver forensic social work practice at the micro, mezzo, and macro levels. Intensive case management provides links to obtain mental and physical health services, education support, mentoring, job training, employment, housing, and outreach for young girls. The groups utilize a gender-specific curriculum known as VOICES that includes sessions on self-discovery, connecting with others, healthy living, and the journey ahead (Covington, 2017). The systems-level macro intervention includes the establishment of an advisory council, represented by members of community organizations, mental health and juvenile justice professionals, policy advocates, and research institutions. This macro-level initiative aims to address and advocate against systemic barriers for reentry. Additionally, the program offers mental health first aid, secondary trauma trainings, human trafficking awareness trainings, and monthly check-ins to juvenile justice professionals. Change Happens recognizes the impact of poverty and distressed environments on justice involvement. Hence, the wraparound case management prioritizes girls who live within opportunity/poverty zones for 6 to 12 months of follow-up. In this process, Change Happens works with opportunity zone partners to help revitalize the area and identify assets within these areas. This includes an asset mapping project where the assets of these opportunity zones will be identified and developed as protective factors that can build prosocial community engagement among justice-involved girls (Change Happens, 2021).

Trauma-Informed Care

The U.S. Department of Justice has charged juvenile justice systems in the United States to develop trauma-informed infrastructure and programs to counter the deleterious impact of trauma on justice-involved youth (Branson et al., 2017). In 2016, the *Journal of Juvenile Justice* featured trauma-informed care in juvenile justice and highlighted the professional consensus to develop four areas of forensic practice for a more trauma-informed juvenile justice system: (a) screening, assessment, and intervention; (b) workforce development; (c) vulnerable populations; and (d) system reform (Dierkhising & Branson, 2016). It is important to address the adversity and trauma experienced by justice-involved youth within correctional settings. Programs developed for this population need to be not only trauma informed but trauma responsive, which will provide healing from ACEs and the stunted neurological development from trauma (Evans-Chase, 2014).

Young people with an extensive traumatic history require extensive trauma support that will help them to process and overcome the trauma meaningfully (Herringa et al., 2013). This trauma support involves conscious attention to the emotional and sensory responses and carefully investigating the reasons behind the responses. This will allow the young person to recollect and meaningfully reconstruct their past experiences (Zilberstein, 2014). Trauma-informed therapy is a slow process where the therapist paces the client with caution and care. The dysregulation of affective states must be complemented by coping skills (Blaustein & Kinniburgh, 2010). Older children require added competencies to handle their dysregulated states, which are necessary for increasing their memory, logical thinking, emotional regulation, and future orientation, and monitoring their thoughts and triggers (Bumge & Wright, 2007).

Multiple studies have identified maladaptive ways of coping with traumatic experiences among the justice-involved youth population. These maladaptive coping mechanisms, such as substance use, running away from home, weapon possession, or gang involvement, often function as a form of self-preservation or protection, although they often result in arrest (Ford et al., 2006; Kerig & Becker, 2010). This presents an opportunity for treatment, where there is a practical focus on enhancing positive coping skills (Blaustein & Kinniburgh, 2010).

Trauma-responsive intervention is pivotal to forensic social work practice. However, scarce resources and a lack of funding impede the development of trauma-informed programs within the juvenile justice system (Ford et al., 2012). Alternatives to juvenile residential placements can be considered for youth who have experienced a high level of trauma so that the trauma will not be exacerbated by the conditions in custody (Sedlak et al., 2013).

Healing-Centered Engagement

Healing-centered engagement, an extension of trauma-informed care, is often recommended to engage young people of color (Ginwright, 2018). A healing-centered approach is an asset-driven model that regards young people who have experienced trauma as agents of change for themselves rather than as victims. There are three underlying values to this approach: interdependence, collective engagement, and service to others. The holistic restoration of young people's well-being cannot happen by only working individually with the youth but must also include the environment and engaging with the systemic injustices they have faced (Ginright, 2018). Though individual services are important, such as mental health treatment, this approach goes further by suggesting the use of rituals that are grounded within cultures, collective strengths, and intentional activities that will restore one's well-being (Martinez, 2001). Healing-centered engagement is a future-oriented approach that accounts for one's future hopes and goals, rather than treating trauma symptoms alone.

Culturally Relevant Interventions

Culturally promotive curricula within alternative schools, such as the New Directions in LA, were said to be meaningful for young Black men as the students described it as a way of "teaching the truth—which refers to pedagogies that incorporate the histories, texts, values, beliefs, and perspectives of people from diverse cultural backgrounds" (Lea et al., 2020, p. 11). Another example of a liberative healing practice can be found within the Truth Telling Project of Ferguson (TTP), which was founded to engage the community through storytelling about the oppressive and violent histories of racial injustice (Ragland, 2021). The author situates the truth-telling process as a "decolonial process attuned to the human dignity of communities silenced by U.S. settler colonial heteropatriarchal social, economic and political worldviews and values" (Ragland, 2021, p. 2). Programs such as these also work to center the experience of youth of color, recognize differential processing, and even reduce factors that contribute to the school-to-prison pipeline (McCarter, 2017).

Forensic Social Work Settings and the Role of Social Workers

Forensic social workers who want to work with justice-involved youth have myriad placement options, many of which have been highlighted in this chapter. Forensic social workers work in intake, diversion, juvenile, and alternative courts; child advocacy centers; alternative learning placements; group homes; corrections; probation; parole; and more. They can provide micro, mezzo, and macro practice in roles such as mitigation specialists, expert witnesses, justice reform advocates, etc. (Scheyett et al., 2012). Consider also the inclusion of juvenile justice in the Achieve Equal Opportunity and Justice grand challenge for social work (http://www.grandchallengesforsocialwork.org).

Social workers serving justice-involved youth must be able to navigate and finesse through competing systems, employ a wide range of skills, and understand the presence of intersectional identities in both their clients and themselves. The ability to consider the multiple systems, identities, and outcomes for youthful offenders can foster the best possible outcomes and experiences. Social workers will act as brokers for service and care coordination, advocates for youth and their families, mediators between agencies and the family, and agents for change in the overall juvenile justice system.

Case Study

Savan (fictitious name representing an actual youth) and her family relocated from Laos when she was an infant. Although Savan speaks English as her primary language, her parents are still learning the language. Savan experienced what might be categorized as a "normal" early childhood but recalls feeling isolated from her peers beginning in middle school. Other students teased her, made fun of her, and began bullying her. Savan admits that at this time she began self-mutilation and often thought about suicide. Her parents report that they didn't know how to help Savan as they weren't familiar with the community and services, and they didn't feel any services would be culturally relevant to help Savan. The forensic social worker first met Savan and her family at a detention hearing after she was charged with assault with a deadly weapon at school. Savan admitted to the misdemeanor charge of simple assault after injuring a school peer during a fight, a fight that Savan and witnesses report happened after a week-long incident of teasing and bullying. The forensic social worker assisted the family in scheduling a medical physical, a mental health assessment, and a psychiatric assessment with a local adolescent-focused clinic. The forensic social worker also assisted Savan and her family in a school system hearing regarding her charges. This was extremely helpful as the parents are not proficient in English and there was no offer to secure a translator. The forensic social worker was able to slow the meeting/process down so that both Savan and her mother understood the educational process as related to the charge. Savan thrived at the clinic and within a few months was transitioned into a dialectical behavior therapy group at the behavioral health center to continue to address her feelings of depression and self-injurious behaviors. She began school in the fall of 2020 at the alternative learning placement for justice-involved youth, excelled in this placement, and has been an exemplary student. She was able to complete all of her community service hours through a local organization serving immigrants and refugees and was successfully discharged from probation in April of 2021.

References

Abrams, L. S., & Terry, D. (2017). *Everyday desistance: The transition to adulthood Among formerly incarcerated youth*. Rutgers University Press.

Adams, E. (2010, July). *Healing invisible wounds: Why investing in trauma-informed care for children makes sense*. Justice Policy Institute. http://www.justicepolicy.org/ images/upload/10-07_REP_HealingInvisibleWounds_JJ-PS.pdf

Altschuler, D. M., & Brash, R. (2004). Adolescent and teenage offenders confronting the challenges and opportunities of reentry. *Youth Violence and Juvenile Justice, 2*(1), 72–87. doi:10.1177/1541204003260048

Baglivio, M. T., Epps, N., Swartz, K., Huq, M. S., Sheer, A., & Hardt, N. S. (2014). The prevalence of adverse childhood experiences (ACE) in the lives of juvenile offenders. *Journal of Juvenile Justice, 3*(2), 12–34.

Beck, A. J., Cantor, D., Hartge, J., & Smith, T. (2013). *Sexual victimization in juvenile facilities reported by youth, 2012* (Report No. NCJ 241708). Bureau of Justice Statistics. http://www.bjs.gov/content/pub/pdf/svjfry12.pdf

Birckhead, T. R. (2012). Delinquent by reason of poverty. *Washington University Journal of Law & Policy*, *38*, 53.

Blaustein, M., & Kinniburgh, K. (2010). *Treating traumatic stress in children and adolescents: How to foster resilience through attachment, self-regulation, and competency*. Guilford Press.

Bouffard, J. A., & Bergseth, K. J. (2008). The impact of reentry services on juvenile offenders' recidivism. *Youth Violence and Juvenile Justice, 6*(3), 295–318.

Branson, C., Baetz, C., Horwitz, S., & Hoagwood, K. (2017). Trauma-informed juvenile justice systems: A systematic review of definitions and core components. *Psychological Trauma, 9*(6), 635–646. https://doi.org/10.1037/tra0000255

Bright, C. L., & Johnson-Reid, M. (2008). Onset of juvenile court involvement: Exploring gender-specific associations with maltreatment and poverty. *Children and Youth Services Review, 30*, 914–927. https://doi.org/10.1016/j.childyouth.2007.11.015

Bruns, E. J., Walker, J. S., Adams, J., Miles, P., Osher, T. W., Rast, J., VanDenBerg, J. D., & National Wraparound Initiative Advisory Group. (2004). *Ten principles of the wraparound process*. Portland State University, National Wraparound Initiative. https://nwi.pdx.edu/pdf/TenPrincWAProcess.pdf

Bumge, S., & Wright, S. (2007). Neurodevelopmental changes in working memory and cognitive control. *Current Opinion in Neuroscience, 17*, 243–250.

Butts, J. A., Bazemore, G., & Meroe, A. S. (2010). *Positive youth justice—Framing justice interventions using the concepts of positive youth development*. Coalition for Juvenile Justice.

Butts, J. A., & Schiraldi, V. N. (2018). *Recidivism reconsidered: Preserving the community justice mission of community corrections*.

Change Happens. (2021). *Voices program*. https://www.changehappenstx.org/voices

Chassin, L. (2008). Juvenile justice and substance use. *Future of Children, 18*(2), 165–183. http://www.jstor.org/stable/20179983

Chesney-Lind, M., Morash, M., & Stevens, T. (2008). Girls' trouble, girls' delinquency, and gender-responsive programming: A review. *Australian and New Zealand Journal of Criminology, 41*, 162–189.

Cochran, J. C., & Mears, D. P. (2014). Race, ethnic, and gender divides in juvenile court sanctioning and rehabilitative intervention. *Journal of Research in Crime and Delinquency, 52*, 181–212.

Cocozza, J. J., & Shufelt, J. L. (2006, June). *Juvenile mental health courts: An emerging strategy*. National Center for Mental Health and Juvenile Justice Research and Program Brief. https://www.issuelab.org/resources/9972/9972.pdfColes, J. A., & Powell, T. (2020). A BlackCrit analysis on Black urban youth and suspension disproportionality as anti-Black symbolic violence. *Race Ethnicity and Education, 23*(1), 113–133. https://doi.org/10.1080/13613324.2019.1631778

Conger, D., & Ross, T. (2001). *Reducing the foster care bias in juvenile detention decisions: The impact of Project Confirm* [Report]. Vera Institute of Justice.

Covington, S. S. (2017). *Voices Curriculum: A program of self-discovery and empowerment for girls*. The Change Companies.Crenshaw, K. W., Ocen, P., & Nanda, J. (2015). *Black girls matter: Pushed out, overpoliced, and underprotected*. African American Policy Forum, Center for Intersectionality and Social Policy Studies.

Crosby, R., Salazar, L. F., DiClemente, R. J., Yarber, W. L., Caliendo, A. M., & Staples-Horne, M. (2004). Health risk factors among detained adolescent females. *American Journal of Preventative Medicine, 27*, 404–410. https://doi.org/10.1016/j.amepre.2004.07.017

Crosland, K., & Dunlap, G. (2015). Running away from foster care: What do we know and what do we do? *Journal of Child and Family Studies, 24*(6), 1697–1706. doi:10.1007/s10826-014-9972-x

Cuevas, C., Wolff, K. T., & Baglivio, M. T. (2019). Dynamic risk factors and timing of recidivism for youth in residential placement. *Journal of Criminal Justice, 60*, 154–166. https://doi.org/10.1016/j.jcrimjus.2018.10.003

Dawson-Edwards, C., Tewksbury, R., & Nelson, N. T. (2020). The causes and pervasiveness of DMC: Stakeholder perceptions of disproportionate minority contact in the juvenile justice system. *Race and Justice, 10*(2), 223–242.

Dierkhising, C. B., & Branson, C. E. (2016). Looking forward: A research & policy agenda for creating trauma-informed juvenile justice systems. *Journal of Juvenile Justice, 5*(1), 14–30.

Dmitrieva, J., Monahan, K. C., Cauffman, E., & Steinberg, L. (2012). Arrested development: The effects of incarceration on the development of psychosocial maturity. *Development and Psychopathology, 24*(3), 1073–1090. doi:10.1017/S0954579412000545

Espinosa, E. M., Sorensen, J. R., & Walfield, S. (2019). Youth pathways: Evaluating the influence of gender, involvement with the public mental health system, perceived mental health need, and traumatic experiences on juvenile justice system processing. *Youth Violence and Juvenile Justice, 18*(3), 215–234. https://doi.org/10.1177/1541204019889664

Esthappan, S., Lacoe, J., & Young, D. (2019). *Juvenile probation transformation: Applying the approach in Lucas County, OH, and Pierce County, WA.* Urban Institute. https://www.urban.org/research/publication/juvenile-probation-transformation/view/full_report

Evans-Chase, M. (2014). Addressing trauma and psychosocial development in juvenile justice-involved youth: A synthesis of the developmental neuroscience, juvenile justice and trauma literature. *Laws, 3*(4), 744–758.

Fader, J. J., Kurlychek, M. C., & Morgan, K. A. (2014). The color of juvenile justice: Racial disparities in dispositional decisions. *Social Science Research, 44*, 126–140.

Fazel, S. M., Doll, H. M., & Långström, N. M. (2008). Mental disorders among adolescents in juvenile detention and correctional facilities: A systematic review and metaregression analysis of 25 surveys. *Journal of the American Academy of Child and Adolescent Psychiatry, 47*(9), 1010–1019. doi:10.1097/CHI.0b013e31817eecf3

Ford, J. (2009). Neurobiological and developmental research: Clinical implications. In C. Courtis & J. Ford (Eds.), *Treating complex traumatic stress disorders: An evidence-based guide* (pp. 31–58). Guilford Press.

Ford, J. D., Steinberg, K. L., Hawke, J., Levine, J., & Zhang, W. (2012). Randomized trial comparison of emotion regulation and relational psychotherapies for PTSD with girls involved in delinquency. *Journal of Clinical Child and Adolescent Psychology, 41*(1), 27–37.

Friedman, M. S., Marshal, M. P., Guadamuz, T. E., Wei, C., Wong, C. F., Saewyc, E. M., & Stall, R. (2011). A meta-analysis of disparities in childhood sexual abuse, parental physical abuse, and peer victimization among sexual minority and sexual nonminority individuals. *American Journal of Public Health, 101*(8), 1481–1494. doi:10.2105/AJPH.2009.190009

Ginwright, S. (2018). The future of healing: Shifting from trauma informed care to healing centered engagement. *Occasional Paper, 25.*

Goshe, S. (2019). How contemporary rehabilitation fails youth and sabotages the American juvenile justice system: A critique and call for change. *Critical Criminology, 27*(4), 559–573. https://doi.org/10.1007/s10612-019-09473-5

Herringa, R., Birn, R., Ruttle, P., Burghy, C., Stodola, D., Davidson, R., & Essex, M. (2013). Childhood maltreatment is associated with altered fear circuitry and increased internalizing symptoms by late adolescence. *PNAS Early Edition, 110*(47), 19119–19124. http://www.pnas.org. ezproxy.lib.uh.edu/content/early/2013/10/30/1310766110.full.pdf+html

Hicks, S. S. (2011). Behind prison walls: The failing treatment choice for mentally ill minority youth. *Hofstra Law Review, 39*(4), 979–1010.

Himmelstein, K. E. W., & Brückner, H. (2011). Criminal-justice and school sanctions against nonheterosexual youth: A national longitudinal study. *Pediatrics, 127*(1), 49–57. doi:10.1542 /peds.2009-2306

Hockenberry, S. (2018). *Juvenile justice Statistics.* National Report Series Bulletin. U.S. Department of Justice, Office of Justice Programs.

Hockenberry, S., & Puzzanchera, C. (2020). *Juvenile court statistics 2018.* National Center for Juvenile Justice. https://www.ojjdp.gov/ojstatbb/njcda/pdf/jcs2018.pdf

Howell, J. C., Kelly, M. R., Palmer, J., & Mangum, R. L. (2004). Integrating child welfare, juvenile justice, and other agencies in a continuum of services. *Child Welfare*, 143–156.

Irvine, A. (2010). "We've had three of them": Addressing the invisibility of lesbian, gay, bisexual and gender non-conforming youths in the juvenile justice system. *Columbia Journal of Gender and Law, 19*(3), 675–701. doi:10.7916/cjgl.v19i3.2603

Irvine, A., & Canfield, A. (2016). The overrepresentation of lesbian, gay, bisexual, questioning, gender nonconforming and transgender youth within the child welfare to juvenile justice crossover population. *American University Journal of Gender, Social Policy & the Law, 24*(2), 243–261.

Javdani, S., & Allen, N. E. (2016). An ecological model for intervention for juvenile justice-involved girls: Development and preliminary prospective evaluation. *Feminist Criminology, 11*(2), 135–162.

Kann, L., Olsen, E. O., McManus, T., Harris, W. A., Shanklin, S. L., Flint, K. H., . . . Zaza, S. (2016). Sexual identity, sex of sexual contacts, and health-related behaviors among students in grades 9–12 — U.S. and selected sites, 2015. *Morbidity and Mortality Weekly Report: Surveillance Summaries, 65*(9), 1–202. doi:10.15585/mmwr.ss6509a1

Kazemian, L. (2015). *Straight lives: The balance between human dignity, public safety, and desistance from crime.* City University of New York, John Jay College of Criminal Justice, Research & Evaluation Center.

Kerig, P. K. (2018). Polyvictimization and girls' involvement in the juvenile justice system: Investigating gender-differentiated patterns of risk, recidivism, and resilience. *Journal of Interpersonal Violence, 33*(5), 789–809. https://doi.org/10.1177/0886260517744843

Kerig, P. K., & Becker, S. P. (2010). From internalizing to externalizing: Theoretical models of the processes linking PTSD to juvenile delinquency. In S. J. Egan (Ed.), *Posttraumatic stress disorder (PTSD): Causes, symptoms and treatment* (pp. 33–78). Nova Science.

Kim, B. K. E., Quinn, C. R., Logan-Greene, P., DiClemente, R., & Voisin, D. (2020). A longitudinal examination of African American adolescent females detained for status offense. *Children & Youth Services Review, 108*, 1–5. doi:10.1016/j.childyouth.2019.104648

King, S., & Bracy, N. L. (2019). School security in the post-Columbine era: Trends, consequences, and future directions. *Journal of Contemporary Criminal Justice, 35*(3), 274–295. https://doi.org/10.1177/10439 86219840188

Kjellstrand, J. M., & Eddy, J. (2011a). Mediators of the effect of parental incarceration on adolescent externalizing behaviors. *Journal of Community Psychology, 39*(5), 551–565. https://doi.org/10.1002/jcop.20451.PMID21673828

Lambie, I., & Randell, I. (2013). The impact of incarceration on juvenile offenders. *Clinical Psychology Review, 33*(3), 448–459. doi:10.1016/j.cpr.2013.01.007

Langton, C. M., Ford, J. D., Chapman, J., Connor, D. F., & Cruise, K. R. (2012). Complex trauma and aggression in secure juvenile justice settings. *Criminal Justice and Behavior, 39*, 694–724. https://doi.org/10.1177/0093854812436957

Lea, C. H., Crumé, H. J., & Hill, D. (2020). "Traditions are not for me": Curriculum, alternative schools, and formerly incarcerated young Black men's academic success. *Social Sciences, 9*(12), 233.

Leve, L. D., & Chamberlain, P. (2004). Female juvenile offenders: Defining an early-onset pathway for delinquency. *Journal of Child and Family Studies, 13*(4), 439–452. doi:10.1023/b:jcfs.0000044726.07272.b5

Liebenberg, L., & Ungar, M. (2014). A comparison of service use among youth involved with juvenile justice and mental health. *Children and Youth Services Review, 39*, 117–122. doi:10.1016/j.childyouth.2014.02.007

Lipsey, M. W., & Cullen, F. T. (2007). The effectiveness of correctional rehabilitation: A review of systematic reviews. *Annual Review of Law and Social Science, 3*, 297–320. doi:10.1146/annurev.lawsocsci.3.081806.112833

Logan-Greene, P., Kim, B. K. E., & Nurius, P. S. (2020). Adversity profiles among court involved youth: Translating system data into trauma-responsive programming. *Child Abuse & Neglect, 104*, 104465. doi:10.1016/j.chiabu.2020.104465

MacDonald, J., & Chesney-Lind, M. (2001). Gender bias & juvenile justice revisited: A multi- year analysis. *Crime & Delinquency, 47*(2), 173–195. doi:10.1177/001112870104 7002002

Majd, K., Marksamer, J., & Reyes, C. (2009). *Hidden injustice: Lesbian, gay, bisexual, and transgender youth in juvenile courts.* Center for HIV Law & Policy. http://www.hivlawandpolicy.org/sites/default/files/hidden_injustice.pdf

Martinez, M. E. (2001). The process of knowing: A biocognitive epistemology. *Journal of Mind and Behavior, 22*(4), 407–426.

Maruna, S. (2001). *Making good: How ex-convicts reform and rebuild their lives.* American Psychological Association.

McCarter, S. A. (2017). The school-to-prison pipeline: A primer for social workers. *Social Work, 62*(1), 53–61. doi:10.1093/sw/sww078

McCarter, S. A. (2018). Adolescence. In E. D. Hutchison (Ed.), *Dimensions of human behavior: The changing life course* (6th ed., pp. 189–230). Sage.

McCarter, S. A. (2019). Intersection of mental health, education, and juvenile justice: The role of mental health providers in reducing the school-to-prison pipeline. *Ethical Human Psychology and Psychiatry, 21*(1), 7–18. doi:10.1891/1559-4343.21.1.7 https://connect.springerpub.com/content/sgrehpp/21/1/7

McNeill, F., & Maruna, S. (2007). Giving up and giving back: Desistance, generativity, and social work with offenders. *Developments in Social Work With Offenders, 48*, 224–339.

Mears, D. P., & Siennick, S. E. (2016). Young adult outcomes and the life-course penalties of parental incarceration. *Journal of Research in Crime and Delinquency, 53*(1), 3–35. https://doi.org/10.1177/0022427815592452

Menon, S. E., & Cheung, M. (2018). Desistance-focused treatment and asset-based programming for juvenile offender reintegration: A review of research evidence. *Child and Adolescent Social Work Journal, 35*(5), 459–476.

Mok, P., Antonsens, S., Pedersen, C., Carr, M., Kapur, N., Nazroo, J., & Webb, R., (2018). Family income inequalities and trajectories through childhood and self-harm and violence in young adults: A population-based, nested case control study. *The Lancet, 3*(10), E498–E507.

National Center for Juvenile Justice. (n.d.). *Easy access to juvenile court statistics.* http://www.ojjdp.gov/ojstatbb/ezajcs/

National Research Council. (2013). *Reforming juvenile justice: A developmental approach.* Committee on Law and Justice, Division of Behavioral and Social Sciences and Education. National Academies Press.

Office of Juvenile Justice and Delinquency Prevention (OJJDP). (2019). *Girls and the juvenile justice system.* https://www.ojjdp.gov/pubs/251486.pdf

Office of Juvenile Justice and Delinquency Prevention (OJJDP). (2020). *The decline in arrests of juveniles continued through 2019.* https://www.ojjdp.gov/ojstatbb/snapshots/DataSnapshot_UCR2019.pdf

Pearce, S. (2019). "It was the small things": Using the concept of racial microaggressions as a tool for talking to new teachers about racism. *Teaching and Teacher Education, 79*, 83–92. https://doi.org/10.1016/j.tate.2018.12.009

Peralta, R., Yeannakis, G., Ambrose, K., Yule, D., & Walker, S. C. (2012). *Washington Judicial Colloquies Project: A guide for improving communication and understanding in juvenile court* (TeamChild Report). Washington State Administrative Office of the Courts and the National Juvenile Defender Center.

Piquero, A. R., Hawkins, J. D., & Kazemian, L. (2012). Criminal career patterns. In R. Loeber & D. P. Farrington (Eds.), *From juvenile delinquency to adult crime: Criminal careers, justice policy, and prevention* (pp. 14–46). Oxford University Press.

Potter, H. (2015). *Intersectionality and criminology: Disrupting and revolutionizing studies of crime.* Routledge.

Proctor, S. L., Li, K., Chait, N., Owens, C., Gulfaraz, S., Sang, E., Prosper, G., & Ogundiran, D. (2020). Preparation of school psychologists to support black students exposed to police violence: Insight and guidance for critical training areas. *Contemporary School Psychology, 25*(3), 377–393. https://doi.org/10.1007/s40688-020-00317-6

Ragland, D. (2021). Truth-telling as decolonial human rights education in the movement for Black liberation. *International Journal of Human Rights Education, 5*(1), 5.

Ryan, J. P., Testa, M. F., & Zhai, F. (2008). African American males in foster care & the risk of delinquency: The values of social bonds & permanence. *Child Welfare, 87*(1), 115–140.

Scheyett, A., Pettus-Davis, C., McCarter, S., & Brigham, R. (2012). Social work and criminal justice: Are we meeting in the field? *Journal of Teaching in Social Work, 32*(4), 438–450. https://doi.org/10.1080/08841233.2012.705241

Schubert, C. A., Mulvey, E. P., & Glasheen, C. (2011). Influence of mental health and substance use problems and criminogenic risk on outcomes in serious juvenile offenders. *Journal of American Academy of Child & Adolescent Psychiatry, 50*(9), 925–937. doi:10.1016/j.jaac.2011.06.006

Sedlak, A. J., & McPherson, K. S. (2010). *Conditions of confinement: Findings from the survey of youth residential placement.* OJJDP Juvenile Justice Bulletin. http://www.ncjrs.gov/pdffiles1/ojjdp/227729.pdf

Sedlak, A. J., McPherson, K. S., & Basena, M. (2013). *Conditions of confinement: Findings from the Survey of Youth in Residential Placement.* OJJDP Juvenile Justice Bulletin. http://www.ncjrs.gov/pdffiles1/ojjdp/227729.pdf

Seigle, E., Walsh, N., & Weber, J. (2014). *Core principles for reducing recidivism and improving other outcomes for youth in the juvenile justice system.* Council of State Governments Justice Center. http://www.modelsforchange.net/publications/640

Tam, C. C., Abrams, L. S., Freisthler, B., & Ryan, J. P. (2016). Juvenile justice sentencing: Do gender and child welfare involvement matter? *Children and Youth Services Review, 64,* 60–65. https://doi.org/10.1016/j.childyouth.2016.02.028.

Teplin, L. A., Welty, L. J., Abram, K. M., Dulcan, M. K., & Washburn, J. J. (2012). Prevalence and persistence of psychiatric disorders in youth after detention: A prospective longitudinal study. *Archives of General Psychiatry, 69*(10), 1031–1043. doi:10.1001/archgenpsychiatry.2011.2062

Wasserman, G. A., McReynolds, L. S., Lucas, C. P., Fisher, P., & Santos, L. (2002). The voice DISC-IV with incarcerated male youths: Prevalence of disorder. *Journal of the American Academy of Child & Adolescent Psychiatry, 41*(3), 314–321. doi:10.1097/00004583-200203000-00011

Weaver, R. D., & Campbell, D. (2015). Fresh start: A meta-analysis of aftercare programs for juvenile offenders. *Research on Social Work Practice, 25*(2), 201–212.

Widom, C. S., Fisher, J. H., Nagin, D. S., & Piquero, A. R. (2018). A prospective examination of criminal career trajectories in abused and neglected males and females followed up into middle adulthood. *Journal of Quantitative Criminology, 34*(3), 831–852.

Zahn, M. A., Agnew, R., Fishbein, D., Miller, S., Winn, D. M., Dakoff, G., & Chesney-Lind, M. (2010) *Causes and correlates of girls' delinquency* (NCJ 226358). U.S. Department of Justice, Office of Justice Programs, Office of Juvenile Justice, and Delinquency Prevention.

Zahn, M. A., Hawkins, S. R., Chiancone, J., & Whitworth, A. (2008). *The Girls Study Group—Charting the way to delinquency prevention for girls* [Bulletin]. http://www.ncjrs.gov/pdffiles1/ojjdp/223434.pdf

Zajac, K., Sheidow, A. J., & Davis, M. (2015). Juvenile justice, mental health, and the transition to adulthood: A review of service system involvement and unmet needs in the U.S. *Children and Youth Services Review, 56,* 139–148. doi:10.1016/j.childyouth.2015.07.014

Zara, G., & Farrington, D. P. (2016). *Criminal recidivism: Explanation, prediction and prevention.* Routledge.

Zilberstein, K. (2014). Trauma's neurobiological toll: Implications for clinical work with children. *Smith College Studies in Social Work, 84*(2–3), 292–309.

26

Drug Court

John R. Gallagher and Anne Nordberg

Theoretical Underpinnings of Drug Court

Drug court and other treatment courts, such as mental health court and veterans court, are guided by therapeutic jurisprudence (TJ), which was first conceptualized through a mental health law perspective by Wexler and Winick (1996). The foundational premise of TJ as "therapy through law," with the law as an agent of behavioral change (Backhouse, 2016, pp. 9–10), has been used considerably in the criminal justice system in recent years. TJ proposes that the criminal justice system, a primarily punitive system, could have a positive, therapeutic impact on some individuals who get involved in the system. According to Wexler (2011), TJ considers the therapeutic and anti-therapeutic consequences of systemic rules and processes, as well as how the behaviors and interactions of legal professionals impact defendants' progress through the system. There is an understanding that poor social conditions may contribute to justice involvement (Winick, 2003), and hence the provision of social services is a key feature of drug courts.

Drug courts are part of contemporary judicial interventions that aim to improve outcomes for individuals, families, and communities that face chronic problems (e.g., opioid epidemic) by explicitly humanizing people who have drug offenses and offering them a holistic alternative to traditional criminal justice (Berman & Feinblatt, 2001). Therefore, an applied framework of TJ includes the diversion of defendants from a system of law to drug court that is focused on solving the core problem (e.g., substance use disorder) that led to their justice involvement. Specifically, many people with substance use disorders are charged with minor, nonviolent offenses that can be better addressed through housing, job training, and especially treatment programs. Therefore, the drug court team, especially the judge, may be regarded as therapeutic agents (Winick & Wexler, 2003) who are essential in treating substance use disorders while simultaneously promoting public safety.

John R. Gallagher and Anne Nordberg, *Drug Court* In: *Handbook of Forensic Social Work*. Edited by: David Axlyn McLeod, Anthony P. Natale, and Kristin W. Mapson, Oxford University Press. © Oxford University Press 2024. DOI: 10.1093/oso/9780197694732.003.0026

Punishment and therapy may seem contradictory, but as Tiger (2011) explains, drug courts are rather prominent examples of coerced treatment. By merging the punitive system of justice with the therapeutic alignment of addiction interventions, drug courts merge the conceptual underpinnings of TJ with the current conceptualization of addiction and recovery. Namely, the power of the court is used to encourage participants to adhere to evidence-based treatment informed by medical and behavioral theories of addiction and recovery, while also reducing the burden on the courts and society (Tiger, 2011). In fact, drug courts operate in an environment that is remarkably caring, as shared by a participant in Tiger's (2011) study:

> Drug courts become very personal. Drug court judges become very involved with these people. The clinical people do. The defense does. The prosecutors do. They care about these people. And when you care about people, you want to do more and more and more for them. (p. 176)

Conceptualizing Drug Courts and Their Key Components

Drug court programming, as discussed previously, has a theoretical foundation that guides social work practice and utilizes the criminal justice system as an avenue to promote recovery from substance use disorders and enhance individuals' health and well-being. To conceptualize drug courts from a theoretical model to evidence-based intervention, it was essential that key components of the intervention be clearly and concisely articulated. In 1997, the National Association of Drug Court Professionals (2004) listed and described the 10 key components of drug court and encouraged programs to incorporate the key components into programming to promote fidelity to the model. The 10 key components of drug court are noted in Box 26.1, as well as examples of how each key component is put into practice.

BOX 26.1 10 Key Components of Drug Court

1. Drug courts integrate alcohol and other drug treatment services with justice system case processing (p. 1).
   Practice example: Participants are required to attend treatment for their substance use disorders and clinical social workers provide the judge and other members of the drug court team with weekly updates on participants' progress in treatment.
2. Using a nonadversarial approach, prosecution and defense counsel promote public safety while protecting participants' due process rights (p. 3).
   Practice example: Prosecution and defense counsel collaborate with participants in developing a rehabilitative approach to criminal justice (e.g., treatment), as compared to incarceration or other punitive models of justice.

---

3. Eligible participants are identified early and promptly placed in the drug court program (p. 5).

   Practice example: Participants are admitted to drug court as soon as possible following arrest in order to enhance motivation for change.

4. Drug courts provide access to a continuum of alcohol, drug, and other related treatment and rehabilitation services (p. 7).

   Practice example: Participants are referred, as needed, to a range of services to meet their individualized needs, which may include mental health treatment, referrals to primary care physicians, or testing and treatment for HIV and sexually transmitted diseases.

5. Abstinence is monitored by frequent alcohol and other drug testing (p. 11).

   Practice example: Participants submit two to three drug tests each week randomly and continuously, and drug test results are shared with participants, treatment providers, and the drug court team.

6. A coordinated strategy governs drug court responses to participants' compliance (p. 13).

   Practice example: Participants are given incentives (e.g., praise from the judge, movie passes, reduced time in drug court) for making progress in the program and sanctions (e.g., community service, brief incarceration, essays on specific topics) for noncompliant behaviors.

7. Ongoing judicial interaction with each drug court participant is essential (p. 15).

   Practice example: Participants attend status hearings weekly to review their progress with the judge, and during these interactions, the judge will ask participants about how things are going in their life (e.g., family, schooling, work, treatment).

8. Monitoring and evaluation measure the achievement of program goals and gauge effectiveness (p. 17).

   Practice example: Drug courts collaborate with local colleges and universities to have social work researchers evaluate their programs.

9. Continuing interdisciplinary education promotes effective drug court planning, implementation, and operations (p. 21).

   Practice example: The drug court team, including judges, probation officers, case managers, drug court coordinators, social workers, and attorneys, attend training yearly to learn about best practices.

10. Forging partnerships among drug courts, public agencies, and community-based organizations generates local support and enhances drug court program effectiveness (p. 23).

    Practice example: The local news does a story about drug court to highlight the program's effectiveness and benefit to the community.

Source: National Association of Drug Court Professionals (2004).

Drug Court Evaluations and Meta-Analyses

The first drug court began in 1989 in Miami, Florida (Nolan, 2001). Those accused of drug crimes who agreed to plead guilty to the charges had their cases diverted to the drug court program. Additionally, they agreed to abstain from drug use, submit to periodic urinalysis, follow treatment recommendations, and report to court for supervision (Wexler & Winick, 1996). Evaluation of this first drug court began in the early 1990s and found promising outcomes (Goldkamp, 1994). Criminal recidivism rates are the gold standard outcome, and Goldkamp (1994) found that recidivism rates among drug court graduates were 32% compared to 48% to 55% among comparison groups. There has been a steady stream of evaluative research conducted on drug courts and several meta-analyses and systematic reviews since Goldkamp's foundational work (Lowenkamp et al., 2005; Mitchell et al., 2012; Wilson et al., 2006). Most have confirmed and expanded Goldkamp's initial promising results, notwithstanding contradictory findings from a handful of studies (Brown, 2010; Miethe et al., 2000). For example, a decade after Goldkamp's evaluation, the U.S. Government Accountability Office (U.S. GAO) conducted a large-scale study that confirmed previous findings that drug courts significantly reduce criminal recidivism rates (U.S. GAO, 2005).

Then, the National Institute of Justice conducted a multisite study of drug courts in the United States (called Multisite Adult Drug Court Evaluation) that compared participants in 23 drug courts to matched offenders from six sites without drug courts. Analyses of these data are consistent with previous work; specifically, participation in drug court significantly reduced criminal recidivism rates compared to matched participants who went through traditional court processes (Rempel, Green, & Kralstein, 2012; Rempel, Zweig, et al., 2012). This work also highlighted other benefits to drug court participants beyond recidivism. Rempel, Zweig, and colleagues (2012) found that drug court participants were significantly less likely than comparison participants to report drug and alcohol use. Also, Green and Rempel (2012) used the MADCE data to explore psychosocial outcomes related to drug courts. They found nonsignificant improvements in many areas including socioeconomic well-being, family relationships, homelessness, and living situation (Green & Rempel, 2012). Meta-analytic reports are consistent with these studies that drug courts reduce criminal recidivism rates (Belenko, 2001; Lowenkamp et al., 2005; Mitchell et al., 2012; Shaffer, 2011; Wilson et al., 2006), and we have learned a great deal about drug courts due to their proliferation and a concomitant increase in research about them. Drug courts, for instance, have lower rates of attrition compared with other court-ordered treatment interventions (Belenko, 2001; Marlowe et al., 2016).

There is strong evidence that completing drug court is important to maximize benefit. A U.S. survey determined that graduation rates ranged from 50% to 75%, with an average graduation rate of 59% (Marlowe et al., 2016). Wolfe et al. (2002) conducted a retrospective review of 3 years of administrative records from 618 participants admitted to a Californian drug court. Participants were 71% male with a mean age of 31 years. The sample was predominantly White, non-Hispanic (58%), followed by Hispanic (19%), African American (13%), and other (10%). They determined that the 2-year criminal recidivism rate was significantly lower among graduates (19%) compared to nongraduates (53%). Also, the mean time to arrest was significantly longer for graduates. Multivariate analyses considered a variety of possible predictors of criminal recidivism including age, gender, race and ethnicity, marital status, past convictions, felony versus misdemeanor, drug court process variables, and employment, but only program completion achieved significance.

Similarly encouraging, Bavon (2001) compared criminal recidivism rates among 72 graduates and 85 nongraduates in a Texas drug court and found recidivism during a 1-year follow-up period to be 2.8% for graduates, compared with 21.2% for nongraduates. Finally, work by Gallagher et al. (2014) in an Indiana drug court followed 108 program graduates and 89 nongraduates for 3 years. Consistent with previous studies, they found the criminal recidivism rate for graduates to be 32%, compared to 65% for nongraduates. Notably, program completion was a significant predictor of criminal recidivism, even after controlling for several demographic, clinical, and legal factors (Gallagher et al., 2014).

Recently, work has been done using more sophisticated statistical methods to determine which factors of drug courts are most efficacious for graduates. Roman et al. (2020) circled back to the robust MADCE dataset and performed a multilevel structural equation model that tested theoretical pathways to desistance from drug use and criminal behaviors. They proposed a model that delineated how drug court program practices change perceptions and attitudes among participants, and how these changes impacted drug use and crime. Proposed mediators included changes in court appearances, drug testing, treatment, perceived risk and reward, perceived legitimacy (procedural justice), and motivation to change one's behavior through substance use disorder treatment. Results indicated that one element of procedural justice, the participant's attitude toward the judge, was the most crucial theoretical mediator on the pathway to desistance from drug use and criminal behaviors (Roman et al., 2020).

The lack of randomized experimental designs in evaluation and research in drug courts does present a limitation of many of the studies discussed above, though this is frequently the case due to legal, ethical, and practical restrictions (Farrington & Welsh, 2005). For example, just 3% of 126 drug court evaluations included in a meta-analysis were randomized experiments (Mitchell et al., 2012). Quasi-experimental designs are more commonly found among drug court evaluations. These aim to isolate an intervention's effect through means other than randomization (Weisburd et al., 2001), such as establishing equivalent or matched comparison groups (as was done with the MADCE data) or statistically controlling for group differences (as Gallagher et al., 2014, did). Despite the lack of randomized experiments and the perceived inferiority of quasi-experimental designs (Weisburd et al., 2001), the evidence that drug court participants recidivate less than participants who do other criminal justice interventions (e.g., probation) is staggering and promising in the treatment of substance use disorders.

Racial and Ethnic Minorities

Drug courts have emerged as an effective intervention in treating individuals who have substance use disorders and are involved in the criminal justice system, and drug court participants tend to have lower criminal recidivism rates than control and comparison group participants who did not participate in a drug court (Mitchell et al., 2012). Criminal recidivism rates are a common outcome measured in drug court evaluations, which is not surprising, as the long-term goal of drug courts is to reduce criminal recidivism rates (Gallagher, 2013b). Criminal recidivism rates are, perhaps, one of the best indicators to highlight program effectiveness, as not recidivating suggests that drug court participants have made behavioral changes to support a recovery-based lifestyle, such as abstaining from drugs, gaining and sustaining employment, and utilizing a recovery support system (Alcoholics Anonymous [AA], Narcotics Anonymous [NA], Celebrate Recovery, Smart Recovery). Another key indicator of program effectiveness is graduation rates. Research has consistently shown that participants who graduate drug court are less likely to recidivate than those who were terminated from the program (Gallagher, 2014; Wolfe et al., 2002). While this finding is logical and not surprising, what is alarming is that racial and ethnic disparities exist in graduation rates in some drug courts.

Racial and ethnic disparities in drug court outcomes are a social justice issue that social workers are equipped to address through practice, research, education, and policy advocacy. Social work values and ethics view the problem of racial and ethnic disparities in drug court outcomes from a solution-focused lens, as compared to traditional, punitive models of criminal justice. For instance, traditional approaches of criminal justice may focus on what racial and ethnic minorities are doing wrong that is leading to disparities in outcomes, whereas a social work lens focuses on how drug courts can best serve racial and ethnic minorities. This paradigm shift from blaming populations for disparities in outcomes to identifying how systems (e.g., drug courts) can deliver culturally informed programming is consistent with the social work values of (a) service, (b) social justice, (c) dignity and worth of the person, (d) importance of human relationships, (e) integrity, and (f) competence (National Association of Social Workers [NASW], 2017).

The majority of research on racial disparities in drug court outcomes is related to African Americans. This is important to note because future social work research should assess the impact of programming on the diverse populations that drug courts serve, such as American Indian or Alaska Native, Asian, Hispanic or Latino, and Native Hawaiian or Other Pacific Islander. In regard to African Americans, drug courts have existed for over 30 years, and unfortunately, there has been a trend in disparities in outcomes dating back two decades (Brewster, 2001). In a Pennsylvania drug court, Brewster (2001) found that African Americans were less likely to be successful (e.g., retention) in the program than White participants.

Quantitative studies have documented the problem of racial disparities in outcomes and qualitative research has explored the phenomenon through a phenomenological lens. Quantitatively, White drug court participants in Texas (Gallagher, 2013b) and Missouri (Dannerbeck et al., 2006) had higher graduation rates than African Americans. In Texas, the graduation rates were 65% for White participants and 45% for African Americans (Gallagher, 2013b), and in Missouri, 55% of White participants graduated, compared to only 28% of African American participants (Dannerbeck et al., 2006). Qualitatively, studies have provided a behind-the-scenes and in-depth understanding of drug courts that could not be captured through quantitative methods. The qualitative work from Gallagher (2013a), to our knowledge, was the first to explore the factors that may contribute to racial disparities in drug court outcomes. Notable findings from individual interviews with African American drug court participants ($n = 14$) were that African Americans were dissatisfied with being mandated to AA and NA meetings, felt that they were not receiving individualized treatment, and viewed sanctions as being delivered in a culturally insensitive manner (Gallagher, 2013a). Additionally, when comparing and contrasting the lived experiences of African American and White drug court participants, African Americans shared concerns and limitations related to the quality of treatment they received for their substance use disorders and viewed terms such as "addict" and "alcoholic" as labeling and stigmatizing, both factors that may contribute to lower graduation rates (Gallagher & Nordberg, 2016).

The graduation rate is an important variable in drug court evaluations because, as mentioned previously, those who graduate tend to recidivate less than those who are terminated from the program. However, Marlowe (2013) emphasized that African Americans, and other racial and ethnic minorities, experienced disparities in multiple outcomes, not just graduation rates. Specifically, in some drug courts, racial and ethnic minorities may be underrepresented, receive fewer evidence-based treatments (e.g., manualized cognitive-behavioral therapy [CBT]), and experience more severe sanctions than their White counterparts for similar behaviors (Marlowe, 2013). To address some of the factors that may contribute to racial disparities in drug court outcomes, and to provide best practices for all participants, the following directions are provided (Gallagher, 2019):

1. Social workers and other drug court professionals should use research-based tools to assess for racial and ethnic disparities in outcomes, such as the *RED Program Assessment Tool* (American University, Working Committee, 2019) and the *Equity and Inclusion: Equivalent Access Assessment and Toolkit* (National Association of Drug Court Professionals, n.d.).
2. Drug courts should remove eligibility criteria that is subjective (e.g., opinions about motivation) and other criteria (e.g., ability to pay) that may inadvertently exclude racial and ethnic minorities from the program.
3. Social workers and other drug court professionals should refer participants to treatment providers who are providing evidence-based interventions (e.g., motivational enhancement therapy, the matrix model, 12-step facilitation therapy) that are guided by social work theories and norms (empowerment theory, strengths perspective).
4. Social workers and other drug court professionals should attend training on implicit bias to increase self-awareness on how biases may impact practice and seek clinical supervision to process biases in a nonjudgmental, safe, and confidential environment.
5. Drug courts should encourage participants to develop and utilize recovery support groups, beyond traditional 12-step programs (e.g., AA, NA), that are consistent with participants' cultures and values (e.g., church, family and friends, community activism, volunteering, schooling).

Sexual and Gender Minorities

There is a growing body of literature related to women's lived experiences in drug courts and best practices in treating women who have substance use disorders. Perhaps the most important findings to emerge from the literature is that the treatment needs of women tend to differ from those of men, particularly when it comes to treating the co-occurrence of trauma symptoms and substance use disorder, promoting motherhood while participating in drug court, and offering gender-responsive interventions. A recent qualitative study, guided by phenomenology and grounded theory, found that the majority of female drug court participants reported histories of trauma and being single mothers (Gallagher & Nordberg, 2017). Gallagher and Nordberg (2017) found that 68% of the women reported traumatic experiences and felt that drug court was not effectively treating their trauma symptoms because treatment tended to be focused mostly, or solely, on treating substance use disorders. It is essential that schools of social work develop curricula that will educate and prepare social workers to treat dual diagnoses, such as substance use disorder and posttraumatic stress disorder (PTSD). Women are more likely than men to experience traumas, and best practice involved treating PTSD concurrently with substance use disorders (National Institute on Drug Abuse, 2020; National Resource Center on Justice Involved Women, 2016).

Gallagher and Nordberg (2017) also found that 60% of women interviewed reported being single mothers and they found it challenging to balance the demands of drug court with the responsibility of motherhood. Drug court participants are required to take part in many interventions, such as frequent drug testing, status hearings with the judge, treatment, and employment, and single mothers felt that not only was it overwhelming to participate in all these interventions while also mothering but also it actually made it more difficult for them to graduate from the program (Gallagher & Nordberg, 2017). In another study, it was promising to see that drug courts can support motherhood by providing an environment consistent with social work values, such as the judge sharing affirmations with mothers, showing genuine concern for mothers' well-being and success in the program, and promoting motherhood by adjusting drug court requirements to support parenting time (Gallagher, Nordberg, et al., 2019).

To further improve drug court outcomes for women, drug courts must refer participants to clinical social workers and other treatment professionals who are trained in evidence-based and gender-responsive interventions. Evidence-based interventions, for instance, that can be used to treat the co-occurrence of PTSD and substance use disorder are stress inoculation training, direct therapeutic exposure, cognitive processing therapy, CBT, and eye movement desensitization and reprocessing (Barlow, 2014). Gender-responsive interventions include giving women the option to attend mixed-gender or all-female therapy groups, incorporating objectives into treatment plans that promote mothering, and referring participants to recovery support groups that empower women and promote camaraderie (e.g., all-women AA and NA meetings), to name a few. Providing gender-responsive interventions in drug court has been shown to improve outcomes related to participants' satisfaction with treatment, improve functioning and decrease PTSD symptoms, and result in better performance in treatment, such as engagement in the treatment process and retention in treatment (Messina et al., 2012).

An important limitation to mention, however, is that there is little information on how drug courts serve individuals who identify as lesbian, gay, bisexual, and transgender (LGBT). This limitation, though unfortunate, is not surprising because the criminal justice system has historically dichotomized gender as men and women. As a result, it is recommended that social work researchers prioritize developing research agendas to assess the impact of drug court programming on individuals who identify as LGBT. This may include qualitative studies (e.g., focus groups, individual interviews, satisfaction surveys) that explore LGBT individuals' lived experiences in drug court or more generalizable, quantitative studies that predict graduation and criminal recidivism outcomes for participants who identify as LGBT.

Case Study

This section presents a case study that provides examples of the role of social workers in drug court. Additionally, the challenges and ethical dilemmas social workers may face in working in drug courts are discussed, and the ETHIC model (Evaluate, Think, Hypothesize, Identify, Consult) (Congress, 2000) is recommended to guide ethical decision-making. The pseudonym Morgan is used for the case study. The case study presents practical and expected scenarios from our social work practice experience; however, all of the details are fictitious, hence not associated in any way with a specific drug court participant. In the case study, we discuss Morgan's drug use history and arrest that led to her referral to drug court, present findings from a clinical diagnostic assessment for substance use disorders, provide an example of a treatment plan, and discuss Morgan's progress in treatment and drug court.

Drug Use History and Arrest

Morgan is a 38-year-old, single, heterosexual female whose drug of choice is heroin. She began using drugs in high school, around the age of 16. During high school, Morgan reported that she used alcohol and marijuana, mainly on the weekends with friends, and her drug use had no negative impact on her functioning, as she maintained part-time employment at a grocery store and graduated high school with honors. A similar pattern emerged in college. Morgan completed her bachelor's degree in sociology in 4 years, and during college, she continued to use alcohol and marijuana approximately one to three times a week and it had little to no negative impact on her functioning. When she did experience a negative consequence of drug use in college, it was rare and typically related to being hungover and missing class, but a pattern of this behavior never developed.

After college, she began working for the state police as a sociologist where she monitored and evaluated crime patterns in suburban communities. She stopped using marijuana and reported using alcohol much less than she did in high school and college. During this timeframe, from her mid-20s to early 30s, Morgan maintained abstinence from marijuana and continued a nonproblematic, social pattern of alcohol use. However, at the age of 35, she began dating a man who, unknown to her at the time they started dating, was misusing opioid prescription pills daily and would use heroin intravenously when it was available. Around the same time, Morgan began experiencing symptoms of anxiety, such as excessive worrying that she felt she could not control, difficulties with concentration that were negatively impacting her employment, irritability, and having trouble falling asleep, which resulted in her often feeling fatigued and tired most of the day. Morgan associated her anxiety with being unhappy in her new relationship with her boyfriend and her suspicion that he was using opioids.

Once Morgan confided in her boyfriend that she was experiencing anxiety, he offered her an opioid prescription pill, which he was buying from others, as a way to ease her symptoms. Morgan took the pill and quickly noticed that it improved her mood, provided a sense of euphoria, and minimized her anxiety symptoms. For about 2 years, Morgan continued this pattern of misusing opioid prescription pills to cope with anxiety symptoms, and as her tolerance to the pills increased, she found herself needing more pills to get the desired effect. Due to her tolerance, she needed a more potent opioid, and her boyfriend introduced her to heroin, which she immediately began using intravenously. Shortly after beginning heroin use, she was terminated from her job at the state police for missing work and low productivity. At the age of 38, Morgan was pulled over by the police for speeding and a search of her vehicle found a small amount of heroin. Morgan was charged with felony possession of a controlled substance. This was Morgan's first criminal arrest, and the arrest was clearly related to her personal drug use, as compared to drug dealing. Therefore, her defense attorney referred her to drug court where she could receive treatment for her opioid use disorder and complete the requirements of the program, which would enable her to have the felony arrest dismissed from her criminal record. Before entering drug court, Morgan ended the relationship with her boyfriend.

Diagnoses and Treatment Plan

Morgan was admitted to drug court and referred to treatment for a bio-psycho-social-spiritual assessment. Based on the findings from the assessment, the clinical social worker diagnosed Morgan with opioid use disorder (severe) and generalized anxiety disorder. Morgan was diagnosed with severe opioid use disorder because she met six of 11 diagnostic criteria, according to the *Diagnostic and Statistical Manual of Mental Disorders*, fifth edition (American Psychiatric Association, 2013). Specifically, Morgan reported (a) a history of cravings to use opioids, (b) a pattern of needing more opioids to experience euphoria from the drug (e.g., tolerance), (c) using opioids to avoid withdrawal symptoms (e.g., nausea, muscle aches, insomnia), (d) continuing to use opioids despite knowing it could exacerbate her anxiety symptoms, (e) reducing her involvement in hobbies and family activities as a result of her opioid use, and (f) recurring opioid use that resulted in her being terminated from her job at the state police. Based on Morgan's dual diagnoses of severe opioid use disorder and generalized anxiety disorder, it is essential that social workers receive training in both substance use disorders and mental illnesses. Morgan's case is not unique. Actually, it is estimated that about 50% of adults who have a substance use disorder also have a mental illness, and although less research has been done on children, the prevalence of dual diagnoses with children also appears high (National Institute on Drug Abuse, 2018). The following is an example of a treatment plan a clinical social worker would develop in collaboration with Morgan.

> **Presenting problem**: Morgan was arrested for possession of heroin and referred to treatment by drug court to be assessed for a substance use disorder and generalized anxiety disorder.
>
> **Treatment goals**: Morgan reports that she wants to improve her quality of life by abstaining from heroin and other opioids, developing a support system of family and friends who support her recovery, and completing drug court to have the pending felony arrest dismissed from her criminal record.
>
> **Treatment objectives**:
> 1. Morgan will maintain abstinence from heroin and other opioids, as evidenced by her report and the results of random, frequent, and continuous drug tests.
> 2. Morgan will develop and utilize a recovery support system, as evidenced by attending recovery support groups (e.g., NA, Smart Recovery) and doing activities (e.g., going to the beach, hiking) with family and friends who are supportive of her recovery.
> 3. Morgan will learn about addiction and recovery and transfer the knowledge she gains in treatment to her life, as evidenced by her attendance and participation in group and individual counseling where she will develop recovery skills, such as using healthy coping skills for cravings, utilizing personal strengths to sustain recovery, and practicing cognitive restructuring to promote thought patterns that are conducive to recovery.
> 4. Morgan will learn about anxiety, including the cyclical relationship between drugs and anxiety, and develop healthy behaviors and cognitions to support recovery, as evidenced by her report that her anxiety symptoms have subsided and are having little to no negative impact on her functioning.
> 5. Morgan will have her pending felony arrest dismissed from her criminal record, as evidenced by her ability to complete drug court, which includes a variety of interventions, such as attending status hearings with the judge and completing treatment.
>
> **Interventions**: The clinical social worker will facilitate group and individual therapy with Morgan, assess her progress in treatment in an ongoing manner, and consult with the drug court team, clinical supervisors, colleagues, and Morgan's psychiatrist to provide a comprehensive treatment approach. Motivational interviewing, CBT, and other evidence-based interventions will be used to support Morgan in meeting the goals and objectives of her treatment plan.

Ethical Dilemmas During the Course of Drug Court

This section identifies and processes two ethical dilemmas related to the practice of clinical social work in drug courts. The ethical dilemmas are discussed in reference to the case study. The first ethical dilemma is related to the exchange of information between the clinical social worker and the drug court. As noted previously, drug courts are conceptualized by their 10 key components (National Association of Drug Court Professionals, 2004). Consistent with the key components, drug court participants are required to attend and complete treatment for substance use disorders, and in order for the judge and other criminal justice professionals (e.g., drug court coordinator) to know that participants are complying with this requirement, treatment providers, such as clinical social workers, provide the drug court team with updates on participants' progress in treatment.

In regard to the case study, Morgan signed a confidentiality release form where her clinical social worker could share information with the drug court team, such as her attendance, diagnoses, treatment plan, and progress in meeting the goals and objectives of her treatment plan. As a result, Morgan knew that if she shared information with her clinical social worker that was noncompliant with drug court rules, such as drug use, the clinical social worker would most likely share that information with the drug court team and Morgan could receive a sanction (e.g., brief incarceration, community service). Knowing this information, at one point in treatment, Morgan relapsed on heroin and chose not to tell her clinical social worker about the relapse. This dynamic can be viewed from multiple perspectives, two of which are discussed here. First, the responsibility may be placed on Morgan. For example, Morgan may be, unfortunately, labeled as a liar and viewed as being dishonest because she omitted, or lied about, important information related to her treatment, such as a relapse on heroin. Second, the responsibility may be placed on the clinical social worker and drug court. For instance, from the moment Morgan signed the confidentiality release form, she knew that her clinical social worker could share sensitive information, such as drug use, with the drug court team. As a result, Morgan viewed her clinical social worker as untrustworthy and the treatment setting as an unsafe environment to be honest; after all, being honest about her relapse on heroin may have resulted in her incarceration.

As social workers, we are ethically responsible to provide a safe, nonjudgmental, empathetic, and confidential environment for the individuals we work with. Providing this environment, however, for individuals who are involved in drug courts, and other criminal justice programs, is challenging, and recent studies have emphasized this challenge (Gallagher et al., 2017; Gallagher & Nordberg, 2018). A qualitative study of 42 drug court participants found that the majority of participants viewed treatment providers as judgmental and punitive, as compared to providing a therapeutic environment where they felt they could be honest (Gallagher et al., 2017). Similar to Morgan's experience in the case study, Gallagher and colleagues (2017) also noted that some drug court participants did not disclose drug use to their counselors because they feared being judged and receiving a sanction because counselors would share relapses with the drug court team.

The dynamic of what information clinical social workers should share with the drug court team is clearly complex. Social workers want to collaborate with the drug court team to provide a holistic, team-based approach in treating substance use disorders while also promoting public safety, which is consistent with the drug court model. Conversely, clinical social workers are ethically required to promote participants' self-determination and behave in a trustworthy manner; however, participants can view clinical social workers as untrustworthy if they share information outside of the treatment setting. The following recommendations are offered to assist clinical social workers in addressing this challenge and practicing in an ethical manner:

1. When drug court participants are asked to sign the confidentiality release form, clinical social workers should explain what information will and will not be shared with the drug court team. This information should be reviewed frequently in treatment so participants are reminded of what information will be shared with others.
2. Clinical social workers should advocate for participants by having a dialogue with the drug court team to educate judges, probation officers, and other members of the team on the importance of maintaining a trustworthy, empathetic, and therapeutic relationship in the treatment of substance use disorders.
3. Clinical social workers should be granted discretion in what they share with the drug court team. This will promote individualized treatment and prevent a one-size-fits-all approach in exchanging information, which is consistent with competent social work practice and respecting the dignity and worth of drug court participants.
4. When information is shared with the drug court team that may result in participants receiving a sanction from drug court, such as positive drug tests, participants should be involved in the exchange of information (e.g., the clinical social worker and participant should call the drug court team together to inform them of a positive drug test, the clinical social worker and participant should collaboratively write a letter or email to the drug court team documenting progress in treatment).
5. The clinical social worker should use the ETHIC model (Congress, 2000) to resolve ethical dilemmas that arise in criminal justice settings. The ETHIC model enables social workers to resolve ethical dilemmas by examining values (e.g., personal, professional), thinking about social work values and ethical principles (e.g., importance of human relationships), hypothesizing the decision-making process and possible outcomes, identifying the potential benefits and harms to participants, and consulting with clinical supervisors and colleagues to identify the most ethical choice.

The second ethical dilemma is related to the use of medication-assisted treatment (MAT) in drug courts to treat opioid use disorders. Three medications are approved to treat opioid use disorders: methadone, buprenorphine, and naltrexone. These medications, particularly when combined with treatment, have been shown to reduce opioid withdrawal symptoms; minimize cravings for opioids; decrease opioid use, overdoses, and deaths; improve retention in treatment; and have many other positive outcomes (Gordon et al., 2014; Kinlock et al., 2009; Lee et al., 2016; Magura et al., 2009; Substance Abuse and Mental Health Services Administration, 2020). Despite the evidence that MAT combined with treatment improves well-being, many drug courts do not allow MAT in programming. Matusow and colleagues (2013) found in their survey that nearly all drug courts served participants who had opioid use disorders, which was not surprising, but only 56% of the drug courts offered MAT. Most concerning is that some drug courts do not allow MAT for unscientific reasons. Key drug court stakeholders may have subjective, negative beliefs about MAT, misinformation, and their own personal views of recovery (e.g., participants using MAT may be seen as not being in *real* recovery), which prevents some programs from using MAT (Gallagher, Whitmore, et al., 2019; Matusow et al., 2013). Additionally, drug court participants are often referred to recovery support groups, such as NA, and participants who are taking MAT may be treated in an unfriendly manner at some meetings because MAT is seen, by some members of recovery support groups, as inconsistent with their abstinence-based philosophy (Narcotics Anonymous World Services, 2016).

In regard to the case study, Morgan had several relapses on opioids while receiving treatment. This pattern of relapses, coupled with her diagnosis of severe opioid use disorder, history of opioid withdrawal symptoms, and tolerance to opioids, suggested that she may benefit from MAT. Therefore, the clinical social worker referred Morgan to an addictionologist to be evaluated for MAT. The addictionologist prescribed Morgan buprenorphine. The clinical social worker supported this intervention, as science has shown that MAT is an effective way to treat opioid use disorders, and using buprenorphine as prescribed was added to Morgan's treatment plan. However, the drug court informed the clinical social worker that Morgan could not take buprenorphine while in the program, even if it was prescribed by an addictionologist.

This was an ethical dilemma for the clinical social worker because she was practicing competently and drug court was a potential barrier to Morgan being successful in the program. The ethical dilemma was to inform Morgan that she could not take buprenorphine, as directed by the drug court, or encourage Morgan to follow the recommendations given by the medical professional. The clinical social worker used research to guide her practice, referred Morgan to a professional (e.g., addictionologist) who had expertise in MAT, and knew that MAT was an evidence-based intervention, and despite these best practices, Morgan may be denied the care she needed to treat her opioid use disorder. This, as with most ethical dilemmas, is a complex scenario because several systems are involved (e.g., drug court, treatment provider, addictionologist, Morgan), and similar to the first ethical dilemma, the ETHIC model (Congress, 2000) is recommended to support social workers in providing best practices. In addition to using the ETHIC model, the following recommendations are offered to assist clinical social workers in addressing this challenge and practicing in an ethical manner. Myths, misinformation, and stigma related to MAT are often barriers to incorporating MAT into drug court programming; therefore, the recommendations are focused on eliminating these barriers:

1. Clinical social workers should advocate for participants who are taking MAT by educating key drug court stakeholders on the benefits of incorporating MAT into treatment planning. Additionally, social workers should collaborate with the drug court team in developing policies and procedures for MAT service delivery that are consistent with best practices, such as ensuring a continuation in care, drug testing, monitoring participants' functioning in major life areas (e.g., social, employment, schooling), and educating participants and families on MAT and how it works (Substance Abuse and Mental Health Services Administration, 2020).
2. Clinical social workers should collaborate with schools of social work to facilitate community forums on topics such as MAT, local resources in treating opioid use disorders,

and other important topics related to substance use disorders and recovery. Community forums will help disseminate accurate information and, hopefully, eliminate stigma and other negative beliefs related to MAT (Gallagher, Marlowe, & Minasian, 2019).

3. Clinical social workers should only refer participants who are taking MAT to recovery support groups (e.g., NA) that are supportive of MAT and will not stigmatize, judge, or otherwise convey negative views toward those who are taking methadone, buprenorphine, or naltrexone (Narcotics Anonymous World Services, 2016).

References

American Psychiatric Association. (2013). *Diagnostic and statistical manual of mental disorders* (5th ed.).

American University, Working Committee. (2019). *RED program assessment tool*. https://redtool.org/

Backhouse, C. (2016). An introduction to David Wexler, the person behind therapeutic jurisprudence. *International Journal of Therapeutic Jurisprudence, 1*, 1–21.

Barlow, D. H. (Ed.). (2014). *Clinical handbook of psychological disorders: A step-by-step treatment manual* (5th ed.). Guilford Press.

Bavon, A. (2001). The effect of the Tarrant County drug court project on recidivism. *Evaluation and Program Planning, 24*, 13–22.

Belenko, S. (2001). Research on drug courts: A critical review 2001 update. *National Drug Court Institute Review, 4*, 1–60.

Berman, G., & Feinblatt, J. (2001). Problem-solving courts: A brief primer. *Law and Policy, 23*, 125–140.

Brewster, M. P. (2001). An evaluation of the Chester County (PA) drug court program. *Journal of Drug Issues, 31*, 177–206.

Brown, R. T. (2010). Systematic review of the impact of adult drug-treatment courts. *Translational Research, 155*, 263–274.

Congress, E. P. (2000). What social workers should know about ethics: Understanding and resolving practice dilemmas. *Advances in Social Work, 1*, 1–22.

Dannerbeck, A., Harris, G., Sundet, P., & Lloyd, K. (2006). Understanding and responding to racial differences in drug court outcomes. *Journal of Ethnicity in Substance Abuse, 5*, 1–22.

Farrington, D., & Welsh, B. (2005). Randomized experiments in criminology: What have we learned in the last two decades? *Journal of Experimental Criminology, 1*, 9–38.

Gallagher, J. R. (2013a). African American participants' views on racial disparities in drug court outcomes. *Journal of Social Work Practice in the Addictions, 13*, 143–162.

Gallagher, J. R. (2013b). Drug court graduation rates: Implications for policy advocacy and future research. *Alcoholism Treatment Quarterly, 31*, 241–253.

Gallagher, J. R. (2014). Predicting criminal recidivism following drug court: Implications for drug court practice and policy advocacy. *Journal of Addictions and Offender Counseling, 35*, 15–29.

Gallagher, J. R. (2019). *Issue brief: Racial and ethnic disparities (RED) in treatment courts*. American University, Justice Programs Office, School of Public Affairs.

Gallagher, J. R., Ivory, E., Carlton, J., & Miller, J. W. (2014). The impact of an Indiana (United States) drug court on criminal recidivism. *Advances in Social Work, 15*, 507–521.

Gallagher, J. R, Marlowe, D. B., & Minasian, R. M. (2019). Participant perspectives on medication-assisted treatment for opioid use disorders in drug court. *Journal for Advancing Justice, 2*, 39–54.

Gallagher, J. R., & Nordberg, A. (2016). Comparing and contrasting white and African American participants' lived experiences in drug court. *Journal of Ethnicity in Criminal Justice, 14*, 100–119.

Gallagher, J. R., & Nordberg, A. (2017). A phenomenological and grounded theory study of women's experiences in drug court: Informing practice through a gendered lens. *Women & Criminal Justice, 27*, 327–340.

Gallagher, J. R., & Nordberg, A. (2018). African American participants' suggestions for eliminating racial disparities in graduation rates: Implications for drug court practice. *Journal for Advancing Justice, 1*, 89–107.

Gallagher, J. R., Nordberg, A., Deranek, M. S., & Minasian, R. M. (2019). Drug court through the lenses of African American women: Improving graduation rates with gender-responsive interventions. *Women & Criminal Justice, 29*, 323–337.

Gallagher, J. R., Nordberg, A., & Lefebvre, E. (2017). Improving graduation rates in drug court: A qualitative study of participants' lived experiences. *Criminology & Criminal Justice, 17*, 468–484.

Gallagher, J. R., Whitmore, T. D., Horsley, J., Marshall, B., Deranek, M., Callantine, S., & Woodward Miller, J. (2019). A perspective from the field: Five interventions to combat the opioid epidemic and ending the dichotomy of harm reduction versus abstinence-based programs. *Alcoholism Treatment Quarterly, 37*, 404–417.

Goldkamp, J. S. (1994). Treatment drug court for felony defendants: Some implications of assessment findings. *Prison Journal, 74*, 110–166.

Gordon, M. S., Kinlock, T. W., Schwartz, R. P., Fitzgerald, T. T., O'Grady, K. E., & Vocci, F. J. (2014). A randomized controlled trial of prison-initiated buprenorphine: Prison outcomes and community treatment entry. *Drug and Alcohol Dependence, 142*, 33–40.

Green, M., & Rempel, M. (2012). Beyond crime and drug use: Do adult courts produce other psychosocial benefits? *Journal of Drug Use, 42*, 156–177.

Kinlock, T. W., Gordon, M. S., Schwartz, R. P., Fitzgerald, T. T., & O'Grady, K. E. (2009). A randomized clinical trial of methadone maintenance for prisoners: Results at 12 months postrelease. *Journal of Substance Abuse Treatment, 37*, 277–285.

Lee, J. D., Friedmann, P. D., Kinlock, T. W., Nunes, E. V., Boney, T. Y., Hoskinson, R. A., Wilson, D., McDonald, R., Rotrosen, J., Gourevitch, M. N., Gordon, M., Fishman, M., Chen, D. T., Bonnie, R. J., Cornish, J. W., Murphy, S. M., & O'Brien, C. P. (2016). Extended-release naltrexone to prevent opioid relapse in criminal justice offenders. *New England Journal of Medicine, 374*, 1232–1242.

Lowenkamp, C. T., Holsinger, A. M., & Latessa, E. J. (2005). Are drug courts effective? A meta-analytic review. *Journal of Community Corrections, 15*, 5–28.

Magura, S., Lee, J. D., Hershberger, J., Joseph, H., Marsch, L., Shropshire, C., & Rosenblum, A. (2009). Buprenorphine and methadone maintenance in jail and post-release: A randomized clinical trial. *Drug and Alcohol Dependence, 99*, 222–230.

Marlowe, D. B. (2013). Achieving racial and ethnic fairness sin drug courts. *Court Review, 49*, 40–47.

Marlowe, D. B., Hardin, C. D., & Fox, C. L. (2016). *Painting the current picture: A national report on drug courts and other problem-solving court programs in the United States.* National Drug Court Institute.

Matusow, H., Dickman, S. L., Rich, J. D., Fong, C., Dumont, D. M., Hardin, C., . . . Rosenblum, A. (2013). Medication assisted treatment in US drug courts: Results from a nationwide survey of availability, barriers and attitudes. *Journal of Substance Abuse Treatment, 44*, 473–480.

Messina, N., Calhoun, S., & Warda, U. (2012). Gender-responsive drug court treatment: A randomized controlled trial. *Criminal Justice and Behavior, 39*, 1539–1558.

Miethe, T. D., Lu, H., & Reese, E. (2000). Reintegrative shaming and recidivism risks in drug court: Explanations for some unexpected findings. *Crime & Delinquency, 46*, 522–541.

Mitchell, O., Wilson, D. B., Eggers, A., & MacKenzie, D. L. (2012). Assessing the effectiveness of drug courts on recidivism: A meta-analytic review of traditional and non-traditional drug courts. *Journal of Criminal Justice, 40*, 60–71.

Narcotics Anonymous World Services. (2016). *Narcotics Anonymous and persons receiving medication-assisted treatment.*

National Association of Drug Court Professionals. (n.d.). *Equity and inclusion: Equivalent access assessment and toolkit.*

National Association of Drug Court Professionals. (2004). *Defining drug courts: The key components.* https://www.ncjrs.gov/pdffiles1/bja/205621.pdf

National Association of Social Workers. (2017). *Read the code of ethics.* https://www.socialworkers.org/About/Ethics/Code-of-Ethics/Code-of-Ethics-English

National Institute on Drug Abuse. (2018). *Comorbidity: Substance use disorders and other mental illnesses.* https://www.drugabuse.gov/sites/default/files/drugfacts-comorbidity.pdf

National Institute on Drug Abuse. (2020). *Substance use in women research report: Summary.* https://www.drugabuse.gov/publications/research-reports/substance-use-in-women

National Resource Center on Justice Involved Women. (2016). *Fact sheet on justice involved women in 2016.* http://cjinvolvedwomen.org/wp-content/uploads/2016/06/Fact-Sheet.pdf

Nolan, J. L. (2001). *Reinventing justice: The American drug court movement.* Princeton University Press.

Rempel, M., Green, M., & Kralstein, D. (2012). The impact of adult drug courts on crime and incarceration: Findings from a multi-site quasi-experimental design. *Journal of Experimental Criminology, 8,* 165–192.

Rempel, M., Zweig, J. M., Lindquist, C. H., Roman, J. K., Rossman, S. B., & Kralstein, D.(2012). Multi-site evaluation demonstrates effectiveness of adult drug courts. *Judicature, 95,* 154–157.

Roman, J. K., Yahner, J., & Zweig, J. (2020). How do drug courts work? *Journal of Experimental Criminology, 16,* 1–25.

Shaffer, D. K. (2011). Looking inside the black box of drug courts: A meta-analytic review. *Justice Quarterly, 28,* 493–521.

Substance Abuse and Mental Health Services Administration. (2020). *Medications for opioid use disorder.* Treatment Improvement Protocol (TIP) Series 63. Publication No. PEP20-02-01-006.

Tiger, R. (2011). Drug courts and the logic of coerced treatment. *Sociological Forum, 26,* 169–182.

U.S. Government Accountability Office. (2005). *Adult drug courts: Evidence indicates recidivism reductions and mixed results for other outcomes* [No. GAO-05-219].

Weisburd, D., Lum, C., & Petrosino, A. (2001). Does research design affect study outcomes in criminal justice? *Annals of the American Academy of Political and Social Science, 578,* 50–70.

Wexler, D. B. (2011). The relevance of therapeutic jurisprudence and its literature. *Federal Sentencing Reporter, 23,* 278–279.

Wexler, D. B., & Winick, B. J. (1996). *Law in a therapeutic key: Developments in therapeutic jurisprudence.* Carolina Academic Press.

Wilson, D. B., Mitchell, O., & MacKenzie, D. L. (2006). A systematic review of drug court effects on recidivism. *Journal of Experimental Criminology, 2,* 459–487.

Winick, B. J. (2003). Outpatient commitment: A therapeutic jurisprudence analysis. *Psychology, Public Policy, and Law, 5,* 795–799.

Winick, B. J., & Wexler, D. B. (Eds.). (2003). *Judging in a therapeutic key: Therapeutic jurisprudence and the courts.* Carolina Academic Press.

Wolfe, E., Guydish, J., & Termondt, J. (2002). A drug court outcome evaluation comparing arrests in a two year follow-up period. *Journal of Drug Issues, 32,* 1155–1171.

27

Veteran Court

Jessica D. Strong and Kathleen Ray

Veterans Treatment Courts

The wars in Iraq and Afghanistan propelled an influx of young veterans into civilian communities in the early 2000s. This cohort of veterans, due to their war-related experiences, were at a higher risk of service-related health disorders such as traumatic brain injury (TBI) and posttraumatic stress disorder (PTSD; Helmer et al., 2009). These veterans also struggled with multiple psychosocial concerns, including a lack of social support (Strong et al., 2014). High rates of substance use can also be found in post-9/11 veterans (Helmer et al., 2009; Seal et al., 2009), especially alcohol use (McDevitt-Murphy et al., 2010). Consequently, these veterans were at a higher risk of involvement with the judicial system. Veterans treatment courts (VTCs), which are specialty courts focused on rehabilitative treatment for veterans with service-related disabilities and modeled after other problem-solving courts, began surfacing in the United States in response.

It is not uncommon for veterans to be involved in the justice system, and there are approximately 181,500 of them in jails and prisons (Finlay et al., 2019). Furthermore, since over two-thirds of criminal offenders will recidivate within 3 years of their prison release, and over three-fourths will recidivate within 5 years of their prison release (Durose et al., 2014), these veterans may not desist from crime. While veterans are less likely to be incarcerated than nonveterans, the veterans who do become involved in the legal system are likely to have comorbid disorders impacting criminal behavior. Tsai et al.'s (2018) study found that 55% had an alcohol use disorder, 38% had a drug use disorder, 38% had PTSD, and 34% had a history of psychiatric hospitalization. Other specialty courts, such as drug courts, family courts, and juvenile justice courts, have been established to "problem-solve" social issues, and the number of VTCs following this model proliferated rapidly. The first designated court appeared in 2008 (Russell, 2009), and this number grew to over 450 by 2016 (Flatley et al., 2017). Early studies noted that this specialty court approach appeared

Jessica D. Strong and Kathleen Ray, *Veteran Court* In: *Handbook of Forensic Social Work*. Edited by: David Axlyn McLeod, Anthony P. Natale, and Kristin W. Mapson, Oxford University Press. © Oxford University Press 2024. DOI: 10.1093/oso/9780197694732.003.0027 promising in terms of both outcomes and cost savings. By 2012, over 7,700 veterans had participated in VTCs, with over two-thirds attending all of their regular court appearances and completing their treatment within an average of 15 to 18 months (McGuire et al., 2013). Jones (2014) reported that besides the cultural and health benefits from VTCs, there is a cost savings of between $4,000 and $12,000 per offender involved in a problem-solving court. There remains, however, significant variability in the implementation of these courts and outcomes, as well as in the potential ethical issues for social workers to consider.

History of the Movement

As noted, VTCs are specialty courts that are a composite of drug courts and mental health courts (Hartley, 2019). They were created in response to the many veterans returning from Operation Enduring Freedom and Operation Iraqi Freedom in the early 2000s who had become involved in the legal system (Frederick, 2014), reflecting an increased awareness of their reintegration difficulties (Baldwin, 2015). This cohort of veterans struggled with mental health, substance use, and other reintegration issues that put them at a higher risk of arrest and incarceration (Greenberg & Rosenheck, 2009). The first informal VTC was established in Anchorage, Alaska, in 2004 by Judge Sigurd Murphy and Judge Jack Smith (Hawkins, 2010). Judge Robert Russell established the first official VTC in Buffalo, New York, in 2008 (Edelman, 2016). The goal was to divert eligible veterans with substance use and/or mental health issues charged with felonies or misdemeanors from the traditional criminal court system to a specialized criminal court docket. Veterans were invited to participate in a program that connected them to health care professionals, mental health care professionals, veteran mentors, and court staff. As interest in VTCs grew, the Substance Abuse and Mental Health Services Administration issued 13 grants between 2008 and 2009 to develop VTCs in the United States using trauma-informed care, infrastructure, and sustainability (Slattery et al., 2013). The movement expanded from 24 VTCs in January 2010 to 168 by December 2012 and reached more than 300 by January 2014 (Johnson et al., 2016). To date, there are over 461 specialized VTCs or dockets in most states in the United States.

VTCs were modeled after the problem-solving court movement that began in the late 1980s. These specialty courts were developed to address the underlying problems that caused recidivism in chronic criminal offenders (Farole et al., 2005), beginning with a drug treatment court in Miami, Florida, in 1989 (Frederick, 2014). The goal was to prevent veterans from entering or reentering the legal system by providing them with care to treat issues relating to substance use, assuming that there would be fewer interactions with law enforcement if the substance use were treated. Due to the success of drug treatment courts, other types of problem-solving courts were created, including teen courts, child abuse courts, mental health courts, homeless courts, and domestic violence courts (Becker & Corrigan, 2002). The goal of all problem-solving courts is to treat the underlying problems, target the psychological and behavioral causes, provide treatment, and reduce recidivism and incarceration rates (Wexler & Winick, 2008).

Subpopulations

During the height of the conflicts in Iraq and Afghanistan, service members faced longer, extended, and multiple deployments and often had shorter breaks in between deployments (Tanielian et al., 2008), putting them at an increased risk of psychological and physical injury. Additionally, the Reserves and National Guard had been deployed more frequently. Personnel in these components of the U.S. military must transition from civilian to military life and then back to civilian life without the benefit of many of the resources available to active-duty families who live on or near military installations. This limited support may also place these service members at a higher risk of engaging in antisocial and criminal behavior.

While recent research has demonstrated a link between military service and criminal activity (Snowden et al., 2017), there are variances among subsets of the population. Snowden and colleagues (2017) have suggested that the greater prevalence of criminal behavior may be attributed to a subset of veterans who "did not fit in with the military culture and were discharged from the military early in their careers" (p. 605). People who have chosen the military as a career have fewer interactions with the legal system. More extended military service was associated with fewer lifetime arrests among incarcerated veterans (Brooke & Gau, 2018). Additionally, within the military structure, officers have lower odds of being imprisoned or of violent offending than enlisted troops (Black et al., 2005). There appear to be protective factors within the military against interaction with the legal system. Still, scant research is done on the links between certain aspects of military service and involvement in the criminal justice system (Finlay et al., 2019).

The VTCs were created and expanded to meet the unique needs of post-9/11 veterans, meaning those who served after September 2001. Today, there are 4.2 million post-9/11 veterans (U.S. Department of Veterans Affairs, 2018), and this population will continue to grow as the conflicts in Iraq, Afghanistan, and other parts of the world continue. This population is younger and more diverse than previous generations of veterans: About 17% are women, 15.3% are Black, and 12.1% are Hispanic. They also have the highest percentage of any wartime cohort with a service-connected disability at 36.1% (United States Census Bureau, 2018).

These service-connected disabilities often take the form of TBI and PTSD, which are the signature injuries of post-9/11 veterans (Tanielian et al., 2008). TBI is defined as damage to the brain from an external force. TBI is often caused by exposure to an improvised explosive device and can cause dizziness, headache, vision problems, and long-term cognitive impairment (Tanielian et al., 2008). Between 2000 and 2019, 414,000 U.S. service members were diagnosed with TBI, with the majority having mild TBI (DVBIC, 2019). Veterans diagnosed with TBI have difficulty reintegrating into civilian life postdeployment (Sayer et al., 2010) and often struggle with civilian social norms (Libin et al., 2017).

PTSD diagnosis rates have been higher in post-9/11 veterans than in previous cohorts of veterans (Fulton et al., 2015), and this places them at a higher risk of violence and criminal involvement (Donley et al., 2012; MacManus et al., 2015; Trevillion et al., 2015). PTSD is a psychological disorder resulting from exposure to trauma and can result in flashbacks, hypervigilance, and nightmares. It is important to note that it is not military service itself but rather the exposure to trauma and subsequent development of PTSD while serving in the military that increases veterans' rates of criminal behavior (Holbrook & Anderson, 2011). Complicating the diagnosis and treatment of these injuries, there is an overlap of symptoms experienced by both diagnoses of TBI and PTSD, such as fatigue, insomnia, depression, anxiety, and irritability (Stein & McAllister, 2009). This may lead to incorrect diagnoses and treatment, thereby increasing the risk of veteran involvement in the criminal justice system.

Substance misuse, however, may be the strongest predictor of veteran involvement in the legal system (S. K. Erickson et al., 2008). Alcohol use and cocaine use, for example, are linked to higher risks of physical aggression and increased rates of violent offenses (Valdez et al., 2007). These risk factors may also be interrelated as there is substantial comorbidity between PTSD and substance use disorders (McCauley et al., 2012). This comorbidity leads to chronic problems, including higher rates of involvement in the legal system (Borsari et al., 2014).

In addition to a greater prevalence of risk factors, such as TBI, PTSD, and substance misuse, veterans may benefit from fewer protective factors to encourage prosocial behavior. Eakman (2015) found that post-9/11 veterans with service-connected injuries in postsecondary education reported lower levels of protective factors—such as social support, meaningful occupation, and academic self-efficacy—and higher levels of health-related vulnerability factors, such as mild TBI, PTSD, depression, and somatic symptoms. Drawing a line between the increased risks and lower protective factors that can result in criminal behavior situated crime as a consequence of war and provided the initial justification for creating VTCs.

Theoretical Underpinnings

VTCs were established based on four assumptions, as described by Baldwin and Brooke (2019). The first assumption for this approach aimed to honor veterans for carrying the burden of the consequences of war; VTCs were founded on the premise that certain veterans' criminal behavior is a response to the physical or psychological trauma they acquired during their military service (Cavanaugh, 2011). These include the two most commonly diagnosed disorders for incoming VTC veterans: substance use disorder and PTSD (Tsai et al., 2018). These two issues are connected; veterans coping with the symptoms of PTSD may turn to drugs or alcohol to numb their symptoms or engage in risky—and potentially illegal—behavior to compensate for their numbed emotions (Cavanaugh, 2011).

However, the literature has not fully substantiated this connection between military service and criminal behavior due to the inherent selection bias of military service. Not all citizens are eligible for military service, and since the implementation of the all-volunteer force, citizens must elect to join military service. While some connections have been found between military service and criminal behavior in Vietnam veterans, these connections are indirect and moderated by other factors such as substance abuse and mental health disorders (Baldwin & Brooke, 2019; Wright et al., 2005).

VTCs were derived from the therapeutic jurisprudence movement based on the concept that courts should enhance the well-being of defendants (Rowen, 2020; Wexler & Winick, 2008), which is similar to the aims of other specialty courts such as mental health and substance abuse courts. Baldwin and Brooke (2019) asserted that the second assumption underlying the creation of VTCs is that traditional courts, and even other specialty courts (such as mental health and substance abuse courts), are unable to address the military experience that is the primary issue at hand. Baldwin and Brooke (2019) also argued that the inadequacy of traditional courts to meet veterans' needs is linked to the third and fourth assumptions: Veterans are a class of people (the third assumption) that is deserving of specialized attention due to their sacrifice and service (the fourth assumption). Indeed, in his justification for creating the VTC approach, Judge Russell (2009) indicated that veterans are a unique population, which calls for tailored care. VTCs represent the justice system's recognition of the unique contributions of military culture and the mental health consequences of engaging in military service. Social workers practicing with military-affiliated populations have long recognized the unique culture of this population (Council on Social Work Education, 2015). Indeed, the military has also highlighted the need for the military justice system to acknowledge how mental health contributes to veterans' misbehavior (Office of the Chief of Public Affairs, 2012).

Structure and Key Components

In his creation of the first official VTC, Judge Russell adapted the following 10 key components from previously established mental health courts (Frederick, 2014):

1. Courts should integrate mental health and substance abuse services.
2. Prosecution and defense should work together to support the veteran's rehabilitation.
3. VTCs should identify and enroll potential beneficiaries as soon as possible.
4. VTCs should also incorporate medical care, education, job training, and counseling as necessary.
5. Sobriety should be monitored via testing throughout program participation.
6. VTCs should reward cooperation and punish noncompliance.
7. Judges should engage with each veteran.
8. VTCs should monitor progress by evaluating established goals regularly.
9. VTC staff should participate in continuing education.
10. VTCs should partner with a variety of community organizations, including government agencies and treatment providers, to foster community-wide participation.

All VTCs require veterans to participate in the program voluntarily. Those who choose not to or do not complete the requirements are returned to the traditional court system (Frederick, 2014). Most courts mandate veteran participation in various components of the program offered, including making regular court appearances, attending treatment sessions, undergoing drug and alcohol testing, and, most importantly, being matched with a volunteer mentor, generally another veteran. This mentor fills various roles but is an essential component of VTCs (Frederick, 2014), building on the concept that veterans will relate best to other veterans with whom they have shared life experiences (Russell, 2009). Several scholars have noted that mentorship is a critical component—the lynchpin—in demonstrating an understanding and appreciation of military culture (Baldwin, 2015; Douds & Ahlin, 2020; Douds et al., 2017; Rowen, 2020).

VTC Participant Characteristics

Tsai et al. (2018) performed a study of over 7,000 VTC-involved veterans and examined the factors associated with an increased risk of recidivism, including alcohol and drug use problems, parole/probation violations, property offenses, and a history of previous incarceration. They found that most VTC participants are White, male, and over 40, with at least a high school education and an income of over $1,000 per month. This is, by many accounts, a privileged group, though not all utilized the veterans benefits available to them. While many were eligible, less than half of the participants received any financial benefits at VTC entry. A similar number were in their own housing or had been employed in the past 2 years.

Efficacy

First, it is crucial to define the outcomes that are targeted for improvement in VTC programs. While the focus, understandably, has been on preventing additional justice system involvement for the veterans, other outcomes are essential for the long-term stability of the veteran. In his initial writings on VTCs, Russell (2009) noted improvements in family relationships, employment, or volunteering. Others have pointed out other positive psychosocial outcomes. Tsai and colleagues (2018) reported greater improvements in housing and employment outcomes and receipt of Veteran Administration (VA) benefits for VTC participants than for other justice-involved veterans, but this was paired with an increased rate of new incarceration. Smelson and colleagues (2015) noted significant improvements in mental health and substance use symptoms and enrollment and use of mental health, physical health, and substance use services as outcomes. Knudsen and Wingenfeld (2016) found significant improvement in PTSD, depression, substance abuse, overall functioning, emotional well-being, relationships with others, recovery status, social connectedness, family functioning, and sleep. VTC programs can improve various outcome variables, including housing, employment, economic security, mental health, and overall functioning, and each of these factors protects against participating in the judicial system.

When focusing strictly on recidivism, rates vary widely, ranging from 2.5% to 56% (McCall et al., 2018). The first report on recidivism was very positive; the original VTC in Buffalo reported a 0% recidivism rate for program graduates (Russell, 2009), though only 14 of the 130 program participants had graduated (Hawkins, 2010). A more recent national survey found that only 2% recidivated (Baldwin, 2013). Reduced recidivism is associated with "graduation" from the VTC program and is less likely for those who drop out (Hartley & Baldwin, 2016; Knudsen & Wingenfeld, 2016; Slattery et al., 2013; J. Smith, 2012). Another study has found increased recidivism among program participants (Tsai et al., 2017), though this study did not account for program graduation. The common theme across these studies is that those who graduate from a VTC program are less likely to reoffend than their noncompleter counterparts.

While VTCs across the country employ a similar framework, variability in both the administration of the programs (Cartwright, 2011; Douds et al., 2017; J. W. Erickson, 2016; Tsai et al., 2018) and the evaluation studies remain a significant challenge in determining their efficacy. Differing eligibility criteria, sampling, comparison groups, and definitions of recidivism all influence whether the program can be deemed a success or failure (McCall et al., 2018).

In terms of eligibility criteria alone, there is considerable variability, including the category and violence of the referring offenses, the combat exposure status of the veteran (McCormick-Goodhart, 2013), and the relationship between the referring offense and the veteran's substance abuse and/or mental health issues (Cartwright, 2011). The majority (66%) of VTCs will accept veterans with either misdemeanor or felony charges, while 20% restrict eligibility to misdemeanors only, and another 14% limit eligibility to felonies only (Flatley et al., 2017). Other factors, such as whether the crime was violent, serve as both inclusion and exclusion criteria in different VTCs. Because of these differences in sampling, it is difficult to compare outcomes across different VTCs. J. W. Erickson (2016) noted that district attorneys served as gatekeepers in each of the VTCs studied, limiting the participants and study sample. Further, some participants were required to plead guilty and participate in a lengthy VTC program that was much longer than typical jail sentences for the types of offenses under review, thereby disincentivizing their participation in the program.

Additional variability in program structure and completion rates also complicates assessing recidivism. Flatley and colleagues (2017) have reported that there are more than 461 VTCs across the country. While the VTCs all follow the same essential procedure, they vary considerably in their eligibility criteria, operations, and placement (Jones, 2014; McCall et al., 2018; J. Smith, 2012). It is difficult to assess their success without consistent program element, placement, eligibility, and recidivism definitions. In J. Smith's (2012) original study of the Anchorage VTC program, 133 veterans were eligible for the program, 74 opted in, but only 38 graduated (50% dropout rate). J. W. Erickson (2016) found that the three VTCs studied reported reduced recidivism. This was among graduates of the program only and did not account for program dropouts, which were the majority of participants.

Studies themselves also vary. Some studies have compared the recidivism rates of VTC participants against a state average (J. Smith, 2012); others have looked at VTC program graduates and compared with participants terminated from the program (Hartley & Baldwin, 2016). Some have defined recidivism as rearrest (Smith, 2012); others have included jail sanctions (Tsai et al., 2017). Because participation in VTCs is voluntary, a true control group cannot be created, so it is impossible to determine the true efficacy of involvement in the program. Baldwin (2015, 2017) urged consideration of program implementation and participant groups in determining program efficacy; variation in program implementation may limit the generalizability of the VTC program. Additional criticism of VTCs is based on their ability to restrict program participation to low-risk offenders, so-called "creaming" (Baldwin, 2015, 2017; Baldwin & Brooke, 2019). This limits the validity of studies in measuring their efficacy since it is difficult to determine if the low-risk offenders were less likely to experience recidivism even without participating in a VTC program.

Ethical Concerns

Baldwin and Brooke (2019) have reported several potentially discriminatory components of VTC programs. VTC program participants often access expedited services. While those services (such as VA services) are available to veterans not enrolled in VTCs, their exped-ited access to services may be seen as discriminatory to veterans in need of VA services but who are not justice involved. Further, specialized courts based on employment status (such as VTCs) are not available for other careers, even those equally dangerous and/or based on public service (e.g., first responders).

Furthermore, Cartwright (2011) noted uneven access to VTCs for veterans across the country; many veterans who may benefit from such programs live outside the catchment area. Early data on the efficacy of VTCs reported that most veterans (79%) treated were between 41 and 60 years of age, which is not representative of the veteran population as a whole or the cohort of post-9/11 veterans for which VTCs were created to serve. Most courts also restrict eligibility to veterans with honorable discharges (Frederick, 2014) be-cause this aligns with both the assumption that veterans deserve special treatment due to their honorable service and their eligibility for VA services. However, this excludes veterans without an honorable discharge, although the cause of their discharge status may also be related to their substance abuse or mental health diagnoses. A veteran with a less than hon-orable discharge status due to a substance abuse problem would also be ineligible for VTCs.

Limitations and Strengths of VTCs

A common criticism of VTCs is their secondary path to justice based solely on veteran status. While other specialty courts, such as juvenile justice courts or drug courts, have di-verted offenders from traditional court systems, these diversions have been based on age or diagnosable mental health conditions (Jones, 2014). Some have criticized VTCs for offering a "free pass based on military status to certain criminal defense rights that others don't have" (Wilson et al., 2011) or argued that they prioritize veteran rehabilitation over retribu-tive justice for victims (Holbrook & Anderson, 2011). Mark Silverstein, an American Civil Liberties Union (ACLU) representative who opposes VTCs, has noted that the criminal justice system should consider PTSD resulting from combat experiences but cannot regu-larly consider PTSD resulting from other life circumstances, such as abuse or interpersonal violence (Wilson et al., 2011). Many veteran offenders have not served in combat positions but may have a diagnosis of PTSD (Frederick, 2014). Civilians can also experience PTSD but receive no such consideration.

Other limitations include access to VTCs in terms of both location (as most VTCs are located in urban areas; Cartwright, 2011) and eligibility (e.g., only accepting veterans with honorable discharges; Frederick, 2014). As stated, the majority of participants are White, male, and over 40, with at least a high school education and an income of over $1,000 per month (Tsai et al., 2018). This would preclude many in the increasingly diverse veteran population from benefiting from this option. The final limitation of VTCs is based on outcome data. There are few standardized measures, recidivism rates are inconsistent (McCall et al., 2018), and the operation of each program is varied (Jones, 2014; McCall et al., 2018; J. Smith, 2012).

Despite disparate access and limited outcome data, the benefits of VTCs may outweigh the limitations (Frederick, 2014). VTC programs can improve various outcome variables, including housing, employment, economic security, mental health, and overall functioning. There also appear to be financial savings for the legal system. To increase the benefits of VTCs, Holbrook and Anderson (2011) have suggested creating consistency across the different treatment courts by employing the following best practices:

- An integrated stakeholder team committed to veterans' rehabilitative interests should be created.
- Prosecutors should play an active role in determining participant eligibility.
- There should be a willingness to maximize the types of offenses that can be heard in VTCs.
- A reliable network should be used to identify participants early in the criminal justice process.
- Tailored and flexible treatment plans and disposition decisions should be implemented.

Social Workers' Role

Social workers are uniquely qualified to play a critical role in VTCs through practice, policy, education, and research. Social workers can connect with veterans and intervene at each point in the VTC process. The VA is the largest employer of social workers, including over 15,000 of them (U.S. Department of Veterans Affairs, 2021). Therefore, the social work profession interacts with veterans while they receive medical care as well as benefits. Since VTCs are voluntary and often only veterans who qualify for VA benefits are eligible to use them, social workers can steer veterans toward this service through their interactions at the VA. The goal of VTCs is to address the underlying issues that have contributed to veterans' interactions with the judicial system, and this goal dovetails with social work practice frameworks. Through their understanding of ecological systems, social workers are trained to understand and support the intersection between veterans and their environment with a strengths-based approach to recovery.

When a veteran is accepted into the program, they are given intensive, community-based treatment; rehabilitative services; and supervision through an interdisciplinary team including a judge, probation officer, caseworker, court administrator, peer mentor, treatment provider, and veterans service representative (Canada & Albright, 2014). Social workers often serve as veteran justice outreach specialists who develop treatment plans with the other VTC members and liaise with the VA. The treatment plan is comprehensive and can include services including mental health, substance use treatment, employment, housing, and peer mentoring (Stiner, 2012). Social workers are well suited to this role because of their strengths-based and ecological approaches, viewing clients at micro, mezzo, and macro levels. This comprehensive approach can help courts better meet the needs of veterans within the court at each point in the continuum of the criminal justice system (Canada & Albright, 2014).

Social workers also have an obligation to advocate at a macro level for more equitable access to programs like VTCs that provide a rehabilitative, community-based approach to justice. This includes increasing the diversity of participants in VTC programs to ensure they represent the growing diversity of the military and are accessible in both urban and rural settings. As the military and veteran population continues to diversify, particularly in post-9/11 veterans, VTC participants should not be limited to predominantly White, non-Hispanic, educated men over 40 with an income. Social workers also have the professional obligation to operate with cultural competency, including military cultural competency, and to bring that cultural awareness to their practice with justice-involved veterans, as indicated by the guidelines for social work practice with veterans and military families (Council on Social Work Education, 2015).

The research on VTCs is inconsistent regarding the effectiveness of VTC interventions (Canada & Albright, 2014) and whether individual factors impact successful completion of treatment. However, social workers have the ability to add to the research on VTCs in multiple ways. Using the systems perspective predominant in social work, interdisciplinary research placing justice-involved veterans in the context of their embedded multiple systems could create new interventions and prevention strategies. Social workers view veterans as both a homogeneous and diverse group, and this perspective could help understand the success of interventions for specific groups within the veteran community. Examining the variation among veterans could lead to better treatment.

Finally, few validated instruments and studies have examined veterans' individual factors and the system factors that may contribute to or undermine the effectiveness of VTCs. This is an area where social work should contribute as it applies an ecological systems perspective.

Social workers have a professional obligation to advance social justice and therefore find it necessary to be sensitive to programs that advantage or disadvantage particular groups. The justice system demonstrates consistent biases in favor of White male defendants at each point in the justice process, from investigation to arrest to conviction and sentencing (R. Smith et al., 2015). Given that most VTC participants are already privileged, the alternative path to justice that the VTC provides is vulnerable to systemic inequalities. Social workers involved with VTCs and the criminal justice system should ensure equitable access and guard against reinforcing privilege. As advocates of social justice, VTC or criminal justice social workers' primary goal should be to enhance equitable access to care and rehabilitation, requiring frequent surveillance and, more importantly, action and advocacy to address inequities.

Conclusion

The evidence base for problem-solving courts, including VTCs, as a whole remains mixed due to persistent methodological problems. Some evidence has shown that other problem-solving courts, like juvenile drug courts, are no more effective than traditional courts in reducing recidivism and drug use but pose no evidence of harm (Tanner-Smith et al., 2016). Other meta-analyses have cautioned against interpreting the programs as successful in preventing recidivism over the long term (Bergseth & Bouffard, 2007). In another meta-analysis of problem-solving courts, Kaiser and Rhodes (2019) found that specialized problem-solving courts, including VTCs, relied on the original court model despite offering specialized services, staff, and procedures. The courts differed in whether felony offenders could participate, if charges were dismissed after completion, and if there was a postadjudication entry. They stated that veteran courts and adult mental health courts were less likely to have an operations manual. Methodological problems arise as the evaluations of problem-solving courts are of poor quality, with very few random assignments, substantial baseline differences, and no measured participant characteristics or drug court features. These challenges limit the conclusions that can be drawn about the efficacy of VTCs in reducing recidivism in particular.

Outside of the methodological concerns in evaluating outcomes, VTCs can be ethically controversial for social workers. On the one hand, they are drawn from therapeutic jurisprudence, which attempts to enhance defendants' well-being to reduce recidivism. This concept aligns with social work's values of service and the dignity and worth of the person. Their focus is on assessing veterans' needs and connecting them with services to meet those needs, which is a critical component of social work. VTCs may be better positioned to serve veterans in the criminal justice system due to the impact of combat, PTSD, or TBI. Still, they can also perpetuate the stereotype of the "traumatized veteran." Additionally, a central criticism of VTCs is the clear advantage that this secondary path to justice provides for veterans, a group that already enjoys many privileges. The majority of veteran participants are male, are White, and have a high school education, some income, and theoretical (if not tangible) access to benefits, including health care, mental health and substance abuse treatment, and financial assistance that is not available to nonveterans (Tsai et al., 2018). It can be argued that this group is already significantly advantaged in the criminal justice system and providing them with further privilege contradicts social workers' obligation to uphold equal rights, protection, opportunity, and social benefits for all.

As the number of VTCs increases, there remains unequal access to the benefits offered by these courts, both for veterans who do not live near a VTC, such as those in rural or remote areas, and for those who are "screened out" before they have the option of utilizing a VTC. The additional challenges in assessing the efficacy and ethical problems associated with VTCs raise concerns about social workers' endorsement of VTCs. These alternative courts have certainly provided benefits for the psychosocial well-being of many veterans. However, the degree to which they lead to tangible, long-term changes and contribute to social work's goal of social justice remains to be seen.

Case Study

Casey is a 45-year-old Army veteran of the Iraq and Afghanistan conflicts. He enlisted in the Army at age 17 and retired at age 39 after working for his entire career as an infantryman, including four deployments to Iraq and Afghanistan. He has a wife, Angie (34 years old), who is estranged from him and lives separately with her two daughters. Her older child from a prior relationship, Kim, is 12 and is deeply distrustful of Casey. Casey and Angie's daughter, Stacie, is 2 and has shown some signs of autism, including irregular posture and gait, limited speech, and poor eye contact. Angie has sought treatment for Stacie, but Casey believes Angie is overreacting and "there's nothing wrong." Having become a father later in his life, Casey takes great joy in spending time with Stacie, and being away from her has been difficult. Angie asked Casey to leave home 7 months ago after Kim told her that Casey had been drinking before driving with the girls in the car.

The transition to postmilitary life has been difficult for Casey, and he has been sporadically employed. He began attending college using his GI Bill benefits to study computer engineering last year but found it challenging to fit in with traditional college students in his classes, so he stopped attending. While in school, he began staying up later to study after the girls went to bed, and he paired caffeinated drinks like Red Bull with alcohol to calm his nerves after a long day with a toddler. This led to him staying up all night, napping during the day, and drinking caffeinated drinks mixed with alcohol for much of the day.

Casey had a difficult childhood and was raised in a physically abusive home. His mother had planned to leave the relationship once her older child had graduated from high school, but she unexpectedly became pregnant with Casey shortly before her daughter's graduation. As a child, Casey displayed symptoms of attention-deficit/hyperactivity disorder. However, his father thought he was "just wild" and addressed Casey's difficulties with physical punishment, including whipping him frequently. These early experiences led Casey to join the military at age 17. He lost several close friends in Afghanistan during his military service and experienced several improvised explosive device bombings on caravans while in Iraq.

Five months ago, Casey was arrested for assault with a deadly weapon. He was on his way to pick up Stacie to take her to a therapy appointment Angie had arranged. He had been drinking for most of the day, but when Angie called with a last-minute request to take Stacie to her appointment, Casey agreed. On the way to Angie's home, Casey encountered unexpected road construction that slowed traffic. Already anxious about being late for Stacie's appointment and triggered by construction sandbags on the side of the road that reminded him of his experiences with improvised explosive device detonations, Casey grew increasingly agitated. As traffic slowed further, a car next to him stopped with the windows open, playing loud rap music. When the track featured sounds of gunshots, Casey grabbed his firearm from the glovebox and jumped out of his vehicle, brandishing the handgun and threatening the driver and passengers of the other vehicle. The police were called, and no one was hurt, but this incident referred Casey to justice.

The presiding judge for the case recommended that Casey participate in a VTC due to his likely (but as-yet-undiagnosed) mental health condition and substance abuse problem, and Casey opted in. Casey was paired with a veteran mentor and a VTC team that connected him with services. Casey was enrolled at the VA and diagnosed with PTSD and alcohol use disorder. He began weekly therapy sessions at the VA to treat his PTSD with prolonged exposure therapy and antidepressant medication. He also began substance abuse treatment through a veteran-specific Alcoholics Anonymous group. The VTC also requires him to make frequent court appearances and have regular and random drug/alcohol testing, and his mentor contacts him every other day to check in. The requirements are rigorous, but Casey seems to be thriving with the structure and camaraderie provided by the VTC. He has failed one random drug test, which has delayed his progress. However, he still makes his court appearances, attends Alcoholics Anonymous meetings and therapy sessions, and is working toward having unsupervised visitation with Stacie.

References

Baldwin, J. (2013). Executive summary: National survey of veterans treatment courts. Available at SSRN 2274138.

Baldwin, J. M. (2015). Investigating the programmatic attack: A national survey of veterans treatment courts. *Journal of Criminal Law and Criminology*, *105*(4) 705–752. https://scholarlycommons.law.north western.edu/jclc/vol105/iss3/4

Baldwin, J. M. (2017). Whom do they serve? A national examination of veterans treatment court participants and their challenges. *Criminal Justice Policy Review*, *28*(6), 515–554. https://doi.org/10.1177/08874 03415606184

Baldwin, J. M., & Brooke, E. J. (2019). Pausing in the wake of rapid adoption: A call to critically examine the veterans treatment court concept. *Journal of Offender Rehabilitation*, *58*(1), 1–29. https://doi.org/ 10.1080/10509674.2018.1549181

Becker, D. J., & Corrigan, M. (2002). Moving problem-solving courts into the mainstream: A report card from the CCJ-COSCA problem-solving courts committee. *Court Review: The Journal of the American Judges Association*, *39*(1), 4–7. https://digitalcommons.unl.edu/ajacourtreview/151/

Bergseth, K. J., & Bouffard, J. A. (2007). The long-term impact of restorative justice programming for juvenile offenders. *Journal of Criminal Justice*, *35*(4), 433–451. https://doi.org/10.1016/j.jcrimjus.2007.05.006

Black, D. W., Carney, C. P., Peloso, P. M., Woolson, R. F., Letuchy, E., & Doebbeling, B. N. (2005). Incarceration and veterans of the first Gulf War. *Military Medicine*, *170*(7), 612–618. https://doi.org/ 10.7205/milmed.170.7.612

Borsari, B., Conrad, S., Mastroleo, N. R., & Tolou-Shams, M. (2014). PTSD, substance use, and veterans' involvement in the legal system: Veterans treatment courts. In P. Ouimette & J. Read (Eds.), *Trauma and substance abuse: Causes, consequences, and treatment of comorbid disorders* (2nd ed., pp. 191–209). American Psychological Association. https://doi.org/10.1037/14273-010

Brooke, E. J., & Gau, J. M. (2018). Military service and lifetime arrests: Examining the effects of the total military experience on arrests in a sample of prison inmates. *Criminal Justice Policy Review*, *29*(1), 24–44. https://doi.org/10.1177/0887403415619007

Canada, K. E., & Albright, D. L. (2014). Veterans in the criminal justice system and the role of social work. *Journal of Forensic Social Work*, *4*(1), 48–62. https://doi.org/10.1080/1936928x.2013.871617

Cartwright, T. (2011). "To care for him who shall have borne the battle": The recent development of veterans treatment courts in America. *Stanford Law and Policy Review*, *22*(295), 295–316.

Cavanaugh, J. M. (2011). Helping those who serve: Veteran treatment courts foster rehabilitation and reduce recidivism for offending combat veterans. *New England Law Review*, *45*(2), 463–465.

Council on Social Work Education. (2015). *2015 EPAS curricular guide resource series: Specialized practice curricular guide for military social work*. https://cswe.org/Education-Resources/2015-Curricular-Guides/ Military-Social-Work/MilitarySW2018.aspx

Donley, M., Habib, L., Jovanovic, T., Kamkwalala, M., Evces, M., Egan, G., Bradley, B., & Ressler, K. (2012). Civilian PTSD symptoms and risk for involvement in the criminal justice system. *Journal of the American Academy of Psychiatry and the Law, 40*(4), 522–529. https://www.ncbi.nlm.nih.gov/pmc/articles/PMC 3752299/pdf/nihms497730.pdf

Douds, A. S., & Ahlin, E. M. (2020). *Veterans treatment court movement: Striving to serve those who served.* Routledge.

Douds, A. S., Ahlin, E. M., Howard, D., & Stigerwalt, S. (2017). Varieties of veterans' courts: A statewide assessment of veterans' treatment court components. *Criminal Justice Policy Review, 28*(8), 740–769. https://doi.org/10.1177/0887403415620633

Durose, M., Cooper, A., Snyder, H., & Cooper, A. D. (2014). *BJS special report: Recidivism of prisoners released in 30 states in 2005: Patterns from 2005 to 2010.* https://bjs.gov/content/pub/pdf/rprts05p0510.pdf

Eakman, A. M. (2015). Resilience protective and vulnerability factors in post-9/11 veterans with service-related trauma in postsecondary education. *American Journal of Occupational Therapy, 69*(Suppl 1), 1111–1113. https://doi.org/10.5014/ajot.2015.69s1-po2114

Edelman, B. (2016). *Veterans treatment courts: A second chance for vets who have lost their way.* National Institute of Corrections.

Erickson, J. W. (2016). Veterans treatment courts: A case study of their efficacy for veterans' needs. *International Journal of Law and Psychiatry, 49*(B), 221–225. https://doi.org/10.1016/j.ijlp.2016.10.009

Erickson, S. K., Rosenheck, R. A., Trestman, R. L., Ford, J. D., & Desai, R. A. (2008). Risk of incarceration between cohorts of veterans with and without mental illness discharged from inpatient units. *Psychiatric Services, 59*(2), 178–183. https://doi.org/10.1176/ps.2008.59.2.178

Farole, D. J., Puffett, N., Rempel, M., & Byrne, F. (2005). Applying problem-solving principles in mainstream courts: Lessons for state courts. *Justice System Journal, 26*(1), 57–75. https://doi.org/10.1080/0098261X.2005.10767738

Finlay, A. K., Owens, M. D., Taylor, E., Nash, A., Capdarest-Arest, N., Rosenthal, J., Blue-Howells, J., Clark, S., & Timko, C. (2019). A scoping review of military veterans involved in the criminal justice system and their health and healthcare. *Health & Justice, 7*(1), 1–18. https://doi.org/10.1186/s40352-019-0086-9

Flatley, B., Clark, S., Rosentah, J., & Blue-Howells, J. (2017). *Veterans court inventory 2016 update: Characteristics of and VA involvement in veterans treatment courts and other veteran-focused court programs from the veterans justice outreach specialist perspective.* Retrieved from Washington, DC.

Frederick, A. (2014). Veterans treatment courts: Analysis and recommendations. *Law and Psychology Review, 38*(2013/2014), 211–230.

Fulton, J., Calhoun, P. S., Wagner, H. R., Schray, A., Hair, L. P., Feeling, N., Elbogen, E., & Beckham, J. C. (2015). The prevalence of posttraumatic stress disorder in Operation Enduring Freedom/Operation Iraqi Freedom (OIF/OIF) veterans: A meta-analysis. *Journal of Anxiety Disorders, 31*, 98–107. https://doi.org/10.1016/j.janxdis.2015.02.003

Greenberg, G. A., & Rosenheck, R. A. (2009). Mental health and other risk factors for jail incarceration among male veterans. *Psychiatric Quarterly, 80*, 41–53.

Hartley, R. D., & Baldwin, J. M. (2016). Waging war on recidivism among justice-involved veterans: An impact evaluation of a large urban veterans treatment court. *Criminal Justice Policy Review, 30*(1), 52–78. https://doi.org/10.1177/0887403416650490

Hawkins, M. D. (2010). *Coming home: Accommodating the special needs of military veterans to the criminal justice system.* http://www.ncdsv.org/images/OSJCL_Coming-Home-Accommodating-the-Special-Needs-of-Military-Veterans-to-the-CJS_2010.pdf

Helmer, D. A., Chandler, H. K., Quigley, K. S., Blatt, M., Teichman, R., & Lange, G. (2009). Chronic widespread pain, mental health, and physical role function in OEF/OIF veterans. *Pain Medicine, 10*(7), 1174–1182. https://doi.org/10.1111/j.1526-4637.2009.00723.x

Holbrook, J. G., & Anderson, S. (2011). *Veterans courts: Early outcomes and key indicators for success* (Widener Law School Legal Studies Research Paper No. 11-25). Widener Law School. Retrieved on August 8, 2021, from https://papers.ssrn.com/sol3/papers.cfm?abstract_id=1912655#.

Johnson, R. S., Stolar, A. G., McGuire, J. F., Clark, S., Coonan, L. A., Hausknecht, P., & Graham, D. P. (2016). US veterans' court programs: An inventory and analysis of national survey data. *Community Mental Health Journal, 52*, 180–186. https://doi.org/10.1007/s10597-015-9972-3

Jones, A. E. (2014). Veterans treatment courts: Do status-based problem-solving courts create an improper privileged class of criminal defendants? *Washington University Journal of Law and Policy*, *43*, 307–331.

Kaiser, K. A., & Rhodes, K. (2019). A drug court by any other name? An analysis of problem-solving court programs. *Law and Human Behavior*, *43*(3), 278–289. https://doi.org/10.1037/lhb0000325

Knudsen, K. J., & Wingenfeld, S. (2016). A specialized treatment court for veterans with trauma exposure: Implications for the field. *Community Mental Health Journal*, *52*(2), 127–135. https://doi.org/10.1007/s10597-015-9845-9

Libin, A. V., Schladen, M. M., Danford, E., Cichon, S., Bruner, D., Scholten, J., Llorente, M., Zapata, S., Dromerick, A. W., Blackman, M. R., & Magruder, K. M. (2017). Perspectives of veterans with mild traumatic brain injury on community reintegration: Making sense of unplanned separation from service. *American Journal of Orthopsychiatry*, *87*(2), 129–138. https://doi.org/10.1037/ort0000253

MacManus, D., Rona, R., Dickson, H., Somaini, G., Fear, N., & Wessely, S. (2015). Aggressive and violent behavior among military personnel deployed to Iraq and Afghanistan: Prevalence and link with deployment and combat exposure. *Epidemiologic Reviews*, *37*(1), 196–212. https://doi.org/10.1093/epirev/mxu006

McCall, J. D., Tsai, J., & Gordon, A. J. (2018). Veterans treatment court research: Participant characteristics, outcomes, and gaps in the literature. *Journal of Offender Rehabilitation*, *57*(6), 384–401. https://doi.org/10.1080/10509674.2018.1510864

McCauley, J. L., Killeen, T., Gros, D. F., Brady, K. T., & Back, S. E. (2012) Posttraumatic stress disorder and co-occurring substance use disorders: Advances in assessment and treatment. *Clinical Psychology Science and Practice*, *19*(3), 283–304. https://doi.org/10.1111/cpsp.12006

McCormick-Goodhart, M. A. (2013). Leaving no veteran behind: Policies and perspectives on combat trauma, veterans courts, and the rehabilitative approach to criminal behavior. *Penn State Law Review*, *117*(3), 895–926. http://www.pennstatelawreview.org/117/3/McCormick-Goodhart%20final.pdf

McDevitt-Murphy, M. E., William, J. L., Bracken, K. L., Field, J. A., Monahan, C. J., & Murphy, J. G. (2010). PTSD symptoms, hazardous drink, and health functioning among U.S. OEF/OIF veterans presenting to primary care. *Journal of Trauma Stress*, *23*(1), 108–111.

McGuire, J., Clark, S., Blue-Howells, J., & Coe, C. (2013). *An inventory of VA involvement in veterans courts, dockets and tracks*. http://www.justiceforvets.org/studies-and-stats.html

Office of the Chief of Public Affairs. (2012, February 17). *Army releases Generating Health and Discipline in the Force Ahead of Strategic Reset Report*. U.S. Army. https://www.army.mil/article/72086/army_releases_generating_health_and_discipline_in_the_force_ahead_of_strategic_reset_report

Rowen, J. (2020). Worthy of justice: A veterans treatment court in practice. *Law & Policy*, *42*(1), 78–100.

Russell, R. T. (2009). Veterans treatment court: A proactive approach. *New England Journal on Criminal and Civil Confinement*, *35*, 357. https://www.american.edu/spa/jpo/initiatives/drug-court/upload/veterans-treatment-court-a-proactive-approach.pdf

Sayer, N. A., Noorbaloochi, S., Frazier, P., Carlson, K., Gravely, A., & Murdoch, M. (2010). Reintegration problems and treatment interests among Iraq and Afghanistan combat veterans receiving VA medical care. *Psychiatric Services*, *61*(6), 589–597. https://doi.org/10.1176/ps.2010.61.6.589

Seal, K. H., Metzler, T. J., Gima, K. S., Bertenthal, D., Maguen, S., & Marmar, C. R. (2009). Trends and risk factors for mental health diagnoses among Iraq and Afghanistan veterans using Department of Veterans Affairs health care, 2002–2008. *American Journal of Public Health*, *99*(9), 1651–1658. https://doi.org/10.2105/ajph.2008.150284

Slattery, M., Dugger, M. T., Lamb, T. A., & Williams, L. (2013). Catch, treat, and release: Veteran treatment courts address the challenges of returning home. *Substance Use & Misuse*, *48*(10), 922–932. https://doi.org/10.3109/10826084.2013.797468

Smelson, D. A., Pinals, D. A., Sawh, L., Fulwiler, C., Singer, S., Guevremont, N., Fisher, W., Steadman, H. J., & Hartwell, S. (2015). An alternative to incarceration: Co-occurring disorders treatment intervention for justice-involved veterans. *World Medical & Health Policy*, *7*(4), 329–348. https://doi.org/10.1002/wmh3.168

Smith, J. (2012). The Anchorage, Alaska veterans court and recidivism: July 6, 2004—December 31, 2010. *Alaska Law Review*, *29*(1), 93–111. https://scholarship.law.duke.edu/alr/vol29/iss1/4/

Smith, R., Levinson, J., & Robinson, Z. (2015). Implicit white favoritism in the criminal justice system. *Alabama Law Review, 871*(2015–2016), 66, 871.

Snowden, D. L., Oh, S., Salas-Wright, C. P., Vaughn, M. G., & King, E. (2017). Military service and crime: New evidence. *Social Psychiatry and Psychiatric Epidemiology, 52*(5), 605–615. https://doi.org/10.1007/s00127-017-1342-8

Stein, M. B., & McAllister, T. W. (2009). Exploring the convergence of posttraumatic stress disorder and mild traumatic brain injury. *American Journal of Psychiatry, 166*(7), 768–776. https://doi.org/10.1176/appi.ajp.2009.08101604

Stiner, M. (2012). *Veterans treatment courts and the U.S. Department of Labor: Putting veterans back to work.* Justice for Vets. https://justiceforvets.org/wp-content/uploads/2017/03/Dispatch-Dept-of-Labor.pdf

Strong, J., Ray, K., Findley, P. A., Torres, R., Pickett, L., & Byrne, R. J. (2014). Psychosocial concerns of veterans of Operation Enduring Freedom/Operation Iraqi Freedom. *Health & Social Work, 39*(1), 17–24. https://doi.org/10.1093/hsw/hlu002

Tanielian, T. L., Jaycox, L. H., & Monica, S. (2008). *Invisible wounds of war. Psychological and cognitive injuries, their consequences, and services to assist recovery.* Rand Center for Military Health Policy.

Tanner-Smith, E. E., Lipsey, M. W., & Wilson, D. B. (2016). Juvenile drug court effects on recidivism and drug use: A systematic review and meta-analysis. *Journal of Experimental Criminology, 12*(4), 477–513. doi:10.1007/s11292-016-9274-y

Trevillion, K., Williamson, E., Thandi, G., Borschmann, R., Oram, S., & Howard, L. M. (2015). A systematic review of mental disorders and perpetration of domestic violence among military populations. *Social Psychiatry and Psychiatric Epidemiology, 50*(9), 1329–1346. https://doi.org/10.1007/s00127-015-1084-4

Tsai, J., Finlay, A., Flatley, B., Kasprow, W. J., & Clark, S. (2018). A national study of veterans treatment court participants: Who benefits and who recidivates. *Administration and Policy in Mental Health and Mental Health Services Research, 45*(2), 236–244. https://doi.org/10.1007/s10488-017-0816-z

Tsai, J., Flatley, B., Kasprow, W. J., Clark, S., & Finlay, A. (2017). Diversion of veterans with criminal justice involvement to treatment courts: Participant characteristics and outcomes. *Psychiatric Services, 68*(4), 375–383. https://doi.org/10.1176/appi.ps.201600233

United States Census Bureau. (2018). They are Half the Size of the Living Vietnam Veteran Population. U.S. Department of Commerce. Retrieved April 27, 2023, from https://data.census.gov/

U.S. Department of Veterans Affairs. (2018) *Veteran population.* https://www.va.gov/vetdata/veteran_population.asp

U.S. Department of Veterans Affairs. (2021). *VA social work.* https://www.socialwork.va.gov/index.asp

Valdez, A., Kaplan, C. D., & Curtis, R. L. (2007). Aggressive crime, alcohol and drug use, and concentrated poverty in 24 U.S. urban areas. *American Journal of Drug and Alcohol Abuse, 33*(4), 595–603. https://doi.org/10.1080/00952990701407637

Wexler, D. B., & Winick, B. J. (2008). *Therapeutic jurisprudence, in principles of addiction medicine* (4th ed.). SSRN. https://ssrn.com/abstract=1101507

Wilson, J. K., Brodsky, S. L., Neal, T. M. S., & Cramer, R. J. (2011). Prosecutor pretrial attitudes and pleas-bargaining behavior toward veterans with posttraumatic stress disorder. *Psychological Services, 8*(4), 319–331. https://doi.org/10.1037/a0025330

Wright, J. P., Carter, D. E., & Cullen, F. T. (2005). A life-course analysis of military service in Vietnam. *Journal of Research in Crime and Delinquency, 42*(1), 55–83. https://doi.org/10.1177/0022427804270436

28

Mental Health Court

Anne Nordberg, John R. Gallagher, and
Meredith Canada

Mental health court (MHC) is a promising intervention used to treat those who have mental illnesses and are involved in the criminal justice system. MHC is a specialized court docket for individuals with mental illnesses (Almquist & Dodd, 2009; Thompson et al., 2007). MHCs differ by type and level of criminal charges accepted, type of mental illnesses accepted, and the court's service capacity. In general, however, all MHCs include judicial supervision, individualized community-based treatment plans for each participant, status hearings with an MHC judge, incentives and rewards for court compliance, and defined criteria for MHC completion. MHCs aim to decrease criminal justice involvement for individuals with mental illnesses by connecting them to community-based resources that promote mental health recovery (Almquist & Dodd, 2009). The main goals of MHCs are to reduce criminal recidivism rates for individuals who have mental illnesses and improve public safety (Canada et al., 2019; Edwards et al., 2020).

Ten essential elements for designing and implementing an effective MHC were developed (Thompson et al., 2007). These elements are rooted in two principles. First, multidisciplinary collaboration between all systems and partners (e.g., criminal justice, mental health treatment, substance use disorder treatment) is required. Second, MHCs are not the main solution in addressing the overrepresentation of individuals with mental illnesses in the criminal justice system. MHCs are one tool in addressing this complex, systemic problem. The 10 essential elements are as follows: (a) planning and administration, which must include stakeholders representing all relevant systems (e.g., criminal justice, mental health treatment, substance use disorder treatment) and community members; (b) clearly defining eligibility criteria for those served by the court; (c) identifying and accepting participants to the court and linking participants to service providers, which must happen in a timely manner; (d) clearly defining terms of participation, imposing the least restrictive

Anne Nordberg, John R. Gallagher, and Meredith Canada, *Mental Health Court* In: *Handbook of Forensic Social Work*. Edited by: David Axlyn McLeod, Anthony P. Natale, and Kristin W. Mapson, Oxford University Press. © Oxford University Press 2024. DOI: 10.1093/oso/9780197694732.003.0028 conditions, and, upon completion, providing participants with a positive legal outcome (e.g., criminal case dismissed); (e) facilitating fully informed consent and access to legal counsel; (f) connecting participants to individualized and comprehensive support and treatment services; (g) protecting participants' legal and health information; (h) facilitating a comprehensive and collaborative MHC team that includes criminal justice, treatment, and other professionals who have been cross-trained in the other disciplines represented; (i) rewarding and sanctioning participants through collaboration between criminal justice and mental health providers based on progress in meeting individualized goals; and (j) regularly collecting and analyzing data to assess court performance and participants' outcomes (Thompson et al., 2007). The development and implementation of these elements are rooted in the history of deinstitutionalization and subsequent criminal justice innovation strongly shaped by therapeutic jurisprudence (TJ).

Deinstitutionalization, MHCs, and Theoretical Innovation

The deinstitutionalization of mental health in North America during the 1960s left many people living with serious and persistent mental health care issues without treatment and frequently resulted in poverty, precarity, and homelessness. Increased visibility on city streets during the 1970s and 1980s resulted in the increased criminalization of people with mental illnesses (Bonfire et al., 2020; Lamb & Bachrach, 2001; Schneider et al., 2007). By the 1990s many people with mental health problems became one of the "revolving door populations" that were cyclically swept into the criminal justice system; passed through courts, many charged with low-level, misdemeanor crimes; and soon released back into communities, only to be swept back into criminal justice contact. Recognizing the negative impact of recurrent criminal justice contact on both the accused and the efficiency of the court system, workers began to seek alternate approaches. Wexler and Winick recognized the possibility and peril of the application of mental health law as it possessed both therapeutic and anti-therapeutic power and sought to maximize therapeutic outcomes (Wexler & Winick, 1996; Winick & Wexler, 2003). Consequently, TJ emerged as an interdisciplinary field of inquiry (Wexler, 2011)—some say theory (Schneider et al., 2007)—that has shaped the application of mental health law, the construction and replication of MHCs, and the outcomes for many justice-involved people with serious and persistent mental health problems.

TJ admits that criminal justice processes and interactions with legal actors *affect* people who are accused of crimes. Traditional punitive responses are deemed inappropriate and ineffective (Schneider et al., 2007) because the reason for the criminal behavior is not individual choice but illness and the poor social conditions that exacerbate it (Schneider, 2010; Slinger & Roesch, 2010). Wexler and Winick (1996) conceptualized the potential of TJ to attend to both the emotional needs of the accused and the psychological impact of the criminal justice process. Their work drew deliberate connections from macro to micro concerns and between systems of care and penalty, linking systemic structures, rehabilitative potential, and individual psychology. MHCs are part of a movement of judicial innovation that attempts to humanize and improve outcomes for defendants and communities that are struggling with complex chronic problems (Berman & Feinblatt, 2001). Thus, TJ focuses a conceptual and practical lens on legal rules, processes, and the behavior of legal actors (Wexler, 2011) and has been a catalyst for reshaping of legal services and defining a generation that has been called "nothing short of phenomenal" (Stolle, 2000, p. xv).

TJ as praxis involves the diversion of defendants away from the system of mainstream or traditional law toward MHCs. Several core concepts help translate and operationalize TJ in MHCs (Marini, 2003; Schneider et al., 2007; Winick & Wexler, 2003): (a) pharmaceutical treatment is the cornerstone of release plans and treatment compliance is a tangible outcome measure (Berman & Feinblatt, 2001), (b) collaboration with mental health professionals and organizations is necessary to positively impact MHC participants and program outcomes (Berman & Feinblatt, 2001), (c) the materialization of the court is based on the assumption that physical and emotional harm may result from the imprisonment of seriously mentally ill people, (d) the usual adversarial court process is replaced by an approach characterized by collaboration between the defense and prosecution (Berman & Feinblatt, 2001; Winick & Wexler, 2003), and finally (e) mental illness is considered the underlying cause of the criminal behaviors among this group of defendants, making treatment of the illness the most impactful deterrent to future criminal justice involvement. MHCs then leverage multiple systems of support (housing, job training, transportation, etc.) to undergird treatment and prevent further criminal justice contact among clients. Woven into MHCs are certain principles that guide the implementation of TJ. For example, Winick (2002) emphasized the importance of autonomy, noncoercion, and voluntary participation for MHC participants. Wiener et al. (2010) suggested that clients' perceptions of TJ concepts such as procedural and distributive justice could positively impact outcomes like mental health and academic success. Social workers and social services are a critical component of the operationalization of TJ, though their roles in program structure vary from court to court, from being embedded in the court both physically and conceptually to being key allies in support through case management, treatment, housing services, and the many ways social workers support vulnerable populations.

Scope of the Problem and Populations Served in MHCs

Approximately one in five adults (19.1%) in the United States had any mental illness (AMI) in the previous year (Substance Abuse and Mental Health Services Administration, 2018); therefore, it is essential that social workers develop expertise in assessing for mental illness and implementing evidence-based interventions that support mental health recovery and individual well-being. AMI is defined as a diagnosable mental, behavioral, or emotional disorder based on criteria defined in the *Diagnostic and Statistical Manual of Mental Disorders*, fifth edition (DSM-5), and excludes developmental and substance use disorders (American Psychiatric Association, 2013). Mental illnesses, if untreated, can have devastating consequences on individuals, families, and other social systems (e.g., employment, schooling), and these consequences are predicted to have significant economic impacts. By 2030, mental disorders are projected to result in a cumulative economic output loss of $16.3 trillion worldwide (Trautman et al., 2016). Cumulative economic output is measured by the estimated impact mental disorders have on a country's gross domestic product. This estimate suggests that mental disorders stifle economic growth at rates similar to cardiovascular diseases and at higher rates than diseases such as cancer and diabetes.

Having a serious mental illness, such as schizophrenia, bipolar disorder, or major depressive disorder, is associated with a decreased life expectancy. In one meta-analysis, for example, it was estimated that individuals with mental illnesses died from any cause a median of 10 years sooner than the general population, with a reduction in life expectancy ranging from 1.4 to 32 years depending on the study (Reisinger Walker et al., 2015). Compared with controls, individuals with schizophrenia ($n = 4,782$) and bipolar disorder ($n = 20,308$) had significantly higher odds for medical comorbidities. For instance, having either illness was associated with greater than two times the odds for having a blood or blood-forming organ disease, digestive system disease, or endocrine/immunity disease (Bahorik et al., 2017). Bipolar disorder and schizophrenia were associated with greater than 1.5 increased odds in all other medical comorbidities measured (e.g., circulatory system, genitourinary, infectious/parasitic, nervous system, and respiratory system). Bipolar disorder and schizophrenia were also associated with 1.5 increased odds for musculoskeletal disorders (Bahorik et al., 2017).

This evidence highlights the importance of social work in addressing the multifaceted consequence related to mental illnesses. Social workers are, perhaps, the best prepared profession to address the complexities of mental health care. Social workers are trained in policy analysis and advocacy; as a result, social workers are prepared to assist policymakers and politicians in developing laws that improve access to mental health care and reduce economic losses related to untreated mental illnesses. Furthermore, social workers have expertise in collaborating with other disciplines and working effectively on multidisciplinary teams, and this is especially important because mental illness often co-occurs with other conditions that require collaboration with primary care physicians, substance use disorder treatment providers, psychiatrists, and vocational counselors, to name a few. Thus, given their training, practice skills, and expertise, it is entirely understandable that social workers are critical personnel in MHCs and in advocating for systemic and policy innovation to support justice-involved people with AMI.

Mental illness and criminal justice involvement impact family systems as well, and social workers seem best equipped to assess family systems from a theoretical lens and use best practices to support families in improving their functioning and quality of life. Mental illness in parents is associated with increased family discord and domestic violence, as well as behavioral, emotional, and social problems in children (Reupert & Maybery, 2016). The directionality of the relationship between parental mental illness, family issues, and children's well-being is not fully understood; mental illness alone is not the sole cause for family disruption. Clearly, though, if children are witnessing domestic violence, for example, this will commonly lead to behavioral, cognitive, emotional, and social problems in kids. As discussed previously, untreated mental illnesses can impact many areas of life, such as physical health and family relationships, and this can lead to noticeable, negative impacts on functioning, such as individuals who have mental illnesses being unable to maintain employment, having limited or no social support system, and having poor intra-personal relationships (e.g., low self-esteem, decreased motivation for change, difficulties with decision-making). Therefore, it is not surprising that some individuals with mental illnesses get involved in the criminal justice system.

There seem to be several challenges in assessing the prevalence of mental illnesses in the criminal justice system. Some of these challenges appear to be that the criminal justice system has historically been underprepared to assess for and treat mental illnesses, been unable or unwilling to tailor interventions to meet the individualized needs of those who have mental illnesses, and been operating under a punitive lens of justice, as compared to a rehabilitative model. A commonly cited study by Steadman et al. (2009) estimated that 17.1% of men and 34.3% of women admitted to jails in the United States had a serious mental illness, which included posttraumatic stress disorder (PTSD), mood disorders, and psychotic disorders. Regardless of prevalence, however, the priority is for social workers to provide evidence-based practices to those who have mental illnesses and are involved in the criminal justice system.

Social workers may interact with MHCs through a variety of means. Social workers, for example, may be part of a multidisciplinary team that develops an MHC in their community, serve as a clinical social worker for the program, or provide leadership by being a court coordinator or clinical supervisor (Tyuse & Linhorst, 2005). Additionally, social work researchers are well suited to evaluate MHCs and use quantitative methodologies to predict graduation and criminal recidivism outcomes and qualitative methodologies to explore MHC participants' lived experiences in the program. From a research lens, however, it is important to note that high variability across MHCs and quasi-experimental research designs make generalizable conclusions about MHC effectiveness difficult (Almquist & Dodd, 2009). This is not surprising because, as mentioned previously, MHCs tend to vary in programming and service delivery. This has both positive and negative outcomes. From a positive standpoint, providing MHCs the flexibility to tailor programming to meet the needs of the community and participants promotes individualized treatment and not a one-size-fits-all approach to mental health recovery. Conversely, variations in MHC programming limit the ability to generalize findings and establish a body of literature highlighting MHCs as an evidence-based practice (Honegger, 2015).

Women

Few studies have examined the experiences and outcomes of women in MHCs. In general, compared to the overall proportion of women involved in the criminal justice system, White women tend to be disproportionately overrepresented in MHCs (Steadman & Redlich, 2006). Women, in general, may be seen as less risky than men for diversion (Luskin, 2001). Kothari et al. (2014) conducted an evaluation of outcomes by gender in

Kalamazoo County, Michigan. Eligible women, compared to eligible men, were more likely to be enrolled (Kothari et al., 2014). Women's mental health diagnoses differed from men's. Women demonstrated higher rates of bipolar disorder and borderline personality disorder. This may reflect the differences in psychosocial stressors and types of trauma women experience. No differences in successful completion were observed between women and men. Women who completed the program demonstrated significantly fewer emergency room visits compared to men. Regardless of completion status, women had significantly fewer days of psychiatric hospitalizations compared to men, as well. No gender differences were observed in the number of jail days served.

Race and Ethnicity

Some studies have examined the outcomes of MHC participants based on race and ethnicity. One difficulty in properly evaluating MHC effectiveness based on race and ethnicity is the difference in demographics by the court's location (Han & Redlich, 2018). Much of the literature focuses on the two largest minority groups, Black/African American and Latino/Hispanic participants. Studies show mixed results on whether racial and ethnic disparities exist at multiple points, such as referral and entry, program completion, and recidivism (Han & Redlich, 2018). Some studies have shown, for example, that minority individuals are less likely to be referred and accepted to MHCs, while others did not (see Han & Redlich, 2018). Some studies have found poorer outcomes (e.g., recidivism, mental health symptoms, hospitalizations, program retention, and successful completion) for minority participants compared to White participants, while others have not. One qualitative study interviewed 12 Black or African American participants and found three important themes related to their experiences (Stare & Fernando, 2019). Participants experienced important internal, relational, and behavioral growth in MHC. They also reported experiencing cognitive dissonance between their previous criminal justice experiences and those in MHC; most importantly, participants felt that the MHC was helpful, and they were receiving what they needed from the program. Finally, participants reported barriers to treatment, including stigma from having a mental health issue and social disconnection from others due to race.

LGBTQ+

No literature currently exists for individuals who are lesbian, gay, bisexual, transgender, questioning, plus (LGBTQ+) in MHCs. However, this population could benefit from diversion from incarceration for several reasons. Research on the experiences of sexual minorities who are incarcerated is also limited. First, LGBTQ+ individuals experience disproportionately higher rates of incarceration compared to the general population. From the 2011–2012 National Inmate Survey, adults who identified as lesbian, gay, or bisexual were incarcerated at a rate of 1,882 persons per 100,000, while the rate of incarceration for adults of the general population in 2014 was 612 persons per 100,000 (Meyer et al., 2017;

U.S. Department of Justice, Bureau of Justice Statistics, 2015). Second, LGBTQ+ individuals report a higher prevalence of mental health conditions compared to the general population. For example, Meyer et al. (2017) found that compared to heterosexual men, sexual minority men reported higher rates of poor mental health; for women, those who identified as lesbian or bisexual reported slightly higher rates of poor mental health than their heterosexual counterparts. Third, these individuals are at substantial risk for physical and sexual victimization while incarcerated. In the same National Inmate Survey, both men and women who identified as a sexual minority reported significantly higher rates of sexual assault from another inmate compared to men and women who identified as heterosexual (Meyer et al., 2017). Males who identified as a sexual minority also demonstrated a higher risk for sexual assault from staff while incarcerated.

Social Workers' Roles

MHCs represent a promising model for serving individuals with mental illness by improving the quality of life for participants while also improving public safety. However, MHCs vary substantially across courts. This in combination with a lack of standard best practices can lead to systematic biases that exclude or harm certain populations, such as women, sexual minorities, and racial and ethnic minorities. For these reasons, social workers have an important role to play through advocacy in ensuring that these individuals have access to MHCs and receive a fair opportunity to experience the positive outcomes MHCs are becoming known for.

MHC Evaluation Research

MHCs are variants of drug treatment courts that began with the first MHC in Broward County, Florida, in 1997 (McGaha et al., 2002 ; Wexler & Winick, 1996). Early evaluation of drug treatment courts provided positive outcomes that informed policy, and similar work was undertaken with the Broward County MHC. McGaha and colleagues (2002), however, reported complications specific to the Broward County MHC. For example, court workers were reluctant to randomly assign participants, which they deemed unethical, process evaluation challenges such as a dynamic environment and complex processes as well as the informality of the court influenced by the application of principles of TJ (McGaha et al., 2002).

Some of the challenges encountered by McGaha and colleagues in their early attempts at evaluation remain relevant because differences between MHCs and drug courts persist that make MHCs more difficult to evaluate and replicate. Drug courts may rely on readily available community-based resources like Alcoholics Anonymous in support of their clients, but no equivalent support exists for people suffering with serious and persistent mental health concerns. Drug treatment court processes are increasingly built upon the key components of drug courts, which were first articulated in the late 1990s (Drug Court Standards Committee, National Association of Drug Court Professionals, 2004), so they are relatively well ordered and easy to follow and evaluate compared with MHC proceedings (McGaha et al., 2002). Serious mental health problems may be chronic in nature and highly individualized (Bureau of Justice Assistance, 2008), and therefore recovery rates are difficult to establish. Finally, drug court participants are easily tracked through urinalysis and other surveillance tests, but MHC treatment compliance is not easily monitored or measured (Bureau of Justice Assistance, 2008). Therefore, MHCs are local manifestations that frequently frustrate replication and complicate evaluation.

Given these challenges, it is perhaps not surprising that evaluation of these MHCs produces varying results. For example, some studies have found that MHCs reduce recidivism (McNiel & Binder, 2007; Moore & Hiday, 2006) and demonstrate improvements in mental health service access (Boothroyd et al., 2003; Herinckx et al., 2005). However, these positive outcomes are not universal among studies, with at least one reporting increased criminal activity among MHC participants (Cosden et al., 2003). Recently, Loong and colleagues conducted a systematic review of the effectiveness of MHCs with respect to recidivism and police contact (Loong et al., 2019). They included 20 studies in their final analysis that included adult defendants and reported on recidivism and/or police contact (Loong et al., 2019). They concluded that there is some evidence that MHCs were effective in reducing recidivism of participants, consistent with other previously published systematic analyses and meta-analytic reviews (Dean, 2017; Honegger, 2015; Lowder et al., 2018). Further, the authors concluded that the involvement of case managers or access to job training and housing services may help reduce rearrest rates (Loong et al., 2019). However, the evidence regarding MHCs' effectiveness in reducing police contact was inconclusive. As noted by the authors, police contact was indirectly measured as either time in the community or time to rearrest and the source study authors were split on whether MHCs reduced police contact or not (Loong et al., 2019). Many reviews focused on effectiveness defined as recidivism while erasing MHC program structures, which might confound results. Canada and colleagues, in response to these limitations, conducted a meta-analysis of the impact of MHCs on communities and individuals and employed a comparative systematic review of MHCs where findings were synthesized by charge type (Canada et al., 2019). They reviewed 29 articles including research on MHC participants with both misdemeanor and felony charges. They concluded that results are generally promising for MHC graduates but that recidivism rates remain high among noncompleters; however, they note a dearth of research in felony-only MHC programs (Canada et al., 2019). The authors reported that recidivism was the primary outcome of interest across all reviewed studies, with less focus on within- or between-group treatment use or mental health differences (Canada et al., 2019). When looking across subgroups, they found that graduates compared to noncompleters had better outcomes in misdemeanor-only or mixed felony/misdemeanor MHCs, though results from misdemeanor-only courts were mixed (Canada et al., 2019).

Only one study, to our knowledge, has examined whether MHC outcomes are predicted by theorized TJ principles of knowledge, perceived voluntariness, and procedural justice (Redlich & Han, 2014). The authors sampled participants from four courts and employed structural equation modeling analytic techniques. They found that higher levels of TJ were significantly associated with higher rates of program success (Redlich & Han,

2014). However, when mediator variables were included, they found that increased levels of initially perceived voluntariness and procedural justice, as well as MHC knowledge, led to positive recidivism outcomes (decreased rates of new arrests, prison, and MHC bench warrants) and increased court compliance, which led to an increased likelihood of MHC graduation (Redlich & Han, 2014).

Evaluation of MHCs remains problematic due to ethical constraints, localized iterations of MHCs, and a focus on recidivism and criminological outcomes despite the acknowledged and foundational importance of mental health among defendants with serious and persistent mental health concerns. Recent reviews indicate only a modest positive impact on recidivism rates among MHC participants and conclude with calls for more evaluation and evaluation of outcomes beyond recidivism.

Case Study

This section presents a case study that provides examples of the role of social workers in MHC. Additionally, the challenges social workers may experience in working in MHCs and the skills needed to practice effectively in forensic settings are discussed. The pseudonym Carley is used for the case study. The case study presents practical and expected scenarios from our social work practice experiences; however, all details are fictitious, hence not associated in any way with a specific MHC participant. In the case study, we discuss Carley's mental health history and arrest that led to her referral to MHC. We also present findings from Carley's clinical diagnostic assessment for mental illnesses, provide an example of Carley's treatment plan, and discuss Carley's progress in treatment and in meeting the goals of MHC.

Mental Health History and Arrest

Carley is a 22-year-old, heterosexual female who is married. She has been married for about 2 years. Carley and her husband have no children, but they do hope to have children in the future. Carley denied any mental health symptoms in her childhood or adolescent years. She reported that her parents divorced when she was 11 years old and she had a difficult time adjusting to this new lifestyle, such as living at two homes, her biological father remarrying, having to begin a relationship with a stepmother, and witnessing frequent arguments between her biological parents. Carley acknowledged that this was a difficult time for her and she reported feeling anxious and depressed at times, but these symptoms did not negatively impact her functioning, as she maintained healthy friendships, was engaged in sports, and sustained honors throughout her middle school and high school education. As a child and adolescent (age birth to 17 years old), she was never diagnosed with a mental illness.

At the age of 20, Carley began experiencing mental health symptoms, and the symptoms were first noticed by her husband. Specifically, her husband noticed that Carley, at times, would be disorganized (e.g., have a difficult time concentrating, be unable to complete household chores and work responsibilities), have paranoid ideations (e.g., she felt that people from the government were trying to harm her), and seem catatonic (e.g., showed little emotion, even in situations that would typically create emotional responses, such as having dinner together or watching a movie). Although Carley's husband noticed these behaviors, he did not mention anything to her, as they were infrequent and he felt that they were isolated events. However, over the following year, the symptoms progressively got worse and started to impact Carley's functioning, as indicated by her being terminated from her job, no longer engaging in hobbies (e.g., painting) that she used to enjoy, isolating herself from family, and having a difficult time maintaining appropriate hygiene (e.g., she stopped going to the dentist, would shower only two or three times a month). Her symptoms, of course, were also negatively impacting the marriage.

Carley's husband encouraged her to see a psychiatrist or other mental health professional (e.g., clinical social worker) for an evaluation, but she refused to do so, noting that she did not feel she had a problem that warranted mental health care. Her symptoms continued to progress, and at the age of 22, she became increasingly paranoid and was adamant that people from the government were going to kidnap her. One day, she stopped at a convenience store near her home to get gas and snacks. While in the store, Carley began shouting statements related to the government watching her and wanting to harm her, and she then went up to other customers demanding that they hide in the back of the store with her. Carley grabbed the arm of one customer and tried to take him to the back of the store. The convenience store clerk observed these behaviors and called the police. When the police arrived, they found Carley in the back of the store alone, continuing to make comments related to the government spying on her. The police attempted to detain Carley for her safety and to remove her from the convenience store, but Carley viewed the police as government officials. Increasingly paranoid, Carley assaulted the police by punching and spitting on the officers. Carley was charged with aggravated assault. This was her first criminal arrest, and she seemed to be a good candidate for MHC, as her arrest seemed to be associated with an undiagnosed mental illness and untreated mental health symptoms. Therefore, her defense attorney referred her to MHC where she could receive mental health treatment.

Diagnosis, Treatment Planning, and the Role of Social Workers

Carley was admitted to MHC and referred to treatment for a bio-psycho-social-spiritual assessment. Based on the findings from the assessment, the clinical social worker diagnosed Carley with schizophrenia. Based on the DSM-5 (American Psychiatric Association, 2013), Carley met the following criteria for schizophrenia: (a) she experienced auditory, visual, and tactile (e.g., false sensation that government officials were touching her in an attempt to kidnap her) hallucinations; (b) she had disorganized speech, mainly related to paranoid thoughts that the government was spying on her, but at times the speech was not understandable; (c) she was grossly disorganized, which negatively impacted her functioning at work, and had catatonic behaviors (e.g., apparent unawareness, at times, of her surrounding environment); and (d) she had negative symptoms, such as frequently having a flat affect, difficulty with speech (e.g., alogia), and reduced motivation (e.g., avolition). Below is an example of a treatment plan a clinical social worker would develop in collaboration with an MHC participant who has been diagnosed with schizophrenia.

> **Presenting problem**: Carley was arrested for aggravated assault and referred to MHC for treatment of schizophrenia.
>
> **Treatment goals**: Carley reports that she wants to learn about schizophrenia, regain employment, develop healthy coping skills that will support her recovery and improve her well-being and quality of life, and complete MHC.
>
> **Treatment objectives**:
>
> 1. Carley will increase her knowledge on schizophrenia to support her in self-diagnosing, as evidenced by her attending group therapy once a week where she will learn about schizophrenia and identify the symptoms of schizophrenia that she can relate to.
> 2. Carley will work collaboratively with the MHC vocational counselor to regain employment, as evidenced by her developing a resume and submitting five job applications within the next month.
> 3. Carley will develop healthy coping skills that will support her recovery and improve her well-being and quality of life, as evidenced by her attending individual therapy once a week where she will develop and utilize a recovery plan and attending appointments with her psychiatrist.
> 4. Carley will have the aggravated assault charge dismissed, as evidenced by her completing all the requirements of the MHC, such as treatment and attending status hearings with the MHC team.
>
> **Interventions**: The clinical social worker will facilitate didactic groups related to schizophrenia to support Carley in self-diagnosing and individual therapy to assist Carley in developing and utilizing healthy coping skills to reduce her symptoms and improve her functioning. Carley will be referred to a psychiatrist for a psychiatric evaluation and medication management sessions if needed. The clinical social worker will consult with the mental health court team weekly to review Carley's progress in the program. Cognitive-behavioral therapy for psychosis (CBTp) will be the primary evidence-based intervention used to assist Carley in meeting the goals and objectives of her treatment plan.

The emergence of MHCs, and other treatment courts, may encourage more social workers to work in forensic settings and more schools of social work to offer classes on social work practice in the criminal justice system. Social workers can make substantial contributions to MHCs, especially because the model promotes a nonadversarial, strengths-based approach to reducing criminal recidivism and promoting mental health recovery. As noted in Carley's treatment plan, clinical social workers must have advanced training in evidence-based interventions used to treat mental illnesses. To receive this advanced training, some social workers may have to do post–master's in social work educational, training, or certificate programs. In treating Carley's schizophrenia, best practices include CBTp, and social workers must have expertise in the range of mental illnesses that MHCs treat. In addition to CBTp, social workers should have expertise in behavioral activation for major depressive disorder, family-focused treatment for bipolar disorder, and cognitive processing therapy for posttraumatic stress disorder, to name a few (Barlow, 2014).

Practicing social work in the criminal justice system has its challenges. The role of social workers in the criminal justice system presents unique challenges, primarily because key values of social work conflict with criminal justice ideology. Social workers are ethically responsible to advocate for clients' rights to self-determination, yet the criminal justice system is designed to limit individuals' liberties. MHCs are marketed as voluntary programs, but from a social work perspective, they are perhaps best described as quasi-voluntary. For instance, as it relates to the case study, if Carley chose not to enroll in MHC, she would have had to do another criminal justice intervention. While there does appear to be some level of decision-making in this process, the other available options for Carley may not have been equivalent to MHC. A felony conviction and long-term prison sentence, for instance, may be the alternative option to MHC.

Social workers who practice within the criminal justice system must recognize and accept their inherit authority, particularly the potential authority to limit the freedom of their clients. MHCs rely on the multidisciplinary team, some of whom may be social workers, to recommend and justify the incarceration of participants when necessary. For social workers who are in positions that could limit the freedom of their clients, it may be difficult to maintain their personal desire to be a helping professional while upholding the punitive expectations of the judicial system. This is particularly challenging in MHCs where some interventions that are designed to enhance motivation for change (e.g., brief incarceration) can actually have negative unintended consequences, such as retraumatization. In Carley's case, she had a history of hallucinations and paranoia related to government officials kidnapping and wanting to harm her. Clearly, brief incarceration ordered by a government official, such as a MHC judge, can have devastating consequences on Carley's well-being. This risk of retraumatization further highlights the need for social workers to have training and expertise in trauma-informed care. Additionally, it is important that social workers utilize clinical supervision and case consultations frequently to assist them in learning about the expectations of their authority and how to utilize their authority consistent with social work values and ethics.

Last, in a classic article relevant to contemporary social work practice, Hutchison (1987) suggests guidelines that social workers can follow when practicing in authoritative settings and with mandated, or what we refer to as quasi-voluntary, clients. The guidelines promote clients' rights to self-determination while also meeting the needs of the criminal justice system. Examples of the guidelines that seem most applicable for social workers who work within mental health and other treatment courts are as follows (Hutchison, 1987):

1. "The social worker should engage the client in explicit discussion of the social worker's mandated authority during the initial phase of work" (p. 594).
2. "Use of authority needs to be based as much as possible on the client's conscious consent; even in coercive actions the client needs to be given some choices" (p. 593).

3. "The client should be informed which decisions the client can make and which decision the social worker will make" (p. 593).

4. "The social worker in mandated transactions should demonstrate respect for client self-determination by addressing problems of concern to the client that are not part of the mandated problem" (p. 594).

5. "The mandated client should always be informed when the social worker does something to, for, or about the client, unless there are compelling safety reasons to withhold such information" (p. 594).

References

Almquist, L., & Dodd, E. (2009). *Mental health courts: A guide to research-informed policy and practice.* https://bja.ojp.gov/sites/g/files/xyckuh186/files/Publications/CSG_MHC_Research.pdf

American Psychiatric Association. (2013). *Diagnostic and statistical manual of mental disorders* (5th ed.).

Bahorik, A. L., Satre, D. D., Kline-Simon, A. H., Weisner, C. M., & Campbell, C. I. (2017). Serious mental illness and medical comorbidities: Findings from an integrated health care system. *Journal of Psychosomatic Research, 100,* 35–45.

Barlow, D. H. (2014). *Clinical handbook of psychological disorders: A step-by-step treatment manual* (5th ed.). Guilford Press.

Berman, G., & Feinblatt, J. (2001). Problem-solving courts: A brief primer. *Law & Policy, 23*(2), 125–140. doi:10.1111/1467-9930.00107

Bonfine, N., Blank Wilson, A., & Munetz, M. R. (2020). Meeting the needs of justice-involved people with serious mental illness within community behavioral health systems. *Psychiatric Services, 71*(4), 355–363.

Boothroyd, R. A., Poythress, N. G., McGaha, A., & Petrila, J. (2003). The Broward Mental Health Court: Process, outcomes, and service utilization. *International Journal of Law and Psychiatry, 26,* 55–71. http://dx.doi.org/10.1016/S0160-2527(02)00203-0

Bureau of Justice Assistance. (2008). *Mental health courts: A primer for policymakers and practitioners.* http://www.ojp.usdoj.gov

Canada, K., Barrenger, S., & Ray, B. (2019). Bridging mental health and criminal justice systems: A systematic review of the impact of mental health courts on individuals and communities. *Psychology, Public Policy, and Law, 25*(2), 73–91.

Cosden, M., Ellens, J. K., Schnell, J. L., Yamini-Diouf, Y., & Wolfe, M. M. (2003). Evaluation of a mental health treatment court with assertive community treatment. *Behavioral Sciences & the Law, 21,* 415–427. http://dx.doi.org/10.1002/bsl.542

Dean, R. (2017). *What is the impact of mental health courts? A systematic literature review.* https://sophia.stkate.edu/msw_papers/721

Drug Court Standards Committee, National Association of Drug Court Professionals. (2017). *Defining drug courts: The key components.* U.S. Department of Justice, Office of Justice Programs, Bureau of Justice Assistance.

Edwards, E. R., Sissoko, D. R., Abrams, D., Samost, D., La Gamma, S., & Geraci, J. (2020). Connecting mental health court participants with services: Process, challenges, and recommendations. *Psychology, Public Policy, and Law, 26*(4), 1–13.

Han, W., & Redlich, A. (2018). A comparison of mental health court and traditional court defendants. *Criminal Justice and Behavior, 45*(2), 173–194.

Herinckx, H. A., Swart, S. C., Ama, S. M., Dolezal, C. D., & King, S. (2005). Rearrest and linkage to mental health services among clients of the Clark County mental health court program. *Psychiatric Services, 56*(7), 853–857.

Honegger, L. N. (2015). Does the evidence support the case for mental health courts? A review of the literature. *Law and Human Behavior, 39*(5), 478–488.

Hutchinson, E. D. (1987). Use of authority in direct social work practice with mandated clients. *Social Service Review*, *61*(4), 581–598.

Kothari, C. L., Butkiewicz, R., Williams, E. R., Jacobson, C., Morse, D. S., & Cerulli, C. (2014). Does gender matter? Exploring mental health recovery court legal and health outcomes. *Health and Justice*, *2*(12), 1–11.

Lamb, H. R., & Bachrach, L. L. (2001). Some perspectives on deinstitutionalization. *Psychiatric Services*, *52*(8), 1039–1045. doi:10.1176/appi.ps.52.8.1039

Loong, D., Bonato, S., Barnsley, J., & Dewa, C. S. (2019). The effectiveness of mental health courts in reducing recidivism and police contact: A systematic review. *Community Mental Health Journal*, *55*(7), 1073–1098. doi:10.1007/s10597-019-00421-9

Lowder, E. M., Rade, C. B., & Desmarais, S. L. (2018). Effectiveness of mental health courts in reducing recidivism: A meta-analysis. *Psychiatric Services*, *69*(1), 15–22. doi:10.1176/appi.ps.201700107

Luskin, M. L. (2001). Who is diverted? Case selection for court-monitored mental health treatment. *Law & Policy*, *23*(2), 217–236.

Marini, R. A. (2003). Mental health court. In B. J. Winick & D. B. Wexler (Eds.), *Judging in a therapeutic key: Therapeutic jurisprudence and the courts* (pp. 59–66). Carolina Academic Press.

McGaha, A., Boothroyd, R. A., Poythress, N. G., Petrila, J., & Ort, R. G. (2002). Lessons from the Broward County mental health court evaluation. *Evaluation and Program Planning*, *25*(2), 125–135. doi:10.1016/S0149-7189(02)00005-8

McNiel, D. E., & Binder, R. L. (2007). Effectiveness of a mental health court in reducing criminal recidivism and violence. *American Journal of Psychiatry*, *164*, 1395–1403. http://dx.doi.org/10.1176/appi.ajp.2007.06101664

Meyer, I. H., Flores, A. R., Stemple, L., Romero, A. P., Wilson, B. D., & Herman, J. L. (2017). Incarceration rates and traits of sexual minorities in the United States: National Inmate Survey, 2011–2012. *American Journal of Public Health Research*, *107*(2), 267–273.

Moore, M. E., & Hiday, V. A. (2006). Mental health court outcomes: A comparison of re-arrest and re-arrest severity between mental health court and traditional court participants. *Law and Human Behavior*, *30*, 659–674. http://dx.doi.org/10.1007/s10979-006-9061-9

Redlich, A. D., & Han, W. (2014). Examining the links between therapeutic jurisprudence and mental health court completion. *Law and Human Behavior*, *38*(2), 109–118. doi:10.1037/lhb0000041

Reisinger Walker, E., McGee, R. E., & Druss, B. G. (2015). Mortality in mental disorders and global disease burden implications: A systematic review and meta-analysis. *JAMA Psychiatry*, *72*(4), 334–341.

Reupert, A., & Maybery, D. (2016). What do we know about families where parents have a mental illness? A systematic review. *Child & Youth Services*, *37*(2), 98–111.

Schneider, R. D. (2010). Mental health courts and diversion programs: A global survey. *International Journal of Law and Psychiatry*, *33*(4), 201–206. doi:10.1016/j.ijlp.2010.07.001

Schneider, R. D., Bloom, H., & Heerema, M. (2007). *Mental health courts: Decriminalizing the mentally ill*. Irwin Law.

Slinger, E., & Roesch, R. (2010). Problem-solving courts in Canada: A review and a call for empirically-based evaluation methods. *International Journal of Law and Psychiatry*, *33*(4), 258–264. doi:10.1016/j.ijlp.2010.06.008

Stare, B. G., & Fernando, D. M. (2019). Black American men's treatment experiences in mental health court: A phenomenological analysis. *Journal of Addictions & Offender Counseling*, *40*, 17–35.Steadman, H. J., Osher, F. C., Clark Robbins, P., Case, B., & Samuels, S. (2009). Prevalence of serious mental illness among jail inmates. *Psychiatric Services*, *60*(6), 761–765.

Steadman, H. J., & Redlich, A. D. (2006, February). *An evaluation of the Bureau of Justice Assistance mental health court initiative*. https://www.ncjrs.gov/pdffiles1/nij/grants/213136.pdf

Stolle, D. P. (2000). Introduction. In D. P. Stolle, D. B. Wexler & B. J. Winick (Eds.), *Practicing therapeutic jurisprudence: Law as a helping profession* (p. xv). Carolina Academic Press.

Substance Abuse and Mental Health Services Administration. (2018). *Results from the 2018 National Survey on Drug Use and Health: Detailed tables*. https://www.samhsa.gov/data/sites/default/files/cbhsq-reports/NSDUHDetailedTabs2018R2/NSDUHDetTabsSect10pe2018.htm

Thompson, M., Osher, F., & Tomasini-Joshi, D. (2007). *Improving responses to people with mental illness: The essential elements of mental health court.* https://bja.ojp.gov/sites/g/files/xyckuh186/files/Publications/MHC_Essential_Elements.pdf

Trautman, S., Rehm, J., & Wittchen, H.-U. (2016). The economic costs of mental disorders: Do our societies react appropriately to the burden of mental disorders? *EMBO Reports, 17*(9), 1245–1249.

Tyuse, S. W., & Linhorst, D. M. (2005). Drug courts and mental health courts: Implications for social work. *Health & Social Work, 30*(3), 233–240.

U.S. Department of Justice, Bureau of Justice Statistics. (2015, September). *US prison population declined one percent in 2014.* https://www.bjs.gov/content/pub/press/p14pr.cfm

Wexler, D. B. (2011). The relevance of therapeutic jurisprudence and its literature. *Federal Sentencing Reporter, 23*(4), 278–279. doi:10.1525/fsr.2011.23.4.278

Wexler, D. B., & Winick, B. J. (1996). *Law in a therapeutic key: Developments in therapeutic jurisprudence.* Carolina Academic Press.

Wiener, R. L., Winick, B. J., Georges, L. S., & Castro, A. (2010). A testable theory of problem solving courts: Avoiding past empirical and legal failures. *International Journal of Law and Psychiatry, 33,* 417–427. doi:10.1016/j.ijlp.2010.09.012

Winick, B. J. (2002). Therapeutic jurisprudence and problem solving courts. *Fordham Urban Law Journal, 30,* 1055–1103.

Winick, B. J., & Wexler, D. B. (Eds.). (2003). *Judging in a therapeutic key: Therapeutic jurisprudence and the courts.* Carolina Academic Press.

29

Probation

Faye S. Taxman

Nearly three times as many people are being supervised by probation (ordered by the court) or parole (after release from prison) as are incarcerated—that is nearly 5 million adults on supervision as compared to 1.5 million incarcerated (Kaeble & Alper, 2020). Yet the policies and practices of probation supervision largely remain unknown in an era that focuses on mass incarceration and addressing the issues related to incarceration. With over 20% of U.S. adults having a criminal arrest, the criminal legal system has a large reach, including an estimated one in 55 adults under supervision at any one time and one in three Black males likely to be involved in the justice system in their lifetime (Public Policy Institute, n.d., adapted from Bureau of Justice Statistics). Mass supervision has emerged as its own policy arena, separate and apart from incarceration, given the sheer volume of individuals exposed to supervision, the liberty restrictions and demands of supervision, and the recycling through the justice system. Failures on supervision account for anywhere from 25% to 75% of new intakes into prison due to violations of program rules and requirements (Horowitz et al., 2018). The stakes of being on supervision are high given that probation tends to be the feeder to incarceration and a test for the supervised as to whether they deserve to have their rights restored.

This chapter is devoted to probation supervision with its competing mission of enforcement and social work, and with its ever-changing tools and strategies to achieve the mission. Probation was originally designed as an alternative or a punishment instead of incarceration, but its roots and contemporary practices borrow from the social work field and enforcement of mandated conditions. Probation has a reputation as being a "slap on the wrist," which resulted in stiffening the conditions of supervision and increasing the requirements. Probation elevated its reputation by demonstrating that it can enforce the ever-growing list of requirements, signaling that probation is "tough." Simultaneous to this focus on accountability and compliance, probation also vacillates in terms of the importance of providing referrals to community treatment programs, offering programs and services, and

Faye S. Taxman, *Probation* In: *Handbook of Forensic Social Work*. Edited by: David Axlyn McLeod, Anthony P. Natale, and Kristin W. Mapson, Oxford University Press. © Oxford University Press 2024. DOI: 10.1093/oso/9780197694732.003.0029 emphasizing goals that support behavior change. Contemporarily, probation now is functioning in a balanced approach with an emphasis on behavior change with accountability. The culture of probation is that it is a punishment first and foremost and then a tool to improve an individual's quality of life and civic responsibilities and promote a crime- or drug-free lifestyle. The secondary goal is challenged in a culture of punishment (Appleton, 2020; Taxman, 2008). The stark realization of comingling punishment and treatment has resulted in a new emphasis on the policies and practices of supervision, including efforts to constrain the bloated supervision requirements. We begin by describing the history of supervision and then discuss current policies and practices and a way forward for probation as a punishment.

Brief History of Probation Supervision

Probation began as a humanitarian effort to prevent individuals with alcohol disorders from being incarcerated. John Augustus, in the 1830s, made the case that incarceration was not appropriate given that the individual had a drinking disorder, and incarceration is unlikely to deal with that. He opened up his home to help the men with drinking disorders to fulfill their societal role as parents, employees, and members of the community. Augustus assisted one man who became proof that this approach was valuable since the man appeared in court sober in a mere 3 weeks. The led to a statute in Massachusetts to formalize probation, meaning that the effort is designed "to prove" (the Latin verb is *probare*, meaning to prove). Probation spread, including in juvenile court, throughout the 1800s and then later to the federal system in 1925. As a formal sentencing option, probation spread to offer nonincarcerated sentencing options. The foundation of Augustus's approach was in social work to help individuals assume law-abiding behavior but also to ensure that the punishment was carried out. The tension between social work and enforcement emerged almost from the inception of supervision, where the emphasis is on helping the individual but also enforcing the conditions ordered by the court.

For nearly a century, probation and parole juggled the social work enforcement hats with altering emphases on different missions and goals. But in the early 1970s, the infamous "nothing works" systematic review questioned the value of rehabilitative services, even in the community, for correctional populations. Robert Martinson (1974) published a review of over 200 articles that reported that treatment interventions did not have better outcomes than punishment ones. Although the article was revised in 1979 and basically proclaimed that "some things work for some people," the emerging retributive justice approach (see the von Hirsch, 1976, treatise on *Doing Justice*) contributed to the unraveling of social work as a predominate feature of supervision. The retributive model focused on punishment that was tailored to the severity of the crime (and person), and therefore probation underwent a continuing transformation to emphasize accountability through required conditions of supervision. The War on Drugs in the 1980s reinforced the greater need for punishment and stiffening the conditions of supervision, thus increasing the conditions of probation, including myriad liberty and spatial restrictions (i.e., curfews, electronic monitoring, etc.), psychological conditions such as evaluation and services, and financial requirements (i.e., fines, fees, restitution, etc.). By the 1990s conditions for probation became commonplace, with the average probationer having 12 to 19 conditions (Corbett, 2015; Taxman, 2012) besides the standard supervision rules regarding face-to-face contacts with officers, not moving without permission, and so on. The probation system resolved the competing social work enforcement tensions by recognizing that enforcement was the dominant punishment goal and focus. The enhanced punishments, which often included treatment and related programs and services offered under stark conditions where services were sparse or inappropriate (see Taxman et al., 2007), altered the perspective of supervision making it difficult for individuals to comply with often difficult and onerous conditions (Taxman et al., 2020).

In the mid-1990s the compliance management model of supervision met with new evidence that increasing conditions and requirements resulted in iatrogenic effects. In one of the largest randomized controlled trials in community corrections, Joan Petersilia and Susan Turner conducted an experiment with intensive supervision probation (ISP) compared to standard supervision. Fourteen sites implemented ISP models that included, at a minimum, increased contacts with the officer, drug testing, and referral to treatment; some sites also included employment and community services. Individuals in ISP across the study sites had similar arrest rates as those in standard supervision and tended to have slightly higher revocation rates including a return to incarceration (Petersilia & Turner, 1993). Commentaries during this era lamented how important these conditions were to ensure that a probation punishment included high levels of accountability and that individuals on supervision were obedient. The stacking-on conditions grew in the 1990s. The Petersilia and Turner study started a discussion about the goals of supervision and alternative models that could blend social work and enforcement. And since treatment and treatment-related issues are a common condition, the social worker enforcement tensions increased, especially in light of increasing revocations from probation. Noncompliance is commonplace on supervision, which leads to revocations and fuels returns to prison. Nearly 25% of new state prison admissions in 2017 (Council of State Governments, 2019) were the result of technical violations, with 75% of prison admissions in Mississippi and North Carolina being probation violations (Pew Charitable Trusts, 2019, p. 2). Individuals with mental illness tend to have higher technical violation rates (Eno Louden & Skeem, 2011). Increased conditions also increase responsibilities, many of which are outside of the control of the probation agency, such as transportation, housing, and discretionary funds to pay for fines, fees, and restitution and treatment services including drug testing. Collectively the "mean" probation period is earmarked by "superhuman" demands on individuals under supervision.

Contemporary Policies and Practices

The risk-need-responsivity (RNR) model of correctional treatment emerged from Canada as a blended approach for merging treatment and punishment under a new theoretical

framework. Andrews and Bonta proffered, supported by meta-analyses and research findings on the value of correctional treatment (see Andrews & Bonta, 2010; Andrews et al.,
1990), that better outcomes could occur from using a three-pronged approach: (a) risk—
getting those individuals who have a higher risk of recidivism into treatment programs
and providing more scrutiny on supervision; (b) need—ensuring that correctional treatment addresses one of the eight "criminogenic needs," which are those directly related to
justice-negative outcomes (such as criminal personality, criminal value system, criminal
peers, substance abuse, deficits in education and employment, dysfunctional families, and
history of justice encounters); and (c) responsivity—ensuring that the programming that is
provided is skills based to help individuals learn to control the thoughts, attitudes, and behaviors that tend to bring them into the justice system and that the programming is tailored
to the individual by being gender and culturally sensitive, working on motivation, dealing
with intellectual disabilities, and so on. The RNR model was primarily applied to carceral
settings, but the early 2000s found the RNR framework adapted for probation supervision
settings. The RNR perspective is viewed as a hybrid model that places a renewed emphasis
on treatment as long as the individual is held accountable for the conditions of supervision.

Taxman (2002, 2008), in her proactive supervision work, identified how the RNR
model can be applied to probation supervision with an emphasis on a working alliance as
the glue to achieve better outcomes. Several models were developed that had similar RNR
components with varying degrees of emphasis: using a standardized risk and need assessment tool, providing case management to link individuals to services, offering treatment
programs that emphasized cognitive-behavioral programming, and using incentives and
sanctions to hold individuals accountable (see Taxman, 2008). A related feature was that the
environment should facilitate a positive working alliance between the officer and person on
supervision (Andrews & Bonta, 2010; Taxman & Ainsworth, 2009), including organization
goals that emphasize treatment and behavioral goals as primary to achieve reductions in
recidivism. In a meta-analysis comparing standard probation, ISP, and RNR-based supervision models, Drake (2011) found that the RNR model reduced recidivism by 16%, whereas
ISP reduced recidivism by 11% and compliance models of supervision had no impact. The
RNR framework has been endorsed by most reform efforts such as the Pew Public Safety
Performance Project and the Bureau of Justice Assistance. RNR-based principles with an
emphasis on a working alliance provide the bridge from mean supervision to meaningful
supervision.

The implementation of the RNR model requires a balancing act, reigniting the enforcement versus social work features of managing individuals in the community. A number
of trainings have emerged to help officers learn the tools, techniques, and strategies of applying social work principles in supervision settings, such as Strategic Training Initiative in
Community Supervision (STICS), Staff Training Aimed at Reducing Re-arrest (STARR),
Effective Practices in Community Supervision (EPICS), and Staff Undertaking Skills To
Advance Innovation (SUSTAIN; see Toronjo & Taxman, 2018, for a discussion of each approach). Each training curriculum reinforces that reductions in recidivism are a result of
targeting medium-/high-risk individuals (risk) for appropriate services, that the interventions should target criminogenic needs (needs), and that those interventions should be

based on cognitive-behavioral and/or social learning models and tailor responses to the individual (responsivity; Bonta et al., 2011; Taxman, 2008). The trainings also prioritize officers creating and maintaining a working relationship with individuals on supervision by using social learning/cognitive-behavioral techniques and by developing trust. Blasko and Taxman (2018) also note the importance of procedural justice where the individual feels they have a voice during supervision and like situations are treated similarly. Chadwick et al. (2015) in a meta-analysis of officers trained in RNR-related strategies (emphasis on a working relationship) found that, regardless of the training curriculum, individuals supervised by trained officers were 13% less likely to be rearrested. The meta-analysis validated that the RNR framework, focusing more on addressing needs (instead of ISP conditions related to surveillance), is more likely to yield positive client outcomes. RNR helps to transform supervision into more of a rehabilitative and meaningful ideal (Taxman et al., 2020).

To deliver a balanced approach using the RNR framework, probation agencies have created innovations to improve supervision. Each offers a set of principles regarding how the officer should proceed and how the officer can achieve the rehabilitative ideals associated with supervision.

Standardized Risk-Need Assessment Tools. Instead of solely relying upon the judgment of the officer (and/or case manager), a number of theoretically and statistically sound tools have been developed to provide officers with the information to identify risk and need factors. These tools (referred to as third-generation tools) include Andrews and Bonta's (2010) eight factors of criminal peers, criminal personality, attitudes and orientation, criminal history, substance abuse, dysfunctional family, and education and employment deficits. More importantly, the tools help to standardize and prioritize the areas that require services and/ or programs to help the individual be successful on supervision. The RNR framework focuses on prioritizing services for criminal behavior attributes and for individuals who are in the moderate- and high-risk categories for future involvement in the justice system; low-risk individuals are generally recommended to have minimal intrusions to reduce demands that might result in noncompliance. The triaging by risk level is promoted to ensure that those with the highest risk (and needs) are able to get the needed resources, particularly in resource-poor supervision settings.

While the goals of standardized instruments are to enhance targeting key areas for intervention, overall, standardized instruments are not necessarily well received by line officers, who find that the instruments interfere with discretion and do not necessarily respect their professionalism (Viglione et al., 2015). In the adult justice literature, the instruments are regarded as information gatherers that can shape the type of information useful for case management, but it is up to the officers to use the information. In the juvenile system, a structured interview process is recommended that integrates the standardized instruments into key decision points. Drawbridge et al. (2019) found that a structured approach facilitates better use of information from risk-need assessment tools than merely providing officers with an instrument.

Another sticking point is the emphasis on triaging moderate- to high-risk individuals with services. This assumes that lower risk individuals do not have needs that should be addressed to be successful on supervision (Viglione & Taxman, 2018). Officers identify various types of lower risk individuals such as those with sex offenses, driving while intoxicated, and numerous other crimes who should be provided services and held to a higher degree of scrutiny. These are considered "high stakes" individuals who tend to score lower on actuarial risk instruments (the risk part of the risk-need assessment tool). Officers tend to use overrides to address these "high stakes" cases, which places individuals in higher risk categories. Overrides serve to label individuals unjustifiably as higher risk (with the assumption that the person is likely going to be risky to the community) as well as to have higher liberty restrictions that increase revocations or further penetration into the justice system. While triaging higher risk individuals for services is common sense, many services are actually geared for individuals who do not have complex needs and therefore the services are not appropriate (Taxman et al., 2007). Given that the array of services *is not* typically geared toward hard-to-treat individuals, more attention should be given to providing a different mix of services.

Recent attention has been raised to whether systematic bias is embedded in the instruments due to how prior arrest, conviction, and incarceration variables are measured (Hannah-Moffat, 2016). Arrests are viewed as determined by law enforcement policing strategies, convictions reflect high rates of plea bargaining without regard for appropriate charging practices, and incarceration is due to systemic bias built into sentencing guidelines, mandatory minimums, and "three strikes and you're out" laws. That is, the historical variables reflect how the justice system functions instead of the behavior of individuals; this is believed to undermine the legitimacy of the risk-need assessment instruments. The debate is whether the variables in risk-need assessment tools measure individual behavior or system behavior since historical factors are affected by justice system operations, both policies and practices.

Further, there is great reoccurring debate over the quality of the measures of "criminogenic needs" since the scales used in many criminal legal risk-need assessment tools are not psychometrically sound and there is variation in definitions of criminogenic needs across the various risk-need instruments (Via et al., 2016). Further, some of the so-called "criminogenic needs" are similar to the factors in the social determinants of health framework that affect individual functioning—where individuals live, work, and/or indulge in recreational activities. Some of the "criminogenic needs" overlap with traits of improvised individuals such as family issues, values, education, employment, and attitudes. The justice system does not necessarily recognize the criminalization of poverty, nor does criminogenic needs. Critics of the tools acknowledge that officers have limited ability to improve the quality of a person's life regarding financial distress, housing, food security, and so on due to limited resources. also, officers do not see it as their role to address these factors since they are not considered to be directly related to justice outcomes or managing conditions. Yet, the intertwining of needs and social determinants of health, with needs perceived as "criminogenic" and the social determinants perceived as "health factors," places the social worker–oriented officer in a dilemma related to case management and enforcement. This is exacerbated by the overemphasis on deciding what is considered criminal instead of realizing how poverty affects the functioning of individuals. In fact, Mulllainathan and Shafir (2013) note that lack of resources, which they refer to as scarcity, can affect decision-making since individuals are preoccupied with food, housing, and other survival needs. This in turn has an impact on an individual's cognitive capacity because it limits the bandwidth of a person to deal with these needs. Deficient bandwidth can lead to impulsivity and carelessness (Corbett, 2015), including missing probation meetings and prioritizing survival needs over supervision demands. The justice system's failure to recognize how individuals under supervision are affected by poverty is generally not incorporated into managing conditions of supervision.

Case Management. In supervision, a supervision plan generally encompasses the requirements of supervision and the services designed to target criminogenic needs. The supervision plan is designed to be similar to the treatment plan, with recommendations to include short-term goals. With a standardized tool, case management strategies can be used to assign individuals to appropriate treatment programs or services and controls as part of a supervision plan. Officers often have to integrate the court- and/or parole board–ordered conditions with the needs of the individual (informed by the risk and need assessment tools). Miller and Maloney (2013) and Viglione et al. (2015) found that officers do not frequently use the risk-need assessment information to inform plans; instead, they rely upon the conditions that are assigned by higher authorities (Thurman et al., 2019). Emphasizing judicially assigned conditions at the sake of tool-informed priorities serves to undermine the RNR framework; it also demonstrates the continuing tensions among compliance and social work emphases. Essentially this reinforces the emphasis on compliance management, where the conditions define the purpose of supervision instead of rehabilitative goals.

Appropriate Treatment and Controls. RNR provides a framework for matching risk and need factors to reduce the likelihood of recidivism. The responsivity component emphasizes treatment that embraces a social learning approach, namely cognitive-behavioral programming. Treatment is viewed as an opportunity to help the individual learn to manage their daily life to reduce the risk of criminal involvement. Cognitive-behavioral programs have been found in primary research studies and meta-analyses to be effective in reducing offending (see Cullen & Gilbert, 2012). Controls (e.g., drug testing, curfews, area restrictions, fines/fees, electronic monitoring, etc.) are used as both therapeutic means and restrictions of liberties to reinforce the punishment message. As a therapeutic tool, controls restrict the movement of the individual and impose psychological constraints. Controls can be considered to structure an individual's movements in such a manner to reinforce treatment goals.

The major challenge to achieving the goal of providing needs-driven treatment services is the limited capacity of existing treatment programs and the limited array of treatment programs. Taxman et al. (2007) found that probation agencies, on any given day, can only provide treatment services to 10% of the probation population, and these programs are unlikely to offer cognitive-behavioral programming (Friedmann et al., 2007). Individuals on probation are often placed in programming that is inconsistent with their needs. A further challenge is that the controls, many of which are conditions mandated by the court, are often overemphasized in the supervision plan (Thurman et al., 2019). The overemphasis on controls can reduce the effectiveness of treatment programming and establish a scenario of "managerial justice," where the rehabilitation programs are symbolic and drowned out by the emphasis on compliance. This is the continuous challenge associated with balancing enforcement and social work roles.

Incentives and Sanctions. Managing conditions of release is a major role of supervision agencies. The stiffening of conditions and probation requirements validates that probation can be tough and individuals can be held accountable for their behavior. The drawback is that the compliance model of ISP efforts sets the bar high for personal conduct, leading to backend sentencing practices (i.e., being sent to prison after failure on supervision affects an individual's further involvement in the justice system through revocations). Probation and justice agencies have responded to the demands of managing conditions by using a number of strategies to incentivize compliance. The use of a "carrot and stick" approach, based on operant conditioning principles where the behavior could be linked to a response (positive or negative), has dominated the response with a goal of preventing revocations.

Various models were implemented as part of efforts to curtail revocations. The favored plan was to use incremental sanctions and/or incentives to show the importance of compliance. Administrative sanctions were the first wave of responses based on the nature of most noncompliant behavior. The grid (type of behavior by response) focused on punitive responses ranging from more drug testing to treatment programming to short periods of time in jail (up to 30 days). The results from these efforts varied from no impact on revocations (Turner et al., 2012) to limited impact on revocations (Hamilton et al., 2017). Most of the grids emphasized sanctions over incentives. The administrative sanctions approach led to some parole officers engaging in enforcement activities including teaming with the police as a means to arrest noncompliant offenders (Rudes, 2012). Another framework included having the judge oversee individuals that were not in compliance. The Hawaii Opportunities Probation with Enforcement (HOPE) program was designed to have the individual appear before a judge to monitor conditions as a reminder of the power of the authority to revoke probation. While HOPE involved some incentives, the judge often used sanctions including increased treatment options (as a sanction) to restate the importance of accountability and compliance. The initial findings from HOPE in Hawaii were promising (see Hawkins & Kleinman, 2009), but replication in four other sites found that the HOPE model did not impact revocations or recidivism. In fact, the study noted the prevalence of noncompliance among probationers in the HOPE and standard supervision groups (Lattimore et al., 2016) given the number of conditions.

One effort to use incentives with sanctions within federal probation had some interesting results. Agencies were given the option to identify the target goals and incentivize these goals with nonmonetary rewards (e.g., reduce time on supervision, reduce drug testing, reduce conditions, reduce face-to-face contacts). Officers were hesitant to incentivize only certain behaviors like treatment attendance, negative drug tests, etc.; instead, they opted to incentivize all conditions but also sanction all conditions (Rudes et al., 2012). This form of "managerial justice" serves to negate incentives by accentuating sanctions. That is, if a person attended treatment and tested positive, the sanction would be issued and the positive behavior would be ignored. Failure to acknowledge small steps reinforces the compliance/enforcement goals. Besides the number of target behaviors, the timing of the incentives affected the impact of the strategy. Some probation agencies did not offer the incentive immediately after the behavior occurred, and others offered it soon after the behavior. Sloas and colleagues (2019) demonstrated that providing the incentive close to when the behavior occurred reduced recidivism. Another modified model is a collaborative behavioral management model where the officers, individuals on probation, and treatment providers meet routinely to review progress and use incentives as a means to make short-term progress. While collaborative behavioral management did not reduce recidivism for all parolees, it did have an impact on those who use "soft drugs" such as alcohol, marijuana, and other similar types of drugs (Friedmann et al., 2012).

Way Forward in Probation Supervision

The cumulative research literature advances the social worker side of the officer's role instead of the enforcer side of correctional interventions on supervision (and carceral settings). The social worker role is focused on more of a person-centered approach to tailor supervision to the needs of the individual and target specific programming needs. Then, the risk level is used to establish the amount of structure to support lifestyle changes. While myriad services are useful, the emphasis on the social learning environment is designed to improve the individual's daily life skills in terms of decisions, attitudes, and behaviors. A meta-analysis by Lipsey and Cullen (2007) found cognitive-behavioral therapy is associated with substantial reductions in recidivism in the range of 10% to 38% (Table 29.1). Control-based interventions are often associated with *increases* in recidivism or, at best, small reductions in the range of 2% to 8%. The more recent meta-analysis on supervision by Drake (2011) reinforces the value of an RNR orientation to supervision with a 16% reduction compared to ISP or standard supervision, although the underlying studies found that RNR is practiced in various ways. RNR supervision can consist of using a validated instrument, case management, cognitive-behavioral therapy, graduated sanctions and incentives, or some combination of these. A supportive environment is also critical to the individual on supervision feeling that probation is not a "nail 'em, jail 'em, and tail 'em" approach.

The tension between enforcement and social work practices is an unresolved issue dating back to the inception of probation as an alternative to incarceration. While the emphasis has been on training officers and on implementing the key features of the RNR model, without attention to the goals and mission of supervision with leadership reinforcing the importance of these goals, the efforts to reform supervision are likely to fail (Blasko et al., 2019; Taxman, 2018). The revised goals and mission must be supported by external stakeholders as well as shifts in policy. Below are some of the reforms that are under consideration.

Reduce the length of supervision. The average probation sentence is 22.4 months, but individuals can be placed on supervision anywhere from 6 months to life. The average probation sentence has increased over the last two decades. Extending the length of the probation sentence has commonly occurred, and since 2000, over one-third of states have increased the average length of supervision (Horowitz et al., 2018).

TABLE 29.1 Meta-Analyses of Treatment and Control Intervention Effects on Recidivism

Meta-Analysis	Age Group	Intervention	Change in Recidivism
Treatment			
Garrett (1985)	Juveniles	Residential treatment	−10%
Whitehead and Lab (1989)	Juveniles	Community and residential treatment	−24%
Andrews et al. (1990)	Juveniles and adults	Community and residential treatment	−20%
	Juveniles	Community and residential treatment	−20%
	Adults	Community and residential treatment	−22%
	Juveniles and adults	Community treatment	−22%
	Juveniles and adults	Residential treatment	−14%
Petrosino (1997)	Juveniles and adults	Community and residential treatment	−20%
	Juveniles	Community and residential treatment	−24%
	Adults	Community and residential treatment	−14%
Cleland et al. (1997)	Juveniles and adults	Community and residential treatment	−16%
	Juveniles	Community and residential treatment	−16%
	Adults	Community and residential treatment	−14%
Lipsey and Wilson (1998)	Juveniles	Community treatment	−26%
	Juveniles	Residential treatment	−14%
Illescas et al. (2001)	Juveniles and adults	Community and residential treatment	−34%
	Juveniles	Community and residential treatment	−38%
	Adults	Community and residential treatment	−20%
Latimer et al. (2003)	Juveniles	Community and residential treatment	−18%
Supervision			
Pearson et al. (1997)	Adults	Community supervision	−8%
Lipsey and Wilson (1998)	Juveniles	Community supervision	−8%
Aos et al. (2001)	Juveniles	Intensive community supervision	−4%
	Adults	Intensive community supervision	−2%
Intermediate Sanctions			
Andrews et al. (1990)	Juveniles and adults	Criminal sanctions	+14%
Petrosino (1997)	Juveniles and adults	Deterrence	0%
Cleland et al. (1997)	Juveniles	Criminal sanctions	−8%
	Adults	Criminal sanctions	−4%
Smith et al. (2002)	Juveniles and adults	Intermediate sanctions	−2%
Lipsey and Wilson (1998)	Juveniles	Prison visitation	+2%
Aos et al. (2001)	Juveniles	Prison visitation	+12%
Petrosino et al. (2003)	Juveniles	Prison visitation	+26%
Confinement			
Pearson et al. (1997)	Adults	Incarceration	+4%
Smith et al. (2002)	Juveniles and adults	Longer vs. shorter prison sentences	+6%
	Juveniles and adults	Incarceration vs. community supervision	+14%
Villettaz et al. (2006)	Juveniles and adults	Custodial vs. noncustodial sentences	+4%
MacKenzie et al. (2001)	Juveniles and adults	Boot camp	0%
Aos et al. (2001)	Juveniles	Boot camp	+10%
	Adults	Boot camp	+0%

Note: Table adapted from Lipsey and Cullen (2007).

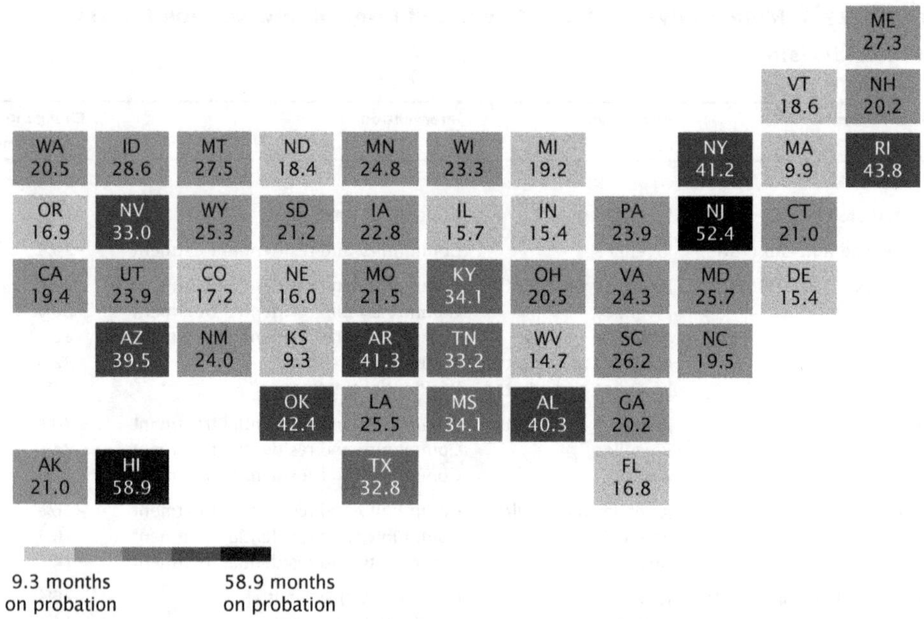

FIGURE 29.1 Where People Are Sentenced Can Dramatically Affect How Long They Spend on Probation Estimated average term by state in months, 2018.

As shown in Figure 29.1, in 2018, the average supervision ranged from 9.9 months to 52.4 months. Extending the length of supervision has the impacts of (a) bulging caseloads, where officers have an average of 100 individuals to supervise, and (b) creating opportunities for revocations and "backend" sentencing (Lin et al., 2010). In 2020, California enacted a new state law (AB 1950) that shortens the length of probation in most misdemeanor cases to 1 year and in most felony cases to 2 years. There has been a push to reduce supervision lengths, which may complicate a social work framework in that individuals have less time for treatment services, giving yield to a push on enforcement. However, the tradeoffs could be that the system finds a way to provide treatment during the period of supervision and continue treatment afterward (preferably with similar funding of the services).

Reduce the number of conditions of supervision. As highlighted earlier, the stiffening of probation includes stacking on conditions to probation. Intensive supervision was built on having standardized conditions, but the 1990s and onward saw judges increase the conditions. Also, many states enacted legislation to increase the standard requirements of supervision, including possession of a firearm, payment of probation fees, drug testing, etc. Ron Corbett (2015), former Massachusetts commissioner of probation, has called for a "zero-based condition setting":

> At the moment an offender is placed on probation, the judge and the probation officer, working collaboratively to set appropriate conditions, would start with a blank sheet. Or almost blank—every probationer should be required to obey the law. Beyond that, any additional conditions would have to be determined, in the instant case, to be necessary in the service of appropriate sanctioning

and treatment. Most importantly, the conditions would need to be determined to be reasonable for the offender. Standard conditions (save the one) would be eliminated, and conditions would optimally be few in number so that probationers (who are often broke and thoroughly preoccupied with survival, as discussed above) would have a decent chance to succeed. Setting conditions, the obtainment of which would be within the reach of the offender, would create opportunities for an experience so seldom available to probationers—a sense of accomplishment for those offenders in dire need of that experience, which would earn them the commendation of the authorities and the pleasure of early termination as a reward for full compliance. (p. 1729)

Corbett makes a compelling case for not only limiting the number of conditions but also ensuring that the conditions are beneficial to the individual. Reducing conditions has the collateral benefit of having fewer opportunities for revocation, which has been identified as a major driver of incarceration rates.

Reduce fines and fees for people on supervision. Probation (and parole) is one of the few sentences that requires the individual to pay for the opportunity to be supervised by the state. States started imposing fees for supervision as a means to generate revenue for cash-stricken states. Fees can start at around $35 and move up in ocst from there. Failure to pay the fees can be used as a reason for revocation. Even more so, Corbett (2015, p. 1711) refers to this as part of "soaking the Poor: the high cost of probation (for probationers)." Probation fees are just one of the many financial penalties, in addition to standard payments such as restitution to individuals, one-time fees, court costs, fines, and other special fees. In fact, officers have the role of bill collector instead of social worker or enforcer (Ruhland, 2020).

Create alternative processes for individuals with substance use and mental health disorders. Over the last four decades, the War on Drugs has resulted in a concentration of individuals with substance use disorders, who tend to be poor and do not have access to health insurance, in the justice system. Nearly half of justice-involved individuals have substance use disorders, and the justice system has implemented substance use treatment in prisons and jails, in the community as part of problem-solving courts, and in probation agencies. As part of probation, treatment, testing, and sanctions became the genre' in the 1990s and clearly is incorporated in all types of initiatives for individuals with substance use disorders. The emphasis on the three-pronged approach has been to ensure that individuals are held accountable, with drug testing and sanctions to ensure that individuals are compliant and that they are drug-free; treatment is the means to help individuals achieve drug-free ends. Since 1994, there has been a push to use problem-solving courts (which also use the treatment, testing, and sanctions model, with the judge overseeing the progress in status hearings), but recently this model has been criticized for its overemphasis on the punishment of individuals who cannot manage their addiction behaviors (Alliance on Drug Policy, 2014). Essentially revocations and reinstatement of incarceration are the unintended consequences of these policies.

Within probation agencies, some have specialized caseloads where officers handle substance use cases, but the majority do not. Instead, cases are distributed over the general population without officers being trained specifically in how to work with substance abusers. There have been few evaluations of specialized caseloads, but Skeem and colleagues (2007, 2017) examined specialized caseloads for supervising individuals with mental health needs and found that there were fewer revocations. The challenge, regardless of specialized or general caseloads, is the availability of services. Few treatment agencies provide services on-site and often rely on services in the community, which are provided by the public health agency or other resources. Therefore, officers often focus on compliance issues. Specialized caseloads with behavioral health officers or counselors probably are the best avenue within the justice system.

A better option is diverting individuals with substance use and/or mental health disorders to community-based treatment services that are offered in lieu of being adjudicated. A number of diversion models have emerged, but one of the fastest-growing approaches is Law Enforcement Assisted Diversion (LEAD), which has recently been retitled Let Everyone Advance with Dignity. LEAD is an alternative to the justice system with officers serving as the decision maker for who should be criminally prosecuted and who should not. LEAD uses an intensive case management approach for low-level offending behavior (i.e., prostitution, drug possession, homelessness, petty shoplifting, etc.). Officers, instead of booking an individual, will refer the individual to a case manager who will work on housing, food security, behavioral health services (if needed), employment, and other factors that affect involvement in low-level offending behavior. A comparison group study found participants of LEAD to have statistically significant fewer arrests (Collins et al., 2017) as well as to be employed, find housing, and have licit income (Clifasefi et al., 2017). LEAD is one of many models to deflect individuals from the justice system. Diversion models require community behavioral health centers that can take individuals "on demand" (24/7) to be successful.

Conclusion

The enforcement versus social work model for probation has been in tension for over 100 years, almost from the inception of probation services. While the tendency leans toward social work as a primary goal of supervision, the punitive culture of supervision often results in enforcing the conditions of release to focus on compliance-based strategies. An emphasis on compliance is a proxy for enforcement. Enforcement became a necessity in a probation environment where the number of requirements (conditions) of supervision increased and the integrity of probation was threatened when requirements were not addressed. That is, societal expectations for a legitimate probation system are to ensure that the individuals on supervision are held accountable for their actions. Otherwise, probation supervision is tainted.

While the culture endorses an enforcement-oriented probation system, the empirical literature counters this with the stark reality that enforcement merely generates more failures (via revocations). Social work approaches consistently generate better justice-related outcomes—fewer arrests, convictions, or reincarcerations. The social work approach has led to new curriculums that train officers to balance their "enforcement cap" with the skills used by social workers and to endorse social learning environments to facilitate better outcomes. The social work skills include empathy, motivational strategies, case management, emphasizing social determinants of health, and small proximal steps. Regardless of the curriculum used, the use of these skills by officers is believed to be the secret to balancing the enforcement aims with individual client–centered progress. While more probation agencies are endorsing the revised RNR framework, the push is to reduce the conditions that an individual is accountable for. This push then creates the capacity within probation agencies to use a social learning framework since the number of conditions to manage is reduced, and with fewer individuals on a caseload, officers have the time to individualize case management services.

Mass supervision, just like the mass incarceration counterpart, is being reinvented through an emphasis on using the criminal legal system to deal with offending behaviors. Public health concerns—behavioral health, social inequities, and so on—are recognized as the greater part of the needs of individuals who are being supervised, and these should be addressed from a public health framework. The punitive features of probation of the past are the focus of efforts to scale back the "meanness" and emphasize meaningful supervision that is devoted to improving an individual's quality of life. The reinvention of supervision calls attention to a more client-centered approach that recognizes the intertwined safety-health dynamics and places emphasis on addressing social determinants of health to achieve supervision outcomes. It is befitting that this approach is more aligned with the principles and ethics of social work, and there is a greater need for social workers to be employed by probation agencies.

Social workers in probation settings can extend the client-centered focus that is embraced by the ethical guidance of the profession. More importantly, the principles of self-determination, informed consent, cultural competency and individuality, and fair procedures (i.e., cost for services, handling clients with limited decision-making capabilities) are embedded in the social work culture and are more commonplace than a compliance or law enforcement perspective. The direction of probation being focused on the individual and advocacy for the individual is part of the ethos of social work.

References

Alliance on Drug Policy. (2014). *Moving away from drug courts: Toward a health-centered approach to drug use.* https://drugpolicy.org/resource/moving-away-drug-courts-toward-health-centered-approach-drug-use-englishspanish

Andrews, D., Zinger, I., Hoge, R. D., Bonta, J., Gendreau, P., & Cullen, F. T. (1990). Does correctional treatment work? A clinically relevant and psychologically informed meta-analysis. *Criminology, 28,* 369–404. https://doi.org/10.1111/j.1745-9125.1990.tb01330.x

Andrews, D. A., & Bonta, J. (2010). *The psychology of criminal conduct* (5th ed.). Anderson Publishing.

Aos, S., Phipps, P., Barnoski, R., Lieb, R. (2001). *The comparative costs and benefits of programs to reduce crime.* Olympia: Washington State Institute for Public Policy.

Appleton, C. (2020). Understanding rapport in supervision settings. In P. K. Lattimore, B. M. Huebner, & F. S. Taxman (Eds.), *Handbook on moving corrections and sentencing forward: Building on the record* (pp. 174–184). Routledge.

Blasko, B., & Taxman, F. S. (2018). Are supervision practices procedurally fair?: Development and predictive utility of a procedural justice measure for use in community corrections settings. *Criminal Justice and Behavior, 45*(3), 402–420. doi.org/10.1177/0093854817749255

Blasko, B., Viglione, J., & Taxman, F. S. (2019). Probation officer-probation agency fit: understanding disparities in the use of motivational interviewing strategies. *Corrections: Policy, Practice and Research, 4*(1), 39–57. https://doi.org/10.1080/23774657.2018.1544471

Bonta, J., Bourgon, G., Rugge, T., Scott, T.-L., Yessine, A. K., Gutierrez, L., & Li, J. (2011). An experimental demonstration of training probation officers in evidence-based community supervision. *Criminal Justice and Behavior, 38*(11), 1127–1148. https://doi.org/10.1177/0093854811420678

Chadwick, N., Dewolf, A., & Serin, R. (2015). Effectively training community supervision officers: A meta-analytic review of the impact on offender outcome. *Criminal Justice and Behavior, 42*(10), 977–989. https://doi.org/10.1177/0093854815595661

Cleland, C. M., Pearson, F. S., Lipton, D. S., Yee, D. (1997). Does age make a difference? A meta-analytic approach to reductions in criminal offending for juveniles and adults. Presented at Annual Meeting of the American Society of Criminology, San Diego.

Clifasefi, S. L., Lonczak, H. S., & Collins, S. E. (2017). Seattle's Law Enforcement Assisted Diversion (LEAD) program: Within-subjects changes on housing, employment and income/benefits outcomes and associations with recidivism. *Crime & Delinquency, 63,* 429–445.

Collins, S. E., Lonczak, H. S., & Clifasefi, S. L. (2017). Seattle's Law Enforcement Assisted Diversion (LEAD): Program effects on recidivism outcomes. *Evaluation and Program Planning, 64,* 49–56. https://doi.org/10.1016/j.evalprogplan.2017.05.008

Corbett, R. P., Jr. (2015). The burdens of leniency: The changing face of probation. *Minnesota Law Review, 99,* 1697–1732.

Council of State Governments. (2019). *Confined and costly: How supervision violations are filling prisons and burdening budgets.* https://csgjusticecenter.org/wp-content/uploads/2020/01/confined-and-costly.pdf

Cullen, F. T., & Gilbert, K. E. (2012). *Reaffirming rehabilitation* (2nd ed.). Routledge.

Drake, E. K. (2011). *"What works" in community supervision: Interim report.* Washington State Institute for Public Policy. https://doi.org/10.13140/RG.2.1.3781.0404

Drawbridge, D. C., Todorovic, K., Winters, G. M., & Vincent, G. M. (2019). Implementation of risk-need-responsivity principles into probation case planning. *Law and Human Behavior, 43*(5), 455–467. https://doi.org/10.1037/lhb0000351

Eno Louden, J., & Skeem, J. L. (2011). *Parolees with mental disorder: Toward evidence-based practice.* UC Irvine Center for Evidence-Based Corrections. https://cpb-us-e2.wpmucdn.com/sites.uci.edu/dist/0/1149/files/2013/06/Parolees-with-Mental-Disorder.pdf

Friedmann, P. D., Green, T. C., Taxman, F. S., Harrington, M., Rhodes, A. G., Katz, E., O'Connell, D., Martin, S. S., Frisman, L. K., Litt, M., Burdon, W., Clarke, J. G., Fletcher, B. W., & the Step'n Out Research Group of CJ-DATS. (2012). Collaborative behavioral management among parolees: Drug use, crime and re-arrest in the Step'n Out randomized trial. *Addiction, 107*(6), 1099–1108. https://doi.org/10.1111/j.1360-0443.2011.03769.x

Friedmann, P. D., Taxman, F. S., & Henderson, C. (2007). Evidence-based treatment practices for drug-involved adults in the criminal justice system. *Journal of Substance Abuse Treatment, 32*(3), 267–277. doi:10.1016/j.jsat.2006.12.020

Garrett, C. J. (1985). Effects of residential treatment on adjudicated delinquents: A meta-analysis. *Journal of Research in Crime and Delinquency, 22,* 287–308.

Hamilton, Z., Tollefsbol, E., Campagna, M., & van Wormer, J. (2017). Customizing criminal justice assessments. In F. S. Taxman (Ed.), *Handbook on risk and need 6 page assessment: Theory and practice, American Society of Criminology, Division of Corrections and Sentencing* (Handbook Series Vol. 1, pp. 333–377). Routledge.

Hannah-Moffat, H. (2016). Purpose and context matters: Creating a space for meaningful dialogues about risk and need. In F. S. Taxman (Ed.), *Handbook on risk and need assessment: Theory and practice* (pp. 312–330). Routledge.

Hawkins, A., & Kleiman, M. (2009). *Managing drug-involved probationers with swift and certain sanctions: Evaluating Hawaii's HOPE. Evaluation Report.* NCJ 229023. National Institute of Justice.

Horowitz, J., Utada, C., & Fuhrmann, M. (2018). *Probation and parole systems marked by high stakes, missed opportunities: 1 in 55 U.S. adults is under community supervision.* Pew Charitable Trusts. https://www.

pewtrusts.org/-/media/assets/2018/09/probation_and_parole_systems_marked_by_high_stakes_misse d_opportunities_pew.pdf

Illescas, S. R., Sanchez-Meca, J. S., Genovés, V. G. (2001). Treatment of offenders and recidivism: Assessment of the effectiveness of programmes applied in Europe. *Psychology in Spain, 5*, 47–62.

Kaeble, D., & Alper, M. (2020). *Probation and parole in the United States, 2017–2018.* Bureau of Justice Statistics. https://www.bjs.gov/content/pub/pdf/ppus1718.pdf

Latimer, J., Dowden, C., Morton-Bourgon, K. E. (2003). Treating youth in conflict with the law: A new meta-analysis. Report RR03YJ-3e. Ottawa, Canada: Department of Justice.

Lattimore, P. K., MacKenzie, D. L., Zajac, G., Dawes, D., Arsenault, E., & Tueller, S. (2016). Outcome findings from the HOPE demonstration field experiment: Is swift, certain, and fair an effective supervision strategy? *Criminology & Public Policy, 15*(4), 1103–1141. https://doi.org/10.1111/1745-9133.12248

Lin, J., Gratter, R., & Petersilia, J. (2010). Back-end sentencing and reimprisonment: Individual, organizational, and community predictors of parole sanctioning decisions. *Criminology, 48*, 759–700.

Lipsey, M. W., & Cullen, F. T. (2007). The effectiveness of correctional rehabilitation: A review of systematic reviews. *Annual Review of Law and Social Science, 3*(1), 297–320. https://doi.org/10.1146/annurev.lawsoc sci.3.081806.112833

Lipsey, M. W., & Wilson, D. B. (1998). Effective intervention for serious juvenile offenders. In R Loeber, DP Farrington (Eds.), *Serious and violent juvenile offenders: Risk factors and successful interventions* (Vol. 13, pp. 313–345). Thousand Oaks, CA: Sage.

Martinson, R. (1974). What works? Questions and answers about prison reform. *Public Interest, 35*, 22–54. https://www.nationalaffairs.com/public_interest/detail/what-works-questions-and-answers-about-pri son-reform

Miller, J., & Maloney, C. (2013). Practitioner compliance with risk/needs assessment tools: A theoretical and empirical assessment. *Criminal Justice and Behavior, 40*(7), 716–736. https://doi.org/10.1177/00938 54812468883

Mulllainathan, E., & Shafir, S. (2013). *Scarcity: Why having so little means so much.* Times Book.

Pearson, F. S., Lipton, D. S., & Cleland, C.M. (1997). Rehabilitative programs in adult corrections: CDATE meta-analysis. Presented at Annual Meeting of the American Society of Criminology, San Diego.

Petersilia, J., & Turner, S. (1993). *Evaluating intensive supervision probation/parole: Results of a nationwide experiment.* National Institute of Justice.

Petrosino, A. (1997). 'What works?' revisited again: A meta-analysis of randomized field experiments in rehabilitation, deterrence, and prevention. PhD diss. Rutgers, State Univ. New Jersey, Newark.

Petrosino, A., Turpin-Petrosino, C., & Buehler, J. (2003). Scared straight and other juvenile awareness programs for preventing juvenile delinquency: a systematic review of the randomized experimental evidence. *Annals of the American Academy of Political and Social Science, 589*, 41–62.

Pew Charitable Trusts. (2019). *To safely cut incarceration, states rethink responses to supervision violations: Evidence-based policies lead to higher rates of parole and probation success.* https://www.pewtrusts. org/-/media/assets/2019/07/pspp_states_target_technical_violations_v1.pdf

Public Policy Institute. (n.d.) *Mass incarceration: The whole pie 2020.* https://www.prisonpolicy.org/reports/ pie2020.html

Rudes, D. S. (2012). Getting technical: Parole officers' continued use of technical violations under California's parole reform agenda. *Journal of Crime and Justice, 35*(2), 249–268. https://doi.org/10.1080/ 0735648X.2012.677572

Rudes, D. S., Taxman, F. S., Portillo, S., Murphy, A., Rhodes, A., Stitzer, M., Luongo, P., & Friedmann, P. D. (2012). Adding positive reinforcements in a criminal justice setting: Acceptability and feasibility. *Journal of Substance Abuse Treatment, 42*(3), 260–270.

Ruhland, E. L. (2020). Social worker, law enforcer, and now bill collector: Probation officers' collection of supervision fees. *Journal of Offender Rehabilitation, 59*, 44–63.

Skeem, J. L., Eno Louden, J., Polaschek, D., & Camp, J. (2007). Assessing relationship quality in mandated community treatment: Blending care with control. *Psychological Assessment, 19*(4), 397–410. https://doi. org/10.1037/1040-3590.19.4.397

Skeem, J. L., Manchak, S., & Montoya, L. (2017). Comparing public safety outcomes for traditional probation vs specialty mental health probation. *JAMA Psychiatry, 74*(9), 942–948. https://doi.org/10.1001/jam apsychiatry.2017.1384

Sloas, L., Murphy, A., Wooditch, A., & Taxman, F. S. (2019). Assessing the use and impact of points and rewards across four federal probation districts: A contingency management approach. *Victims & Offenders, 14*(7), 811–831. https://doi.org/10.1080/15564886.2019.1656691

Smith, P., Goggin, C., & Gendreau, P. (2002). The effects of prison sentences and intermediate sanctions on recidivism: General effects and individual differences. Report JS42–103/2002. Ottawa, Canada: Solicitor General.

Taxman, F. S. (2002). Supervision—Exploring the dimensions of effectiveness. *Federal Probation, 66*(2), 14–27. https://www.uscourts.gov/sites/default/files/66_2_3_0.pdf

Taxman, F. S. (2008). No illusions: Offender and organizational change in Maryland's proactive community supervision efforts. *Criminology & Public Policy, 7*(2), 275–302.

Taxman, F. S. (2018). The partially clothed emperor: Evidence-based practices. *Journal of Contemporary Criminal Justice, 34*(1), 97–114. https://doi.org/10.1177/1043986217750444

Taxman, F. S. (2012). Probation, intermediate sanctions, and community-based corrections. In J. Petersilia & K. R. Reitz (Eds.), *The Oxford handbook of sentencing and corrections* (pp. 363–385). Oxford University Press.

Taxman, F. S., Perdoni, M. L., & Harrison, L. D. (2007). Drug treatment services for adult offenders: The state of the state. *Journal of Substance Abuse Treatment, 32*(3), 239–254.

Taxman, F. S., Smith, L., & Rudes, D. S. (2020). From mean to meaningful probation: The legacy of intensive supervision programs. In P. K. Lattimore, B. M. Huebner, & F. S. Taxman (Eds.), *Handbook on moving corrections and sentencing forward: Building on the record* (pp. 61–78). Routledge.

Taxman, F. S., & Ainsworth, S. (2009). Correctional milieu: The key to quality outcomes. *Victims & Offenders, 4*(4), 334–340.

Toronjo, H., & Taxman, F. (2018). Supervision face-to-face contacts: The emergence of an intervention. In P. Ugwudike, P. Raynor, & J. Annison (Eds.), *Evidence-based skills in criminal justice: International research on supporting rehabilitation and desistance* (pp. 217–242). Policy Press.

Turner, S. F., Braithwaite, H., Kearney, L., & Hearle, D. (2012). Evaluation of the California Parole Violation Decision-Making Instrument (PVDMI). *Journal of Crime and Justice, 35*(2), 269–295.

Thurman, T., Chowdhury, S., & Taxman, F. S. (2019). Fidelity measures for risk need assessment (RNA) tools usage in case plans. *Corrections: Policy, Practice and Research.* https://doi.org/10.1080/23774 657.2019.1696252

Viglione, J., Rudes, D. S., & Taxman, F. S. (2015). Misalignment in supervision: Implementing risk/needs assessment instruments in probation. *Criminal Justice and Behavior, 42*(3), 263–285. https://doi.org/ 10.1177/0093854814548447

Viglione, J., & Taxman, F. S. (2018). Low risk offenders under probation supervision: Risk management and the risk-needs-responsivity framework. *Criminal Justice and Behavior, 45*(12), 1809–1831. https://doi. org/10.1177/0093854818790299

Via, B., Dezember, A., & Taxman, F. S. (2016). Exploring how to measure criminogenic needs: Five instruments and no real answers. In F. S. Taxman (Ed.), *Handbook on risk and need assessment: Theory and practice* (pp. 312–330). Routledge.

Villettaz, P., Killias, M., & Zoder, I. (2006). The effects of custodial vs noncustodial sentences on reoffending. A systematic review of the state of knowledge. Campbell Collaboration Library. http://www. campbellcollaboration.org/frontend.asp

von Hirsch, A. (1976). *Doing justice: The choice of punishments.* Farrar, Strauss, and Giroux.

Whitehead, J. T., & Lab, S. P. (1989). A meta-analysis of juvenile correctional treatment. *Journal of Research in Crime and Delinquency, 26,* 276–295.

30

Restorative Justice

Shannon M. Sliva and Sophia P. Sarantakos

Restorative justice is a community-based approach to harm response that is increasingly used in criminal legal settings as an alternative or supplement to court and correctional procedures. It is uniquely situated for social work practice due to its focus on human relationships. This chapter will offer an introduction to restorative justice and discuss the theoretical bases of this approach. It will then identify the restorative justice practices most commonly used in criminal legal settings and summarize empirical support for their efficacy with justice-involved populations. Finally, it will offer a case study depicting the use of a restorative justice approach to respond to community violence and highlight the challenges and opportunities for social workers in this unique practice arena.

What Is Restorative Justice?

Restorative justice is a philosophy and a set of practices that seek repair and healing when people cause harm. Unlike other approaches in this text, restorative justice is concerned with crime only to the extent that it is one way of conceptualizing harm that has been caused within a community. Restorative justice processes typically bring together people who have a stake in a crime, conflict, or other harmful situation to identify what has happened, who has been impacted, and how the harm can be repaired as much as possible. The people who have a stake are many. They include the person(s) most directly impacted and the person(s) most directly responsible, as well as others who are affected by the harm or have a role in repairing it. These people may include family members, neighbors, or community members such as church leaders, teachers, or elders. Participants in a restorative justice process often create a verbal or written agreement about how the responsible person will make amends and—to the extent possible—how the harm caused will be repaired. Importantly, restorative justice practices are collective processes that put decision-making into the hands of

Shannon M. Sliva and Sophia P. Sarantakos, *Restorative Justice* In: *Handbook of Forensic Social Work*. Edited by: David Axlyn McLeod, Anthony P. Natale, and Kristin W. Mapson, Oxford University Press. © Oxford University Press 2024.
DOI: 10.1093/oso/9780197694732.003.0030

impacted people and seek solutions based on the community's strengths and resources. As such, it offers an approach to crime and violence that is particularly congruent with social work values (Beck, Kropf, & Leonard, 2010).

While the scenario outlined above offers a typical example, the term "restorative justice" has been liberally used to describe a range of ideas and practices—from facilitated personal encounters called victim-offender dialogues (VODs) to community justice processes to peacemaking processes between groups and nations. Key practices used by forensic social workers will be further described later in this chapter, where we will also summarize the body of evidence for each. For now, it is important to understand that restorative justice is what Johnstone and Van Ness (2007) have called a "contested concept" (p. 6), signifying both its internal complexity and its openness to different understandings and influences across time and place. For instance, it has been characterized by some scholars as a "theory of justice" (Van Ness & Strong, 2015) and by others as a "justice mechanism" (Daly, 2016). It has been defined alternatively by its *processes*—namely, transformative encounters between people—and its *outcomes* of repair and restoration (Johnstone & Van Ness, 2007). It has been articulated specifically as a response to crime (Zehr, 1990) and broadly as a way of being in everyday life (Wachtel, 2003).

Restorative justice has been defined perhaps as often by what it is not as what it is. Most commonly, it is positioned opposite of retributive justice. In 1990, Howard Zehr popularized the current application of the term "restorative justice" in a book titled *Changing Lenses: A New Focus for Crime and Justice* (see Gade, 2018, for a complete history of the term). In this text, Zehr argued that the contemporary criminal legal system is characterized by a retributive lens that focuses on what law has been broken, who broke it, and what that person deserves. He described restorative justice as an alternate lens that focuses on the harm that has been caused. According to Zehr, restorative justice processes ask who has been harmed, what their needs are, and who now bears an obligation to meet those needs. Sociologist Kathleen Daly has referred to this dichotomous depiction as "a misleading simplification" and suggests that the ideas of retribution and restoration may be more tangled than advocates prefer to believe (Daly, 2002). Nonetheless, the contrast between restorative and retributive justice has been a useful heuristic for positioning restorative justice within the context of the contemporary criminal legal system.

Johnstone and Van Ness (2007) argue that rather than seeking to agree upon a single unifying definition, we should acknowledge the various, distinct conceptualizations of restorative justice in different contexts. McCold (2000) suggests that the categorization of justice practices as restorative need not be carried out in a binary fashion. In order to be fully restorative, a practice should engage and collaboratively address the needs of a triad of stakeholders: the person(s) harmed, the person(s) responsible, and their respective communities. However, practices that engage one or more of these stakeholders in a restorative manner might be considered partially restorative. Similarly, in his more recent writings, Howard Zehr has suggested that it is necessary to view restorative justice practices on a continuum with several stops (Zehr, 2015). In the third edition of *Changing Lenses* (2005, p. 270), Zehr offered five core characteristics of restorative justice, which we offer as guiding principles for the understanding of restorative justice in forensic social work practice:

1. It focuses on the harms that have occurred and the consequent needs of those who have been impacted, as well as those who have caused harm and the community.
2. It addresses obligations resulting from those harms, including the obligations of the people directly responsible as well as the obligations of the community and society.
3. It involves those with a stake in the situation—the people harmed, the people responsible, community members, and society—in creating a just solution.
4. It uses inclusive, collaborative processes.
5. It seeks to right the wrong by repairing the harm as much as possible.

Human-Centered Language for Restorative Practice

As we will emphasize throughout this chapter, restorative justice is a fundamentally humanist approach. Therefore, this chapter will use humanizing language for justice-involved persons consistent with their role in a restorative justice process. We use the terms "person responsible," "responsible person," or "person who caused the harm" in place of the terms "offender" and "defendant," except when we intend to indicate the defendant's role in a legal process. Similarly, we use the terms "person harmed" or "harmed person" in place of the terms "victim" and "survivor," except when our intention is to indicate their position in the legal context. We note that these terms are embraced by the victim advocacy community and by many victims and survivors who enter into restorative justice processes. Further, we will frequently discuss "harm" instead of "crime," acknowledging that restorative justice is primarily interested in the former. While many crimes are harmful, and many harmful acts are codified as crimes, restorative justice does not assume that these terms are synonymous. Importantly, restorative justice practices are intended to be used in cases where the harm to a person or community can be clearly identified. In this chapter, we primarily use the term "harm" instead of "crime" to discuss the topic of a restorative justice process, except when our intention is to acknowledge the practice of restorative justice in a criminal legal context—in other words, as a response to a harm that is statutorily defined as a crime.

Understanding the Needs Resulting From Crime

The primary aim of restorative justice in the context of the criminal legal system is to meet the needs of people and communities impacted by crime and work toward their healing and restoration (Van Ness & Strong, 2015). This includes the needs of crime victims and survivors, people who have caused harm through a criminal offense, the communities in which they live, and even society at large. Therefore, it is important to understand the nature of these needs. First, restorative justice centers the person or people harmed. Crime victims and survivors may experience the loss of property, physical injury, or death, as well as related personal and financial losses including medical bills, therapy costs, lost time or productivity and work, and damaged social relationships. Of crime victims participating in the Crime Survivors Speak Survey by the Alliance for Safety and Justice, 80% reported experiencing trauma symptoms. Further, victims reported that they felt less safe in their communities and experienced a diminished quality of life as compared to people who were not victimized. These impacts are disproportionately experienced by Black and Latino people, women, and people with lower income and educational attainment (Alliance for Safety and Justice, 2016).

Beyond the initial needs of victims and survivors resulting from a crime, an extensive body of research documents the occurrence of secondary victimization, a term for the further harm caused to victims as a result of interactions with police and adversarial court and correctional processes (Symonds, 2010). Indeed, there are high rates of dissatisfaction with the criminal legal process and its outcomes (Sered, 2019). Victims of crime have little sense of control during the court process, are shielded from important information about their case, and have few avenues to participate (Waller, 2011). The adversarial court process disincentivizes defendants from taking accountability or apologizing, as statements of guilt can be used as evidence to increase punishment. Even in the case of a guilty plea or verdict, victims are unlikely to receive a meaningful apology or have an opportunity to have questions answered by the person who harmed them. Finally, punishment is often in opposition to the wishes of victims, who overwhelmingly state that they prefer treatment and rehabilitation as outcomes in a criminal case and that they prefer investment in education, job creation, and treatment over investment in prisons and jails (Alliance for Safety and Justice, 2016). What many crime survivors deeply wish for is to address the root causes of harmful behavior and stop the cycle of violence (Sered, 2019). This may be why, according to the National Crime Victimization Survey (2020), less than half of violent crimes—and only about a third of property crimes—are ever reported to law enforcement. Restorative justice offers an opportunity for crime victims and survivors to seek help and healing outside of police, courts, and prisons.

While restorative justice centers the needs of people harmed by crime or conflict, it also attends to the needs of people who have caused harm. Criminological research clearly connects acts of violence to both community-level conditions like poverty and oppression and personal experiences such as shame, isolation, exposure to violence, and unmet survival needs (Sered, 2019). In one study of released prisoners, half reported experiencing family violence and 40% said they had witnessed someone being killed (Western, 2015). Estimates of prior victimization for people in prison range from 50% to 80%, with similarly high estimates of mental health conditions and substance abuse patterns. As Danielle Sered, director of the New York restorative justice project Common Justice, points out, contemporary "corrections" inflict upon prisoners the same conditions that led to violence: shame, isolation, violence, and unmet need. It also limits their ability to repair any harms they have caused. Despite popular narratives, incarcerated people often wish to take accountability, apologize, or take action to make things right with the victim of the crime or with their community. Without restorative solutions, there are few opportunities for people under the supervision of the criminal legal system to meet their needs or to fulfill their obligations.

Finally, restorative justice emphasizes that experiences of crime, conflict, and other forms of harm are not isolated to individuals. People harm one another within the context of community and within a larger structure of societal needs and obligations. Restorative justice offers a unique understanding of crime not as an offense against the state, but as a violation of relationships between people, and between people and their communities. Viewed from this perspective, crime—or at least the crimes with which restorative justice is concerned—damages protective social bonds in communities and diminishes trust and safety. In short, crime creates needs at the community level. It also creates obligations, wherein community members in a restorative process are called upon to consider their role in the harm that occurred. This may be personal (like failing to offer support in the early stages of an abusive relationship or substance abuse problem) or social (like examining and responding to the role of poverty, treatment gaps, or racist structures in what has happened).

Restorative Justice and the State

Van Ness and Strong (2015, p. 45) offer as a core principle of restorative justice that practitioners "rethink the relative roles and responsibilities of government and community" in promoting justice. Namely, there was a time before the advent of the contemporary criminal legal system that local communities bore collective responsibility for responding to social harm. Reflecting on the expanded role of the state and of professionals like judges, lawyers, and social workers in the court process, sociologist Nils Christie (1977) bemoans the likelihood that "criminology to some extent has amplified a process where conflicts have been taken away from the parties directly involved and thereby have either disappeared or become other people's property" (p. 1). In its theoretical ideal, restorative justice offers one approach by which people and communities may reclaim their obligations to one another.

However, as Coker (2002) and others have noted, the restorative justice movement in the United States has an "ambiguous relationship with state power." Restorative justice practices are increasingly integrated into contemporary court and correctional processes, where they are in danger of being co-opted and, paradoxically, extending the reach of the state. While originally offered as an alternative system of justice and meant to replace the criminal legal system, it has increasingly been embedded as an "alternative" practice within the landscape of the criminal legal process—in the vein of problem-solving courts, treatment courts, and various diversion schemes (Suzuki & Wood, 2017). While the institutionalization of restorative justice has extended its uses and possibly offered legal safeguards to participants, many practitioners and scholars are concerned about the co-optation of an inherently community-based justice response (see Pavlich, 2005; Schiff, 2013). So iterated, might restorative become, as Boutellier (2013) has suggested, just "another strategy in security politics"?

Restorative justice is often associated with parallel movements including community justice, community accountability, and transformative justice (see Coker, 2002; Kim, 2018; and McCold, 2004, for instance). In particular, the transformative justice movement is a response to the call for more radical, social justice–focused efforts in restorative work. While restorative justice practitioners and scholars have historically focused on "making things right" or returning individuals to right relationships with one another and their communities, the transformative justice movement explicitly recognizes that returning to the social conditions before the harm may be inadequate to attain justice. Rather, it is necessary to challenge social structures and systems as sources of harm. Transformative justice practices are more closely aligned with a prison abolitionist stance and reject cooperation with state systems to address harm (Kim, 2018). For the purposes of this chapter, it is important to understand that restorative justice is practiced both outside and inside of the criminal legal system, and that practitioners, advocates, and skeptics disagree on whether this fundamentally community-driven approach can fulfill its aspirations in partnership with the state.

Theoretical Foundations

We have established that restorative justice is itself widely viewed as a theoretical frame. Even so, it is informed by and associated with a number of philosophical and theoretical frameworks. Here, we will address the Indigenous origins of some aspects of restorative justice, as well as its connection to a wide range of spiritual practices. We then discuss its theoretical linkages to critical criminology and peacemaking criminology (Pepinsky & Quinney, 1991), as well as reintegrative shaming theory (Braithwaite, 1989) and the social discipline window (Wachtel & McCold, 2001).

Indigenous and Spiritual Origins of Restorative Justice

Traditional practices of Indigenous peoples around the world are frequently cited as precursors of modern restorative justice practices. Broadly, scholars and practitioners ground restorative justice in a holistic, communitarian worldview associated with tribal communities (Davis, 2019; Johnstone, 2011; Pranis, 2012). More specifically, Indigenous scholars have written about restorative justice as congruent with the healing justice paradigms and practices of Indigenous peoples, such as Navaho peacemaking (Yazzie, 2005), Maori traditional justice (Thomas, 2005), the African ethic of Ubuntu (Davis, 2019), and many others (see McClasin, 2005).

While Braithwaite (2002) has claimed that "restorative justice has been the dominant model of criminal justice throughout most of human history for all the world's peoples" (p. 5), Fania Davis has suggested that "for most of human history, we have practiced *restorative-type* justice" (Davis, 2005). Criminologist Kathleen Daly (2002) warns against romanticizing or flattening the relationship between contemporary restorative justice and Indigenous practices. For instance, circle practices and the use of talking pieces are associated with Indigenous practices, whereas VODs are more frequently associated with the Christian church and its ethic of redemption. Daly specifically addresses restorative conferencing, describing it as a "fragmented justice form" that "splices white, bureaucratic forms of justice with elements of informal justice that may include non-white (or non-Western) values or methods of judgment, with all the attendant dangers of such 'spliced justice.'" In summary, we suggest that restorative justice practitioners should properly acknowledge practices that are rooted in Indigenous traditions, practicing them with care and with the permission of Indigenous teachers (Davis, 2019). However, they should also be cautious not to overattribute contemporary restorative justice to Indigenous peoples, particularly when this may not be an accurate comparison.

As alluded to above, restorative justice is associated not only with Indigenous practices but also with a number of modern spiritual and religious traditions. Restorative practitioner Kay Pranis connects the "restorative impulse," a term she credits to law professor Howard Vogel, to a shared set of values iterated in most religious and spiritual traditions, "values that describe how to be in good relationship with one another" (Pranis, 2012, p. 33). Indeed, restorative justice has been linked philosophically to depictions of justice in Christianity (Zehr, 1990), Judaism (Segal, 2001), and Islam (Qafisheh, 2012), as well as other religious traditions (see Hadley, 2001). Themes of redemptive reconciliation consistent with the aims and processes of restorative justice can be found across religious texts including the Bible, the Quran, the Tanakh, and the Mishnah (Llewellyn & Philpott, 2014). Restorative justice writings also emphasize universal spiritual constructs including transformation, harmony, interconnectedness and belonging, repentance and forgiveness, the use of ritual, and experiences of "divine intervention" (Bender & Armour, 2007). Though restorative justice is not considered religious in nature, for many practitioners, holding a circle or facilitating dialogue is a spiritually grounded practice.

Critical Criminology and Peacemaking Criminology

Much criminological writing about restorative justice is grounded in critical criminology, a broad category of theorizing that rejects traditional criminological explanations for crime in favor of understanding the economic, social, and political forces that contribute to violence and harm. This includes naming and critiquing the power structures that govern how crime and justice are defined and carried out in society. Situated within this frame, peacemaking criminology (Pepinsky & Quinney, 1991; Quinney, 1989) advances a critical but humanistic view of crime and justice. Peacemaking criminologists seek to reduce harm and alleviate suffering by rejecting violent, harm-producing justice practices in favor of practices rooted in peacemaking and social justice. Peacemaking justice practices are responsive to the assumptions that (a) to live peacefully, we must reduce suffering; (b) humans are fundamentally interconnected, and suffering arises from separation; (c) humans are capable of transcendence and transformation; and (d) the process of peacemaking is essential to the outcome of peace—in other words, violent practices produce violence, while peaceful practices produce peace.

As a critical criminological approach, peacemaking criminology recognizes the role of structural forces in creating suffering and undermining peace. For instance, in seeking to understand the nature of human suffering, peacemaking criminologists may critically examine the role of racial, gendered, and class-based hierarchies on the human condition, or how structural arrangements in society promote separation and alienation (Caulfield, 2019). A peacemaking approach recognizes punishments that produce isolation and suffering—like incarceration—as violent and harmful. The tenets of peacemaking criminology invite a restorative response to conflict and harm that is characterized by principles of interconnectedness, nondomination, and the restoration of peaceful relationships between individuals and their communities.

Braithwaite's Reintegrative Shaming Theory

While critical and peacemaking criminologies offer a broad frame for understanding restorative justice, criminologist John Braithwaite was among the first to offer a formal theory to explain how and why restorative justice works. This theory is known as reintegrative shaming theory (Braithwaite, 1989). Braithwaite argues that we must address harmful behavior to contribute to a just and peaceful society, but that doing so through shame alone will increase—rather than decrease—harm. He describes *reintegrative shaming* as disapproval of crimes and harmful acts, issued within "a continuum of respect" for the person who caused the harm. Importantly, the period of disapproval culminates in a ritual of restoration and reintegration as a member of the community. In a restorative justice process, a generative kind of shame is evoked by discussion of the impacts of the crime on the direct victim, the family of the responsible party, and other members of the community. Braithwaite (2002) emphasizes the importance of relationships in creating the conditions for reintegrative shaming, saying, "It is not the shame of police or judges or newspapers that are most able to get through to us; it is shame in the eyes of those we respect and trust" (p. 74). Restorative justice processes also offer a ritual of completion, in which the people present agree about what must be done to fully rejoin as a community.

The Social Discipline Window

Ted Wachtel and Paul McCold (2001) have developed and advanced an alternative framework for understanding restorative justice called the social discipline window. Wachtel and McCold suggest that discipline occurs at the intersection of two dimensions: control and support. The control dimension consists of limit setting and the expectations for compliance that accompany those limits. Support consists of encouragement and nurture, which assist individuals in reaching expectations or maintaining boundaries. When control is high but support is low, discipline is punitive and authoritarian. This is the quadrant (Figure 30.1) most associated with the contemporary criminal legal system and with exclusionary school discipline.

In contrast, when control is low but support is high, discipline becomes permissive and paternalistic. This might be seen in a classroom or parenting relationship characterized by constant affirmation and accommodation, even when expectations for behavior are not being met. When both control and support are low, discipline is neglectful and irresponsible. Finally, when control and support are both high, Wachtel and McCold consider discipline to be restorative and collaborative. While authoritative discipline is done *to* people and permissive discipline is done *for* people, restorative discipline is done *with* people.

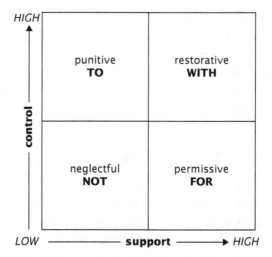

FIGURE 30.1 Social Discipline Window Source: Reprinted from Wachtel and McCold (2001).

Within this quadrant, individuals are held to the limits and expectations of the community with all of the support and nourishment needed to meet those expectations.

The social discipline window has been widely embraced as a useful theoretical frame for restorative practices (RPs), particularly in school discipline settings (Vaandering, 2013). However, school-based practitioner and scholar Dorothy Vaandering has criticized the framework for its emphasis on behavior over relationships. In response, she has offered an amended social relationship window (Figure 30.2), which more clearly articulates the human relationships present in each quadrant (Vaandering, 2013).

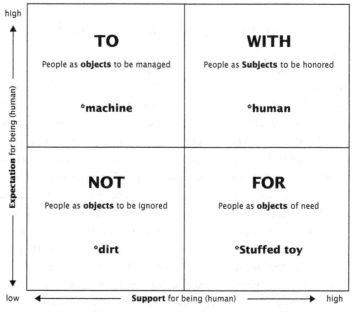

FIGURE 30.2 Social Relationship Window Source: Reprint from Vaandering (2013).

Authoritative relationships treat people as *objects to be managed*, while permissive relationships treat people as *objects of need*. Neglectful relationships treat people as *objects to be ignored*. In contrast, restorative relationships treat people as subjects with agency and inherent human dignity, not objects to be controlled, patronized, or dismissed. Variations on the social discipline window offer a useful framework for situating restorative justice within other approaches to behavioral and crime response.

Empirical Support for Restorative Justice

We have established that restorative justice is broadly defined. The term has been used to describe a number of formal and informal practices in the arenas of criminal justice, school discipline, conflict resolution, and peacemaking. These practices have been measured, tested, and written about to varying degrees. As a result, it is difficult to offer a singular assessment of the evidentiary support for restorative justice as an overarching approach. Instead, it is necessary to consider restorative justice as a set of practices, each with a unique context and set of outcomes. This section will first provide a broad overview of restorative justice practices used in criminal legal contexts, acknowledging that this is a subset of a broader landscape of community accountability and peacemaking practices. We will then introduce four types of restorative justice practices in the criminal legal context that are the most well defined and empirically studied: school-based RPs, restorative justice conferencing, VODs, and Circles of Support and Accountability (CoSAs). We will summarize the body of evidence for each of these approaches, addressing the populations and settings for which they are best indicated, and identifying gaps in what is known about their effectiveness. Finally, we will provide an assessment of the evidence base for restorative justice and discuss the methodological challenges and opportunities associated with restorative justice research.

Restorative Justice Practices in the Criminal Legal Context

The use of restorative justice in criminal matters has been endorsed by the American Bar Association, the National Organization for Victims Assistance (1995), the Council of Europe (1999), and the United Nations The Economic and Social Council (2002). However, restorative justice can best be described as a panorama of practices representing both community-based and system-based responses and spanning every phase of the criminal legal process (Figure 30.3). Previously in this chapter, we have described restorative justice's contentious relationship with the criminal legal system. For these reasons, we remind the reader that restorative justice is practiced not only in the ways emphasized here but also as a community-based harm response, carried out without the partnership of the state. In communities, restorative justice practices such as peacemaking circles and community accountability processes are facilitated by community healers of all sorts (not just professionals) and activate mutual aid structures to address harms and strengthen relationships. They are situated in organizing spaces, religious and spiritual communities, neighborhoods and community centers, and other grassroots settings, and as a result, are not well documented in scholarly literature.

Policing
Restorative language
Community conferencing

Prosecution
Community conferencing
Family group conferencing
Accountability boards

Sentencing
Community conferencing
Sentencing circles

Corrections
Restorative circles
Victim-offender dialogue

Re-Entry
Restorative circles
Victim-offender dialogue
Circles of Support and Accountability (CoSA)

FIGURE 30.3 Typical Restorative Justice Practices at Each Stage of the Criminal Legal System

However, over the past three decades, restorative justice has increasingly been used throughout the criminal legal system as a diversionary or supplemental justice alternative.

The first point of entry is policing, where officers may make direct referrals to community-based restorative justice practices. For instance, the Longmont Community Justice Partnership (LCJP) in Longmont, Colorado, holds restorative justice conferences for people accused of a crime who are referred to the organization by local police officers as an alternative to arrest. Conferences include the person harmed, the person responsible, support persons, and community volunteers, including police officers.

If not diverted at the policing stage, defendants may be offered the opportunity to participate in restorative justice as part of a prefile or pe-adjudication diversion agreement through the district attorney's office. The district attorney's office may refer the crime victim and the defendant to a restorative process—such as community conferencing, family group conferencing, or a neighborhood accountability board—where a completed agreement will result in the dismissal of charges. Impact Justice, a restorative justice organization based in Oakland, California, offers a restorative justice diversion toolkit that outlines one model for this approach (see https://impactjustice.org/). While some district attorneys deliver restorative justice directly within their offices, the more common approach is to refer cases to a community provider who oversees the restorative process and provides documentation of completion. Restorative justice may also be offered at the sentencing stage, where a judge might sentence someone convicted of a crime to be assessed for or to participate in a restorative justice process such as community conferencing or a sentencing circle. Sometimes these requirements are part of a probation agreement.

While the approaches above position restorative justice as an alternative to prosecution or traditional sentencing outcomes, restorative justice is also frequently utilized alongside of or after standard court and sentencing processes. In the postsentencing phase, people convicted of crimes may participate in restorative justice practices—including restorative circles and VODs—while incarcerated, while on parole, or while reentering into the community. These practices typically offer no legal benefits to the person who has been convicted. Their aims are primarily to promote accountability and healing. In prison settings, restorative circles and programming frequently use surrogate models, wherein crime victims participate in RPs with incarcerated people who are not directly responsible for harming them (see Armour & Sliva, 2018). The Insight Prison Project, founded in San Quentin State Prison, and Bridges to Life, founded in Houston, Texas, are two examples of in-prison RPs using surrogate models.

Legal scholars Joseph Robinson and Jennifer Hudson (2015) acknowledge four strands of restorative justice in a typology that is particularly useful for social workers, who may work within or across micro, mezzo, and macro systems to improve justice outcomes for marginalized communities. Robinson and Hudson's reintegrative strand of restorative justice focuses on processes and outcomes for justice-involved people at a micro level. It consists of practices like sentencing circles and restorative conferencing, which are used alongside of or in place of courtroom processes. The psychotherapeutic strand focuses on processes and outcomes for victims and survivors, such as victim impact panels and victim advocacy. These practices are used in courtrooms, as well as in therapeutic settings. The communitarian strand focuses on what Robinson and Hudson (2016) refer to as "communities of meaning" and are associated with the mezzo system. These practices include peacemaking circles and family group conferences. Finally, the insurgent strand represents a macro-level approach to restorative justice and focuses on transforming unjust social and political structures. Insurgent restorative justice practices do not eschew the importance of addressing personal harm but ultimately seek social transformation. While Robinson and Hudson associate the reintegrative strand with criminology and social work, we argue that social workers are uniquely positioned to consider all of these applications and are particularly called to engage with the insurgent strand of restorative justice. Regardless of the arena in which social workers practice, it is important to recognize that restorative justice has both personal and social implications and that it is practiced both inside and outside of state systems.

School-Based Restorative Practices

Perhaps the fastest growing site for restorative justice in the United States is primary and secondary schools. Most often referred to as RPs or restorative approaches (RAs), restorative justice initiatives in K–12 schools offer a key pathway for reducing exclusionary school discipline and school-initiated referrals to law enforcement. In short, one aim of restorative justice in schools is to disrupt the school-to-prison pipeline—the well-documented pathway (walked three times as often by Black students as White ones) from school pushout to carceral system involvement. Situated within parallel educational movements focused on social-emotional learning and positive behavioral interventions and supports (PBISs), school-based RPs are increasingly recommended as a "whole-school approach" to improving relationships, developing a supportive school climate, and resolving conflicts within the classroom community (Hulvershorn & Mulholland, 2018). Schools frequently use a multitier system of supports to frame a progressive slate of RPs. Universal practices are used with all students and are preventative and proactive. These include proactive classroom circle practices, relationship building, and restorative questioning—simple affective statements and questions that explore impacts, needs, and responsibilities in the present situation. Secondary practices are used with selected groups of students in order to manage conflict, resolve differences, and prevent harm. These practices include conflict circles and restorative conversations. Tertiary practices are used with specific students to repair harms, rebuild relationships, and reintegrate students who are separated from the school community for disciplinary or other reasons. These practices include reintegration circles and formal restorative conferences.

RPs in schools are a burgeoning area of research inquiry as well as practice. Much outcomes-focused research on RPs has been published in the past 2 years alone (Weber & Vereenooghe, 2020). The body of literature includes three cluster randomized controlled trials (Acosta et al., 2019; Augustine et al., 2018; Bonell et al., 2018) and two quasi-experimental designs with control conditions (Norris, 2019; Wong et al., 2011), as well as a number of cross-sectional and correlational studies using a combination of quantitative and qualitative data to examine the impacts of RPs on school disciplinary outcomes and student well-being. A number of these studies link schoolwide use of RPs with reduced suspensions and behavioral referrals. In addition, there is at least some support for RPs' influence on secondary outcomes, such as improvements to school climate, connectedness, and engagement, as well as more respectful teacher-student and student-student relationships (see Weber & Vereenooghe, 2020, for a full review). RPs have also been offered as a tool to reduce racial disparities in school discipline. While social work researcher Yolanda Anyon's team (Anyon et al., 2016) found that racial disparities in school discipline persisted despite a whole-school RP approach, their team also found that participation in restorative interventions served as a protective factor against out-of-school suspensions for students of color (Anyon et al., 2014).

Research on school-based restorative justice initiatives consistently suggests that the effective implementation of school-level interventions presents a challenge to realizing the aspirational outcomes of RPs in school settings. While at least some studies have found that whole-school RP implementation is associated with more positive outcomes (Wong et al., 2011, for instance), researchers in another instance found that relatively small numbers of students attending RP intervention schools actually experienced RPs (Acosta et al., 2019). While the latter team was unable to identify statistically significant changes in hypothesized outcomes at the school level, students in their study who self-reported experiences with RPs were much more likely to report perceived improvements in the school climate, connectedness to the school and their peers, and social skills, while reporting reduced victimization from bullying. These findings suggest that there are serious challenges to whole-school implementation, but that—when implemented properly—RPs offer a promising approach for reducing school pushout and improving student well-being.

Restorative Justice Conferencing

Restorative conferencing—sometimes called community conferencing—is the most typical application of restorative justice in the criminal legal system, as well as the most extensively tested (Strang et al., 2013). A restorative justice conference consists of a face-to-face meeting between the harmed person(s), responsible person(s), and their respective communities in order to decide what must be done to repair the harm caused during a crime (Sherman & Strang, 2012). Restorative conferencing is most frequently offered prior to or during the sentencing process, when the restorative agreement made by participants may be used in place of or in combination with traditional sentencing decisions made by the court. It may be used before a charge is filed—following a direct referral from law enforcement to a community justice partner or following referral from a district attorney's office—or as part of a diversion agreement or alternative sentencing process. It may also be recommended as part of a noncustodial sentencing agreement: for instance, as a requirement of probation. In the United States, this form of restorative justice conferencing is most often used for misdemeanors or low-level felonies, for first-time offenses, and with juvenile defendants. However, there are many examples of uses with more serious crimes and/or with adult populations, such as Common Justice in New York. Further, it should be noted that restorative conferencing is frequently used outside of criminal legal contexts entirely, though it has most often been documented and measured within legal settings and in comparison to traditional court and correctional outcomes (Strang et al., 2013).

The empirical literature on restorative justice conferencing or community conferencing is muddied by overlapping conceptualizations of related practices such as family group conferencing, sentencing circles, victim-offender mediation, and VOD (discussed here as a separate approach in the following section), as well as variations in the implementation of each approach. A 2002 review by Umbreit et al. (2002) found 63 empirical studies meeting their definition of restorative justice conferencing, including victim-offender mediation, family group conferencing, and peacemaking circles. These studies examined a range of outcomes including participant satisfaction, procedural justice (participants' sense of fairness in the justice process), completion of restitution agreements, recidivism rates, and cost. Across studies, the authors found that 80% to 90% of participants were satisfied with the restorative conferencing process, found it to be fair, and experienced the fulfillment of any restitution agreement that was made. In addition, studies with comparison groups consistently indicated that those participating in restorative conferencing had more positive experiences and better agreement completion rates than those going through a traditional court process.

In general, restorative justice research is confounded by selection bias. Participants must voluntarily opt into an RP, and there are a number of reasons that participants undertaking a restorative justice approach may have different preferences, attitudes, or beliefs than those who do not. In addition, many practitioners believe that every crime victim who wants a restorative justice process should have access to one; as a result, random assignment to restorative justice is ethically controversial and difficult to achieve. However, there are some studies that inform a clearer comparison between restorative justice conferencing and traditional court processes. In 2013, in Campbell's systematic review, Strang and colleagues examined 10 randomized controlled trials measuring the impact of restorative justice conferencing programs in the United States, United Kingdom, and Australia. The authors found that restorative conferencing "caused a modest but highly cost-effective reduction in repeat offending, with substantial benefits of victims" (p. 2). In summary, there is a wide-ranging but cumulatively compelling body of evidence suggesting that restorative justice conferencing benefits both harmed and responsible parties and offers superior outcomes to traditional court processes.

Victim-Offender Dialogue

VOD is sometimes referred to as victim-offender reconciliation, victim-offender-mediated dialogue, or victim-offender mediation, though it should not be confused with traditional forms of court mediation. VOD is a facilitated process between the person harmed and the person responsible. Support persons may also be present; however, their role is limited to supporting the experiences of the primary participants. Unlike court mediation, the goal of a VOD is not negotiation or compromise. It is to facilitate a healing encounter that allows the victim to express the impacts of the crime on their life, be heard, receive direct accountability, and have their questions answered. Unlike the restorative justice conferencing models described above, VOD is typically offered in cases of serious violent crime after formal sentencing is already completed. Therefore, participants rarely discuss a diversion plan and may or may not discuss other forms of reparations or repair. How can the harm of a life lost be repaired? Instead, the VOD focuses on personal healing and redemption in the face of irreparable loss.

There is a small but consistent body of research exploring the outcomes of VODs in cases of serious violent crime (see Armour & Umbreit, 2018; Flaten, 1996; Roberts, 1995; Sliva et al., 2021; Umbreit, 1989; Umbreit et al., 2006). These studies, spanning four decades, rely on mostly small samples ranging from four to 40 cases. All but the two most recent rely on some combination of simple satisfaction surveys and qualitative interviews with primary participants. Harmed persons across studies most frequently express that they feel heard, that they regain a sense of control over their life, that they can begin to see the offender as a human being, that they regain feelings of trust and safety, and that they feel less anger and more peace. Responsible persons have reported that they were able to see the victim as a person, better understand the impact of their actions, show accountability and remorse, and have the opportunity to give something back. Forgiveness is one possible but contentious outcome of restorative justice processes. A VOD is not a process of forgiveness, and facilitators emphasize that responsible persons should neither request nor expect forgiveness (Umbreit & Armour, 2010). Even so, participants across studies are satisfied—nearly unanimously—with their experience in the dialogue and rate it as a positive encounter.

Recently, social work scholars Marilyn Armour and Mark Umbreit have further explored the construct of "energy shifts" in VOD—a term they use to capture participants' frequent descriptions of a weight or burden being lifted, transferred, or transformed. In one of the few studies to utilize psychometric scales in addition to qualitative interviewing, Shannon Sliva and colleagues (2021) have focused on understanding energy shifts as an expression of trauma response and resolution, noting that in postdialogue interviews, crime victims described no longer being "stuck" in feelings or experiences that characterize trauma response. Indeed, crime victims participating in a dialogue experienced declines in depression, anger, and fear, as compared to a control group of crime victims over a similar period of time (Sliva et al., 2021). There is growing evidence that dialogues support participants in making meaning of their experiences or rewriting their story of loss as one of redemption.

Circles of Support and Accountability

We have demonstrated that restorative justice offers an alternative to court and correctional processes, as well as a parallel opportunity for healing and redemption. In addition, reentry is a viable arena for restorative justice approaches in the context of the U.S. criminal legal system. Without a restorative approach to reentry, these community members may lack pathways to full reintegration. CoSAs are a restorative justice approach to reentry that originated in Canada in the mid-1990s as an intervention to support the integration of people convicted of sex offenses into the community following incarceration. While most commonly used with people convicted of sex offenses, CoSAs may also be formed for other reentering people who are considered to be at increased risk of reoffending and face a particularly isolating reentry experience. In a CoSA, the core member is supported by a group of community volunteers who offer encouragement, mutual aid (e.g., assistance with securing a job or housing), and accountability for goals determined in collaboration with the core member. CoSAs differ distinctly from the other restorative justice approaches we have described because they do not include the person(s) harmed by the core member. However, the CoSA model is based in restorative justice principles, including the core objective that "no one is disposable" (CoSA Canada website), and allows the community to be directly involved in the restoration of harms and the reintegration of its members.

There is a growing body of empirical evidence focused on understanding the outcomes of the CoSA model, including at least one randomized controlled trial and three quasi-experimental studies offering control conditions. Empirical research comparing the outcomes of CoSAs with matched control groups has consistently identified reduced recidivism among CoSA core members (Duwe, 2012; Wilson et al., 2005, 2009). Several other studies have used quantitative and qualitative methods to examine psychosocial outcomes for CoSA participants (see Clark et al., 2015). Sociologist Kathryn Fox's (2015) research with CoSA participants in Vermont—including core members, community members, and staff—has suggested that the circle provides a sense of belonging and a shared moral space while mitigating the exclusion and isolation experienced by many people reentering the community following incarceration. In addition, circles may support core members in "de-labeling" and building a positive self-identity by validating their humanity and personal worth. Other researchers have successfully measured improvements in prosocial attitudes and behaviors and emotional well-being (Bates et al., 2014; McCartan et al., 2014). Additionally, research in the United States and the United Kingdom has estimated modest to substantial returns on investment using cost-benefit analyses of the CoSA model (Duwe, 2012; Elliot & Beech, 2013).

Research on the use of CoSAs in the United States remains fairly sparse and largely focuses on core members who are convicted of sex offenses, neglecting more generalized approaches. Elliott et al. (2013) note that the existing body of research has a "myopic focus on recidivism" at the cost of other outcomes of interest and that people convicted of sex offenses have low baseline rates of reoffending already—between 4% and 12%. In addition, as with other restorative justice approaches, variation in program implementation plagues efforts to generalize findings of individual studies to the CoSA model as a whole. In 2013, an evaluability assessment of five U.S. sites delivering CoSAs observed significant differences in program implementation across sites and found that only the site demonstrated the fidelity necessary for rigorous evaluation (Elliott et al., 2013). Despite these limitations, research on the CoSA model is promising and deserves additional attention.

Challenges and Opportunities for Restorative Justice Research

Restorative justice approaches are supported by an expansive but disjointed body of evidence. As we have noted, the range of practices constituting restorative justice and the degree of flexibility in implementation create formidable challenges for building a consistent evidence base. However, it is important to note that flexibility and intuition are valued elements of restorative justice practice. Indeed, practitioners have intentionally resisted the professionalization of restorative justice approaches. Restorative justice inherently seeks a shift in power and control—from systems and their professionals to communities and their people. While most practices require a facilitator or circle keeper, these positions may be held by nonprofessionals, such as elders, healers, or spiritual leaders, who can offer a space of healing to their communities.

Restorative justice is not a manualized intervention, and to a considerable extent, its tenets are incongruent with the requirements of intervention research. For instance, research has explored why some people choose to participate in restorative justice processes when offered and others do not (Choi et al., 2010). These differences make it difficult to recruit meaningful control groups. In addition, the personal nature of decision-making about participating in restorative justice presents ethical challenges to random sampling. Further, the outcomes of restorative justice—constructs like transformation, accountability, and healing—are difficult to distill and measure. Pavlich (2005) notes that as restorative justice is increasingly situated in criminal legal systems, it is increasingly measured by system aims like rehabilitation, compliance, and reoffending. This focus is evident in the review we have provided in this chapter, which attends extensively to outcomes such as recidivism and cost while failing to measure the transformative community impacts promised by restorative justice approaches. In addition, research has largely neglected to address relationships between restorative justice approaches and major system failures in policing and punishment, including widespread racial disparities from arrest to sentencing. We view this as an essential opportunity for researchers to measure not just the internal effectiveness of restorative justice practices but also whether and how it meets its aspirations of system transformation.

Case Study: Restorative Conferencing

Derrick, a young Black man in his 20s, engages in an armed robbery of Kelli, a White college student who is walking home across campus late one night. Derrick points a gun at Kelli and steals her laptop and phone. Shaken, she reports the robbery to the campus police, who are able to identify the young man walking with the stolen items a few blocks away. During the campus police officer's apprehension of the suspect, he notices that the young man seems apologetic and fearful. Derrick has no prior arrests, and the officer remembers a recently formed partnership between the city police department and a local restorative justice agency. Upon his recommendation, the intake officer at the city police department works with their victim advocate team to contact Kelli. While relieved that her property has been recovered, she is angry and afraid that she or others on campus may be victimized in the future. When offered the opportunity to talk with the man who robbed her in a facilitated restorative justice conference, she hesitates but ultimately says yes.

Sheila, a Black woman and an experienced practitioner with the local restorative justice partner, receives a call from the police department and agrees to see if the case is right for restorative justice. Sheila meets with Kelli and with Derrick separately to learn more about their readiness for a restorative conference. After talking with them both, she feels confident that bringing them together will not cause further harm to either of them and that doing so may help bring about justice in this case. The conference takes place on a Saturday morning in the welcoming community room of the restorative justice agency. Sheila has arranged eight chairs in a circle in the middle of the room. Gathered are Derrick and his sister, Kelli and her roommate, the campus police officer who responded to the call, and two other volunteers from the local community. Sheila ensures that at least one of the volunteers that she invites is a person of color and that the other is a woman. In this way, she helps ensure that the volunteers represent Derrick and Kelli's extended "communities."

Sheila opens the conference by reading a poem about facing what is difficult in our lives. She then asks Kelli, Derrick, and, finally, the campus police officer to talk about what happened that night. She asks all of the members of the conference to share how they have been impacted by what happened, including Derrick and his sister. Kelli talks about how afraid she was during the robbery and how afraid she has felt ever since. She has not been able to walk home by herself anymore. Others in the circle share too. Derrick's sister expresses how fearful she is that she will lose him if he goes to jail. The community volunteers talk about feeling afraid in the community and wishing for a safe place to live. Derrick puts his head in his hands and is obviously remorseful. He tells Kelli and the others how sorry he is. He also explains what drove him to commit the robbery. He talks about the pressure of supporting his mom and sister and how hard it is to make ends meet. He even shares, ashamed but angry, that he feels resentful when walking past the college campus on the way home and seeing people his age who look like they have it all.

Together, the members of the circle talk about ways that Derrick can help make things right, as well as ways that they can support Derrick and his family. They all offer ideas, drawing on Derrick's strengths and resources, as well as their own. Derrick is a talented artist, and at Kelli's request, he agrees to create a piece of art for her apartment that will offer a healing memory associated with the night of the robbery. Sheila also suggests that Derrick join a group at the community center that is organizing a series of murals in the city. One of the community volunteers is part of a local business association and offers to help Derrick secure and prepare for some job interviews that will pay a living wage and accommodate his family's needs. The group agrees to come back together in 6 months to assess whether the agreements have been met and make adjustments if needed. At that time, Sheila will also communicate with the city police department about the successful completion of Derrick's restorative justice process.

Derrick and Kelli's case provides an example of how meeting face to face in a restorative process can interrupt cycles of harm. Without restorative intervention, Derrick may have spent time in prison and/or repeated his actions. There would be no effort to address the root causes of his behavior. In addition, a court process would have likely prevented Kelli from receiving a sincere, personal apology and would have done little to alleviate her anger and fear. This case also demonstrates that the robbery occurred in the context of complex social dynamics that would have likely been ignored by the criminal legal system. It points to the race and class divides into many communities, the ways that college campuses and other well-resourced institutions (particularly those that are predominantly White) fail their neighbors, and the anger and resentment this incites. It offers an example of how the community can come together to enact justice and solve social problems more adeptly than the criminal legal system. It also raises a number of questions that may promote a critical understanding of the benefits and risks of restorative justice:

1. What was the role of police discretion in creating access to the restorative process? What might affect decision-making by system professionals about whether to offer restorative justice?
2. What role did race play in this process unfolding the way it did? How might it have gone differently?
3. What if either Kelli or Derrick were unwilling to engage in a restorative process? Are there "partially restorative" options that could be made available to them?
4. How important is it that the case was facilitated by a community-based restorative justice organization? How might it have gone differently if the facilitator were a system-based professional, like a staff facilitator with the police department?
5. How realistic is the agreement created by these participants? What might contribute to less robust—or even problematic—agreements?

Challenges and Opportunities for Social Work

Restorative justice has been increasingly embraced by the social work profession as a collaborative and holistic approach for dealing with harms and conflicts of all kinds. Social workers are often at the helm of implementing restorative justice approaches in schools and child welfare settings. In forensic settings, social workers have an opportunity to design and deliver restorative responses for crime victims and survivors, justice-involved people, and their families and communities. They may seek training and mentoring to facilitate RPs themselves or develop partnerships with community-based organizations, organizers, and healers who practice restorative justice. There is a natural alignment between social work and restorative justice based on a set of shared values, including:

- respecting the dignity and worth of each person and their right to self-determination;
- honoring the importance of human relationships in personal and social well-being;
- sharing power and resources through collaborative processes; and
- demonstrating social responsibility for one another (Umbreit & Armour, 2010).

This section will explore how forensic social workers can engage the profession's unique knowledge and skills to support the effective and ethical use of restorative justice practices. In addition, it will address key ethical dilemmas for social workers practicing in this arena.

Social Work Knowledge and Skills for Restorative Justice Practice

Social work practice—including clinical practice with individuals and groups, as well as organizing and social action—is congruent in many ways with the skills that restorative justice practitioners use. In a restorative conference, for instance, the facilitator engages in setting boundaries and norms, creating safe therapeutic relationships, active listening, reflecting, and generating collaborative solutions. Further, social work's hallmark person-in-environment framework offers a valuable perspective for understanding the interconnected nature of human lives. Employing this lens, social workers understand the complex ways in which individuals are supported and challenged by their interpersonal relationships, their social environment, and the structural features of their community and society. This knowledge is important for the practice of restorative justice, which attends to both personal and social harms. Social workers are likely to be adept in identifying "all those who are impacted"— or the necessary participants in a restorative process. Further, they may easily recognize community-level needs and obligations that are overlooked by clinicians. Restorative justice provides an opportunity to engage both people and communities in responding to and healing from violence, and social workers are uniquely qualified to carry out this work.

Social workers are also well prepared to consider the role of race, gender, sexuality, physical ability, neurodiversity, and other aspects of difference in the practice of restorative justice. In particular, an understanding of race and racism is critical to all work in criminal legal contexts, where Black and Brown people are disproportionately surveilled and punished. Restorative justice practitioner and organizer Fania Davis has noted that restorative justice "is generally perceived as—and too often behave[s] as—a white movement" (Davis, 2012, p. 32). She argues that restorative justice is grounded at least in part in the civil rights movement—in the principles of truth telling, nonviolence, and compassion—yet notes that restorative justice often fails to intentionally engage the issues of race. Dashman et al. (2019), a group of self-identified White practitioners, have called upon their peers to be responsive to these needs and to be intentional about bringing a racial justice consciousness to the restorative justice movement. In addition to prioritizing diversity and addressing disparities, they call for White practitioners to create restorative spaces in which they can critically examine Whiteness and work through their own racial conflicts. Importantly, the responsibilities of White and other non-Indigenous practitioners extend to acknowledging and honoring the role of Indigenous peoples in creating many restorative models that we practice today, openly discussing their relationship to these practices and peoples, and refraining from using sacred objects and rituals that are not theirs to use. Bringing a racial consciousness to restorative justice is an opportunity for a challenging but beneficial alliance between the social work profession and the restorative justice movement.

Despite the many ways in which their professional knowledge, skills, and values align, social workers planning to engage in RPs should seek specialized training and mentorship. This is in alignment with the social work profession's value of competence, which articulates that social workers practice within their areas of expertise. While there is no nationally recognized professional certification for restorative justice, practitioners have diverse skillsets and often hundreds of hours of training or guided experience (Sliva et al., 2019). Many restorative justice programs encourage prospective facilitators to participate as community volunteers first, gradually gaining the knowledge, experience, and intuition required to move into a facilitation role. In addition, there are increasingly academic programs or private training opportunities focused on restorative justice, conflict transformation, and peacemaking that may provide relevant background for social workers seeking to engage in RP (Umbreit & Armour, 2010).

Ethical Dilemmas

In choosing to practice restorative justice, social workers are likely to find deep alignment with their professional values. However, they will also be faced with ethical challenges that require humility and care. In general, social workers should be prepared to apply a critical lens to the use of restorative justice practices in the criminal legal context. Indeed, a number of practitioners and scholars have suggested that practicing restorative justice within the legal system is like fitting a square peg into a round hole (Shah et al., 2017). The criminal legal system is adversarial, coercive, and hierarchical, while restorative justice is collaborative, voluntary, and collective (Figure 30.4).

What does it mean for social workers to engage restorative justice within such a system? In what ways does a partnership between restorative justice and criminal punishment diminish or distort the restorative justice while legitimizing or justifying the harms of the contemporary criminal legal system? For instance, a restorative justice conference

Criminal Legal System	Restorative Justice
adversarial	collaborative
coercive	voluntary
hierarchical	collective
structured	flexible
professionalized	community-based
issues punishment	meets needs
control-oriented	freedom-oriented

FIGURE 30.4 Contrasting Characteristics of the Criminal Legal System and Restorative Justice

offered in a juvenile diversion context may appear voluntary but actually coerce participation and compliance through state supervision. Further, such diversion programs have been linked with net-widening, wherein a "progressive" feature of the legal system captures cases that might have otherwise been dismissed (Sliva & Plassmeyer, 2020).

Social workers should be thoughtful about their role in bringing restorative justice practices to the criminal legal system, weighing the benefits and costs. In addition, they should consider opportunities to design and develop restorative justice approaches that are situated in the community.

And even there—outside of the criminal legal context—social workers have reason to be reflective about their role in restorative justice practice. They must be cautious not to further disenfranchise communities by asserting a professionalized or hierarchical version of restorative justice. Instead, social workers should consider how to create spaces for community members to lead in the design and delivery of RPs that are responsive to their lived experiences.

Summary

Restorative justice is a philosophy of justice that focuses on repairing harms and restoring relationships as the primary pathway to making things right when something damaging has occurred. The term "restorative justice" represents a diverse set of practices that bring together the person(s) harmed, the person(s) responsible, and their respective communities to decide what can be done to address the harm and to repair it as much as possible. Importantly, it emphasizes values of interconnectedness, nondomination, collaboration, and social responsibility. As a result, it is well suited for social work practice. While most recognized as a community-based approach, restorative justice is increasingly practiced as an alternative justice response in criminal legal contexts including police and prosecutorial diversion, alternative sentencing agreements, prisons, and reentry processes. While there is ample opportunity to further understand whether, when, and how restorative justice works, there is a growing body of research that suggests that restorative justice may meet the needs of both the people harmed and the people responsible more effectively than contemporary court and correctional processes. With specialized training and with appropriate attention to the ethical challenges of integrating RPs into a criminal legal context, social workers in forensic settings are well positioned to design and deliver restorative justice responses that offer both justice and healing.

References

Acosta, J., Chinman, M., Ebener, P., Malone, P. S., Phillips, A., & Wilks, A. (2019). Evaluation of a whole-school change intervention: Findings from a two-year cluster-randomized trial of the restorative practices intervention. *Journal of Youth and Adolescence, 48*(5), 876–890. https://doi.org/10.1007/s10 964-019-01013-2

Alliance for Safety and Justice (2016). Crime survivors speak: The first ever national survey of victim's views on safety and justice. https://allianceforsafetyandjustice.org/crimesurvivorsspeak/

Anyon, Y., Gregory, A., Stone, S., Farrar, J., Jenson, J. M., McQueen, J., Downing, B., Greer, E., & JSimmons, J. (2016). Restorative interventions and school discipline sanctions in a large urban school district. *American Educational Research Journal, 53*(6), 1663–1697. https://doi.org/10.3102/0002831216675719

Anyon, Y., Jenson, J. M., Altschul, I., Farrar, J., McQueen, J., Greer, E., . . . Simmons, J. (2014). The persistent effect of race and the promise of alternatives to suspension in school discipline outcomes. *Children and Youth Services Review, 44*, 379–386. https://doi.org/10.1016/j.childyouth.2014.06.025

Armour, M., & Sliva, S. M. (2018). How does it work? Mechanisms of action in an in-prison restorative justice program. *International Journal of Offender Therapy and Comparative Criminology, 62*(3), 759–784. https://doi.org/10.1177/0306624X16669143

Armour, M., & Umbreit, M. S. (2018). *Violence, restorative justice, and forgiveness: Dyadic forgiveness and energy shifts in restorative justice dialogue.* Jessica Kingsley Publishers.

Augustine, C. H., Engberg, J., Grimm, G. E., Lee, E., Wang, E. L., Christianson, K., & Joseph, A. A. (2018). *Can restorative practices improve school climate and curb suspensions? An evaluation of the impact of restorative practices in a mid-sized urban school district.* Rand. https://www.rand.org/content/dam/rand/pubs/research_reports/RR2800/RR2840/RAND_RR2840.pdf

Bates, A., Williams, D., Wilson, C., & Wilson, R. J. (2014). Circles South East: The first 10 years 2002–2012. *International Journal of Offender Therapy and Comparative Criminology, 58*, 861–885. https://doi.org/10.1177/0306624X13485362

Beck, E., Kropf, N. P., & Leonard, P. B. (Eds.). (2010). *Social work and restorative justice: Skills for dialogue, peacemaking, and reconciliation.* Oxford University Press.

Bender, K., & Armour, M. P. (2007). The spiritual components of restorative justice. *Victims and Offenders, 2*(3), 251–267. https://doi.org/10.1080/15564880701403967

Bonell, C., Allen, E., Warren, E., McGowan, J., Bevilacqua, L., Jamal, F., Legood, R., Wiggins, M., Opondo, C., Mathiot, A., & Sturgess, J. (2018). Effects of the Learning Together intervention on bullying and aggression in English secondary schools (INCLUSIVE): A cluster randomised controlled trial. *The Lancet, 392*(10163), 2452–2464. https://doi.org/10.1016/S0140-6736(18)31782-3

Boutellier, H. (2013). The vital context of restorative justice. In I. Aertsen, T. Daems, & L. Robert (Eds.), *Institutionalizing restorative justice* (pp. 25–43) Routledge.

Braithwaite, J. (1989). *Crime, shame, and reintegration.* Cambridge University Press. https://doi.org/10.1017/CBO9780511804618

Braithwaite, J. (2002). *Restorative justice and responsive regulation.* Oxford University Press.

Caulfield, S. L. (2019). Peacemaking criminology: Introduction and implications for the intersection of race, class, and gender. In D. Milovanovic & D. S. Martin (Eds.), *Race, gender, and class in criminology: The intersections* (pp. 91–103). Routledge.

Choi, J. J., Green, D. L., & Kapp, S. A. (2010). Victimization, victims' needs, and empowerment in victim offender mediation. *International Review of Victimology, 17*, 267–290. https://doi.org/10.1177/026975801001700302

Coker, D. (2002). Transformative justice: Anti-subordination processes in cases of domestic violence. In H. Strang & J. Braithwaite (Eds.), *Restorative justice and family violence* (pp. 128–152). Cambridge University Press.

Daly, K. (2002). Restorative justice: The real story. *Punishment & Society 4*(1), 55–79. https://doi.org/10.1177/14624740222228464

Daly, K. (2016). What is restorative justice? Fresh answers to a vexed question. *Victims & Offenders, 11*(1), 9–29. https://doi.org/10.1080/15564886.2015.1107797

Dashman, M., Culberg, K., Dean, D., Lemler, A., Lyubansky, M., & Shackford-Bradley, J. (2019). Bringing a racial justice consciousness to the restorative justice movement: A call to white practitioners. In T. Lewis & C. Stauffer (Eds.), *Listening to the movement: Essays on new growth and new challenges in restorative justice* (pp. 21–35). Wipf & Stock Publishers.

Davis, F. (2005). Reflections on justice as healing. In W. D. McClaslin (Ed.), *Justice as healing: Indigenous ways: Writings on community peacemaking and restorative justice from the Native Law Centre* (inside cover). Living Justice Press.

Davis, F. E. (2012). What's love got to do with it? *Tikkun, 27*(1), 30–33. https://doi.org/10.1215/08879982-2012-1014

Davis, F. E. (2019). *The little book of race and restorative justice: Black lives, healing, and US social transformation*. Simon and Schuster.

Duwe, G. (2012). Can Circles of Support and Accountability (COSA) work in the United States? Preliminary results from a randomized experiment in Minnesota. *Sexual Abuse: A Journal of Research and Treatment, 25*, 143–165. https://doi.org/10.1177/1079063212453942

Elliott, I. A., & Beech, A. R. (2013). A U.K. cost-benefit analysis of Circles of Support and Accountability interventions. *Sexual Abuse: A Journal of Research and Treatment, 25*, 211–229. https://doi.org/10.1177/1079063212443385

Elliott, I. A., Zajac, G., & Meyer, C. A. (2013). *Evaluability assessments of the Circles of Support and Accountability (COSA) model: Cross site report.* https://www. ncjrs.gov/pdffiles1/nij/grants/243832.pdf

Flaten, C. (1996). Victim offender mediation: Application with serious offences committed by juveniles. In B. Galaway & J. Hudson (Eds.), *Restorative justice: International perspectives* (pp. 387–401). Criminal Justice Press.

Fox, K. J. (2015). Theorizing community integration as desistance-promotion. *Criminal Justice and Behavior, 42*(1), 82–94.

Gade, C. B. (2018). "Restorative justice": History of the term's international and Danish use. *Nordic Mediation Research,* 27.

Hadley, M. L. (Ed.). (2001). *The spiritual roots of restorative justice.* Suny Press.

Hulvershorn, K., & Mulholland, S. (2018). Restorative practices and the integration of social emotional learning as a path to positive school climates. *Journal of Research in Innovative Teaching & Learning, 11*(1), 110–123. https://doi.org/10.1108/JRIT-08-2017-0015

Johnstone, G. (2011). Reviving restorative justice traditions. In G. Johnstone (Ed.), *Restorative justice: Ideas, values and debates* (pp. 30–50). Taylor & Francis.

Johnstone, G., & Van Ness, D. (2007). The meaning of restorative justice. In G. Johnstone & D. Van Ness (Eds.), *Handbook of restorative justice* (pp. 5–23). Willan Publishing.

Kim, M. E. (2018). From carceral feminism to transformative justice: Women-of-color feminism and alternatives to incarceration. *Journal of Ethnic & Cultural Diversity in Social Work, 27*(3), 219–233. https://doi.org/10.1080/15313204.2018.1474827

Llewellyn, J. J., & Philpott, D. (Eds.). (2014). *Restorative justice, reconciliation, and peacebuilding.* Oxford University Press.

McCartan, K., Kemshall, H., Westwood, S., Solle, J., MacKenzie, G., Cattel, J., & Pollard, A. (2014). *Circles of Support and Accountability (CoSA): A case file review of two pilots.* Ministry of Justice Analytical Summary.

McClasin, W. D. (2005). *Justice as healing-Indigenous ways: Writings on community peacemaking and restorative justice from the native law centre.* St. Paul: Living Justice Press.

McCold, P. (2000). Toward a holistic vision of restorative juvenile justice: A reply to the maximalist model. *Contemporary Justice Review, 3*(4), 357–414.

McCold, P. (2004). Paradigm muddle: The threat to restorative justice posed by its merger with community justice. *Contemporary Justice Review, 7*(1), 13–35. https://doi.org/10.1080/1028258042000211987

National Crime Victimization Survey. (2020). *Bureau of Justice Statistics.* Washington, DC.

Norris, H. (2019). The impact of restorative approaches on well-being: An evaluation of happiness and engagement in schools. *Conflict Resolution Quarterly, 36*(3), 221–234. https://doi.org/10.1002/crq.21242

Pavlich, G. (2005). *Governing paradoxes of restorative justice.* Psychology Press.

Pepinsky, H. E., & Quinney, R. (Eds.). (1991). *Criminology as peacemaking.* Indiana University Press.

Pranis, K. (2012). The restorative impulse. *Tikkun, 27*(1), 33–34. https://doi.org/10.1215/08879982-2012-1015

Qafisheh, M. (2012). Restorative justice in Islamic Penal Law: A contribution to the global system. *International Journal of Criminal Justice Sciences, 7*(1), 487–507.

Quinney, R. (1989, Winter). The theory and practice of peacemaking in the development of radical criminology. *The Critical Criminologist, 1,* 5.

Roberts, T. (1995). *Evaluation of the victim offender mediation project: Final report.* https://www.publicsafety.gc.ca/lbrr/archives/hv%209509.b7%20r6%201995-eng.pdf

Robinson, J., & Hudson, J. (2015). Restorative justice: A typology and critical appraisal. *Willamette Journal of International Law & Dispute Resolution, 23*, 335.

Schiff, M. (2013). Institutionalizing restorative justice: Paradoxes of power, restoration, and rights. In T. Gavrielides & V. Artinopoulou (Eds.), *Reconstructing restorative justice philosophy* (pp. 153–179). Furnham, UK: Ashgate.

Segal, E. (2001). Jewish perspectives on restorative justice. In M. L. Hadley (Ed.), *The spiritual roots of restorative justice.* (pp. 181–197). Albany, NY: SUNY Press.

Sered, D. (2019). *Until we reckon: Violence, mass incarceration, and a road to repair.* The New Press.

Shah, S., Stauffer, C., & King, S. (2017). *Restorative justice listening project (final report).* Zehr Institute for Restorative Justice. https://zehr-institute.org/images/Restorative-Justice-Listening-Project-Final-Report.pdf

Sherman, L. W., & Strang, H. (2012). Restorative justice as evidence-based sentencing. In J. Pertersilia & K. R. Reitz (Eds.), *The Oxford handbook of sentencing and corrections* (pp. 215–243). Oxford University Press.

Sliva, S. M., Han, T. M., Samimi, C., Golieb, K., McCurdy, J., & Forte, A. (2019). *State of the state: Restorative justice in Colorado.* Colorado Restorative Justice Coordinating Council. https://restorativejusticeontherise.org/state-of-the-state-restorative-justice-in-colorado/

Sliva, S. M., & Plassmeyer, M. (2020). Effects of restorative justice pre-file diversion legislation on juvenile filing rates: An interrupted time-series analysis. *Criminology and Public Policy, 20*(1), 19–40. https://doi.org/10.1111/1745-9133.12518

Sliva, S. M., Samimi, C., Han, T. M., McClain, T., & Albright, K. (2021). *Effects of victim offender dialogue on mental health and trauma appraisals* (Working paper). http://portfolio.du.edu/ssliva

Strang, H., Sherman, L. W., Mayo-Wilson, E., Woods, D., & Ariel, B. (2013). Restorative justice conferencing (RJC) using face-to-face meetings of offenders and victims: Effects on offender recidivism and victim satisfaction. A systematic review. *Campbell Systematic Reviews, 9*(1), 1–59. https://doi.org/10.4073/csr.2013.12

Suzuki, M., & Wood, W. R. (2017). Co-option, coercion and compromise: Challenges of restorative justice in Victoria, Australia. *Contemporary Justice Review, 20*(2), 274–292. https://doi.org/10.1080/10282580.2017.1311194

Symonds, M. (2010). The "second injury" to victims of violent acts. *American Journal of Psychoanalysis, 70*(1), 34–41.

Thomas, E. W. (2005). *The judicial process: Realism, pragmatism, practical reasoning and principles.* Cambridge University Press.

Umbreit, M. (1989). Crime victims seeking fairness, not revenge: Toward restorative justice. *Federal Probation, 53*(3), 52–57.

Umbreit, M., & Armour, M. P. (2010). *Restorative justice dialogue: An essential guide for research and practice.* Springer Publishing Company.

Umbreit, M. S., Coates, R. B., & Vos, B. (2002). *The impact of restorative justice conferencing: A review of 63 empirical studies in 5 countries.* University of Minnesota Center for Restorative Justice & Peacemaking, School of Social Work, University of Minnesota. http://www.antoniocasella.eu/restorative/Umbreit_impact_2002.pdf

Umbreit, M. S., Vos, B., Coates, R. B., & Armour, M. P. (2006). Victims of severe violence in mediated dialogue with offender: The impact of the first multi-site study in the US. *International Review of Victimology, 13*, 27–48. https://doi.org/10.1177/026975800601300102

Vaandering, D. (2013). A window on relationships: Reflecting critically on a current restorative justice theory. *Restorative Justice, 1*(3), 311–333.

Van Ness, D. W., & Strong, K. H. (2015). *Restoring justice: An introduction to restorative justice* (5th ed.). Elsevier.

Wachtel, T. (2003). Restorative justice in everyday life: Beyond the formal ritual. *Reclaiming Children and Youth, 12*(2), 83–87.

Wachtel, T., & McCold, P. (2001). Restorative justice in everyday life. In J. Braithwaite & H. Strang (Eds.), *Restorative justice in civil society* (pp. 114–129). Cambridge University Press.

Waller, I. (2011). *Rights for victims of crime: Rebalancing Justice.* New York City: Rowman & Littlefield.

Western, B. (2015). *Lifetimes of violence in a sample of released prisoners.* Boston Reentry Study (working papers). https://scholar.harvard.edu/brucewestern/working-papers

Wilson, R. J., Cortoni, F., & McWhinnie, A. J. (2009). Circles of Support & Accountability: A Canadian national replication of outcome findings. *Sexual Abuse, 21*(4), 412–430. https://doi.org/10.1177/10790 63209347724

Wilson, R. J., Picheca, J. E., & Prinzo, M. (2005). *Circles of Support & Accountability: An evaluation of the pilot project in South-Central Ontario* (Research Report No. R-168). Correctional Service of Canada. https://www.csc-scc.gc.ca/research/r168-eng.shtml

Wong, D. S., Cheng, C. H., Ngan, R. M., & Ma, S. K. (2011). Program effectiveness of a restorative whole-school approach for tackling school bullying in Hong Kong. *International Journal of Offender Therapy and Comparative Criminology, 55*(6), 846–862. https://doi.org/10.1177/0306624X10374638

Yazzie, R. (2005) . Life Comes from It. Navajo Nation Peacemaking: Living Traditional Justice, 42. https://books.google.com/books/about/Navajo_Nation_Peacemaking.html?id=ai1rOrd4qVkC

Zehr, H. (1990). A restorative lens. In *Changing lenses: A new focus for crime and justice.* Waterloo, Ontario: Herald Press.

Zehr, H. (2015). *The little book of restorative justice (revised and updated).* Good Books.

31

Correctional Settings

Rachel C. Casey

Social Work Practice in Correctional Settings

When learning about the origin of the social work profession, students often read about the noteworthy efforts of Jane Addams and her service to immigrants and people in poverty through the Chicago settlement house movement. However, contemporaries of Addams in the burgeoning social work field were also dedicating their efforts to criminal justice reform, with a particular focus on corrections. Indeed, the organization now known as the National Association of Social Workers was once named the National Conference of Charities and Corrections (Zenderland, 1998) and included among its charges both prison reform and care for so-called "delinquent children" (Hart, 1893). Social workers were largely responsible for the creation of separate correctional facilities for youth, with the aim of ensuring their protection and humane treatment (Maschi & Killian, 2011; Roberts & Brownell, 1999; Rosenthal, 1987). Since the Progressive Era, social workers have maintained their commitment to justice-involved populations, and they continue to serve in a variety of capacities within correctional contexts.

This chapter will first describe the correctional environments in which social workers engage with clients, specifically jails and prisons, providing information about the physical and cultural characteristics of those environments, as well as vocabulary used within these contexts. The chapter will also discuss the tasks social workers often perform within correctional settings and highlight the assessment tools and evidence-based treatment models social workers use. Finally, this chapter will explore some of the ethical dilemmas that may present themselves to correctional social workers. Importantly, the individual facilities in which social workers find themselves inevitably reflect the systemic injustices of the broader criminal justice system. Readers are encouraged to review other chapters in this book, especially Chapter 14, Mass Incarceration and For-Profit Prisons, to better understand the theoretical and political landscape in which correctional social workers find themselves.

Rachel C. Casey, *Correctional Settings* In: *Handbook of Forensic Social Work*. Edited by: David Axlyn McLeod, Anthony P. Natale, and Kristin W. Mapson, Oxford University Press. © Oxford University Press 2024. DOI: 10.1093/oso/9780197694732.003.0031

Correctional Environments

As social workers, we emphasize the role of the environment in understanding human behavior. The physical and cultural environment of correctional facilities is especially unique and invariably impacts both incarcerated people and correctional staff. Innumerable films, television programs, and books have depicted jails and prisons, providing audiences harrowing glimpses into the lives of incarcerated people. Except for a handful of documentary and reality series, these depictions tend to exaggerate or even glamorize aspects of the correctional environment, spawning inaccurate stereotypes about jails and prisons and the realities of the people incarcerated and employed within them. In actuality, correctional facilities vary widely in terms of their physical structure, policies, and populations. Much of this variation results from differences in purpose and security level across facilities.

Physical Settings

Although many people use the terms "jail" and "prison" interchangeably, these terms actually refer to two distinct types of correctional facilities. Jail facilities house people awaiting trial or serving shorter sentences, typically up to 1 year. Jails are operated at the county or municipal level, usually under the oversight of the local sheriff. On the other hand, prisons are operated at either the state or federal level by the state Department of Corrections (DOC) or the Federal Bureau of Prisons, respectively. State and federal facilities incarcerate people serving sentences of longer than 1 year, including life sentences. Depending on the size and needs of the population served, both jails and prisons may feature specialized units designed for rehabilitative programs, ranging from sex offender treatment to community reintegration. Some detention and diversion programs operated by municipal courts may also be housed within correctional facilities.

The most significant distinguishing characteristic of a correctional facility is its security classification. Although these classifications vary across jurisdictions, there are generally three security levels: minimum-security, medium-security, and maximum-security facilities. There are a few facilities across the United States designated as super-maximum security, colloquially referred to as "supermax" facilities. The vast majority of incarcerated people do not require the intensive security measures of supermax facilities, or may only require them for a limited time. Instead of transferring inmates to supermax facilities, many institutions temporarily house inmates in specialized units that provide supermax levels of security, including solitary confinement of inmates. These units, officially termed "restrictive housing units" or "segregated housing units," have become proverbially known as "the hole" because of the extreme physical and social isolation inmates experience there. Because the negative emotional and psychological impacts of solitary confinement have been well documented (Ahalt et al., 2017; Cloud et al., 2015), correctional social workers may be tasked with visiting and assessing inmates housed in these units on a routine—often daily—basis. The security level of an institution may also dictate what type of sleeping arrangements are provided to inmates, such as individual cells or open bunk rooms. Generally, inmates are assigned to facilities within a correctional system according to the security level required to detain them safely, as well as other factors such as the length of their sentence, time until release, and even location of relatives in the community.

Security protocols and facility layouts vary widely based on security classification. For example, most prisons have fences or walls with escape prevention mechanisms, but there are also minimum-security facilities with no physical barriers whatsoever. Some facilities consist of a single building, while others may have numerous buildings spread across larger grounds. Regardless of the security classification of a facility, security screening proced- ures are generally required for all persons entering a facility, including staff. Unfortunately, there have been many instances of correctional staff bringing contraband materials such as alcohol or drugs into facilities and supplying it to inmates. There have also been instances of correctional staff supplying inmates with materials to facilitate their escape, such as the now-infamous case of Joyce Mitchell, a former staff member at the Clinton Correctional Facility in New York (Taylor, 2015). Because of such security concerns, staff may not be per- mitted to bring any personal items into the facility or may be limited to only a small, clear container of personal items. Electronic devices, including cell phones, are generally pro- hibited, a potentially difficult adjustment for correctional social workers who have grown accustomed to the immediate access to information and interpersonal connection that technology provides.

As one might expect, jails and prisons vary dramatically in the condition of their fa- cilities depending on the age of the institution and the funding available for maintenance. Within the United States, some facilities have become notorious for the poor living con- ditions afforded to inmates, especially in terms of cleanliness and temperature control. Changes to facilities over time may result in questionable repurposing of some spaces within a facility; for example, this writer once worked in a prison office that had been converted from a shower room, complete with (mercifully inoperable) showerheads and drains! The derelict nature of some facilities has appropriately prompted intervention from human rights organizations (Liebling & Arnold, 2004; Shalev, 2011).

In his landmark study of a maximum-security prison, American sociologist Gershman Sykes (1958) characterized correctional institutions as environments of deprivation, citing how the "pains of imprisonment" wielded a negative impact on inmate health and behavior. Specifically, Sykes identified five fundamental losses that people experience during incar- ceration: loss of liberty, desirable goods and services, heterosexual relationships, autonomy, and security. Incarcerated people generally have little control over their surroundings or their schedule, as these are dictated by institutional security protocols and resources. Like many institutional settings, correctional facilities generally have designated times for meals, administering medication, exercise, and other recreational activities. Movement within the institution is closely monitored and often restricted, for inmates as well as staff. Access to preferred food or personal items is severely limited. While such unfavorable conditions in correctional facilities create unparalleled hardship for the people incarcerated within them, correctional social workers and other staff must also contend with these realities during working hours.

Culture of the Correctional Environment

Numerous sociological and ethnographic studies have explored the unique culture that exists among incarcerated people. This culture has also been showcased in popular entertainment just as the physical environment of correctional facilities has been. Prison lingo has even permeated everyday conversations, with sayings such as "snitches get stitches" becoming colloquial punchlines. Some stereotypes about inmate culture find basis in reality; inmates do tend to develop strong bonds with one another despite demands for a tough exterior. As in most institutional settings, cliques and hierarchies inevitably form among inmates, often fueling interpersonal conflicts that occasionally escalate to violence (Winfree et al., 2002). Loyalty and honesty tend to be valued highly (Bronson, 2006). The restrictions and stressors of the correctional environment are such that seemingly insignificant incidents—the theft of a snack item, for example—can have monumental social ramifications for inmates. Some criminal offenses, such as sexual offenses against children, are highly stigmatized, which can result in significant difficulties for perpetrators of those offenses, including bullying, ostracization, and violent victimization (Winfree et al., 2002). Sexual interactions between inmates do take place, sometimes in the context of a romantic relationship, but just as often in a transactional capacity or as assault. While some encounters may appear consensual, all sexual activity is strictly prohibited by the Prison Rape Elimination Act of 2003 (PREA). Importantly, power between individual inmates is often unbalanced, which minimizes the likelihood of genuine consent among the parties involved in a sexual encounter. Importantly, PREA also prohibits any sexual interaction between inmates and correctional staff, as does the social work code of ethics (National Association of Social Workers, 2017). Unfortunately, such violations do take place, and correctional social workers may be in the position to report such transgressions or support inmates during the aftermath of an assault.

The prioritization of security within correctional facilities necessitates a highly regimented environment, and the culture among correctional staff often reflects this. Security staff receive training akin to that of law enforcement officers and adhere to a strict chain of command organized according to military-style ranks (Crawley & Crawley, 2013). As a result, aspects of military culture permeate the correctional environment, such as addressing security staff according to their rank and using "military time" in the documentation. Correctional social workers may be expected to use a more formal tone when interacting with security staff and demonstrate respect to higher ranking officers. Although their professional values may sometimes seem at odds, correctional social workers and security staff collaborate very closely throughout much of the workday. Maintaining congenial relationships with security staff proves advantageous for correctional social workers, who typically rely on security staff to provide them with access to locked units or escort inmates to appointments in an efficient manner. Importantly, correctional officers experience tremendous job-related stress and have lower than average life expectancies and higher rates of suicide as a result (Brower, 2013). An appreciation for the difficulties associated with employment as a correctional officer can help correctional social workers engage more effectively and compassionately with these essential colleagues.

Like social workers in every practice context, correctional social workers use specific vocabulary in their practice. One of the terms that has been revised most often is the one used to refer to incarcerated people. Once referred to by more stigmatizing terms such as "convicts" and "felons," incarcerated people are now more often referred to as "inmates." While "prisoner" is similar to the term "inmate" insofar as it reflects the environment in which the person finds themself, "prisoner" would be a misnomer for people incarcerated in jail facilities, which are distinct from prisons in the ways described above. Within some settings, "offender" has been adopted as the preferred term. Such terminology is often dictated at an administrative level to ensure consistent use of language among staff. Notably, the universally preferred term for members of security staff is "correctional officer." Although sometimes used in popular media or by inmates, "guard" is no longer an appropriate term, and may even be considered disrespectful to correctional officers when used by other staff. Facilities often have individualized standards around language use, both formal and informal, with which correctional social workers quickly become accustomed. Such standards may include the appropriate means of addressing inmates, which may be by the last name only, for example.

Correctional Rehabilitation and Treatment Services

As detailed in other chapters of this book, philosophical and political approaches to the management of crime have shifted over time. The latter half of the 20th century witnessed an era of "tough on crime" policies that, most scholars agree, contributed significantly to creating the current state of mass incarceration (Alexander, 2012; Mackenzie, 2001). However, the pendulum of correctional philosophy has slowly swung away from punitive approaches and back toward what was originally termed the "rehabilitative ideal" (Allen, 1959, p. 226). Although the availability of programming and treatment services varies across correctional institutions, most institutions typically offer an array of medical, mental health, educational, and vocational services. A national survey of prison health care services across 45 states found that most correctional institutions offer outpatient, inpatient, and emergency medical care as well as dental and optometric care (Chari et al., 2016). The majority of female institutions also offer gynecological services either on-site or off-site (Chari et al., 2016). The same study found that inpatient and outpatient mental health care is also available at almost all state correctional facilities (Chari et al., 2016). Available mental health services range from cursory mental health screenings and suicide risk assessments to traditional outpatient therapy or intensive inpatient stabilization (Chari et al., 2016; Manderscheid et al., 2004). Psychotherapy is provided in both individual and group treatment modalities to address a range of mental health concerns, including symptom management, skill development, and substance abuse treatment (Bewley & Morgan, 2011; Boothby & Clements, 2000; Morgan et al., 1999). Interestingly, incarcerated people seem to prefer individual interventions to group interventions (Morgan et al., 2004). Mental health services may also address specific criminogenic needs—that is, characteristics related to offending behavior—in an effort to reduce recidivism. Educational programming represents another readily available form of services, which ranges from literacy support to secondary education programs to college courses (Stephan, 2008). Most prisons have access to vocational activities, including employment programs for inmates (Stephan, 2008). Many female correctional facilities also offer prenatal and parenting programs, including parenting classes or programming that involves visitation with minor children (Hoffmann et al., 2010). While research attests to the wide range of programming ostensibly available in correctional facilities, there may also be challenges around the accessibility and quality of correctional programming and treatment due to resource limitations.

Roles and Tasks of Correctional Social Workers

Social workers provide a variety of services within correctional facilities, including case management, rehabilitative and educational programming, and clinical mental health services. The responsibilities of a social worker will depend upon their education level and licensure status. Typical tasks include conducting assessments of risk and need and the provision of therapeutic interventions in individual and group treatment modalities (Sheehan, 2012). Social workers are often among those staff charged with responding to mental health crises or behavioral disruptions. More than 15% of correctional mental health professionals identify as social workers, affirming that social workers play a central role in the provision of mental health treatment in correctional settings (Bewley & Morgan, 2011). Because many correctional facilities also offer medical services, social workers will often be a member of an interdisciplinary team of service providers within the facility.

A trend that has emerged alongside the for-profit prison industry is the outsourcing of prison services. In the past, social workers and other staff were employed directly by the governing agency of a facility, such as the state Department of Corrections. However, medical professionals, mental health professionals, case managers, and educators are now more commonly employed by external vendors. Although this employment structure has little bearing on the daily tasks of the correctional social worker, it may impact training requirements or compensation packages. When seeking employment in the correctional field, social workers may need to investigate what external vendors provide staffing to various facilities to locate appropriate job listings.

Assessment

Correctional social workers, especially those providing clinical mental health services, often conduct a wide range of assessments to understand the needs of incarcerated clients, as well as significant risk factors. Assessment is especially important when an inmate has newly arrived at a facility, even more so if they have arrived directly from the community, such as when an inmate arrives at jail following an arrest. Initial assessments of newly admitted inmates enable service providers to understand their immediate needs to ensure their safety and the safety of others. Social workers may also conduct assessments aimed at identifying longer term needs for treatment during incarceration. Table 31.1 outlines some

TABLE 31.1 Evidence-Based Assessment Tools for Correctional Populations

Assessment Aim	Assessment Tool	Description
Mental Health Assessment and Diagnosis	Brief Jail Mental Health Screen	8-item instrument to determine whether further mental health assessment is needed
	Global Appraisal of Individual Needs-Short Screener (GAIN-SS)	16-item instrument to identify needs for further assessment in the areas of mental health, substance abuse, and anger management
	Psychopathy Checklist-Revised (PCLR)	20-item instrument to assess psychopathic traits that may indicate risk of violent behavior
Suicide Risk	Prison Suicide Risk Assessment Checklist	27-category interview guide to assess risk of suicide among prison inmates
	Jail Suicide Assessment Tool	24-category interview guide to assess risk of suicide among jail inmates
	Columbia-Suicide Severity Rating Scale (C-SSRS)	6-item instrument to assess immediate suicide risk among correctional populations
Recidivism Risk	Proxy Risk Triage Screener	3-item instrument to assess risk of recidivism on an 8-point scale
	Level of Service/Case Management Inventory (LS/CMI)	124-item inventory to assess risk of recidivism and determine optimal case management plan
	Correctional Offender Management Profiling for Alternative Sanctions (COMPAS)	98-item inventory to assess risk of general recidivism, violent recidivism, noncompliance, and failure to appear
	Inventory of Offender Risk, Needs, and Strengths (IORNS)	130-item inventory to assess risk of recidivism according to static and dynamic risk factors as well as protective factors
	Static-99	10-item instrument to assess risk of recidivism among adult male sexual offenders based on static characteristics

evidence-based tools used for a variety of assessment purposes. Additional commentary has been provided below to highlight special considerations when conducting assessments with correctional populations.

Mental Health Assessment and Diagnosis

As detailed in Chapter 10, Mental Health and Forensic Settings, correctional facilities have become the "new asylums" for people with serious mental illnesses since the so-called deinstitutionalization movement of the 1960s (Barnao & Ward, 2015; Barrenger & Draine, 2013; Kondrat et al., 2013). Studies have consistently shown that incarcerated people disproportionately experience mental health difficulties (James & Glaze, 2006; Steadman et al., 2009; Torrey et al., 2014), and incarceration typically exacerbates existing difficulties (Harner & Riley, 2013). Of course, thorough assessment and accurate diagnosis of mental health difficulties provide the foundation for effective treatment during incarceration.

Correctional social workers may face unique challenges around mental health assessment, in part because incarceration is rarely conducive to optimal mental health. Thus, correctional social workers must often parse out which symptoms reflect a normal response to incarceration versus which symptoms indicate more specific mental health concerns.

Obtaining a detailed mental health history and cross-referencing that information with re-cords from community service providers can assist tremendously in the diagnostic process. However, incarcerated people may not have accessed mental health services in the commu-nity, instead managing their symptoms without formal treatment, perhaps self-medicating with alcohol or drugs. Incarceration may present their first opportunity for engagement with mental health service providers. As such, the absence of a *documented* mental health difficulty does not necessarily indicate the absence of mental health issues.

Especially in jail settings where inmates may have arrived directly from the commu-nity, assessment should include screening for current intoxication and substance use. Often, arrests are prompted by dangerous behavior resulting from substance use, so determining the current level of intoxication may indicate what security measures are appropriate for ensuring the safety of the newly admitted person, other inmates, and correctional staff. Thorough substance use screening can help indicate whether medical intervention is re-quired for detoxification, which is often the case for people with opioid or alcohol depend-ence. Some hallucinogenic substances can prompt mental states that mimic psychosis, so in-depth mental health assessment should only take place once an inmate is no longer ex-hibiting substance-related symptoms.

Another important factor to consider when conducting mental health assessment is the extremely high exposure to trauma among correctional populations. Indeed, the vast majority of incarcerated people have experienced some form of trauma, such as childhood abuse or neglect, physical or sexual assault, community violence, or poverty (Baranyi et al., 2018; Fazel et al., 2016). Due to the pervasive nature of racism in society, incarcerated people of color have likely experienced trauma during their daily lived experiences (Kirkinis et al., 2018). Correctional mental health assessment should account for trauma, and correctional social workers must use a trauma-informed approach in responding to and assessing in-mate behavior. Some behaviors deemed problematic or inappropriate in the correctional environment may constitute a trauma response. For example, refusal to submit to a body cavity search—a routine security procedure in many correctional facilities—may indicate a history of sexual trauma. Some correctional clients who exhibit frequent mental distress or experience emotional dysregulation may report a past diagnosis of bipolar disorder; while not always the case, a more accurate diagnosis for this presentation is likely a trauma-related disorder or a personality disorder rather than a mood disorder. Understanding the impact of trauma on symptomatology and behavior is especially important for social workers en-gaging with correctional populations.

Considering the high correlation that exists between trauma and personality disorders (Berenz et al., 2014), it is not surprising that correctional populations demonstrate higher rates of personality disorders compared to both community and in-patient psychiatric sam-ples (Conn et al., 2016). Within the correctional environment, behaviors that indicate di-agnosable mental health difficulties may be mislabeled as "criminal" traits because they involve manipulation of others or apparent deceitfulness. While the potentially harmful nature of these behaviors should not be minimized, a trauma-informed and strengths-based approach might prompt a more accurate (and compassionate) interpretation of these behaviors as indicative of a personality disorder or other mental health difficulty.

Manipulative or deceitful behaviors may have functioned as survival mechanisms or coping skills for some incarcerated people with histories of interpersonal trauma. Borderline personality disorder and antisocial personality disorder, specifically, are more prevalent among correctional populations. Differential diagnosis of these two disorders can prove especially challenging given the similarity in the presentation of some symptoms. Ultimately, distinguishing between these two diagnoses may not have a significant bearing on treatment, especially considering some research indicating common cognitive and emotional processes underlying the two disorders (Chun et al., 2017).

Social workers are probably more likely to encounter a client with antisocial personality disorder in a correctional setting than any other practice context. Although not included as a diagnosis in the *Diagnostic and Statistical Manual of Mental Disorders,* fifth edition (DSM-5) (American Psychiatric Association, 2022), or the *International Classification of Diseases,* 10th revision, Clinical Modification, psychopathy has received much attention from clinicians and researchers, especially in forensic contexts (Andersen & Kiehl, 2015). Several assessments exist to ascertain the presence of psychopathic traits, such as callousness, grandiosity, and antisocial behavior; the most widely used of these assessments is the Psychopathy Checklist-Revised (PCL-R), developed by Robert Hare, a pioneer in this field of study (Hare, 1996, 1999, 2003). These assessments are considered especially helpful for understanding the criminogenic treatment needs of incarcerated persons, as individuals deemed psychopathic may be more likely to recidivate after their release (Hare et al., 2000; Porter et al., 2009).

In the correctional environment, diagnosis with a mental health condition may afford inmates privileges to which they would not otherwise be entitled, such as access to programming or psychotropic medication. As such, inmates occasionally fabricate or exaggerate mental health symptoms; the DSM-5 refers to this behavior as "malingering." While malingering is not a disorder, it may become the focus of clinical attention. Indeed, additional attention from correctional staff may incentivize malingering among inmates. Many mental health assessment tools designed for forensic populations include items to screen for possible malingering, and correctional social workers quickly become attuned to the distinctions between malingered and genuine presentations of mental health symptoms.

Suicide Risk

Suicide represents a leading cause of death among incarcerated people in the United States (Mumola, 2005). Incarceration may exacerbate the risk for self-directed violence, including suicide, among already vulnerable populations, such as people with serious mental illness (Way et al., 2005). Often, social workers perform suicide risk assessments as part of the initial processing of an inmate upon their arrival at a facility or as part of a response to mental health crises. In addition to typical risk factors for suicide, some unique risk factors may exist for incarcerated people. Social workers should consider the circumstances surrounding the client's legal proceedings, including any publicity around their case. Some people may be especially vulnerable leading up to and following court appearances related to their alleged offense, especially if that court appearance results in a conviction or unfavorable sentence. Due to limited contact with family and loved ones in the community, visitation can be emotionally fraught for some incarcerated people, potentially contributing to elevated risk for suicide, particularly around the holidays or significant anniversaries and events. All of these factors may increase the already elevated risk of suicide for an incarcerated person.

Recidivism Risk

The vast majority of incarcerated people will reenter the community at some point. As such, correctional social workers may be tasked with assessing recidivism risk, especially if an inmate is under consideration for probation or parole. Several assessment tools exist for measuring recidivism risk, including some tools designed for special populations, such as sex offenders. In general, violent offenders, and especially sex offenders, are considered to be at highest risk for recidivism (Prescott et al., 2019), and their potential recidivism would pose the most significant threat to the safety of the community. However, no assessment tool is infallible in its ability to predict future offending. As with any diagnostic or assessment process, correctional social workers must view the client from a holistic and strengths-based perspective, while also exercising their clinical judgment. Additionally, many assessment tools require specialized training to administer, so credentialing beyond a graduate degree or clinical licensure may be necessary for some correctional social workers. Some facilities employ psychologists specifically for their training and expertise in assessment.

Intervention

Once assessment has been completed, correctional social workers often engage with an interdisciplinary team to determine appropriate intervention options, if any are indicated. Social workers often implement those interventions as well. This section provides a brief overview of some evidence-based interventions used within correctional contexts. Detailed instructions for implementing these interventions are beyond the scope of this chapter, but many of the interventions mentioned below have manualized implementation models that have been cited below when available.

Suicide and Self-Harm Prevention

In recent decades, tremendous efforts have been made to reduce the rates of suicide within correctional facilities. The high level of control within the correctional environment allows for the implementation of extensive suicide prevention measures when necessary. When an inmate is assessed as being at a heightened risk for suicide, they will often be placed under "mental health watch," meaning a member of security staff will be assigned to make visual contact with the inmate at regular intervals, or perhaps watch them at all times. Many facilities now have specialized units in which cells are situated to allow for unimpeded viewing from a centralized security station. Facilities may also have suicide-resistant cells that have been specially designed with features to reduce the risk of self-directed violence, such as padded walls or plastic furniture with soft, sloping edges.

Incarcerated people have a reputation for ingenuity in their use of everyday items for alternative purposes; unfortunately, in the case of inmates experiencing suicidality, such ingenuity can lead to seemingly benign objects—underwear, a toothbrush, a book—being used for self-directed violence. Because bedding and clothing can be used as strangulation devices, an inmate deemed at increased risk of suicide may be given tear-resistant blankets and clothing (typically a smock-style garment). If an inmate is engaging in self-directed violence through scratching with their hands, they may be required to wear specially de-signed hand coverings that look like large mittens. To prevent the use of everyday objects for self-harm, inmates deemed at increased risk of suicide usually have very limited access to personal property, such as hygiene products or leisure materials; often, these items can only be used under direct supervision. In exceptionally rare cases, an inmate may be phys-ically restrained with fabric straps to prevent self-directed violence; this is often necessary in the case of repeated head-banging, for example.

The wide array of resources and strategies available to prevent suicide and other self-directed violence can alleviate some anxiety for the correctional social worker; rarely do mental health professionals have such control over the implementation of prevention meas-ures for clients experiencing suicidality. However, many of the prevention measures de-scribed above may also have a deleterious impact on mental health. The removal of clothing and personal property can be experienced as degrading, and the limited privacy that comes with a "mental health watch" can feel invasive or even traumatizing. In consultation with colleagues, correctional social workers must carefully weigh the potential positive and neg-ative impact of each individual prevention measure to both prevent self-directed violence and promote mental wellness.

Interventions for Mental Health–Related Needs

Many of the mental health interventions social workers use with community populations are appropriate to use with correctional populations as well. This section will briefly high-light some mental health interventions that are either unique to corrections or especially appropriate for correctional populations because of the specific needs of incarcerated people. Given the high rates of trauma and substance use among incarcerated populations, interventions focused on those needs may be particularly relevant for correctional so-cial workers. Especially in correctional facilities for women and girls, dialectical behavior therapy (DBT; Linehan, 1993) is used to address trauma and related personality disorders. One manualized intervention with demonstrated effectiveness for treating co-occurring trauma-related symptomatology and substance use in correctional populations specifi-cally is *Seeking Safety*, typically offered in a group treatment modality (Zlotnick et al., 2003, 2009).

As a means of alleviating the strain on mental health resources within prisons and jails, several program models have emerged for peer-led services, ranging from structured emo-tional support and psychoeducational groups to mentorship to crisis intervention (Bagnall et al., 2015; Devilly et al., 2005). Several studies have noted the positive outcomes associ-ated with peer-led services in correctional environments, finding that such programs can promote prosocial attitudes (Collica, 2010), reduce symptomatology (Woodall et al., 2015), and prevent self-directed violence (Griffiths & Bailey, 2015; Halls & Gabor, 2004). Another noteworthy strength of peer-led interventions is their potential for addressing disparities in mental health service use among inmates who are Black, Indigenous, or people of color (Corrigan et al., 2017; Weng & Spaulding-Givens, 2017). Drawing upon the tenets of 12-step programs like Alcoholics Anonymous, therapeutic communities—sometimes referred to as residential substance abuse treatment in corrections—use a model of mutual self-help to address substance use in a residential setting (Stohr et al., 2003). Correctional social workers may be tasked with supervising peer mentors to facilitate such programs.

Interventions for Criminogenic Needs

Several evidence-based theoretical and intervention models provide a foundation for addressing offending behavior among incarcerated people, especially those with violent offenses and/or extensive histories of repeated offending. Most notably, the risk-need-responsivity model (RNR), which has been implemented in correctional facilities worldwide, is designed to identify and target dynamic attributes of offenders that contribute to their criminal behavior (Andrews & Bonta, 2010). The central principles of RNR assert that antisocial cognitive patterns combine with certain lifestyle choices to result in criminal behavior. As such, cognitive-behavioral therapy is a popular intervention approach to target these "criminal thinking errors" (Bush et al., 2003). *Thinking for a Change* is a manualized cognitive-behavioral program designed specifically for justice-involved populations and has been implemented across many correctional facilities in the United States (Bush et al., 2003). Although not developed for correctional populations specifically, the stages of change model—sometimes referred to as the transtheoretical model—also guides the practice of correctional social workers as they engage with inmates aiming to change a range of behaviors (Prochaska et al., 1992; Yong et al., 2015). Rooted in the stages of change model, motivational interviewing is a popular intervention approach among correctional social workers because it supports clients in resolving ambivalence around behavioral change (Miller & Rollnick, 2012).

Approximately 36% of correctional facilities offer specialized treatment for people convicted of sexually based offenses (Stephan, 2008). Participation in these treatment programs is often mandated at sentencing as a condition for reentry to the community. Like the models delineated above, most sex offender treatment models utilize a cognitive-behavioral framework (Yates, 2012). Interventions based on the self-regulation model of sexual offending guide participants in evaluating the cognitive and behavioral processes that led to their offending behavior (Kingston et al., 2012, 2013). Participants develop skills in challenging cognitive distortions, managing emotions, and problem-solving. Such programs also encourage participants to develop empathy for their potential victims and respond appropriately to sexual arousal. Designed to augment the RNR model described above, the Good Lives Model provides a more strengths-based approach to sex offender treatment by focusing on well-being; sexual offending is understood as a barrier to obtaining "primary human goods," such as independence, peace of mind, meaningful relationships, and community (Willis, Prescott, & Yates, 2013; Wills, Ward, & Levenson, 2014). Participants develop goals focused on both attainment of primary goods and avoidance of offending behaviors and cultivate strategies for achieving those goals (Whitehead et al., 2007).

Culturally Responsive Interventions

Increased awareness of mass incarceration has also prompted an increased awareness of the unique needs of those disproportionately impacted by it, especially Black, Indigenous, and people of color in jails and prisons. Just as gender-responsive interventions have become a standard of best practice for working with women and girls in forensic settings, culturally responsive interventions present an emerging avenue for social workers to respond more effectively to their incarcerated clients. For example, the Maine Department of Corrections has partnered with Maine-Wabanaki REACH: Reconciliation, Engagement, Advocacy, Change, and Healing, an advocacy and service organization serving Indigenous people in Maine, to provide culturally responsive services to incarcerated Indigenous people. In correctional facilities across the state, volunteers from REACH hold healing circles, a traditional practice intended to cultivate connection within Indigenous communities (Maine-Wabanaki REACH, n.d.; Casey, 2017). Correctional social workers who are not themselves members of the cultural group in need of services might advocate for partnerships with outside service organizations to provide culturally responsive services.

Ethical Dilemmas for Correctional Social Workers

Social workers must always attend to power dynamics within their practice, and this is especially important in the correctional context. Incarcerated people experience unique forms of disempowerment as a result of their incarceration, so the power imbalance between social workers and the client may be even more pronounced in correctional environments compared to community settings. Correctional social workers often function as gatekeepers to privileges, programming, and resources within the facility, and their decision-making about access to those may have significant practical and emotional repercussions for their incarcerated clients. For example, correctional social workers may be tasked with determining which inmates will receive individual therapy, a limited mental health resource in most correctional facilities; while most inmates would likely benefit tremendously from this treatment, very few will have access to it.

As described above, security and safety are prioritized above most other considerations within the correctional environment. However, many security protocols degrade or dehumanize incarcerated people in addition to ostensibly promoting safety. For example, pregnant women were routinely shackled while giving birth until recent activism and legislative efforts challenged this practice (King, 2018). Over time, security protocols have been adjusted to ensure the humane treatment of incarcerated people, but the restrictive nature of the correctional environment is in some ways inherently inhumane. The degrading effect of limited agency cannot be underestimated. Frankly stated, social workers may value the dignity and worth of the person, but most correctional environments do not. Although correctional social workers can use their position to advocate for more humane treatment of incarcerated people, they often have little power over the implementation of security protocols or the treatment of inmates by security staff. This reality can be especially disheartening when security protocols seem to exacerbate an inmate's current emotional distress or contribute to the deterioration of their overall well-being.

Since the construction of the first correctional institutions, the prison abolition movement has challenged their existence. Today, abolitionists consider mass incarceration a human rights atrocity and call for the dismantling of the "prison industrial complex" (Davis, 2003). Correctional social workers must consider the extent to which they function as an agent of the criminal justice system, potentially enabling the perpetuation of a grossly unjust system. Most correctional social workers recognize the necessity of some correctional system to promote public safety through incarceration of legitimately dangerous offenders; however, we also confront the realities of mass incarceration as we interact with people incarcerated for minor offenses resulting from poverty, substance use, or mental illness. Many incarcerated people have entered the criminal justice system because other systems—the child welfare system, the education system, the health care system—have failed them. Correctional social workers have a valuable opportunity to serve some of the most vulnerable members of our society and envision with them a meaningful path forward.

Case Study

You are a social worker in the city jail of a midsized metropolitan area, and you are the mental health provider currently on duty to respond to mental health crises. You receive a call from security staff asking you to report to the intake unit, where a recently admitted inmate has been exhibiting signs of mental distress. When you arrive at the intake unit, the correctional officer completing intake documentation provides you with information about Stanley Pierre, a 34-year-old man who has been arrested for alleged child sexual abuse. Mr. Pierre has an extensive criminal history, with 14 prior arrests for nonviolent offenses, including petty theft, check forgery, and possession of marijuana.

Because Mr. Pierre has been detained at this facility previously, you have access to records detailing his biopsychosocial history. Mr. Pierre is the son of Haitian immigrants and identifies as Black. When Mr. Pierre was 12 years old, his mother died of ovarian cancer. Shortly thereafter, Mr. Pierre and his two younger siblings entered foster care because child protective services deemed their father an unfit parent due to his substance use. Mr. Pierre remained in foster care until age 18, at which point he became homeless for approximately 6 months. Although he did not graduate high school, Mr. Pierre earned his GED at age 23 while incarcerated at a state correctional facility. He has been employed in various entry-level jobs throughout his adulthood, though typically for less than 1 year at a time because incarceration often disrupted his employment. According to notes from another correctional social worker, Mr. Pierre has two school-aged children who have served as a source of positive motivation when he has participated in correctional programming during prior incarcerations. Mr. Pierre has a diagnosis of Crohn's disease but has no other history of health issues. Records indicate no prior mental health diagnoses or treatment. His most recent detainment at this jail facility was 24 months ago before he was convicted of check forgery and sentenced to 18 months in state prison. You calculate that he has been in the community for approximately 6 months since completing that most recent sentence.

You ask the correctional officers processing his intake about their observations of Mr. Pierre so far. They report Mr. Pierre was crying "loudly and inconsolably" for almost an hour before you arrived. Although Mr. Pierre complied with all security protocols, including the strip search, he required significant prompting and moved clumsily, as if under the influence of substances. The medical staff conducted a rapid drug test using a urine sample, which was positive for THC and benzodiazepines. The correctional officers also report smelling body odor and marijuana when within close proximity to Mr. Pierre. Except to answer direct questions from correctional staff, Mr. Pierre has not spoken to anyone, and he has refused all offers of food and water. One officer who is familiar with Mr. Pierre from a prior incarceration tells you, "He's just not acting like himself. In the past, he's always seemed pretty easygoing. Then again, it's a more serious offense this time around."

You meet with Mr. Pierre in a small cell used to house inmates temporarily during the intake process. Mr. Pierre has shackles on his arms and legs, and he is slumped in his plastic chair, quiet and motionless. You notice what appears to be recent bruising on his neck. You sit across from Mr. Pierre and introduce yourself, explaining that you are a social worker and hope to provide him with some emotional support. Mr. Pierre does not respond for several seconds, but then looks up to meet your gaze as he quietly says, "There is nothing you can do for me." You nod empathetically but continue by saying, "I'd really like to help if I can. Why is it you say there is nothing I can do?" His voice grows louder as he responds, "Because nothing can change what happened to my little girl. It is unforgivable! This whole situation is just crazy! I can't be back here again. I can't even—" Mr. Pierre begins crying again before he can finish his last sentence.

Guiding Questions

- How would you respond to Mr. Pierre in this moment? What are your primary concerns?
- Which assessment tool(s) would you administer during this initial conversation with Mr. Pierre?
- Which assessment tool(s) would you plan to administer to Mr. Pierre during a follow-up appointment 1 week from now?
- What interventions, both immediate and long term, might be appropriate for Mr. Pierre while he is incarcerated at the jail?

References

Ahalt, C., Haney, C., Rios, S., Fox, M. P., Farabee, D., & Williams, B. (2017). Reducing the use and impact of solitary confinement in corrections. *International Journal of Prisoner Health, 13*(1), 41–48. https://doi.org/10.1108/IJPH-08-2016-0040

Alexander, M. (2012). *The new Jim Crow: Mass incarceration in the age of colorblindness.* New Press.

Allen, F. A. (1959). Criminal justice, legal values and the rehabilitative ideal. *Journal of Criminal Law, Criminology and Police Science, 50*(3), 226–232. https://doi.org/10.2307/1141037

American Psychiatric Association. (2022). *Diagnostic and statistical manual of mental disorders* (5th ed., text rev.). https://doi.org/10.1176/appi.books.9780890425787

Andersen, N. E., & Kiehl, K. A. (2015). Psychopathy: Developmental perspectives and their implications for treatment. *Restorative Neurology and Neuroscience, 32*(1), 103–117. https://doi.org/*10.3233/RNN-139001*

Andrews, D. A., & Bonta, J. L. (2010). *The psychology of criminal conduct* (5th ed.). Anderson.

Bagnall, A., South, J., Hulme, C., Woodall, J., Vinall-Collier, K., Raine, G., Kinsella, K., Dixey, R., Harris, L., & Wright, N. M. (2015). A systematic review of the effectiveness and cost-effectiveness of peer education and peer support in prisons. *BMC Public Health, 15*(290), 1–30. https://doi.org/10.1186/s12 889-015-1584-x

Baranyi, G., Cassidy, M., Fazel, S., Priebe, S., & Mundt, A. P. (2018). Prevalence of posttraumatic stress disorder in prisoners. *Epidemiologic Reviews, 40*(1), 134–145. https://doi.org/10.1093/epirev/mxx015

Barnao, M., & Ward, T. (2015). Sailing uncharted seas without a compass: A review of interventions in forensic mental health. *Aggression and Violent Behavior, 22*, 77–86. https://doi.org/10.1016/j.avb.2015.04.009

Barrenger, S. L., & Draine, J. (2013). "You don't get no help": The role of community context in effectiveness of evidence-based treatments for people with mental illness leaving prison for high risk environments. *American Journal of Psychiatric Rehabilitation, 16*(2), 154–178. https://doi.org/10.1080/15487 768.2013.789709

Berenz, E. C., Amstadter, A. B., Aggen, S. H., Knudsen, G. P., Reichborn-Kjennerud, T., Gardner, C. O., & Kendler, K. S. (2014). Childhood trauma and personality disorder criterion counts: A co-twin control analysis. *Journal of Abnormal Psychology, 122*(4), 1070–1076. https://doi.org/10.1037/a0034238

Bewley, M. T., & Morgan, R. D. (2011). A national survey of mental health services available to offenders with mental illness: Who is doing what? *Law and Human Behavior, 35*, 351–363. https://doi.org/10.1007/ s10979-010-9242-4

Boothby, J. L., & Clements, C. B. (2000). A national survey of correctional psychologists. *Criminal Justice and Behavior, 27*(6), 716–732. https://doi.org/10.1177/0093854800027006003

Bronson, E. F. (2006). Medium security prisons and inmate subcultures: The "normal prison." *Southwest Journal of Criminal Justice, 3*(2), 61–85.

Brower, J. (2013). *Correctional officer wellness and safety literature review.* U.S. Department of Justice Office of Justice Programs Diagnostic Center. https://s3.amazonaws.com/static.nicic.gov/Public/244831.pdf

Bush, J., Glick, B., & Taymans, J. (2003). *Thinking for a change: Integrated cognitive behavior change program.* National Institute of Corrections. https://nicic.gov/thinking-for-a-change

Casey, R. C. (2017). Hard time: A content analysis of incarcerated women's personal accounts. *Affilia: Journal of Women and Social Work, 33*(1), 126–138. doi:10.1177/0886109917718233

Chari, K. A., Simon, A. E., DeFrances, C. J., & Maruschak, L. (2016). *National survey of prison health care: Selected findings* (National Health Statistics Report No. 96). U.S. Department of Health and Human Services. https://www.bjs.gov/content/pub/pdf/nsphcsf.pdf

Chun, S., Harris, A., Carrion, M., Rojas, E., Stark, S., Lejuez, C., Lechner, W. V., & Bornovalova, M. A. (2017). A psychometric investigation of gender differences and common processes across borderline and antisocial personality disorders. *Journal of Abnormal Psychology, 126*(1), 76–88. https://doi.org/10.1037/ abn0000220

Cloud, D. H., Drucker, E., Browne, A., & Parsons, J. (2015). Public health and solitary confinement in the United States. *American Journal of Public Health, 105*(1), 18–26. https://doi.org/10.2105/AJPH.2014.302205

Collica, K. (2010). Surviving incarceration: Two prison-based peer programs build communities of support for female offenders. *Deviant Behavior, 31*, 314–347. https://doi.org/10.1080/01639620903004812

Conn, C., Warden, R., Stuewig, J., Kim, E. H., Harty, L., Hastings, M., & Tangney, J. P. (2016). Borderline personality disorder among jail inmates: How common and how distinct? *Corrections Compendium, 35*(4), 6–13.

Corrigan, P. W., Torres, A., Lara, J. L., Sheehan, L., & Larson, J. E. (2017). The healthcare needs of Latinos with serious mental illness and the potential of peer navigators. *Administration and Policy in Mental Health, 44*(4), 547–557. https://doi.org/10.1007/s10488-016-0737-2

Crawley, E., & Crawley, P. (2013). Understanding prison officers: Culture, cohesion and conflicts. In J. Bennett, B. Crewe, & A. Wahidin (Eds.), *Understanding prison staff* (pp. 19–37). Routledge. https://doi. org/10.4324/9781843925491

Davis, A. Y. (2003). *Are prisons obsolete?* Seven Stories.

Devilly, G. J., Sorbello, L., Eccleston, L., & Ward, T. (2005). Prison-based peer-education schemes. *Aggression and Violent Behavior, 10*(2), 219–240. https://doi.org/10.1016/j.avb.2003.12.001

Fazel, S., Hayes, A. J., Bartellas, K., Clerici, M., & Trestman, R. (2016). Mental health of prisoners: Prevalence, adverse outcomes and interventions. *Lancet Psychiatry, 3*(9), 871–881. http://doi.org/10.1016/S2215-0366(16)30142-0

Griffiths, L., & Bailey, D. (2015). Learning from peer support schemes—Can prison listeners support offenders who self-injure in custody? *International Journal of Prisoner Health, 11*(3), 157–168. https://doi.org/10.1108/IJPH-01-2015-0004

Halls, B., & Gabor, P. (2004). Peer suicide prevention in a prison. *Crisis, 25*(1), 19–26. https://doi.org/10.1027/0227-5910.25.1.19

Hare, R. D. (1996). Psychopathy: A clinical construct whose time has come. *Criminal Justice and Behavior, 23*(1), 25–54. https://doi.org/10.1177/0093854896023001004

Hare, R. D. (1999). *Without conscience: The disturbing world of the psychopaths among us.* Guilford Press.

Hare, R. D. (2003). *The psychopathy checklist–Revised.* Toronto, ON, 412.

Hare, R. D., Clark, D., Grann, M., & Thornton, D. (2000). Psychopathy and the predictive validity of the PCL-R: An international perspective. *Behavioral Sciences & the Law, 18*(5), 623–645. https://doi.org/10.1002/1099-0798(200010)18:5<623::AID-BSL409>3.0.CO;2-W

Harner, H. M., & Riley, S. (2013). The impact of incarceration on women's mental health: Responses from women in a maximum-security prison. *Qualitative Health Research, 23*(1), 26–42. https://doi.org/10.1177/1049732312461452

Hart, H. A. (1893). *Proceedings of the national conference on charities and correction* [President's address]. National Conference on Charities and Correction, Chicago, IL, United States.

Hoffmann, H. C., Byrd, A. L., & Kightlinger, A. M. (2010). Prison programs and services for incarcerated parents and their underage children: Results from a national survey of correctional facilities. *Prison Journal, 90*(4), 397–416. https://doi.org/10.1177/0032885510382087

James, D. J., & Glaze, L. E. (2006). *Mental health problems of prison and jail inmates* (Report No. NCJ213600). Bureau of Justice Statistics.

King, L. (2018). Labor in chains: The shackling of pregnant inmates. *Policy Perspectives, 25*, 55–68. https://doi.org/10.4079/pp.v25i0.18348

Kingston, D. A., Yates, P. M., & Firestone, P. (2012). The self-regulation model of sexual offending: Relationship to risk and need. *Law and Human Behavior, 36*(3), 215–224. https://doi.org/10.1037/h0093960

Kingston, D. A., Yates, P. M., & Olver, M. E. (2013). The self-regulation model of sexual offending: Intermediate outcomes and posttreatment recidivism. *Sexual Abuse, 26*(5), 429–449. https://doi.org/10.1177/1079063213495896

Kirkinis, K., Pieterse, A. L. Martin, C., Agiliga, A., & Brownell, A. (2018). Racism, racial discrimination, and trauma: A systematic review of the social science literature. *Ethnicity & Health, 26*(3), 392–412. https://doi.org/10.1080/13557858.2018.1514453

Kondrat, D. C., Rowe, W. S., & Sosinski, M. (2013). An exploration of specialty programs for inmates with severe mental illness: The United States and the United Kingdom. *Best Practices in Mental Health, 8*(2), 99–108.

Liebling, A., & Arnold, H. (2004). *Prisons and their moral performance: A study of values, quality, and prison life.* Oxford University Press.

Linehan, M. M. (1993). *Diagnosis and treatment of mental disorders: Cognitive-behavioral treatment of borderline personality disorder.* Guildford Press.

Mackenzie, D. L. (2001). *Sentencing and corrections in the 21st century: Setting the stage for the future.* US Department of Justice. https://www.ncjrs.gov/pdffiles1/nij/189106-2.pdf

Maine-Wabanaki REACH. (n.d.). Retrieved 4/7/2019, from http://www.mainewabanakireach.org/

Manderscheid, R. W., Gravesande, A., & Goldstrom, I. D. (2004). Growth of mental health services in state adult correctional facilities, 1988 to 2000. *Psychiatric Services, 55*, 869–872. https://doi.org/10.1176/appi.ps.55.8.869

Maschi, T., & Killian, M. L. (2011). The evolution of forensic social work in the United States: Implications for 21st century practice. *Journal of Forensic Social Work, 1*(8), 8–36. https://doi.org/10.1080/19369 28X.2011.541198

Miller, W. R., & Rollnick, S. (2012). *Motivational interviewing: Helping people change* (3rd ed.). Guilford Press.

Morgan, R. D., Rozycki, A. T., & Wilson, S. (2004). Inmate perceptions of mental health services. *Professional Psychology: Research and Practice, 35*(4), 389–396. https://doi.org/10.1037/0735-7028.35.4.389

Morgan, R. D., Winterowd, C. D., & Ferrell, S. W. (1999). A national survey of group psychotherapy services in correctional facilities. *Professional Psychology: Research and Practice, 30*, 600–606. https://doi.org/10.1037/0735-7028.30.6.600

Mumola, C. (2005). *Suicide and homicide in state prisons and local jails* (NCJ Report No. 210036). Bureau of Justice Statistics.

National Association of Social Workers. (2006). *Code of ethics.* https://www.socialworkers.org/About/Eth ics/Code-of-Ethics/Code-of-Ethics-English

Porter, S., Brinke, L., & Wilson, K. (2009). Crime profiles and conditional release performance of psychopathic and non-psychopathic sexual offenders. *Legal and Criminological Psychology, 14*(1), 109–111. https://doi.org/10.1348/135532508X284310

Prescott, J. J., Pyle, B., & Starr, S. B. (2019). Understanding violent-crime recidivism. *Notre Dame Law Review, 95*(4), 1643–1698.

Prison Rape Elimination Act, 42 U.S.C. ch. 147 § 15601 et seq. (2003).

Prochaska, J. O., DiClemente, C. C., & Norcross, J. C. (1992). In search of how people change: Applications to the addictive behaviors. *American Psychologist, 47*, 1102–1114. https://doi.org/10.1037//0003-066x.47.9.1102

Roberts, A. R., & Brownell, P. (1999). A century of forensic social work: Bridging the past to the present. *Social Work, 44*(4), 359–369. https://doi.org/10.1093/sw/44.4.359

Rosenthal, M. G. (1987). Reforming the juvenile correctional institution: Efforts of the U.S. Children's Bureau in the 1930s. *Journal of Sociology & Social Welfare, 14*(4), 47–73. https://www.ojp.gov/ncjrs/virt ual-library/abstracts/reforming-juvenile-correctional-institution-efforts-us-childrens

Shalev, S. (2011). Solitary confinement and supermax prisons: A human rights and ethical analysis. *Journal of Forensic Psychology Practice, 11*(2), 151–183. https://doi.org/10.1080/15228932.2011.537582

Sheehan, R. (2012). Forensic social work: A distinctive framework for intervention. *Social Work in Mental Health, 10*(5), 409–425. https://doi.org/10.1080/15332985.2012.678571

Steadman, H. J., Osher, F. C., Robbins, P. C., Case, B., & Samuels, S. (2009). Prevalence of serious mental illness among jail inmates. *Psychiatric Services, 60*(6), 761–765. https://doi.org/10.1176/ps.2009.60.6.761

Stephan, J. J. (2008). *Census of state and federal correctional facilities, 2005* (NCJ Report No. 222182). Bureau of Justice Statistics.

Stohr, M. K., Hemmens, C., Baune, D., Dayley, J., Gornik, M., Kjaer, K., & Noon, C. (2003). *Residential substance abuse treatment for state prisoners: Breaking the drug-crime cycle among parole violators.* National Institute of Justice. https://www.ncjrs.gov/pdffiles1/nij/199948.pdf

Sykes, G. M. (1958). *The society of captives: A study of a maximum security prison.* Princeton University Press.

Taylor, K. (2015, September 14). Joyce Mitchell, who helped prisoners escape, says she was driven by fear and depression. *New York Times.* https://www.nytimes.com/2015/09/15/nyregion/joyce-mitchell-ex-pri son-worker-says-in-interview-she-was-driven-by-depression.html

Torrey, E. F., Zdanowicz, M. T., Kennard, A. D., Lamb, H. R., Eslinger, D. F., Biasotti, M. I., & Fuller, D. A. (2014). *The treatment of persons with mental illness in prisons and jails: A state survey.* Treatment Advocacy Center. https://www.treatmentadvocacycenter.org/storage/documents/treatment-behind-bars/treatment-behind-bars.pdf

Way, B. B., Miraglia, R., Sawyer, D. A., Beer, R., & Eddy, J. (2005). Factors related to suicide in New York state prisons. *International Journal of Law and Psychiatry, 28*(3), 207–221. https://doi.org/10.1016/j.ijlp.2004.09.003

Weng, S. S., & Spaulding-Givens, J. (2017). Informal mental health support in the Asian American community and culturally appropriate strategies for community-based mental health organizations. *Human*

Service Organizations: Management, Leadership, & Governance, 41(2), 119–132. https://doi.org/10.1080/23303131.2016.1218810

Whitehead, P. R., Ward, T., & Collie, R. M. (2007). Time for a change: Applying the Good Lives Model of rehabilitation to a high-risk violent offender. *International Journal of Offender Therapy and Comparative Criminology, 51*(5), 578–598. https://doi.org/10.1177/0306624X06296236

Willis, G. M., Prescott, D. S., & Yates, P. M. (2013). The Good Lives Model (GLM) in theory and practice. *Sexual Abuse in Australia and New Zealand, 5*(1), 3–9.

Willis, G. M., Ward, T., & Levenson, J. S. (2014). The Good lives model (GLM) an evaluation of GLM operationalization in North American treatment programs. *Sexual Abuse, 26*(1), 58–81.

Winfree, L. T., Newbold, G., & Tubb, S. H. (2002). Prisoner perspectives on inmate culture in New Mexico and New Zealand: A descriptive case study. *Prison Journal, 82*(2), 213–233. https://doi.org/10.1177/003288550208200204

Woodall, J., South, J., Dixey, R., de Viggiani, N., & Penson, W. (2015). Expert views of peer-based interventions for prisoner health. *International Journal of Prisoner Health, 11*(2), 87–97. https://doi.org/10.1108/IJPH-10-2014-0039

Yates, P. M. (2012). Models of sexual offender treatment. In A. Phenix & H. Hoberman (Eds.), *Sexual offending* (pp. 591–604). Springer.

Yong, A. D., Williams, M. W. M., Provan, H., Clarke, D., & Sinclair, G. (2015). How do offenders move through the stages of change? *Psychology, Crime & Law, 21*(4), 375–397.

Zenderland, L. (1998). *Measuring minds*. Cambridge University Press.

Zlotnick, C., Johnson, J., & Najavits, L. M. (2009). Randomized controlled pilot study of cognitive-behavioral therapy in a sample of incarcerated women with substance use disorder and PTSD. *Behavior Therapy, 40*(4), 325–336. https://doi.org/10.1016/j.beth.2008.09.004

Zlotnick, C., Najavits, L. M., Rohsenow, D. J., & Johnson, D. M. (2003). A cognitive-behavioral treatment for incarcerated women with substance abuse disorder and posttraumatic stress disorder: Findings from a pilot study. *Journal of Substance Abuse Treatment, 25*(2), 99–105. https://doi.org/10.1016/s0740-5472(03)00106-5

32

Human Trafficking

Kathleen M. Preble and Andrea Nichols

Human trafficking has garnered political and public interest since the passage of the U.S. Trafficking Victims Protection Act (TVPA) in 2000. While social work practice and related interventions precede this legislation, only within the last 20 years have funding streams, community activism, interagency partnerships, research, and best practices been a focal point of social work and criminal justice interventions. In contemporary times, human trafficking is viewed as an emerging practice area, with little empirical research examining interventions specific to service populations experiencing human trafficking. Modern-day responses to human trafficking are rooted in theoretical paradigms that span more than five decades and continue to impact policy and practice. Feminist paradigms focus on sex trafficking, involving radical feminists who view all commercial sex as oppressive and in need of abolition, compared to liberal feminists who see commercial sex as variable, and as a form of empowerment under conditions of autonomy. Radical and abolitionist feminists' abolitionist views set the stage for interventions focused on abstinence from commercial sex under ideologies of the oppression paradigm, thereby "rescuing and restoring" an individual involved in commercial sex. In contrast, liberal feminists' theoretical underpinnings support the empowerment paradigm, with interventions focused on supporting people's choices to engage in commercial sex, following principles of harm reduction. Individual experiences with interventions and other aspects of the trafficking experience will also be impacted by legal definitions of human trafficking, as well as criminal justice policy surrounding prostitution more broadly. With a deep chasm in the relationship between sex trafficking and labor trafficking research, scant scholarship examines social work practice and policy interventions related to labor trafficking victimization. Furthermore, practice paradigms and their theoretical roots enhance our understandings of the ways in which individuals experience social work and criminal justice interventions in distinct intersectional ways by race, ethnicity, citizenship, age, gender identity, sexual orientation, and social class. The present chapter largely focuses on sex trafficking of adult domestic survivors in

Kathleen M. Preble and Andrea Nichols, *Human Trafficking* In: *Handbook of Forensic Social Work*. Edited by: David Axlyn McLeod, Anthony P. Natale, and Kristin W. Mapson, Oxford University Press. © Oxford University Press 2024. DOI: 10.1093/oso/9780197694732.003.0032 order to illustrate key themes. Surprisingly, adult survivors accessing services in the United States are most commonly domestically sex-trafficked adults, but they are marginalized in the current academic and practice-related discourse. Specifically, this chapter critically examines practice paradigms, their theoretical underpinnings, promising practice interventions and related empirical support, and the role of social workers in responding to human trafficking victimization.

Definitions and Common Manifestations

Human trafficking is a severe form of interpersonal violence and a human rights abuse. According to the U.S. TVPA, a severe form of human trafficking is currently defined as:

a) a commercial sex act induced by force, fraud, or coercion, or in which the person induced to perform such act has not attained 18 years of age; or
b) the recruitment, harboring, transportation, provision, or obtaining of a person for labor or services, through the use of force, fraud, or coercion for the purpose of subjection to involuntary servitude, peonage, debt bondage, or slavery (TVPA, Section 103, 8a and 8b).

The requirement to prove force, fraud, or coercion sets this abuse apart from other forms of intimate partner violence (IPV). The definition includes all minors involved in commercial sex, regardless of consent or the presence of force, fraud, or coercion. A minor trading any sex act (e.g., intercourse, oral sex, pornography, stripping, erotic massage) for anything of value (e.g., money, shelter, clothing, food) is legally considered a sex trafficking survivor. For adults, the legal definition is limited, in that adults must be willing and able to prove force, fraud, or coercion to be considered sex trafficking survivors. If they are unable to demonstrate that one of these elements occurred, they are treated as criminals in the legal system in violation of existing prostitution laws. This leads to a host of vulnerabilities, including returning to the sex trade, revictimization, legal and social service barriers, and a continued cycle of retrafficking.

Force is typically construed as use of various forms of physical violence, as well as trafficking involving kidnapping and abduction. While often a focal point of the public discourse, as well as professionalized and community education and training endeavors, kidnapping and abduction are rare, and research suggests they compose between 7% and 11% of identified sex trafficking cases in the United States (Polaris Project, 2013, 2015). Fraud can include things such as false promises, withholding wages, misrepresenting work conditions, bait-and-switch tactics (e.g., the promise of a job as a nanny, but the job is actually commercial sex), and use of blackmail or extortion. Occurring with greater frequency is the element of coercion (Baldwin et al., 2015; Preble, 2019, 2020). Coercion involves the threat of harm; this may include things like threatening violence to the trafficked individual and their family members, friends, or even pets. Threats of deportation and detainment also are forms of coercion. Coercion also includes intimidation, such as modeling abusive behaviors, displaying weapons, and using debt bondage and economic dependency (Baldwin et al., 2015).

Common forms of sex trafficking include trafficking as an extension of IPV, survival sex involving minors, familial trafficking (e.g., foster parent sex trafficking a foster child), child pornography, an overlap with labor trafficking (e.g., trafficked massage labor combined with commercial sex), or trafficking by another third party (e.g., managerial pimp). Common forms of labor trafficking include trafficking in agriculture, livestock, construction, restaurant, landscaping, hospitalities, carnival and mining industries, and panhandling/forced begging. Vulnerabilities are rooted in identity-based oppression, such as structural oppression disproportionately experienced by gender identity, sexual orientation, race and ethnicity, citizenship, disabilities, and social class. Labor trafficking has similar vulnerabilities and background as sex trafficking and often survivors experience similar types of coercive exploitation. However, specific aftercare and intervention for survivors of labor trafficking are rare in the United States, and as such little evidence-based practice is available to guide social work practice with such survivors. Because of this, our chapter focuses on what is available for work with *adult* survivors of sex trafficking. The following sections depict intervention paradigms and their theoretical underpinnings, followed by a discussion of intersectionality and its importance for inclusion in interventions.

Treatment Programs: Theoretical and Empirical Foundations

While human trafficking has been legally condemned in the United States for two decades, the inclusion of adult U.S. citizens in interventions has only recently begun. Since the Progressive Era, women involved in the commercial sex trade have been viewed as morally corrupt participants in a "victimless crime," and as criminals who should be punished accordingly (Bromfield, 2016; Wahab, 2002). Indeed, for nearly the first decade after the establishment of the TVPA, interventions and funding streams largely focused on trafficking victimization experienced by foreign-born women and men who were coerced, forced, or defrauded into commercial sex or other nonsexual labor, as well as children involved in commercial sex.

It was not until after the domestic minor sex trafficking (DMST) movement successfully advocated for the commercial sexual exploitation (CSE) of U.S. citizen children to be protected by the TVPA that the possibility for CSE of U.S. citizen adults to be included as a part of anti-trafficking efforts could occur, as trafficking of adults was largely ignored and/or tolerated. Still, there is a tremendous amount of controversy surrounding the idea that adult citizens, fully aware of their rights as citizens; knowledgeable about U.S. political, legal, and social systems; and native English speakers, could be trafficked through force, fraud, or coercion into commercial sex or nonsexual forms of compelled labor in the United States. Increasingly, since around 2010, advocates, politicians, and rights groups have been fervently negotiating definitions of human trafficking and who should be included within the protections of the TVPA, particularly when considering sex trafficking of women, children, and men alike (Alvarez & Alessi, 2012). While some have urged for all (cis- and White) *adult* women involved in the sex trade to be considered trafficking victims, since all commercial sex is an exploitative result of patriarchy (i.e., oppression paradigm; Farley, 2004), others have cautioned that diluting the definition of trafficking could cause unintended consequences and weaken the TVPA (Todres & Diaz, 2019).

Anti-trafficking treatment programs have been developed and operate through several underlying ideologies, which is not unique in the world of IPV response. For example, most sexual and domestic violence (DSV) response programs have historically adhered to feminist models to undergird their approaches to working with survivors of physical and sexual violence (McPhail et al., 2007). However, there are many forms of feminist thought, all situating gender at the center of experiences with oppression and marginalization. Radical feminists tend to view all commercial sex as exploitation and victimization, rooted in gendered power dynamics reflecting and reproducing patriarchy (Ekberg, 2004; Madden-Dempsey, 2011). In contrast, some liberal feminists suggest that criminalization of prostitution is state control of women's bodies and centers gender equality on the ability to make autonomous choices; thus, sex trading involving autonomy and free will is viewed as a legitimate economic opportunity that can be empowering and/or reflective of desire, whereas sex trading that is forced or coerced is deemed trafficking (Doezema, 2005; Weitzer, 2010). Furthermore, like the IPV and rape and sexual assault (R&SA) movements, anti-trafficking and anti-prostitution initiatives often work to create partnerships with law enforcement. In fact, the funding streams and language utilized in anti-trafficking government grants and initiatives are highly parallel to that seen in the IPV movement of the 1980s and 1990s, including a focus on the "4Ps"—prosecution, prevention, protection, and interagency partnerships (Gerassi & Nichols, 2017). Also, strikingly similar to the history of the IPV/R&SA movements, various feminist paradigms view the partnership with law enforcement in different ways, with some highlighting revictimization and coercive services and others focusing on the need to hold traffickers/abusers and purchasers of commercial sex accountable for the greater societal good. In addition, IPV response programs often utilize criminal justice–based interventions and theories, which assume that deviance requires rehabilitation and incapacitation and satisfies carceral feminist desires to seek restitution from trafficking perpetrators. In the following section, we will explore various theoretical underpinnings of popular response programs for survivors of human trafficking, of which there are generally three: abstinence/supportive services, diversion programs, and harm reduction interventions. The treatment approaches will be discussed in conjunction with the underlying theoretical perspective that undergirds the approach. Finally, we will critique the approaches, paying particular attention to the notable views of the approach and the methodology and evidence behind the use of the approach pertaining to work with adult U.S. citizen survivors. We will also take care to include survivor voices when possible.

Abstinence and Support Services Programs/Oppression Paradigm

Sex trafficking abstinence-only and supportive services programs are designed to facilitate exit from the sex trade and to deter them from ever engaging in the sex trade again (Cimino, 2018; Preble et al., 2016). These programs typically espouse radical feminist views, which emphasize the idea that sex trading is inherently exploitative and subordinates the female body to sexual objects made to serve the sexual voracity of men. Hence, they typically believe that all sex trading is sex trafficking and that women engaging in the sex trade do not have a rational choice when engaging in such commerce. Philosophically, these programs replicate the ideals and missions of Progressive Era abolitionists and social workers who saw their work as a moral imperative to set the course right for women involved in sex trading "for their own good" (Alvarez & Alessi, 2012; Bromfield, 2016; Hu, 2019; Smolak, 2013; Wahab, 2002).

Abstinence-only/supportive services programs offer clients a holistic repertoire of supportive services including housing (crisis and transitional), financial assistance, job readiness and placement, case management, and therapy (group and individual; Preble, 2016). These programs are found in secular and nonsecular environments and typically are not associated with governmental bureaucracies. In general, these agencies are known to provide a wide variety of professional services and have a variety of treatment modalities. Some establish a tiered approach toward "graduating" from a program in which the new participants are given more intense and structured services, which are gradually reduced until they have completed programming requirements, at which point they graduate (Preble et al., 2016). Other programs have a period of assessment in which the participants are assessed for readiness to exit and fulfill the requirements of the programming.

While their privatization allows for freedom of innovation and flexibility to serve the underserved within the target population, some agencies have also been found to employ coercive measures on participants "for their own good," which is a major criticism of sex trafficking social service response in general. These programs have also been criticized for requiring participants to assume the label of a "victim" in order to receive services, whether or not participants identified as such (Wahab & Panichelli, 2013). They have also been criticized for failing to meet the needs of potential participants due to the reliance on stereotypical assumptions about the population and requiring abstinence from these behaviors in order to receive services (Gerassi, 2020; Preble et al., 2016). For example, it is common for such agencies to advertise that they work with sexually exploited and trafficked women but also only serve women dealing with substance use disorders (SUDs) but who are sober, excluding CSE women who do not have SUDs or are currently using substances. Similar issues exist at the intersection of CSE and IPV—agencies serve women experiencing CSE only if they have also experienced IPV or are willing to leave their abuser (trafficker).

Additionally, there are few academic outcome evaluations of these programs (Baker et al., 2010; Mayhew & Mossman, 2007; Preble et al., 2016). The studies that do exist suggest a low success rate of around 25% (see Cimino, 2018, for discussion). Reasons for such low success are in part due to faulty methodology used to assess these programs, limited standardized assessments available to measure the progress of clients, and inconsistent operationalization of success in treatment (Cimino, 2018). Other reasons for the lack of success among these programs has to do with a failure to address the structural barriers (i.e., poverty) and stigma that women exiting the sex trade face (Cimino, 2018). Further, some survivors who have received services from these programs report feeling compelled to adhere to faith traditions different from their own, or minimize their own, in order to receive services, which raises ethical questions for social work practitioners engaging in these services.

Diversion Courts/Criminal Justice

As a consequence of ongoing debates about the oppressive or empowering nature of commercial sex trade, dubbed the "sex wars," criminal justice policy responses to sex trading generally fall into one of three different categories: criminalization, decriminalization, or legalization (Cimino, 2018). Cimino (2018) examines in great detail the various policy approaches and their positive and negative consequences. While there is evidence that all three policy remedies are present across the United States, the criminalization of prostitution, which seeks harsh penalties for engaging in the buying and/or selling of sex, is by far the most common. Though most advocates and the general public agree that trafficking survivors are victims of a crime and not the criminals, anti-trafficking responses must exist within a landscape that seeks to criminalize all individuals involved in sex trading *before* seeing the aspects of their victimization. Moreover, it is reasonably well documented that adults with commercial sex involvement are often overlooked as sex trafficking victims. First, with prostitution charges or other charges tied to their trafficking experiences, law enforcement is less likely to identify or investigate trafficking in such cases (Egyes, 2019). Thus, initial misreporting and misidentification can result in further misreporting and misidentification and subsequent systemic revictimization in the justice system. In addition, commercial sex involvement is fluid, and experiences with agency and victimization/oppression and empowerment can vary significantly along individuals' trajectories (Cimino, 2018). Someone may experience trafficking and then trade sex on their own autonomously; someone may trade sex autonomously and become involved in a trafficking situation. The reality is that commercial sex involvement doesn't always fit neatly into boxes of "trafficking" or autonomous "sex trading." Lack of knowledge in this area results in justice system challenges in which those who have been exploited through commercial sex and trafficking survivors alike experience arrest, fines, jail time, and criminal records, which impedes future help seeking. Therefore, those who are identified as trafficking survivors typically experience systemic revictimization and coerced services before being viewed as such. For example, access to diversion programming, which diverts individuals from the justice system into social services, occurs after a survivor has already interacted with the justice system.

Diversion programs, such as New York State's Human Trafficking Intervention Courts; the Changing Actions to Changing Habits Court in Columbus, Ohio; the RISE program in Tarrant County, Texas; and Project ROSE in Phoenix, Arizona, offer court-supervised intervention for individuals arrested on prostitution-related offenses (Cimino, 2012). In general (and not specific to the aforementioned programs), these programs are available to first-time offenders, and hence, those with prior offenses are not eligible (Wahab & Panichelli, 2014). Central to the success of diversion programs is the client's willingness to adhere to a "prostitution-free" lifestyle upon completing the diversion programming, which could include case management, housing assistance, and mental and physical health treatments (Cimino, 2012). Though treatment-based or specialized courts have gained popularity in recent years, they often do not realize the positive outcomes they seek to find (Roe-Sepowitz et al., 2014). Studies have found that because women involved in these programs may not be ready to exit and may be more motivated to avoid criminal charges (Cimino, 2018), the recidivism rates are as high as 83% (Felini et al., 2011). These poor outcomes have led some scholars to call for a re-examination of what should be considered "success" in these programs (Luminais, Lovell, & McGuire, 2019).

Bernstein (2010) coined the term "carceral feminism" to describe the pairing of feminist groups with criminal justice system responses as a means to address gender-based violence. Challenges to this approach involve diversion of resources to criminal justice responses instead of social services, cooptation of nonprofits by carceral institutions through funding initiatives that require this pairing, and revictimization of commercial sex–involved people who experience arrest, fines, jail time, surveillance, detainment, deportation, and criminal records as a result (Bernstein, 2010; Kim, 2020; Shih, 2016; Whalley & Hackett, 2017). Carceral responses also disproportionately target people of color, those experiencing poverty, LGBTQ+ people, and immigrants, who may be treated as criminals rather than victims (Musto, 2010; Schwarz et al., 2017; Shih, 2016). Diversion programs have been criticized because of their ability to coercively engage clients in the programs to avoid formal charges (Roe-Sepowitz et al., 2014) and engage clients when they are not ready to exit the industry (Cimino, 2012, 2018; Wahab & Panichelli, 2014). These criticisms have ignited debates about the violation of basic human rights and dignity and worth of individuals involved in sex trading to autonomously make choices regarding their bodies and live free from externally coercive influences. In a particularly poignant public debate, Wahab and Panichelli (2014) argued that some sex trading intervention programs, like Project ROSE, have done more harm than good "under the cover of kindness" by arresting people involved in commercial sex and then offering diversion programming as an alternative to criminal charges (Wahab & Panichelli, 2014).

Moreover, it is well established that having a criminal record of prostitution limits one's ability to find certain kinds of employment and even can restrict one's ability to find housing (Preble et al., 2016). By usurping the rational decision-making capabilities of women involved in sex trading and trafficked women "for their own good," one could construe that the willingness of these participants was coerced by the carrot of avoiding a formal criminal charge outweighing their desire for autonomy. Wahab and Panichelli (2014) challenge that this form of assistance violates several ethical standards by targeting an oppressed group, encouraging structural violence against this population, and then coercing participants to accept services they may not actually want or face criminal arrest. Moreover, this strategy runs the risk of overlooking sex trafficking as the power to determine victim status is in the hands of the service provider—not the people involved in commercial sex. It also runs the risk of imposing barriers to successful exit from sex trading by creating a criminal justice record that may not have existed before through the specific targeting of this oppressed population. Courts also assume sex traders will always see criminal justice interventions positively, thus ignoring the historic and current abuses of power experienced by people of color through the criminal justice system.

Harm Reduction/Empowerment Paradigm

Harm reduction treatment programs designed for trafficked populations are not particularly common in the United States, primarily due to the underlying ideological foundation of our nation, which assumes that deviant behavior stems from moral ineptitude, proving an individual unworthy of charity (Berquist, 2015; Smolak, 2013; Zimmerman, 2010). Harm reduction programs (HRPs) approach social deviance by mediating risk-taking behavior through behavioral, environmental, and, at times, pharmaceutical modifications while not requiring complete abstinence from the risk-taking behavior (Brocato & Wagner, 2003; Preble et al., 2016). Drawing from the empowerment paradigm's principles to utilize an individual's strengths to overcome oppression, HRPs attempt to recognize the inherent resilience of an individual and their environment to help them stay safe while working toward a personal goal—which could be to permanently exit the commercial sex trade.

HRPs typically employ five principles in guiding their approach. The first is to *educate* people about risk and risk taking so they can make informed decisions about their behavior and take *pragmatic steps* toward mitigating these risks. HRP practitioners work with individuals to establish incremental *client-centered goals* toward reducing harms associated with the risk-taking behavior, which *empowers* individuals to achieve reduction or complete elimination of the dangerous behavior. The practitioner also *engages community support* to assist individuals through their transition from risk-taking to risk elimination behavior through support programs, drop-in centers, and other support mechanisms (Blume & Logan, 2013; Brocato & Wagner, 2003; Hickle & Hallett, 2016). As discussed, abstinence-only programs have a host of challenges in combating risk-taking behavior—primarily having to do with substance use and HIV/AIDS treatment—which HRPs actively work to mitigate. As Rekart (2005) suggests, effective HRPs should be rights based and include aspects of education, empowerment, prevention, care (including sexually transmitted disease detection), occupational health and safety, and decriminalization of individuals involved in sex trading.

Though HRPs are relatively rare in the United States, it appears that interest in these programs has grown over the last few years around the world (Bungay et al., 2013; Decker et al., 2015; Hickle & Hallett, 2015; Open Society Institute/International Harm Reduction Development, 2015; Preble et al., 2016;). HRPs typically focus on substance abuse treatment, which can alienate non-substance-using commercial sex traders (Cusick, 2006). However, harm reduction models have begun broadening their services to include the needs of nonsubstance users, non-IPV victims, and a more diverse population of CSE victims such as males, sexual and gender minorities (WHO, 2013), and First Nations peoples (Pierce, 2012). As noted in Hynes (2015), social workers in Sweden, where the solicitation of sex trading is expressly illegal and few HRPs exist for survivors of CSE, have lamented that the criminalization of sex trading has reduced their ability to assist survivors of CSE. Perhaps more troubling, they have seen funds be diverted to prosecutorial actions in lieu of preventive outreach, resulting in "deteriorating conditions" for survivors of CSE and the denial of their right to self-determination by forcing them to accept a "victim" status to receive services (Hynes, 2015). The schism between the realities that frontline social workers see and the policies directed toward this population appear to create a paradoxical equation for which real solutions are difficult to find when practitioners are focused on ideological ideals and not actual practice solutions.

Because HRPs are not commonly utilized in responses to sex trading, there are few evidence-based evaluations of existing programs by which to gauge their effectiveness. However, the evaluations that exist suggest a significant increase in engagement with safe behavior and reduced exposures to harms such as substance use, incarceration, and even time engaged in sex trading (Wilson et al., 2015). Other evaluations have found similar results and have found that participants in these programs have articulated that they feel respected and valued, leading to their continued engagement (Gerassi, 2020; Rabinovich & Strega, 2004). These positive feelings regarding service acquisition are important because they have been found to lead to a 25% increase in participant engagement over time, whereas other exiting programs tend to see a significant drop or increased recidivism rates (Cimino, 2018). Hence, HRPs may see better continuity of care among participants over the long term than other interventions, which is an important element of ethical social work practice.

Intersectional Critique

The lack of inclusive response has long plagued the anti-trafficking movement (Razack, 1998; Smolak, 2013). Critiques around the erasure of women of color, particularly Black and Indigenous women, and gender and sexual minorities; the failure of the movement to fully embrace the vulnerability of men to becoming trafficked in general, and in particular for sex; and the lack of inquiry around the trafficker have paralyzed the movement and weakened its message.

Core assumptions within oppression paradigms about the function of sex and gender in maintaining the dynamics that allow trafficking to occur may make it difficult to account for the experiences of transgender or genderqueer individuals within sex trafficking (Razack, 1998). Moreover, the placement of heteronormative gender dichotomies makes invisible oppressions by race, class, and nationality. As such, the traditional feminist ability to be inclusive is diminished. Razack (1998) maintains that this paradigm assumes that the female need for economic independence drives her choice to engage in sex trading. Further, this stance suggests a consensual, contractual agreement in which sex trading allows violence to occur (Razack, 1998). These whitewashed assumptions about the nature of sex trading and gender hide the experiences of women of color, particularly Black women, who have been socially caged in a choiceless frame in which heterosexual, White males have the right, almost duty, to subjugate, violate, and penetrate women of color to maintain their supremacy in society (Razack, 1998). "[A] central problem in considering how prostitution sustains, and is sustained by, multiple systems of domination (of which white supremacy is one) is the difficulty of understanding social relations from several angles at once" (Razack, 1998, p. 355). White women, on the other hand, have the choice to emulate virtuous morality or fall from grace—forever.

As such, White men are able to escape punishment otherwise due as well as navigate simultaneously moral and immoral worlds with ease (Razack, 1998). Such demonstrations of Razack's point have been displayed repeatedly as illustrated by numerous historical accounts of slave masters sexually brutalizing slave women, Recy Taylor's gang rape in 1944 in which the six White men (and their accomplices) who admitted to raping her were never held accountable, and the more recent advocacy surrounding the #sayhername movement in which Black women and women of color have been killed in connection with police brutality with little accountability. Many in our society have never heard of their stories, unlike their male counterparts, many of whom have become iconic representations of modern police brutality.

The opposing views of radical feminist oppression paradigms and liberal feminist empowerment paradigms have created a philosophical polarity (the "sex wars") in understanding sex trading and sexual exploitation that, perhaps, impedes understanding the complexities between sex trafficking victims and their interpersonal relationships with their abusers as well as with would-be service providers (Sloan & Wahab, 2000; Weitzer, 2012). Moreover, these debates distract us from understanding the nuances of the experiences and risks those engaged with sex trading and trafficked persons have while in the sex industry, such as the differences between outdoor and indoor sex trading or between those who are cis- and transgender and genderqueer (Cimino, 2012; Lutnick & Cohan, 2009). These complexities of human experience have their own rules of engagement that are driven, in part, by societal norms, as well as by the norms developed within the community of people engaged with sex trading themselves and the people with whom they engage. It is our view that an ideological battle, driven largely by people with little personal experience in trading sex or sexual exploitation themselves, about the nature of sex trading distracts us from understanding how the personal, multiple, and intersected identities of sex trafficking victims and those engaged in sex trading may significantly influence their relationships. Rather, this ideological battle places energy upon outlining *our* (White, middle-class women) agendas instead of focusing on how sex trading and sex trafficking victims define their own realities. Illustrating this danger, Wahab and Panichelli's (2014) editorial pointed to ethical and rights-based dilemmas posed by ideologically driven social work practice and research with people engaging in the sex trade and trafficked individuals. Moreover, the "ideological capture" (Chuang, 2009) of sex and exploitation leaves little room for examining the experiences of labor trafficking victims, or perhaps considering how sex and labor trafficking may at times overlap with one another (see Alvarez & Alessi, 2012; Preble et al., 2020). Instead, these rather dominant theoretical perspectives, and the debates that occur between their adherents, have contributed to the popular myths that sex trading is synonymous with sex trafficking, that sex trafficking is synonymous with human trafficking rather than one subcategory of the phenomenon, and that only (White) females are trafficked rather than individuals of all genders and minority statuses (see, e.g., Jackson, 2016).

Characteristics of Survivors and Aftercare Settings

Characteristics of U.S. adult sex trafficking survivors are difficult to find; however, the field has added a body of knowledge over the last several years about this population. According to the Polaris Project's Human Trafficking Resource and Hotline, in 2019 the tipline revealed that 22,326 survivors had been identified nationally. Of these survivors, the vast majority were identified as sex trafficking survivors (65.3%, $n = 14,597$). When age at the time of trafficking was ascertained, 1,435 (6.4%) were categorized as an adult (69.5%, $n = 15,532$ were categorized as "unknown"). Over 1,300 survivors were U.S. citizens (6.2%, $n = 1,388$), and the top recruitment tactic reported to the tipline was intimate partner/marriage proposition (7.3%, $n = 1,067$) followed by familial relationships (6.7%, $n = 981$), suggesting a strong intimate partner or family violence pattern.

Academic studies have begun to report demographic trends of identified survivors of sex trafficking as well. Though the field is developing more concrete understandings about the phenomenon and survivors, there are several important critiques that limit the generalizability of these understandings and their potential implications. Perhaps one of the most important issues the field faces is a lack of standardized acceptance of who is or is not a victim of sex trafficking. As explained earlier, much of this issue reflects the ideological biases of practitioners and researchers. The result of this ideological divide is that there is not a comprehensive way to compare data across agencies or disciplines. This issue leads to another major problem the field has, which is that there is not a centralized national data repository in the United States currently. This further limits our ability to examine typologies of survivors and, potentially, of their traffickers across criminal justice, health care, social service, child welfare, homelessness, and other structures that may intersect with survivors of trafficking regularly. These two major limitations obfuscate virtually every other nuance one might want to explore.

Additionally, the field has very limited knowledge about the differences and similarities between urban settings and more rural settings. Characteristics of survivors, types of sex trafficking experienced, and gaps in services may all be influenced by these geographic indicators in important ways. We are only now beginning to explore these nuances (Nichols et al., 2019). Recent studies have also begun to explore characteristics and experiences of survivors who identify as part of the gender and sexual minority community. Knowledge about the general risks these induvial experience for interpersonal and community-based violence logically implies they may have heightened risk for trafficking victimization. In fact, recent studies have shown that survivors of sex trafficking who identify as LGBTQ+ have regularly been denied services because of others' reactions to their gender or sexual identity or have been told to hide their identities to receive needed services (Dank et al., 2015; Murphy, 2017).

Empirical evidence has shown that trafficking may intersect with other victimization experiences (de Vries & Farrell, 2018). For example, it is established that as much as 10% of dating violence experiences also include sexual exploitation at the hands of the abuser (Rothman & Xuan, 2014; Rothman et al., 2015). Many survivors of dating violence are known to become involved in other abusive relationships, yet it is unknown how much of the sexual exploitation experienced in the dating violence context could in fact be categorized as sex trafficking or evolve into a sex trafficking scenario. Yet, we hear anecdotal evidence that such relationships exist.

Practice Interventions and Empirical Support

Interventions for sex trafficking survivors are viewed as part of an emerging practice area. There are some promising practice interventions, although very little rigorous empirical research supports their use with sex trafficking survivors. Importantly, one-size-fits-all approaches are deemed ineffective, as the experiences of sex trafficking survivors vary considerably. As a result, interventions must vary according to individual cases and needs. For example, in cases involving minors who want to remain with their trafficker, due to love relationships or other reasons, practices such as motivational interviewing and the stages of change model may be beneficial (Gerassi & Esbensen, 2020; Lloyd, 2018). In contrast, in the rare instances in which sex trafficking survivors experience kidnapping or abduction (Polaris Project, 2013, 2015), such interventions are inappropriate (Gerassi & Nichols, 2017). Instead, trauma-related therapies, such as eye movement desensitization (EMDR) or cognitive-behavioral therapy (CBT0 are more promising (Edmond, 2018). For adults who may view their trafficking situation as the best available option (e.g., adults involved in survival sex that is a result of debt bondage due to addiction) and who are not ready to leave their situation, engaging in aspects of harm reduction, such as safety planning, is viewed as a better response (Preble, 2018).

The stages of change model is utilized by organizations serving survivors of sex trafficking, such as Girls' Education and Mentoring Services (GEMS) and Acknowledge, Commit, and Transform (ACT). Empirical evidence drawing from organizations utilizing the approach suggests this intervention is successful, but only if the survivor is already in the contemplation stage (e.g., ready to make a change; Lloyd, 2018). Emerging scholarship is recommending longer term (e.g., 2 years or more) interventions for survivors of sex trafficking (Gerassi & Nichols, 2017; Oselin, 2014). Empirical research on use of this intervention more broadly is limited, but the approach is criticized for being overly broad, oversimplifying and overemphasizing distinct stages, and facing challenges in accurately determining an individual's stage (Littell & Girvin, 2002, 2004; Sylva et al., 2012). Moreover, long-term changes are unclear; prior research shows that short-term changes are accomplished, but there is lack of support for the attainment of long-term changes (Sylva et al., 2012). Empirical research is extremely limited in evaluating this intervention specifically with sex trafficking/CSE service populations, so this intervention is best viewed as a promising practice in need of further research. This intervention is used in abstinence and harm reduction approaches alike.

Motivational interviewing is a practice technique that also aims to reduce harm associated with risky behaviors and is commonly engaged in as a principle of harm reduction. Empirical research examining its use in the area of sex trafficking or CSE indicates positive outcomes, such as reducing the frequency of high-risk behaviors tied to drug use, unsafe sex (e.g., not using a condom), and risky sex trade behaviors (Champion & Collins, 2012; Yahne et al., 2002). The approach has also been shown to enhance therapeutic relationships and increase goal accomplishments of the service population (Roe-Sepowitz et al., 2012). Because the intervention shows positive outcomes among trafficking/CSE survivors, as well as in the broader service population, motivational interviewing can be considered a best practice. However, because the research is limited in its examination of use specifically with sex trafficking/CSE populations, further research is needed to better understand both the outcomes and the ways in which the intervention is implemented (Gerassi, 2020).

Cultural competency is necessary to enhance therapeutic relationships and to improve interventions and organizational practices. Drawing from principles of intersectionality and understandings of identity-based oppression can enhance cultural competency in practices with sex trafficking survivors. Gerassi and Nichols (2017) maintain that social workers can act as cultural brokers in resource referrals, interagency and wraparound services, and working to uncover needs specific to various cultures. Lack of cultural competency has been identified as a barrier to service access and utilization by sex trafficking and labor trafficking survivors, in terms of language barriers, LGBTQ+ identities, and race and ethnicity (Gerassi, 2019; Heil & Nichols, 2019). Thus, cultural competency, due to its existing empirical support combined with identified needs among trafficking survivors, can be viewed as a best practice (Clifford et al., 2015; Ferreira et al., 2010; Gaston, 2013; Robey et al., 2013).

Survivor-centered (also referred to as person-centered, client-centered, survivor-defined, victim-centered, or woman-centered) practices hold empirical support in other areas of study, such as IPV and R&SA (Bennet Catteneo et al., 2011; Goodman & Epstein, 2008; Kulkarni et al., 2012), but also among trafficked populations (Busch-Armendariz et al., 2014; Hotaling et al., 2004), and can be viewed as a best practice. Similarly, strengths-based practices, rapport building, and other commonly accepted practice techniques also have an evidence base and can be viewed as best practices (Heffernan & Blyth, 2014; Okech et al., 2018).

In terms of specific trauma-focused mental health treatments, the evidence examining such treatments among those experiencing human trafficking is extremely limited. However, there is evidence supporting use of EMDR and CBT/cognitive processing therapy (CPT) among those with posttraumatic stress disorder (PTSD) in other areas of study (Gaughran et al., 2013; van Dam et al., 2013). PTSD or complex PTSD is a common diagnosis for those experiencing trafficking; as such, related interventions, regardless of the area of study, provide some level of support for their use with trafficking survivors (Cole, 2014; Heffernan & Blyth, 2014). Findings more broadly show that clients experience significant improvement with CPT, in that 50% to 70% will no longer meet the diagnostic criteria for PTSD by the end of treatment (Bradley et al., 2005; Resick et al., 2002). Empirical support shows that EMDR reduces trauma symptoms with adult women who are survivors of childhood sexual abuse (Edmond et al., 1999) and also reduces trauma symptoms caused by other forms of sexual violence and trauma (Allon, 2015; Jarero & Artigas, 2010). Because of the reasonably strong empirical support of trauma-focused mental health treatments such as CBT/CPT and EMDR, these interventions can also be viewed as best practices for use among those experiencing human trafficking, although further research is needed to enhance the empirical support specifically with this service population.

Case Study

In this section, we will offer a vignette related to an adult sex trafficking victim seeking services initially through a domestic violence agency. We will address social work competency and ethics throughout the response reflection following the scenario.

Intimate Partner Violence and Sex Trafficking

Thalia is working as a social worker doing case management for an organization providing a multitude of anti-violence services to the community. She meets with a client who has sought assistance in leaving an abusive partner. In developing a safety plan, 27-year-old Kelsey indicates that her boyfriend has a criminal record involving violent crimes and prior abuse both to her and to past girlfriends of his. Thalia recommends a confidential shelter, in light of Kelsey's increased concern for safety, and asks what she thinks about this option. Kelsey agrees and tells Thalia that would make her feel more comfortable and increase her feeling of safety. Kelsey also discloses that she has a job but doesn't quite have the money yet for a downpayment on an apartment and is afraid of serious physical abuse if she returns to their home. Thalia continues to meet with her weekly over the next 2 months while Kelsey stays in the confidential shelter and gets a new full-time job at a department store making more money than she did at her previous part-time job. Through subsequent conversations, it becomes clear that Kelsey suffers from anxiety and depression. At one meeting, Kelsey disclosed that her boyfriend sometimes coerced her into having sex for money to pay their bills, and she isn't sure if that or the physical or emotional abuse is the source of her anxiety and depression. Kelsey explained that he became angry if she didn't bring money into the household, verbally abused her, and minimized her financial contributions to the household coming from her part-time job as a door greeter at Walmart. He also threatened to throw her dog out of the house because of the cost of its food and said that if she didn't want that to happen, she needed to bring in some money through trading sex. Kelsey indicated that occasionally, he either threatened to hit her or hit her if she refused to trade sex for money.

In this situation, because the commercial sex involvement was an extension of IPV and manifested due to coercive behaviors on the part of Kelsey's partner, Kelsey's situation can be viewed as sex trafficking. Coercion typically involves threats of harm or intimidating behaviors. Threats to hit her and to take her dog away are both viewed as forms of coercion as well. The physical violence Kelsey experienced also shows some level of force used by her boyfriend as a means to facilitate trading sex for money. Kelsey described physical, verbal, emotional, and economic abuses that were intertwined with her commercial sex involvement. In many cases of sex trafficking, as seen in Kelsey's case, elements of coercive control (e.g., economic abuse, emotional abuse, threats, intimidation) parallel those often experienced in situations of IPV; particularly, when the sex trafficking is happening within the context of already existing IPV, the sex trafficking can be viewed as another manifestation of IPV.

A criminal justice response focused on Kelsey's commercial sex involvement as a *perpetrator* for violating prostitution laws would revictimize her through arrest, fines, and jail time. This response would not meet the intended goals of deterrence or rehabilitation. First, if she'd been arrested and charged with prostitution as a deterrent, this would be ineffective, as Kelsey already does not want to engage in commercial sex; she's experiencing trafficking, and thus preventing further commercial sex involvement through punishment would be ineffective. This approach also would violate the social worker code of ethics in several ways as explained by Wahab and Panichelli (2013), in that it undermines self-determination to seek exiting services when the participant is ready and violates fundamental human rights to live free from targeted aggression (i.e., discrimination and oppression). Moreover, this method of intervention violates the spirit of social work best practices that seeks to be strengths based and empowerment focused. Finally, social workers should not seek to prevent desired change among their clients; rather, they should promote it. Second, principles of rehabilitation would not be met through this response, as Kelsey does not need rehabilitation—her commercial sex involvement is rooted in the abuse she is experiencing. A criminal justice response focused on deterrence or rehabilitation to coerce compliance with abstaining from commercial sex would do little to help her. Furthermore, if Kelsey had been arrested and charged, and eligible for a diversion program, she would experience revictimization through her criminalization before ever accessing the diversion program. In addition, diversion would not be the response needed, as her situation involved coerced commercial sex involvement; thus, this response would not benefit her and would cause harm through a criminal record negatively impacting her ability to gain employment and housing. It would also create an additional hurdle: The time needed to go through the programming would have made it more difficult for her to apply for and obtain her new department store job and find her new apartment. Coerced services are oftentimes consuming and take away from utilization of other services that may be more needed depending on the context. Similarly, programs focused on abstinence are not particularly applicable in Kelsey's situation. Her rational choice to engage in commercial sex involved mitigating her abuse.

If the criminal justice response focused on Kelsey as a trafficking and/or IPV *victim/ survivor* instead of as violating prostitution laws, there may be some benefit. Kelsey may be able to access a restraining order, which is known to benefit survivors of IPV, depending on the contextual dynamics of the IPV. Further, Kelsey may be able to access legal interventions related to the trafficking; for example, she may be able to engage in prosecuting her boyfriend for trafficking her. In Kelsey's case, decriminalization of prostitution and maintaining criminalization of trafficking would benefit her as well as others with similar experiences. Because IPV-related trafficking is known to be among the most commonly experienced forms of sex trafficking (e.g., Nichols et al., 2019), such legislative endeavors could potentially help trafficking and CSE survivors alike. This would prevent revictimization through arrest, fines, and jail time while offering legal recourse for victimization. At the same time, wraparound services that are often a part of organizations engaged in case management, including those maintaining oppression and empowerment paradigms alike, work to meet survivors where they are and individualize services to needs. When wraparound services meet principles of harm reduction, with a focus on empowerment, they offer more benefit to survivors. These actions seek to promote self-determination and empower the survivor while positioning the social worker in the role of a broker for service referral rather than a broker of punishment.

Principles of harm reduction are more promising in Kelsey's case. In particular, Thalia must engage in person-centered practice. Individually tailoring services to meet Kelsey's wants and needs and viewing Kelsey as the expert of her own situation are called for. Hence, Thalia must clearly embody the ideals of strengths-based and empowerment social work practice. Person-centered practice is to be viewed as a collaboration, involving Kelsey's knowledge of her own situation and what assets she has available to her to strengthen her exit, in combination with Thalia's knowledge and ability to educate Kelsey about available resources and safety considerations. By focusing on what Kelsey can do to improve her situation and providing related information and resources, such as assistance obtaining a higher paying full-time job and getting her own apartment, Thalia is supporting Kelsey's empowerment. Engaging community support to eliminate risks, such as discussing options for safety by utilizing the confidential shelter while Kelsey was working on job attainment and permanent housing, also supported Kelsey's empowerment.

As a social worker, Thalia can develop an ethical response to Kelsey's situation by drawing from social work's core values of service, social justice, dignity and worth of the person, importance of human relationships, integrity, and competence (i.e., National Association of Social Workers [NASW] Code of Ethics [COE] 1.01 Commitment to Clients; 1.04 Competence; and 1.05 Cultural Awareness and Social Diversity). In this scenario, Thalia should engage in acknowledging and encouraging Kelsey's expression of feelings. This involves active listening, nonjudgment, and facilitating and encouraging further expression of feelings and thoughts (NASW COE 1.01 Commitment to Clients). Such practices can result in fine-tuning interventions and further uncovering Kelsey's wants and needs, facilitating further individualization (NASW COE 1.02 Self-Determination; 1.04 Competence). Controlled emotional involvement requires sensitivity to and empathy for the client's expression of feelings, working to understand their meaning, and maintaining objectivity. In this scenario, Kelsey discloses, after 2 months, that her partner was trafficking her by facilitating commercial sex involvement through coercion as an extension of the IPV Kelsey was experiencing. It is important that Thalia does not place her own feelings about the situation onto Kelsey; rather, she should work with Kelsey's comfort level and allow her to talk about her experience in her own words and with her own emotional expression, and then discuss therapeutic interventions related to the anxiety and depression (NASW 1.04 Competence). Acknowledging the dignity and worth of the person involves the recognition of the client's wants and needs and their innate dignity and worth (NASW COE 1.01 Commitment to Clients). Even when the social worker does not approve of the client's choices, respecting the client's choices as their own and/or on their own terms is key to self-determination (NASW COE 1.02 Self-Determination; 1.05 Cultural Awareness and Social Diversity). In this situation, Thalia should use the same language Kelsey uses to talk about her situation—having sex for money to pay bills, and as coerced by her partner. Thalia should not use trafficking language or language of modern slavery (NASW COE 1.05 Cultural Awareness and Social Diversity). Thalia can ask if Kelsey wants to take legal action against her former partner and explain legal options with regard to trafficking. If Kelsey does not want to take legal action, Thalia must respect her choice. Principles of self-determination work to respect the rights of individuals to shape their own present and future. This involves supporting individuals' choices and needs rather than dictating them. Taking control away from clients is antithetical to self-determination and individualization, and thus unethical. Nonjudgment is particularly important, as victim-blaming attitudes toward IPV survivors, as well as stigma tied to trading sex, is a well-documented barrier to accessing and continued utilization of services. As such, it is imperative that Thalia does not express judgment or facilitate stigma (NASW COE 1.01 Commitment to Clients; 1.12 Derogatory Language). Feelings of guilt and shame are commonly expressed among sex trafficking survivors, and nonjudgmental attitudes are particularly important to continued service engagement. Integrity involves behaving in a trustworthy manner, illustrating honesty. For example, making it known to the client that the social worker will keep all information disclosed as private is viewed as a basic right of the client (NASW COE 1.07 Confidentiality). At times, confidentiality must be violated. For example, in cases involving children, mandated reporting supersedes confidentiality. For adults, with few exceptions, written permission is needed before any disclosure can be shared with other organizations, agencies, or professionals. By sharing this with Kelsey, Thalia may create an environment where she feels more comfortable disclosing, which may be important to therapeutic interventions. When Kelsey is in a place of stability, screening for PTSD and offering related trauma therapy is viewed as a best practice, as PTSD and related symptoms, such as the anxiety and depression Kelsey disclosed, are associated with both IPV and sex trafficking victimization. Thalia should engage in ongoing safety planning and work with Kelsey to continue conversations about the need to individually tailor services as Kelsey's needs change. See Table 32.1.

TABLE 32.1 Social Work Principles in Relation to Work With Exiting Adult Sex Trafficking Survivors

Social Work Principles	Recommendations	Social Work Action
Dignity and Worth of the Person Social Justice	Recognize the human rights of people involved in commercial sex by choice, by circumstance, or through trafficking.	1. Recognize the self-determination and dignity and worth of people involved in commercial sex (Decker et al., 2015). 2. Recognize agency in the sex trade (Benoit & Millar, 2001) and their need to exercise free will (Mayhew & Mossman, 2007; Rabinovich & Strega, 2004).
	Refrain from requiring an implicit victim status from people involved in commercial sex.	1. Recognize that this requirement implies there are "worthy" and "unworthy" clients (Hynes, 2015; Wahab & Panichelli, 2013). 2. Provide services regardless of clients' intent to leave the sex trade.
	Recognize the need for improved public and service professional education surrounding the realities of commercial sex to reduce stigma.	1. Create a CSE- and sex trafficking survivor–informed public awareness effort (Mayhew & Mossman, 2007; Rabinovich & Strega, 2004; Twis-McCoy & Preble, 2020). 2. Create a CSE- and sex trafficking survivor–informed service professional (social, legal, and health) training (Benoit & Millar, 2001).
Importance of Human Relationships Service	Facilitate access to needed services.	1. Create an advisory board of clients who can assist agencies and policymakers to understand gaps and needed improvements to existing services. 2. Ensure that clients and potential clients have access to services anytime they might need them (flexible hours and multiple locations; Bodkin et al., 2015). 3. Ensure that clients have necessary support structures to effectively engage in services being provided (i.e., childcare, transportation, education; Preble, 2015; Rabinovic & Strega, 2004). 4. Allow clients to receive services without an abstinence requirement or promise to leave the sex trade (Preble, 2016).

TABLE 32.1 Continued

Social Work Principles	Recommendations	Social Work Action
	Recognize that exiting commercial sex–involved people return to the sex trade on average five times before ultimately leaving.	1. Exercise patience, without the requirements to abstain from their main source of income (Mayhew & Mossman, 2007; Cimino, 2012). 2. Create programming with this fact in mind. Address the needs of the client as they articulate in small achievable goals. 3. Focus on strength-building principles in practice (Preble, 2016; Rabinovich & Strega, 2004).
	Recognize the need for commercial sex–involved people to create a community.	1. Create systems for commercial sex–involved people (current and former) to advocate for societal and structural reform (Benoit & Millar, 2001; Rabinovich & Strega, 2004; Twis & Preble, 2020).
Competence Integrity	Recognize that commercial sex–involved people are the experts of their lived experience and so know how best to achieve the goals they establish for themselves.	1. Focus treatment goals on the individual needs and desires of the client—not funder- or program-originated goals (Preble, 2016; Rabinovich & Strega, 2004).
	Recognize that CSE potentially have access to and knowledge about sexually trafficked individuals.	1. Create partnerships between CSE and anti-trafficking groups to assist each other in identifying and responding to individuals being trafficked in the sex trade (Preble, 2016). 2. Establish safe housing for commercial sex–involved people who are currently and formerly engaged in the sex trade (Benoit & Millar, 2001).

References

Allon, M. (2015). EMDR group therapy with women who were sexually assaulted in the Congo. *Journal of EMDR Practice and Research, 9*, 28–34.

Alvarez, M., & Alessi, E. (2012). Human trafficking is more than sex trafficking and prostitution: Implications for Social Work. *Affilia: Journal of Women and Social Work, 27*, 142–152.

Andrasik, M. P., & Ro, Y. (2013). Exploring barriers and facilitators to participation of male-to-female transgender persons in preventive HIV vaccine clinical trials. *Preventative Science, 15*, 268–276. http://doi.org/10.1007/s11121-013-0371-0

Baker, L. M., Dalla, R. L., & Williamson, C. (2010). Exiting prostitution: An integrated model. *Violence Against Women, 16*(5), 579–600.

Baldwin, S. B., Fehrenbacher, A. E., & Eisenman, D. P. (2015). Psychological coercion in human trafficking: An application of Biderman's framework. *Qualitative Health Research, 25*(9), 1171–1181.

Bennett Cattaneo, L., Cho, S., & Botuck, S. (2011). Describing intimate partner stalking over time: An effort to inform victim-centered service provision. *Journal of Interpersonal Violence, 26*(17), 3428–3454. http://doi.org/10.1177/0886260511403745

Bernstein, E. (2010). Militarized humanitarianism meets carceral feminism: The politics of sex, rights, and freedom in contemporary antitrafficking campaigns. *Signs, 36*(1), 45–71.

Berquist, K. J. S. (2015). Criminal, victim, or ally? Examining the role of sex workers in addressing minor sex trafficking. *Journal of Women and Social Work, 30*(3), 314–327. doi:10.1177/0886109915572844

Bradley, R., Green, J., Russ, E., Dutra, L., & Westen, D. (2005). A multidimensional meta-analysis of psychotherapy for PTSD. *American Journal Psychiatry, 162*, 214–227.

Brocato, J., & Wagner, E. F. (2003). Harm reduction: A social work practice model and social justice agenda. *Health & Social Work, 28*(2), 117.

Bromfield, N. F. (2016). Sex slavery and sex trafficking of women in the United States: Historical and contemporary parallels, policies, and perspectives in social work. *Affilia, 31*(1), 129–139. https://doi.org/10.1177/0886109915616437

Bungay, V., Kolar, K., Thindal, S., Remple, V. P., Johnston, C. L., & Ogilvie, G. (2013). Community-based HIV and STI prevention in women working in indoor sex markets. *Health Promotion Practice, 14*(2), 247–255.

Busch-Armendariz, N., Nsonwu, M. B., & Heffron, L. C. (2014). A kaleidoscope: The role of the social work practitioner and the strength of social work theories and practice in meeting the complex needs of people trafficked and the professionals that work with them. *International Social Work, 57*(1), 7–18. http://doi.org/10.1177/0020872813505630

Champion, J. D., & Collins, J. L. (2012). Comparison of a theory-based (AIDS Risk Reduction Model) cognitive behavioral intervention versus enhanced counseling for abused ethnic minority adolescent women on infection with sexually transmitted infection: Results of a randomized controlled trial. *International Journal of Nursing Studies, 49*(2), 138–150. http://doi.org/10.1016/j.ijnurstu.2011.08.010

Chuang, J. A. (2009). Rescuing trafficking from ideological capture: Prostitution reform and anti-trafficking law and policy. *University of Pennsylvania Law Review, 158*, 1655.

Cimino, A. N. (2012). A predictive theory of intentions to exit street-level prostitution. *Violence Against Women, 18*(10), 1235–1252. http://doi.org/10.1177/1077801212465153

Cimino, A. N. (2018). Sex work and adult prostitution: From entry to exit. In M. Bourke & V. Van Hasselt (Eds.), *Handbook of behavioral criminology: Contemporary strategies and issues*. New York, NY: Springer Publishing.

Clifford, A., Mccalman, J., Bainbridge, R., & Tsey, K. (2015). Interventions to improve cultural competency in health care for Indigenous peoples of Australia, New Zealand, Canada and the USA: A systematic review. *International Journal for Quality in Health Care, 27*, 89–98. http://doi.org/10.1093/intqhc/mzv010

Cole, J., Sprang, G., Lee, R., & Cohen, J. (2014). The trauma of commercial sexual exploitation of youth: A comparison of CSE victims to sexual abuse victims in a clinical sample. *Journal of Interpersonal Violence, 31*(1), 1–25.

Cusick, L. (2006). Widening the harm reduction agenda: From drug use to sex work. *International Journal of Drug Policy, 17*(1), 3–11.

Dank, M., Yu, L., Yahner, J., Pelletier, E., Mora, M., & Conner, B. (2015). *Locked in: Interactions with the criminal justice and child welfare systems for LGBTQ youth, YMSM, and YWSE who engage in survival sex*. Urban Institute. https://www.urban.org/sites/default/files/publication/71446/2000424-Locked-In-Interactions-with-the-Criminal-Justice-and-Child-Welfare-Systems-for-LGBTQ-Youth-YMSM-and-YWSW-Who-Engage-in-Survival-Sex.pdf

Decker, M. R., Crago, A. L., Chu, S. K., Sherman, S. G., Seshu, M. S., Buthelezi, K., . . . Beyrer, C. (2015). Human rights violations against sex workers: Burden and effect on HIV. *The Lancet, 385*(9963), 186–199.

de Vries, I., & Farrell, A. (2018). Labor trafficking victimizations: Repeat victimization and polyvictimization. *Psychology of Violence, 8*(5), 630.

Doezema, J. (2005). Now you see her, now you don't: Sex workers at the UN trafficking protocol negotiation. *Social & Legal Studies, 14*(1), 61–89. doi:10.1177/0964663905049526.

Edmond, T. (2018). Evidence based trauma treatments for survivors of sex trafficking and commercial sexual exploitation. In A. Nichols, T. Edmond, & E. Heil (Eds.) *Social work practice with survivors of sex trafficking and commercial sexual exploitation* (pp. 70–96). Columbia University Press.

Egyes, L. (2019). Borders and intersections: The unique vulnerabilities of LGBTQ immigrants to trafficking. In E. Heil & A. Nichols (Eds.), *Broadening the scope of human trafficking* (2nd ed.). Carolina Academic Press.

Ekberg, G. (2004). The Swedish law that prohibits the purchase of sexual services best practices for prevention of prostitution and trafficking in human beings. *Violence Against Women, 10*(10), 1187–1218. doi:10.1177/1077801204268647

Farley, M. (2004). Bad for the body, bad for the heart: Prostitution harms women even if legalized or decriminalized. *Violence Against Women, 10*(10), 1087–1125. http://doi.org/10.1177/1077801204268607

Felini, M., Ryan, E., Frick, J., Bangara, S., Felini, L., & Breazeale, R. (2011). *Prostitute diversion initiative: Annual report 09-10.* Dallas, TX: Dallas Police Department.

Ferreira, J. F., Vallier, N., Roulin, D., Dominice, M. I., Hirschel, B., & Calmy, A. (2010). Health perceptions of African HIV-infected patients and their physicians. *Patient Education and Counseling, 80,* 185–190. http://doi.org/10.1016/j.pec.2009.10.023

Gaston, G. B. (2013). African-Americans' perceptions of health care provider cultural competence that promote HIV medical self-care and antiretroviral medication adherence. *AIDS Care, 25*(9), 1159–1166.

Gaughran, F., Stahl, D., Ismail, K., Atakan, Z., Lally, J., Gardner-Sood, P., Patel, A., David, A., Hopkins, D., Harries, B., & Lowe, P. (2013). Improving physical health and reducing substance use in psychosis—randomised control trial (IMPACT RCT): Study protocol for a cluster randomised controlled trial. *BMC Psychiatry, 13,* 263. http://doi.org/10.1186/1471-244X-13-263

Gerassi, L. B. (2019). Experiences of racism and racial tensions among African American Women impacted by commercial sexual exploitation in practice: A qualitative study. *Violence Against Women, 26,* 438–457. doi:10.1177/1077801219835057

Gerassi, L. B. (2020). How adult women who trade sex navigate social services: A grounded theory study. *Feminist Criminology, 15*(2), 196–216. https://doi.org/10.1177/1557085119885444

Gerassi, L. B., & Esbensen, K. (2021). Motivational interviewing with individuals at risk of sex trafficking. *Journal of Social Work, 21*(4), 676–695.

Gerassi, L., & Nichols, A. (2017). *Sex trafficking and commercial sexual exploitation: Prevention, advocacy, and trauma-informed practice.* Springer.

Gilbert, A. R., Domino, M. E., Morrissey, J. P., & Gaynes, B. N. (2012). Differential service utilization associated with trauma-informed integrated treatment for women with co-occurring disorders. *Administration and Policy in Mental Health, 39*(6), 426–439. http://doi.org/10.1007/s10488-011-0362-z

Goodman, L. A., & Epstein, D. (2008). *Listening to battered women: A survivor centered approach to advocacy, mental health, and justice.* American Psychological Association.

Heffernan, K., & Blythe, B. (2014). Evidence-based practice: Developing a trauma-informed lens to case management for victims of human trafficking. *Global Social Welfare, 1,* 169–177.

Heil, E., & Nichols, A. (2019). *Human trafficking in the Midwest: A case study of St. Louis and the bi-state area.* Carolina Academic Press.

Hickle, K., & Hallett, S. (2016). Mitigating harm: Considering harm reduction principles in work with sexually exploited young people. *Children & Society, 30*(4), 302–313.

Hotaling, N., Burris, A., Johnson, B. J., Bird, Y. M., & Melbye, K. A. (2004). Been there done that: SAGE, a peer leadership model among prostitution survivors. *Journal of Trauma Practice, 2,* 255–265. http://doi.org/10.1300/J189v02n03_15

Hu, R. (2019). Examining social service providers' representation of trafficking victims: A feminist postcolonial lens. *Affilia, 34*(4), 421–438. https://doi.org/10.1177/0886109919868832

Hynes, M. (2015). Sex Work and the Law in South Africa, Sweden and New Zealand: an evidence-based argument for decriminalization. *The Columbia University Journal of Global Health, 5*(2), 24–30.

Jackson, C. A. (2016). Framing sex worker rights: How US sex worker rights activists perceive and respond to mainstream anti–sex trafficking advocacy. *Sociological Perspectives, 59*(1), 27–45.

Jarero, I., & Artigas, L. (2010). EMDR integrative group treatment protocol: Application with adults during ongoing geopolitical crisis. *Journal of EMDR Practice and Research, 4*(4), 148–155.

Kim, M. (2020). The carceral creep: Gender-based violence, race, and the expansion of the punitive state, 1973–1983. *Social Problems, 67,* 251–269. doi:10.1093/socpro/spz013

Kulkarni, S., Bell, H., & Rhodes, D. (2012). Back to basics: Essential qualities of services for survivors of intimate partner violence. *Violence Against Women, 18,* 85–101.

Littell, J. H., & Girvin, H. (2002). Stages of change: A critique. *Behavior Modification, 26*(2), 223–273.

Littell, J. H., & Girvin, H. (2004). Ready or not: Uses of the stages of change model in child welfare. *Child Welfare League of America, 83*(4), 341–366.

Lloyd, R. (2018). Change is a process: Using the transtheoretical model with commercially sexually exploited and trafficked youth and adults. In A. Nichols, T. Edmond, & E. Heil (Eds.), *Social work practice with survivors of sex trafficking and commercial sexual exploitation* (pp. 51–69). Columbia University Press.

Luminais, M., Lovell, R., & McGuire, M. (2019). A safe harbor is temporary shelter, not a pathway forward: How court-mandated sex trafficking intervention fails to help girls quit the sex trade. *Victims & Offenders, 14*(5), 540–560.

Lutnick, A., & Cohan, D. (2009). Criminalization, legalization or decriminalization of sex work: What female sex works say in San Francisco, USA. *Reproductive Health Matters, 17*(34), 38–46. doi:10.1016/S0968-8080(09)34469-9

Madden-Dempsey, M. (2011). Sex trafficking and criminalization: In defense of feminist abolitionism. *University of Pennsylvania Law Review., 158*, 1729–1778

Mayhew, P., & Mossman, E. (2007). Exiting prostitution: Models of best practice. Retrieved from http://www.justice.govt.nz/policy/commercial-property-and-regulatory/prostitution/prostitution-law-review-committee/publications/exiting- prositution-models/documents/report.pdf [Google Scholar].

McPhail, B. A., Busch, N. B., Kulkarni, S., & Rice, G. (2007). An integrative feminist model: The evolving feminist perspective on intimate partner violence. *Violence Against Women, 13*(8), 817–841. https://doi.org/10.1177/1077801207302039

Murphy, L. (2017). *Labor and sex trafficking among homeless youth.* https://static1.squarespace.com/static/5887a2a61b631bfbbc1ad83a/t/59498e69197aea24a33a640b/1497992809780/CovenantHouseReport.pdf

Musto, J. (2010). Carceral protectionism and multi-professional anti-trafficking human rights work in the Netherlands. *International Feminist Journal of Politics, 12*(3–4), 381–400.

National Association of Social Workers. (2021). Preamble to the code of ethics. Retrieved May 4, 2021, from http://www.socialworkers.org/pubs/ Code/code.asp

Okech, D., Choi, Y. J., Elkins, J., & Burns, A. C. (2018). Seventeen years of human trafficking research in social work: A review of the literature. *Journal of Evidence-Informed Social Work, 15*(2), 103–122. doi:10.1080/23761407.2017.1415177

Oselin, S. (2014). *Leaving prostitution: Getting out and staying out of sex work.* New York University Press.

Pierce, A. (2012). American Indian adolescent girls: Vulnerability to sex trafficking, intervention strategies. *American Indian and Alaska Native Mental Health Research: The Journal of the National Center, 19*(1), 37–56.

Polaris Project. (2013). *Human trafficking trends in the United States National Human Trafficking Resource Center 2007–2012.* https://polarisproject.org/resources/human-trafficking-trends-2007-2012

Polaris Project. (2015). *Sex trafficking in the U.S.—A closer look at U.S. citizen victims.* http://www.polaris project.org/human-trafficking/sex-trafficking-in-the-us/us-citizen-sex-trafficking-closer-look

Preble, K. (2018). Client centered harm reduction, commercial sex, and trafficking: Implications for rights based social work practice. In A. Nichols, T. Edmond, & E. Heil (Eds.), *Social work practice with survivors of sex trafficking and commercial sexual exploitation* (pp. 97–116). Columbia University Press.

Preble, K. M. (2019). Under Their "Control": Perceptions of traffickers' power and coercion among international female trafficking survivors. *Victims & Offenders, 14*(2), 199–122. doi:10.1080/15564886.2019.1567637

Preble, K. M. (2020). Influence of survivors' entrapment factors and traffickers' characteristics on perceptions of interpersonal social power while being recruited to be trafficked. *Journal of Violence Against Women*, online first, 1–24. https://doi.org/10.1177/1077801220920376

Preble, K., Nichols, A., & Cox, A. (2020). Labor trafficking in Missouri: Revelations from a statewide needs assessment. *Journal of Human Trafficking, 9*(1), 15–32. doi:10.1080/23322705.2020.1855900

Preble, K. M., Peatorius, R. T., & Cimino, A. N. (2016). Supportive exits: A best practices report for a sex worker intervention. *Journal of Human Behavior and the Social Environment, 26*(2), 162–178. doi:10.1080/10911359.2015.1082852

Pyra, M., Weber, K., Wilson, T. E., Cohen, J., Murchison, L., Goparaju, L., & Cohen, M. H. (2014). Sexual minority status and violence among HIV infected and at-risk women. *Journal of General Internal Medicine, 29*(8), 1131–1138. http://doi.org/10.1007/s11606-014-2832-y

Rabinovitch, J., & Strega, S. (2004). The PEERS story: Effective services sidestep the controversies. *Violence Against Women, 10*, 140–159.

Razack, S. (1998). Race, space, and prostitution: The making of the bourgeois subject. *Canadian Journal of Women & the Law, 10*, 338.

Rekart, M. L. (2005). Sex-work harm reduction. *The Lancet, 366*(9503), 2123–2134.

Resick, P. A., Nishith, P., Weaver, T. L., Astin, M. C., & Feuer, C. A. (2002). A comparison of cognitive-processing therapy with prolonged exposure and a waiting condition for the treatment of chronic posttraumatic stress disorder in female rape victims. *Journal of Consulting and Clinical Psychology, 70*(4), 867–879. https://doi.org/10.1037/0022-006X.70.4.867

Robey, K. L., Minihan, P. M., Long-Bellil, L. M., . . . Edde, G. E. (2013). Teaching health care students about disability within a cultural competency context. *Disability and Health Journal, 6*(4), 271–279. http://doi.org/10.1016/j.dhjo.2013.05.002

Roe-Sepowitz, D. E., Gallagher, J., Hickle, K. E., Pérez Loubert, M., & Tutelman, J. (2014). Project ROSE: An arrest alternative for victims of sex trafficking and prostitution. *Journal of Offender Rehabilitation, 53*(1), 57–74. http://doi.org/10.1080/10509674.2013.861323

Roe-Sepowitz, D. E., Hickle, K. E., & Cimino, A. (2012). The impact of abuse history and trauma symptoms on successful completion of a prostitution-exiting program. *Journal of Human Behavior in the Social Environment, 22*(1), 65–77. http://doi.org/10.1080/10911359.2011.598830

Rothman, E. F., Bazzi, A. R., & Bair-Merritt, M. (2015). "I'll do whatever as long as you keep telling me that I'm important": A case study illustrating the link between adolescent dating violence and sex trafficking victimization. *Journal of Applied Research on Children: Informing Policy for Children at Risk, 6*(1), Article 8.

Rothman, E. F., & Xuan, Z. (2014). Trends in physical dating violence victimization among US high school students, 1999–2011. *Journal of School Violence, 13*(3), 277–290.

Sausa, L., Keatley, J., & Operario, D. (2007). Perceived risks and benefits of sex work among transgender women of color in San Francisco. *Archives of Sexual Behavior, 36*(6), 768–777. http://doi.org/10.1007/s10508-007-9210-3

Schwarz, C., Kennedy, E., & Britton, H. (2017). Aligned across difference: Structural injustice, sex work, and human trafficking. *Feminist Formations, 29*(2), 1–25. https://doi.org/10.1353/ff.2017.0014

Shih, E. (2016). Not in my "backyard abolitionism": Vigilante rescue against American sex trafficking. *Sociological Perspectives, 59*(1), 66–90. https://doi.org/10.1177/0731121416628551

Sloan, L., & Wahab, S. (2000). Feminist voices on sex work: Implications for social work. *Affilia, 15*(4), 457–479.

Smolak, A. (2013). White slavery, whorehouse riots, venereal disease, and saving women: Historical context of prostitution interventions and harm reduction in New York City during the Progressive Era. *Social Work in Public Health, 28*(5), 496–508. http://doi.org/10.1080/19371918.2011.592083

Sylva, F. D., Graffam, J., Hardcastle, L., & Shinkfield, A. J. (2012). Analysis of the stages of change model of drug and alcohol treatment readiness among prisoners. *International Journal of Offender Therapy and Comparative Criminology, 56*(2), 265–280. http://doi.org/10.1177/0306624X10392531

Taylor, V., & Rupp, L. J. (1993). Women's culture and lesbian feminist activism: A reconsideration of cultural feminism. *Chicago Journals, 19*(1), 32–61.

Todres, J., & Diaz, A. (2019). *Preventing child trafficking: a public health approach.* Johns Hopkins University Press.

Trafficking Victims Protection Act of 2000, Pub. L. No. 106-386, 114 Stat. 1464 (2000). http://www.state.gov/documents/organization/10492.pdf

Twis-McCoy, M. K., & Preble, K. M. (2020). Intersectional-standpoint method: Toward a participatory framework for human trafficking study and social change. *Violence & Victims, 35*(3), 418–439.

Van Dam, D., Ehring, T., Vedel, E., & Emmelkamp, P. M. G. (2013). Trauma-focused treatment for post-traumatic stress disorder combined with CBT for severe substance use disorder: A randomized controlled trial. *BMC Psychiatry, 13*, 172. http://doi.org/10.1186/1471-244X-13-172

Wahab, S. (2002). For their own good?: Sex work, social control and social workers, a historical perspective. *Journal of Sociology & Social Welfare, 29*(4), Article 4. https://scholarworks.wmich.edu/jssw/vol29/iss4/4

Wahab, S., & Panichelli, M. (2013). Ethical and human rights issues in coercive interventions with sex workers. *Affilia: Journal of Women and Social Work, 28*(4), 344–349.

Weitzer, R. (2010). *The movement to criminalize sex work in the United States.* SSRN Scholarly Paper ID 1558068. Social Science Research Network. http://papers.ssrn.com/abstract=1558068

Whalley, E., & Hackett, C. (2017). Carceral feminisms: The abolitionist project and undoing dominant feminisms. *Contemporary Justice Review, 20*(4), 456–473. doi:10.1080/10282580.2017.1383762

Yahne, C. E., Miller, W. R., Irvin-Vitela, L., & Tonigan, J. S. (2002). Magdalena pilot project: Motivational outreach to substance abusing women street sex workers. *Journal of Substance Abuse Treatment, 23*, 49–53.

33

Decarceration and Advocacy

Carrie Pettus and Stephanie Kennedy

Introduction

Smart decarceration of the U.S. criminal justice system requires a dramatic shift in the way our criminal justice system is viewed and used. Nearly 13 million individuals cycle through jails and prisons across the nation every year (Carson, 2020; Zeng, 2019). In the 2010s, the United States reached a place where the country had the moral, fiscal, and political will to end the era of mass incarceration that began in the 1980s and enact the era of smart decarceration, which began in the 2010s. Smart decarceration refers to a comprehensive decarceration approach that is effective, sustainable, and socially just. Social workers are increasingly at the forefront of generating new approaches to criminal justice and are active participants in the smart decarceration movement. Social workers serve advocacy organizations that aim to prevent incarceration and they enact policy and practice reforms through criminal justice and correctional organizations. Social workers function as interventionists and researchers who generate evidence-driven innovations for policy and practice designed to transform how justice is approached in the United States. As nearly all fields of practice in which social workers engage (e.g., child welfare, schools, health, military, and aging) intersect with criminal justice, it is important for social workers to understand the transformative movement of our time, the context of criminal justice reform, and how to implement smart decarceration strategies.

Although many social workers were actively engaged in prison reform work in the 19th and early 20th centuries, the field moved away from criminal justice work as mass incarceration grew throughout the latter half of the 20th century. In 2012, social workers were urged to re-engage in intervening with individuals and families involved in the criminal justice system as well as with the political, organizational, and macro structures that surround the justice system (Pettus-Davis, 2012). Nearly a decade later, social workers have demonstrated a profound re-engagement within the criminal justice field, and as a result, a

Carrie Pettus and Stephanie Kennedy, *Decarceration and Advocacy* In: *Handbook of Forensic Social Work*. Edited by: David Axlyn McLeod, Anthony P. Natale, and Kristin W. Mapson, Oxford University Press. © Oxford University Press 2024. DOI: 10.1093/oso/9780197694732.003.0033 growing number of social workers are leaders in smart decarceration approaches to criminal justice reform. Social workers have offered new conceptual models for thinking about a decarceration-oriented approach to criminal justice reform, have established an evidence base with which to examine criminal justice from a trauma-informed and family systems perspective, and have begun to organize the field around smart decarceration. This chapter provides an overview of smart decarceration scholarship, examines policy and practice strategies for achieving smart decarceration goals, and explores the intersectionality of social justice, civil rights, public health, and the criminal justice system in its current form. The chapter concludes with case examples of how social workers can work within the decarceration paradigm and anticipate and overcome common challenges to the work.

Foundational Model for Decarceration Approaches

Widespread mass incarceration practices hit their tipping point during the first decade of the 21st century, and the second decade ushered in the era of smart decarceration in the United States. While skeptics suggested the appetite for reform was fleeting as the recession resolved, politicians across the political spectrum called for reforms, famous philanthropists and activists engaged, multichannel media bloomed, and public will consistently shifted toward reform. The fact that the criminal justice system would have to change could no longer be avoided. Numerous papers and texts have documented the evolution of decarceration and the devolution of support for the criminal justice system as we know it, so this chapter does not review that phenomenon (see National Research Council, 2014; Petersilia & Cullen, 2014; Travis et al., 2014; Western, 2006). Instead, this chapter focuses on the contemporary guiding principles and concepts of a predominant model for decarceration in social work—smart decarceration. Thus, a few definitional distinctions are warranted. Decarceration is the process of removing people from institutions such as prisons or psychiatric hospitals—the opposite of incarceration (Oxford Reference, n.d.). Criminal justice reform is broadly conceptualized as the examination of structural and policy reforms needed across the criminal justice spectrum—from an individual's first contact with law enforcement, court procedures, in-prison programming, and reentry to reforming factors that drive disparities that concentrate along race, socioeconomic class, and behavioral health status. Smart decarceration was coined by Pettus-Davis and Epperson (2015) and combines the definitions of decarceration and criminal justice reform. Smart decarceration was defined as effective, sustainable, and socially just decarceration achieved when three outcomes are concurrently accomplished: (a) the incarcerated population in U.S. jails and prisons is substantially decreased, (b) existing racial and economic disparities in the criminal justice system are redressed, and (c) community safety and public well-being are maximized. As criminal justice policies vary widely by jurisdiction, criminal justice is hyperlocal and reforms must be designed to the specific local context of a given criminal justice system. Thus, Epperson and Pettus-Davis (2017) described smart decarceration as an approach designed to *build community capacity in order to develop community-driven responses to local issues that do not resort to the default incarceration approach. Smart decarceration also posits that local jails and state and federal prisons should no longer be used to address society's greatest problems—including limited access to behavioral and physical health services, inadequate education and employment opportunities, and lack of affordable housing and health care.*

The foundational model for smart decarceration was first articulated by Pettus-Davis and Epperson (2015) in a proposal to the American Academy of Social Work and Social Welfare in response to the academy's effort to launch a decade-long grand challenge effort. The grand challenge initiative sought to identify major focal areas for the social work profession to organize around and to generate sustainable solutions over a 10-year period (Sherraden et al., 2014). The social work grand challenges were modeled after the grand challenges initiative of the engineering profession, which resulted in significant successes in tackling some of the world's most intractable infrastructure problems. A grand challenge for smart decarceration, entitled Promote Smart Decarceration, was established along with 11 others. The Promote Smart Decarceration grand challenge articulates that in order to ensure effective and sustainable decarceration, the country must prepare for and do the difficult work of developing a "smart" approach—one that is evidence driven and grounded in a social justice orientation. Pettus-Davis and Epperson (2015) underscore how the three outcomes of dramatically reducing the incarcerated population, ameliorating racial disparities, and promoting public health and safety must be achieved simultaneously. They argue that only by achieving all three outcomes could the criminal justice system be truly transformed. For example, if the incarcerated population was substantially reduced but racial disparities increased, then smart decarceration is not achieved. This did occur in juvenile justice reform efforts—the detained juvenile population decreased substantially, but existing racial disparities among youth who remained in confinement were amplified (D. M. Washington et al., 2021). As noted by Epperson and Pettus-Davis (2015), "Existing paradigms and small adjustments to existing approaches will not achieve these aims—new perspectives, transformed approaches, and transdisciplinary paradigms are needed to achieve smart decarceration."

As the smart decarceration construct was taking shape, other scholars proposed principles to guide criminal justice reform. Travis et al. (2014) suggested four principles needed to limit the scale of incarceration: (a) proportionality, suggesting that criminal sentences should be responsive to the seriousness of the crime; (b) parsimony, underscoring how the length of incarceration should not be greater than necessary to achieve the goals of the sentencing policy; (c) citizenship, indicating that incarceration should not violate any individual's fundamental status as a member of society; and (d) social justice, highlighting how the collective effect of incarceration should promote a fair distribution of rights, resources, and opportunities across the population. Petersilia and Cullen (2014) also generated principles to "downsize prisons," which included setting state limits on prison capacity, referred to as "inmate caps"; using assessment tools and data to monitor recidivism; adequately resourcing community corrections to provide rehabilitation support; providing consultation to states willing to reduce the incarcerated population; and building an evidence base for downsizing prisons.

While noting the benefits of principles proposed by other scholars, Epperson and Pettus-Davis (2015) argued that making small adjustments to existing paradigms would not achieve the aims of smart decarceration and that transformed approaches using transdisciplinary-produced paradigms were needed to achieve smart decarceration. Thus, smart decarceration work is aligned with four principles: It seeks to change the narrative on incarceration and the incarcerated; it produces innovations that span the spectrum of the criminal justice system; it disseminates or implements transdisciplinary policy and practice interventions; and it employs evidence-driven strategies. Expanding on these four principles, Epperson and Pettus-Davis (2015) further articulated 10 assumptions of smart decarceration. These assumptions are that incarceration cannot be the default response to crime; incarceration should be used as a last resort; formerly incarcerated individuals need a leadership voice; the stigma of criminal justice involvement must be redressed; smart decarceration requires a comprehensive, system-wide reform approach and each segment of the criminal justice system must fully appreciate its impact on the next segment of the criminal justice system; exit points are needed throughout the criminal justice system and each sector of the system should acknowledge its impact on driving incarceration rates; community capacity to promote behavioral and physical health, housing, education, employment, and civic engagement must be increased in order to support incarceration becoming a last resort—thus, there must be an array of multidisciplinary-developed and -delivered replacement prevention and interventions to incarceration; transdisciplinary perspectives are needed to redefine what constitutes criminal behavior and when incarceration is truly necessary; there should be continual evaluation on whether the smart decarceration policy and practice innovations had their intended effects; and existing innovations are insufficient and new strategies should be continuously proposed and refined and interventions should strive to achieve the highest standard.

In subsequent work, Pettus-Davis and Epperson convened and surveyed advocates, scholars, practitioners, and policymakers about how to operationalize into actionable steps the four guiding concepts of smart decarceration. In a concept mapping study (Pettus-Davis & Epperson, 2017; Pettus-Davis, Epperson, Taylor, & Grier, 2017) with 307 advocates, practitioners, reformers, and researchers, 12 guideposts were generated for the implementation of smart decarceration strategies. The 12 guideposts are to (a) reform contributors to incarceration to reduce incarceration rates; (b) change when and how incarceration is used; (c) employ cross-sector training within the criminal justice system; (d) improve integration between the criminal justice system and the community; (e) develop a talent pipeline of professionals versed in smart decarceration strategies; (f) create universal reentry/transitional program models to be adopted in jail and prison settings; (g) re-evaluate and repeal policy-driven collateral consequences prompted when an individual receives a felony conviction; (h) build community capacity for social innovation to better prevent people from becoming incarcerated and to receive them when they are released from incarceration; (i) address gaps in knowledge about the most effective policy and practice approaches through research; (j) refine research-practice-policy partnerships to create feedback loops that drive effective and socially just innovations; (k) maximize measurement and data collection to promote continual evaluation of reforms; and (l) package and disseminate information to targeted audiences to share widely knowledge development and promote further innovation. The Promote Smart Decarceration grand challenge working group further articulated four initial policy considerations for smart decarceration (American Academy of Social Work and Social Welfare, n.d.): (a) using incarceration primarily for incapacitation of the most dangerous; (b) foregrounding the reduction of racial, economic, and behavioral health disparities as a key outcome in decarceration efforts; (c) removing civic and legal exclusions; and (d) reallocating resources to community-based supports. Combined, smart decarceration offers a framework for the social work academic and practice fields to follow in order to rapidly develop a body of knowledge on how to transform the criminal justice system to achieve equitable, just, and well-being outcomes for the country.

Emergent Topics and Populations in the Era of Smart Decarceration

As the second decade of the 21st century began, attention was drawn to the intersectionality of public health, social justice, civil rights, and criminal justice reform. A burgeoning body of theoretical and empirical scholarship underscored how the U.S. criminal justice system could no longer be viewed solely through the lens of public safety. Rather, it became clear that our criminal justice system had become the default response to public health and interpersonal crises and was driving social injustice and threatening individual civil rights. The need for system-wide reforms to promote smart decarceration was clear as the nation awakened to the vast reach of the criminal justice system and its devastating effects for individuals, families, and communities across the nation.

Public Health

Substantial literature exploring the intersection of public health and criminal justice focuses on how the transinstitutionalization of individuals (e.g., the movement of individuals between psychiatric hospitals and jail/prison) and the War on Drugs drove mass incarceration (e.g., Ben-Moshe, 2020; Parsons, 2018; Primeau et al., 2013; Raphael & Stoll, 2013). The lack of accessible community-based physical and behavioral health services has long been posited to contribute to the mortality that occurs inside correctional facilities and in the community after individuals return home. However, as the smart decarceration movement was taking shape, scholarly attention turned to the impact of trauma and mental health and substance use disorders on justice-involved individuals and how, as a result, criminal justice involvement shortens lives and leads to premature death.

Lifetime experiences of traumatic events are rampant among individuals involved in the criminal justice system. Across the spectrum of criminal justice—from those under community supervision to those in jail and prison to those who have reentered communities after an incarceration experience—more than 90% of individuals involved in any segment of the criminal justice system report lifetime traumatic experiences (e.g., DeHart et al., 2014; Komarovskaya et al., 2011; Morrison et al., 2018; Pettus-Davis et al., 2020; Wolff et al., 2014). According to the American Psychiatric Association (2013), lifetime traumatic experiences include direct personal experiences of victimization, threat or experience of serious injury, the threat of death, learning of a serious injury or death occurring to a loved one, or witnessing an event that involves death or serious injury/threat to another person in childhood, adolescence, or adulthood. The prevalence of lifetime traumatic experiences among justice-involved individuals is important because trauma symptoms are correlated with a range of negative life outcomes that span behavioral health, physical health, social relationships, and criminal behavior. Untreated trauma symptoms can include aggression, impulsivity, sensation and risk seeking, increased sensitivity to stress, inadequate assessments of risk, high levels of negative emotions, and difficulties with interpersonal relationships (e.g., Brady, 2006; Clark et al., 2013; Dube et al., 2003; Jaycox et al., 2004; Medrano et al., 2002; Swogger et al., 2011).

Research suggests that untreated trauma symptoms are associated with engagement in both violent and nonviolent criminal behavior (Forsman & Langstrom, 2012; Nyamathi et al., 2012) Compared to their nonvictimized peers, formerly incarcerated men with lifetime traumatic experiences have higher rates of reported violence prior to their incarceration and are at greater risk of engaging in violence (Burnette et al., 2008; Hill & Nathan, 2008; Van Buren et al., 2014; Wolff et al., 2014). For incarcerated women, lifetime traumatic experiences increase risk for in-prison suicide attempts (E. M. Wright et al., 2007), completed suicides (Mennicke et al., 2021), and reincarceration after release (Cloyes et al., 2010). Higher rates of lifetime traumatic experiences are associated with early onset of aggression, and criminal justice system involvement may exacerbate symptoms of trauma (Kubiak, 2004; Messina et al., 2014; Moloney et al., 2009). Experiences of trauma are also correlated with substance use disorders (e.g., Sindicich et al., 2014). The number of times an individual has experienced incarceration is correlated with the number of lifetime traumatic experiences a person reports (Mersky et al., 2012; Messina et al., 2007; Nyamathi et al., 2012), and as the number of lifetime traumatic experiences increases in a person's life, the odds of arrest, incarceration, and recidivism increase (Cloyes et al., 2010; Jennings et al., 2012; Sadeh & McNiel, 2014). Recent research underscores the pernicious nature of trauma indicating that lifetime traumatic experiences do not cease after an incarceration experience, and rather, nearly half of individuals released from incarceration experience at least one additional lifetime traumatic event in the months after they return home (Boxer et al., 2011; Pettus-Davis et al., 2020). In one study, of those individuals who experienced trauma after release, 20% lost a loved one to homicide, nearly 25% were violently assaulted, 31% witnessed a serious injury or death, 31% were diagnosed with a life-threatening illness or sustained a serious injury, and 60% learned of the serious injury or death of a loved one.

Trauma symptoms can progress into more serious behavioral health problems including posttraumatic stress disorder (PTSD), a mental health condition characterized by flashbacks, nightmares, and severe anxiety, as well as uncontrollable thoughts about the traumatic event, and substance use disorders (National Alliance on Mental Illness, n.d.). The presence of PTSD is much higher among individuals with incarceration histories when compared to a range of individuals who have never experienced incarceration. For example, PTSD prevalence is estimated at 13% of incarcerated men and 40% of incarcerated women compared to 7% of male veterans, 13% of female veterans, 5% of men in the general public, and 10% of women in the general public (Breslau, 2009; Dobie et al., 2004; Komarovskaya et al., 2011; U.S. Department of Veterans Affairs, 2015; Wisco et al., 2014; Wolff et al., 2014).

Due to the growing awareness of the prevalence and consequences of lifetime traumatic events among those involved in the criminal justice system—particularly those who become incarcerated—a burgeoning number of scholars have documented the consequences and trajectories of those with lifetime traumatic experiences (e.g., Kennedy et al., 2016; Messina & Grella, 2006; Morrison et al., 2019; Tripodi & Pettus-Davis, 2013; Wolff et al., 2014). Scholars have suggested a variety of intervention methods to promote healing from trauma and stabilize individuals during and after criminal justice system involvement. Broadly, these recommendations have included (a) creating a trauma-informed justice system in order to reduce the number of people who become convicted and the length of time individuals are under supervision once sentenced (e.g., N. A. Miller & Najavits, 2012); (b) delivering gender-tailored trauma treatment or psychoeducation during or after confinement (Najavits, 2004; Pettus-Davis et al., 2019; Zlotnick et al., 2009); (c) adapting evidence-based trauma treatment designed for the general population for those who are involved in the criminal justice system (Pettus-Davis et al., 2019); and (d) addressing trauma in the context of alternative to incarceration programs such as police deflection efforts and prosecutorial-led diversion (e.g., Lowry & Kerodal, 2019). Although prevention of lifetime traumatic experiences is of utmost importance, researchers and practitioners now recognize that these experiences should be responded to with supports to prevent involvement in the justice system and to promote successful exits from the criminal justice system. The next decade is likely to have a proliferation of programmatic and policy attention to trauma- and justice culture–specific adapted interventions.

Mental Health and Substance Use Disorders and Behavioral Health Disparities

The U.S. criminal justice system is the default response to most public health crises. A divestment in preventing and treating mental health and substance use disorders by both the private and public sectors removed the health safety net for millions of Americans (Parsons, 2016; Primeau et al., 2013; Raphael & Stoll, 2013). In turn, untreated mental health and substance use disorders among the U.S. population drove the growth of criminal justice involvement and incarceration throughout the era of mass incarceration. More than half of those incarcerated in prisons and 64% of jail inmates are diagnosed with a mental health disorder; these rates are higher among incarcerated women when compared to incarcerated men (73% compared to 55%; Bronson & Berzofsky, 2017). The prevalence of serious mental illness is estimated at nearly 15%—more than double the rate in the general population (National Institute of Mental Health, 2021). Nearly three-quarters of incarcerated men and women are diagnosed with substance use disorders (Bronson et al., 2017).

Individuals with behavioral health disorders are often incarcerated for crimes associated with public nuisances, homelessness, and being under the influence of drugs and alcohol; these individuals are also more likely reincarcerated for violating the terms of their probation (Califano, 2010). When compared to individuals charged with similar crimes who do not have mental health or substance use disorders, those who do are more likely to be held pretrial and to receive longer sentences (Karberg & Glaze, 2005). After release from incarceration, individuals with serious mental illness are reincarcerated more quickly and likely to make multiple contacts with jails and prisons (Veeh et al., 2018). Further, more than half (52%) of incarcerated adults with substance use disorders have at least one prior incarceration compared to fewer than a third (31%) of those without substance use disorders (King et al., 2018; Veeh et al., 2018). Individuals with substance use disorders are reincarcerated more quickly after release from incarceration; 20% to 25% of those with substance use disorders are reincarcerated within the first year after release (Califano, 2010) compared to 9% to 12% of those without substance use disorders (Mallik-Kane & Visher, 2008). Approximately 68% of individuals released from county jail who have co-morbid mental health and substance use disorders end up being reincarcerated within 4 years, a much higher rate when compared to individuals with either a mental health disorder or a substance use disorder and to those with no disorder (Wilson et al., 2011).

Although correctional supervision agencies provide the majority of referrals to mental health and substance use disorder treatment, they have very little capacity to provide such treatment during custody (Taxman et al., 2007). In fact, existing in-prison drug treatment programs are only able to serve 10% of the incarcerated individuals identified as needing treatment (Taxman et al., 2013). The majority of services are psychoeducational in nature or use 12-step group-based models, which are only suitable for individuals with low-threshold substance use disorders. A third of those incarcerated are identified with severe substance dependence, which requires more intensive services for treatment (Taxman et al., 2013). In essence, although the majority of correctional agencies are responsible for assisting individuals under their supervision with mental health—and substance use—related needs, they do not have the infrastructure or capacity to do so.

The uniform responsibility of correctional agencies is to supervise and secure individuals involved in the system in the name of public safety. Most corrections professionals are not cross-trained to provide mental health and substance use disorder support. Yet, because of the prevalence of these disorders among the justice-involved population, corrections professionals are often expected to have behavioral health expertise. The capacity of community-based clinics to prevent and treat mental health and substance use disorders is also limited; as agencies are not cross-trained in corrections strategies, they lack expertise to respond to a client's criminal behavior should it arise. Thus, the country faces a quandary in which neither the public health nor the public safety systems have the expertise or capacity to address the common intersection of mental health, problematic substance use, and crime. Currently, social workers and other professionals are exploring how to remediate this intersection when prevention strategies have failed. There are several prominent and ongoing debates. First, national conversations are exploring who the appropriate first responders should be to address behavioral health crises that require emergency supports. The "defund the police" movement argues that mental health professionals rather than law enforcement should respond; the counterargument posits that public safety often requires a law enforcement response (Weichselbaum & Lewis, 2020). Second, some suggest that social work–law enforcement professionals should be developed with cross-training; they are countered by arguments that helping professionals should remain distinct from law enforcement (Jacobs et al., 2021). Third, there are lively debates on the definition of "true" criminal justice transformation. For example, the prison abolition movement posits how three approaches, dubbed the three pillars of abolitionism, are needed for societal transformation: *moratorium*—stop building correctional facilities, *decarceration*—release people from prisons, and *excarceration*—decriminalize mental health and substance use disorders and provide adequate treatment (Bagaric et al., 2021; J. Washington, 2018). Taken together, these conversations are re-envisioning the role and purpose of the criminal justice system, identifying strategies to disentangle crime from the criminalization of mental health and substance use disorders, and generating viable alternatives for humanely responding to undesirable behaviors.

Death

The COVID-19 pandemic reignited scholarship and public awareness of how incarceration increases risk for illness and death, which in turn has increased a sense of urgency to decarcerate American jails and prisons (Abraham et al., 2020). Incarcerated individuals are at greater risk than members of the general public of dying from cancer and liver disease and are significantly more likely to die from homicide (twice the rate of the general population) or to die by suicide (Carson, 2021). Incarceration settings appear to have become more volatile in the past 20 years; in 2018, state prisons reported the highest rates of homicide and suicide in decades (Carson, 2021). The relationship between incarceration and death, however, extends well beyond prison fences. The most frequent causes of death after release from incarceration are homicide, suicide, chronic illness, and drug overdose (Binswanger et al., 2007; Ranapurwala et al., 2018; Zlodre & Fazel, 2012). Formerly incarcerated individuals are 3.5 times more likely to die than those who have never been incarcerated (Bingswanger et al., 2007); during the first 2 weeks after release, they are 13 times more likely to die (Merrall et al., 2010). Rates of death nearly double for those who have been incarcerated multiple times (Lize et al., 2015).

Although incarceration is largely invisible to many in American society, these death rates demonstrate incarceration as a potential life-or-death experience. Criminal justice involvement is trajectory changing for both individuals and the family systems in which they are embedded; it exacerbates racial, economic, and health disparities and may result not just in the loss of freedom, but in the loss of life. To wit, the prevalence of chronic illness, long sentences, and an aging incarcerated population has led to the proliferation of in-prison hospice programs to help incarcerated individuals to die with dignity (e.g., Hoffman & Dickinson, 2011). As additional data and analyses explore the intersection of incarceration and premature death, ideally incarceration will come to be seen as a last resort for responding to criminal behavior.

Social Justice and Civil Rights

There is a large body of research and scholarship that documents historical and modern-day disparities among those with criminal justice system involvement across race, socioeconomic class, and behavioral health status. Disparities begin at the front end of the criminal justice system (i.e., with law enforcement) and are perpetuated through individuals' attempt to remain free of future criminal justice involvement after release from incarceration (i.e., the reentry period). Race, economic, and behavioral health disparities lead to significant social disadvantage for individuals during their incarceration and after release; the burden of disparities, however, also extends to their children, families, and communities. Both the existence of disparities and their resultant ripple-out impacts have catalyzed social work's renewed engagement in criminal justice reform and smart decarceration work. Increasingly, social workers are choosing to refer to the criminal justice system as the "criminal legal system" to underscore the lack of justice and presence of pervasive disparities and broken practices. As many scholars have documented these injustices (e.g., Lofstrom & Raphael, 2016; Tonry, 2010), only a brief synopsis of the statistics is provided below.

Racial disparities in criminal justice contact and outcomes have been empirically established beginning with juvenile justice system and law enforcement contact, arrest rates and prosecutorial dispositions, pretrial outcomes, sentencing, incarceration, and reentry. In the juvenile justice system, Black/African American and Indigenous/American Indian youth are incarcerated at a rate three times that of White youth, most often for low-level offenses (Sickmund et al., 2021). Further, Black/African American youth are over four times more likely to be incarcerated compared to White youth (Sickmund et al., 2021). Although attempts were made to shrink the juvenile justice population, these reductions resulted in the growth of racial disparities by 10% across 11 states (Sickmund et al., 2021).

Racial disparities have also been empirically documented for law enforcement contact. Black, Indigenous, and people of color (BIPOC) men are more likely to be stopped for minor infractions and, once stopped, more likely to be searched but less likely to have contraband when compared to White men (Pierson et al., 2020). Further, the odds of receiving a traffic citation are 44% higher for Black/African American men and 82% higher for Latinx men than for White men (Fletcher, 2018). Once individuals come into contact with law enforcement, BIPOC individuals are 30% more likely to be arrested than their White counterparts (Baumgartner et al., 2018; Kochel, 2011).

Disparities continue for BIPOC individuals in the court system. Among those charged with drug offenses, Black/African American defendants and Latinx defendants are 80% and 67% more likely to be denied bail when compared to White defendants, respectively (Carson, 2018). Pretrial release is more frequently granted to White defendants (67%) than Black/African American defendants (55%) or Latinx defendants (50%; Carson, 2018). Among those who are granted bail, more Whites are able to secure bail (54%) compared to Blacks/African Americans (40%) and Latinx (28%; Carson, 2018). Disparities persist in plea deals—White defendants receive, on average, a 28% sentence reduction compared to an average 13% reduction for Black/African American individuals (Federal Bureau of Investigation, 2017). BIPOC individuals are disproportionately represented in our local jails; they make up 69% of the jail population compared to just 32% of the total U.S. population (Zeng, 2019). Among prison residents, Black/African American males and females are admitted to prison at a rate six and four times higher respectively than their White counterparts; Indigenous/American Indian males and females are admitted at four and six times higher rates; and Latinx are admitted at a rate two times higher (Burch, 2015). BIPOC individuals return to incarceration as a result of parole revocation at similarly dispropor-tionately higher rates (Burch, 2015).

The Black Lives Matter movement, founded in 2013, was thrust back into the spotlight in June 2020 after the murder of George Floyd in Minneapolis. The movement's years of advocacy coupled with media attention have attracted the attention of scholars, advocates, policymakers, practitioners, and members of the general public to existing racial dispar-ities in criminal justice in a way that has not been seen in decades (Howard University Law Library, n.d.). Researchers, policymakers, and practitioners are assessing the evidence and re-examining contributors to racial disparities such as overpolicing, biased disciplinary ap-proaches in schools, intergenerational transmission of disadvantage, social determinants of health, intergenerational trauma, and other pernicious factors. Within these contexts, the field is taking a renewed look at risk assessment tools and other screening processes that perpetuate racial bias from arrest to sentencing to reentry (e.g., Mayson, 2019; Van Eijk, 2017). Further, the small reductions achieved in the overall incarcerated population over the past decade are now being explored for racial equity to ensure that prevention and decarceration is not disproportionately experienced by White individuals. Although sub-stantial work remains to be done in this area, social workers are uniquely well positioned to lead the charge. The progress and increased openness to acknowledging racially biased justice system approaches in recent years suggest that achieving equity is possible, but this goal will require significant effort, time, scholarship, and advocacy.

Economic inequities are also rampant in the U.S. criminal justice system, and soci-oeconomic bias contributes to people becoming ensnared in the criminal justice system, becoming incarcerated, and enduring significant economic disadvantage after release from incarceration. The economic burden of criminal justice involvement spreads to the families of justice-involved individuals and keeps or pushes those families into poverty. The factors driving these disparities include the criminalization of poverty (e.g., loitering, sleeping, and camping); overpolicing of economically disadvantaged communities; fines and fees that lead to incarceration (e.g., traffic tickets and supervision feels); public defender burden; plea bargains; and an inability to pay bail (Edelman, 2019). Those men and women who become incarcerated are disproportionately low-income prior to incarceration and have ap-proximately half the median annual income of those individuals who are nonincarcerated (Rabuy & Kopf, 2015). In 2016–2017, 65% of those under probation supervision had an annual income of less than $20,000 compared to just under 40% of individuals not under supervision; conversely, fewer than 10% of those under supervision had an annual income above $50,000 compared to nearly 30% of those not under supervision (Finkel, 2019). Monthly supervision fees required by most probation or parole offices exacerbate poverty. In addition, having a felony conviction results in employment restrictions (see the National Inventory of Collateral Consequences [n.d.] website for state-level inventory), loss of gov-ernment identification (particularly driver's licenses), and supervision requirements and court-mandated treatment that can interfere with the ability to obtain or maintain employ-ment (Pew Charitable Trusts, 2020). Not surprisingly, economic disadvantage continues after incarceration. Compared to men who have never been incarcerated, incarcerated men experience a 21% decline in the likelihood of obtaining employment after release, 11%

lower hourly wages, and a 40% reduction in annual earnings (Couloute & Kopf, 2018). The economic burden of incarceration is also borne by families of incarcerated loved ones—family income declines by 22% during the years that a loved one is incarcerated (de Vuono-Powell et al., 2015). In addition to lost wages while their loved one is incarcerated, families also incur incarceration costs as the incarcerated individual needs to access toiletries, canteen, and telecommunications; families also often pay an incarcerated loved one's debts and must pay for transportation to visit their loved ones during custody (de Vuono-Powell et al., 2015).

An individual's socioeconomic status currently influences the way they experience the criminal justice system, but as smart decarceration approaches flourish, this phenomenon should wane. Growing numbers of approaches to reducing disparities are being adopted, such as alternatives to fines and fees that can drive someone toward incarceration. For example, amnesty is now being offered in some municipal courts to prevent further justice involvement for individuals unable to pay fines, fees, tickets, and the costs of supervision (Edelman, 2019). Although the movement away from cash payments is positive, it is important that proposed alternatives (which include community service) do not displace costs to the individual in the form of transportation expenses, childcare costs, and lost wages. Further, community bail funds are proliferating across the nation; bail funds offer a mechanism for local governments or philanthropic organizations to make payments for individuals unable to afford cash bail (Steinberg et al., 2018). Additionally, both prosecutors' offices and law enforcement departments are building out diversion and deflection programs to move people away from arrest, incarceration, and supervision and connect them with community-based treatment and supports (e.g., Collins et al., 2019; R. F. Wright & Levine, 2021),

Although less common, other alternative measures implemented to reduce disparities include integrating poverty considerations during sentencing, reducing probation and parole sentences as a means to reduce supervision fees, reinstating individuals' driver's licenses (when revoked for failure to pay fines and fees associated with noncriminal traffic citations) to ensure individuals have transportation to employment, and removing professional licensure restrictions that exist for individuals with arrest or conviction records. Given social work's profession-long history of working to alleviate poverty through structural reforms, the profession is well positioned to develop and facilitate substantial reforms at this intersection.

Evaluation of Research Methodologies

Ample theoretical and empirical scholarship exists on the contributors to criminal behavior, desistance from criminal behavior, and systemic flaws (e.g., Laub & Boonstoppel, 2012; Laub & Sampson, 2001; Lopez-Aguado, 2016; R. J. Miller, 2013; Tanner-Smith et al., 2013). However, few best practices have been established to guide prevention of the overreliance on incarceration to address social and public health issues and effective intervention with individuals once they are involved with the criminal justice system. Beginning in the

1980s, the criminal justice system shifted from a goal of rehabilitation to focus instead on incapacitation and retribution. This shift resulted in reduced scholarly attention to the generation of data-driven prevention, intervention, and remediation solutions for those who become embroiled in the criminal justice system. Thus, the bulk of what we know explores *why* individuals commit crime (e.g., risk factors for crime and delinquency); we lack a robust evidence base on *how* to effectively prevent criminal justice contact, divert individuals away from incarceration after first contact, and set them up to succeed after release from incarceration.

Although there has been an ample amount of evaluation work done on specialty courts, in-prison programming, and reentry programs, these evaluations lack causal rigor and results across studies have produced mixed findings. Typically, as study rigor increases, the evidence base decreases. As growing numbers of practitioners and policymakers seek evidence-based solutions to implement, they find they are limited, not by lack of access, but by lack of established evidence-based practices due to limited rigor in studies. Fraser et al. (2009) define interventions as "intentional change strategies" (p. 5); intervention research is thus the dynamic process of evaluating these intentional change strategies—a process that must involve researchers, agencies, and practitioners. Social workers, as natural change agents, are perfectly situated to design and implement policy and practice interventions and evaluate the effectiveness of those interventions using rigorous methodologies.

Social work researchers and researcher-practitioner collaborators must consider several factors when developing and implementing interventions designed to achieve smart decarceration. First, all stakeholders must recognize that we do not have one overarching criminal justice system in the United States—instead, we have thousands of criminal justice systems, each one hyperlocal and complicated by its own unique political and geographic factors. Within each of these hyperlocal criminal justice systems, an individual's experience and outcomes after first law enforcement contact are heavily influenced by their own racial, socioeconomic, and behavioral health status as well as the status of the criminal justice professionals with whom they interact. Thus, implementing an intervention study at one site or local jurisdiction is imperative, although external generalizability of the findings will be limited. Multisite studies that include and transcend jurisdictional boundaries are more difficult to conduct but allow for the identification and tailoring of foundational intervention components. Then, researchers and practitioners must allow for those identified core intervention components to be tailored without losing potency back into the local context to ensure feasibility of the intervention and maximize impact. Second, although almost every state in the country has adopted criminal justice–related policy reforms over the past decade, few policy evaluations explore whether these reforms have resulted in their stated goals. For example, "ban the box" policies, which remove the disclosure of a criminal record on an initial application for employment, have political momentum and have proliferated. Although preliminary evidence on how ban-the-box policies increased opportunity is favorable, these policies also appear to drive racial inequity (e.g., Agan & Starr, 2018). Additionally, some scholars have explored the impact of certificates of rehabilitation on whether an individual with a conviction history will receive a call-back from a potential employer or landlord; the evidence is limited, but positive (Leasure & Andersen, 2016;

Leasure & Martin, 2017). Further, while the expungement of criminal records is effective in reducing the collateral consequences of criminal convictions, universal policies allowing individuals to qualify after completing their requirements do not exist, the expungement process is confusing and often prohibitively expensive, and multiyear waiting periods hamper broad application (Burton et al., 2021).

From a smart decarceration perspective, at a minimum, policy reforms should be evaluated for whether they significantly reduce the reach of the criminal justice system; promote racial, economic, and behavioral health equity; and facilitate public well-being and public safety. For more than four decades we have relied upon recidivism—rearrest or reincarceration—as the primary outcome with which to evaluate the success of individuals leaving incarceration and the behavioral interventions designed to improve their trajectories. As of 2021, we have yet to definitively identify a high-impact, comprehensive, continuum-of-care reentry model despite the fact that current statistics indicate that millions of individuals are transitioning into or out of incarceration annually. Rearrest rates after an incarceration event are high; 71% of individuals released from state prisons experience another arrest within 5 years (Durose & Antenangeli, 2021). There are many factors that contribute to the limited impact of existing reentry service models to decrease rearrest and reincarceration among individuals who are released from incarceration. While a small proportion of individuals do get released from incarceration and commit new crimes, recidivism is largely driven by factors including an individual's inability to pay fines and fees, screening positive for drug use during required urinalyses, or not meeting supervision requirements (e.g., not seeking out or securing employment, failing to access or complete required treatment programs), or for minor supervision infractions including failing to update an address or missing required meetings (Travis et al., 2014). Despite the fact that the recidivism construct does not solely measure an individual's engagement in subsequent crime, recidivism has been the default measure of reentry services' success for decades. Additional outcomes used to gauge program effectiveness are as varied as the programs themselves and may include employment, education, housing, or mental health and substance use disorder symptoms (Visher et al., 2017). The establishment of a new set of outcomes that measure individual behavior and progress are needed, and work identifying these outcomes has begun.

Social Workers: The Opportunity and the Dilemmas

Michael Sherraden, one of the most prolific thought leaders in the field of social work, wrote in the opening to the first book on *Smart Decarceration* (Epperson & Pettus-Davis, 2017) the following statement:

> Social innovation has made what we think of as human development, progress, and civilization possible. Social innovation has made possible all of the social systems and institutions that we take for granted. Unfortunately, not all human social

innovations are successful. Arguably, mass incarceration in the United States today is one of those wayward innovations. Humans created mass incarceration, and we have the ability to uncreate it. (pp. vii–viii)

The field of social work is deeply rooted in a code of ethics inextricably linked with racial justice, social justice, and human rights. We are trained as interventionists and perform as such in our professional work settings including advocacy work, policy work, organizational and social administration, individual and behavioral therapies, and research and scholarship. Over the next decade, forensic social workers will be relied upon as experts in smart decarceration and will be responsible not only for enacting reforms but also for educating all stakeholders on the complexities and injustices of the criminal justice system. Although the need for system-wide reforms is clear, those who support reform efforts often lack comprehensive understanding of how the criminal justice system functions, which increases the risk for reforms to result in a range of unintended negative consequences. Therefore, forensic social workers must simultaneously promote and critique decarceration approaches to ensure that criminal justice system transformation is sustainable, is humane, and will not need to be revisited in 20 years because disparities and other negative consequences persist.

A commitment to smart decarceration as a social worker comes with many dilemmas and challenges. A smart decarceration social worker, regardless of the setting in which they work, must view the criminal justice system as their primary client and, consistent with social work therapeutic approaches, must meet that client where they are to begin the work. To achieve this perspective shift, social workers must first decide where they are going to situate themselves in the social movement of criminal justice transformation. Will they operate outside the system to advance the pillars of abolition or other social justice principles? Or will they work within the system and strive for incremental change, working alongside correctional or other stakeholders who might be engaged in harmful practices but who are open to change? Regardless of this primary positionality, engaging in collaborative smart decarceration work means that smart decarceration social workers will interact with, or work alongside, many individuals and systems who challenge their own value system and who are misaligned with social work's code of ethics. Social workers in this field of practice will need to continually negotiate the space while seizing opportunities for change and being open to the inevitable policy or practice sacrifices inherent to dramatic paradigm shifts. The changes required of the criminal justice system to enact reform of the magnitude of smart decarceration will require social workers to find common ground with people who hold opposing viewpoints, espouse stigmatizing ideas, or otherwise challenge our shared values as social workers. Further, it may be necessary for those social workers who position themselves inside the system to accept a paycheck from the very entity they are working to dismantle and to understand that some—including one's own individual clients—may view the worker as part of the problem rather than an agent of change. Enacting smart decarceration, however, means that work with individual clients is possible, and through that individual work, a sustainable pathway for thousands of others can be created for those who follow. As with many fields of practice in social work, smart decarceration social workers will undoubtedly struggle to manage the slow and incremental pace of reform, face gut-wrenching setbacks to progress, bear witness to unthinkable human suffering, and reflect deeply on the unnecessary destruction of lives. However, at the same time, working in the smart decarceration arena means that social workers can face each day with hope, passion, and dedication, knowing that their work is helping individuals to develop their full human potential and to thrive, while simultaneously participating in the civil rights movement of our time—using data-driven solutions to dismantle mass incarceration and promote equity and change.

References

Abraham, L. A., Brown, T. C., & Thomas, S. A. (2020). How COVID-19's disruption of the US correctional system provides an opportunity for decarceration. *American Journal of Criminal Justice, 45*(4), 780–792.

Agan, A., & Starr, S. (2018). Ban the box, criminal records, and racial discrimination: A field experiment. *Quarterly Journal of Economics, 133*(1), 191–235.

American Psychiatric Association. (2013). *Diagnostic and statistical manual of mental disorders* (5th ed.). https://doi.org/10.1176/appi.books.9780890425596

Bagaric, M., Hunter, D., & Svilar, J. (2021). Prison abolition. *Journal of Criminal Law and Criminology (1973-), 111*(2), 351–406. https://www.jstor.org/stable/pdf/48614943.pdf

Baumgartner, F., Epp, D., & Shoub, K. (2018). *Suspect citizens: What 20 million traffic stops tell us about policing and race.* Cambridge University Press. doi:10.1017/9781108553599

Ben-Moshe, L. (2020). *Decarcerating disability: Deinstitutionalization and prison abolition.* University of Minnesota Press.Binswanger, I. A., Stern, M. F., Deyo, R. A., Heagerty, P. J., Cheadle, A., Elmore, J. G., & Koepsell, T. D. (2007). Release from prison-a high risk of death for former inmates. *New England Journal of Medicine, 356*(2), 157–165.

Boxer, P., Schappell, A., Middlemass, K., & Mercado, I. (2011). Cognitive and emotional covariates of violence exposure among former prisoners: Links to antisocial behavior and emotional distress and implications for theory. *Aggressive Behavior, 37*(5), 465–475.

Brady, S. S. (2006). Lifetime community violence exposure and health risk behavior among young adults in college. *Journal of Adolescent Health, 39*(4), 610–613.

Breslau, N. (2009). The epidemiology of trauma, PTSD, and other posttrauma disorders. *Trauma, Violence, & Abuse, 10,* 198–210. doi:10.1177/1524838009334448

Bronson, J., & Berzofsky, M. (2017). *Indicators of mental health problems reported by prisoners and jail inmates, 2011–12* (NCJ 250612). Bureau of Justice Statistics. https://bjs.ojp.gov/content/pub/pdf/imhprpji1112.pdf

Bronson, J., Stroop, J., Zimmer, S., & Berzofsky, M. (2017). *Drug use, dependence, and abuse among state prisoners and jail inmates, 2007–2009* (NCJ 250546). U.S. Department of Justice, Office of Juvenile Justice and Delinquency Prevention.

Burch, T. (2015). Skin color and the criminal justice system: Beyond Black-White disparities in sentencing. *Journal of Empirical Legal Studies, 12*(3), 395–420. doi:10.1111/jels.12077

Burnette, M. L., Ilgen, M., Frayne, S. M., Lucas, E., Mayo, J., & Weitlauf, J. C. (2008). Violence perpetration and childhood abuse among men and women in substance abuse treatment. *Journal of Substance Abuse Treatment, 35,* 217–222. doi:10.1016/j.jsat.2007.10.002

Burton, A. L., Cullen, F. T., Pickett, J. T., Burton, V. S., Jr., & Thielo, A. J. (2021). Beyond the eternal criminal record: Public support for expungement. *Criminology & Public Policy, 20*(1), 123–151.

Califano, J. (2010). *Behind bars II: Substance abuse and America's prison population.* U.S. Department of Justice. https://www.ojp.gov/ncjrs/virtual-library/abstracts/behind-bars-ii-substance-abuse-and-americas-prison-population

Carson, E. A. (2018). *Prisoners in 2016* (NCJ 251149). Bureau of Justice Statistics. https://www.bjs.gov/content/pub/pdf/p16.pdf

Carson, E. A. (2020). *Prisoners in 2019* (NCJ 255115). Bureau of Justice Statistics. https://bjs.ojp.gov/content/pub/pdf/p19.pdf

Carson, E. A. (2021). *Mortality in state and federal prisons, 2001–2018—Statistical tables* (NCJ 255970). Bureau of Justice Statistics. https://bjs.ojp.gov/content/pub/pdf/msfp0118st.pdf

Clark, C. B., Reiland, S., Thorne, C., & Cropsey, K. L. (2013). Relationship of trauma exposure and substance abuse to self-reported violence among men and women in substance abuse treatment. *Journal of Interpersonal Violence, 29,* 1514–1530. doi:10.1177/0886260513507138

Cloyes, K. G., Wong, B., Latimer, S., & Abarca, J. (2010). Women, serious mental illness and recidivism: A gender-based analysis of recidivism risk for women with SMI released from prison. *Journal of Forensic Nursing, 6*(1), 3–14. https://doi.org/10.1111/j.1939-3938.2009.01060.x

Collins, S. E., Lonczak, H. S., & Clifasefi, S. L. (2019). Seattle's law enforcement assisted diversion (LEAD): Program effects on criminal justice and legal system utilization and costs. *Journal of Experimental Criminology, 15*(2), 201–211.

Couloute, L., & Kopf, D. (2018). *Out of prison & out of work: Unemployment among formerly incarcerated people.* https://www.prisonpolicy.org/reports/outofwork.html

de Vuono-Powell, S., Schweidler, C., Walters, A., & Zohrabi, A. (2015). *Who pays? The true cost of incarceration on families.* Ella Baker Center, Forward Together, Research Action Design. http://whopaysreport.org/who-pays-full-report/

DeHart, D., Lynch, S., Belknap, J., Dass-Brailsford, P., & Green, B. (2014). Life history models of female offending: The roles of serious mental illness and trauma in women's pathways to jail. *Psychology of Women Quarterly, 38*(1), 138–151. https://doi.org/10.1177/0361684313494357

Dobie, D. J., Kivlahan, D. R., Maynard, C., Bush, K. R., Davis, T. M., & Bradley, K. A. (2004). Posttraumatic stress disorder in female veterans: Association with self-reported health problems and functional impairment. *Archives of Internal Medicine, 164*(4), 394–400.

Dube, S. R., Felitti, V. J., Dong, M., Chapman, D. P., Giles, W. H., & Anda, R. F. (2003). Childhood abuse, neglect, and household dysfunction and the risk of illicit drug use: The adverse childhood experiences study. *Pediatrics, 111,* 564–572. doi:10.1542/peds.111.3.564

Durose, M., & Antenangeli, L. (2021). *Recidivism of prisoners released in 34 states in 2012: A 5-year follow-up period (2012–2017)* (NCJ 255947). Bureau of Justice Statistics.

Edelman, P. (2019). *Not a crime to be poor: The criminalization of poverty in America.* New Press.

Epperson, M. W., & Pettus-Davis, C. (2015). *Smart decarceration: Guiding concepts for an era of criminal justice transformation.* (CSD Working Paper No. 15-53). Washington University in St. Louis, Center for Social Development.

Epperson, M. W., & Pettus-Davis, C. (Eds.). (2017). *Smart decarceration: Achieving criminal justice transformation in the 21st century.* Oxford University Press.

Federal Bureau of Investigation. (2017). *2017: Crime in the United States.* https://ucr.fbi.gov/crime-in-the-u.s/2017/crime-in-the-u.s.-2017/tables/table-43

Finkel, M. (2019). *New data: Low incomes—but high fees—for people on probation.* https://www.prisonpolicy.org/blog/2019/04/09/probation_income/

Fletcher, M. A. (2018). For Black motorists, a never-ending fear of being stopped. *National Geographic.*

Forsman, M., & Långström, N. (2012). Child maltreatment and adult violent offending: Population-based twin study addressing the "cycle of violence" hypothesis. *Psychological Medicine, 42,* 1977–1983. doi:10.1017/S0033291711003060

Fraser, M. W., Richman, J. M., Galinsky, M. J., & Day, S. H. (2009). *Intervention research: Developing social programs.* Oxford University Press.

Hill, J., & Nathan, R. (2008). Childhood antecedents of serious violence in adult male offenders. *Aggressive Behavior, 34,* 329–338. doi:10.1002/ab.20237

Hoffman, H. C., & Dickinson, G. E. (2011). Characteristics of prison hospice programs in the United States. *American Journal of Hospice and Palliative Medicine, 28*(4), 245–252.

Howard University Law Library. (n.d.). *Black Lives Matter movement.* https://library.law.howard.edu/civilrightshistory/BLM

Jacobs, L. A., Kim, M. E., Whitfield, D. L., Gartner, R. E., Panichelli, M., Kattari, S. K., . . . Mountz, S. E. (2021). Defund the police: Moving towards an anti-carceral social work. *Journal of Progressive Human Services, 32*(1), 37–62.

Jaycox, L. H., Marshall, G. N., & Schell, T. (2004). Use of mental health services by men injured through community violence. *Psychiatric Services, 55*(4), 415–420.

Jennings, W. G., Piquero, A. R., & Reingle, J. M. (2012). On the overlap between victimization and offending: A review of the literature. *Aggression and Violent Behavior, 17*(1), 16–26.

Karberg, J., & James, D. J. (2005). *Substance dependence, abuse, and treatment of jail inmates, 2002* (NCJ 209588). Bureau of Justice Statistics.

Kennedy, S. C., Tripodi, S. J., Pettus-Davis, C., & Ayers, J. (2016). Examining dose–response relationships between childhood victimization, depression, symptoms of psychosis, and substance misuse for incarcerated women. *Women & Criminal Justice, 26*(2), 77–98. https://doi.org/10.1080/08974454.2015.1023486

King, E. A., Tripodi, S. J., & Veeh, C. A. (2018). The relationship between severe mental disorders and recidivism in a sample of women released from prison. *Psychiatric Quarterly, 89*(3), 717–731. doi:10.1007/s11126-018-9572-9

Kochel, T. R., Wilson, D. B., & Mastrofski, S. D. (2011). Effect of suspect race on officers' arrest decisions. *Criminology, 49*(2), 473–512. https://doi.org/10.1111/j.1745-9125.2011.00230.x

Komarovskaya, I. A., Booker Loper, A., Warren, J., & Jackson, S. (2011). Exploring gender differences in trauma exposure and the emergence of symptoms of PTSD among incarcerated men and women. *Journal of Forensic Psychiatry & Psychology, 22*(3), 395–410.

Kubiak, S. P. (2004). The effects of PTSD on treatment adherence, drug relapse, and criminal recidivism in a sample of incarcerated men and women. *Research on Social Work Practice, 14*, 424–433. doi:10.1177/1049731504265837

Laub, J. H., & Boonstoppel, S. L. (2012). Understanding desistance from juvenile offending: Challenges and opportunities. In *The Oxford handbook of juvenile crime and juvenile justice* (pp. 373–394).

Laub, J. H., & Sampson, R. J. (2001). Understanding desistance from crime. *Crime and Justice, 28*, 1–69.

Leasure, P., & Andersen, T. S. (2016). The effectiveness of certificates of relief as collateral consequence relief mechanisms: An experimental study. *Yale Law & Policy Review, 35*, 11.

Leasure, P., & Martin, T. (2017). Criminal records and housing: An experimental study. *Journal of Experimental Criminology, 13*(4), 527–535.

Lize, S. E., Scheyett, A. M., Morgan, C. R., Proescholdbell, S. K., Norwood, T., & Edwards, D. (2015). Violent death rates and risk for released prisoners in North Carolina. *Violence and Victims, 30*, 1019–1036.

Lofstrom, M., & Raphael, S. (2016). Crime, the criminal justice system, and socioeconomic inequality. *Journal of Economic Perspectives, 30*(2), 103–126.

Lopez-Aguado, P. (2016). The collateral consequences of prisonization: Racial sorting, carceral identity, and community criminalization. *Sociology Compass, 10*(1), 12–23. doi:10.1111/soc4.12342

Lowry, M., & Kerodal, A. (2019). *Prosecutor-led diversion.* Center for Court Innovation. https://www.courtinnovation.org/sites/default/files/media/document/2019/prosecutor-led_diversion.pdf

Mallik-Kane, K., & Visher, C. A. (2008). *Health and prisoner reentry: How physical, mental, and substance abuse conditions shape the process of reintegration.* Urban Institute. https://www.urban.org/sites/default/files/publication/31491/411617-Health-and-Prisoner-Reentry.PDF

Mayson, S. (2019). Bias in, bias out. *Yale Law Journal, 128*, 2218–2300. https://digitalcommons.law.uga.edu/fac_artchop/1293/

Medrano, M. A., Hatch, J. P., Zule, W. A., & Desmond, D. P. (2002). Psychological distress in childhood trauma survivors who abuse drugs. *American Journal of Drug and Alcohol Abuse, 28*, 1–13. doi:10.1081/ADA-120001278

Mennicke, A., Daniels, K., & Rizo, C. F. (2021). Suicide completion among incarcerated women. *Journal of Correctional Health Care, 27*(1), 14–22.

Merrall, E. L., Kariminia, A., Binswanger, I. A., Hobbs, M. S., Farrell, M., Marsden, J., . . . Bird, S. M. (2010). Meta-analysis of drug-related deaths soon after release from prison. *Addiction, 105*, 1545–1554.

Mersky, J. P., Topitzes, J., & Reynolds, A. J. (2012). Unsafe at any age: Linking childhood and adolescent maltreatment to delinquency and crime. *Journal of Research in Crime and Delinquency, 49*, 295–318. doi:10.1177/0022427811415284

Messina, N. P., Calhoun, S., & Braithwaite, J. (2014). Trauma-informed treatment decreases PTSD among women offenders. *Drug and Alcohol Dependence, 140,* e147. doi:10.1016/j.drugalcdep.2014.02.416

Messina, N., & Grella, C. (2006). Childhood trauma and women's health outcomes in a California prison population. *American Journal of Public Health, 96*(10), 1842–1848. https://doi.org/10.2105/AJPH.2005.082016

Messina, N., Grella, C., Burdon, W., & Prendergast, M. (2007). Childhood adverse events and current traumatic distress: A comparison of men and women drug dependent prisoners. *Criminal Justice and Behavior, 34,* 1385–1401. doi:10.1177/0093854807305150

Miller, N. A., & Najavits, L. M. (2012). Creating trauma-informed correctional care: A balance of goals and environment. *European Journal of Psychotraumatology, 3*(1), 17246.

Miller, R. J. (2013). Race, hyper-incarceration, and US poverty policy in historic perspective. *Sociology Compass, 7*(7), 573–589. https://doi.org/10.1111/soc4.12049

Moloney, K. P., van den Bergh, B. J., & Moller, L. F. (2009). Women in prison: The central issues of gender characteristics and trauma history. *Public Health, 123*(6), 426–430. doi:10.1016/j.puhe.2009.04.002

Morrison, M., Pettus-Davis, C., Renn, T., Veeh, C., & Weatherly, C. (2019). What trauma looks like for incarcerated men: A study of men's lifetime trauma exposure in two state prisons. *Journal of Traumatic Stress Disorders & Treatment, 8*(1), 1–7. doi:10.4172/2324-8947.1000192

Najavits, L. M. (2004). Treatment of posttraumatic stress disorder and substance abuse: Clinical guidelines for implementing Seeking Safety therapy. *Alcoholism Treatment Quarterly, 22*(1), 43–62.

National Alliance on Mental Illness. (n.d.). *Posttraumatic stress disorder.* https://www.nami.org/About-Mental-Illness/Mental-Health-Conditions/Posttraumatic-Stress-Disorder

National Institute of Mental Health. (2021). *Mental illness.* https://www.nimh.nih.gov/health/statistics/mental-illness.shtml

National Inventory of Collateral Consequences of Conviction. (n.d.). https://niccc.nationalreentryresourcecenter.org/

National Research Council. (2014). *The Growth of Incarceration in the United States: Exploring Causes and Consequences.* Washington, DC: The National Academies Press.

Nyamathi, A., Marlow E., Zhang, S., Hall, E., Farabee, D., Marfisee, M., . . . Leake, B. (2012). Correlates of serious violent crime for recently released parolees with a history of homelessness. *Violence and Victims, 27,* 793–810. doi:10.1891/08866708.27.5.793

Oxford Reference. (n.d.). *Decarceration.* https://www.oxfordreference.com/view/10.1093/oi/authority.20110803095705401

Parsons, A. E. (2018). *From asylum to prison: Deinstitutionalization and the rise of mass incarceration after 1945.* UNC Press Books.

Petersilia, J., & Cullen, F. T. (2014, June). Liberal but not stupid: Meeting the promise of downsizing prisons. *Stanford Journal of Criminal Law and Policy, 2,* 1–43.

Pettus-Davis, C. (2012). Reverse social work's neglect of justice-involved adults: The intersection and an agenda. *Social Work Research, 36,* 3–7. doi:10.1093/swr/svs036

Pettus-Davis, C., & Epperson, M. W. (2015). *From mass incarceration to smart decarceration* (Grand Challenges for Social Work Initiative Concept Paper No. 4). American Academy of Social Work and Social Welfare.

Pettus-Davis, C., & Epperson, M. (2017). *Policy recommendations for grand challenge to promote smart decarceration.* American Academy of Social Work and Social Welfare.

Pettus-Davis, C., Epperson, M. W., & Grier, A. (2017a). Reforming civil disability policy to facilitate effective and sustainable decarceration. In M. W. Epperson & C. Pettus-Davis (Eds.), *Smart decarceration: Achieving criminal justice transformation in the 21st century* (pp. 3–28). Oxford University Press.

Pettus-Davis, C., Epperson, M., & Grier, A. (2017b). *Reverse civil and legal exclusions for persons with criminal charges and convictions: A policy action to promote smart decarceration.* American Academy of Social Work and Social Welfare. https://aaswsw.org/wp-content/uploads/2017/03/PAS.9.1.pdf.

Pettus-Davis, C., Epperson, M. W., Taylor, S., & Grier, A. (2017). Guideposts for the American era of smart decarceration: Recommendations from a national collection of researchers, practitioners, and formerly incarcerated leaders. In M. W. Epperson & C. Pettus-Davis (Eds.), *Smart decarceration: Achieving criminal justice transformation in the 21st century* (pp. 250–270). Oxford University Press.

Pettus-Davis, C., Renn, T., & Kennedy, S. C. (2020, May). *Trauma and loss during reentry.* https://ijrd.csw.fsu.edu/sites/g/files/upcbnu1766/files/Publications/Trauma_During_Reentry.pdf

Pettus-Davis, C., Renn, T., Lacasse, J. R., & Motley, R. (2019). Proposing a population-specific intervention approach to treat trauma among men during and after incarceration. *Psychology of Men & Masculinities, 20*(3), 379.

Pettus-Davis, C., Veeh, C., & Hickman, S. (2017). *Reforms of policy barriers to positive and productive community engagement of individuals with felony histories: Preliminary report.* Institute for Advancing Justice Research & Innovation, Washington University in St. Louis.

Pew Charitable Trusts. (2020). *Policy reforms can strengthen community supervision: A framework to improve probation and parole.* https://www.pewtrusts.org/-/media/assets/2020/04/policyreform_communitysupervision_report_final.pdf

Pierson, E., Simoiu, C., Overgoor, J., Corbett-Davies, S., Jenson, D., Shoemaker, A., . . . Goel, S. (2020). A large-scale analysis of racial disparities in police stops across the United States. *Nature Human Behaviour, 4*(7), 736–745. https://doi.org/10.1038/s41562-020-0858-1

Primeau, A., Bowers, T. G., Harrison, M. A., & XuXu. (2013). Deinstitutionalization of the mentally ill: Evidence for transinstitutionalization from psychiatric hospitals to penal institutions. *Comprehensive Psychology, 2*, 16–02.

Rabuy, B., & Kopf, D. (2015). *Prisons of poverty: Uncovering the pre-incarceration incomes of the imprisoned.* https://www.prisonpolicy.org/reports/income.html

Ranapurwala, S. I., Shanahan, M. E., Alexandridis, A. A., Proescholdbell, S. K., Naumann, R. B., Edwards, D., & Marshall, S. W. (2018). Opioid overdose mortality among former North Carolina inmates: 2000–2015. *American Journal of Public Health, 108*, 1207–1213.

Raphael, S., & Stoll, M. A. (2013). Assessing the contribution of the deinstitutionalization of the mentally ill to growth in the US incarceration rate. *Journal of Legal Studies, 42*(1), 187–222.

Sadeh, N., & McNiel, D. E. (2014). Posttraumatic stress disorder increases risk of criminal recidivism among justice-involved persons with mental disorders. *Criminal Justice and Behavior, 42*(6), 573–586. doi:10.1177/0093854814556880

Sherraden, M., Barth, R. P., Brekke, J., Fraser, M., Madershied, R., & Padgett, D. (2014). *Social is fundamental: Introduction and context for grand challenges for social work* (Grand Challenges for Social Work Initiative Working Paper No. 1). American Academy of Social Work and Social Welfare. https://grandchallengesforsocialwork.org/wp-content/uploads/2015/04/FINAL-GCSW-Intro-and-Context-4-2-2015-formatted-final.pdf

Sickmund, M., Sladky, T. J., Puzzanchera, C., & Kang, W. (2021). *Easy access to the census of juveniles in residential placement.* National Center for Juvenile Justice. https://www.ojjdp.gov/ojstatbb/ezacjrp/

Sindicich, N., Mills, K. L., Barrett, E. L., Indig, D., Sunjic, S., Sannibale, C., . . . Najavits, L. M. (2014). Offenders as victims: Post-traumatic stress disorder and substance use disorder among male prisoners. *Journal of Forensic Psychiatry & Psychology, 25*(1), 44–60.

Steinberg, R., Kalish, L., & Ritchin, E. (2018). Freedom should be free: A brief history of bail funds in the United States. *UCLA Criminal Justice Law Review, 2*(1), 79–95.

Swogger, M. T., You, S., Cashman-Brown, S., & Conner, K. R. (2011). Childhood physical abuse, aggression, and suicide attempts among criminal offenders. *Psychiatry Research, 185*, 363–367. doi:10.1016/j.psychres.2010.07.036

Tanner-Smith, E. E., Wilson, S. J., & Lipsey, M. W. (2013). Risk factors and crime. In *The Oxford handbook of criminological theory* (pp. 89–111). F. T. Cullen P. Wilcox: Oxford University Press.

Taxman, F. S., & Kitsantas, P. (2009). Availability and capacity of substance abuse programs in correctional settings: A classification and regression tree analysis. *Drug and Alcohol Dependence, 103*, S43–S53. https://doi.org/10.1016/j.drugalcdep.2009.01.008

Taxman, F. S., Perdoni, M. L., & Caudy, M. (2013). The plight of providing appropriate substance abuse treatment services to offenders: Modeling the gaps in service delivery. *Victims & Offenders, 8*(1), 70–93. https://doi.org/10.1080/15564886.2012.747459

Taxman, F. S., Perdoni, M. L., & Harrison, L. D. (2007). Drug treatment services for adult offenders: The state of the state. *Journal of Substance Abuse Treatment, 32*(3), 239–254. https://doi.org/10.1016/j.jsat.2006.12.019Get

Tonry, M. (2010). The social, psychological, and political causes of racial disparities in the American criminal justice system. *Crime and Justice, 39*(1), 273–312.

Travis, J., Western, B., & Redburn, F. S. (2014). The growth of incarceration in the United States: Exploring causes and consequences. *Federal Probation, 78*(2), 71–74.

Tripodi, S. J., & Pettus-Davis, C. (2013). Histories of childhood victimization and subsequent mental health problems, substance use, and sexual victimization for a sample of incarcerated women in the US. *International Journal of Law and Psychiatry, 36*(1), 30–40.

U.S. Department of Veterans Affairs. (2015). *Men and sexual trauma.* http://www.ptsd.va.gov/public/types/ violence/men-sexual-trauma.asp

Van Buren, T. M., Stocke, T. L., Wunderlich, T. L., & Thurston-Snoha, B.-J. (2014). Incarcerated men and trauma: Treatment gap. *American Jails, 28,* 53–56, 58. Retrieved from http://libproxy.wustl.edu/ login?url=http://search.proquest.com/docview/1644456262?accountid=1515

Van Eijk, G. (2017). Socioeconomic marginality in sentencing: The built-in bias in risk assessment tools and the reproduction of social inequality. *Punishment & Society, 19,* 463–481. https://doi.org/10.1177/ 1462474516666282

Veeh, C. A., Tripodi, S. J., Pettus-Davis, C., & Scheyett, A. M. (2018). The interaction of serious mental disorder and race on time to reincarceration. *American Journal of Orthopsychiatry, 88*(2), 125.

Visher, Christy A., Pamela K. Lattimore, Kelle Barrick, & Stephen Tueller. (2017). Evaluating the long-term effects of prisoner reentry services on recidivism: What types of services matter? *Justice Quarterly, 34*(1), 136–165.

Washington, D. M., Harper, T., Hill, A. B., & Kern, L. J. (2021). Achieving juvenile justice through abolition: A critical review of social work's role in shaping the juvenile legal system and steps toward achieving an antiracist future. *Social Sciences, 10*(6), 211.

Washington, J. (2018, July 31). *What is prison abolition?* https://www.thenation.com/article/what-is-prison-abolition/

Weichselbaum, S., & Lewis, N. (2020, June 9). *Support for defunding the police department is growing: Here's why it's not a silver bullet.* Marshall Project. https://www.scribd.com/article/464950542/Support-For-Defunding-The-Police-Department-Is-Growing-Here-s-Why-It-s-Not-A-Silver-Bullet

Western, B. (2006). *Punishment and inequality in America.* Russell Sage.

Wilson, A. B., Draine, J., Hadley, T., Metraux, S., & Evans, A. (2011). Examining the impact of mental illness and substance use on recidivism in a county jail. *International Journal of Law & Psychiatry, 34*(4), 264–268. doi:10.1016/j.ijlp.2011.07.004

Wisco, B. E., Marx, B. P., Wolf, E. J., Miller, M. W., Southwick, S. M., & Pietrzak, R. H. (2014). Posttraumatic stress disorder in the US veteran population: Results from the National Health and Resilience in Veterans Study. *Journal of Clinical Psychiatry, 75,* 1338–1346. doi:10.4088/JCP.14m09328

Wolff, N., Huening, J., Shi, J., & Frueh, B. C. (2014). Trauma exposure and posttraumatic stress disorder among incarcerated men. *Journal of Urban Health, 91,* 707–719. doi:10.1007/s11524-014-9871-x

Wright, R. F., & Levine, K. L. (2021). Models of prosecutor-led diversion programs in the United States and beyond. *Annual Review of Criminology, 4,* 331–351.

Wright, E. M., Salisbury, E. J., & Van Voorhis, P. (2007). Predicting the prison misconducts of women offenders: The importance of gender-responsive needs. *Journal of Contemporary Criminal Justice, 23*(4), 310–340. https://doi.org/10.1177/1043986207309595

Zeng, Z. (2019). *Jail inmates in 2017* (NCJ 251774). Bureau of Justice Statistics.

Zlodre, J., & Fazel, S. (2012). All-cause and external mortality in released prisoners: Systematic review and meta-analysis. *American Journal of Public Health, 102*(12), e67–e75.

Zlotnick, C., Johnson, J., & Najavits, L. M. (2009). Randomized controlled pilot study of cognitive-behavioral therapy in a sample of incarcerated women with substance use disorder and PTSD. *Behavior Therapy, 40*(4), 325–336.

Index

civil commitment policy, 334–35
decarceration, 578–81
immigration policy, 237
intimate partner violence, 350
mental health policies, 303
racial and ethnic disparities, 128–29
social justice system approach, 128–29
social policy development, 28–37
  ideas to laws, 29–30
  issues, policy practice, 36–37
  policymaking levels, 29
  policymaking process, 30–34, 31*f*
    agenda setting, 31*f*, 31–32
    policy adoption, 31*f*, 32–33
    policy evaluation, 31*f*, 33–34
    policy formation, 31*f*, 32
    policy implementation, 31*f*, 33
  policy types, 34–36, 35*t*
    constituent and symbolic, 35*t*, 36
    distributive, 34–35, 35*t*
    redistributive, 35–36, 35*t*
    regulatory, 35, 35*t*
  terminology, 28, 29*t*
social stress theory, 175
social work practice
  immigration policy on, 236–37
    ethics, education, and practice, 237–38
  transgender and nonconforming people, 116–17
*Social Work Speaks, Policy Statements by the
    National Association of Social Work*, 284
Societies for the Prevention of Cruelty to Children,
    345
socioeconomic status, on criminal justice
    involvement, 581
solitary confinement, 530–31
  capital punishment, 274
  LGB, 87–88, 89, 90–91, 94–95, 97–98
  mental illness, 290, 299–300
  prisons, COVID-19 infection, 357–58
  transgender and gender nonconforming, 107,
    110, 112–13, 115
*Solitary Confinement: A Clinical Social Work
    Perspective* (National Association of Social
    Workers), 300
Special Rule Cancellation of Removal for Battered
    Spouses and Children, 230–31
specific responsivity, 141
spiraling marginalization, 52*f*, 52–53
stacking-on conditions, probation, 488, 496
stages of change model, 540, 559
  sex trafficking survivors, 559
standardized risk-need assessment tools, 490–92
state courts, 19–23, 20*f*, 25*t*
  civil courts, 20–21
  criminal cases source, 19, 20*f*

criminal courts, 20
  felony caseload composition, 19–20
  phases, civil and criminal courts, 21–23, 22*f*
Steadman, H. J., 475
Steib, S. D., 391
Steiker, C. S., 266–67, 268, 271, 277
Steiker, J. M., 266–67, 268, 271, 277
stereotypes
  correctional settings, 530, 532
  homophobia, 88, 89
  immigrants, 227–28
  mental illness, 142, 289–90, 302
  poverty, 389
  stigma and focal concerns theory, 142
stigma, mental illness. *See* mental illness, stigma
strain theories, 178–80
Strang, H., 516–17
stress
  relational violence, 401–2, 409*f*, 410
  tolerable, 173–75, 174*f*
  toxic, 173–75, 174*f*, 176–77, 179, 184
  vs. positive/tolerable, 173–75, 175*f*
Strong, K. H., 507
structural heterosexism, 89–90
Stryker, S., *Transgender History*, 106–7
student loans, 369–70
subjective application, 3
subject matter jurisdiction, 13
substance abuse/substance use disorder. *See
    also* drug court; drug policy; therapeutic
    jurisprudence
  assessment, correctional settings, 536
  child abuse and, 339, 390
  civil commitment, vulnerable
    populations, 330
  correctional settings, 531
  decarceration, 576–78
  drug courts, 254
  juvenile justice, 421
  mass incarceration, 576
  mental health, 535–36
  older adults, 73
  post-traumatic stress disorder, 58, 458
  Reagan administration, 312
  trauma experiences, lifetime, 445–46, 575
  treatment
    justice-involved, 358, 360*t*, 361*t*
    residential, 539–40
  veterans, 455–56, 458, 459–60
  women
    drug court outcomes, 445–46
    forensic settings, 57–58
    gender-responsive interventions, 445–46
    trauma and post-traumatic stress disorder,
      445–46